INTRODUCTION TO ETHICS

INTRODUCTION TO ETHICS

Personal and Social Responsibility in a Diverse World

Edited by

Gary Percesepe

PRENTICE HALL, Englewood Cliffs, New Jersey 07632

Library of Congress Cataloging-in-Publication Data

Percesepe, Gary John
Introduction to ethics: personal and social responsibility in a diverse world/
Gary Percesepe.
p. cm.
Includes bibliographical references.
ISBN 0-02-393891-9
1. Ethics. 2. Ethical problems. 3. Multiculturalism. I. Title.
BJ1031.P47 1995
170—dc20 94-4826
CIP

Editorial/production supervision: Bonnie Jo Collins
Acquisitions editor: Ted Bolen
Cover design: Tom Nery
Cover illustration: Jose Ortega
Buyer: Lynn Pearlman

Printed in the United States of America
10 9 8 7 6 5 4 3 2 1

ISBN 0-02-393891-9

Prentice-Hall International (UK) Limited, *London*
Prentice-Hall of Australia Pty. Limited, *Sydney*
Prentice-Hall Canada Inc., *Toronto*
Prentice-Hall Hispanoamericana, S. A., *Mexico*
Prentice-Hall of India Private Limited, *New Delhi*
Prentice-Hall of Japan, Inc., *Tokyo*
Simon & Schuster Asia Pte. Ltd., *Singapore*
Editora Prentice-Hall do Brasil, Ltda., *Rio de Janeiro*

Dedicated
to the Memory of
THOMAS PERCESEPE

my brother

22 June 1947 to 17 February 1958

Contents

Preface

Introduction to Ethics: Personal and Social Responsibility in a Diverse World is designed as a text for general ethics courses that wish to stress the integration of ethical theory with contemporary moral issues that have a gendered, multicultural focus.

The first chapter of the text, on ethical theory, is preceded by an introduction to ethical theory that aims to introduce students to the working vocabulary, central concepts, and organizing principles of ethics. The stress here is on normative ethics. The discussion of metaethics is brief; instructors and their students who wish to do more in this area can refer to the "For Further Study" section at the end of Chapter One. The introduction is meant to be neither exhaustive nor sufficient in itself; it should be read as an aid to understanding the ethical theories presented in this book. Because ethical theory in the political realm is best understood against the background of some social practice, there is a treatment of civil disobedience immediately following the section on social contract theory. A glossary is provided at the end of the book.

Chapter One introduces students to some of the more important moral theories. Again, no anthology can hope to be exhaustive—the hope, rather, is that these theories are *tools* that can be used to construct meaning, assisting in the interpretation of the essays that follow in the remaining nine chapters of the book and, more generally, to help make sense of the bewildering moral choices that we face. I have selected contemporary authors to represent historical positions in ethics. Thus, Alasdair MacIntyre writes in support of virtue ethics, James Rachels of utilitarianism, and Onora O'Neill of Kant and respect for persons. Ronald Dworkin discusses taking rights seriously, and John Rawls's theory of justice, crucial to understanding liberal democracy in the modern welfare state, is likewise included. The chapter concludes with Carol Gilligan's rotation of the axis of discussion to include a "different voice," a call for the inclusion of women's voices in the ethical arena.

In selecting the nine issues that constitute the remainder of the book I have been guided by these criteria:

1. The issues should be relevant to the experience of both instructors and students.
2. The issues should put into question the relation of private to public morality.
3. Attention must be paid to the complex matrix of race, class, and gender.
4. Attention must be paid to the role religion plays in the shaping of moral discourse.

These criteria grow out of my (admittedly postmodern) conviction that all philosophical issues are socially constructed from some concrete historical situation. The very way that we identify "issues" arises from our particular "worldview," our "take" on reality. All worldviews attempt to answer four fundamental questions: Who are we? Where are we? What is wrong? What is the remedy? The nine issues I have selected, then, all deal in some way with what is perceived by many to be wrong in us and wrong in our society, and with possible remedies for these wrongs.

There is a wide spectrum of opinion on what is wrong and what remedies exist. In selecting authors for this anthology I have tried to be as inclusive as possible, realizing that no anthology can be *completely* inclusive: Our values are revealed in what is excluded as well as what is included, and the best one can do is to try to make clear the grounds for inclusion. And so I sought selections that would work well in the classroom, that I myself have had success in teaching, that were accessible yet substantive, and that related to other selections in the chapter or in the text as a whole. I also wanted to include essays that some might not call "philosophical" in the strictest sense of the term but that still shed valuable light on the issue in question, such as the selections by Henry David Thoreau, Jesus of Nazareth, Martin Luther King Jr., Oliver North, Adrienne Rich, Mohandas Gandhi, Shulamith Firestone, Peter Marin, Margaret B. Wilkerson and Jewell Handy Gresham, Shelby Steele, a Vatican declaration, a Supreme Court decision, and the like.

Chapter Two, Ethics of Community, suggests that the stress on individualism in Western culture has produced a kind of "cultural disconnect," resulting in factions of every kind, tribalism, and what some have called "culture wars." Must issues of race, class, and gender continue to divide us until there is no common good left to unite us? Has the social fabric of America been stretched so far that we resign ourselves to documenting its ripping? Or is there a remedy? The selection by Kwame Gyekye presents a non-Western model of community. Martin Luther King Jr., and Cornel West and bell hooks present a nuanced Western approach to community and love of neighbor that is also Christian and politically progressive. David Kirp and his coeditors attempt to situate discussions of community in the context of gender, and Emmanuel Levinas (writing from a Jewish perspective) suggests that our common suffering, our "face-to-face" encounter with the suffering of the Other, unites us.

Chapter Three explores the ethics of friendship, love, and caring. Although he wrote in the nineteenth century, Thoreau's wisdom about friendship still seems contemporary. The philosopher and novelist William H. Gass draws upon the poet Rilke to articulate a philosophy of "nonpossessive love." Robert Solomon's essay, "The Virtue of (Erotic) Love," provides a useful history of the treatment of love in Western literature, while Nel Noddings details an ethics of care. Shulamith Firestone's essay illustrates how romantic love may become an instrument of power leading to the silencing and marginalizing of women.

Chapter Four seeks to understand the linkage of truth, power, and lying. The essays by Charles Fried, Michel Foucault, and Václev Havel, taken together, demonstrate how the personal becomes the political, shattering the idea of a merely private moral space. The transcript of the Iran–Contra hearings, featuring excerpts of an important exchange between Oliver North and his congressional interlocutors, provides a wonderful occasion to examine Sissela Bok's comments in "Lies for the Public Good." Finally, the poet Adrienne Rich offers her thoughts on lying and honor, from a woman's perspective.

Chapter Five explores war, violence, and peace. William V. O'Brien's article is a traditional defense of just-war theory, while Cheyney C. Ryan's is a discussion of the logic of pacifism, violence, and self-defense. Hannah Arendt's essay is important for its analysis of the necessary and sufficient conditions of violence and power, and the relationship between them. Sissela Bok examines Kant's classic work, *Perpetual Peace* (published in 1795), a prophetic and passionate plea for a change in international relations. Both Ryan and Arendt mention and discuss the views of Gandhi, whose meditations on a philosophy of nonviolence, included here as selection 27, have influenced many, including Martin Luther King Jr.

Chapter Six, on hunger, welfare, and homelessness, begins with the words of Jesus of Nazareth. Almost two thousand years old, they continue to provide moral guidance for millions today. Peter Singer and Garrett Hardin present contrasting positions, both from a utilitarian perspective, while Peter Marin's essay explores the social, geographic, and psychological terrain of homelessness. Margaret B. Wilkerson and Jewell Handy Gresham, meanwhile, take the discussion into the political realm, citing disturbing statistics on race and poverty and highlighting the special challenges that face black women in America.

Chapter Seven, on the ethics of race and power, features two essays from Cornel West's bestseller, *Race Matters*. In the first selection, West claims that to engage in a serious discussion of race in America we must begin not with the problems of black people but with the flaws of American society, as West puts it, "flaws rooted in historic inequalities and longstanding cultural stereotypes." The title of Shelby Steele's essay raises an important question: "I'm Black, You're White, Who's Innocent?" Richard Wasserstrom's essay explicitly links sexism with racism, in an analysis of both; Elizabeth V. Spelman engages critically with Wasserstrom in her essay, "The Erasure of Black Women." Lisa Newton's essay explores the phenomenon of "reverse discrimination" and provides an important counterpoint to the concluding essay by West, which is a defense of affirmative action.

Chapter Eight, on the ethics of sex and power, opens with the Vatican's "Declaration on Sexual Ethics." It is followed by Sandra Bartky's essay, which explores the implications of Michel Foucault's thought for a feminist analysis of femininity and power. Christina Sommers argues that much contemporary moral theory seems to be hostile to the family; she criticizes "radical feminists" for being out of touch with what women really want. John Stoltenberg, in "Rapist Ethics," offers reflections on the disquieting question of why men rape women. Finally, in "Sex and Violence," the noted feminist legal scholar Catharine MacKinnon broadens the question of violence against women to include not only rape but also sexual harassment, pornography, and battery.

Chapter Nine, on abortion, highlights an issue that has proven to be extremely divisive in America. It begins with excerpts from the highly controversial Supreme Court decision of 1973, *Roe v. Wade*, which is followed by John T. Noonan Jr.'s affirmation of the sacredness of human life. Judith Jarvis Thomson's classic defense of abortion and Mary Anne Warren's thoughtful critique provide a useful contrast to Stanley Hauerwas, who desires to shift the discussion from personhood to the Kingdom of God, in articulating a Christian response to abortion.

Chapter Ten, on the ethics of animals and the nonhuman environment, begins with Thoreau's aesthetic of walking. Susan Power Bratton appropriates the Bible in articulating a responsible approach to the environment. Joel Feinberg's essay "The Rights of Animals and Unborn Generations" is a classic, and Tom Regan, best known as a champion of animal rights, takes up the question of the possibility of an environmental ethic. Barry Commoner tries to answer those who insist we must choose between care of the environment and economic growth. Finally, Karen J. Warren's essay shows the linkage between the domination of women and the domination of nature; it also shows the promise of ecofeminism for healing relationships in both areas.

Here then are fifty-four selected readings, organized into ten topics, with additional readings suggested at the end of each chapter for those who wish to further examine these issues. Study questions appear at the end of each selection; these may be used by instructors to stimulate class discussion. Pedagogically, instructors may wish to begin with the discussion in Chapter One of ethical theory and then move topically through the remaining chapters, selecting those issues and articles that seem most helpful. (It is unlikely that *all* of the reading selections could be covered in one semester, impossible in a quarter system.) Alternatively, one may choose to traverse chapters, pursuing a more thematic approach: Themes that suggest themselves include power, truth, gender, race, class, caring, religion, and community.

It is my sincere hope that this text may prove to be useful to my colleagues and their students. I am solely responsible for its flaws and indebted to many for whatever virtues it may possess. I am grateful to Macmillan Publishing Company for permission to reprint a revised version of part 8 of my book *Philosophy: An Introduction to the Labor of Reason*, on ethics. I am particularly grateful to my student assistants Paige Wolfanger and Jim Donahue, who assisted with the permissions, study questions, and preparation of the manuscript. Judy Johnson, Darla Kennedy, Sherrie Wood, and Ami Johnston also helped prepare the manuscript, and have my gratitude. Special thanks are due to my readers, including Bob Long and Patrick Nnoromele, who provided valuable guidance and helpful suggestions. I would also like to thank the following reviewers: Duane H. Davis, *Xavier University*; Thomas L. Benson, *St. Andrews Presbyterian College*; Thomas J. Loughran, *University of Portland*; Al Denman, *Antioch College*; Jere Paul Surber, *University of Denver*; Jim Friel, *SUNY Farmingdale*; Douglas R. Anderson, *Pennsylvania State University*; Richard G. Henson, *Rutgers University*; and Merold Westphal, *Fordham University*. Their criticisms have helped to make this a better book. I also wish to thank my editor, Maggie Barbieri, who saw the need for this book from the start and worked hard to see that it was published. Finally, I wish to thank my wife, Suzanne, and my children, Jae and Vinny, for their love and encouragement.

Gary Percesepe

INTRODUCTION TO ETHICS

An Introduction to Ethical Theory

Whether we are aware of it or not, each of us has a set of values that we live by. Life forces us constantly to make choices: When we choose, we are expressing our values, rating things as better or worse, important or unimportant, right or wrong, good or bad, beautiful or ugly. Some choices seem trivial: It is of little lasting importance whether you choose to wear red rather than brown this morning. Other choices are monumental, affecting our entire life: Will we marry, become politically active, profess a religion, have children? Since choice is inevitable (to remain undecided is itself a choice), the question is not whether we shall have preferences, loyalties, standards, or ideals—the real question is, "Will our choices be consistent or inconsistent, life-enhancing or life-destroying?" Ignoring the role of value judgments in life leads to a lack of wholeness and perspective in our lives. If we are to choose well, we must take up the study of values, both personal and social.

This textbook is designed to help you do just that. Chapter one deals with ethical theory. It is designed to acquaint you with the leading contemporary ethical theories and the philosophers who espouse them. The subsequent nine chapters are devoted to contemporary issues in normative ethics.

Our treatment of ethics in this introduction is divided into the following sections: the nature of ethics, moral principles, ethical relativism, ethical subjectivism, morality and religion, consequentialist ethical theories, nonconsequentialist ethical theories, social contract theory, moral and legal rights, civil disobedience, virtue-based ethics, ethics and metaphysics, and feminist ethics.

THE NATURE OF ETHICS

Definitions of Ethics and Morality

Ethics may be defined as that branch of philosophy that seeks to analyze systematically moral concepts (such as "good," "bad," "right," "wrong," "duty," "responsibility," "rights," and so on) and to justify moral principles and theories. Ethics endeavors to establish principles of right conduct that can serve as a decision-making guide for individuals and groups. In its search for those values and virtues that are life-enhancing, ethics constructs and criticizes arguments that state valid moral principles (for example, "Kill no innocent human being," "Be a truth-teller," "Always keep promises") and the relationship between these principles (for example, are there occasions when saving a human life presents a valid reason for breaking a promise or telling a lie?).

Whereas the natural sciences are descriptive, concerned with empirical facts, ethics is prescriptive, concerned with normative values. As a normative-value-based discipline, ethics is more concerned with *what ought to be* than *what is*. Ethics is a practical, action-oriented discipline that seeks to effect change—from *the world as it is* to *the world as it ought to be*. Studying ethics requires a serious commitment to think honestly and soberly about how we ought to live our lives. Should we always tell the truth regardless of the consequences? Must we always keep our promises? Is it ever morally permissible to take a human life? What about abortion? Is there such a thing as a just war? No wonder Plato could say in the *Republic,* "We are discussing no small matter, but how we ought to live."

Ethics is frequently referred to as moral philosophy. *Moral,* derived from the Latin word *moralis,* and *ethics,* derived from the Greek word *ethikos,* both mean conduct or custom; the terms, while frequently used interchangeably, do have slightly different meanings. We shall follow the generally accepted practice of using *moral* to refer to principles or rules of conduct that govern (or ought to govern) an individual life or society and *ethics* to designate the systematic endeavor to understand moral concepts and to justify moral principles and theories.

Normative Ethics and Metaethics

Philosophers typically make a distinction between *normative ethics* and *metaethics.* Normative ethics constructs ethical theories based on valid moral principles; normative ethical statements are actual moral statements, such as "Apartheid is a glaring social evil," "Abortion is always wrong," "You should honor your promise to your friend." Thus normative ethics tries systematically to establish the general principles for determining right and wrong. By contrast, metaethics is a theoretical study centered on the analysis and meaning of the language used in ethical discourse and the logic used to justify ethical reasoning. Conceptual analysis and inquiry into the correct method for answering moral questions are two of the major concerns of metaethics. There is a close relationship between metaethics and normative ethics; by clarifying crucial moral concepts, metaethics makes normative ethics possible. This textbook is devoted primarily to normative ethics. Those interested in metaethics should consult with their instructor, and see the "For Further Study" selections at the end of this chapter.

MORAL PRINCIPLES

The central feature of normative ethics is the moral principle. Principles are general guidelines for right conduct; the principles in ethical theories are intentionally general so that they may apply to every situation we are likely to encounter. The Golden Rule of Jesus ("Do unto others as you would have others do unto you") is a good example of a principle with the desired level of generality; from it we can work out more specific principles and area rules for truth telling, giving, killing, honoring, and so on, which enable us to apply it as a useful guide to specific cases.

In his book *Ethics: Discovering Right and Wrong,* Louis Pojman observes that moral principles are practical guides to action possessing the following features:

1. Prescriptivity
2. Universalizability
3. Overridingness

4. Publicity
5. Practicability[1]

Prescriptivity

Prescriptivity refers to the action-guiding nature of morality. Generally, moral principles are posed as injunctions or imperatives (for example, "Do not kill," "Love your neighbor," "Do no unnecessary harm").

Universalizability

The Golden Rule exemplifies the notion of universalizability, for it prescribes that what is right for one person is right also for another, in a relatively similar situation. From the moral point of view, there are no privileged persons; we must acknowledge that other people's welfare is just as important as our own. Justice would seem to require that we avoid partiality, the arbitrary favoring of one person over another. Henry Sedgwick formalized the Principle of Justice in this way: "It cannot be right for A to treat B in a manner in which it would be wrong for B to treat A, merely on the ground that they are different individuals, and without there being any difference between the natures and circumstances of the two that can be stated as a reasonable ground for difference of treatment."[2] Universalizability, then, is at bottom the requirement of impartiality: when formulated as a principle, it functions as a rule that forbids us from treating one person differently from another when there is no good reason to do so. It is an important feature that helps us to explain what is wrong with racism and sexism.

Overridingness

Moral principles take precedence over other kinds of considerations, including aesthetic, prudential, and legal ones. Consider the example of the artist Paul Gauguin:

> Paul Gauguin may have been aesthetically justified in abandoning his family in order to devote his life to painting beautiful Pacific island pictures, but morally, or all things considered, he probably was not justified. It may be prudent to lie to save my reputation, but it probably is morally wrong to do so, in which case I should tell the truth. When the law becomes egregiously immoral, it may be my moral duty to exercise civil disobedience. There is a general moral duty to obey the law, because the law serves an overall moral purpose, and this overall purpose may give us reasons to obey laws that may not be moral or ideal; however, there may come a time when the injustice of a bad law is intolerable and hence calls for illegal but moral defiance (such as the antebellum laws in the South requiring citizens to return slaves to their owners). Religion is a special case, and the religious person may be morally justified in following a perceived command from God to break a normal moral rule. The Quakers' pacifist religious beliefs may cause them to renege on an obligation to fight for their country. Religious morality is morality, and ethics recognizes its legitimacy.[3]

Legal justice and moral justice do not necessarily coincide, since laws themselves may be morally unjust. Imagine a nation that had a law that unfairly discriminated against some of its inhabitants because of their gender. Suppose such a law denied that women have a legal right to life but guarantees that right to all males. In this case, legal justice would be done in this nation if this law is enforced. But it does not necessarily follow that moral justice is done. Legal justice depends not on whether there is a law in this nation but on the *overriding* question of whether the law recognizes and protects the moral rights of all of the nation's inhabitants.

Publicity

Since we use principles to play an action-guiding role in our lives, it would be self-defeating to keep them secret. To be maximally effective, moral principles must be made public.

Practicability

A moral system must be workable; its rules must not lay too heavy a burden on moral agents. Overly idealistic principles may produce overwhelming guilt, moral despair, and ineffective action. Most ethical systems take human limitations into consideration.

ETHICAL RELATIVISM

Ethnocentrism, the uncritical belief of a group or a people in the superiority of its own culture, is today rightly condemned as a form of prejudice similar to racism or sexism. It is wrong, for example, to suppose that all American preferences are based on some absolute rational standard, while the preferences of other cultures are not. The rejection of ethnocentrism coupled with an increased awareness of other cultures has led many to hold a version of *ethical relativism,* the theory that there are no universally valid principles, since all moral principles are valid relative to cultural or individual choice. It should be distinguished from *moral skepticism,* the view that there are no valid moral principles (or at least we cannot know that there are any), and from all forms of *moral absolutism* and *moral objectivism.* Moral absolutism is the theory that there is one true morality with a consistent set of moral principles that never conflict and never need to be overridden. Kant's approach to ethics is an example of this type of moral theory. Moral objectivism, defended by W. D. Ross and others, holds that moral principles have universal objective validity but admits that many of its principles may be overridden by other principles in certain cases.

John Ladd states the theory of ethical relativism in this way:

> Ethical relativism is the doctrine that the moral rightness and wrongness of an action varies from society to society and that there are no absolute universal moral standards binding on all men [*sic*] at all times. Accordingly, it holds that whether or not it is right for an individual to act in a certain way depends on or is relative to the society to which he belongs.

Cultural Relativism

The most common expression of ethical relativism is found in *cultural relativism,* an anthropological thesis that acknowledges the fact that moral beliefs and practices differ from society to society. From this descriptive observation (which is doubtlessly correct), the cultural relativist wishes to draw a normative conclusion that is very questionable: that there is no universal or objective truth in ethics, there are only various cultural codes. Furthermore, our moral code is but one of many, and thus has no special status.

At first glance, cultural relativism seems very plausible. It is only when we examine the structure of its argumentation that we discover problems. The strategy used by cultural relativists is to argue from facts about cultural diversity to a conclusion about the nature of morality. Is there reason to believe that all moral practices are as diverse as the cultural relativist claims? At least two objections may be made at the level of facts and the interpretations of those facts. In the discussion that follows, remember that the mere existence of objections to a position does not by itself establish grounds for not taking a position seriously; it merely establishes that there is a philosophical problem that must be addressed.

First, it seems that the facts really do not establish ethical relativism. Recent research in anthropology has documented universal prescriptions against incest, for example, and against wanton killing within one's social group. Even where particular moral practices and rules vary, universal areas of value related to human need have been identified: life and health, marriage and family, economic sufficiency.

Second, it would appear that the diversity thesis of cultural relativism fails to distinguish between diversity in particular moral practices and diversity in the principles implicit in such concerns. Practices are always guided by more general concerns. For example, how societies define property rights or how they punish wrongdoers may vary greatly, but they may still be equally concerned about both preserving property and punishing offenders, and equally concerned about having an ordered society.

Finally, we might ask the question "What would it be like if cultural relativism were true?" James Rachels[4] has identified three undesirable consequences of taking cultural relativism seriously.

1. *We could no longer say that the customs of other countries are morally inferior to our own.* While this at first may appear to be desirable and enlightened, suppose a country waged war on its neighbors for the purpose of taking slaves. Or suppose a nation set out systematically to eliminate all Jews? Cultural relativism would preclude us from saying that either of these practices was wrong. As Rachels points out, we would not even be able to say that a society tolerant of Jews is better than the anti–Semitic society, for that would imply some sort of transcultural standard of comparison, inadmissible in cultural relativism. Cultural relativism, then, would appear to have the undesirable consequence of forcing us to give up our convictions that these two practices are wrong.
2. *We could decide whether actions are right or wrong just by consulting the standards of our own society.* Cultural relativism is exceedingly conservative in that it endorses whatever moral views happen to be current within society. A simple test for determining what is right and wrong: an action is right if it is in accord with the code of one's society. But suppose a resident of South Africa wonders whether her society's practice of apartheid—rigid racial separation—is morally correct. All she has to do is ask whether this policy conforms to her society's moral code. If it does, than all is well. Clearly, this is a disturbing consequence: few of us actually believe that our society is free from flaws. Cul-

tural relativism, if true, would not only stop us from criticizing the moral codes of other countries, it would stop us from criticizing our own. This is profoundly undemocratic.

3. *The idea of progress is called into doubt.* Throughout most of Western history, the role of women has been narrowly defined. Women could not own property, vote, or hold political office; for the most part, they were not permitted to have paying jobs; and they were under the almost absolute control of their husbands. Much has changed in recent times, and most people think of this change as progress. But if cultural relativism is correct, can we legitimately think of this as progress? After all, progress means replacing an inferior way of doing things with an improved way. But by what standard do we judge the new way as better? If the old ways were in accordance with the social standards of their time, then cultural relativism would say it is a mistake to judge them by the standards of a different time. To say that we have made progress implies a judgment that present-day society is better, and that is precisely the sort of transcultural judgment that, according to this theory, is impermissible.

These three undesirable consequences have led many thinkers to reject cultural relativism as implausible. Faced with the choice of (a) accepting cultural relativism or (b) giving up the belief in moral progress, or the conviction that slavery and anti–Semitism are wrong, most people choose to reject (a) and embrace (b).

ETHICAL SUBJECTIVISM

Ethical subjectivism is the view that right and wrong are relative, not to the standards of culture but to the attitudes of each individual person. Our moral opinions are based on our feelings, and nothing more. A subjectivist would claim that anyone who declares something to be right or wrong is expressing nothing more than a personal preference or attitude. Whereas factual statements (for example, "The cat is on the mat") are either true or false, moral judgments (for example, "Abortion is wrong") are neither true nor false. They are matters of opinion, or statements expressing preference, not knowledge; hence, people can disagree about them without being mistaken.

The outstanding defender of ethical subjectivism is David Hume (1711–76), who thought that ethics could only be accounted for on the basis of sentiment (or feeling), not on reason. For example, reason may tell you that if you give someone poison to drink, he will die. But after your reason has told you this, it is necessary for your sentiments to come into play—how do you feel about this person dying, do you want it or not?—in order for you to decide what you will do. If you want the person to die, you give him the poison; if you do not want him to die, you do not poison him. All decisions are like this, in that they depend on our passions, not merely on our reason. As Hume put it, "Reason is, and ought to be, the slave of our passions."

Hume was led to this position by three persuasive arguments. In the first place, reason lacks the motivational power of moral judgments. Second, the origin of our moral judgments lies not in some action itself—for instance, the act of murder—but in the feeling of disapproval that we experience toward this action. Third, ethical judgments are concerned with what we *ought* to do, whereas reason informs us only of what *is* the case. Because there is a logical chasm between *is* and *ought,* we can never derive ought from is; hence, ethics cannot be a deduction from reason alone.

Some philosophers find problems with ethical subjectivism. If ethical subjectivism is correct, then as long as a person is truly reporting how she feels, could she ever be mistaken in her moral views? Wouldn't this theory, if correct, make us all infallible? Furthermore, on this theory it is difficult to see how it is possible for people to disagree. If I say that something is right, I am merely saying that I have certain positive feelings on the subject; and if you say it is wrong, you are only saying that you have different feelings. Since both of us are entitled to our feelings (which, being feelings, are neither true nor false), what then could we disagree about?

MORALITY AND RELIGION

Divine Command Theory

Does morality depend upon religion? Do moral standards depend upon God for their validity, or is there an autonomy of ethics, such that even God is subject to the moral order? Plato raised this issue in one of his dialogues when Socrates asked the pious Euthyphro, "Do the gods love holiness because it is holy, or is it holy because the gods love it?"

Divine command theory provides the most obvious way of connecting morality with religion. According to this theory, ethical principles are simply the commands of God. Since morality originates with God, it is argued, "moral rightness" simply means "willed by God," and "moral wrongness" means "against the will of God." According to this theory, a moral statement such as "adultery is morally wrong" means "adultery is forbidden by God."

Divine command theory faces two serious problems. First, it would seem to make the attribute of the goodness of God redundant. When we say "God is good," we normally think that we are attributing a property to God; but if "good" simply means "what God wills or commands," then we are not attributing any property to God. Our statement "God is good" would merely translate into "God does whatever God wills to do," and the statement "God commands us to do what is good" is merely the logical tautology "God commands us to do what God commands us to do."

A second problem, equally serious, is that divine command theory seems to make morality into something arbitrary. If nothing was wrong with adultery prior to God's command, then God could have no reason to forbid it; if something was wrong with it, then its wrongness is based on some standard of judgment independent of God's command. If God's fiat is the sole standard of right and wrong, it would seem logically possible for such acts as rape, murder, and incest to become morally praiseworthy if God suddenly decided to command us to do these things. If there is no independent measure or reason for moral action, this means that there are no constraints on what God can command; thus anything can become a moral duty and our moral duties can switch from moment to moment. In the Middle Ages, this position was known as *voluntarism.* For voluntarists like William Ockham (ca. 1285–?1349) moral law, as it is revealed, is binding simply because it is God's will. Had God chosen otherwise, the law then revealed would bind us with equal force. Thus religion is prior to ethics. This is precisely the sort of situation that is recorded in the Bible (Genesis 22), when God commands Abraham to kill his son Isaac. According to voluntarists, God's very request makes this otherwise odious act morally permissible.

A defender of divine command theory may object that the will of God has been revealed in the Bible, which forbids things like rape, incest, or murder. But how is one to know that God is not lying? (You may be tempted to respond, "But God would never command us to be liars!" But why not? If God did endorse lying, it would not be commanding us to do wrong, since God's command makes lying right!) The point is, if there is no independent criterion of right and wrong except whatever God happens to will, then how can we know that God isn't willing to make lying into a duty? In such a case, believers would have no reason to believe the Bible's pronouncements on these matters. Suppose we had two sets of commands, one from God and the other from Satan. How could we ever know which set was which? Could they be identical? What exactly would make them different? Once again, if there were no independent criterion by which to judge right and wrong, it is difficult to see how we could know which was which.

There have been numerous attempts to modify divine command theory in order to rescue it from these and other objections.[5] But many religious thinkers argue that it is perfectly permissible to accept the other horn of Euthyphro's dilemma—that God commands the Good because it is good. This position accepts the notion of autonomous ethics, and argues (1) that rightness and wrongness are not based simply on God's will and (2) that there are reasons for acting one way or another that can be known independently of God's will. The autonomy of ethics means that even God must obey the moral law, which exists independently, as do the laws of logic and mathematics. Just as God cannot make a four-sided triangle or commit suicide, so even God cannot make what is intrinsically good evil or make what is evil good. Since God's sovereignty and omnipotence (which the divine command theorist is intent on upholding at all costs) are not threatened by the fact that the laws of logic exist independently, why must it be threatened by the notion of an autonomous ethics?

Natural Law Theory

In the history of Christian thought, the dominant alternative to divine command theory has been *natural law theory.* The most influential natural law theorist was Saint Thomas Aquinas (1224–74), who argued that both natural and divine law are expressions of the one basic law established by God, namely, the eternal law. Hence, they must be compatible with one another. Aquinas held this position, sometimes called *intellectualism,* against the voluntarism of the defenders of the divine command theory.

According to Aquinas, moral judgments are "dictates of reason." In any circumstance, the best thing to do is whatever course of conduct has the best reasons on its side. The believer and the unbeliever are in exactly the same position when it comes to making moral judgments. Since both are endowed with powers of reason and conscience, both may make responsible decisions by heeding reason and remaining true to their conscience. God, who is by nature a perfectly rational being, has created the world as a rational order; men and women, in the image and likeness of God, are rational agents. Just as the realm of nature operates in conformity with natural laws discoverable by reason (such as gravity), so there are natural laws that govern how we ought to conduct ourselves. Since all people—not merely Christians—are rational creatures, even nonbelievers are able to function as rational beings. Their lack of faith prevents them from realizing that God is the ultimate source of the rational order in which they participate, yet their capacity for moral judgment is itself revelatory of God.

Drawing out the implications of natural law theory, one can see that both science and morality are autonomous enterprises. Science has its own questions, its own methods, and its own standards of truth. To the scientist intent on understanding and explaining the workings of the world, religious authority is nonbinding. (There was, of course, a time when the Roman Catholic Church claimed the right to judge science in the name of faith; Galileo was forced to recant his astronomical findings because they were deemed incompatible with Christian doctrine. This episode has been quite an embarrassment to the church, and recently, Pope John Paul II exonerated Galileo completely.)

Like science, morality is autonomous. It too has a set of questions, its own methods of answering them, and its own standards of truth. A person facing a moral decision must ask what reason and conscience demand of her, and religious considerations are often not decisive. Thus even a person who accepts the moral authority of the Bible has much to gain from the study of philosophical ethics. Arthur Holmes presents this view:

> [T]he Bible gives us a vast repertoire of ethical material in different literary forms and from different historical and cultural contexts. We have a succinct summary in the Ten Commandments, extended casuistry (case applications) in the Mosaic code, epigrammatic wisdom in Proverbs, reflections on life's meaning and values in Ecclesiastes, preaching of social justice in the prophets, down-to-earth homilies in the Gospels, and systematic statements in Paul's letters. . . . But Christians do not claim that the Bible is exhaustive, that it tells us everything we can know or can benefit ethically from knowing. It is silent about many things, including many moral problems that we face today—problems in bio and medical ethics, for example, problems about responsibility to unborn generations and about population control. . . . We are confronted at times with moral dilemmas in which every available option is morally undesirable and a decision cannot be avoided or postponed. Suppose that in Nazi-occupied Holland you are hiding Jews in your attic and the Gestapo comes searching for them. Do you lie to save innocent lives, or do you forfeit innocent lives to save lying? Whatever you do will violate some moral rule or another. How then do you choose, and to what extent are you blameworthy?[6]

Natural law theory thus leaves morality independent, in the sense that religious belief does not necessarily affect the calculation of what is morally best in a given situation. Believing souls and nonbelievers may approach moral questions in the same way, sharing common ground; if both conscientiously seek good reasons for their conduct, they may arrive at the same answers. They will part company only when theorizing about the nature of the moral choices they have made. Believing souls, of course, will regard the results of their moral inquiry as revealing God's will—the voice of God is heard in the call of conscience. Unbelievers, according to Aquinas, do not have this advantage; nevertheless, through the grace of God, they may make good moral choices. Thus, even though the believer and unbeliever may disagree about religion, natural law theory enables them to inhabit the same moral universe.

CONSEQUENTIALIST ETHICAL THEORIES

Earlier, normative ethics was characterized as the construction of ethical theories based on valid moral principles. But what are these valid principles, and how have philosophers arrived at them? One way to think about moral principles is to imagine a situation in which everyone would agree that something wrong has been done. For example, imagine that Suzanne has a favorite tennis racket. She enjoys using it and on occasion has lent it out to her friends. Jane likes the tennis racket too; she could afford to buy one but then she wouldn't have enough money to buy something she really wants but does not need. One day when Suzanne is out of town, Jane steals the tennis racket. As a result, Suzanne experiences some unhappiness. Whenever she thinks about the missing racket, she is upset and frustrated.

Or, imagine a country that forbids black people from being in public after six o'clock. Robert, who is black, could get a job and support his family if the law did not restrict his movements solely because he is black. As it is, he is unable to find work, and he and his family suffer because of it.[7]

In both of these examples—stealing and racial injustice—what stands out is that some action leads to bad consequences. Generalizing, these philosophers argue that what is common to all right actions is that they lead to good results, and what is common to all wrong actions is that they lead to bad results. The frustration and disappointment that Suzanne and Robert experience are negative consequences—these negative consequences are what make stealing and racial injustice wrong.

Philosophers who take this view are called *consequentialists,* since they stress the consequences or results of actions. Consequentialist theories are sometimes called *teleological* theories.[8] There are many varieties of consequentialist theories in ethics. What they all have in common is that they regard a wrong action as something that leads to bad consequences and a good action as something that leads to good consequences. Where such theories differ, among other things, is in what counts as "good," and in the scope of consequences that must be considered—that is to say, consequences for whom?

Two consequentialist theories are especially important: *ethical egoism* and *utilitarianism.* Whereas egoism asks me to consider the consequences of my actions for one person only (namely, myself), utilitarianism asks me to consider the consequences of my actions for everyone concerned, myself included.

Psychological Egoism

Ethical egoism, which will be discussed in the following section, should be distinguished from *psychological egoism,* with which it is sometimes confused. Psychological egoism is a theory that states that everyone as a matter of fact always performs that act which they perceive to be in their own best interest. Whereas psychological egoism is a theory of human nature concerned with how people *do* behave, ethical egoism is a normative theory about how we *ought* to behave. In effect, psychological egoism defines the possibility of non-selfish behavior out of existence, since it reinterprets every piece of behavior as rooted in selfishness. There is good reason to believe that psychological egoism is counterfactual, and therefore wrong.

Ethical Egoism

Ethical egoism is a theory based on an ultimate principle of self-interest: Everyone ought to serve his or her own self-interest. According to this theory, the only real duty we have in life is to promote our own self-interest; this we ought to pursue, even if it conflicts with the interests of others or causes harm to others.

The practical implications of ethical egoism are startling. For instance, if this theory is correct, then we have no moral obligation to help others in need unless there is some benefit to be gained for us. But why should we be so exclusively preoccupied with good consequences for ourselves? Isn't this showing extreme partiality to one person (myself)? Is such partiality morally justifiable in a world awash in need?

In criticizing ethical egoism we do not need to go all the way over to *altruism*—the view that asks us to engage in only those actions that bring about good consequences for everyone except ourselves. Rather than be narrowly focused on our own welfare, to the exclusion of others (egoism), or on others, to the exclusion of ourselves (altruism), why shouldn't we be concerned with the welfare of all people? Thoughts like these lead naturally into the most popular consequentialist theory, *utilitarianism.*

Utilitarianism

Utilitarianism, first proposed by David Hume but worked out more systematically by Jeremy Bentham (1748–1832) and John Stuart Mill (1806–73), is based upon an ultimate moral principle known as the Principle of Utility. This principle has been expressed in a variety of ways. Here is one common formulation:

> *Everyone ought to act so as to bring about the greatest possible balance of intrinsic good over intrinsic evil for everyone concerned.*

Utilitarians, however, often do not agree on what is intrinsically good and evil. Some, like Bentham, defend *ethical hedonism* (from the Greek *hedone,* meaning pleasure), the view that pleasure and pleasure alone is intrinsically good (or good in itself), whereas pain—the absence of pleasure—is intrinsically evil. Bentham even devised a scheme for measuring pleasure and pain that he called the "hedonic calculus." According to this system, the value of any experience could be obtained by adding up the amounts of pleasure and pain for seven aspects of the experience: its intensity, duration, certainty, nearness, fruitfulness, purity, and extent.

Bentham's version of utilitarianism was criticized by John Stuart Mill as being too simplistic. It was sometimes referred to as the "pig philosophy," since a pig enjoying its life would constitute a higher moral state than a slightly dissatisfied Socrates! Mill made a distinction between happiness and mere sensual pleasure. His version of utilitarianism, eudaimonistic utilitarianism (from the Greek word for "happiness"), defines happiness in terms of higher-order pleasures such as intellectual, aesthetic, and social enjoyments. Here is how Mill stated his version of the Principle of Utility in his *Utilitarianism* (1861): "According to the Greatest Happiness Principle . . . the ultimate end, with reference to and for the sake of which all other things are desirable (whether we are considering our good or that of other people), is an existence exempt as far as possible from pain, and as rich as possible in enjoyments." Three separate ideas may be identified in Mill's formulation:

1. Actions are to be judged as right or wrong solely by virtue of their consequences.
2. When assessing consequences, the only thing that matters is the amount of happiness or unhappiness that is caused.
3. Each person's happiness is equally important; no one's happiness is to be counted as more important than anyone else's. (This feature separates utilitarianism from egoism and altruism, which both arbitrarily privilege the happiness of the self (egoism) or the other (altruism), thus violating the notion of universalizability mentioned earlier as essential to valid moral principles.)

In its own way, this is a very radical and modern thesis; gone are all references to divine moral commands or some divinely implanted code of natural law imprinted on the soul. The utilitarians were secular social reformers concerned with promoting happiness and minimizing suffering in *this* world.

Utilitarians also disagree about how the Principle of Utility should be applied to individual actions. It is important in this regard to make a distinction between *act utilitarianism* and *rule utilitarianism.* Act utilitarianism is the view that the Principle of Utility should be applied to *individual actions.* Rule utilitarianism states that the Principle of Utility should be applied mainly to *rules of action.* The act utilitarian argues that whenever people must decide what to do, they ought to perform that act bringing about the greatest possible balance of intrinsic good over intrinsic evil. The rule utilitarian argues something quite different: People ought to do whatever is required by justified moral rules. These are rules that would lead to the best possible consequences, all things considered, if everyone were to abide by them. Under rule utilitarianism, a person who chooses to do what a moral rule requires might perform an act that in that particular situation might not lead to the best possible circumstances. Thus act and rule utilitarians can reach opposing moral judgments about the same action.

It appears that act utilitarianism, consistently followed, could lead to a situation where an obviously wrong action might be considered right. The rightness or wrongness of an act, remember, depends solely on whether or not the net consequences of the act are at least as good as the consequences that would have resulted if another act had been done. Richard Brandt criticizes act utilitarianism on precisely this point:

> It implies that if you have employed a boy to mow your lawn and he has finished the job and asks for his pay, you should pay him what you promised only if you cannot find a better use for your money. It implies that when you bring home your monthly paycheck you should use it to support your family and yourself only if it cannot be used more effectively to supply the needs of others. It implies that if your father is ill and has no prospect of good in his life, and maintaining him is a drain on the energy and enjoyment

> of others, then, if you can end his life without provoking any public scandal or setting a bad example, it is your positive duty to take matters into your own hands and bring his life to a close.[9]

One of the most important objections to rule utilitarianism turns on considerations about justice. It appears that rule utilitarianism could justify rules that would be manifestly unjust. Suppose, says Tom Regan, there were a rule that discriminated against persons because of the color of their skin:

> Imagine this rule (R): "No one with black skin will be permitted in public after six o'clock." If we think about R, its unfairness jumps out at us. It is unjust to discriminate against people simply on the basis of skin color. However, although it is clear that R would be unjust, might not R conceivably be justified by appealing to the Principle of Utility? Certainly it seems possible that everyone's acting according to R might bring about the greatest possible balance of intrinsic good over intrinsic evil. True, black people are not likely to benefit from everyone's acting according to R. Nevertheless, their loss might be more than outweighed by non-blacks' gains, especially if blacks are a small minority. Thus, if rule-utilitarianism could be used to justify flagrantly unjust behavior, it is not a satisfactory theory.[10]

NONCONSEQUENTIALIST ETHICAL THEORIES

Nonconsequentialism is a name frequently associated with normative ethical theories that are not forms of consequentialism. Hence, any theory holding that right and wrong are *not* determined solely by the relative balance of intrinsic good over intrinsic evil commonly is called nonconsequentialist. Some theories answering this description are also called *deontological* theories, from the Greek *deon,* meaning "duty."

Nonconsequentialist theories may be either extreme or moderate. An extreme nonconsequentialist theory holds that the intrinsic good and evil of consequences are totally irrelevant to determining what is morally right or wrong. A moderate nonconsequentialist theory holds that the intrinsic good and evil of consequences are relevant to determining what is morally right and wrong, but they are not the only things that are relevant and may not be of greatest importance in some cases.

Kant's Categorical Imperative: The Formula of Universal Law

The great German philosopher Immanuel Kant (1724–1804) called his ultimate moral principle the *categorical imperative.* In his *Fundamental Principles of the Metaphysics of Morals* (1785) Kant expressed this principle in two different formulations. The first he called the *Formula of Universal Law.* Before we state it, let us define two Kantian terms: *maxim* and *law.* By *maxim,* Kant means a general rule by which the agent intends to act; by *law,* he means an objective principle that passes the test of universalizability:

> *Act only on that maxim whereby thou canst at the same time will that it should become a universal law.*

Kant is specifying a three-step procedure here:

1. When you are thinking about performing a particular action, you are required to ask yourself what rule you could be following if you were to do that action. (This rule will be the "maxim" of the act.)
2. Next, you are to ask whether you are willing for that rule to be followed by everyone all of the time (that is, are you willing to universalize your maxim).
3. If you are willing for everyone to follow the rule, then the act you're contemplating is permissible; if not, then the maxim must be rejected as self-defeated, and the act is morally impermissible.

By way of example, think back to Suzanne and her tennis racket. Suppose one day Suzanne's friend comes to her with a broken racket and asks to borrow Suzanne's. If Suzanne refuses, then she would be following this rule: "Don't lend out a tennis racket to a person who has broken his tennis racket." But would Suzanne wish to follow this rule all of the time? What if Suzanne's tennis racket broke on the morning of an important match and she desperately needed to borrow one? Would Suzanne want her neighbor to adopt the policy of not lending out tennis rackets? No, she wouldn't. In refusing her friend's request, Suzanne could not, in Kant's terms, "will that the maxim of her act be made into universal law." Therefore, Suzanne should not refuse her friend's request.

In addition to the case of refraining from helping others, Kant applies his Formula of Universal Law to three test cases: making a lying promise, suicide, and neglecting one's talent. Unsurprisingly, lying promises, suicide, and neglecting one's talent are found to be morally impermissible because they are based on defective (nonuniversalizable) maxims.

Kant's Formula of the End in Itself

Kant states the *Formula of the End in Itself* as follows:

> *Act in such a way that you always treat humanity, whether in your own person or in the person of any other, never simply as a means but always at the same time as an end.*

Let us be clear about what Kant is *not* saying. He is not saying that there is anything wrong about using someone as a means. If you order a meal in a restaurant, you are using the cook and server as means to accomplish your end (eating); the cook and server in turn uses you as a means to accomplish their ends (earning a living). In this case each party has consented to his or her part in the transaction. To use someone as a *mere* means, however, is to involve them in a scheme of action *to which they could not in principle give consent.*

One very obvious way to use a person as a mere means is by deceiving them. For example, if we get someone involved in a business scheme or criminal activity on false pretenses, or by giving him or her a misleading or incomplete account of what is going on (or if we construct a false chronology of events), we are involving that person in something to which he or she in principle cannot give consent, since the scheme requires that the person be kept in the dark.

> If a rich or powerful person threatens a debtor with bankruptcy unless he or she joins in some scheme, then the creditor's intention is to coerce; and the debtor, if coerced, cannot consent to his or her part in the creditor's scheme. If a moneylender in an Indian village threatens not to renew a vital loan unless he is given the debtor's land, then he uses the debtor as a mere means. He coerces the debtor, who cannot truly consent to this "offer he cannot refuse."[11]

Are there problems and limitations to Kant's approach to ethics? Many philosophers have thought so. Particularly troublesome is Kant's insistence that moral rules are exceptionless. For example, Kant believed that the rule against lying was absolute; that is, lying under *any* circumstances is "the obliteration of one's dignity as a human being." This is an extremely strong statement. What led Kant to this view, as we have seen, is his Formula of Universal Law. We could never will that lying be made a universal law, since people would quickly learn that they could not rely on what other people said; thus, the lies would not be believed. There is certainly a compelling logic to this argument; in order for a lie to be successful, people must believe that others are telling the truth. Therefore, the success of a lie depends upon there *not* being a "universal law" permitting it.

But couldn't we construct a successful counterexample to Kant's treatment of "truth telling" as an absolute duty? Suppose a man is fleeing from a murderer and tells you he is going home to hide. The murderer then comes to you and asks where the man went. You have reason to believe that if you tell the truth, the murderer will find his victim and kill him. Should you tell the truth or lie? (Life, unfortunately, is filled with real-life examples of this kind. During World War II, Dutch fishing boats smuggling Jewish refugees to safety would frequently be stopped by Nazi patrol boats. The Nazi captain would call out, asking who was on board the Dutch ship; the fisherman would lie and be allowed to pass. In these cases the fishermen had only two alternatives: to lie or to allow their passengers—and possibly themselves—to be taken and shot. No third alternative, such as remaining silent, or outrunning the Nazis, existed.)

In fact, Kant has an answer to our counterexample of "The Inquiring Murderer," for the example originally is his! In an essay entitled "On a Supposed Right to Lie from Altruistic Motives," Kant has this to say:

> After you have honestly answered the murderer's question as to whether his intended victim is at home, it may be that he has slipped out so that he does not come in the way of the murderer, and thus that the murder may not be committed. But if you had lied and said he was not at home when he had really gone out without your knowing it, and if the murderer had then met him as he went away and murdered him, you might justly be accused as the cause of his death. For if you had told the truth as far as you knew it, perhaps the murderer might have been apprehended by the neighbors while he searched the house and thus the deed might have been prevented. Therefore, whoever tells a lie, however well intentioned he might be, must answer for the consequences, however unforeseeable they were, and pay the penalty for them. . . .
>
> To be truthful, (honest) in all deliberations, therefore, is a sacred and absolutely commanding decree of reason, limited by no expediency.

Some philosophers find Kant's argument unconvincing. Kant argues that since we can never know what the consequences of our actions will be—the results of lying might be unexpectedly bad, perhaps worse than if we had told the truth—the best policy is to avoid the known evil of lying, and let the consequences come as they may. Even if the consequences are bad, they will not be our fault, for we will have done our moral duty.

The problems with Kant's argument, stated here by James Rachels, seem obvious:

> In the first place, the argument depends upon an unreasonably pessimistic view of what we can know. Sometimes we can be quite confident of what the consequences of our action will be, and justifiably so; in which case, we need not hesitate because of uncertainty. Moreover . . . Kant seems to assume that although we would be morally responsible for any bad consequences of lying, we would *not* be similarly responsible for any bad consequences of telling the truth. Suppose, as a result of our telling the truth, the murderer found his victim and killed him. Kant seems to assume that we would be blameless. But can we escape blame so easily? After all, we aided the murderer. This argument, then . . . is not very convincing.[12]

SOCIAL CONTRACT THEORY

Social contract theory, advocated by Thomas Hobbes (1588–1679), John Locke (1632–1704), and Jean-Jacques Rousseau (1712–78), attempts to explain the purpose of the state as well as the nature of morality. Contemporary American contractarians who have focused on the political implications of the theory include John Rawls and Robert Nozick.

Social contract theory offers a different approach to morality than any of the other approaches mentioned thus far. The basic idea is that moral rules are rules that human beings must accept if they are to live peaceably together in society. Since humans are social animals, bound to live together rather than in isolation from one another, there must be general agreement on the rules of social living; if there is no general agreement, the result is chaos and anarchy, a condition that Hobbes, Locke, and Rousseau called the *state of nature.*

The foremost British philosopher of the seventeenth century, Hobbes described how dreadful the state of nature would be in this classic passage from the *Leviathan:*

> [There would be] no place for industry, because the fruit thereof is uncertain: and consequently, no navigation, nor use of the commodities that may be imported by sea; no commodious building; no instruments of moving, such things as require much force; no knowledge of the face of the earth; no account of time; no arts; no letters; no society; and which is worst of all, continual fear, and danger of violent death; and the life of man solitary, poor, nasty, brutish, and short.[13]

To picture what life would be like in the state of nature that Hobbes depicts, imagine waking up tomorrow to a nation whose government had collapsed completely, so that there was no law, no police, no courts, and no justice. Might makes right. People would begin to hoard food and other commodities essential to life. Everyone, of necessity, would be thrown into a continual war of one against all. There would be no time for anything besides the daily war to seize what one needed for life, defending it from others. We would all be at each other's throats, armed, suspicious, afraid, lawless, and miserable. To escape the state of nature, then, people must agree to give up some of their independence, trading it for safety. Such an agreement, to which every citizen is a party, is called the social contract.

Having established that government is needed, what about morality? James Rachels states the social contract conception of morality: "Morality consists in the set of rules, governing how people are to treat one another, that rational people will agree to accept, for their mutual benefit, on the condition that others will follow those rules as well."[14] On this view, morally binding rules are those that are necessary for social living. We agree to follow these rules because it is in our self-interest to do so. We agree to obey the rules only on condition that others agree as well. The state sees to it that these laws are enforced, punishing those who break them.

Like all ethical theories, social contract theory is not without its problems. One major problem has to do with the issue of civil disobedience. Social contract theory requires us to obey the law. But what if the law is unjust? Are we ever justified in breaking or defying the law? And what if the morally binding rules adopted by government have been set up to arbitrarily benefit one race or class or gender? In this case, when "justice" is administered by government, whose interests are served? Whose justice, whose sense of rationality should prevail?

A second problem is that the theory seems to rest on a historical fiction. Hobbes and Rousseau, for instance, both ask us to believe that people once lived in isolation from one another; finding this situation unacceptable, they eventually bonded together, agreeing to follow rules for the good of all. But there is no evidence that any of this actually happened. Was this agreement consummated in a mythical prehistory? If so, how have we come to know of it? And even if the "contract" was agreed to by our ancestors long ago, why would it be binding on us? If it is not a real historical agreement, can it be an "implicit contract," renewed in each new generation? Is it a "useful fiction" that still provides a framework for understanding morality? (John Rawls, in a selection that follows, argues that this indeed is the case.)

A third problem has to do with the implications of the theory for beings who are not able to participate in the contract, although they are affected by it. Nonhuman animals lack the capacity to enter into agreements with us; nevertheless, isn't it wrong to torture animals? Must animals be excluded from moral consideration? Hobbes thought so, as did his contemporary René Descartes. But if animals can be excluded because they can't enter into agreements, can't mentally retarded humans be excluded for the same reason? From a moral point of view, this is undesirable; an ethical theory that cannot extend moral considerations to these two important classes is seriously flawed. In recent years philosophers have attempted to extend the moral point of view to include animals and the nonhuman environment. Notable in this regard are Peter Singer's pathbreaking book, *Animal Liberation: New Ethics for Our Treatment of Animals,* and Tom Regan's *Case for Animal Rights.*

MORAL AND LEGAL RIGHTS

At this point it might be helpful to clarify what philosophers mean when they speak of *rights.* Not surprisingly, the concept of rights has been analyzed differently by philosophers from different traditions. Some analyses of rights center on an individual's entitlements to be treated in a certain way (or the right not to be treated in a certain way, that is, the right to not be harmed). Other analyses have focused on rights as valid claims that an individual can make (or have made on her behalf), to have one's interests and well-being taken into account.

As Tom Regan points out, what is common to all of these analyses is that a right involves the idea of a justified constraint upon how others may act.

> If Beth has a right to x, then others are constrained not to interfere with her pursuit or possession of x, at least so long as her pursuit or possession of x does not come into conflict with the rights of others. If it does, Beth may be exceeding her rights, and a serious moral question would arise. But aside from cases of exceeding one's rights and, as may sometimes be the case, of forfeiting them, the possession of a right by one individual places a justified limit on how others may treat the person possessing the right.[15]

Basic moral rights are those that are not dependent upon any other moral principle. Thomas Jefferson, in the Declaration of Independence, identified three basic moral rights possessed by all people and went on to say that these three rights were inalienable, meaning they could not be transferred to another or taken away by another individual or by the government. The three rights he identified were the rights to life, liberty, and the pursuit of happiness. According to our treatment of rights, then, the right of life is basic—it places a justified constraint on the actions of others, such that no one can justifiably take the life of another.

We must make an important distinction between moral rights and legal rights, however. Moral rights are universal, whereas legal rights needn't be. Legal rights are determined by the legislative bodies of particular nations, and may vary from place to place. Eighteen-year-old citizens have a legal right to vote in the United States, but this is not the case in every nation. If, however, a person has a basic moral right to life, then that right obtains even if the state does not recognize it as a legal right.

Certainly, there have been laws, even in the United States, that have been unjust; think of the laws regulating and enforcing slavery in America or apartheid in South Africa. Legal justice and moral justice are not the same, and may not always coincide. For example, if it is the law of the land that persons of color cannot be out on the streets after ten o'clock at night, then legal justice is accomplished if such a law is enforced by police. But it in no way follows that moral justice has been done. That would depend on whether or not the law recognized and protected the basic moral rights of its citizens. If the law does this, then it is both legally and morally just; if it fails to do this, then it may be morally unjust even though it is legally just. Hence, *the law itself may be the object of moral scrutiny.* (In this regard, see Catharine MacKinnon's essay in chapter eight, "Sex and Violence," as well as the selections in chapter nine, on abortion.) This leads to the question of civil disobedience, which is discussed in the next section.

Of course, there is tremendous controversy in the area of rights. Must rights be restricted to humans, or are they open to other beings who exhibit purposeful behavior, have intentions, are capable of being harmed—for example, animals? Does the right to life extend to unborn humans? That is, do human fetuses have basic moral rights, or are these rights restricted to those who have been born? And is it possible to forfeit one's right to life? If, for example, I murder another human being, have I forfeited my right to life? If so, is the state justified in taking my life, in what is termed "capital punishment"? If I kill for my country in a war, do I not terminate someone's right to life? Can such an act ever be justified? If it could somehow be determined that life begins at conception, would abortion be a capital crime? If I assist a person who wishes to end his or her life because of a terminal disease, am I guilty of murder? Who gets to decide such matters? These are questions that will be taken up at some length in the remaining chapters of this book. Ronald Dworkin's article in chapter one, "Taking Rights Seriously," will lay the groundwork for considering these and other questions about rights.

CIVIL DISOBEDIENCE

No person can be said to be perfectly just. The same can be said of any institution or society. For this reason, as we have said, occasions arise where moral justice and legal justice do not coincide. Recall the institution of slavery in the United States. In the Dred Scott decision of 1857, the Supreme Court of the United States ruled that even in a free state a slave did not have the rights of a citizen but was to be treated as the property of his or her owner. Laws were enacted that made it illegal to give aid to a runaway slave; citizens who wished to be law-abiding were obligated to return runaway slaves to their masters. Ask yourself this question: Who were the heroes of this period, the people who returned runaway slaves or the people who worked with the Underground Railroad helping slaves to escape to freedom? Posing the question should give you some insight into the question of civil disobedience. What would you have done?

Civil disobedience may be defined as nonviolent resistance to the law aimed at changing laws deemed unjust. The folks who worked on the Underground Railroad did so secretly.[16] But often civil disobedience takes the form of public disobedience to the law. In the 1960s, public acts of civil disobedience were common in America, prompted both by segregation laws and by an unpopular war in Vietnam. In the 1980s and 1990s, "Operation Rescue" protesters have engaged in this tactic in an attempt to gain the support of lawmakers to outlaw abortion.

Although people who engage in civil disobedience break particular laws because they think them unjust, this does not mean that they do not believe in the rule of law. Martin Luther King Jr. was arrested on numerous occasions for breaking segregation laws that he deemed unjust. He was frequently asked, "How can you advocate breaking some laws and obeying others?" King responded by making a distinction between a just law and an unjust law. He made it clear that he believed he had a moral obligation to obey just laws and a moral obligation to disobey unjust laws. One who breaks an unjust law, he said, must do so openly, lovingly, and with a willingness to accept the penalty. *Isn't this the highest respect for law?* In King's words, "I submit that an individual who breaks a law that conscience tells him is unjust, and who willingly accepts the penalty of imprisonment in order to arouse the conscience of the community over its injustice, is in reality expressing the highest respect for law."

Civil disobedience is a highly controversial issue and has been repeatedly criticized for a wide variety of reasons. Let us consider a few of the most important objections:

1. Many object that civil disobedience is inappropriate behavior in a democracy. We should all try to "work within the system." As long as we have the right to make our views known to our elected officials, there is no need for civil disobedience. Why resort to breaking the law when we have the freedom to change the law?
2. Innocent people are harmed or inconvenienced by civil disobedience. During the 1960s, service was often disrupted at "white" restaurants that refused to recognize or wait on black customers. Why should someone who merely wishes to order a sandwich and coffee be penalized by demonstrators who disrupt service at a lunch counter? Why should I be late for an important job interview because demonstrators are blocking the street protesting some law?
3. Civil disobedience can lead to anarchy. When people publicly break the law in large numbers, there is an inevitable breakdown in respect for the law, even if protestors are willing to be punished.

Proponents of civil disobedience respond to the first objection by agreeing that traditional means of changing the law must first be tried. But there are occasions when laws are fundamentally unjust and traditional means do not work. Sometimes elected representatives and the courts remain unresponsive to peaceful petitioning, and voters cannot be convinced to replace these officials by "normal means." This being the case, something must be done to call attention to the injustice of the law, and civil disobedience is required.

Advocates point out that civil disobedience is a form of moral persuasion, not an act of coercion. When lawmakers and citizens see that decent, otherwise law-abiding members of their community are willing to be jailed for their convictions, *attention shifts from the law itself to the moral principle behind the law.* During the height of the civil rights debate in this country, millions of television viewers were shocked to see students, ministers, and ordinary working people dragged off to jail for the "crime" of refusing to sit in the back of a bus or the "crime" of sitting at a "white" lunch counter. Outraged Americans witnessed the police turning powerful water hoses and fierce dogs on men, women, and children, while elected officials looked on with approval and even merriment. In this way, public attitudes toward segregation laws were changed, and the way cleared for the passage of important civil rights legislation.

Concerning the second objection, civil disobedience advocates argue that some social disruption is bound to occur. But when the goal is the abolition of a fundamentally unjust social arrangement (for example, segregation or apartheid), such nonviolent disruption is morally permissible. Perhaps the innocent people whose lunch has been disturbed at the lunch counter will reflect on the ways that the existing law benefits them to the exclusion of others who are made to suffer unjustly.

What about the third objection—the threat of anarchy? Most defenders of civil disobedience deny that this is a real threat. If acts of civil disobedience are restricted to cases of fundamental injustice, and if protestors show their respect for the law by consenting peacefully to their imprisonment, anarchy will not result.

In 1849 Henry David Thoreau was arrested for refusing to pay a poll tax. His refusal was his way of protesting slavery and the Mexican War. In his famous essay "On the Duty of Civil Disobedience," Thoreau contends that if enough people follow his lead, slavery and the war would end. The government could not continue indefinitely putting decent citizens in prison. Thoreau put it this way: "Under a government which imprisons any unjustly, the true place for a just man is also a prison." It was rumored that when Thoreau was imprisoned, his friend Ralph Waldo Emerson had looked in through a prison window and asked, "Henry, what are you doing in there?" Thoreau is rumored to have responded, "The question is, what are you doing out there?"

Thoreau's question was very much on Martin Luther King's mind on April 16, 1963. As he sat in a Birmingham, Alabama, jail, King was troubled by a public statement directed to him by a group of eight Birmingham clergymen. That statement, in part, reads as follows:

> [W]e are now confronted by a series of demonstrations by some of our Negro citizens, directed and led in part by outsiders. We recognize the natural impatience of people who feel that their hopes are slow in being realized. But we are convinced that these demonstrations are unwise and untimely.
>
> We . . . strongly urge our own Negro community to withdraw support from these demonstrations, and to unite in working peacefully for a better Birmingham. When rights are consistently denied, a cause should be pressed in the courts and in negotiations among local leaders, and not in the street. We appeal to both our white and Negro citizenry to observe the principles of law and order and common sense.

King's response to the eight clergymen, "Letter from a Birmingham Jail," is a classic defense of civil disobedience and an eloquent plea for social justice in America. King begins by explaining why he is in Birmingham. Speaking with the courage and conviction of a moral prophet, King explains, "I am in Birmingham because injustice is here." He then sets forth his theory of civil disobedience, making a distinction between just and unjust laws and affirming his respect for the rule of law. He reminds his correspondents of some memorable cases of civil disobedience in the Bible and expresses his regret that the Christian churches of the South, with a few notable exceptions, have not identified themselves with the call of justice. He concludes by expressing his desire to meet with his correspondents as fellow Christians.

We sense the importance of King's legacy and the widespread acceptance of his views on civil disobedience when we ask this question: Who today recalls the identity of those eight clergymen? History, in its inexorable march forward, has submerged their memory while elevating that of King.

Nevertheless, we do well to ask other questions. Are King's criteria for distinguishing between just and unjust laws valid? What are the criteria for acts of civil disobedience? Where do we draw the line between what is acceptable and what is unacceptable? Must we be utilitarian in deciding the good we hope to accomplish by our actions outweighs the negative consequences of our actions? Finally, how can we be sure that our sense of what is an unjust law is not just our own sense of bigotry?

VIRTUE-BASED ETHICS

Whereas most ethical theories have been either duty-based (nonconsequentialism) or action-based (utilitarian theories), there is a third option that goes back to Aristotle and that received the support of the early Christian church. Virtue-based ethical systems are sometimes called *aretaic ethics* (from the Greek *arete,* meaning "excellence" or "virtue"). Whereas consequentialist and nonconsequentialist theories emphasize *doing* (following moral rules), virtue ethics emphasizes *being*—it is the character of a person that lies at the heart of this approach to ethics. Whereas action-based and duty-based ethics ask "What should I do?", virtue-based ethics asks, "What sort of person should I become?" Aretaic ethics seeks to produce, very simply, good people. The focus is on the proper goal of life: living well and achieving moral excellence. According to virtue ethics, merely doing right is not enough; it is also important to have the right dispositions, motivations, and emotions when being good and doing right. We will enjoy doing good because we *are* good.

According to Aristotle, humans are social beings, made for living in community. Virtues are simply those excellences of character that enable individuals to live well in community. Humanity has an essence or function. Just as the function of a doctor is to cure the sick and the function of a knife is to cut, the function of humans is to use reason in pursuit of the good life. In order to achieve a state of well-being, or happiness (from the Greek *eudaimonia*), proper social institutions are necessary. Because moral persons cannot exist apart from a political setting, Aristotle considered ethics to be a branch of politics. The virtues, then, are the political and moral characteristics necessary for people to attain happiness.

According to Aristotle, there is general agreement that the end toward which all human acts are directed is happiness. Happiness is the highest human good, he argues, because it is sought for its own sake and not for the sake of anything else. The "good" of humans is to engage in "activity of the soul which is in accordance with virtue and which follows a rational principle."

Virtues may be classified into two types: moral and intellectual. Generally speaking, the intellectual virtues (such as rationality, skill in mathematics, or philosophy) may be taught directly, while the moral virtues (courage, honesty, generosity, and so on) must be lived in order to be learned. The morally virtuous life consists of living in moderation, according to what Aristotle calls the Golden Mean. By this Aristotle means that the virtues lie midway between excess and deficiency. For example, when facing danger, a person can act with excess, that is, show too much fear; this is cowardice. Or one can act deficiently by showing too little fear; this is foolhardiness. Courage (showing the right amount of fear) lies midway between cowardice and foolhardiness.

Unfortunately, Aristotle was an elitist who believed that not everyone was capable of achieving the virtues; some people (for instance, the one hundred thousand slaves in Athens who enabled Aristotle to have the leisure to formulate his ethical theories, not to mention women, whom he conveniently excluded from his account!) were seemingly incapable of developing moral dispositions. Furthermore, he believed that the moral virtues were a necessary but not sufficient condition of happiness. Certain material conditions must be in place before one can achieve happiness, Aristotle believed. In addition to being virtuous, a person also needed health, wealth, high birth, good looks, good fortune, and the freedom from having to perform manual labor, in order to have happiness. (In fairness to Aristotle, it should be pointed out that his moral theory remains largely intact even after his elitist bias is deleted.)

Critics of virtue-based ethics point out that ethical theories ought to provide some kind of guidance for decision making. They contend that Aristotle's approach is just not very helpful when facing moral dilemmas. Aristotle's advice to a person facing a moral dilemma would simply seem to be "Do whatever a good person would do," which doesn't tell us what we need to know. What seems to be required is the translation of particular virtues into action-guiding principles. Currently, virtue theorists are at work on this very problem.

After years of neglect, virtue ethics has reemerged as a major ethical theory, largely due to the dissatisfaction with rule- and action-governed ethical systems. Alasdair MacIntyre has carried on the Aristotelian project of grounding morality in the virtues, arguing that a core set of virtues is necessary for the successful functioning of society.[17] MacIntyre argues that we all begin our moral inquiry in a historical and social context. We are "situated," for example, as a daughter, a son, a parent, a citizen. Our situation gives us a moral starting point, a place from which we weave a personal narrative or story. The meaning of a person's act can be understood only in terms of that person's life story. Virtue, MacIntyre argues, is best taught through storytelling. What is missing in most modern moral theory is a sense of unity and wholeness. By neglecting history, tradition, and the value of storytelling or narrative, modern moral theory has become dangerously abstract. What is needed (as MacIntyre puts it in his essay in chapter one) is "the virtue of having an adequate sense of the traditions to which one belongs or which confront one."

ETHICS AND METAPHYSICS

Philosophy in the Western tradition has always been concerned with the true, the good, and the beautiful. The relationship between the true and the good is an interesting one. If forced to choose between them, which would you choose: knowledge or goodness? Our choice has consequences. If we choose to prioritize knowledge over goodness, then our philosophy will emphasize epistemology, and questions of cognition and conditions of knowing will take priority over moral principles and standards. Where knowledge interests dominate in a philosophical tradition, truth will absorb and transform goodness according to its own purposes. That is to say, such a prioritization of truth over ethics will yield a discourse and practice that bend the good to the true. We are well acquainted with the privileging of the true over the good in our culture: think of scientists who claim that their scientific discourse is "value-free," that is, answerable to no moral principle, only to itself: so long as it is true it is, ipso facto, good.

But suppose we privileged the good over the true, what then? Suppose the true were bent to the good? Suppose goodness came first, and knowledge were viewed as insufficient and inadequate in itself? Contemporary moral theory, particularly in Europe, is in the grip of this debate. A central figure in the debate is the French philosopher Emmanuel Levinas. Richard A. Cohen interprets the significance of Levinas's approach to ethics in this way:

> [I]s an ethical philosophy primarily philosophical, a true discourse that happens to be about moral phenomena? Or is such a philosophy primarily ethical, an edifying discourse designed to stimulate good behavior, an exhortation, instruction or prescription rather than an explanation, description or denotation? Knowing that the drowning child must be saved, even when coupled with knowing how to save the child, is not the same as saving the child, unless knowing and doing are synonymous, which in our world they are not. For Levinas goodness comes first. His philosophy aims to pronounce this goodness, to articulate and emphasize it, and thus to realign its relation to the true.[18]

Totality and Infinity[19] contains Levinas's extended critique of the "totalizing" vision of the West, which has privileged knowing over goodness, thus marginalizing ethics as being inferior to metaphysics, ontology, and epistemology. In *Totality and Infinity* Levinas rejects the synthesizing of phenomena so characteristic of the West from Plato to Husserl and the birth of phenomenology, in favor of a kind of thought that is open to the *face of the other.* By "face" Levinas means the way in which the *presentation* of the Other exceeds all *idea* of the Other in me. When I encounter the Other in a face-to-face relation, this relation cannot be analyzed totally; something always escapes the totalizing knowledge gesture, thus opening me to the *infinite* rather than the *total.* Unlike philosophy, the face does not signify. Absolutely present, in the face-to-face relation; the Other faces me. As Jacques Derrida remarks in his influential essay on Levinas, "The other is not signalled by his face, he is this face."[20] The face of the Other is not a metaphor, not a concept, not a symbol, not a sign, not an allegory, not a figure, not a trope, not an occasion, not an accident. My presence before the Other is an epiphany, a revelation. The face of the Other is a moral summons. I am indebted to the Other, an asymmetrical indebtedness that is based not on prior knowledge but rather on the primacy of the Other's right to exist. Ethics thus arises from the presence of infinity in the ethical relation of the face-to-face; ethics occurs as an unsettling of being and essence, what Levinas calls "otherwise than being or beyond essence," that cannot be thematized in a totalizing way because goodness is both prior to and better than the true and the false. As Cohen points out, "This is not because ethics makes some truths better and others worse, but because it disrupts the entire project of knowing with a higher call, a more severe "condition": responsibility."[21]

Clearly, this way of approaching the question of the relation between ethics and metaphysics is disturbing and will seem excessive—as excessive as the famous remark of Alyosha Karamozov in Dostoyevsky's *Brothers Karamozov:* "We are all responsible for everyone else—but I am more responsible than all the others." To be sure, the ethical relation for Levinas is excessive, but Levinas believes that only exorbitant claims such as Alyosha's can hope to contest the totalizing of knowledge in our culture, and thus point up the seriousness of the ethical situation itself. For Levinas, responsibility for the Other is not an attribute of the self; rather, it is the self itself. *To be oneself is to be for the Other.* Responding to the Other is thus made an infinite responsibility, and one that increases the more it is fulfilled, for the Other is not an end that can ever be totally satisfied. We are responsible, endlessly, for all the frailties of the Other—his or her hunger, wounds, and desires; nor are we released by death, for the Other must not die alone, forsaken.

Many of the articles in this book are concerned with justice, and this is altogether fitting. Levinas is also concerned with justice, for the demands of justice arise out of the face-to-face relation as well. "The danger of justice, *injustice,* is the forgetting of the human face."[22]

In summary, ethics for Levinas is not a "side issue" coming after our (more important) metaphysical labors are done. Ethics is *first philosophy* (the traditional name for metaphysics, since Aristotle), because the face-to-face relation is an encounter with transcendence, with the infinite, beyond being or essence. The Other always exceeds my grasp, because he or she cannot be viewed merely as an extension of myself and my needs. In this approach to ethics, knowledge is not degraded. On the contrary, knowledge is *situated;* it emerges from the ethical situation owing to the inexplicable within the situation itself; it emerges as a chastened knowledge disturbed by the good.

FEMINIST ETHICS

Elizabeth V. Spelman, playfully paraphrasing the sixteenth-century philosopher Thomas Hobbes, has written, "What philosophers have had to say about women typically has been nasty, brutish and short. A page or two of quotations from those considered among the great philosophers (Aristotle, Hume, and Nietzsche, for example) constitute a veritable litany of contempt."[23]

A careful study of the history of philosophy supports Spelman's claim. In her book *The Man of Reason: "Male" and "Female" in Western Philosophy,*[24] Genevieve Lloyd reviews the history of philosophy from Plato to Simone de Beauvoir, cataloging the ways in which rationality has come to be associated with "maleness." In the course of Lloyd's book, some astoundingly misogynistic claims made by male philosophers are unearthed, including the following:

> The woman has [the deliberative faculty] but is without authority.—Aristotle (384–322 B.C.)

> The male is more complete, more dominant than the female, closer akin to causal activity, for the female is incomplete and in subjection and belongs to the category of the passive rather than the active. So too with the two ingredients which constitute our life-principle, the rational and the irrational; the rational which belongs to mind and reason is of the masculine gender, the irrational, the province of sense, is of the feminine. Mind belongs to a genus wholly superior to sense as man is to woman.—Philo (20 B.C.–A.D. 40)

> Nature herself has decreed that woman, both for herself and her children, should be at the mercy of man's judgments.—Jean-Jacques Rousseau (1712–1778)

> Womankind—the everlasting irony (in the life) of the community—changes by intrigue the universal end of the government into a private end, transforms its universal activity into a work of some particular individual, and perverts the universal property of the state into a possession and ornament for the Family.—G. W. F. Hegel (1770–1831)

> Woman is more closely related to Nature than man and in all her essentials she remains ever herself. Culture is with her always something external, a something which does not touch the kernel that is eternally faithful to Nature.—Friedrich Nietzsche (1844–1900)

In these remarks, and in scores of others, male philosophers echo a set of cultural and conceptual oppositions that have ancient origins and still exercise enormous influence in today's world. These dualities, consciously (and unconsciously) assimilated and passed along to succeeding generations, help account for the marginalization of women. It is instructive to list these cultural and conceptual oppositions that are the hallmark of Western thought:

Superior/Good	*Inferior/Less Good*
male	female
mind (soul)	body (flesh)
heaven	earth
husband	wife
active	passive
culture	nature
spirit	matter
original	copy
harmony	discord
One/unity	many/plurality
eternity/permanence	mutability/change

Feminist ethics begins with the realization that much of what the Western philosophical tradition has said—a tradition overwhelmingly dominated by men, in which women's voices are not heard—*either has not applied or does not apply to women.*

To the question "What is feminist ethics," Hestor Eisenstein responds: "A woman-centered analysis which presupposes the centrality, normality, and value of women's experience and women's culture." Feminist ethics, therefore, poses the question, "Is it good for women?"[25] It seeks nothing less than the reenvisioning of moral philosophy, beginning with challenging the hegemony of male ethical theory and subsequently addressing issues that arise directly out of women's lives, such as reproductive rights, maternal thinking, women's sexuality, discrimination against and sexual harassment of women, women as objects of science, violence against women, and the like.

Carol Gilligan, in her book *In a Different Voice,*[26] suggests that women's moral development may be different from men's. Traditional moral theories (including that of Gilligan's own mentor at Harvard, Lawrence Kohlberg) have not accounted for this difference. In the course of her empirical research, listening to people talk about morality and about themselves, Gilligan began to hear two distinctive voices; two ways of speaking about moral problems; two modes of describing the relationship between self and Other. Her research showed her that women's voices were distinctive. Gilligan argues that women's morality differs from men's in that it places a premium on caring, responsibility, and maintaining relationships. She contrasts this with theorists like Kohlberg and others whose work emphasizes so-called standards of right and wrong—an ethics of rules and rights that men have formulated and that men apply. When this "standard" view of morality is imposed on women, it is unsurprising that women do not measure up to the "male-stream" standards and practices that dominate the psychological field. As Gilligan puts it:

> The disparity between women's experience and the representation of human development, noted throughout the psychological literature, has generally been seen to signify a problem in women's development. Instead, the failure of women to fit existing models of human growth may point to a problem in the representation, a limitation in the conception of the human condition, an omission of certain truths about life.[27]

Rather than denigrate women as being "less ethical" than men, Gilligan suggests that we need to rethink the old male-dominated standards and recognize that women's moral development must be acknowledged and valorized in its own right. By including Gilligan as an ethical theorist in chapter one, and by including feminist analyses of issues and ideas in each of the subsequent chapters, this book aims to let the voices of women be heard.

NOTES

1. Louis P. Pojman, *Ethics: Discovering Right and Wrong* (Belmont, Calif.: Wadsworth, 1990), 5–7.
2. Henry Sedgwick, *The Methods of Ethics,* 7th ed. (London: Macmillan, 1907), 380.
3. Pojman, *Ethics,* 6
4. See James Rachels, *The Elements of Moral Philosophy* (New York: Random House, 1986), 17–19. I am indebted to Professor Rachels for his critique of cultural relativism.
5. See Robert M. Adams, "A Modified Divine Command Theory of Ethical Wrongness," in *Religion and Morality: A Collection of Essays,* ed. Gene Outka and John P. Reeder (San Angelo, Tex.: Anchor, 1973); and Philip Quinn, *Divine Commands and Moral Requirements* (Oxford: Oxford University Press, 1978).
6. Arthur F. Holmes, *Ethics: Approaching Moral Decisions* (Downers Grove, Ill.: InterVarsity Press, 1984), 12–13.
7. I am indebted to Tom Regan for these examples (which I have modified slightly), and for the framework of his discussion of consequentialism and nonconsequentialism in the introduction to his book *Matters of Life and Death: New Introductory Essays in Moral Philosophy*, ed. (New York: Random House, 1980), 15–22.
8. *Teleological* comes from the Greek word *telos,* meaning "end" or "purpose." Such theories regard actions as right or wrong if they promote or frustrate the purpose of morality, which is to bring about the greatest possible balance of good over evil.
9. Richard Brandt, "Towards a Credible Form of Utilitarianism," in *Morality and the Language of Conduct,* ed. H. Castaneda and G. Nakhnikian (Detroit: Wayne State University Press, 1963), 109–10.
10. Regan, *Matters of Life and Death,* 19.
11. Onora O'Neill, "The Perplexities of Famine Relief," in *Matters of Life and Death: New Introductory Essays in Moral Philosophy,* ed. Tom Regan (New York: Random House, 1980), 287.
12. James Rachels, *The Elements of Moral Philosophy* (New York: Random House, 1986), 109–10.
13. Thomas Hobbes, *Leviathan* (Indianapolis: Bobbs-Merrill, 1958), 107.
14. Rachels, *The Elements of Moral Philosophy,* 129
15. Regan, *Matters of Life and Death,* 23
16. For the gripping story of how one former slave escaped to freedom on the Underground Railroad, read Frederick Douglass's autobiography *Narrative of the Life of Frederick Douglass, An American Slave,* ed. Benjamin Quarles (Cambridge, Mass.: Belknap Press, 1960).

17. See Alasdair MacIntyre, *After Virtue* (Notre Dame, Ind.: Notre Dame University Press, 1981).
18. Richard A. Cohen, *Face to Face with Levinas* (Albany: State University of New York Press, 1986), 1.
19. Emmanuel Levinas, *Totality and Infinity,* tr. Alphonso Lingis (Pittsburgh: Duquesne University Press), 1992.
20. Jacques Derrida, "Violence and Metaphysics: An Essay on the Thought of Emmanuel Levinas," in *Writing and Difference* (Chicago: University of Chicago Press, 1978), 100.
21. Cohen, *Face to Face with Levinas,* 5.
22. Ibid., 9.
23. Elizabeth V. Spelman, "Woman as Body," *Feminist Studies* 8, no. 1 (Spring 1982): 109.
24. Genevieve Lloyd, *The Man of Reason: "Male" and "Female" in Western Philosophy* (Minneapolis: University of Minnesota Press, 1984).
25. Marilyn Pearsall, *Women and Values* (Belmont, Calif.: Wadsworth, 1986), 266.
26. Carol Gilligan, *In A Different Voice: Psychological Theory and Women's Development* (Cambridge, Mass.: Harvard University Press, 1982).
27. Ibid., 1–2.

Chapter One

Ethical Theories

1

Tradition and the Virtues

Alasdair MacIntyre

Alasdair MacIntyre teaches philosophy at Notre Dame University and is the author of many books and articles, including *After Virtue* and *Against the Self: Images of the Age.*

Any contemporary attempt to envisage each human life as a whole, as a unity, whose character provides the virtues with an adequate *telos* encounters two different kinds of obstacle, one social and one philosophical. The social obstacles derive from the way in which modernity partitions each human life into a variety of segments, each with its own norms and modes of behavior. So work is divided from leisure, private life from public, the corporate from the personal. So both childhood and old age have been wrenched away from the rest of human life and made over into distinct realms. And all these separations have been achieved so that it is the distinctiveness of each and not the unity of the life of the individual who passes through those parts in terms of which we are taught to think and to feel.

The philosophical obstacles derive from two distinct tendencies, one chiefly, though not only, domesticated in analytical philosophy and one at home in both sociological theory and in existentialism. The former is the tendency to think atomistically about human action and to analyze complex actions and transactions in terms of simple components. Hence the recurrence in more than one context of the notion of a "basic action." That particular actions derive their character as parts of larger wholes is a point of view alien to our dominant ways of thinking and yet one which it is necessary at least to consider if we are to begin to understand how a life may be more than a sequence of individual actions and episodes.

Equally the unity of a human life becomes invisible to us when a sharp separation is made either between the individual and the roles he or she plays . . . or between the different role . . . enactments of an individual life so that the life comes to appear as nothing but a series of unconnected episodes—a liquidation of the self. . . .

[T]he liquidation of the self into a set of demarcated areas of role-playing allows no scope for the exercise of dispositions which could genuinely be accounted virtues in any sense remotely Aristotelian. For a virtue is not a disposition that makes for success only in some one particular type of situation. What are spoken of as the virtues of a good committee man or of a good administrator or of a gambler or a pool hustler are professional skills professionally deployed in those situations where they can be effective, not virtues. Someone who genuinely possesses a virtue can be expected to manifest it in very different types of situations, many of them situations where the practice of a virtue cannot be expected to be effective in the way that we expect a professional skill to be. Hector exhibited one and the same courage in his parting from Andromache and on the battlefield with Achilles; Eleanor Marx exhibited one and the same compassion in her relationship with her father, in her work with trade unionists and in her entanglement with Aveling. And the unity of a virtue in someone's life is intelligible only as a characteristic of a unitary life, a life that can be conceived and evaluated as a whole. Hence just as in [an earlier] discussion of the changes in and fragmentation of morality which accompanied the rise of modernity, each stage in the emergence of the characteristically modern views of the moral judgment was accompanied by a corresponding stage in the emergence of the characteristically modern conceptions of selfhood; so now, in defining the particular premodern concept of the virtues with which I have been preoccupied, it has become necessary to say something of the concomitant concept of selfhood, a concept of a self whose unity resides in the unity of a narrative which links birth to life to death as narrative beginning to middle to end.

Such a conception of the self is perhaps less unfamiliar than it may appear at first sight. Just because it has played a key part in the cultures which are historically predecessors of our own, it would not be surprising if it turned out to be still an unacknowledged presence in many of our ways of thinking and acting. Hence it is not inappropriate to begin by scrutinizing some of our most taken-for-granted, but clearly correct conceptual insights about human actions and selfhood in order to show how natural it is to think of the self in a narrative mode.

It is a conceptual commonplace, both for philosophers and for ordinary agents, that one and the same segment of human behavior may be correctly characterized in a number of different ways. To the question "What is he doing?" the answers may with equal truth and appropriateness be "Digging," "Gardening," "Taking exercise," "Preparing for winter" or "Pleasing his wife." Some of these answers will characterize the agent's intentions, other unintended consequences of his actions, and of these unintended consequences some may be such that the agent is aware of them and others not. What is important to notice immediately is that any answer to the questions of how we are to understand or to explain a given segment of behavior will presuppose some prior answer to the question of how these different correct answers to the question "What is he doing?" are related to each other. For if someone's primary intention is to put the garden in order before the winter and it is only incidentally the case that in so doing he is taking exercise and pleasing his wife, we have one type of behavior to be explained; but if the agent's primary intention is to please his wife by taking exercise, we have quite another type of behavior to be explained and we will have to look in a different direction for understanding and explanation.

In the first place the episode has been situated in an annual cycle of domestic activity, and the behavior embodies an intention which presupposes a particular type of household-cum-garden setting with the peculiar narrative history of that setting in which this segment of behavior now becomes an episode. In the second instance the episode has been situated in the narrative history of a marriage, a very different, even if related, social setting. We cannot, that is to say, characterize behavior independently of intentions, and we cannot characterize intentions independently of the settings which make those intentions intelligible both to agents themselves and to others.

I use the word "setting" here as a relatively inclusive term. A social setting may be an institution, it may be what I have called a practice, or it may be a milieu of some other human kind. But it is central to the notion of a setting as I am going to understand it that a setting has a history, a history within which the histories of individual agents not only are, but have to be, situated, just because without the setting and its changes through time the history of the individual agent and his changes through time will be unintelligible. Of course one and the same piece of behavior may belong to more than one setting. There are at least two different ways in which this may be so.

In my earlier example the agent's activity may be part of the history both of the cycle of household activity and of his marriage, two histories which have happened to intersect. The household may have its own history stretching back through hundreds of years, as do the histories of some European farms, where the farm has had a life of its own, even though different families have in different periods inhabited it; and the marriage will certainly have its own history, a history which itself presupposes that a particular point has been reached in the history of the institution of marriage. If we are to relate some particular segment of behavior in any precise way to an agent's intentions and thus to the settings which that agent inhabits, we shall have to understand in a precise way how the variety of correct characterizations of the agent's behavior relate to each other first by identifying which characteristics refer us to an intention and which do not and then by classifying further the items in both categories.

Where intentions are concerned, we need to know which intention or intentions were primary, that is to say, of which it is the case that, had the agent intended otherwise, he would not have performed that action. Thus if we know that a man is gardening with the self-avowed purposes of healthful exercise and of pleasing his wife, we do not yet know how to understand what he is doing until we know the answer to such questions as whether he would continue gardening if he continued to believe that gardening was healthful exercise, but discovered that his gardening no longer pleased his wife, *and* whether he would continue gardening, if he ceased to believe that gardening was healthful exercise, but continued to believe that it pleased his wife, *and* whether he would continue gardening if he changed his beliefs on both points. That is to say, we need to know both what certain of his beliefs are and which of them are causally effective; and, that is to say, we need to know whether certain contrary-to-fact hypothetical statements are true or false. And until we know this, we shall not know how to characterize correctly what the agent is doing. . . .

Consider what the argument so far implies about the interrelationships of the intentional, the social and the historical. We identify a particular action only by invoking two kinds of context, implicitly if not explicitly. We place the agent's intentions, I have suggested, in causal and temporal order with reference to their role in his or her history; and we also place them with reference to their role in the history of the setting or settings to which they belong. In doing this, in determining what causal efficacy the agent's intentions had in one or more directions, and how his short-term intentions succeeded or failed to be constitutive of long-term intentions, we ourselves write a further part of these histories. Narrative history of a certain kind turns out to be the basic and essential genre for the characterization of human action. . . .

At the beginning of this chapter I argued that in successfully identifying and understanding what someone else is doing we always move towards having a particular episode in the context of a set of narrative histories, histories both of the individuals concerned and of the settings in which they act and suffer. It is now becoming clear that we render the actions of others intelligible in this way because action itself has a basically historical character. It is because we all live out narratives in our lives and because we understand our own lives in terms of the narratives that we live out that the form of narrative is appropriate for understanding the actions of others. Stories are lived before they are told—except in the case of fiction. . . .

A central thesis then begins to emerge: man is in his actions and practice, as well as in his fictions, essentially a story-telling animal. He is not essentially, but becomes through his history, a teller of stories that aspire to truth. But the key question for men is not about their own authorship; I can only answer the question "What am I to do?" if I can answer the prior question "Of what story or stories do I find myself a part?" We enter human society, that is, with one or more imputed characters—roles into which we have been drafted—and we have to learn what they are in order to be able to understand how others respond to us and how our responses to them are apt to be construed. It is through hearing stories about wicked stepmothers, lost children, good but misguided kings, wolves that suckle twin boys, youngest sons who receive no inheritance but must make their own way in the world and eldest sons who waste their inheritance on riotous living and go into exile to live with the swine, that children learn or mislearn both what a child and what a parent is, what the cast of characters may be in the drama into which they have been born and what the ways of the world are. Deprive children of stories and you leave them unscripted, anxious stutterers in their actions as in their words. Hence there is no way to give us an understanding of any society, including our own, except through the stock of stories which constitute its initial dramatic resources. Mythology, in its original sense, is at the heart of things. Vico was right and so was Joyce. And so too of course is that moral tradition from heroic society to its medieval heirs according to which the telling of stories has a key part in educating us into the virtues.

To be the subject of a narrative that runs from one's birth to one's death is, I remarked earlier, to be accountable for the actions and experiences which compose a narratable life. It is, that is, to be open to being asked to give a certain kind of account of what one did or what happened to one or what one witnessed at any earlier point in one's life than the time at which the question is posed. Of course someone may have forgotten or suffered brain damage or simply not attended sufficiently at the relevant time to be able to give the relevant account. But to say of someone under some one description ("The prisoner of the Chateau d'If") that he is the same person as someone characterized quite differently ("The Count of Monte Cristo") is precisely to say that it makes sense to ask him to give an intelligible narrative account enabling us to understand how he could at different times and different places be one and the same person and yet be so differently characterized. Thus personal identity is just that identity presupposed by the unity of the character which the unity of a narrative requires. Without such unity there would not be subjects of whom stories could be told.

The other aspect of narrative selfhood is correlative: I am not only accountable, I am one who can always ask others for an account, who can put others to the question. I am part of their story, as they are part of mine. The narrative of any one life is part of an interlocking set of narratives. Moreover this asking for and giving of accounts itself plays an important part in constituting narratives. Asking you what you did and why, saying what I did and why, pondering the differences between your account of what I did and my account of what I did, and *vice versa,* these are essential constituents of all but the very simplest and barest of narratives. Thus without the accountability of the self those trains of events that constitute all but the simplest and barest of narratives could not occur; and without that same accountability narratives would lack that continuity required to make both them and the actions that constitute them intelligible. . . .

It is now possible to return to the question from which this enquiry into the nature of human action and identity started: In what does the unity of an individual life consist? The answer is that its unity is the unity of a narrative embodied in a single life. To ask "What is the good for me?" is to ask how best I might live out that unity and bring it to completion. To ask "What is the good for man?" is to ask what all answers to the former question must have in common. But now it is important to emphasize that it is the systematic asking of these two questions and the attempt to answer them in deed as well as in word which provide the moral life with its unity. The unity of a human life is the unity of a narrative quest. Quests sometimes fail, are frustrated, abandoned or dissipated into distractions; and human lives may in all these ways also fail. But the only criteria for success or failure in a human life as a whole are the criteria of success or failure in a narrated or to-be-narrated quest. A quest for what?

Two key features of the medieval conception of a quest need to be recalled. The first is that without some at least partly determinate conception of the final *telos* there could not be any beginning to a quest. Some conception of the good for man is required. Whence is such a conception to be drawn? Precisely from those questions which led us to attempt to transcend that limited conception of the virtues which is available in and through practices. It is in looking for a conception of *the* good which will enable us to order other goods, for a conception of *the* good which will enable us to extend our understanding of the purpose and content of the virtues, for a conception of *the* good which will enable us to understand the place of integrity and constancy in life, that we initially define the kind of life which is a quest for the good. But secondly it is clear the medieval conception of a quest is not at all that of a search for something already adequately characterized, as miners search for gold or geologists for oil. It is in the course of the quest and only through encountering and coping with the various particular harms, dangers, temptations and distractions which provide any quest with its episodes and incidents that the goal of the quest is finally to be understood. A quest is always an education both as to the character of that which is sought and in self-knowledge.

The virtues therefore are to be understood as those dispositions which will not only sustain practices and enable us to achieve the goods internal to practices, but which will also sustain us in the relevant kind of quest for the good, by enabling us to overcome the harms, dangers, temptations and distractions which we encounter, and which will furnish us with increasing self-knowledge and increasing knowledge of the good. The catalogue of the virtues will therefore include the virtues required to sustain the kind of households and the kind of political communities in which men and women can seek for the good together and the virtues necessary for philosophical enquiry about the character of the good. We have then arrived at a provisional conclusion about the good life for man: the good life for man is the life spent in seeking for the good life for man, and the virtues necessary for the seeking are those which will enable us to understand what more and what else the good life for man is. We have also completed the second stage in our account of the virtues, by situating them in relation to the good life for man and not only in relation to practices. But our enquiry requires a third stage.

For I am never able to seek for the good or exercise the virtues only *qua* individual. This is partly because what it is to live the good life concretely varies from circumstance to circumstance even when it is one and the same conception of the good life and one and the same set of virtues which are being embodied in a human life. What the good life is for a fifth-century Athenian general will not be the same as what it was for a medieval nun or a seventeenth-century farmer. But it is not just that different individuals live in different social circumstances; it is also that we all approach our own circumstances as bearers of a particular social identity. I am someone's son or daughter, someone else's cousin or uncle; I am a citizen of this or that city, a member of this or that guild or profession; I belong to this clan, that tribe, this nation. Hence what is good for me has to be the good for one who inhabits these roles. As such, I inherit from the past of my family, my city, my tribe, my nation, a variety of debts, inheritances, rightful expectations and obligations. These constitute the given of my life, my moral starting point. This is in part what gives my life its own moral particularity.

This thought is likely to appear alien and even surprising from the standpoint of modern individualism. From the standpoint of individualism I am what I myself choose to be. I can always, if I wish to, put in question what are taken to be the merely contingent social features of my existence. I may biologically be my father's son; but I cannot be held responsible for what he did unless I choose implicitly or explicitly to assume such responsibility. I may legally be a citizen of a certain country; but I cannot be held responsible for what my country does or has done unless I choose implicitly or explicitly to assume such responsibility. Such individualism is expressed by those modern Americans who deny any responsibility for the effects of slavery upon black Americans, saying "I never owned any slaves." It is more subtly the standpoint of those other modern Americans who accept a nicely calculated responsibility for such effects measured precisely by the benefits they themselves as individuals have indirectly received from slavery. In both cases "being an American" is not in itself taken to be part of the moral identity of the individual. And of course there is nothing peculiar to modern Americans in this attitude: the Englishman who says, "*I* never did any wrong to Ireland; why bring up that old history as though it had something to do with *me?*" or the young German who believes that being born after 1945 means that what Nazis did to Jews has no moral relevance to his relationship to his Jewish contemporaries, exhibit the same attitude, that according to which the self is detachable from its social and historical roles and statuses. And the self so detached is of course a self very much at home in either Sartre's or Goffman's perspective, a self that can have no history. The contrast with the narrative view of the self is clear. For the story of my life is always embedded in the story of those communities from which I derive my identity. I am born with a past; and to try to cut myself off from that past, in the individualist mode, is to deform my present relationships. The possession of an historical identity and the possession of a social identity coincide. Notice that rebellion against my identity is always one possible mode of expressing it.

Notice also that the fact that the self has to find its moral identity in and through its membership in communities such as those of the family, the neighborhood, the city and the tribe does not entail that the self has to accept the moral *limitations* of the particularity of those forms of community. Without those moral particularities to begin from there would never be anywhere to begin; but it is in moving forward from such particularity that the search for the good, for the universal, consists. Yet particularity can never be simply left behind or obliterated. The notion of escaping from it into a realm of entirely universal maxims which belong to man as such, whether in its eighteenth-century Kantian form or in the presentation of some modern analytical moral philosophies, is an illusion and an illusion with painful consequences. When men and women identify what are in fact their partial and particular causes too easily and too completely with the cause of some universal principle, they usually behave worse than they would otherwise do.

What I am, therefore, is in key part what I inherit, a specific past that is present to some degree in my present. I find myself part of a history and that is generally to say, whether I like it or not, whether I recognize it or not, one of the bearers of a tradition. It was important when I characterized the concept of a practice to notice that practices always have histories and that at any given moment what a practice is depends on a mode of understanding it which has been transmitted often through many generations. And thus; insofar as the virtues sustain the relationships required for practices, they have to sustain relationships to the past—and to the future—as well as in the present. But the traditions through which particular practices are transmitted and reshaped never exist in isolation for larger social traditions. What constitutes such traditions?

We are apt to be misled here by the ideological uses to which the concept of a tradition has been put by conservative political theorists. Characteristically such theorists have followed Burke in contrasting tradition with reason and the stability of tradition with conflict. Both contrasts obfuscate. For all reasoning takes place within the context of some traditional mode of thought, transcending through criticism and invention the limitations of what had hitherto been reasoned in that tradition; this is as true of modern physics as of medieval logic. Moreover when a tradition is in good order it is always partially constituted by an argument about the goods the pursuit of which gives to that tradition its particular point and purpose.

So when an institution—a university, say, or a farm, or a hospital—is the bearer of a tradition of practice or practices, its common life will be partly, but in a centrally important way, constituted by a continuous argument as to what a university is and ought to be or what good farming is or what good medicine is. Traditions, when vital, embody continuities of conflict. Indeed when a tradition becomes Burkean, it is always dying or dead. . . .

A living tradition then is an historically extended, socially embodied argument, and an argument precisely in part about the goods which constitute that tradition. Within a tradition the pursuit of goods extends through generations, sometimes through many generations. Hence the individual's search for his or her good is generally and characteristically conducted within a context defined by those traditions of which the individual's life is a part, and this is true both of those goods which are internal to practices and of the goods of a single life. Once again the narrative phenomenon of embedding is crucial: the history of a practice in our time is generally and characteristically embedded in and made intelligible in terms of the larger and longer history of the tradition through which the practice in its present form was conveyed to us; the history of each of our own lives is generally and characteristically embedded in and made intelligible in terms of the larger and longer histories of a number of traditions. I have to say "generally and characteristically" rather than "always," for traditions decay, disintegrate and disappear. What then sustains and strengthens traditions? What weakens and destroys them?

The answer in key part is: the exercise or the lack of exercise of the relevant virtues. The virtues find their point and purpose not only in sustaining those relationships necessary if the variety of goods internal to practices are to be achieved and not only in sustaining the form of an individual life in which that individual may seek out his or her good as the good of his or her whole life, but also in sustaining those traditions which provide both practices and individual lives with their necessary historical context. Lack of justice, lack of truthfulness, lack of courage, lack of the relevant intellectual virtues—these corrupt traditions, just as they do those institutions and practices which derive their life from the traditions of which they are the contemporary embodiments. To recognize this is of course also to recognize the existence of an additional virtue, one whose importance is perhaps most obvious when it is least present, the virtue of having an adequate sense of the traditions to which one belongs or which confront one. . . .

STUDY QUESTIONS

1. What does MacIntyre mean by "the liquidation of the self"? What might be the consequences of such a liquidation?
2. How are the stories we tell linked, and important to, our behavior?
3. How is narrative important to the moral life? What does this mean for people, especially parents?

2

Utilitarianism

James Rachels

James Rachels is a professor of philosophy at the University of Alabama at Birmingham. His most recent book is entitled *The End of Life.*

The utilitarian doctrine is that happiness is desirable, and the only thing desirable, as an end; all other things being desirable as means to that end.

John Stuart Mill, *Utilitarianism* (1861)

Man does not strive after happiness; only the Englishman does that.

Friedrich Nietzsche, *Twilight of the Idols* (1889)

THE RESILIENCE OF THE THEORY

Classical Utilitarianism—the theory defended by Bentham and Mill—can be summarized in three propositions:

First, actions are to be judged right or wrong solely in virtue of their consequences. Nothing else matters. Right actions are, simply, those that have the best consequences.

Second, in assessing consequences, the only thing that matters is the amount of happiness or unhappiness that is caused. Everything else is irrelevant. Thus right actions are those that produce the greatest balance of happiness over unhappiness.

Third, in calculating the happiness or unhappiness that will be caused, no one's happiness is to be counted as more important than anyone else's. Each person's welfare is equally important. As Mill put it in his *Utilitarianism,*

> the happiness which forms the utilitarian standard of what is right in conduct, is not the agent's own happiness, but that of all concerned. As between his own happiness and that of others, utilitarianism requires him to be as strictly impartial as a disinterested and benevolent spectator.

Thus right actions are those that produce the greatest possible balance of happiness over unhappiness, with each person's happiness counted as equally important.

The appeal of this theory to philosophers, economists, and others who theorize about human decision making has been enormous. The theory continues to be widely accepted, even though it has been challenged by a number of apparently devastating arguments. These antiutilitarian arguments are so numerous, and so persuasive, that many have concluded the theory must be abandoned. But the remarkable thing is that so many have *not* abandoned it. Despite the arguments, a great many thinkers refuse to let the theory go. According to these contemporary utilitarians, the antiutilitarian arguments show only that the classical theory needs to be *modified;* they say the basic idea is correct and should be preserved, but recast into a more satisfactory form.

In what follows, we will examine some of these arguments against Utilitarianism, and consider whether the classical version of the theory may be revised satisfactorily to meet them. These arguments are of interest not only for the assessment of Utilitarianism but for their own sakes, as they raise some additional fundamental issues of moral philosophy.

IS HAPPINESS THE ONLY THING THAT MATTERS?

The question *What things are good?* is different from the question *What actions are right?* and Utilitarianism answers the second question by referring back to the first one. Right actions, it says, are the ones that produce the most good. But what is good? The classical utilitarian reply is: one thing, and one thing only, namely happiness. As Mill put it, "The utilitarian doctrine is that happiness is desirable, and the only thing desirable, as an end; all other things being desirable as means to that end."

The idea that happiness is the one ultimate good (and unhappiness the one ultimate evil) is known as **Hedonism.** Hedonism is a perennially popular theory that goes back at least as far as the ancient Greeks. It has always been an attractive theory because of its beautiful simplicity, and because it expresses the intuitively plausible notion that things are good or bad only on account of the way they make us *feel.* Yet a little reflection reveals serious flaws in the theory. The flaws stand out when we consider examples like these:

1. A promising young pianist's hands are injured in an automobile accident so that she can no longer play. Why is this a bad thing for her? Hedonism would say it is bad because it causes her unhappiness. She will feel frustrated and upset whenever she thinks of what might have been, and *that* is her misfortune. But this way of explaining the misfortune seems to get things the wrong way around. It is not as though, by feeling unhappy, she has made an otherwise neutral situation into a bad one. On the contrary, her unhappiness is a rational response to a situation that *is* unfortunate. She could have had a career as a concert pianist, and now she cannot. *That* is the tragedy. We could not eliminate the tragedy just by getting her to cheer up.

2. You think someone is your friend, but really he ridicules you behind your back. No one ever tells you, so you never know. Is this situation unfortunate for you? Hedonism would have to say no, because you are never caused any unhappiness by the situation. Yet we do feel that there is something bad going on here. You *think* he is your friend, and you are "being made a fool," even though you are not aware of it and so suffer no unhappiness.

Both these examples make the same basic point. We value all sorts of things, including artistic creativity and friendship, for their own sakes. It makes us happy to have them, but only because we *already* think them good. (We do not think them good *because* they make us happy—this is what I meant when I said that Hedonism "gets things the wrong way around.") Therefore we think it a misfortune to lose them, independently of whether or not the loss is accompanied by unhappiness.

In this way, Hedonism misunderstands the nature of happiness. Happiness is not something that is recognized as good and sought for its own sake, with other things appreciated only as means of bringing it about. Instead, happiness is a response we have to the attainment of things that we recognize *as* goods, independently and in their own right. We think that friendship is a good thing, and so having friends makes us happy. That is very different from first setting out after happiness, then deciding that having friends might make us happy, and then seeking friends as a means to this end.

Today, most philosophers recognize the truth of this. There are not many contemporary hedonists. Those sympathetic to Utilitarianism have therefore sought a way to formulate their view without assuming a hedonistic account of good and evil. Some, such as the English philosopher G. E. Moore (1873–1958), have tried to compile short lists of things to be regarded as good in themselves. Moore suggested that there are three obvious **intrinsic goods**—pleasure, friendship, and aesthetic enjoyment—and that right actions are those that increase the world's supply of such things. Other utilitarians have tried to bypass the question of how many things are good in themselves, leaving it an open question and saying only that right actions are the ones that have the best results, *however* goodness is measured. (This is sometimes called **Ideal Utilitarianism.**) Still others try to bypass the question in another way, holding only that we should act so as to maximize the satisfaction of people's *preferences*. (This is called **Preference Utilitarianism.**) It is beyond the scope of this book to discuss the merits or demerits of these varieties of Utilitarianism. I mention them only in order to note that although the hedonistic assumption of the classical utilitarians has largely been rejected, contemporary utilitarians have not found it difficult to carry on. They do so by urging that Hedonism was never a necessary part of the theory in the first place.

ARE CONSEQUENCES ALL THAT MATTER?

The claim that only consequences matter *is*, however, a necessary part of Utilitarianism. The most fundamental idea underlying the theory is that in order to determine whether an action would be right, we should look at *what will happen as a result of doing it*. If it were to turn out that some *other* matter is also important in determining rightness, then Utilitarianism would be undermined at its very foundation.

The most serious antiutilitarian arguments attack the theory at just this point: they urge that various other considerations, in addition to utility, are important in determining whether actions are right. We will look briefly at three such arguments.

1. *Justice*. Writing in the academic journal *Inquiry* in 1965, H. J. McCloskey asks us to consider the following case:

> Suppose a utilitarian were visiting an area in which there was racial strife, and that, during his visit, a Negro rapes a white woman, and that race riots occur as a result of the crime, white mobs, with the connivance of the police, bashing and killing Negroes, etc. Suppose too that our utilitarian is in the area of the crime when it is committed such that his testimony would bring about the conviction of a particular Negro. If he knows that a quick arrest will stop the riots and lynchings, surely, as a utilitarian, he must conclude that he has a duty to bear false witness in order to bring about the punishment of an innocent person.

This is a fictitious example, but that makes no difference. The argument is only that *if* someone were in this position, then on utilitarian grounds he should bear false witness against the innocent person. This might have some bad consequences—the innocent man might be executed—but there would be enough good consequences to outweigh them: the riots and lynchings would be stopped. The best consequences would be achieved by lying; therefore, according to Utilitarianism, lying is the thing to do. But, the argument continues, it would be wrong to bring about the execution of the innocent man. Therefore, Utilitarianism, which implies it would be right, must be incorrect.

According to the critics of Utilitarianism, this argument illustrates one of the theory's most serious shortcomings: namely, that it is incompatible with the ideal of justice. Justice requires that we treat people fairly, according to their individual needs and merits. The innocent man has done nothing wrong; he did not commit the rape and so he does not deserve to be punished for it. Therefore, punishing him would be unjust. The example illustrates how the demands of justice and the demands of utility can come into conflict, and so a theory that says utility is the *whole* story cannot be right.

2. *Rights*. Here is a case that is *not* fictitious; it is from the records of the U.S. Court of Appeals, Ninth Circuit (Southern District of California), 1963, in the case of *York v. Story:*

> In October, 1958, appellant [Ms. Angelynn York] went to the police department of Chino for the purpose of filing charges in connection with an assault upon her. Appellee Ron Story, an officer of that police department, then acting under color of his authority as such, advised appellant that it was necessary to take photographs of her. Story then took appellant to a room in the police station, locked the door, and directed her to undress, which she did. Story then directed appellant to assume various indecent positions, and photographed her in those positions. These photographs were not made for any lawful purpose.
>
> Appellant objected to undressing. She stated to Story that there was no need to take photographs of her in the nude, or in the positions she was directed to take, because the bruises would not show in any photograph. . . .
>
> Later that month, Story advised appellant that the pictures did not come out and that he had destroyed them. Instead, Story circulated these photographs among the personnel of the Chino police department. In April, 1960, two other officers of that police department, appellee Louis Moreno and defendant Henry Grote, acting under color of their authority as such, and using police photographic equipment located at the police station made additional prints of the photographs taken by Story. Moreno and Grote then circulated these prints among the personnel of the Chino police department. . . .

Ms. York brought suit against these officers and won. Her *legal* rights had clearly been violated. But what of the *morality* of the officers' behavior?

Utilitarianism says that actions are defensible if they produce a favorable balance of happiness over unhappiness. This suggests that we consider the amount of unhappiness caused to Ms. York and compare it with the amount of pleasure taken in the photographs by Officer Story and his cohorts. It is at least possible that more happiness than unhappiness was caused. In that case, the utilitarian conclusion apparently would be that their actions were morally all right. But this seems to be a perverse way to approach the case. Why should the pleasure afforded Story and his cohorts matter at all? Why should it even count? They had no right to treat Ms. York in that way, and the fact that they enjoyed doing so hardly seems a relevant defense.

To make the point even clearer, consider an (imaginary) related case. Suppose a Peeping Tom spied on Ms. York by peering through her bedroom window, and secretly took pictures of her undressed. Further suppose that he did this without ever being detected and that he used the photographs entirely for his own amusement, without showing them to anyone. Now under these circumstances, it seems clear that the *only* consequence of his action is an increase in his own happiness. No one else, including Ms. York, is caused any unhappiness at all. How, then, could Utilitarianism deny that the Peeping Tom's actions are right? But it is evident to moral common sense that they are not right. Thus, Utilitarianism appears to be an incorrect moral view.

The moral to be drawn from this argument is that Utilitarianism is at odds with the idea that people have *rights* that may not be trampled on merely because one anticipates good results. This is an extremely important notion, which explains why a great many philosophers have rejected Utilitarianism. In the above cases, it is Ms. York's right to privacy that is violated; but it would not be difficult to think of similar cases in which other rights are at issue—the right to freedom of religion, to free speech, or even the right to life itself. It may happen that good purposes are served, from time to time, by ignoring these rights. But we do not think that our rights *should* be set aside so easily. The notion of a personal right is not a utilitarian notion.

Quite the reverse: it is a notion that places limits on how an individual may be treated, regardless of the good purposes that might be accomplished.

3. *Backward-Looking Reasons.* Suppose you have promised someone you will do something—say, you promised to meet him downtown this afternoon. But when the time comes to go, you don't want to do it—you need to do some work and would rather stay home. What should you do? Suppose you judge that the utility of getting your work accomplished slightly outweighs the inconvenience your friend would be caused. Appealing to the utilitarian standard, you might then conclude that it is right to stay home. However, this does not seem correct. The fact that *you promised* imposes an obligation on you that you cannot escape so easily. Of course, if the consequences of not breaking the promise were *great*—if, for example, your mother had just been stricken with a heart attack and you had to rush her to the hospital—you would be justified in breaking it. But a *small* gain in utility cannot overcome the obligation imposed by the fact that you promised. Thus Utilitarianism, which says that consequences are the only things that matter, seems mistaken.

There is an important general lesson to be learned from this argument. Why is Utilitarianism vulnerable to this sort of criticism? It is because the only kinds of considerations that the theory holds relevant to determining the rightness of actions are considerations having to do with the *future.* Because of its exclusive concern with consequences, Utilitarianism has us confine our attention to what *will happen* as a result of our actions. However, we normally think that considerations about the *past* also have some importance. The fact that you promised your friend to meet him is a fact about the past, not the future. Therefore, the general point to be made about Utilitarianism is that it seems to be an inadequate moral theory because it excludes what we might call backward-looking considerations.

Once we understand this point, other examples of backward-looking considerations come easily to mind. The fact that someone did not commit a crime is a good reason why he should not be punished. The fact that someone once did you a favor may be a good reason why you should now do him a favor. The fact that you did something to hurt someone may be a reason why you should now make it up to her. These are all facts about the past that are relevant to determining our obligations. But Utilitarianism makes the past irrelevant, and so it seems deficient for just that reason.

THE DEFENSE OF UTILITARIANISM

Taken together, the above arguments form an impressive indictment of Utilitarianism. The theory, which at first seemed so progressive and commonsensical, now seems indefensible: it is at odds with such fundamental moral notions as justice and individual rights, and seems unable to account for the place of backward-looking reasons in justifying conduct. The combined weight of these arguments has prompted many philosophers to abandon the theory altogether.

Many thinkers, however, continue to believe that Utilitarianism, in some form, is true. In reply to the arguments, three general defenses have been offered.

The First Line of Defense

The first line of defense is to point out that the examples used in the antiutilitarian arguments are unrealistic and do not describe situations that come up in the real world. Since Utilitarianism is designed as a guide for decision making in the situations we actually face, the fanciful examples are dismissed as irrelevant. . . .

The Second Line of Defense

The first line of defense contains more bluster than substance. While it can plausibly be maintained that *most* acts of false witness and the like have bad consequences in the real world, it cannot reasonably be asserted that *all* such acts have bad consequences. Surely, in at least some real-life cases, one can bring about good results by doing things that moral common sense condemns. Therefore, in at least some real-life cases Utilitarianism will come into conflict with common sense. Moreover, even if the antiutilitarian arguments had to rely exclusively on fictitious examples, those arguments would nevertheless retain their power; for showing that Utilitarianism has unacceptable consequences in hypothetical cases is a perfectly valid way of pointing up its theoretical defects. The first line of defense, then, is weak.

The second line of defense admits all this and proposes to save Utilitarianism by giving it a new formulation. In revising a theory to meet criticism, the trick is to identify precisely the feature of the theory that is causing the trouble and to change *that,* leaving the rest of the theory undisturbed as much as possible.

The troublesome aspect of the theory was this: the classical version of Utilitarianism implied that *each individual action* is to be evaluated by reference to its own particular consequences. If on a certain occasion you are tempted to lie, whether it would be wrong is determined by the consequences of *that particular lie.* This, the theory's defenders said, is the point that causes all the trouble; even though we know that *in general* lying has bad consequences, it is obvious that sometimes particular acts of lying can have good consequences.

Therefore, the new version of Utilitarianism modifies the theory so that individual actions will no longer be judged by the Principle of Utility. Instead, *rules* will be established by reference to the principle, and individual acts will then be judged right or wrong by reference to the rules. This new version of the theory is called *Rule–Utilitarianism,* to contrast it with the original theory, now commonly called *Act–Utilitarianism.*

Rule–Utilitarianism has no difficulty coping with the three antiutilitarian arguments. An act-utilitarian, faced with the situation described by McCloskey, would be tempted to bear false witness against the innocent man because the consequences of *that particular act* would be good. But the rule-utilitarian would not reason in that way. He would first ask, "What *general rules of conduct* tend to promote the greatest happiness?" Suppose we imagine two societies, one in which the rule "Don't bear false witness against the innocent" is faithfully adhered to, and one in which this rule is not followed. In which society are people likely to be better off? Clearly, from the point of view of utility, the first society is preferable. Therefore, the rule against incriminating the innocent should be accepted, and *by appealing to this rule,* the rule-utilitarian concludes that the person in McCloskey's example should not testify against the innocent man.

Analogous arguments can be used to establish rules against violating people's rights, breaking promises, lying, and so on. We should accept such rules because following them, as a regular practice, promotes the general welfare. But once having appealed to the Principle of Utility to establish the rules, we do not have to invoke the principle again to determine the rightness of particular actions. Individual actions are justified simply by appeal to the already-established rules.

Thus Rule–Utilitarianism cannot be convicted of violating our moral common sense, or of conflicting with ordinary ideas of justice, personal rights, and the rest. In shifting emphasis from the justification of acts to the justification of rules, the theory has been brought into line with our intuitive judgments to a remarkable degree.

The Third Line of Defense

Finally, a small group of contemporary utilitarians has had a very different response to the antiutilitarian arguments. Those arguments point out that the classical theory is at odds with ordinary notions of justice, individual rights, and so on; to this, their response is, essentially, "So what?" In

1961 the Australian philosopher J. J. C. Smart published a monograph entitled *An Outline of a System of Utilitarian Ethics;* reflecting on his position in that book, Smart said:

> Admittedly utilitarianism does have consequences which are incompatible with the common moral consciousness, but I tended to take the view "so much the worse for the common moral consciousness." That is, I was inclined to reject the common methodology of testing general ethical principles by seeing how they square with our feelings in particular instances.

Our moral common sense is, after all, not necessarily reliable. It may incorporate various irrational elements, including prejudices absorbed from our parents, our religion, and the general culture. Why should we simply assume that our feelings are always correct? And why should we reject a plausible, rational theory of ethics such as Utilitarianism simply because it conflicts with those feelings? Perhaps it is the feelings, not the theory, that should be discarded.

In light of this, consider again McCloskey's example of the person tempted to bear false witness. McCloskey argues that it would be wrong to have a man convicted of a crime he did not commit, because it would be unjust. But wait: such a judgment serves *that man's* interests well enough, but what of the *other* innocent people who will be hurt if the rioting and lynchings are allowed to continue? What of them? Surely we might hope that we never have to face a situation like this, for the options are all extremely distasteful. But if we *must* choose between (a) securing the conviction of one innocent person and (b) allowing the deaths of several innocent people, is it so unreasonable to think that the first option, bad as it is, is preferable to the second?

On this way of thinking, Act–Utilitarianism is a perfectly defensible doctrine and does not need to be modified. Rule–Utilitarianism, by contrast, is an unnecessarily watered-down version of the theory, which gives rules a greater importance than they merit. Act–Utilitarianism is, however, recognized to be a radical doctrine which implies that many of our ordinary moral feelings may be mistaken. In this respect, it does what good philosophy always does—it challenges us to rethink matters that we have heretofore taken for granted.

WHAT IS CORRECT AND WHAT IS INCORRECT IN UTILITARIANISM

There is a sense in which no moral philosopher can completely reject Utilitarianism. The consequences of one's actions—whether they promote happiness, or cause misery—must be admitted by all to be extremely important. John Stuart Mill once remarked that, insofar as we are benevolent, we must accept the utilitarian standard; and he was surely right. Moreover, the utilitarian emphasis on impartiality must also be a part of any defensible moral theory. The question is whether these are the *only* kinds of considerations an adequate theory must acknowledge. Aren't there *other* considerations that are also important?

If we consult what Smart calls our "common moral consciousness," it seems that there are *many* other considerations that are morally important. But I believe the radical act-utilitarians are right to warn us that "common sense" cannot be trusted. Many people once felt that there is an important difference between whites and blacks, so that the interests of whites are somehow more important. Trusting the "common sense" of their day, they might have insisted that an adequate moral theory should accommodate this "fact." Today, no one worth listening to would say such a thing. But who knows how many *other* irrational prejudices are still a part of our moral common sense? At the end of his classic study of race relations, *An American Dilemma* (1944), the Swedish sociologist Gunnar Myrdal reminds us:

> There must be still other countless errors of the same sort that no living man can yet detect, because of the fog within which our type of Western culture envelops us. Cultural influences have set up the assumptions about the mind, the body, and the universe with which we begin; pose the questions we ask; influence the facts we seek; determine the interpretation we give these facts; and direct our reaction to these interpretations and conclusions.

The strength of Utilitarianism is that it firmly resists "corruption" by possibly irrational elements. By sticking to the Principle of Utility as the *only* standard for judging right and wrong, it avoids all danger of incorporating into moral theory prejudices, feelings, and "intuitions" that have no rational basis.

The warning should be heeded. "Common sense" can, indeed, mislead us. At the same time, however, there might be at least some nonutilitarian considerations that an adequate theory *should* accept, because there *is* a rational basis for them. Consider, for example, the matter of what people deserve. A person who has worked hard in her job may deserve a promotion more than someone who has loafed, and it would be unjust for the loafer to be promoted first. This is a point that we would expect any fair-minded employer to acknowledge; we would all be indignant if we were passed over for promotion in favor of someone who had not worked as hard or as well as we. Now utilitarians might agree with this, and say that it can be explained by their theory—they might argue that it promotes the general welfare to encourage hard work by rewarding it. But this does not seem to be an adequate explanation of the importance of desert. The woman who worked harder has a superior claim to the promotion, *not* because it promotes the general welfare for her to get it, but *because she has earned it*. The reason she should be promoted has to do with *her* merits. This does not appear to be the kind of consideration a utilitarian could admit.

Does this way of thinking express a mere prejudice, or does it have a rational basis? I believe it has a rational basis, although it is not one that utilitarians could accept. We ought to recognize individual desert as a reason for treating people in certain ways—for example, as a reason for promoting the woman who has worked harder—because that is the principal way we have of treating individuals as autonomous, responsible beings. If in fact people have the power to choose their own actions, in such a way that they are *responsible* for those actions and what results from them, then acknowledging their deserts is just a way of acknowledging their standing as autonomous individuals. In treating them as they deserve to be treated, we are responding to the way they have freely chosen to behave. Thus in some instances we will not treat everyone alike, because people are not just members of an undifferentiated crowd. Instead, they are individuals who, by their own choices, show themselves to deserve different kinds of responses. . . .

STUDY QUESTIONS

1. What is the foundation of utilitarianism?
2. Why does the first line of defense fail? Think about how the example of Ms. York may pertain to this problem, and explain the failure in terms of her experience.
3. How is rule–utilitarianism superior to act–utilitarianism? Consider this question in light of the third line of defense.
4. Do nonhuman animals and the environment have moral status? Ought they to, on a utilitarian account?

3

Kant's Ethics

Onora O'Neill

Onora O'Neill teaches philosophy at the University of Essex in Colchester, England. She has published extensively in the field of ethics, including *Acting on Principle* and *Faces of Hunger.*

Kant's moral theory has acquired the reputation of being forbiddingly difficult to understand and, once understood, excessively demanding in its requirements. I don't believe that this reputation has been wholly earned, and I am going to try to undermine it. . . . I shall try to reduce some of the difficulties. . . . Finally, I shall compare Kantian and utilitarian approaches and assess their strengths and weaknesses.

The main method by which I propose to avoid some of the difficulties of Kant's moral theory is by explaining only one part of the theory. This does not seem to me to be an irresponsible approach in this case. One of the things that makes Kant's moral theory hard to understand is that he gives a number of different versions of the principle that he calls the Supreme Principle of Morality, and these different versions don't look at all like one another. They also don't look at all like the utilitarians' Greatest Happiness Principle. But the Kantian principle is supposed to play a similar role in arguments about what to do.

Kant calls his Supreme Principle the *Categorical Imperative;* its various versions also have sonorous names. One is called the Formula of Universal Law; another is the Formula of the Kingdom of Ends. The one on which I shall concentrate is known as the *Formula of the End in Itself.* To understand why Kant thinks that these picturesquely named principles are equivalent to one another takes quite a lot of close and detailed analysis of Kant's philosophy. I shall avoid this and concentrate on showing the implications of this version of the Categorical Imperative.

THE FORMULA OF THE END IN ITSELF

Kant states the Formula of the End in Itself as follows:

> Act in such a way that you always treat humanity, whether in your own person or in the person of any other, never simply as a means but always at the same time as an end.

To understand this we need to know what it is to treat a person as a means or as an end. According to Kant, each of our acts reflects one or more *maxims.* The maxim of the act is the principle on which one sees oneself as acting. A maxim expresses a person's policy, or if he or she has no settled policy, the principle underlying the particular intention or decision on which he or she acts. Thus, a person who decides "This year I'll give 10 percent of my income to famine relief" has as a maxim the principle of tithing his or her income for famine relief. In practice, the difference between intentions and maxims is of little importance, for given any intention, we can formulate the corresponding maxim by deleting references to particular times, places, and persons. In what follows I shall take the terms 'maxim' and 'intention' as equivalent.

Whenever we act intentionally, we have at least one maxim and can, if we reflect, state what it is. (There is of course room for self-deception here—"I'm only keeping the wolf from the door" we may claim as we wolf down enough to keep ourselves overweight, or, more to the point, enough to feed someone else who hasn't enough food.)

When we want to work out whether an act we propose to do is right or wrong, according to Kant, we should look at our maxims and not at how much misery or happiness the act is likely to produce, and whether it does better at increasing happiness than other available acts. We just have to check that the act we have in mind will not use anyone as a mere means, and, if possible, that it will treat other persons as ends in themselves.

USING PERSONS AS MERE MEANS

To use someone as a *mere means* is to involve them in a scheme of action *to which they could not in principle consent.* Kant does not say that there is anything wrong about using someone as a means. Evidently we have to do so in any cooperative scheme of action. If I cash a check I use the teller as a means, without whom I could not lay my hands on the cash; the teller in turn uses me as a means to earn his or her living. But in this case, each party consents to her or his part in the transaction. Kant would say that though they use one another as means, they do not use one another as *mere* means. Each person assumes that the other has maxims of his or her own and is not just a thing or a prop to be manipulated.

But there are other situations where one person uses another in a way to which the other could not in principle consent. For example, one person may make a promise to another with every intention of breaking it. If the promise is accepted, then the person to whom it was given must be ignorant of what the promisor's intention (maxim) really is. If one knew that the promisor did not intend to do what he or she was promising, one would, after all, not accept or rely on the promise. It would be as though there had been no promise made. Successful false promising depends on deceiving the person to whom the promise is made about what one's real maxim is. And since the person who is deceived doesn't know that real maxim, he or she can't in principle consent to his or her part in the proposed scheme of action. The person who is deceived is, as it were, a prop or a tool—a mere means—in the false promisor's scheme. A person who promises falsely treats the acceptor of the promise as a prop or a thing and not as a person. In Kant's view, it is this that makes false promising wrong.

One standard way of using others as mere means is by deceiving them. By getting someone involved in a business scheme or a criminal activity on false pretenses, or by giving a misleading account of what one is about, or by making a false promise or a fraudulent contract, one involves another in something to which he or she in principle cannot consent, since the scheme requires that he or she doesn't know what is going on. Another standard way of using others as mere means is by coercing them. If a rich or powerful person threatens a debtor with bankruptcy unless he or she joins in some scheme, then the creditor's intention is to coerce; and the debtor, if coerced, cannot consent to his or her part in the creditor's scheme. To make the example more specific: If a moneylender in an Indian village threatens not to renew a vital loan unless he is given the debtor's land, then he uses the debtor as a mere means. He coerces the debtor, who cannot truly consent to this "offer he can't refuse." (Of course the outward form of such transactions may look like ordinary commercial dealings, but we know very well that some offers and demands couched in that form are coercive.)

In Kant's view, acts that are done on maxims that require deception or coercion of others, and so cannot have the consent of those others (for consent precludes both deception and coercion), are wrong. When we act on such maxims, we treat others as mere means, as things rather than as ends in themselves. If we act on such maxims, our acts are not only wrong but unjust: such acts wrong the particular others who are deceived or coerced.

TREATING PERSONS AS ENDS IN THEMSELVES

Duties of justice are, in Kant's view (as in many others'), the most important of our duties. When we fail in these duties, we have used some other or others as mere means. But there are also cases where, though we do not use others as mere means, still we fail to use them as ends in themselves in the fullest possible way. To treat someone as an end in him- or herself requires in the first place that one not use him or her as mere means, that one respect each as a rational person with his or her own maxims. But beyond that, one may also seek to foster others' plans and maxims by sharing some of their ends. To act beneficently is to seek others' happiness, therefore to intend to achieve some of the things that those others aim at with their maxims. If I want to make others happy, I will adopt maxims that not merely do not manipulate them but that foster some of their plans and activities. Beneficent acts try to achieve what others want. However, we cannot seek everything that others want; their wants are too numerous and diverse, and, of course, sometimes incompatible. It follows that beneficence has to be selective.

There is then quite a sharp distinction between the requirements of justice and of beneficence in Kantian ethics. Justice requires that we act on *no* maxims that use others as mere means. Beneficence requires that we act on *some* maxims that foster others' ends, though it is a matter for judgment and discretion which of their ends we foster. Some maxims no doubt ought not to be fostered because it would be unjust to do so. Kantians are not committed to working interminably through a list of happiness-producing and misery-reducing acts; but there are some acts whose obligatoriness utilitarians may need to debate as they try to compare total outcomes of different choices, to which Kantians are stringently bound. Kantians will claim that they have done nothing wrong if none of their acts is unjust, and that their duty is complete if in addition their life plans have in the circumstances been reasonably beneficent.

In making sure that they meet all the demands of justice, Kantians do not try to compare all available acts and see which has the best effects. They consider only the proposals for action that occur to them and check that these proposals use no other as mere means. If they do not, the act is permissible; if omitting the act would use another as mere means, the act is obligatory. Kant's theory has less scope than utilitarianism. Kantians do not claim to discover whether acts whose maxims they don't know fully are just. They may be reluctant to judge others' acts or policies that cannot be regarded as the maxim of any person or institution. They cannot rank acts in order of merit. Yet, the theory offers more precision than utilitarianism when data are scarce. One can usually tell whether one's act would use others as mere means, even when its impact on human happiness is thoroughly obscure.

THE LIMITS OF KANTIAN ETHICS: INTENTIONS AND RESULTS

Kantian ethics differs from utilitarian ethics both in its scope and in the precision with which it guides action. Every action, whether of a person or of an agency, can be assessed by utilitarian methods, provided only that information is available about all the consequences of the act. The theory has unlimited scope, but, owing to lack of data, often lacks precision. Kantian ethics has a more restricted scope. Since it assesses actions by looking at the maxims of agents, it can only assess intentional acts. This means that it is most at home in assessing individuals' acts; but it can be extended to assess acts of agencies that (like corporations and governments and student unions) have decision-making procedures. It can do nothing to assess patterns of action that reflect no intention or policy, hence it cannot assess the acts of groups lacking decision-making procedures, such as the student movement, the women's movement, or the consumer movement.

It may seem a great limitation of Kantian ethics that it concentrates on intentions to the neglect of results. It might seem that all conscientious Kantians have to do is to make sure that they never intend to use others as mere means, and that they sometimes intend to foster other's ends. And, as we all know, good intentions sometimes lead to bad results and correspondingly, bad intentions sometimes do no harm, or even produce good. If Hardin is right, the good intentions of those who feed the starving lead to dreadful results in the long run. If some traditional arguments in favor of capitalism are right, the greed and selfishness of the profit motive have produced unparalleled prosperity for many.

But such discrepancies between intentions and results are the exception and not the rule. For we cannot just *claim* that our intentions are good and do what we will. Our intentions reflect what we expect the immediate results of our action to be. Nobody credits the "intentions" of a couple who practice neither celibacy nor contraception but still insist "we never meant to have (more) children." Conception is likely (and known to be likely) in such cases. Where people's expressed intentions ignore the normal and predictable results of what they do, we infer that (if they are not amazingly ignorant) their words do not express their true intentions. The Formula of the End in Itself applies to the intentions on which one acts—not to some prettified version that one may avow. Provided this intention—the agent's real intention—uses no other as mere means, he or she does nothing unjust. If some of his or her intentions foster others' ends, then he or she is sometimes beneficent. It is therefore possible for people to test their proposals by Kantian arguments even when they lack the comprehensive causal knowledge that utilitarianism requires. Conscientious Kantians can work out whether they will be doing wrong by some act even though it blurs the implications of the theory. If we peer through the blur, we see that the utilitarian view is that lives may indeed be sacrificed for the sake of a greater good even when the persons are not willing. There is nothing wrong with using another as a mere means provided that the end for which the person is so used is a happier result than could have been achieved any other way, taking into account the misery the means have caused. In utilitarian thought, persons are not ends in themselves. Their special moral status derives from their being means to the production of happiness. Human life has therefore a high though derivative value, and one life may be taken for the sake of greater happiness in other lives, or for ending of misery in that life. Nor is there any deep difference between ending a life for the sake of others' happiness by not helping (e.g., by triaging) and doing so by harming. Because the distinction between justice and beneficence is not sharply made within utilitarianism, it is not possible to say that triaging is a matter of not benefiting, while other interventions are a matter of injustice.

Utilitarian moral theory has then a rather paradoxical view of the value of human life. Living, conscious humans are (along with other sentient beings) necessary for the existence of everything utilitarians value. But it is not their being alive but the state of their consciousness that is of value. Hence, the best results may require certain lives to be lost—by whatever means—for the sake of the total happiness and absence of misery that can be produced.

KANT AND RESPECT FOR PERSONS

Kantians reach different conclusions about human life. Human life is valuable because humans (and conceivably other beings, e.g., angels or apes) are the bearers of rational life. Humans are able to choose and to plan. This capacity and its exercise are of such value that they ought not to be sacrificed for anything of lesser value. Therefore, no one rational or autonomous creature should be treated as mere means for the enjoyment or even the happiness of another. We may in Kant's view justifiably—even nobly—risk or sacrifice our lives for others. For in doing so we follow our own maxim and nobody uses us as mere means. But no others may use either our lives or our bodies for a scheme that they have either coerced or deceived us into joining. For in doing so they would fail to treat us as rational beings; they would use us as mere means and not as ends in ourselves.

It is conceivable that a society of Kantians, all of whom took pains to use no other as mere means, would end up with less happiness or with fewer persons alive than would some societies of complying utilitarians. For since the Kantians would be strictly bound only to justice, they might without wrongdoing be quite selective in their beneficence and fail to maximize either survival rates or happiness, or even to achieve as much of either as a strenuous group of utilitarians, who know that their foresight is limited and that they may cause some harm or fail to cause some benefit. But they will not cause harms that they can foresee without this being reflected in their intentions.

UTILITARIANISM AND RESPECT FOR LIFE

From the differing implications that Kantian and utilitarian moral theories have for our actions towards those who do or may suffer famine, we can discover two sharply contrasting views of the value of human life. Utilitarians value happiness and the absence or reduction of misery. As a utilitarian one ought (if conscientious) to devote one's life to achieving the best possible balance of happiness over misery. If one's life plan remains in doubt, this will be because the means to this end are often unclear. But whenever the causal tendency of acts is clear, utilitarians will be able to discern the acts they should successively do in order to improve the world's balance of happiness over unhappiness.

This task is not one for the faint-hearted. First, it is dauntingly long, indeed interminable. Second, it may at times require the sacrifice of happiness, and even of lives, for the sake of a greater happiness. Such sacrifice may be morally required not only when the person whose happiness or even whose life is at stake volunteers to make the sacrifice. It may be necessary to sacrifice some lives for the sake of others. As our control over the means of ending and preserving human life has increased, analogous dilemmas have arisen in many areas for utilitarians. Should life be preserved at the cost of pain when modern medicine makes this possible? Should life be preserved without hope of consciousness? Should triage policies, because they may maximize the number of survivors, be used to determine who should be left to starve? Should population growth be fostered wherever it will increase the total of human happiness—or on some views so long as average happiness is not reduced? All these questions can be fitted into utilitarian frameworks and answered *if* we have the relevant information. And sometimes the answer will be that human happiness demands the sacrifice of lives, including the sacrifice of unwilling lives. Further, for most utilitarians, it makes no difference if the unwilling sacrifices involve acts of injustice to those whose lives are to be lost. It might, for example, prove necessary for maximal happiness that some persons have their allotted rations, or their hard-earned income, diverted for others' benefit. Or it might turn out that some generations must sacrifice comforts or liberties and even lives to rear "the fabric of felicity" for their successors. . . . On the other hand, nobody will have been made an instrument of others' survival or happiness in the society of complying Kantians.

STUDY QUESTIONS

1. In Kant's system, according to the Formula of the End in Itself, what is required of an individual for that person to fulfill the duties of justice?
2. In Kant, what is the difference between justice and beneficence?
3. According to O'Neill, does a Kantian's attention to maxim (intention) preclude attention to result? Why or why not?
4. What difference is there between the Kantian respect for persons and the utilitarian respect for life?
5. Some think Kant buries the particular in the universal. O'Neill does not seem to agree. How does she come to this conclusion?
6. Does Kant's theory appeal to you more than utilitarianism? Why or why not?

4

Taking Rights Seriously

Ronald Dworkin

Ronald Dworkin is a professor of law at New York University. He has published extensively in the areas of law and ethics, and is the author of *Life's Dominion: An Argument about Abortion, Euthanasia, and Individual Freedom.*

THE RIGHTS OF CITIZENS

The language of rights now dominates political debate in the United States. Does the Government respect the moral and political rights of its citizens? Or does the Government's foreign policy, or its race policy, fly in the face of these rights? Do the minorities whose rights have been violated have the right to violate the law in return? Or does the silent majority itself have rights, including the right that those who break the law be punished? It is not surprising that these questions are now prominent. The concept of rights, and particularly the concept of rights against the Government, has its most natural use when a political society is divided, and appeals to co-operation or a common goal are pointless.

The debate does not include the issue of whether citizens have *some* moral rights against their Government. It seems accepted on all sides that they do. Conventional lawyers and politicians take it as a point of pride that our legal system recognizes, for example, individual rights of free speech, equality, and due process. They base their claim that our law deserves respect, at least in part, on that fact, for they would not claim that totalitarian systems deserve the same loyalty.

Some philosophers, of course, reject the idea that citizens have rights apart from what the law happens to give them. Bentham thought that the idea of moral rights was 'nonsense on stilts'. But that view has never been part of our orthodox political theory, and politicians of both parties appeal to the rights of the people to justify a great part of what they want to do. I shall not be concerned, in this essay, to defend the thesis that citizens have moral rights against their governments; I want instead to explore the implications of that thesis for those, including the present United States Government, who profess to accept it.

It is much in dispute, of course, what *particular* rights citizens have. Does the acknowledged right to free speech, for example, include the right to participate in nuisance demonstrations? In practice the Government will have the last word on what an individual's rights are, because its police will do what its officials and courts say. But that does not mean that the Government's view is necessarily the correct view; anyone who thinks it does must believe that men and women have only such moral rights as Government chooses to grant, which means that they have no moral rights at all.

All this is sometimes obscured in the United States by the constitutional system. The American Constitution provides a set of individual *legal* rights in the First Amendment, and in the due process, equal protection, and similar clauses. Under present legal practice the Supreme Court has the power to declare an act of Congress or of a state legislature void if the Court finds that the act offends these provisions. This practice has led some commentators to suppose that individual moral rights are fully protected by this system, but that is hardly so, nor could it be so.

The Constitution fuses legal and moral issues, by making the validity of a law depend on the answer to complex moral problems, like the problem of whether a particular statute respects the inherent equality of all men. This fusion has important consequences for the debates about civil disobedience; . . . But it leaves open two prominent questions. It does not tell us whether the Constitution, even properly interpreted, recognizes all the moral rights that citizens have, and it does not tell us whether, as many suppose, citizens would have a duty to obey the law even if it did invade their moral rights. . . .

Even if the Constitution were perfect, of course, and the majority left it alone, it would not follow that the Supreme Court could guarantee the individual rights of citizens. A Supreme Court decision is still a legal decision, and it must take into account precedent and institutional considerations like relations between the Court and Congress, as well as morality. And no judicial decision is necessarily the right decision. Judges stand for different positions on controversial issues of law and morals and, as the fights over Nixon's Supreme Court nominations showed, a President is entitled to appoint judges of his own persuasion, provided that they are honest and capable.

So, though the constitutional system adds something to the protection of moral rights against the Government, it falls far short of guaranteeing these rights, or even establishing what they are. . . .

RIGHTS AND THE RIGHT TO BREAK THE LAW

. . . In most cases when we say that someone has a 'right' to do something, we imply that it would be wrong to interfere with his doing it, or at least that some special grounds are needed for justifying any interference. I use this strong sense of right when I say that you have the right to spend your money gambling, if you wish, though you ought to spend it in a more worthwhile way. I mean that it would be wrong for anyone to interfere with you even though you propose to spend your money in a way that I think is wrong.

There is a clear difference between saying that someone has a right to do something in this sense and saying that it is the 'right' thing for him to do, or that he does no 'wrong' in doing it. Someone may have the right to do something that is the wrong thing for him to do, as might be the case with gambling. Conversely, something may be the right thing for him to do and yet he may have no right to do it, in the sense that it would not be wrong for someone to interfere with his trying. If our army captures an enemy soldier, we might say that the right thing for him to do is to try to escape, but it would not follow that it is wrong for us to try to stop him. . . .

These distinctions enable us to see an ambiguity in the orthodox question: Does a man ever have a right to break the law? Does that question mean to ask whether he ever has a right to break the law in the strong sense, so that the Government would do wrong to stop him, by arresting and prosecuting him? Or does it mean to ask whether he ever does the right thing to break the law, so that we should all respect him even though the Government should jail him? . . .

Conservatives and liberals do agree that sometimes a man does not do the wrong thing to break a law, when his conscience so requires. They disagree, when they do, over the different issue of what the State's response should be. Both parties do think that sometimes the State should prosecute. But this is not inconsistent with the proposition that the man prosecuted did the right thing in breaking the law. . . .

I said that in the United States citizens are supposed to have certain fundamental rights against their Government, certain moral rights made into legal rights by the Constitution. If this idea is significant, and worth bragging about, then these rights must be rights in the strong sense I just described. The claim that citizens have a right to free speech must imply that it would be wrong for the Government to stop them from speaking, even when the Government believes that what they will say will cause more harm than good. The claim cannot mean, on the prisoner-of-war analogy, only that citizens do no wrong in speaking their minds, though the Government reserves the right to prevent them from doing so.

This is a crucial point, and I want to labour it. Of course a responsible government must be ready to justify anything it does, particularly when it limits the liberty of its citizens. But normally it is a sufficient justification, even for an act that limits liberty, that the act is calculated to increase what the philosophers call general utility—that it is calculated to produce more over-all benefit than harm. So, though the New York City government needs a justification for forbidding motorists to drive up Lexington Avenue, it is sufficient justification if the proper officials believe, on sound evidence, that the gain to the many will outweigh the inconvenience to the few. When individual citizens are said to have rights against the Government, however, like the right of free speech, that must mean that this sort of justification is not enough. Otherwise the claim would not argue that individuals have special protection against the law when their rights are in play, and that is just the point of the claim.

Not all legal rights, or even Constitutional rights, represent moral rights against the Government. I now have the legal right to drive either way on Fifty-seventh Street, but the Government would do no wrong to make that street one-way if it thought it in the general interest to do so. I have a Constitutional right to vote for a congressman every two years, but the national and state governments would do no wrong if, following the amendment procedure, they made a congressman's term four years instead of two, again on the basis of a judgment that this would be for the general good.

But those Constitutional rights that we call fundamental, like the right of free speech, are supposed to represent rights against the Government in the strong sense; that is the point of the boast that our legal system respects the fundamental rights of the citizen. If citizens have a moral right of free speech, then governments would do wrong to repeal the First Amendment that guarantees it, even if they were persuaded that the majority would be better off if speech were curtailed.

I must not overstate the point. Someone who claims that citizens have a right against the Government need not go so far as to say that the State is *never* justified in overriding that right. He might say, for example, that although citizens have a right to free speech, the Government may override that right when necessary to protect the rights of others, or to prevent a catastrophe, or even to obtain a clear and major public benefit (though if he acknowledged this last as a possible justification he would be treating the right in question as not among the most important or fundamental). What he cannot do is to say that the Government is justified in overriding a right on the minimal grounds that would be sufficient if no such right existed. He cannot say that the Government is entitled to act on no more than a judgment that its act is likely to produce, overall, a benefit to the community. That admission would make his claim of a right pointless, and would show him to be using some sense of 'right' other than the strong sense necessary to give his claim the political importance it is normally taken to have. . . .

I said that any society that claims to recognize rights at all must abandon the notion of a general duty to obey the law that holds in all cases. This is important, because it shows that there are no short cuts to meeting a citizen's claim to right. If a citizen argues that he has a moral right not to serve in the Army, or to protest in a way he finds effective, then an official who wants to answer him, and not simply bludgeon him into obedience, must respond to the particular point he makes, and cannot point to the draft law or a Supreme Court decision as having even special, let alone decisive, weight. Sometimes an official who considers the citizen's moral arguments in good faith will be persuaded that the citizen's claim is plausible, or even right. It does not follow, however, that he will always be persuaded or that he always should be.

I must emphasize that all these propositions concern the strong sense of right, and they therefore leave open important questions about the right thing to do. If a man believes he has the right to break the law, he must then ask whether he does the right thing to exercise that right. He must remember that reasonable men can differ about whether he has a right against the Government, and therefore the right to break the law, that he thinks he has; and therefore that reasonable men can oppose him in good faith. He must take into account the various consequences his acts will have, whether they involve violence, and such other considerations as the context makes relevant; he must not go beyond the rights he can in good faith claim, to acts that violate the rights of others. . . .

CONTROVERSIAL RIGHTS

The argument so far has been hypothetical: if a man has a particular moral right against the Government, that right survives contrary legislation or adjudication. But this does not tell us what rights he has, and it is notorious that reasonable men disagree about that. There is wide agreement on certain clearcut cases; almost everyone who believes in rights at all would admit, for example, that a man has a moral right to speak his mind in a non-provocative way on matters of political concern, and that this is an important right that the State must go to great pains to protect. But there is great controversy as to the limits of such paradigm rights, and the so-called 'anti-riot' law involved in the famous Chicago Seven trial of the last decade is a case in point.

The defendants were accused of conspiring to cross state lines with the intention of causing a riot. This charge is vague—perhaps unconstitutionally vague—but the law apparently defines as criminal emotional speeches which argue that violence is justified in order to secure political equality. Does the right of free speech protect this sort of speech? That, of course, is a legal issue, because it invokes the free-speech clause of the First Amendment of the Constitution. But it is also a moral issue, because, as I said, we must treat the First Amendment as an attempt to protect a moral right. It is part of the job of governing to 'define' moral rights through statutes and judicial decisions, that is, to declare officially the extent that moral rights will be taken to have in law. Congress faced this task in voting on the anti-riot bill, and the Supreme Court has faced it in countless cases. How should the different departments of government go about defining moral rights?

They should begin with a sense that whatever they decide might be wrong. History and their descendants may judge that they acted unjustly when they thought they were right. If they take their duty seriously, they must try to limit their mistakes, and they must therefore try to discover where the dangers of mistakes lie.

They might choose one of two very different models for this purpose. The first model recommends striking a balance between the rights of the individual and the demands of society at large. If the Government *infringes* on a moral right (for example, by defining the right of free speech more narrowly than justice requires), then it has done the individual a wrong. On the other hand, if the Government *inflates* a right (by defining it more broadly than justice requires), then it cheats society of some general benefit, like safe streets, that there is no reason it should not have. So a mistake on one side is as serious as a mistake on the other. The course of government is to steer to the middle, to balance the general good and personal rights, giving to each its due. . . .

The first model, described in this way, has great plausibility, and most laymen and lawyers, I think, would respond to it warmly. The metaphor of balancing the public interest against personal claims is established in our political and judicial rhetoric, and this metaphor gives the model both familiarity and appeal. Nevertheless, the first model is a false one, certainly in the case of rights generally regarded as important, and the metaphor is the heart of its error.

The institution of rights against the Government is not a gift of God, or an ancient ritual, or a national sport. It is a complex and troublesome practice that makes the Government's job of securing the general benefit more difficult and more expensive, and it would be a frivolous and wrongful practice unless it served some point. Anyone who professes to take rights seriously, and who praises our Government for respecting them, must have some sense of what that point is. He must accept, at the minimum, one or both of two important ideas. The first is the vague but powerful idea of human dignity. This idea, associated with Kant, but defended by philosophers of different schools, supposes that there are ways of treating a man that are inconsistent with recognizing him as a full member of the human community, and holds that such treatment is profoundly unjust.

The second is the more familiar idea of political equality. This supposes that the weaker members of a political community are entitled to the same concern and respect of their government as the more powerful members have secured for themselves, so that if some men have freedom of decision whatever the effect on the general good, then all men must have the same freedom. I do not want to defend or elaborate these ideas here, but only to insist that anyone who claims that citizens have rights must accept ideas very close to these.[1]

It makes sense to say that a man has a fundamental right against the Government, in the strong sense, like free speech, if that right is necessary to protect his dignity, or his standing as equally entitled to concern and respect, or some other personal value of like consequence. It does not make sense otherwise.

So if rights make sense at all, then the invasion of a relatively important right must be a very serious matter. It means treating a man as less than a man, or as less worthy of concern than other men. The institution of rights rests on the conviction that this is a grave injustice, and that it is worth paying the incremental cost in social policy or efficiency that is necessary to prevent it. But then it must be wrong to say that inflating rights is as serious as invading them. If the Government errs on the side of the individual, then it simply pays a little more in social efficiency than it has to pay; it pays a little more, that is, of the same coin that it has already decided must be spent. But if it errs against the individual it inflicts an insult upon him that, on its own reckoning, it is worth a great deal of that coin to avoid. . . .

It cannot be an argument for curtailing a right, once granted, simply that society would pay a further price for extending it. There must be something special about that further cost, or there must be some other feature of the case, that makes it sensible to say that although great social cost is warranted to protect the original right, this particular cost is not necessary. Otherwise, the Government's failure to extend the right will show that its recognition of the right in the original case is a sham, a promise that it intends to keep only until that becomes inconvenient.

How can we show that a particular cost is not worth paying without taking back the initial recognition of a right? I can think of only three sorts of grounds that can consistently be used to limit the definition of a particular right. First, the Government might show that the values protected by the original right are not really at stake in the marginal case, or are at stake only in some attenuated form. Second, it might show that if the right is defined to include the marginal case, then some competing right, in the strong sense I described earlier, would be abridged. Third, it might show that if the right were so defined, then the cost to society would not be simply incremental, but would be of a degree far beyond the cost paid to grant the original right, a degree great enough to justify whatever assault on dignity or equality might be involved. . . .

But what of the individual rights of those who will be destroyed by a riot, of the passerby who will be killed by a sniper's bullet or the shopkeeper who will be ruined by looting? To put the issue in this way, as a question of competing rights, suggests a principle that would undercut the effect of uncertainty. Shall we say that some rights to protection are so important that the Government is justified in doing all it can to maintain them? Shall we therefore say that the Government may abridge the rights of others to act when their acts might simply increase the risk, by however slight or speculative a margin, that some person's right to life or property will be violated?

Some such principle is relied on by those who oppose the Supreme Court's recent liberal rulings on police procedure. These rulings increase the chance that a guilty man will go free, and therefore marginally increase the risk that any particular member of the community will be murdered, raped, or robbed. Some critics believe that the Court's decisions must therefore be wrong.

But no society that purports to recognize a variety of rights, on the ground that a man's dignity or equality may be invaded in a variety of ways, can accept such a principle. If forcing a man to testify against himself, or forbidding him to speak, does the damage that the rights against self-incrimination and the right of free speech assume, then it would be contemptuous for the State to tell a man that he must suffer this damage against the possibility that other men's risk of loss may be marginally reduced. If rights make sense, then the degrees of their importance cannot be so different that some count not at all when others are mentioned.

Of course the Government may discriminate and may stop a man from exercising his right to speak when there is a clear and substantial risk that his speech will do great damage to the person or property of others, and no other means of preventing this are at hand, as in the case of the man shouting 'Fire!' in a theater. But we must reject the suggested principle that the Government can simply ignore rights to speak when life and property are in question. So long as the impact of speech on these other rights remains speculative and marginal, it must look elsewhere for levers to pull.

WHY TAKE RIGHTS SERIOUSLY?

I said at the beginning of this essay that I wanted to show what a government must do that professes to recognize individual rights. It must dispense with the claim that citizens never have a right to break its law, and it must not define citizens' rights so that these are cut off for supposed reasons of the general good. Any Government's harsh treatment of civil disobedience, or campaign against vocal protest, may therefore be thought to count against its sincerity.

One might well ask, however, whether it is wise to take rights all that seriously after all. America's genius, at least in her own legend, lies in not taking any abstract doctrine to its logical extreme. It may be time to ignore abstractions, and concentrate instead on giving the majority of our citizens a new sense of their Government's concern for their welfare, and of their title to rule.

That, in any event, is what former Vice-President Agnew seemed to believe. In a policy statement on the issue of 'weirdos' and social misfits, he said that the liberals' concern for individual rights was a headwind blowing in the face of the ship of state. That is a poor metaphor, but the philosophical point it expresses is very well taken. He recognized, as many liberals do not, that the majority cannot travel as fast or as far as it would like if it recognizes the rights of individuals to do what, in the majority's terms, is the wrong thing to do.

Spiro Agnew supposed that rights are divisive, and that national unity and a new respect for law may be developed by taking them more skeptically. But he is wrong. America will continue to be divided by its social and foreign policy, and if the economy grows weaker again the divisions will become more bitter. If we want our laws and our legal institutions to provide the ground rules within which these issues will be contested then these ground rules must not be the conqueror's law that the dominant class imposes on the weaker, as Marx supposed the law of a capitalist society must be. The bulk of the law—that part which defines and implements social, economic, and foreign policy—cannot be neutral. It must state, in its greatest part, the majority's view of the common good. The institution of rights is therefore crucial, because it represents the majority's promise to the minorities that their dignity and equality will be respected. When the divisions among the groups are most violent, then this gesture, if law is to work, must be most sincere.

The institution requires an act of faith on the part of the minorities, because the scope of their rights will be controversial whenever they are important, and because the officers of the majority will act on their own notions of what these rights really are. Of course these officials will disagree with many of the claims that a minority makes. That makes it all the more important that they take their decisions gravely. They must show that they understand what rights are, and they must not cheat on the full implications of the doctrine. The Government will not re-establish respect for law without giving the law some claim to respect. It cannot do that if it neglects the one feature that distinguishes law from ordered brutality. If the Government does not take rights seriously, then it does not take law seriously either.

NOTE

1. He need not consider these ideas to be axiomatic. He may, that is, have reasons for insisting that dignity or equality are important values, and these reasons may be utilitarian. He may believe, for example, that the general good will be advanced, *in the long run,* only if we treat indignity or inequality as very great injustices, and never allow our *opinions* about the general good to justify them. I do not know of any good arguments for or against this sort of 'institutional' utilitarianism, but it is consistent with my point, because it argues that we must treat violations of dignity and equality as special moral crimes, beyond the reach of ordinary utilitarian justification.

STUDY QUESTIONS

1. Is Dworkin correct in saying that a government is wrong to try to follow the fine line between infringing on a right and inflating a right? Why or why not?
2. Is there tension between Kant's idea of human dignity and the idea of political equality? How might they conflict?
3. Does a legal right necessarily imply a moral right? Do legal rights and moral rights ever conflict? When they do, how does one decide which of the two should win?
4. Dworkin states, "If this idea is significant, and worth bragging about, then these rights must be rights in the strong sense I have just described." What does he mean by this statement? Are there limits? Should there be?

5

A Theory of Justice

John Rawls

John Rawls is a professor of philosophy at Harvard University. He is the author of a pathbreaking book in political philosophy, *A Theory of Justice,* from which this excerpt is taken.

THE MAIN IDEA OF THE THEORY OF JUSTICE

My aim is to present a conception of justice which generalizes and carries to a higher level of abstraction the familiar **theory of the social contract** as found, say, in Locke, Rousseau, and Kant.[1] In order to do this we are not to think of the original contract as one to enter a particular society or to set up a particular form of government. Rather, the guiding idea is that the principles of justice for the basic structure of society are the object of the original agreement. They are the principles that free and rational persons concerned to further their own interests would accept in an initial position of equality as defining the fundamental terms of their association. These principles are to regulate all further agreements; they specify the kinds of social cooperation that can be entered into and the forms of government that can be established. This way of regarding the principles of justice I shall call justice as fairness.

Thus we are to imagine that those who engage in social cooperation choose together, in one joint act, the principles which are to assign basic rights and duties and to determine the division of social benefits. Men are to decide in advance how they are to regulate their claims against one another and what is to be the foundation charter of their society. Just as each person must decide by rational reflection what constitutes his good, that is, the system of ends which it is rational for him to pursue, so a group of persons must decide once and for all what is to count among them as just and unjust. The choice which rational men would make in this hypothetical situation of equal liberty, assuming for the present that this choice problem has a solution, determines the principles of justice.

In justice as fairness the original position of equality corresponds to the state of nature in the traditional theory of the social contract. This original position is not, of course, thought of as an actual historical state of affairs, much less as a primitive condition of culture. It is understood as a purely hypothetical situation characterized so as to lead to a certain conception of justice.[2] Among the essential features of this situation is that no one knows his place in society, his class position or social status, nor does any one know his fortune in the distribution of natural assets and abilities, his intelligence, strength, and the like. I shall even assume that the parties do not know their conceptions of the good or their special psychological propensities. The principles of justice are chosen behind a veil of ignorance. This ensures that no one is advantaged or disadvantaged in the choice of principles by the outcome of natural chance or the contingency of social circumstances. Since all are similarly situated and no one is able to design principles to favor his particular condition, the principles of justice are the result of a fair agreement or bargain. For given the circumstances of the original position, the symmetry of everyone's relations to each other, this initial situation is fair between individuals as moral persons, that is, as rational beings with their own ends and capable, I shall assume, of a sense of justice. The original position is, one might say, the appropriate initial status quo, and thus the fundamental agreements reached in it are fair. This explains the propriety of the name "justice as fairness": it conveys the idea that the principles of justice are agreed to in an initial situation that is fair. The name does not mean that the concepts of justice and fairness are the same, any more than the phrase "poetry as metaphor" means that the concepts of poetry and metaphor are the same.

Justice as fairness begins, as I have said, with one of the most general of all choices which persons might make together, namely, with the choice of the first principles of a conception of justice which is to regulate all subsequent criticism and reform of institutions. Then, having chosen a conception of justice, we can suppose that they are to choose a constitution and a legislature to enact laws, and so on, all in accordance with the principles of justice initially agreed upon. Our social situation is just if it is such that by this sequence of hypothetical agreements we would have contracted into the general system of rules which defines it. Moreover, assuming that the original position does determine a set of principles (that is, that a particular conception of justice would be chosen), it will then be true that whenever social institutions satisfy these principles those engaged in them can say to one another that they are cooperating on terms to which they would agree if they were free and equal persons whose relations with respect to one another were fair. They could all view their arrangements as meeting the stipulations which they would acknowledge in an initial situation that embodies widely accepted and reasonable constraints on the choice of principles. The general recognition of this fact would provide the basis for a public acceptance of the corresponding principles of justice. No society can, of course, be a scheme of cooperation which men enter voluntarily in a literal sense; each person finds himself placed at birth in some particular position in some particular society, and the nature of this position materially affects his life prospects. Yet a society satisfying the principles of justice as fairness comes as close as a society can to being a voluntary scheme, for it meets the principles which free and equal persons would assent to under circumstances that are fair. In this sense its members are autonomous and the obligations they recognize self-imposed.

One feature of justice as fairness is to think of the parties in the initial situation as rational and mutually disinterested. This does not mean that the parties are egoists, that is, individuals with only certain kinds of interests, say in wealth, prestige, and domination. But they are conceived as not taking an interest in one another's interests. They are to presume that even their spiritual aims may be opposed, in the way that the aims of those of different religions may be opposed. Moreover, the concept of rationality must be interpreted as far as possible in the narrow sense, standard in economic theory, of taking the most effective means to given ends. I shall modify this concept to some extent . . . but one must try to avoid introducing into it any controversial ethical elements. The initial situation must be characterized by stipulations that are widely accepted.

In working out the conception of justice as fairness one main task clearly is to determine which principles of justice would be chosen in the original position. To do this we must describe this situation in some detail and formulate with care the problem of choice which it presents. . . . It may be observed, however, that once the principles of justice are thought of as arising from an original agreement in a situation of equality, it is an open question whether the principle of utility would be acknowledged. Offhand it hardly seems likely that persons who view themselves as equals, entitled to press their claims upon one another, would agree to a principle which may require lesser life prospects for some simply for the sake of a greater sum of advantages enjoyed by others. Since each desires to protect his interests, his capacity to advance his conception of the good, no one has a reason to acquiesce in an enduring loss for himself in order to bring about a greater net balance of satisfaction. In the absence of strong and lasting benevolent impulses, a rational man would not accept a basic structure merely because it maximized the algebraic sum of advantages irrespective of its permanent effects on his own basic rights and interests. Thus it seems that the principle of utility is incompatible with the conception of social cooperation among equals for mutual advantage. It appears to be inconsistent with the idea of reciprocity implicit in the notion of a well-ordered society. Or, at any rate, so I shall argue.

I shall maintain instead that the persons in the initial situation would choose two rather different principles: the first requires equality in the assignment of basic rights and duties, while the second holds that social and economic inequalities, for example inequalities of wealth and authority, are just only if they result in compensating benefits for everyone, and in particular for the least advantaged members of society. These principles rule out justifying institutions on the grounds that the hardships of some are offset by a greater good in the aggregate. It may be expedient but it is not just that some should have less in order that others may prosper. But there is no injustice in the greater benefits earned by a few provided that the situation of persons not so fortunate is thereby improved. The intuitive idea is that since everyone's well-being depends upon a scheme of cooperation without which no one could have a satisfactory life, the division of advantages should be such as to draw forth the willing cooperation of everyone taking part in it, including those less well situated. Yet this can be expected only if reasonable terms are proposed. The two principles mentioned seem to be a fair agreement on the basis of which those better endowed, or more fortunate in their social position, neither of which we can be said to deserve, could expect the willing cooperation of others when some workable scheme is a necessary condition of the welfare of all.[3] Once we decide to look for a conception of justice that nullifies the accidents of natural endowment and the contingencies of social circumstance as counters in quest for political and economic advantage, we are led to these principles. They express the result of leaving aside those aspects of the social world that seem arbitrary from a moral point of view.

The problem of the choice of principles, however, is extremely difficult. I do not expect the answer I shall suggest to be convincing to everyone. It is, therefore, worth noting from the outset that justice as fairness, like other contract views, consists of two parts: (1) an interpretation of the initial situation and of the problem of choice posed there, and (2) a set of principles which, it is argued, would be agreed to. One may accept the first part of the theory (or some variant thereof), but not the other, and conversely. The concept of the initial contractual situation may seem reasonable although the particular principles proposed are rejected. To be sure, I want to maintain that the most appropriate conception of this situation does lead to principles of justice contrary to utilitarianism and perfectionism, and therefore that the contract doctrine provides an alternative to these views. . . .

A final remark. Justice as fairness is not a complete contract theory. For it is clear that the contractarian idea can be extended to the choice of more or less an entire ethical system, that is, to a system including principles for all the virtues and not only for justice. Now for the most part I shall consider only principles of justice and others closely related to them; I make no attempt to discuss the virtues in a systematic way. Obviously if justice as fairness succeeds reasonably well, a next step would be to study the more general view suggested by the name "rightness as fairness." But even this wider theory fails to embrace all moral relationships, since it would seem to include only our relations with other persons and to leave out of account how we are to conduct ourselves toward animals and the rest of nature. I do not contend that the contract notion offers a way to approach these questions which are certainly of the first importance; and I shall have to put them aside. We must recognize the limited scope of justice as fairness and of the general type of view that it exemplifies. How far its conclusions must be revised once these other matters are understood cannot be decided in advance. . . .

TWO PRINCIPLES OF JUSTICE

I shall now state in a provisional form the two principles of justice that I believe would be chosen in the original position. In this section I wish to make only the most general comments, and therefore the first formulation of these principles is tentative. As we go on I shall run through several formulations and approximate step by step the final statement to be given much later. I believe that doing this allows the exposition to proceed in a natural way.

The first statement of the two principles reads as follows.

> First: each person is to have an equal right to the most extensive basic liberty compatible with a similar liberty for others.
>
> Second: social and economic inequalities are to be arranged so that they are both (a) reasonably expected to be to everyone's advantage, and (b) attached to positions and offices open to all. . . .

By way of general comment, these principles primarily apply, as I have said, to the basic structure of society. They are to govern the assignment of rights and duties and to regulate the distribution of social and economic advantages. As their formulation suggests, these principles presuppose that the social structure can be divided into two more or less distinct parts, the first principle applying to the one, the second to the other. They distinguish between those aspects of the social system that define and secure the equal liberties of citizenship and those that specify and establish social and economic inequalities. The basic liberties of citizens are, roughly speaking, political liberty (the right to vote and to be eligible for public office) together with freedom of speech and assembly; liberty of conscience and freedom of thought; freedom of the person along with the right to hold (personal) property; and freedom from arbitrary arrest and seizure as defined by the concept of the rule of law. These liberties are all required to be equal by the first principle, since citizens of a just society are to have the same basic rights.

The second principle applies, in the first approximation, to the distribution of income and wealth and to the design of organizations that make use of differences in authority and responsibility, or chains of command. While the distribution of wealth and income need not be equal, it must be to everyone's advantage, and at the same time, positions of authority and offices of command must be accessible to all. One applies the second principle by holding positions open, and then, subject to this constraint, arranges social and economic inequalities so that everyone benefits.

These principles are to be arranged in a serial order with the first principle prior to the second. This ordering means that a departure from the institutions of equal liberty required by the first principle cannot be justified by, or compensated for, by greater social and economic advantages. The distribution of wealth and income, and the hierarchies of authority, must be consistent with both the liberties of equal citizenship and equality of opportunity.

It is clear that these principles are rather specific in their content, and their acceptance rests on certain assumptions that I must eventually try to explain and justify. A theory of justice depends upon a theory of society in ways that will become evidence as we proceed. For the present, it should be observed that the two principles (and this holds for all formulations) are a special case of a more general conception of justice that can be expressed as follows.

> All social values—liberty and opportunity, income and wealth, and the bases of self-respect—are to be distributed equally unless an unequal distribution of any, or all, of these values is to everyone's advantage.

Injustice, then, is simply inequalities that are not to the benefit of all. Of course, this conception is extremely vague and requires interpretation.

As a first step, suppose that the basic structure of society distributes certain primary goods, that is, things that every rational man is presumed to want. These goods normally have a use whatever a person's rational plan of life. For simplicity, assume that the chief primary goods at the disposition of society are rights and liberties, powers and opportunities, income and wealth. . . . These are the social primary goods. Other primary goods such as health and vigor, intelligence and imagination, are natural goods; although their possession is influenced by the basic structure, they are not so directly under its control. Imagine, then, a hypothetical initial arrangement in which all the social primary goods are equally distributed: everyone has similar rights and duties, and income and wealth are evenly shared. This state of affairs provides a benchmark for judging improvements. If certain inequalities of wealth and organizational powers would make everyone better off than in this hypothetical starting situation, then they accord with the general conception.

Now it is possible, at least theoretically, that by giving up some of their fundamental liberties men are sufficiently compensated by the resulting social and economic gains. The general conception of justice imposes no restrictions on what sort of inequalities are permissible; it only requires that everyone's position be improved. We need not suppose anything so drastic as consenting to a condition of slavery. Imagine instead that men forego certain political rights when the economic returns are significant and their capacity to influence the course of policy by the exercise of these rights would be marginal in any case. It is this kind of exchange which the two principles as stated rule out; being arranged in serial order they do not permit exchanges between basic liberties and economic and social gains. The serial ordering of principles expresses an underlying preference among primary social goods. When this preference is rational so likewise is the choice of these principles in this order.

In developing justice as fairness I shall, for the most part, leave aside the general conception of justice and examine instead the special case of the two principles in serial order. The advantage of this procedure is that from the first the matter of priorities is recognized and an effort made to find principles to deal with it. One is led to attend throughout to the conditions under which the acknowledgment of the absolute weight of liberty with respect to social and economic advantages, as defined by the lexical order of the two principles, would be reasonable. Offhand, this ranking appears extreme and too special a case to be of much interest; but there is more justification for it than would appear at first sight. Or at any rate, so I shall maintain. . . . Furthermore, the distinction between fundamental rights and liberties and economic and social benefits marks a difference among primary social goods that one should try to exploit. It suggests an important division in the social system. Of course, the distinctions drawn and the ordering proposed are bound to be at best only approximations. There are surely circumstances in which they fail. But it is essential to depict clearly the main lines of a reasonable conception of justice; and under many conditions anyway, the two principles in serial order may serve well enough. When necessary we can fall back on the more general conception.

The fact that the two principles apply to institutions has certain consequences. Several points illustrate this. First of all, the rights and liberties referred to by these principles are those which are defined by the public rules of the basic structure. Whether men are free is determined by the rights and duties established by the major institutions of society. Liberty is a certain pattern of social forms. The first principle simply requires that certain sorts of rules, those defining basic liberties, apply to everyone equally and that they allow the most extensive liberty compatible with a like liberty for all. The only reason for circumscribing the rights defining liberty and making men's freedom less extensive than it might otherwise be is that these equal rights as institutionally defined would interfere with one another.

Another thing to bear in mind is that when principles mention persons, or require that everyone gain from an inequality, the reference is to representative persons holding the various social positions, or offices, or whatever, established by the basic structure. Thus in applying the second principle I assume that it is possible to assign an expectation of well-being to representative individuals holding these positions. This expectation indicates their life prospects as viewed from their social station. In general, the expectations of representative persons depend upon the distribution of rights and duties throughout the basic structure. When this changes, expectations change. I assume, then, that expectations are connected: by raising the prospects of the representative man in one position we presumably increase or decrease the prospects of representative men in other positions. Since it applies to institutional forms, the second principle (or rather the first part of it) refers to the expectations of representative individuals. As I shall discuss below, neither principle applies to distributions of particular goods to particular individuals who may be identified by their proper names. The situation where someone is considering how to allocate certain commodities to needy persons who are known to him is not within the scope of the principles. They are meant to regulate basic institutional arrangements. We must not assume that there is much similarity from the standpoint of justice between an administrative allotment of goods to specific persons and the appropriate design of society. Our common sense intuitions for the former may be a poor guide to the latter.

Now the second principle insists that each person benefit from permissible inequalities in the basic structure. This means that it must be reasonable for each relevant representative man defined by this structure, when he views it as a going concern, to prefer his prospects with the inequality to his prospects without it. One is not allowed to justify differences in income or organizational powers on the ground that the disadvantages of those in one position are outweighed by the greater advantages of those in another. Much less can infringements of liberty be counterbalanced in this way. Applied to the basic structure, the principle of utility would have us maximize the sum of expectations of representative men (weighted by the number of persons they represent, on the classical view); and this would permit us to compensate for the losses of some by the gains of others. Instead, the two principles require that everyone benefit from economic and social inequalities. It is obvious, however, that there are indefinitely many ways in which all may be advantaged when the initial arrangement of equality is taken as a benchmark. How then are we to choose among these possibilities? The principles must be specified so that they yield a determinate conclusion. I now turn to this problem. . . .

NOTES

1. As the text suggests, I shall regard Locke's *Second Treatise of Government,* Rousseau's *The Social Contract,* and Kant's ethical works beginning with *The Foundations of the Metaphysics of Morals* as definitive of the contract tradition. For all of its greatness, Hobbes's *Leviathan* raises special problems. A general historical survey is provided by J. W. Gough, *The Social Contract,* 2nd ed. (Oxford, The Clarendon Press, 1957), and Otto Gierke, *Natural Law and*

the Theory of Society, trans. with an introduction by Ernest Barker (Cambridge, The University Press, 1934). A presentation of the contract view as primarily an ethical theory is to be found in G. R. Grice, *The Grounds of Moral Judgment* (Cambridge, The University Press, 1967). See also § 19, note 30. [The footnotes have been renumbered—Ed.]

2. Kant is clear that the original agreement is hypothetical. See *The Metaphysics of Morals,* pt. I (*Rechtslehre*), especially §§ 47, 52; and pt. II of the essay "Concerning the Common Saying: This May Be True in Theory but It Does Not Apply in Practice," in *Kant's Political Writings,* ed. Hans Reiss and trans. by H. B. Nisbet (Cambridge, The University Press, 1970), pp. 73–87. See Georges Vlachos, *La Pensée politique de Kant* (Paris, Presses Universitaires de France, *1962*), pp. 326–335; and J. G. Murphy, *Kant: The Philosophy of Right* (London, Macmillan, 1970), pp. 109–112, 133–136, for a further discussion.

3. For the formulation of this intuitive idea I am indebted to Allan Gibbard.

STUDY QUESTIONS

1. Carefully state Rawls's view of the "original position."
2. How do Rawls's two principles of justice mediate the dispute between "left-wing" and "right-wing" thinkers?
3. What does Rawls mean by the "veil of ignorance"? Why is this concept important to his argument?

6

In a Different Voice: Women's Conceptions of Self and of Morality

Carol Gilligan

Carol Gilligan teaches at Harvard University. She is the author of *In a Different Voice,* the book that grew out of this article.

The arc of developmental theory leads from infantile dependence to adult autonomy, tracing a path characterized by an increasing differentiation of self from other and a progressive freeing of thought from contextual constraints. The vision of Luther, journeying from the rejection of a self defined by others to the assertive boldness of "Here I stand" and the image of Plato's allegorical man in the cave, separating at last the shadows from the sun, have taken powerful hold on the psychological understanding of what constitutes development. Thus, the individual, meeting fully the developmental challenges of adolescence as set for him by Piaget, Erikson, and Kohlberg, thinks formally, proceeding from theory to fact, and defines both the self and the moral autonomously, that is, apart from the identification and conventions that had comprised the particulars of his childhood world. So equipped, he is presumed ready to live as an adult, to love and work in a way that is both intimate and generative, to develop an ethical sense of caring and a genital mode of relating in which giving and taking fuse in the ultimate reconciliation of the tension between self and other.

Yet the men whose theories have largely informed this understanding of development have all been plagued by the same problem, the problem of women, whose sexuality remains more diffuse, whose perception of self is so much more tenaciously embedded in relationships with others and whose moral dilemmas hold them in a mode of judgment that is insistently contextual. The solution has been to consider women as either deviant or deficient in their development.

That there is a discrepancy between concepts of womanhood and adulthood is nowhere more clearly evident than in the series of studies on sex-role stereotypes reported by Broverman, Vogel, Broverman, Clarkson, and Rosenkrantz (1972). The repeated finding of these studies is that the qualities deemed necessary for adulthood—the capacity for autonomous thinking, clear decision making, and responsible action—are those associated with masculinity but considered undesirable as attributes of the feminine self. The stereotypes suggest a splitting of love and work that relegates the expressive capacities requisite for the former to women while the instrumental abilities necessary for the latter reside in the masculine domain. Yet, looked at from a different perspective, these stereotypes reflect a conception of adulthood that is itself out of balance, favoring the separateness of the individual self over its connection to others and leaning more toward an autonomous life of work than toward the interdependence of love and care.

This difference in point of view is the subject of this essay, which seeks to identify in the feminine experience and construction of social reality a distinctive voice, recognizable in the different perspective it brings to bear on the construction and resolution of moral problems. The first section begins with the repeated observation of difference in women's concepts of self and of morality. This difference is identified in previous psychological descriptions of women's moral judgments and described as it again appears in current research data. Examples drawn from interviews with women in and around a university community are used to illustrate the characteristics of the feminine voice. The relational bias in women's thinking that has, in the past, been seen to compromise their moral judgment and impede their development now begins to emerge in a new developmental light. Instead of being seen as a developmental deficiency, this bias appears to reflect a different social and moral understanding.

This alternative conception is enlarged in the second section through consideration of research interviews with women facing the moral dilemma of whether to continue or abort a pregnancy. Since the research design allowed women to define as well as resolve the moral problem, developmental distinctions could be derived directly from the categories of women's thought. The responses of women to structured interview questions regarding the pregnancy decision formed the basis for describing a developmental sequence that traces progressive differentiations in their understanding and judgment of conflicts between self and other. While the sequence of women's moral development follows the three-level progression of all social developmental theory, from an egocentric through a societal to a universal perspective, this progression takes place within a distinct moral conception. This conception differs from that derived by Kohlberg from his all-male longitudinal research data.

This difference then becomes the basis in the third section for challenging the current assessment of women's moral judgment at the same time that it brings to bear a new perspective on developmental assessment in general. The inclusion in the overall conception of development of those categories derived from the study of women's moral judgment enlarges developmental understanding, enabling it to encompass better the thinking of both sexes. This is particularly true with respect to the construction and resolution of the dilemmas of adult life. Since the conception of adulthood retrospectively shapes the theoretical understanding of the development that precedes it, the changes in that conception that follow from the more central inclusion of women's judgments recast developmental understanding and lead to a reconsideration of the substance of social and moral development.

CHARACTERISTICS OF THE FEMININE VOICE

The revolutionary contribution of Piaget's work is the experimental confirmation and refinement of Kant's assertion that knowledge is actively constructed rather than passively received. Time, space, self, and other, as well as the categories of developmental theory, all arise out of the active interchange between the individual and the physical and social world in which he lives and of which he strives to make sense. The development of cognition is the process of reappropriating reality at progressively more complex levels of apprehension, as the structures of thinking expand to encompass the increasing richness and intricacy of experience.

Moral development, in the work of Piaget and Kohlberg, refers specifically to the expanding conception of the social world as it is reflected in the understanding and resolution of the inevitable conflicts that arise in the relations between self and others. The moral judgment is a statement of priority, an attempt at rational resolution in a situation where, from a different point of view, the choice itself seems to do violence to justice.

Kohlberg (1969), in his extension of the early work of Piaget, discovered six stages of moral judgment, which he claimed formed an invariant sequence, each successive stage representing a more adequate construction of the moral problem, which in turn provides the basis for its more just resolution. The stages divide into three levels, each of which denotes a significant expansion of the moral point of view from an egocentric through a societal to a universal ethical conception. With this expansion in perspective comes the capacity to free moral judgment from the individual needs and social conventions with which it had earlier been confused and anchor it instead in principles of justice that are universal in application. These principles provide criteria upon which both individual and societal claims can be impartially assessed. In Kohlberg's view, at the highest stages of development morality is freed from both psychological and historical constraints, and the individual can judge independently of his own particular needs and of the values of those around him.

That the moral sensibility of women differs from that of men was noted by Freud (1925/1961) in the following by now well-quoted statement:

> I cannot evade the notion (though I hesitate to give it expression) that for women the level of what is ethically normal is different from what it is in man. Their superego is never so inexorable, so impersonal, so independent of its emotional origins as we require it to be in men. Character-traits which critics of every epoch have brought up against women—that they show less sense of justice than men, that they are less ready to submit to the great exigencies of life, that they are more often influenced in their judgments by feelings of affection or hostility—all these would be amply accounted for by the modification in the formation of their super-ego which we have inferred above.

While Freud's explanation lies in the deviation of female from male development around the construction and resolution of the Oedipal problem, the same observations about the nature of morality in women emerge from the work of Piaget and Kohlberg. Piaget (1932/1965), in his study of the rules of children's games, observed that, in the games they played, girls were "less explicit about agreement [than boys] and less concerned with legal elaboration." In contrast to the boys' interest in the codification of rules, the girls adopted a more pragmatic attitude, regarding "a rule as good so long as the game repays it." As a result, in comparison to boys, girls were found to be "more tolerant and more easily reconciled to innovations."

Kohlberg (1971) also identifies a strong interpersonal bias in the moral judgments of women, which leads them to be considered as typically at the third of his six-stage developmental sequence. At that stage, the good is identified with "what pleases or helps others and is approved of by them." This mode of judgment is conventional in its conformity to generally held notions of the good but also psychological in its concern with intention and consequence as the basis for judging the morality of action.

That women fall largely into this level of moral judgment is hardly surprising when we read from the Broverman et al. (1972) list that prominent among the twelve attributes considered to be desirable for women are tact, gentleness, awareness of the feelings of others, strong need for security, and easy expression of tender feelings. And yet, herein lies the paradox, for the very traits that have traditionally defined the "goodness" of women, their care for and sensitivity to the needs of others, are those that mark them as deficient in moral development. The infusion of feeling into their judgments keeps them from developing a more independent and abstract ethical conception in which concern for others derives from principles of justice rather than from compassion and care. Kohlberg, however, is less pessimistic than Freud in his assessment, for he sees the development of women as extending beyond the interpersonal level, following the same path toward independent, principled judgment that he discovered in the research on men from which his stages were derived. In Kohlberg's view, women's development will proceed beyond Stage Three when they are challenged to solve moral problems that require them to see beyond the relationships that have in the past generally bound their moral experience.

What then do women say when asked to construct the moral domain; how do we identify the characteristically "feminine" voice? A Radcliffe undergraduate, responding to the question, "If you had to say what morality meant to you, how would you sum it up?" replies:

> When I think of the word morality, I think of obligations. I usually think of it as conflicts between personal desires and social things, social considerations, or personal desires of yourself versus personal desires of another person or people or whatever. Morality is that whole realm of how you decide these conflicts. A moral person is one who would decide, like by placing themselves more often than not as equals, a truly moral person would always consider another person as their equal . . . in a situation of social interaction, something is morally wrong where the individual ends up screwing a lot of people. And it is morally right when everyone comes out better off.*

Yet when asked if she can think of someone whom she would consider a genuinely moral person, she replies, "Well, immediately I think of Albert Schweitzer because he has obviously given his life to help others." Obligation and sacrifice override the ideal of equality, setting up a basic contradiction in her thinking.

Another undergraduate responds to the question, "What does it mean to say something is morally right or wrong?," by also speaking first of responsibilities and obligations:

> Just that it has to do with responsibilities and obligations and values, mainly values. . . . In my life situation I relate morality with interpersonal relationships that have to do with respect for the other person and myself. [Why respect other people?] Because they have a consciousness or feelings that can be hurt, an awareness that can be hurt.

The concern about hurting others persists as a major theme in the responses of two other Radcliffe students:

> [Why be moral?] Millions of people have to live together peacefully. I personally don't want to hurt other people. That's a real criterion, a main criterion for me. It underlies my sense of justice. It isn't nice to inflict pain. I empathize with anyone in pain. Not hurting others is important in my own private morals. Years ago, I would have jumped out of a window not to hurt my boyfriend. That was pathological. Even today though, I want approval and love and I don't want enemies. Maybe that's why there is morality—so people can win approval, love and friendship.

> My main moral principle is not hurting other people as long as you aren't going against your own conscience and as long as you remain true to yourself. . . . There are many moral issues such as abortion, the draft, killing, stealing, monogamy, etc. If something is a controversial issue like these, then I always say it is up to the individual. The individual has to decide and then follow his own conscience. There are no moral absolutes. . . . Laws are pragmatic instruments, but they are not absolutes. A viable society can't make exceptions all the time, but I would personally. . . . I'm afraid I'm heading for some big crisis with my boyfriend someday, and someone will get hurt, and he'll get more hurt than I will. I feel an obligation to not hurt him, but also an obligation to not lie. I don't know if it is possible to not lie and not hurt.

The common thread that runs through these statements, the wish not to hurt others and the hope that in morality lies a way of solving conflicts so that no one will get hurt, is striking in that

* The Radcliffe women whose responses are cited were interviewed as part of a pilot study on undergraduate moral development conducted by the author in 1970.

it is independently introduced by each of the four women as the most specific item in their response to a most general question. The moral person is one who helps others; goodness is service, meeting one's obligations and responsibilities to others, if possible, without sacrificing oneself. While the first of the four women ends by denying the conflict she initially introduced, the last woman anticipates a conflict between remaining true to herself and adhering to her principle of not hurting others. The dilemma that would test the limits of this judgment would be one where helping others is seen to be at the price of hurting the self.

The reticence about taking stands on "controversial issues," the willingness to "make exceptions all the time" expressed in the final example above, is echoed repeatedly by other Radcliffe students, as in the following two examples:

> I never feel that I can condemn anyone else. I have a very relativistic position. The basic idea that I cling to is the sanctity of human life. I am inhibited about impressing my beliefs on others.

> I could never argue that my belief on a moral question is anything that another person should accept. I don't believe in absolutes. . . . If there is an absolute for moral decisions, it is human life.

Or as a thirty-one-year-old Wellesley graduate says, in explaining why she would find it difficult to steal a drug to save her own life despite her belief that it would be right to steal for another: "It's just very hard to defend yourself against the rules. I mean, we live by consensus, and you take an action simply for yourself, by yourself, there's no consensus there, and that is relatively indefensible in this society now."

What begins to emerge is a sense of vulnerability that impedes these women from taking a stand, what George Eliot (1860/1965) regards as the girl's "susceptibility" to adverse judgments of others, which stems from her lack of power and consequent inability to do something in the world. While relativism in men, the unwillingness to make moral judgments that Kohlberg and Kramer (1969) and Kohlberg and Gilligan (1971) have associated with the adolescent crisis of identity and belief, takes the form of calling into question the concept of morality itself, the women's reluctance to judge stems rather from their uncertainty about their right to make moral statements or, perhaps, the price for them that such judgment seems to entail. This contrast echoes that made by Matina Horner (1972), who differentiated the ideological fear of success expressed by men from the personal conflicts about succeeding that riddled the women's responses to stories of competitive achievement.

> Most of the men who responded with the expectation of negative consequences because of success were not concerned about their masculinity but were instead likely to have expressed existential concerns about finding a "non-materialistic happiness and satisfaction in life." These concerns, which reflect changing attitudes toward traditional kinds of success or achievement in our society, played little, if any, part in the female stories. Most of the women who were high in fear of success imagery continued to be concerned about the discrepancy between success in the situation described and feminine identity.

When women feel excluded from direct participation in society, they see themselves as subject to a consensus or judgment made and enforced by the men on whose protection and support they depend and by whose names they are known. A divorced middle-aged woman, mother of adolescent daughters, resident of a sophisticated university community, tells the story as follows:

> As a woman, I feel I never understood that I was a person, that I can make decisions and I have a right to make decisions. I always felt that that belonged to my father or my husband

> in some way or church which was always represented by a male clergyman. They were the three men in my life; father, husband, and clergyman, and they had much more to say about what I should or shouldn't do. They were really authority figures which I accepted. I didn't rebel against that. It only has lately occurred to me that I never even rebelled against it, and my girls are much more conscious of this, not in the militant sense, but just in the recognizing sense. . . . I still let things happen to me rather than make them happen, than to make choices, although I know all about choices. I know the procedures and the steps and all. [Do you have any clues about why this might be true?] Well, I think in one sense, there is less responsibility involved. Because if you make a dumb decision, you have to take the rap. If it happens to you, well, you can complain about it. I think that if you don't grow up feeling that you ever had any choices, you don't either have the sense that you have emotional responsibility. With this sense of choice comes this sense of responsibility.

The essence of the moral decision is the exercise of choice and the willingness to accept responsibility for that choice. To the extent that women perceive themselves as having no choice, they correspondingly excuse themselves from the responsibility that decision entails. Childlike in the vulnerability of their dependence and consequent fear of abandonment, they claim to wish only to please but in return for their goodness they expect to be loved and cared for. This, then, is an "altruism" always at risk, for it presupposes an innocence constantly in danger of being compromised by an awareness of the trade-off that has been made. Asked to describe herself, a Radcliffe senior responds:

> I have heard of the onion skin theory. I see myself as an onion, as a block of different layers, the external layers for people that I don't know that well, the agreeable, the social, and as you go inward there are more sides for people I know that I show. I am not sure about the innermost, whether there is a core, or whether I have just picked up everything as I was growing up, these different influences. I think I have a neutral attitude towards myself, but I do think in terms of good and bad. . . . Good—I try to be considerate and thoughtful of other people and I try to be fair in situations and be tolerant. I use the words but I try and work them out practically. . . . Bad things—I am not sure if they are bad, if they are altruistic or I am doing them basically for approval of other people. [Which things are these?] The values I have when I try to act them out. They deal mostly with interpersonal type relations. . . . If I were doing it for approval, it would be a very tenuous thing. If I didn't get the right feedback, there might go all my values.

Ibsen's play *A Doll House* (1879/1965) depicts the explosion of just such a world through the eruption of a moral dilemma that calls into question the notion of goodness that lies at its center. Nora, the "squirrel wife," living with her husband as she had lived with her father, puts into action this conception of goodness as sacrifice and, with the best of intentions, takes the law into her own hands. The crisis that ensues, most painfully for her in the repudiation of that goodness by the very person who was its recipient and beneficiary, causes her to reject the suicide that she had initially seen as its ultimate expression and chose instead to seek new and firmer answers to the adolescent questions of identity and belief.

The availability of choice and with it the onus of responsibility has now invaded the most private sector of the woman's domain and threatens a similar explosion. For centuries, women's sexuality anchored them in passivity, in a receptive rather than active stance, where the events of conception and childbirth could be controlled only by a withholding in which their own sexual needs were either denied or sacrificed. That such a sacrifice entailed a cost to their intelligence as well was seen by Freud (1908/1959) when he tied the "undoubted intellectual inferiority of so many women" to "the inhibition of thought necessitated by sexual suppression." The strategies of withholding and denial that women have employed in the politics of sexual relations appear similar to their evasion or withholding of judgment in the moral realm. The hesitance expressed in the previous examples to impose even a belief in the value of human life on others, like the reluctance to claim one's sexuality, bespeaks a self uncertain of its strength, unwilling to deal with consequence, and thus avoiding confrontation.

Thus women have traditionally deferred to the judgment of men, although often while intimating a sensibility of their own which is at variance with that judgment. Maggie Tulliver, in *The Mill on the Floss* (Eliot, 1860/1965), responds to the accusations that ensue from the discovery of her secretly continued relationship with Philip Wakeham by acceding to her brother's moral judgment while at the same time asserting a different set of standards by which she attests her own superiority:

> I don't want to defend myself. . . . I know I've been wrong—often continually. But yet, sometimes when I have done wrong, it has been because I have feelings that you would be the better for if you had them. If *you* were in fault ever, if you had done anything very wrong, I should be sorry for the pain it brought you; I should not want punishment to be heaped on you.

An eloquent defense, Kohlberg would argue, of a Stage Three moral position, an assertion of the age-old split between thinking and feeling, justice and mercy, that underlies many of the clichés and stereotypes concerning the difference between the sexes. But considered from another point of view, it is a moment of confrontation, replacing a former evasion, between two modes of judging, two differing constructions of the moral domain—one traditionally associated with masculinity and the public world of social power, the other with femininity and the privacy of domestic interchange. While the developmental ordering of these two points of view has been to consider the masculine as the more adequate and thus as replacing the feminine as the individual moves toward higher stages, their reconciliation remains unclear.

THE DEVELOPMENT OF WOMEN'S MORAL JUDGMENT

Recent evidence for a divergence in moral development between men and women comes from the research of Haan (Note 1) and Holstein (1976) whose findings lead them to question the possibility of a "sex-related bias" in Kohlberg's scoring system. This system is based on Kohlberg's six-stage description of moral development. Kohlberg's stages divide into three levels, which he designates as preconventional, conventional, and postconventional, thus denoting the major shifts in moral perspective around a center of moral understanding that equates justice with the maintenance of existing social systems. While the preconventional conception of justice is based on the needs of the self, the conventional judgment derives from an understanding of society. This understanding is in turn superseded by a postconventional or principled conception of justice where the good is formulated in universal terms. The quarrel with Kohlberg's stage scoring does not pertain to the structural differentiation of his levels but rather to questions of stage and sequence. Kohlberg's stages begin with an obedience and punishment orientation (Stage One), and go from there in invariant order to instrumental hedonism (Stage Two), interpersonal concordance (Stage Three), law and order (Stage Four), social contract (Stage Five), and universal ethical principles (Stage Six).

The bias that Haan and Holstein question in this scoring system has to do with the subordination of the interpersonal to the societal definition of the good in the transition from Stage Three to Stage Four. This is the transition that has repeatedly been found to be problematic for women. In 1969, Kohlberg and Kramer identified Stage Three as the characteristic mode of women's moral judgments, claiming that, since women's lives were interpersonally based, this stage was not only "functional" for them but also adequate for resolving the moral conflicts that they faced. Turiel (1973) reported that while girls reached Stage Three sooner than did boys, their judgments tended to remain at that stage while the boys' development continued further along Kohlberg's scale. Gilligan, Kohlberg, Lerner, and Belenky (1971) found a similar association between sex and moral-judgment stage in a study of high-school students, with the girls' responses being scored predominantly at Stage Three while the boys' responses were more often scored at Stage Four.

This repeated finding of developmental inferiority in women may, however, have more to do with the standard by which development has been measured than with the quality of women's thinking per se. Haan's data (Note 1) on the Berkeley Free Speech Movement and Holstein's (1976) three-year longitudinal study of adolescents and their parents indicate that the moral judgments of women differ from those of men in the greater extent to which women's judgments are tied to feelings of empathy and compassion and are concerned more with the resolution of "real-life" as opposed to hypothetical dilemmas (Note 1, p. 34). However, as long as the categories by which development is assessed are derived within a male perspective from male research data, divergence from the masculine standard can be seen only as a failure of development. As a result, the thinking of women is often classified with that of children. The systematic exclusion from consideration of alternative criteria that might better encompass the development of women indicates not only the limitations of a theory framed by men and validated by research samples disproportionately male and adolescent but also the effects of the diffidence prevalent among women, their reluctance to speak publicly in their own voice, given the constraints imposed on them by the politics of differential power between the sexes.

In order to go beyond the question, "How much like men do women think, how capable are they of engaging in the abstract and hypothetical construction of reality?" it is necessary to identify and define in formal terms developmental criteria that encompass the categories of women's thinking. Such criteria would include the progressive differentiations, comprehensiveness, and adequacy that characterize higher-stage resolution of the "more frequently occurring, real-life moral dilemmas of interpersonal, empathic, fellow-feeling concerns" (Haan, Note 1, p. 34), which have long been the center of women's moral judgments and experience. To ascertain whether the feminine construction of the moral domain relies on a language different from that of men, but one which deserves equal credence in the definition of what constitutes development, it is necessary first to find the places where women have the power to choose and thus are willing to speak in their own voice.

When birth control and abortion provide women with effective means for controlling their fertility, the dilemma of choice enters the center of women's lives. Then the relationships that have traditionally defined women's identities and framed their moral judgments no longer flow inevitably from their reproductive capacity but become matters of decision over which they have control. Released from the passivity and reticence of a sexuality that binds them in dependence, it becomes possible for women to question with Freud what it is that they want and to assert their own answers to that question. However, while society may affirm publicly the woman's right to choose for herself, the exercise of such choice brings her privately into conflict with the conventions of femininity, particularly the moral equation of goodness with self-sacrifice. While independent assertion in judgment and action is considered the hallmark of adulthood and constitutes as well the standard of masculine development, it is rather in their care and concern for others that women have both judged themselves and been judged.

The conflict between self and other thus constitutes the central moral problem for women, posing a dilemma whose resolution requires a reconciliation between femininity and adulthood. In the absence of such a reconciliation, the moral problem cannot be resolved. The "good woman" masks assertion in evasion, denying responsibility by claiming only to meet the needs of others, while the "bad woman" forgoes or renounces the commitments that bind her in self-deception and betrayal. It is precisely this dilemma—the conflict between compassion and autonomy, between virtue and power—which the feminine voice struggles to resolve in its effort to reclaim the self and to solve the moral problem in such a way that no one is hurt.

When a woman considers whether to continue or abort a pregnancy, she contemplates a decision that affects both self and others and engages directly the critical moral issue of hurting. Since the choice is ultimately hers and therefore one for which she is responsible, it raises precisely those questions of judgment that have been most problematic for women. Now she is asked whether she wishes to interrupt that stream of life which has for centuries immersed her in the passivity of dependence while at the same time imposing on her the responsibility for care. Thus the abortion decision brings to the core of feminine apprehension, to what Joan Didion (1972) calls "the irreconcilable difference of it—that sense of living one's deepest life underwater, that dark involvement with blood and birth and death," the adult questions of responsibility and choice.

How women deal with such choices has been the subject of my research, designed to clarify, through considering the ways in which women construct and resolve the abortion decision, the nature and development of women's moral judgment. Twenty-nine women, diverse in age, race, and social class, were referred by abortion and pregnancy counseling services and participated in the study for a variety of reasons. Some came to gain further clarification with respect to a decision about which they were in conflict, some in response to a counselor's concern about repeated abortions, and others out of an interest in and/or willingness to contribute to ongoing research. Although the pregnancies occurred under a variety of circumstances in the lives of these women, certain commonalities could be discerned. The adolescents often failed to use birth control because they denied or discredited their capacity to bear children. Some of the older women attributed the pregnancy to the omission of contraceptive measures in circumstances where intercourse had not been anticipated. Since the pregnancies often coincided with efforts on the part of the women to end a relationship, they may be seen as a manifestation of ambivalence or as a way of putting the relationship to the ultimate test of commitment. For these women, the pregnancy appeared to be a way of testing truth, making the baby an ally in the search for male support and protection or, that failing, a companion victim of his rejection. There were, finally, some women who became pregnant either as a result of a failure of birth control or intentionally as part of a joint decision that later was reconsidered. Of the twenty-nine women, four decided to have the baby, one miscarried, twenty-one chose abortion, and three remained in doubt about the decision.

In the initial part of the interview, the women were asked to discuss the decision that confronted them, how they were dealing with it, the alternatives they were considering, their reasons for and against each option, the people involved, the conflicts entailed, and the ways in which making this decision affected their self-concepts and their relationships with others. Then, in the second part of the interview, moral judgment was assessed in the hypothetical mode by presenting for resolution three of Kohlberg's standard research dilemmas.

While the structural progression from a preconventional through a conventional to a postconventional moral perspective can readily be discerned in the women's responses to both actual and hypothetical dilemmas, the conventions that shape women's moral judgments differ from those that apply to men. The construction of the abortion dilemma, in particular, reveals the existence of a distinct moral language whose evolution informs the sequence of women's development. This is the language of selfishness and responsibility, which defines the moral problem as one of obligation to exercise care and avoid hurt. The infliction of hurt is considered selfish and immoral in its reflection of unconcern, while the expression of care is seen as the fulfillment of moral responsibility. The reiterative use of the language of selfishness and responsibility and the underlying moral orientation it reflects sets the women apart from the men whom Kohlberg studied and may be seen as the critical reason for their failure to develop within the constraints of his system.

In the developmental sequence that follows, women's moral judgments proceed from an initial focus on the self at the *first level* to the discovery, in the transition to the *second level*, of the concept of responsibility as the basis for a new equilibrium between self and others. The elaboration of this concept of responsibility and its fusion with a maternal concept of morality, which seeks to ensure protection for the dependent and unequal, characterizes the *second level* of judgment. At this level the good is equated with caring for others. However, when the conventions of feminine goodness legitimize only others as the recipients of moral care, the logical inequality between self and other and the psychological violence that it engenders create the disequilibrium that initiates the *second* transition. The relationship between self and others is then reconsidered in an effort to sort out the confusion between conformity and care inherent in the conventional definition of feminine goodness and to establish a new equilibrium, which dissipates the tension between selfishness and responsibility. At the *third level*, the self becomes the arbiter of an independent judgment that now subsumes both conventions and individual needs under the moral principle of nonviolence. Judgment remains psychological in its concern with the intention and consequences of action, but it now becomes universal in its condemnation of exploitation and hurt.

Level I: Orientation to Individual Survival

In its initial and simplest construction, the abortion decision centers on the self. The concern is pragmatic, and the issue is individual survival. At this level, "should" is undifferentiated from "would," and others influence the decision only through their power to affect its consequences. An eighteen-year-old, asked what she thought when she found herself pregnant, replies: "I really didn't think anything except that I didn't want it. [Why was that?] I didn't want it, I wasn't ready for it, and next year will be my last year and I want to go to school."

Asked if there was a right decision, she says, "There is no right decision. [Why?] I didn't want it." For her the question of right decision would emerge only if her own needs were in conflict; then she would have to decide which needs should take precedence. This was the dilemma of another eighteen-year-old, who saw having a baby as a way of increasing her freedom by providing "the perfect chance to get married and move away from home," but also as restricting her freedom "to do a lot of things."

At this first level, the self, which is the sole object of concern, is constrained by lack of power; the wish "to do a lot of things" is constantly belied by the limitations of what, in fact, is being done. Relationships are, for the most part, disappointing: "The only thing you are ever going to get out of going with a guy is to get hurt." As a result, women may in some instances deliberately choose isolation to protect themselves against hurt. When asked how she would describe herself to herself, a nineteen-year-old, who held herself responsible for the accidental death of a younger brother, answers as follows:

> I really don't know. I never thought about it. I don't know. I know basically the outline of a character. I am very independent. I don't really want to have to ask anybody for anything and I am a loner in life. I prefer to be by myself than around anybody else. I manage to keep my friends at a limited number with the point that I have very few friends. I don't know what else there is. I am a loner and I enjoy it. Here today and gone tomorrow.

The primacy of the concern with survival is explicitly acknowledged by a sixteen-year-old delinquent in response to Kohlberg's Heinz dilemma, which asks if it is right for a desperate husband to steal an outrageously overpriced drug to save the life of his dying wife:

> I think survival is one of the first things in life and that people fight for. I think it is the most important thing, more important than stealing. Stealing might be wrong, but if you have to steal to survive yourself or even kill, that is what you should do. . . . Preservation of oneself, I think, is the most important thing; it comes before anything in life.

The First Transition: From Selfishness to Responsibility

In the transition which follows and criticizes this level of judgment, the words selfishness and responsibility first appear. Their reference initially is to the self in a redefinition of the self-interest which has thus far served as the basis for judgment. The transitional issue is one of attachment or connection to others. The pregnancy catches up the issue not only by representing an immediate, literal connection, but also by affirming, in the most concrete and physical way, the capacity to assume adult feminine roles. However, while having a baby seems at first to offer respite from the loneliness of adolescence and to solve conflicts over dependence and independence, in reality the continuation of an adolescent pregnancy generally compounds these problems, increasing social isolation and precluding further steps toward independence.

To be a mother in the societal as well as the physical sense requires the assumption of parental responsibility for the care and protection of a child. However, in order to be able to care for another, one must first be able to care responsibly for oneself. The growth from childhood to adulthood, conceived as a move from selfishness to responsibility, is articulated explicitly in these terms by a seventeen-year-old who describes her response to her pregnancy as follows:

> I started feeling really good about being pregnant instead of feeling really bad, because I wasn't looking at the situation realistically. I was looking at it from my own sort of selfish needs because I was lonely and felt lonely and stuff. . . . Things weren't really going good for me, so I was looking at it that I could have a baby that I could take care of or something that was part of me, and that made me feel good . . . but I wasn't looking at the realistic side . . . about the responsibility I would have to take on . . . I came to this decision that I was going to have an abortion [because] I realized how much responsibility goes with having a child. Like you have to be there, you can't be out of the house all the time which is one thing I like to do . . . and I decided that I have to take on responsibility for myself and I have to work out a lot of things.

Stating her former mode of judgment, the wish to have a baby as a way of combating loneliness and feeling connected, she now criticizes that judgment as both "selfish" and "unrealistic." The contradiction between wishes for a baby and for the freedom to be "out of the house all the time"—that is, for connection and also for independence—is resolved in terms of a new priority, as the criterion for judgment changes. The dilemma now assumes moral definition as the emergent conflict between wish and necessity is seen as a disparity between "would" and "should." In this construction the "selfishness" of willful decision is counterposed to the "responsibility" of moral choice:

> What I want to do is to have the baby, but what I feel I should do which is what I need to do, is have an abortion right now, because sometimes what you want isn't right. Sometimes what is necessary comes before what you want, because it might not always lead to the right thing.

While the pregnancy itself confirms femininity—"I started feeling really good; it sort of made me feel, like being pregnant, I started feeling like a woman"—the abortion decision becomes an opportunity for the adult exercise of responsible choice.

> [How would you describe yourself to yourself?] I am looking at myself differently in the way that I have had a really heavy decision put upon me, and I have never really had too many hard decisions in my life, and I have made it. It has taken some responsibility to do this. I have changed in that way, that I have made a hard decision. And that has been good. Because before, I would not have looked at it realistically, in my opinion. I would have gone by what I wanted to do, and I wanted it, and even if it wasn't right. So I see myself as I'm becoming more mature in ways of making decisions and taking care of myself, doing something for myself. I think it is going to help me in other ways, if I have other decisions to make put upon me, which would take some responsibility. And I would know that I could make them.

In the epiphany of this cognitive reconstruction, the old becomes transformed in terms of the new. The wish to "do something for myself" remains, but the terms of its fulfillment change as the decision affirms both femininity and adulthood in its integration of responsibility and care. Morality, says another adolescent, "is the way you think about yourself . . . sooner or later you have to make up your mind to start taking care of yourself. Abortion, if you do it for the right reasons, is helping yourself to start over and do different things."

Since this transition signals an enhancement in self-worth, it requires a conception of self which includes the possibility for doing "the right thing," the ability to see in oneself the potential for social acceptance. When such confidence is seriously in doubt, the transitional questions may be raised but development is impeded. The failure to make this first transition, despite an understanding of the issues involved, is illustrated by a woman in her late twenties. Her struggle with the conflict between selfishness and responsibility pervades but fails to resolve her dilemma of whether or not to have a third abortion.

> I think you have to think about the people who are involved, including yourself. You have responsibilities to yourself . . . and to make a right, whatever that is, decision in this depends on your knowledge and awareness of the responsibilities that you have and whether you can survive with a child and what it will do to your relationship with the father or how it will affect him emotionally.

Rejecting the idea of selling the baby and making "a lot of money in a black market kind of thing . . . because mostly I operate on principles and it would just rub me the wrong way to think I would be selling my own child," she struggles with a concept of responsibility which repeatedly turns back on the question of her own survival. Transition seems blocked by a self-image which is insistently contradictory:

> [How would you describe yourself to yourself?] I see myself as impulsive, practical—that is a contradiction—and moral and amoral, a contradiction. Actually the only thing that is consistent and not contradictory is the fact that I am very lazy which everyone has always told

> me is really a symptom of something else which I have never been able to put my finger on exactly. It has taken me a long time to like myself. In fact there are times when I don't, which I think is healthy to a point and sometimes I think I like myself too much and I probably evade myself too much, which avoids responsibility to myself and to other people who like me. I am pretty unfaithful to myself . . . I have a hard time even thinking that I am a human being, simply because so much rotten stuff goes on and people are so crummy and insensitive.

Seeing herself as avoiding responsibility, she can find no basis upon which to resolve the pregnancy dilemma. Instead, her inability to arrive at any clear sense of decision only contributes further to her overall sense of failure. Criticizing her parents for having betrayed her during adolescence by coercing her to have an abortion she did not want, she now betrays herself and criticizes that as well. In this light, it is less surprising that she considered selling her child, since she felt herself to have, in effect, been sold by her parents for the sake of maintaining their social status.

The Second Level: Goodness as Self-Sacrifice

The transition from selfishness to responsibility is a move toward social participation. Whereas at the first level, morality is seen as a matter of sanctions imposed by a society of which one is more subject than citizen, at the second level, moral judgment comes to rely on shared norms and expectations. The woman at this level validates her claim to social membership through the adoption of societal values. Consensual judgment becomes paramount and goodness the overriding concern as survival is now seen to depend on acceptance by others.

Here the conventional feminine voice emerges with great clarity, defining the self and proclaiming its worth on the basis of the ability to care for and protect others. The woman now constructs the world perfused with the assumptions about feminine goodness reflected in the stereotypes of the Broverman et al. (1972) studies. There the attributes considered desirable for women all presume an other, a recipient of the "tact, gentleness and easy expression of feeling" which allow the woman to respond sensitively while evoking in return the care which meets her own "very strong need for security." The strength of this position lies in its capacity for caring; its limitation is the restriction it imposes on direct expression. Both qualities are elucidated by a nineteen-year-old who contrasts her reluctance to criticize with her boyfriend's straightforwardness:

> I never want to hurt anyone, and I tell them in a very nice way, and I have respect for their own opinions, and they can do the things the way that they want, and he usually tells people right off the bat. . . . He does a lot of things out in public which I do in private. . . . it is better, the other [his way], but I just could never do it.

While her judgment clearly exists, it is not expressed, at least not in public. Concern for the feelings of others imposes a deference which she nevertheless criticizes in an awareness that, under the name of consideration, a vulnerability and a duplicity are concealed.

At the second level of judgment, it is specifically over the issue of hurting that conflict arises with respect to the abortion decision. When no option exists that can be construed as being in the best interest of everyone, when responsibilities conflict and decision entails the sacrifice of somebody's needs, then the woman confronts the seemingly impossible task of choosing the victim. A nineteen-year-old, fearing the consequences for herself of a second abortion but facing the opposition of both her family and her lover to the continuation of the pregnancy, describes the dilemma as follows:

> I don't know what choices are open to me; it is either to have it or the abortion; these are the

> choices open to me. It is just that either way I don't . . . I think what confuses me is it is a choice of either hurting myself or hurting other people around me. What is more important? If there could be a happy medium, it would be fine, but there isn't. It is either hurting someone on this side or hurting myself.

While the feminine identification of goodness with self-sacrifice seems clearly to dictate the "right" resolution of this dilemma, the stakes may be high for the woman herself, and the sacrifice of the fetus, in any event, compromises the altruism of an abortion motivated by a concern for others. Since femininity itself is in conflict in an abortion intended as an expression of love and care, this is a resolution which readily explodes in its own contradiction.

"I don't think anyone should have to choose between two things that they love," says a twenty-five-year-old woman who assumed responsibility not only for her lover but also for his wife and children in having an abortion she did not want:

> I just wanted the child and I really don't believe in abortions. Who can say when life begins. I think that life begins at conception and . . . I felt like there were changes happening in my body and I felt very protective . . . [but] I felt a responsibility, my responsibility if anything ever happened to her [his wife]. He made me feel that I had to make a choice and there was only one choice to make and that was to have an abortion and I could always have children another time and he made me feel if I didn't have it that it would drive us apart.

The abortion decision was, in her mind, a choice not to choose with respect to the pregnancy—"That was my choice, I had to do it." Instead, it was a decision to subordinate the pregnancy to the continuation of a relationship that she saw as encompassing her life—"Since I met him, he has been my life. I do everything for him; my life sort of revolves around him." Since she wanted to have the baby and also to continue the relationship, either choice could be construed as selfish. Furthermore, since both alternatives entailed hurting someone, neither could be considered moral. Faced with a decision which, in her own terms, was untenable, she sought to avoid responsibility for the choice she made, construing the decision as a sacrifice of her own needs to those of her lover. However, this public sacrifice in the name of responsibility engendered a private resentment that erupted in anger, compromising the very relationship that it had been intended to sustain.

> Afterwards we went through a bad time because I hate to say it and I was wrong, but I blamed him. I gave in to him. But when it came down to it, I made the decision, I could have said, "I am going to have this child whether you want me to or not," and I just didn't do it.

Pregnant again by the same man, she recognizes in retrospect that the choice in fact had been hers, as she returns once again to what now appears to have been missed opportunity for growth. Seeking, this time, to make rather than abdicate the decision, she sees the issue as one of "strength" as she struggles to free herself from the powerlessness of her own dependence:

> I think that right now I think of myself as someone who can become a lot stronger. Because of the circumstances, I just go along like with the tide. I never really had anything of my own before . . . [this time] I hope to come on strong and make a big decision, whether it is right or wrong.

Because the morality of self-sacrifice had justified the previous abortion, she now must suspend that judgment if she is to claim her own voice and accept responsibility for choice.

She thereby calls into question the underlying assumption of Level Two, which leads the woman to consider herself responsible for the actions of others, while holding others responsible for the choices she makes. This notion of reciprocity, backwards in its assumptions about control, disguises assertion as response. By reversing responsibility, it generates a series of indirect actions, which leave everyone feeling manipulated and betrayed. The logic of this position is confused in that the morality of mutual care is embedded in the psychology of dependence. Assertion becomes personally dangerous in its risk of criticism and abandonment as well as potentially immoral in its power to hurt. This confusion is captured by Kohlberg's (1969) definition of Stage Three moral judgment, which joins the need for approval with the wish to care for and help others.

When thus caught between the passivity of dependence and the activity of care, the woman becomes suspended in an immobility of both judgment and action. "If I were drowning, I couldn't reach out a hand to save myself, so unwilling am I to set myself up against fate," begins the central character of Margaret Drabble's novel, *The Waterfall* (1971), in an effort to absolve herself of responsibility as she at the same time relinquishes control. Facing the same moral conflict which George Eliot depicted in *The Mill on the Floss*, Drabble's heroine proceeds to relive Maggie Tulliver's dilemma but turns inward in her search for the way in which to retell that story. What is initially suspended and then called into question is the judgment which "had in the past made it seem better to renounce myself than them."

The Second Transition: From Goodness to Truth

The second transition begins with the reconsideration of the relationship between self and other, as the woman starts to scrutinize the logic of self-sacrifice in the service of a morality of care. In the interview data, this transition is announced by the reappearance of the word selfish. Retrieving the judgmental initiative, the woman begins to ask whether it is selfish or responsible, moral or immoral, to include her own needs within the compass of her care and concern. This question leads her to reexamine the concept of responsibility, juxtaposing the outward concern with what other people think with a new inner judgment.

In separating the voice of the self from those of others, the woman asks if it is possible to be responsible to herself as well as to others and thus to reconcile the disparity between hurt and care. The exercise of such responsibility, however, requires a new kind of judgment whose first demand is for honesty. To be responsible, it is necessary first to acknowledge what it is that one is doing. The criterion for judgment thus shifts from "goodness" to "truth" as the morality of action comes to be assessed not on the basis of its appearance in the eyes of others, but in terms of the realities of its intention and consequence.

A twenty-four-year-old married Catholic woman, pregnant again two months following the birth of her first child, identifies her dilemma as one of choice: "You have to now decide; because it is now available, you have to make a decision. And if it wasn't available, there was no choice open; you just do what you have to do." In the absence of legal abortion, a morality of self-sacrifice was necessary in order to insure protection and care for the dependent child. However, when such sacrifice becomes optional, the entire problem is recast.

The abortion decision is framed by this woman first in terms of her responsibilities to others: having a second child at this time would be contrary to medical advice and would strain both the emotional and financial resources of the family. However, there is, she says, a third reason for having an abortion, "sort of an emotional reason. I don't know if it is selfish or not, but it would really be tying myself down and right now I am not ready to be tied down with two."

Against this combination of selfish and responsible reasons for abortion is her Catholic belief that

> . . . it is taking a life, and it is. Even though it is not formed, it is the potential, and to me it is still taking a life. But I have to think of mine, my son's and my husband's, to think about, and at first I think that I thought it was for selfish reasons, but it is not. I believe that too, some of it is selfish. I don't want another one right now; I am not ready for it.

The dilemma arises over the issue of justification for taking a life: "I can't cover it over, because I believe this and if I do try to cover it over, I know that I am going to be in a mess. It will be denying what I am really doing." Asking "Am I doing the right thing; is it moral?," she counterposes to her belief against abortion her concern with the consequences of continuing the pregnancy. While concluding that "I can't be so morally strict as to hurt three other people with a decision just because of my moral beliefs," the issue of goodness still remains critical to her resolution of the dilemma:

> The moral factor is there. To me it is taking a life, and I am going to take that upon myself, that decision upon myself and I have feelings about it, and talked to a priest . . . but he said it is there and it will be from now on, and it is up to the person if they can live with the idea and still believe they are good.

The criteria for goodness, however, move inward as the ability to have an abortion and still consider herself good comes to hinge on the issue of selfishness with which she struggles to come to terms. Asked if acting morally is acting according to what is best for the self or whether it is a matter of self-sacrifice, she replies:

> I don't know if I really understand the question. . . . Like in my situation where I want to have the abortion and if I didn't it would be self-sacrificing, I am really in the middle of both those ways . . . but I think that my morality is strong and if these reasons—financial, physical reality and also for the whole family involved—were not here, that I wouldn't have to do it, and then it would be a self-sacrifice.

The importance of clarifying her own participation in the decision is evident in her attempt to ascertain her feelings in order to determine whether or not she was "putting them under" in deciding to end the pregnancy. Whereas in the first transition, from selfishness to responsibility, women made lists in order to bring to their consideration needs other than their own, now, in the second transition, it is the needs of the self which have to be deliberately uncovered. Confronting the reality of her own wish for an abortion, she now must deal with the problem of selfishness and the qualification that she feels it imposes on the "goodness" of her decision. The primacy of this concern is apparent in her description of herself:

> I think in a way I am selfish for one thing, and very emotional, very . . . and I think that I am a very real person and an understanding person and I can handle life situations fairly well, so I am basing a lot of it on my ability to do the things that I feel are right and best for me and whoever I am involved with. I think I was very fair to myself about the decision, and I really think that I have been truthful, not hiding anything, bringing out all the feelings involved. I feel it is a good decision and an honest one, a real decision.

Thus she strives to encompass the needs of both self and others, to be responsible to others and thus to be "good" but also to be responsible to herself and thus to be "honest" and "real."

While from one point of view, attention to one's own needs is considered selfish, when looked at from a different perspective, it is a matter of honesty and fairness. This is the essence of the transitional shift toward a new conception of goodness which turns inward in an acknowledgement of the self and an acceptance of responsibility for decision. While outward justification, the concern with "good reasons," remains critical for this particular woman: "I still think abortion is wrong, and it will be unless the situation can justify what you are doing." But the search for justification has produced a change in her thinking, "not drastically, but a little bit." She realizes that in continuing the pregnancy she would punish not only herself but also her husband, toward whom she had begun to feel "turned off and irritated." This leads her to consider the consequences self-sacrifice can have both for the self and for others. "God," she says, "can punish, but He can also forgive." What remains in question is whether her claim to forgiveness is compromised by a decision that not only meets the needs of others but that also is "right and best for me."

The concern with selfishness and its equation with immorality recur in an interview with another Catholic woman whose arrival for an abortion was punctuated by the statement, "I have always thought abortion was a fancy word for murder." Initially explaining this murder as one of lesser degree—"I am doing it because I have to do it. I am not doing it the least bit because I want to," she judges it "not quite as bad. You can rationalize that it is not quite the same." Since "keeping the child for lots and lots of reasons was just sort of impractical and out," she considers her options to be either abortion or adoption. However, having previously given up one child for adoption, she says: "I knew that psychologically there was no way that I could hack another adoption. It took me about four-and-a-half years to get my head on straight; there was just no way I was going to go through it again." The decision thus reduces in her eyes to a choice between murdering the fetus or damaging herself. The choice is further complicated by the fact that by continuing the pregnancy she would hurt not only herself but also her parents, with whom she lived. In the face of these manifold moral contradictions, the psychological demand for honesty that arises in counseling finally allows decision:

> On my own, I was doing it not so much for myself; I was doing it for my parents. I was doing it because the doctor told me to do it, but I had never resolved in my mind that I was doing it for me. Because it goes back to the fact that I never believed in abortions. . . . Actually, I had to sit down and admit, no, I really don't want to go the mother route now. I honestly don't feel that I want to be a mother, and that is not really such a bad thing to say after all. But that is not how I felt up until talking to Maureen [her counselor]. It was just a horrible way to feel, so I just wasn't going to feel it, and I just blocked it right out.

As long as her consideration remains "moral," abortion can be justified only as an act of sacrifice, a submission to necessity where the absence of choice precludes responsibility. In this way, she can avoid self-condemnation, since, "When you get into moral stuff then you are getting into self-respect and that stuff, and at least if I do something that I feel is morally wrong, then I tend to lose some of my self-respect as a person." Her evasion of responsibility, critical to maintaining the innocence necessary for self-respect, contradicts the reality of her own participation in the abortion decision. The dishonesty in her plea of victimization creates the conflict that generates the need for a more inclusive understanding. She must now resolve the emerging contradiction in her thinking between two uses of the term right: "I am saying that abortion is morally wrong, but the situation is right, and I am going to do it." But the thing is that eventually they are going to have to go together, and I am going to have to put them together somehow." Asked how this could be done, she replies:

> I would have to change morally wrong to morally right. [How?] I have no idea. I don't think you can take something that you feel is morally wrong because the situation makes it right and put the two together. They are not to-

gether, they are opposite. They don't go together. Something is wrong, but all of a sudden because you are doing it, it is right.

This discrepancy recalls a similar conflict she faced over the question of euthanasia, also considered by her to be morally wrong until she "took care of a couple of patients who had flat EEGs and saw the job that it was doing on their families." Recalling that experience, she says:

> You really don't know your black and whites until you really get into them and are being confronted with it. If you stop and think about my feelings on euthanasia until I got into it, and then my feelings about abortion until I got into it, I thought both of them were murder. Right and wrong and no middle but there is a gray.

In discovering the gray and questioning the moral judgments which formerly she considered to be absolute, she confronts the moral crisis of the second transition. Now the conventions which in the past had guided her moral judgment become subject to a new criticism, as she questions not only the justification for hurting others in the name of morality but also the "rightness" of hurting herself. However, to sustain such criticism in the face of conventions that equate goodness with self-sacrifice, the woman must verify her capacity for independent judgment and the legitimacy of her own point of view.

Once again transition hinges on self-concept. When uncertainty about her own worth prevents a woman from claiming equality, self-assertion falls prey to the old criticism of selfishness. Then the morality that condones self-destruction in the name of responsible care is not repudiated as inadequate but rather is abandoned in the face of its threat to survival. Moral obligation, rather than expanding to include the self, is rejected completely as the failure of conventional reciprocity leaves the woman unwilling any longer to protect others at what is now seen to be her own expense. In the absence of morality, survival, however "selfish" or "immoral," returns as the paramount concern.

A musician in her late twenties illustrates this transitional impasse. Having led an independent life which centered on her work, she considered herself "fairly strong-willed, fairly in control, fairly rational and objective" until she became involved in an intense love affair and discovered in her capacity to love "an entirely new dimension" in herself. Admitting in retrospect to "tremendous naiveté and idealism," she had entertained "some vague ideas that some day I would like a child to concretize our relationship . . . having always associated having a child with all the creative aspects of my life." Abjuring, with her lover, the use of contraceptives because, "as the relationship was sort of an ideal relationship in our minds, we liked the idea of not using foreign objects or anything artificial," she saw herself as having relinquished control, becoming instead "just simply vague and allowing events to just carry me along." Just as she began in her own thinking to confront "the realities of that situation"—the possibility of pregnancy and the fact that her lover was married—she found herself pregnant. "Caught" between her wish to end a relationship that "seemed more and more defeating" and her wish for a baby, which "would be a connection that would last a long time," she is paralyzed by her inability to resolve the dilemma which her ambivalence creates.

The pregnancy poses a conflict between her "moral" belief that "once a certain life has begun, it shouldn't be stopped artificially" and her "amazing" discovery that to have the baby she would "need much more [support] than I thought." Despite her moral conviction that she "should" have the child, she doubts that she could psychologically deal with "having the child alone and taking the responsibility for it." Thus a conflict erupts between what she considers to be her moral obligation to protect life and her inability to do so under the circumstances of this pregnancy. Seeing it as "my decision and my responsibility for making the decision whether to have or have not the child," she struggles to find a viable basis on which to resolve the dilemma.

Capable of arguing either for or against abortion "with a philosophical logic," she says, on the one hand, that in an overpopulated world one should have children only under ideal conditions for care but, on the other, that one should end a life only when it is impossible to sustain it. She describes her impasse in response to the question of whether there is a difference between what she wants to do and what she thinks she should do:

> Yes, and there always has. I have always been confronted with that precise situation in a lot of my choices, and I have been trying to figure out what are the things that make me believe that these are things I should do as opposed to what I feel I want to do. [In this situation?] It is not that clear cut. I both want the child and feel I should have it, and I also think I should have the abortion and want it, but I would say it is my stronger feeling, and that I don't have enough confidence in my work yet and that is really where it is all hinged, I think . . . [the abortion] would solve the problem and I know I can't handle the pregnancy.

Characterizing this solution as "emotional and pragmatic" and attributing it to her lack of confidence in her work, she contrasts it with the "better thought out and more logical and more correct" resolution of her lover who thinks that she should have the child and raise it without either his presence or financial support. Confronted with this reflected image of herself as ultimately giving and good, as self-sustaining in her own creativity and thus able to meet the needs of others while imposing no demands of her own in return, she questions not the image itself but her own adequacy in filling it. Concluding that she is not yet capable of doing so, she is reduced in her own eyes to what she sees as a selfish and highly compromised fight

> for my survival. But in one way or another, I am going to suffer. Maybe I am going to suffer mentally and emotionally having the abortion, or I would suffer what I think is possibly something worse. So I suppose it is the lesser of two evils. I think it is a matter of choosing which one I know that I can survive through. It is really. I think it is selfish, I suppose, because it does have to do with that. I just realized that. I guess it does have to do with whether I would survive or not. [Why is this selfish?] Well, you know, it is. Because I am concerned with my survival first, as opposed to the survival of the relationship or the survival of the child, another human being . . . I guess I am setting priorities, and I guess I am setting my needs to survive first. . . . I guess I see it in negative terms a lot . . . but I do think of other positive things; that I am still going to have some life left, maybe. I don't know.

In the face of this failure of reciprocity of care, in the disappointment of abandonment where connection was sought, survival is seen to hinge on her work which is "where I derive the meaning of what I am. That's the known factor." While uncertainty about her work makes this survival precarious, the choice for abortion is also distressing in that she considers it to be "highly introverted—that in this one respect, having an abortion would be going a step backward; going outside to love someone else and having a child would be a step forward." The sense of retrenchment that the severing of connection signifies is apparent in her anticipation of the cost which abortion would entail:

> Probably what I will do is I will cut off my feelings, and when they will return or what would happen to them after that, I don't know. So that I don't feel anything at all, and I would probably just be very cold and go through it very coldly. . . . The more you do that to yourself, the more difficult it becomes to love again or to trust again or to feel again. . . . Each time I

> move away from that, it becomes easier, not more difficult, but easier to avoid committing myself to a relationship. And I am really concerned about cutting off that whole feeling aspect.

Caught between selfishness and responsibility, unable to find in the circumstances of this choice a way of caring which does not at the same time destroy, she confronts a dilemma which reduces to a conflict between morality and survival. Adulthood and femininity fly apart in the failure of this attempt at integration as the choice to work becomes a decision not only to renounce this particular relationship and child but also to obliterate the vulnerability that love and care engender.

The Third Level: The Morality of Nonviolence

In contrast, a twenty-five-year-old woman, facing a similar disappointment, finds a way to reconcile the initially disparate concepts of selfishness and responsibility through a transformed understanding of self and a corresponding redefinition of morality. Examining the assumptions underlying the conventions of feminine self-abnegation and moral self-sacrifice, she comes to reject these conventions as immoral in their power to hurt. By elevating nonviolence—the injunction against hurting—to a principle governing all moral judgment and action, she is able to assert a moral equality between self and other. Care then becomes a universal obligation, the self-chosen ethic of a post-conventional judgment that reconstructs the dilemma in a way that allows the assumption of responsibility for choice.

In this woman's life, the current pregnancy brings to the surface the unfinished business of an earlier pregnancy and of the relationship in which both pregnancies occurred. The first pregnancy was discovered after her lover had left and was terminated by an abortion experienced as a purging expression of her anger at having been rejected. Remembering the abortion only as a relief, she nevertheless describes that time in her life as one in which she "hit rock bottom." Having hoped then to "take control of my life," she instead resumed the relationship when the man reappeared. Now, two years later, having once again "left my diaphragm in the drawer," she again becomes pregnant. Although initially "ecstatic" at the news, her elation dissipates when her lover tells her that he will leave if she chooses to have the child. Under these circumstances, she considers a second abortion but is unable to keep the repeated appointments she makes because of her reluctance to accept the responsibility for that choice. While the first abortion seemed an "honest mistake," she says that a second would make her feel "like a walking slaughter-house." Since she would need financial support to raise the child, her initial strategy was to take the matter to "the welfare people" in the hope that they would refuse to provide the necessary funds and thus resolve her dilemma:

> In that way, you know, the responsibility would be off my shoulders, and I could say, it's not my fault, you know, the state denied me the money that I would need to do it. But it turned out that it was possible to do it, and so I was, you know, right back where I started. And I had an appointment for an abortion, and I kept calling and cancelling it and then remaking the appointment and cancelling it, and I just couldn't make up my mind.

Confronting the need to choose between the two evils of hurting herself or ending the incipient life of the child, she finds, in a reconstruction of the dilemma itself, a basis for a new priority that allows decision. In doing so, she comes to see the conflict as arising from a faulty construction of reality. Her thinking recapitulates the developmental sequence, as she considers but rejects as inadequate the components of earlier-stage resolutions. An expanded conception of responsibility now reshapes moral judgment and guides resolution of the dilemma, whose pros and cons she considers as follows:

> Well, the pros for having the baby are all the admiration that you would get from, you know, being a single woman, alone, martyr, struggling, having the adoring love of this beautiful Gerber baby . . . just more of a home life than I have had in a long time, and that basically was it, which is pretty fantasyland; it is not very realistic. . . . Cons against having the baby: it was going to hasten what is looking to be the inevitable end of the relationship with the man I am presently with. . . . I was going to have to go on welfare, my parents were going to hate me for the rest of my life, I was going to lose a really good job that I have, I would lose a lot of independence . . . solitude . . . and I would have to be put in a position of asking help from a lot of people a lot of the time. Cons against having the abortion is having to face up to the guilt . . . and pros for having the abortion are I would be able to handle my deteriorating relation with S. with a lot more capability and a lot more responsibility for him and for myself . . . and I would not have to go through the realization that for the next twenty-five years of my life I would be punishing myself for being foolish enough to get pregnant again and forcing myself to bring up a kid just because I did this. Having to face the guilt of a second abortion seemed like, not exactly, well, exactly the lesser of the two evils but also the one that would pay off for me personally in the long run because by looking at why I am pregnant again and subsequently have decided to have a second abortion, I have to face up to some things about myself.

Although she doesn't "feel good about having a second abortion," she nevertheless concludes,

> I would not be doing myself or the child or the world any kind of favor having this child. . . . I don't need to pay off my imaginary debts to the world through this child, and I don't think that it is right to bring a child into the world and use it for that purpose.

Asked to describe herself, she indicates how closely her transformed moral understanding is tied to a changing self-concept:

> I have been thinking about that a lot lately, and it comes up different than what my usual subconscious perception of myself is. Usually paying off some sort of debt, going around serving people who are not really worthy of my attentions because somewhere in my life I think I got the impression that my needs are really secondary to other people's, and that if I feel, if I make any demands on other people to fulfill my needs, I'd feel guilty for it and submerge my own in favor of other people's, which later backfires on me, and I feel a great deal of resentment for other people that I am doing things for, which causes friction and the eventual deterioration of the relationship. And then I start all over again. How would I describe myself to myself? Pretty frustrated and a lot angrier than I admit, a lot more aggressive than I admit.

Reflecting on the virtues which comprise the conventional definition of the feminine self, a definition which she hears articulated in her mother's voice, she says, "I am beginning to think that all these virtues are really not getting me anywhere. I have begun to notice." Tied to this recognition is an acknowledgement of her power and worth, both previously excluded from the image she projected:

> I am suddenly beginning to realize that the things that I like to do, the things I am interested in, and the things that I believe and the kind of person I am is not so bad that I have to constantly be sitting on the shelf and letting it gather dust. I am a lot more worthwhile than what my past actions have led other people to believe.

Her notion of a "good person," which previously was limited to her mother's example of hard work, patience and self-sacrifice, now changes to include the value that she herself places on directness and honesty. Although she believes that this new self-assertion will lead her "to feel a lot better about myself" she recognizes that it will also expose her to criticism:

> Other people may say, 'Boy, she's aggressive, and I don't like that,' but at least, you know, they will know that they don't like that. They are not going to say, 'I like the way she manipulates herself to fit right around me.' . . . What I want to do is just be a more self-determined person and a more singular person.

While within her old framework abortion had seemed a way of "copping out" instead of being a "responsible person [who] pays for his mistakes and pays and pays and is always there when she says she will be there and even when she doesn't says she will be there is there," now, her "conception of what I think is right for myself and my conception of self-worth is changing." She can consider this emergent self "also a good person," as her concept of goodness expands to encompass "the feeling of self-worth; you are not going to sell yourself short and you are not going to make yourself do things that, you know, are really stupid and that you don't want to do." This reorientation centers on the awareness that:

> I have a responsibility to myself, and you know, for once I am beginning to realize that that really matters to me . . . instead of doing what I want for myself and feeling guilty over how selfish I am, you realize that that is a very usual way for people to live . . . doing what you want to do because you feel that your wants and your needs are important, if to no one else, then to you, and that's reason enough to do something that you want to do.

Once obligation extends to include the self as well as others, the disparity between selfishness and responsibility is reconciled. Although the conflict between self and other remains, the moral problem is restructured in an awareness that the occurrence of the dilemma itself precludes nonviolent resolution. The abortion decision is now seen to be a "serious" choice affecting both self and others: "This is a life that I have taken, a conscious decision to terminate, and that is just very heavy, a very heavy thing." While accepting the necessity of abortion as a highly compromised resolution, she turns her attention to the pregnancy itself, which she now considers to denote a failure of responsibility, a failure to care for and protect both self and other.

As in the first transition, although now in different terms, the conflict precipitated by the pregnancy catches up the issues critical to development. These issues now concern the worth of the self in relation to others, the claiming of the power to choose, and the acceptance of responsibility for choice. By provoking a confrontation with these issues, the crisis can become "a very auspicious time; you can use the pregnancy as sort of a learning, teeing-off point, which makes it useful in a way." This possibility for growth inherent in a crisis which allows confrontation with a construction of reality whose acceptance previously had impeded development was first identified by Coles (1964) in his study of the children of Little Rock. This same sense of possibility is expressed by the women who see, in their resolution of the abortion dilemma, a reconstructed understanding which creates the opportunity for "a new beginning," a chance "to take control of my life."

For this woman, the first step in taking control was to end the relationship in which she had considered herself "reduced to a nonentity," but to do so in a responsible way. Recognizing hurt as the inevitable concomitant of rejection, she strives to minimize that hurt "by dealing with [his] needs as best I can without compromising my own . . . that's a big point for me, because the thing in my life to this point has been always compromising, and I am not willing to do that any more." Instead, she seeks to act in a "decent, human kind of way . . . one that leaves maybe a slightly shook but not totally destroyed person." Thus the "nonentity" confronts her power to destroy which formerly had impeded any assertion, as she considers the possibility for a new kind of action that leaves both self and other intact.

The moral concern remains a concern with hurting as she considers Kohlberg's Heinz dilemma in terms of the question, "who is going to be hurt more, the druggist who loses some money or the person who loses their life?" The right to property and right to life are weighed not in the abstract, in terms of their logical priority, but rather in the particular, in terms of the actual consequences that the violation of these rights would have in the lives of the people involved. Thinking remains contextual and admixed with feelings of care, as the moral imperative to avoid hurt begins to be informed by a psychological understanding of the meaning of non-violence.

Thus, release from the intimidation of inequality finally allows the expression of a judgment that previously had been withheld. What women then enunciate is not a new morality, but a moral conception disentangled from the constraints that formerly had confused its perception and impeded its articulation. The willingness to express and take responsibility for judgment stems from the recognition of the psychological and moral necessity for an equation of worth between self and other. Responsibility for care then includes both self and other, and the obligation not to hurt, freed from conventional constraints, is reconstructed as a universal guide to moral choice.

The reality of hurt centers the judgment of a twenty-nine-year-old woman, married and the mother of a preschool child, as she struggles with the dilemma posed by a second pregnancy whose timing conflicts with her completion of an advanced degree. Saying that "I cannot deliberately do something that is bad or would hurt another person because I can't live with having done that," she nevertheless confronts a situation in which hurt has become inevitable. Seeking that solution which would best protect both herself and others, she indicates, in her definition of morality, the ineluctable sense of connection which infuses and colors all of her thinking:

> [Morality is] doing what is appropriate and what is just within your circumstances, but ideally it is not going to affect—I was going to say, ideally it wouldn't negatively affect another person, but that is ridiculous, because decisions are always going to affect another person. But you see, what I am trying to say is that it is the person that is the center of the decision making, of that decision making about what's right and what's wrong.

The person who is the center of this decision making begins by denying, but then goes on to acknowledge, the conflicting nature both of her own needs and of her various responsibilities. Seeing the pregnancy as a manifestation of the inner conflict between her wish, on the one hand, "to be a college president" and, on the other, "to be making pottery and flowers and having kids and staying at home," she struggles with contradiction between femininity and adulthood. Considering abortion as the "better" choice—because "in the end, meaning this time next year or this time two weeks from now, it will be less of a personal strain on us individually and on us as a family for me not to be pregnant at this time," she concludes that the decision has

> got to be, first of all, something that the woman can live with—a decision that the woman can live with, one way or another, or at least try to

> live with, and that it be based on where she is at and other people, significant people in her life, are at.

At the beginning of the interview she had presented the dilemma in its conventional feminine construction, as a conflict between her own wish to have a baby and the wish of others for her to complete her education. On the basis of this construction she deemed it "selfish" to continue the pregnancy because it was something "I want to do." However, as she begins to examine her thinking, she comes to abandon as false this conceptualization of the problem, acknowledging the truth of her own internal conflict and elaborating the tension which she feels between her femininity and the adulthood of her work life. She describes herself as "going in two directions" and values that part of herself which is "incredibly passionate and sensitive"—her capacity to recognize and meet, often with anticipation, the needs of others. Seeing her "compassion" as "something I don't want to lose" she regards it as endangered by her pursuit of professional advancement. Thus the self-deception of her initial presentation, its attempt to sustain the fiction of her own innocence, stems from her fear that to say that *she* does not want to have another baby at this time would be

> an acknowledgement to me that I am an ambitious person and that I want to have power and responsibility for others and that I want to live a life that extends from 9 to 5 every day and into the evenings and on weekends, because that is what the power and responsibility means. It means that my family would necessarily come second . . . there would be such an incredible conflict about which is tops, and I don't want that for myself.

Asked about her concept of "an ambitious person" she says that to be ambitious means to be

> power hungry [and] insensitive. [Why insensitive?] Because people are stomped on in the process. A person on the way up stomps on people, whether it is family or other colleagues or clientele, on the way up. [Inevitably?] Not always, but I have seen it so often in my limited years of working that it is scary to me. It is scary because I don't want to change like that.

Because the acquisition of adult power is seen to entail the loss of feminine sensitivity and compassion, the conflict between femininity and adulthood becomes construed as a moral problem. The discovery of the principle of nonviolence begins to direct attention to the moral dilemma itself and initiates the search for a resolution that can encompass both femininity and adulthood.

DEVELOPMENTAL THEORY RECONSIDERED

The developmental conception delineated at the outset, which has so consistently found the development of women to be either aberrant or incomplete, has been limited insofar as it has been predominantly a male conception, giving lip-service, a place on the chart, to the interdependence of intimacy and care but constantly stressing, at their expense, the importance and value of autonomous judgment and action. To admit to this conception the truth of the feminine perspective is to recognize for both sexes the central importance in adult life of the connection between self and other, the universality of the need for compassion and care. The concept of the separate self and of the moral principle uncompromised by the constraints of reality is an adolescent ideal, the elaborately wrought philosophy of a Stephen Daedalus, whose flight we know to be in jeopardy. Erikson (1964), in contrasting the ideological morality of the adolescent with the ethics of adult care, attempts to grapple with this problem of integration, but is impeded by the limitations of his own previous developmental conception. When his developmental stages chart a path where the sole precursor to the intimacy of adult relationships is the trust established in infancy and all intervening experience is marked only as steps toward greater independence, then separation itself becomes the model and the measure of growth. The observation that for women, identity has as much to do with connection as with separation led Erikson into trouble largely because of his failure to integrate this insight into the mainstream of his developmental theory (Erikson, 1968).

The morality of responsibility which women describe stands apart from the morality of rights which underlies Kohlberg's conception of the highest stages of moral judgment. Kohlberg (Note 3) sees the progression toward these stages as resulting from the generalization of the self-centered adolescent rejection of societal morality into a principled conception of individual natural rights. To illustrate this progression, he cites as an example of integrated Stage Five judgment, "possibly moving to Stage Six," the following response of a twenty-five-year-old subject from his male longitudinal sample:

> [What does the word morality mean to you?] Nobody in the world knows the answer. I think it is recognizing the right of the individual, the rights of other individuals, not interfering with those rights. Act as fairly as you would have them treat you. I think it is basically to preserve the human being's right to existence. I think that is the most important. Secondly, the human being's right to do as he pleases, again without interfering with somebody else's rights. (p. 29)

Another version of the same conception is evident in the following interview response of a male college senior whose moral judgment also was scored by Kohlberg (Note 4) as at Stage Five or Six:

> [Morality] is a prescription, it is a thing to follow, and the idea of having a concept of morality is to try to figure out what it is that people can do in order to make life with each other livable, make for a kind of balance, a kind of equilibrium, a harmony in which everybody feels he has a place and an equal share in things, and it's doing that—doing that is kind of contributing to a state of affairs that go beyond the individual in the absence of which, the individual has no chance for self-fulfillment of any kind. Fairness; morality is kind of essential, it seems to me, for creating the kind of environment, interaction between people, that is prerequisite to this fulfillment of most individual goals and so on. If you want other people to not interfere with your pursuit of whatever you are into, you have to play the game.

In contrast, a woman in her late twenties responds to a similar question by defining a morality not of rights but of responsibility:

> [What makes something a moral issue?] Some sense of trying to uncover a right path in which to live, and always in my mind is that the world is full of real and recognizable trouble, and is it heading for some sort of doom and is it right to bring children into this world when we currently have an overpopulation problem, and is it right to spend money on a pair of shoes when I have a pair of shoes and other people are shoeless. . . . It is part of a self-critical view, part of saying, how am I spending my time and in what sense am I working? I think I have a real drive to, I have a real maternal drive to take care of someone. To take care of my mother, to take care of children, to take care of other people's children, to take care of my own children, to take care of the world. I think that goes back to your other question, and when I am dealing with moral issues, I am sort of saying to myself constantly, are you taking care of all the things that you think are important and in what ways are you wasting yourself and wasting those issues?

While the postconventional nature of this woman's perspective seems clear, her judgments of Kohlberg's hypothetical moral dilemmas do not meet his criteria for scoring at the principled level. Kohlberg regards this as a disparity between normative and metaethical judgments which he sees as indicative of the transition between conventional and principled thinking. From another perspective, however, this judgment represents a different moral conception, disentangled from societal conventions and raised to the principled level. In this conception, moral judgment is oriented toward issues of responsibility. The way in which the responsibility orientation guides moral decision at the postconventional level is described by the following woman in her thirties:

> [Is there a right way to make moral decisions?] The only way I know is to try to be as awake as possible, to try to know the range of what you feel, to try to consider all that's involved, to be as aware as you can be to what's going on, as conscious as you can of where you're walking. [Are there principles that guide you?] The principle would have something to do with responsibility, responsibility and caring about yourself and others. . . . But it's not that on the one hand you choose to be responsible and on the other hand you choose to be irresponsible—both ways you can be responsible. That's why there's not just a principle that once you take hold of you settle—the principle put into practice here is still going to leave you with conflict.

The moral imperative that emerges repeatedly in the women's interviews is an injunction to care, a responsibility to discern and alleviate the "real and recognizable trouble" of this world. For the men Kohlberg studied, the moral imperative appeared rather as an injunction to respect the rights of others and thus to protect from interference the right to life and self-fulfillment. Women's insistence on care is at first self-critical rather than self-protective, while men initially conceive obligation to others negatively in terms of noninterference. Development for both sexes then would seem to entail an integration of rights and responsibilities through the discovery of the complementarity of these disparate views. For the women I have studied, this integration between rights and responsibilities appears to take place through a principled understanding of equity and reciprocity. This understanding tempers the self-destructive potential of a self-critical morality by asserting the equal right of all persons to care. For the men in Kohlberg's sample as well as for those in a longitudinal study of Harvard undergraduates (Gilligan & Murphy, Note 5) it appears to be the recognition through experience of the need for a more active responsibility in taking care that corrects the potential indifference of a morality of noninterference and turns attention from the logic to the consequences of choice. In the development of a postconventional ethic understanding, women come to see the violence generated by inequitable relationships, while men come to realize the limitations of a conception of justice blinded to the real inequities of human life.

Kohlberg's dilemmas, in the hypothetical abstraction of their presentation, divest the moral actors from the history and psychology of their individual lives and separate the moral problem from the social contingencies of its possible occurrence. In doing so, the dilemmas are useful for the distillation and refinement of the "objective principles of justice" toward which Kohlberg's stages strive. However, the reconstruction of the dilemma in its contextual particularity allows the understanding of cause and consequence which engages the compassion and tolerance considered by previous theorists to qualify the feminine sense of justice. Only when substance is given to the skeletal lives of hypothetical people is it possible to consider the social injustices which their moral problems may reflect and to imagine the individual suffering their occurrence may signify or their resolution engender.

The proclivity of women to reconstruct hypothetical dilemmas in terms of the real, to request or supply the information missing about the nature of the people and the places where they live, shifts their judgment away from the hierarchical ordering of principles and the formal procedures of decision making that are critical for scoring at Kohlberg's highest stages. This insistence on the particular signifies an orientation to the dilemma and to moral problems in general that differs from any of Kohlberg's stage descriptions. Given the constraints of Kohlberg's system and the biases in his research sample, this different orientation can only be construed as a failure in development. While several of the women in the research sample clearly articulated what Kohlberg regarded as a postconventional metaethical position, none of them were considered by Kohlberg to be principled in their normative moral judgments of his hypothetical moral dilemmas (Note 4). Instead, the women's judgments pointed toward an identification of the violence inherent in the dilemma itself which was seen to compromise the justice of any of its possible resolutions. This construction of the dilemma led the women to recast the moral judgment from a consideration of the good to a choice between evils.

The woman whose judgment of the abortion dilemma concluded the developmental sequence presented in the preceding section saw Kohlberg's Heinz dilemma in these terms and judged Heinz's action in terms of a choice between selfishness and sacrifice. For Heinz to steal the drug, given the circumstances of his life (which she inferred from his inability to pay two thousand dollars), he would have "to do something which is not in his best interest, in that he is going to get sent away, and that is a supreme sacrifice, a sacrifice which I would say a person truly in love might be willing to make." However, not to steal the drug "would be selfish on his part . . . he would just have to feel guilty about not allowing her a chance to live longer." Heinz's decision to steal is considered not in terms of the logical priority of life over property which justifies its rightness, but rather in terms of the actual consequences that stealing would have for a man of limited means and little social power.

Considered in the light of its probable outcomes—his wife dead, or Heinz in jail, brutalized by the violence of that experience and his life compromised by a record of felony—the dilemma itself changes. Its resolution has less to do with the relative weights of life and property in an abstract moral conception than with the collision it has produced between two lives, formerly conjoined but now in opposition, where the continuation of one life can now occur only at the expense of the other. Given this construction, it becomes clear why consideration revolves around the issue of sacrifice and why guilt becomes the inevitable concomitant of either resolution.

Demonstrating the reticence noted in the first section about making moral judgments, this woman explains her reluctance to judge in terms of her belief

> that everybody's existence is so different that I kind of say to myself, that might be something I wouldn't do, but I can't say that it is right or wrong for that person. I can only deal with what is appropriate for me to do when I am faced with specific problems.

Asked if she would apply to others her own injunction against hurting, she says:

> See, I can't say that it is wrong. I can't say that it is right or that it's wrong because I don't know what the person did that the other person did something to hurt him . . . so it is not right that the person got hurt, but it is right that the person who just lost the job has got to get that anger up and out. It doesn't put any bread on his table, but it is released. I don't mean to be copping out. I really am trying to see how to answer these questions for you.

Her difficulty in answering Kohlberg's questions, her sense of strain with the construction which they impose on the dilemma, stems from their divergence from her own frame of reference:

> I don't even think I use the words right and wrong anymore, and I know I don't use the word moral, because I am not sure I know what it means. . . . We are talking about an unjust society, we are talking about a whole lot of things that are not right, that are truly wrong, to use the word that I don't use very often, and I have no control to change that. If I could change it, I certainly would, but I can only make my small contribution from day to day, and if I don't intentionally hurt somebody, that is my contribution to a better society. And so a chunk of that contribution is also not to pass judgment on other people, particularly when I don't know the circumstances of why they are doing certain things.

The reluctance to judge remains a reluctance to hurt, but one that stems now not from a sense of personal vulnerability but rather from a recognition of the limitations of judgment itself. The deference of the conventional feminine perspective can thus be seen to continue at the postconventional level, not as moral relativism but rather as part of a reconstructed moral understanding. Moral judgment is renounced in an awareness of the psychological and social determinism of all human behavior at the same time as moral concern is reaffirmed in recognition of the reality of human pain and suffering.

> I have a real thing about hurting people and always have, and that gets a little complicated at times, because, for example, you don't want to hurt your child. I don't want to hurt my child but if I don't hurt her sometimes, then that's hurting her more, you see, and so that was a terrible dilemma for me.

Moral dilemmas are terrible in that they entail hurt; she sees Heinz's decision as "the result of anguish, who am I hurting, why do I have to hurt them." While the morality of Heinz's theft is not in question, given the circumstances which necessitated it, what is at issue is his willingness to substitute himself for his wife and become, in her stead, the victim of exploitation by a society which breeds and legitimizes the druggist's irresponsibility and whose injustice is thus manifest in the very occurrence of the dilemma.

The same sense that the wrong questions are being asked is evident in the response of another woman who justified Heinz's action on a similar basis, saying "I don't think that exploitation should really be a right." When women begin to make direct moral statements, the issues they repeatedly address are those of exploitation and hurt. In doing so, they raise the issue of nonviolence in precisely the same psychological context that brought Erikson (1969) to pause in his consideration of the truth of Gandhi's life.

In the pivotal letter, around which the judgment of his book turns, Erikson confronts the contradiction between the philosophy of nonviolence that informed Gandhi's dealing with the British and the psychology of violence that marred his relationships with his family and with the children of the ashram. It was this contradiction, Erikson confesses,

> which almost brought *me* to the point where I felt unable to continue writing *this* book because I seemed to sense the presence of a kind of untruth in the very protestation of truth; of something unclean when all the words spelled out an unreal purity; and, above all, of displaced violence where nonviolence was the professed issue.

In an effort to untangle the relationship between the spiritual truth of Satyagraha and the truth of his own psychoanalytic understanding, Erikson reminds Gandhi that "truth, you once said, 'excludes the use of violence because man is not capable of knowing the absolute truth and therefore is not competent to punish.'" The affinity between Satyagraha and psychoanalysis lies in their shared commitment to seeing life as an "experiment in truth," in their being

> somehow joined in a universal "therapeutics," committed to the Hippocratic principle that one can test truth (or the healing power inherent in a sick situation) only by action which avoids harm—or better, by action which maximizes mutuality and minimizes the violence caused by unilateral coercion or threat.

Erikson takes Gandhi to task for his failure to acknowledge the relativity of truth. This failure is manifest in the coercion of Gandhi's claim to exclusive possession of the truth, his "unwillingness to learn from *anybody anything* except what was approved by the 'inner voice.'" This claim led Gandhi, in the guise of love, to impose his truth on others without awareness or regard for the extent to which he thereby did violence to their integrity.

The moral dilemma, arising inevitably out of a conflict of truths, is by definition a "sick situation" in that its either/or formulation leaves no room for an outcome that does not do violence. The resolution of such dilemmas, however, lies not in the self-deception of rationalized violence—"I was" said Gandhi, "a cruelly kind husband. I regarded myself as her teacher and so harassed her out of my blind love for her"—but rather in the replacement of the underlying antagonism with a mutuality of respect and care.

Gandhi, whom Kohlberg has mentioned as exemplifying Stage Six moral judgment and whom Erikson sought as a model of an adult ethical sensibility, instead is criticized by a judgment that refuses to look away from or condone the infliction of harm. In denying the validity of his wife's reluctance to open her home to strangers and in his blindness to the different reality of adolescent sexuality and temptation, Gandhi compromised in his everyday life the ethic of nonviolence to which in principle and in public he was so steadfastly committed.

The blind willingness to sacrifice people to truth, however, has always been the danger of an ethics abstracted from life. This willingness links Gandhi to the biblical Abraham, who prepared to sacrifice the life of his son in order to demonstrate the integrity and supremacy of his faith. Both men, in the limitations of their fatherhood, stand in implicit contrast to the woman who comes before Solomon and verifies her motherhood by relinquishing truth in order to save the life of her child. It is the ethics of an adulthood that has become principled at the expense of care that Erikson comes to criticize in his assessment of Gandhi's life.

This same criticism is dramatized explicitly as a contrast between the sexes in *The Merchant of Venice* (1598/1912), where Shakespeare goes through an extraordinary complication of sexual identity (dressing a male actor as a female character who in turn poses as a male judge) in order to bring into the masculine citadel of justice the feminine plea for mercy. The limitation of the contractual conception of justice is illustrated through the absurdity of its literal execution, while the "need to make exceptions all the time" is demonstrated contrapuntally in the matter of the rings. Portia, in calling for mercy, argues for that resolution in which no one is hurt, and as the men are forgiven for their failure to keep both their rings and their word, Antonio in turn forgoes his "right" to ruin Shylock.

The research findings that have been reported in this essay suggest that women impose a distinctive construction on moral problems, seeing moral dilemmas in terms of conflicting responsibilities. This construction was found to develop through a sequence of three levels and two transitions, each level representing a more complex understanding of the relationship between self and other and each transition involving a critical reinterpretation of the moral conflict between selfishness and responsibility. The development of women's moral judgment appears to proceed from an initial concern with survival, to focus on goodness, and finally to a principled understanding of nonviolence as the most adequate guide to the just resolution of moral conflicts.

In counterposing to Kohlberg's longitudinal research on the development of hypothetical moral judgment in men a cross-sectional study of women's responses to actual dilemmas of moral conflict and choice, this essay precludes the possibility of generalization in either direction and leaves to further research the task of sorting out the different variables of occasion and sex. Longitudinal studies of women's moral judgments are necessary in order to validate the claims of stage and sequence presented here. Similarly, the contrast drawn between the moral judgments of men and women awaits for its confirmation a more systematic comparison of the responses of both sexes. Kohlberg's research on moral development has confounded the variables of age, sex, type of decision, and type of dilemma by presenting a single configuration (the responses of adolescent males to hypothetical dilemmas of conflicting rights) as the basis for a universal stage sequence. This paper underscores the need for systematic treatment of these variables and points toward their study as a critical task for future moral development research.

For the present, my aim has been to demonstrate the centrality of the concepts of responsibility and care in women's constructions of the moral domain, to indicate the close tie in women's thinking between conceptions of the self and conceptions of morality, and, finally, to argue the need for an expanded developmental theory that would include, rather than rule out from developmental consideration, the difference in the feminine voice. Such an inclusion seems essential, not only for explaining the development of women but also for understanding in both sexes the characteristics and precursors of an adult moral conception.

NOTES

1. Haan, N. *Activism as moral protest: Moral judgments of hypothetical dilemmas and an actual situation of civil disobedience.* Unpublished manuscript, University of California at Berkeley, 1971.
2. Turiel, E. *A comparative analysis of moral knowledge and moral judgment in males and females.* Unpublished manuscript, Harvard University, 1973.
3. Kohlberg, L. *Continuities and discontinuities in childhood and adult moral development revisited.* Unpublished paper, Harvard University, 1973.
4. Kohlberg, L. Personal communication, August, 1976.
5. Gilligan, C., & Murphy, M. *The philosopher and the "dilemma of the fact": Moral development in late adolescence and adulthood.* Unpublished manuscript, Harvard University, 1977.

STUDY QUESTIONS

1. Is there a difference between a "feminine" morality and a traditional morality based on moral rules or laws?
2. What are the characteristics of this "altruism" some women shoulder? How does altruism tie in with goodness and approval?
3. What role does honesty, or self-awareness, play in Gilligan's model?
4. What is universal nonviolence? How is it implemented?
5. What does Gilligan mean when she calls this nonviolent morality not a new morality but rather a morality "disentangled"? From what is it disentangled?
6. Must "femininity" somehow be sacrificed in order to become adult?

FOR FURTHER STUDY

Cole, Eve Browning. *Explorations in Feminist Ethics: Theory and Practice.* Bloomington, Ind.: Indiana University Press, 1992.

Frankena, William K. *Ethics,* 2nd ed. Englewood Cliffs, N.J.: Prentice-Hall, 1973.

Hardin, Russell. *Morality Within the Limits of Reason.* Chicago: University of Chicago Press, 1988.

Helm, Paul, ed. *The Divine Command Theory of Ethics.* Oxford: Oxford University Press, 1979.

Hospers, John. *Human Conduct: Problems of Ethics.* New York: Harcourt, Brace, Jovanovich, 1972.

MacIntyre, Alasdair. *After Virtue.* Notre Dame, Ind.: University of Notre Dame Press, 1981.

Moore, G. E. *Principia Ethica.* Cambridge: Cambridge University Press, 1903.

Murdoch, Iris. *The Sovereignty of Good.* London: Routledge, 1970.

Nelson, Kai. *Ethics Without God.* Pemberton Books, 1973.

O'Conner, D. J. *Aquinas and Natural Law.* London: Macmillan, 1968.

Olson, Robert G. *The Morality of Self-Interest.* New York: Harcourt, Brace, Jovanovich, 1965.

Rawls, John. *A Theory of Justice.* Cambridge, Mass.: Harvard University Press, 1971.

Regan, Tom. *The Case for Animal Rights.* Berkeley: University of California Press, 1983.

Ross, W. D. *Kant's Ethical Theory.* London: Clarendon Press, 1954.

Taylor, Charles. *Sources of the Self: The Making of Modern Identity.* Cambridge, Mass.: Harvard University Press, 1989.

Chapter Two

Ethics of Community

7

African Communalism

Kwame Gyekye

Kwame Gyeke teaches philosophy at Howard University. An Akan himself, he is the author of *An Essay on African Philosophical Thought: The Akan Conceptual Scheme,* from which this selection is taken.

THE CONCEPTS OF GOOD AND EVIL

I shall begin with the Akan moral concepts of good (or goodness: *papa*) and evil (*bōne*), which are fundamental in the moral thought and practice of any culture. In Akan thought goodness is not defined by reference to religious beliefs or supernatural beings. What is morally good is not that which is commanded by God or any spiritual being; what is right is not that which is pleasing to a spiritual being or in accordance with the will of such being. In the course of my field research none of my discussants referred to Onyame (God) or other spiritual entities in response to the questions What is good? What is evil? None of them held that an action was good or evil because Onyame had said so. On the contrary, the views that emerge in discussions of these questions reveal an undoubted conviction of a nonsupernaturalistic—a humanistic—origin of morality. Such views provide insight into the Akan conception of the criterion of moral value.

In Akan moral thought the sole criterion of goodness is the welfare or well-being of the community. Thus, in the course of my field research, the response I had to the question, "What do the Akan people mean by 'good' (or, goodness)?" invariably included a list of goods, that is, a list of deeds, habits, and patterns of behavior considered by the society as worthwhile because of their consequences for human well-being. The list of such goods invariably included: kindness (generosity: *ayamyie*), faithfulness (honesty, truthfulness: *nokwaredi*), compassion (*mmōbrōhunu*), hospitality (*ahōhoyē, adōe*), that which brings peace, happiness, dignity, and respect (*nea ede asomdwee, ahomeka, anuonyam ne abuo ba*), and so on. The good comprehends all the above, which is to say that the good (*papa*) is explained in terms of the qualities of things (actions, behavioral patterns). Generosity, hospitality, justice are considered (kinds of) good. Generosity is a good thing, but it is not identical with goodness. Goodness (or the good), then, is considered in Akan moral thinking as a concept comprehending a number of acts, states, and patterns of behavior that exemplify certain characteristics.

On what grounds are some acts (etc.) considered good? The answer is simply that each of them is supposed (expected or known) to bring about or lead to social well-being. Within the framework of Akan social and humanistic ethics, what is morally good is generally that which promotes social welfare, solidarity, and harmony in human relationships. Moral value in the Akan system is determined in terms of its consequences for mankind and society. "Good" is thus used of actions that promote human interest. The good is identical with the welfare of the society, which is expected to include the welfare of the individual. This appears to be the meaning or definition of "good" in

Akan ethics. It is clear that this definition does not at all refer to the will or commands of God. That which is good is decreed not by a supernatural being as such, but by human beings within the framework of their experiences in living in society. So that even though an Akan maxim says

> I am doing the *good* (thing) so that my way to the world of spirits might not be blocked,
>
> (*mereye papa na ankosi me nsaman kwan*)

what constitutes the good is determined not by spiritual beings but by human beings.

Just as the good is that action or pattern of behavior which conduces to well-being and social harmony, so the evil (*bōne;* that is, moral evil) is that which is considered detrimental to the well-being of humanity and society. The Akan concept of evil, like that of good, is definable entirely in terms of the needs of society. Thus, even though one often hears people say "God does not like evil" (*Onyame mpē bōne*), yet what constitutes evil is determined by the members of the community, not by Onyame.

Akan ethics recognizes two categories of evil, *bōne* and *musuo,* although *bōne* is the usual word for evil. The first category, *bōne,* which I shall call "ordinary," includes such evils as theft, adultery, lying, backbiting (*kōkōnsa*), and so on. The other category of evil, *musuo,* I shall call "extraordinary." As described by a group of discussants, "*musuo* is an evil which is great and which brings suffering (*ōhaw, ahokyerē:* disaster, misfortune) to the whole community, not just to the doer alone." Another discussant also stated that "the consequences of committing *musuo* affect the whole community." *Musuo* was also defined as an "uncommon evil" (*bōne a wōntaa nhu*), and as an "indelible evil" (*ade a woye a wompepa da*), "remembered and referred to by people even many years after the death of the doer." Thus, *musuo* is generally considered to be a great, extraordinary moral evil; it is viewed by the community with particular abhorrence and revulsion because its commission is believed not only to bring shame to the whole community, but also, in the minds of many ordinary people, to invite the wrath of the supernatural powers.

The category of *musuo* includes such acts as suicide, incest, having sexual intercourse in the bush, rape, murder, stealing things dedicated to the deities or ancestral spirits, etc. Moral evils that are *musuo* are also considered as taboos (*akyiwade:* abominations, prohibitions), a taboo being, to most people, an act that is forbidden or proscribed just because it is supposedly hateful to some supernatural being. That *musuo* are classifiable as taboos was in fact the view of some discussants: "*musuo* is something we abominate" (*musuo ye ade a yekyi*); "*musuo* is a taboo" (*akyiwade*). Now, it is remarkable that the same evils considered as taboos by Bishop Sarpong, such as murder, sexual intercourse with a woman impregnated by another man, suicide, incest, words of abuse against the chief, and stealing from among the properties of a deity, are all *musuo.* This gives the impression that the category of extraordinary moral evils (*musuo*) is coextensive with the category of taboos (*akyiwade*). But in reality this is not so. The *musuo* are indeed taboos, but from this we can only infer that some taboos are *musuo;* since *musuo* are moral evils, such taboos (as are *musuo*) are also moral evils. It seems to me that extraordinary moral evils (which include both *musuo* and moral taboos) are the kinds of moral evil that are *never* to be committed under any circumstances. This view is based on the force of the word *kyi,* to abhor, hate, from which *akyiwade* (hateful things, taboos) derives. Henceforth, I shall simply use the expression "moral taboos" to cover both *musuo* and *akyiwade. . . .*

How would the traditional Akan thinker explain the origin and role of taboos in Akan morality? In connection with taboo, Bishop Sarpong observed: "If one were to ask the Ashanti why he keeps these taboos, he will probably not be able to give the reasons I have propounded. All he is likely to assert is that they existed from time immemorial, that the ancestors want him to observe them." Bishop Sarpong is right as far as the ordinary Akan is concerned; but the wise persons (*anyansafo*) among them would be able to furnish the underlying reasons for considering such acts as moral evils of a high order. Their statements quoted above indicate clearly that they believe that committing a taboo act affects the welfare of the whole community. Moral taboos are thus explained by reference to their social function and purpose. Communal well-being, then, appears to be the principal reason for the proscription of the category of moral evils referred to as moral taboos (*musuo* and *akyiwade*). The following explanation given by Bishop Sarpong for tabooing sexual intercourse in the bush is in line with the thinking of the Akan thinkers:

> Those who indulge in it expose themselves to the risk of being bitten by venomous creatures like the snake, the scorpion, and the spider. (It should be borne in mind that Ashanti is a forested region with dangerous creatures whose bites may easily be fatal.) Let a mishap of this nature take place and there is every likelihood that misapprehensions are conceived about the conjugal act itself. That this would be detrimental to the human species is too obvious to emphasize.

In the view of Akan thinkers, the real, underlying reason for regarding sexual intercourse in the bush as a great moral evil and thus for tabooing it is not that it is hated by the earth goddess (*Asase Yaa*), but that it has undesirable social consequences. Their position is plainly that the acts classified as moral taboos were so regarded simply because of the *gravity* of their consequences for human society, not because those acts were hateful to any supernatural beings.

MORALITY IN THE CONTEXT OF A NONREVEALED RELIGION

. . . to the question asked by Socrates (in Plato's *Euthyphro*) whether something is good because God approves of it or whether God approves of it because it is good, the response of the Akan moral thinker would be that God approves of the good because it is good. The reason is, if something is good because God approves of it, how would that good thing be known to them (that is, Akans)? How would they know what God approves in a nonrevealed religion? On the contrary, their ascription of moral attributes to God and the sanctions that he is believed to apply . . . in the event of a breach of the moral law clearly suggest the Akan conviction that God approves of the good because it is good and eschews the evil because it is evil.

RELIGION, SANCTIONS, AND MORAL PRACTICE

. . . Akan thought conceives the human being as a social animal and society as a necessary condition for human existence. . . . This thought is expressed in the proverb

> When a man descends from heaven, he descends into human society.

But the person who descends into human society has desires, aims, interests, and will, and these have to be reconciled with those of others. An Akan proverb such as

> One man's curse is another man's fortune
>
> (lit: What appears sour on one man's palate appears sweet on another man's palate),

indicates the view that the desires, interests, and passions of individual members of a society differ and may conflict with one another. One often hears the ordinary Akan say *obi mpē a obi pē:* "If one does not desire it, the other does"; that is, people have different desires, preferences, and choices. One Akan motif shows a "siamese" crocodile with two heads but a common stomach. The saying that goes with the symbol is that, although they have one stomach, the heads fight over the food that will eventually nourish both of them. The symbol . . . points to the conflicts that result from the existence of individual desires and needs. The problem is how to minimize such conflicts and at the same time allow room for the realization of individual desires and needs. The need for a system of rules to regulate the conduct of individuals and, consequently, for social harmony and cooperative living, thus becomes urgent. It is this social need that gives rise to morality, according to Akan ethics.

Thus considerations for human well-being and for an ideal type of social relationships—both of which are generated by the basic existential conditions of man—these, not divine pronouncements, constitute the crucible in which Akan morality is fashioned. Whatever the moral virtues possessed by, or ascribed to, God and the other spiritual powers, it should now be clear that the compelling reason of the Akan for pursuing the good is not that it is pleasing to the supernatural beings or approved by them, but rather that it will lead to the attainment of human well-being. This *humanistic* moral outlook of the Akan is something that, I think, is worth being cherished, for its goal, from the moral point of view, is ultimate and, thus, self-justifying. . . .

THE CENTRALITY OF CHARACTER (*suban*) IN AKAN ETHICS

Morality is generally concerned with right and wrong conduct or behavior and good and bad character. We speak not only of a moral act but also of a moral person; we speak not only of an honest or generous or vicious act but also of an honest or generous or vicious person. When a person is generally honest or generous the Akans judge him or her to be a good person, by which they mean that he or she has a good character (*ōwō suban papa*), and when the person is wicked or dishonest they judge him or her to be a bad person, that is, to have a bad character. It is on the basis of a person's conduct (deeds, *nneyēe*) that the Akans judge one to be good or bad, to have good character or bad character. According to them, the character of a person is basic. The performance of good or bad acts depends on the state of one's character; inasmuch as good deeds reflect good character, character (*suban*) appears as the focal point of the ethical life. It is, in Akan moral thought, the crucial element in morality, for it profits a society little if its moral system is well articulated intellectually and the individuals in that system nevertheless have bad character and so do the wrong things. A well-articulated moral system does not necessarily produce good character; neither does knowledge of moral rules make one a good person or produce good character.

For the Akans, and perhaps also for the Greeks and Arabs, ethics has to do principally with character. Ethics, according to Akan thinkers, deals essentially with the quality of the individual's character. This is a remarkable assertion, for after all the ethical response, that is, the response or attitude to a moral rule, is an individual, private affair. All that a society can do regarding morality is to provide or impart moral knowledge to its members, making them aware of the moral rules that are applicable to all living in it. But granted this, it does not follow that the individual members of the society will lead lives in conformity with the moral rules. A man may know and may even accept a moral rule such as, say, it is wrong to seduce someone's wife. But he may fail to apply this rule to a particular situation. He is not able to effect the transition from knowledge to action. According to the Akan thinkers, to be able to act in accord with the moral rules of the society requires the possession of a good character (*suban*).

What, then, is character? How do Akan thinkers define character? The root of *suban* is *su* or *esu,* meaning nature, which might imply that character is associated with a person's nature, that character develops from a set of inborn traits. . . . Overall, one might conclude that character is a state or condition of the soul which "causes" it to perform its actions spontaneously and easily. This implies that the moral habits are innate, that we are born virtuous and are not responsible for our character. That impression, however, is false. Despite its etymological link with nature, the *suban* of a person is not wholly innate. . . .

Akan thinkers define character in terms of habits, which originate from a person's deeds or actions; character is the configuration of (individual) acts. Thus, several of my discussants opined that "Character is your deeds" (actions: *nneyēe*); "Character comes from your deeds" (*suban firi wo nneyēe*). Moreover, sometimes the Akans use the sentence, "He has a bad character" (*ōwō suban bōne*) when they want to say "He does bad things" (*ōyē nneēma bōne*). The thought here is that moral virtues arise through habituation, which is consonant with the empirical orientation of Akan philosophy. This is, I think, the reason for the teaching of moral values embedded in proverbs and folktales to children in the process of their socialization; the moral instructions are meant to habituate them to moral virtues. If moral habits were thought to be acquired by nature or through birth it would be senseless to pursue moral instruction. But it is believed and expected that the narratives are one way by which children acquire and internalize moral virtues.

I hold the view that in general society presents us with a variety of modes of behavior. We see and are told what is good behavior and what is bad, what is praiseworthy and what is blameworthy. We are given a choice. To acquire virtue, a person must practice good deeds so that they become habitual. The newly acquired good habit must be strengthened by repetition. A single good deed may initiate further good deeds, and in this way virtue is acquired. Over time such an acquired virtue becomes a habit. This is the position of Akan philosophy, for this is what they mean by saying *aka ne hō,* "It is left (or has remained) with him," "It has become part of him," "It has become his habit." Such practice and performance emphasize the relevance and importance of action in the acquisition of virtue. To be just, for instance, one must first behave in a just manner. The emphasis placed by Akan thinkers on the influence of actions on character illustrates their conviction that one is in some sense responsible for the sort of person one is; the person is responsible for the state of his or her character. The unjust man may be held responsible for becoming unjust, because his character is the result of repeated (*aka hō*) voluntary acts of injustice. He had the choice between committing acts of injustice and refraining from such acts.

The emphasis on the relevance of actions for states of character is reflected in the way that abstract terms for "goodness," "virtue," are formed. The usual words for "goodness" in Akan are *yieyē* and *papayē* (the latter also appears sometimes as *papa*). The last syllable of each word means to do or perform. Thus, the two words literally mean "good-doing" (that is, doing good).

This analysis of the Akan concept of character supports, as far as the Akan position goes, Mbiti's view that "the essence of African morality is that it is a morality of 'conduct' rather than a morality of 'being' . . . a person is what he is because of what he does, rather than that he does what he does because of what he is." This view is repeated by Bishop Sarpong: "For it would appear that for the Akan what a man is is less important than what a man does. To put it more concretely, a person is what he is because of his deeds. He does not perform those deeds because of what he is." The emphasis on deeds (*nneyēe*) is appropriate, for it agrees with the Akan belief that a person is not born virtuous or vicious. The previously quoted proverb

> One is not born with a bad "head," but one takes it on the earth

implies, among other things, that a bad habit is not an inborn characteristic, but one that is acquired. The Akan position thus is that the original nature of human beings was morally neutral. If this were not the case, there would be no such thing as a moral person. The person's original moral neutrality later comes to be affected by actions, habits, responses to moral instruction, and so on. Consequently, what a person does or does not do is crucial to the formation of the character. A virtuous character is the result of the performance of virtuous *acts*. . . .

. . . But then the question is: If a person is not born virtuous, how can he or she perform virtuous acts? The answer is through moral instruction, which in traditional Akan society was normally done by means of ethical proverbs and folktales. In this way the growing child and young adult become aware of what is a virtuous or vicious act and become virtuous by performing virtuous acts. . . .

COMMUNALISM AS A SOCIAL THEORY

. . . Communalism, which is a doctrine about social organization and relations, is an offshoot of the Akan concept of humanism. It is perhaps indisputable that social institutions embody a philosophical perspective about human nature and social relationships. One way in which the Akan concept of humanism is made explicit is in its social organization. Ensuring the welfare and interests of each member of society—the essential meaning of Akan humanism—can hardly be accomplished outside the communal system.

Communalism may be defined as the doctrine that the group (that is, the society) constitutes the focus of the activities of the individual members of the society. The doctrine places emphasis on the activity and success of the wider society rather than, though not necessarily at the expense of, or to the detriment of, the individual.

Aristotle proclaimed many centuries ago that man is by nature a social animal, and that it is impossible for him to live outside society. Akan thinkers agree that society is not only a necessary condition for human existence, but it is natural to man. This idea is expressed in an already-quoted proverb:

> When a man descends from heaven, he descends into a human society.
>
> (*onipa firi soro besi a, obesi onipa kurom*)

[The idea of man descending from heaven stems from the belief that man is created by the Supreme Being, Onyame, in heaven (*soro*).]

This proverb rejects the concept of the state of nature, as explicated by those eighteenth-century European philosophers who asserted the existence of an original presocial character of man. In the state of nature, people lived solitary and uncooperative lives, with undesirable consequences that in time led to the formation of society. Akan thought, however, sees humans as originally born into a human society (*onipa kurom*), and therefore as social beings from the outset. In this conception, it would be impossible for people to live in isolation. For not only is the person not born to live a solitary life, but the individual's capacities are not sufficient to meet basic human requirements. For the person, as another proverb has it, is not a palm tree that he or she should be complete or self-sufficient. Consequently, the individual inevitably requires the succor and the relationships of others in order to realize or satisfy basic needs. As another proverb states it:

> The prosperity [or well-being] of man depends upon his fellow man.
>
> (*obi yiye firi obi*)

Human sociality, then, is seen as a consequence of basic human nature, but it is also seen as that which makes for personal well-being and worth. Because community life is natural to man, the kind of society that permits the full realization of human capacities, needs, and aspirations should be communal.

Communalism as conceived in Akan thought is not a negation of individualism; rather, it is the recognition of the limited character of the possibilities of the individual, which limited possibilities whittle away the individual's self-sufficiency. Thus, we have the following proverbs:

> One finger cannot lift up a thing.
>
> If one man scrapes the bark of a tree for medicine, the pieces fall down.
>
> The left arm washes the right arm and the right arm washes the left arm.

The above proverbs, and many more similar to these in content, clearly underscore the rationale behind communalism. They indicate, on the one hand, the failures and frustrations of extreme individualism; that in spite of individual talents and capacities, the individual ought to be aware of his or her insufficiency to achieve his welfare through solitary effort. On the other hand, the proverbs also indicate the value of collective action, mutual aid, and interdependence as necessary conditions not only for an individual's welfare, but also for the successful achievement of even the most difficult undertakings. Communalism insists that the good of all determines the good of each or, put differently, the welfare of each is dependent on the welfare of all. This requires that the individual should work for the good of all, which of course includes his or her own good.

Thus, it is implicit in communalism that the success and meaning of the individual's life depend on identifying oneself with the group. This identification is the basis of the reciprocal relationship between the individual and the group. It is also the ground of the overriding emphasis on the individual's obligation to the members of the group; it enjoins upon him or her the obligation to think and act in terms of the survival of the group as a whole. In fact one's personal sense of responsibility is measured in terms of responsiveness and sensitivity to the needs and demands of the group. Since this sense of responsibility is enjoined equally upon each member of the group—for all the members are expected to enhance the welfare of the group as a whole—communalism maximizes the interests of all the individual members of the society. . . .

But inherent in the communal enterprise is the problem of contribution and distribution. The communal enterprise tends to maximize the common good because each individual is expected to contribute to it, but obviously individuals are not equal in their capacities and talents—a fact explicitly recognized in Akan thought. . . . It follows therefore that individual contributions to the common good will be unequal. Now, the question is: Should inequality in contribution lead to inequality in distribution? Akan social thought, with its social and humanistic thrust, answers this question in the negative. It may be objected that this leads to an unfair treatment of those who have contributed more, to which one may respond that those who have contributed more must have been endowed with greater talents and capacities—natural characteristics and assets for which they were not responsible. This counterargument is perhaps implicit in the proverbs, "The left arm washes the right arm and the right arm washes the left arm" and "The fingers of the hand are not equal in length." Even though the power or effort of one arm may not be as great as that of the other, nevertheless it is able to make *some* contribution. The natural assets of human beings are, as the two proverbs imply, different and should therefore not be made the basis of unequal distribution, even though the second proverb rejects the idea of absolute equality.

The Akan position is defensible for, irrespective of an individual's contribution to the common good, it is fair and reasonable that everyone's *basic* human needs be satisfied by the society: From each according to *whatever contribution* one can make to each according to one's *basic* needs will be the new slogan. . . .

THE TENSIONS OF INDIVIDUALISM

. . . The common good, I take it, is not merely the sum of the various individual goods. The concept implies, I think, that there are certain needs that are *basic* to the enjoyment and fulfillment of the life of each individual. Such needs include shelter, food, health, equality of opportunity, and liberty. Thus conceived, the common good is predicated on a true or essential universal, the good of *all,* that which is essentially good for human beings as such. The common good, therefore, is not conceptually opposed to the individual good of any member of the society. It embraces his or her individual good as it embraces the goods of other members. If the common good is attained, then logically the individual good is also attained. Strictly speaking, there can or should be no conflict between the two, for the individual and the common goods are tied up together and overlap. Therefore, any conflict stems from a misconception either of the common good, of the individual good, or of the relationship between the two.

Thus, the symbol of the crossed crocodiles with two heads and a common stomach has great significance for Akan social thought. While it suggests the rational underpinnings of the concept of communalism, it does not do so to the detriment of individuality. The concept of communalism, as it is understood in Akan thought, therefore does not overlook individual rights, interests, desires, and responsibilities, nor does it imply the absorption of the individual will into the "communal will," or seek to eliminate individual responsibility and accountability. Akan social thought attempts to establish a delicate balance between the concepts of communality and individuality. Whether it succeeds in doing so in practice is of course another question.

The Akan acceptance of individualism is also indicated by their understanding of an important feature of the group. We see it expressed in the proverb,

> The clan (group) is (merely) a *multitude* (crowd).
>
> (*abusua yē dōm*)

This proverb does not say that the group is amorphous or unreal, but that the individual cannot always and invariably depend on the group for everything. The proverb is thus intended to deepen the individual's sense of responsibility for oneself. The proverb suggests that the relevance and importance of the group (clan) are exaggerated even by the Akan people themselves. This gives the lie to the supposition that the individual in a communal social order is a parasite. The individual is supposed to have a dual responsibility: for oneself as an individual as well as to the group. This is not easy to do successfully, and the balance between individuality and communality is a precarious one indeed.

In striking the right balance between individualism and communalism, Akan social thought seeks to promote social arrangements that allow for the adequate expression of the individual's worth and self-fulfillment. If one is by nature a social being, and not merely an atomized entity, then the development of one's full personality and identity can best be achieved only within the framework of social relationships that are realizable within a communal social system. That is to say, the conception and development of an individual's full personality and identity cannot be separated from his or her role in the group. The interaction between the individual and the group is thus conceived in Akan social thought to be basic to the development and enhancement of the individual's personality.

STUDY QUESTIONS

1. In what ways does Akan morality differ from Western utilitarianism?
2. How, in Akan philosophy, is an individual responsible for his or her own character? Why is character important to the Akan?
3. How is one to reconcile his or her individual needs with the conflicting needs of another or of the community itself?

8

On Being a Good Neighbor

Martin Luther King Jr.

Martin Luther King Jr. (1929–68), pastor, civil rights leader, and conscience of his generation, was awarded the Nobel Prize for Peace in 1964. He is the author of *Why We Can't Wait* and *Strength to Love,* from which this selection is taken.

And who is my neighbour?
Luke 10:29

I should like to talk with you about a good man, whose exemplary life will always be a flashing light to plague the dozing conscience of mankind. His goodness was not found in a passive commitment to a particular creed, but in his active participation in a life-saving deed; not in a moral pilgrimage that reached its destination point, but in the love ethic by which he journeyed life's highway. He was good because he was a good neighbor.

The ethical concern of this man is expressed in a magnificent little story, which begins with a theological discussion on the meaning of eternal life and concludes in a concrete expression of compassion on a dangerous road. Jesus is asked a question by a man who had been trained in the details of Jewish law: "Master, what shall I do to inherit eternal life." The retort is prompt: "What is written in the law? how readest thou?" After a moment the lawyer recites articulately: "Thou shalt love the Lord thy God with all thy heart, and with all thy soul, and with all thy strength, and with all thy mind; and thy neighbour as thyself." Then comes the decisive word from Jesus: "Thou hast answered right: this do, and thou shalt live."

The lawyer was chagrined. "Why," the people might ask, "would an expert in law raise a question that even the novice can answer?" Desiring to justify himself and to show that Jesus' reply was far from conclusive, the lawyer asks, "And who is my neighbour?" The lawyer was now taking up the cudgels of debate that might have turned the conversation into an abstract theological discussion. But Jesus, determined not to be caught in the "paralysis of analysis," pulls the question from mid-air and places it on a dangerous curve between Jerusalem and Jericho.

He told the story of "a certain man" who went down from Jerusalem to Jericho and fell among robbers who stripped him, beat him, and, departing, left him half dead. By chance a certain priest appeared, but he passed by on the other side, and later a Levite also passed by. Finally, a certain Samaritan, a half-breed from a people with whom the Jews had no dealings, appeared. When he saw the wounded man, he was moved with compassion, administered first aid, placed him on his beast, "and brought him to an inn, and took care of him."

Who is my neighbor? "I do not know his name," says Jesus in essence. "He is anyone toward whom you are neighborly. He is anyone who lies in need at life's roadside. He is neither Jew nor Gentile; he is neither Russian nor American; he is neither Negro nor white. He is 'a certain man'—

any needy man—on one of the numerous Jericho roads of life." So Jesus defines a neighbor, not in a theological definition, but in a life situation.

What constituted the goodness of the good Samaritan? Why will he always be an inspiring paragon of neighborly virtue? It seems to me that this man's goodness may be described in one word—altruism. The good Samaritan was altruistic to the core. What is altruism? The dictionary defines altruism as "regard for, and devotion to, the interest of others." The Samaritan was good because he made concern for others the first law of his life.

I

The Samaritan had the capacity for a *universal altruism.* He had a piercing insight into that which is beyond the eternal accidents of race, religion, and nationality. One of the great tragedies of man's long trek along the highway of history has been the limiting of neighborly concern to tribe, race, class, or nation. The God of early Old Testament days was a tribal god and the ethic was tribal. "Thou shalt not kill" meant "Thou shalt not kill a fellow Israelite, but for God's sake, kill a Philistine." Greek democracy embraced a certain aristocracy, but not the hordes of Greek slaves whose labors built the city-states. The universalism at the center of the Declaration of Independence has been shamefully negated by America's appalling tendency to substitute "some" for "all." Numerous people in the North and South still believe that the affirmation, "All men are created equal," means "All white men are created equal." Our unswerving devotion to monopolistic capitalism makes us more concerned about the economic security of the captains of industry than for the laboring men whose sweat and skills keep industry functioning.

What are the devastating consequences of this narrow, group-centered attitude? It means that one does not really mind what happens to the people outside his group. If an American is concerned only about his nation, he will not be concerned about the peoples of Asia, Africa, or South America. Is this not why nations engage in the madness of war without the slightest sense of penitence? Is this not why the murder of a citizen of your own nation is a crime, but the murder of the citizens of another nation in war is an act of heroic virtue? If manufacturers are concerned only in their personal interests, they will pass by on the other side while thousands of working people are stripped of their jobs and left displaced on some Jericho road as a result of automation, and they will judge every move toward a better distribution of wealth and a better life for the working man to be socialistic. If a white man is concerned only about his race, he will casually pass by the Negro who has been robbed of his personhood, stripped of his sense of dignity, and left dying on some wayside road.

A few years ago, when an automobile carrying several members of a Negro college basketball team had an accident on a Southern highway, three of the young men were severely injured. An ambulance was immediately called, but on arriving at the place of the accident, the driver, who was white, said without apology that it was not his policy to service Negroes, and he drove away. The driver of a passing automobile graciously drove the boys to the nearest hospital, but the attending physician belligerently said, "We don't take niggers in this hospital." When the boys finally arrived at a "colored" hospital in a town some fifty miles from the scene of the accident, one was dead and the other two died thirty and fifty minutes later respectively. Probably all three could have been saved if they had been given immediate treatment. This is only one of thousands of inhuman incidents that occur daily in the South, an unbelievable expression of the barbaric consequences of any tribal-centered, national-centered, or racial-centered ethic.

The real tragedy of such narrow provincialism is that we see people as entities or merely as things. Too seldom do we see people in their true *humanness.* A spiritual myopia limits our vision to external accidents. We see men as Jews or Gentiles, Catholics or Protestants, Chinese or American, Negroes or whites. We fail to think of them as fellow human beings made from the same basic stuff as we, molded in the same divine image. The priest and the Levite saw only a bleeding body, not a human being like themselves. But the good Samaritan will always remind us to remove the cataracts of provincialism from our spiritual eyes and see men as men. If the Samaritan had considered the wounded man as a Jew first, he would not have stopped, for the Jews and the Samaritans had no dealings. He saw him as a human being first, who was a Jew only by accident. The good neighbor looks beyond the external accidents and discerns those inner qualities that make all men human and, therefore, brothers.

II

The Samaritan possessed the capacity for a *dangerous altruism.* He risked his life to save a brother. When we ask why the priest and the Levite did not stop to help the wounded man, numerous suggestions come to mind. Perhaps they could not delay their arrival at an important ecclesiastical meeting. Perhaps religious regulations demanded that they touch no human body for several hours prior to the performing of their temple functions. Or perhaps they were on their way to an organizational meeting of a Jericho Road Improvement Association. Certainly this would have been a real need, for it is not enough to aid a wounded man on the Jericho Road; it is also important to change the conditions which make robbery possible. Philanthropy is commendable, but it must not cause the philanthropist to overlook the circumstances of economic injustice which make philanthropy necessary. Maybe the priest and the Levite believed that it is better to cure injustice at the causal source than to get bogged down with a single individual effect.

These are probable reasons for their failure to stop, yet there is another possibility, often overlooked, that they were afraid. The Jericho Road was a dangerous road. When Mrs. King and I visited the Holy Land, we rented a car and drove from Jerusalem to Jericho. As we traveled slowly down that meandering, mountainous road, I said to my wife, "I can now understand why Jesus chose this road as the setting for his parable." Jerusalem is some two thousand feet above and Jericho one thousand feet below sea level. The descent is made in less than twenty miles. Many sudden curves provide likely places for ambushing and expose the traveler to unforeseen attacks. Long ago the road was known as the Bloody Pass. So it is possible that the Priest and the Levite were afraid that if they stopped, they too would be beaten. Perhaps the robbers were still nearby. Or maybe the wounded man on the ground was a faker, who wished to draw passing travelers to his side for quick and easy seizure. I imagine that the first question which the priest and the Levite asked was: "If I stop to help this man, what will happen to me?" But by the very nature of his concern, the good Samaritan reversed the question: "If I do not stop to help this man, what will happen to him?" The good Samaritan engaged in a dangerous altruism.

We so often ask, "What will happen to my job, my prestige, or my status if I take a stand on this issue? Will my home be bombed, will my life be threatened, or will I be jailed?" The good man always reverses the question. Albert Schweitzer did not ask, "What will happen to my prestige and security as a university professor and to my status as a Bach organist, if I work with the people of Africa?" but rather he asked, "What will happen to these millions of people who have been wounded by the forces of injustice, if I do not go to them?" Abraham Lincoln did not ask, "What will happen to me if I issue the Emancipation Proclamation and bring an end to chattel slavery?" but he asked, "What will happen to the Union and to millions of

Negro people, if I fail to do it?" The Negro professional does not ask, "What will happen to my secure position, my middle-class status, or my personal safety, if I participate in the movement to end the system of segregation?" but "What will happen to the cause of justice and the masses of Negro people who have never experienced the warmth of economic security, if I do not participate actively and courageously in the movement?"

The ultimate measure of a man is not where he stands in moments of comfort and convenience, but where he stands at times of challenge and controversy. The true neighbor will risk his position, his prestige, and even his life for the welfare of others. In dangerous valleys and hazardous pathways, he will lift some bruised and beaten brother to a higher and more noble life.

III

The Samaritan also possessed *excessive altruism.* With his own hands he bound the wounds of the man and then set him on his own beast. It would have been easier to pay an ambulance to take the unfortunate man to the hospital, rather than risk having his neatly trimmed suit stained with blood.

True altruism is more than the capacity to pity; it is the capacity to sympathize. Pity may represent little more than the impersonal concern which prompts the mailing of a check, but true sympathy is the personal concern which demands the giving of one's soul. Pity may arise from interest in an abstraction called humanity, but sympathy grows out of a concern for a particular needy human being who lies at life's roadside. Sympathy is fellow feeling for the person in need—his pain, agony, and burdens. Our missionary efforts fail when they are based on pity, rather than true compassion. Instead of seeking to do something *with* the African and Asian peoples, we have too often sought only to do something *for* them. An expression of pity, devoid of genuine sympathy, leads to a new form of paternalism which no self-respecting person can accept. Dollars possess the potential for helping wounded children of God on life's Jericho Road, but unless those dollars are distributed by compassionate fingers they will enrich neither the giver nor the receiver. Millions of missionary dollars have gone to Africa from the hands of church people who would die a million deaths before they would permit a single African the privilege of worshiping in their congregation. Millions of Peace Corps dollars are being invested in Africa because of the votes of some men who fight unrelentingly to prevent African ambassadors from holding membership in their diplomatic clubs or establish residency in their particular neighborhoods. The Peace Corps will fail if it seeks to do something *for* the underprivileged peoples of the world; it will succeed if it seeks creatively to do something *with* them. It will fail as a negative gesture to defeat Communism; it will succeed only as a positive effort to wipe poverty, ignorance, and disease from the earth. Money devoid of love is like salt devoid of savor, good for nothing except to be trodden under the foot of men. True neighborliness requires personal concern. The Samaritan used his hands to bind up the wounds of the robbed man's body, and he also released an overflowing love to bind up the wounds of his broken spirit.

Another expression of the excessive altruism on the part of the Samaritan was his willingness to go far beyond the call of duty. After tending to the man's wounds, he put him on his beast, carried him to an inn, and left money for his care, making clear that if further financial needs arose he would gladly meet them. "Whatsoever thou spendest more, when I come again, I will repay thee." Stopping short of this, he would have more than fulfilled any possible rule concerning one's duty to a wounded stranger. He went beyond the second mile. His love was complete.

Dr. Harry Emerson Fosdick has made an impressive distinction between enforceable and unenforceable obligations. The former are regulated by the codes of society and the vigorous implementation of law-enforcement agencies. Breaking these obligations, spelled out on thousands of pages in law books, has filled numerous prisons. But unenforceable obligations are beyond the reach of the laws of society. They concern inner attitudes, genuine person-to-person relations, and expressions of compassion which law books cannot regulate and jails cannot rectify. Such obligations are met by one's commitment to an inner law, written on the heart. Man-made laws assure justice, but a higher law produces love. No code of conduct ever persuaded a father to love his children or a husband to show affection to his wife. The law court may force him to provide bread for the family, but it cannot make him provide the bread of love. A good father is obedient to the unenforceable. The good Samaritan represents the conscience of mankind because he also was obedient to that which could not be enforced. No law in the world could have produced such unalloyed compassion, such genuine love, such thorough altruism.

In our nation today a mighty struggle is taking place. It is a struggle to conquer the reign of an evil monster called segregation and its inseparable twin called discrimination—a monster that has wandered through this land for well-nigh one hundred years, stripping millions of Negro people of their sense of dignity and robbing them of their birthright of freedom.

Let us never succumb to the temptation of believing that legislation and judicial decrees play only minor roles in solving this problem. Morality cannot be legislated, but behavior can be regulated. Judicial decrees may not change the heart, but they can restrain the heartless. The law cannot make an employer love an employee, but it can prevent him from refusing to hire me because of the color of my skin. The habits, if not the hearts, of people have been and are being altered every day by legislative acts, judicial decisions, and executive orders. Let us not be misled by those who argue that segregation cannot be ended by the force of law.

But acknowledging this, we must admit that the ultimate solution to the race problem lies in the willingness of men to obey the unenforceable. Court orders and federal enforcement agencies are of inestimable value in achieving desegregation, but desegregation is only a partial, though necessary, step toward the final goal which we seek to realize, genuine intergroup and interpersonal living. Desegregation will break down the legal barriers and bring men together physically, but something must touch the hearts and souls of men so that they will come together spiritually because it is natural and right. A vigorous enforcement of civil rights laws will bring an end to segregated public facilities which are barriers to a truly desegregated society, but it cannot bring an end to fears, prejudice, pride, and irrationality, which are the barriers to a truly integrated society. These dark and demonic responses will be removed only as men are possessed by the invisible, inner law which etches on their hearts the conviction that all men are brothers and that love is mankind's most potent weapon for personal and social transformation. True integration will be achieved by true neighbors who are willingly obedient to unenforceable obligations.

More than ever before, my friends, men of all races and nations are today challenged to be neighborly. The call for a worldwide good-neighbor policy is more than an ephemeral shibboleth; it is the call to a way of life which will transform our imminent cosmic elegy into a psalm of creative fulfillment. No longer can we afford the luxury of passing by on the other side. Such folly was once called moral failure; today it will lead to universal suicide. We cannot long survive spiritually separated in a world that is geographically together. In the final analysis, I must not ignore the wounded man on life's Jericho Road, because he is a part of me and I am a part of him. His agony diminishes me, and his salvation enlarges me.

In our quest to make neighborly love a reality, we have, in addition to the inspiring example of the good Samaritan, the magnanimous life of our

Christ to guide us. His altruism was universal, for he thought of all men, even publicans and sinners, as brothers. His altruism was dangerous, for he willingly traveled hazardous roads in a cause he knew was right. His altruism was excessive, for he chose to die on Calvary, history's most magnificent expression of obedience to the unenforceable.

STUDY QUESTIONS

1. Is the altruism that King describes possible in today's world?
2. What is the difference between pity and compassion, according to King? In what way is this difference important? What makes compassion indispensible in King's theory of altruism?
3. How does altruism, in order to work, need to be excessive and dangerous?
4. King asserts that rules or laws, although helping to alleviate the visible effects, cannot solve the problem at heart. What does he mean, exactly? What is the solution to this problem?
5. Why do you think King chose the parable of the good Samaritan to make his case for altruism?

9

Breaking Bread

bell hooks and *Cornel West*

---

bell hooks is the pen name of Gloria Watkins. She teaches at Oberlin College and is the author of *Yearning: Race, Gender, and Cultural Politics* and *Sisters of the Yam: Black Women and Self-Recovery.*

Cornel West is a professor of religion and the director of Afro-American Studies at Princeton University. He is the author of *The American Evasion of Philosophy* and *Race Matters.*

---

b.h.

I requested that Charles sing "Precious Lord" because the conditions that led Thomas Dorsey to write this song always make me think about gender issues, issues of black masculinity. Mr. Dorsey wrote this song after his wife died in childbirth. That experience caused him to have a crisis of faith. He did not think he would be able to go on living without her. That sense of unbearable crisis truly expresses the contemporary dilemma of faith. Mr. Dorsey talked about the way he tried to cope with this "crisis of faith." He prayed and prayed for a healing and received the words to this song. This song has helped so many folk when they are feeling low, feeling as if they can't go on. It was my grandmother's favorite song. I remembered how we sang it at her funeral. She died when she was almost ninety. And I am moved now as I was then by the knowledge that we can take our pain, work with it, recycle it, and transform it so that it becomes a source of power.

Let me introduce to you my "brother," my comrade Cornel West.

C.W.

First I need to just acknowledge the fact that we as black people have come together to reflect on our past, present, and objective future. That, in and of itself, is a sign of hope. I'd like to thank the Yale African-American Cultural Center for bringing us together. bell and I thought it would be best to present in dialogical form a series of reflections on the crisis of black males and females. There is a state of siege raging now in black communities across this nation linked not only to drug addiction but also consolidation of corporate power as we know it, and redistribution of wealth from the bottom to the top, coupled with the ways with which a culture and society centered on the market, preoccupied with consumption, erode structures of feeling, community, tradition. Reclaiming our heritage and sense of history are prerequisites to any serious talk about black freedom and black liberation in the twenty-first century. We want to try to create that kind of community here today, a community that we hope will be a place to promote understanding. Critical understanding is a prerequisite for any serious talk about coming together, sharing, participating, creating bonds of solidarity so that black people and other progressive people can continue to hold up the blood-stained banners that were raised when that song was sung in the civil rights movement. It was one of Dr. Martin Luther King's favorite songs, reaffirming his own struggle and that of many others who have tried to link some sense of faith, religious faith, political faith, to the struggle for freedom. We thought it would be best to have a dialogue to put forth analysis and provide a sense of what form a praxis would take. That praxis will be necessary for us to talk seriously about black power, black liberation in the twenty-first century.

b.h.

Let us say a little bit about ourselves. Both Cornel and I come to you as individuals who believe in God. That belief informs our message.

C.W.

One of the reasons we believe in God is due to the long tradition of religious faith in the black community. I think, that as a people who have had to deal with the absurdity of being black in America, for many of us it is a question of God and sanity, or God and suicide. And if you are serious about black struggle you know that in many instances you will be stepping out on nothing, hoping to land on something. That is the history of black folks in the past and present, and it continually concerns those of us who are willing to speak out with boldness and a sense of the importance of history and struggle. You speak knowing that you won't be able to do that for too long because America is such a violent culture. Given those conditions you have to ask yourself what links to a tradition will sustain you given the absurdity and insanity we are bombarded with daily. And so the belief in God itself is not to be understood in a noncontextual manner. It is understood in relation to a particular context, to specific circumstances.

b.h.

We also come to you as two progressive black people on the left.

C.W.

Very much so.

b.h.

I will read a few paragraphs to provide a critical framework for our discussion of black power, just in case some of you may not know what black power means. We are gathered to speak with one another about black power in the twenty-first century. In James Boggs's essay, "Black Power: A Scientific Concept Whose Time Has Come," first published in 1968, he called attention to the radical political significance of the black power movement, asserting: "Today the concept of black power expresses the revolutionary social force which must not only struggle against the capitalist but against the workers and all who benefit by and support the system which has oppressed us." We speak of black power in this very different context to remember, reclaim, revision, and renew. We remember first that the historical struggle for black liberation was forged by black women and men who were concerned about the collective welfare of black people. Renewing our commitment to this collective struggle should provide a grounding for new direction in contemporary political practice. We speak today of political partnership between black men and women. The late James Baldwin wrote in his autobiographical preface to *Notes of a Native Son:* "I think that the past is all that makes the present coherent and further that the past will remain horrible for as long as we refuse to accept it honestly." Accepting the challenge for this prophetic statement as we look at our contemporary past as black people, the space between the sixties and the nineties, we see a weakening of political solidarity between black men and women. It is crucial for the future black liberation struggle that we remain ever mindful that ours is a shared struggle, that we are each other's faith.

C.W.

I think we can even begin by talking about the kind of existentialist chaos that exists in our own lives and our inability to overcome the sense of alienation and frustration we experience when we try to create bonds of intimacy and solidarity with one another. Now part of this frustration is to be understood again in relation to structures and institutions. In the way in which our culture of consumption has promoted an addiction to stimulation—one that puts a premium on bottled commodified stimulation. The market does this in order to convince us that our consumption keeps oiling the economy in order for it to reproduce itself. But the effect of this addiction to stimulation is an undermining, a waning of our ability for qualitatively rich relationships. It's no accident that crack is the postmodern drug, that it is the highest form of addiction known to humankind, that it provides a feeling ten times more pleasurable than orgasm.

b.h.

Addiction is not about relatedness, about relationships. So it comes as no surprise that as addiction becomes more pervasive in black life it undermines our capacity to experience community. Just recently, I was telling someone that I would like to buy a little house next door to my parent's house. This house used to be Mr. Johnson's house but he recently passed away. And they could not understand why I would want to live near my parents. My explanation that my parents were aging did not satisfy. Their inability to understand or appreciate the value of sharing family life intergenerationally was a sign to me of the crisis facing our communities. It's as though as black people we have lost our understanding of the importance of mutual interdependency, of communal living. That we no longer recognize as valuable the notion that we collectively shape the terms of our survival is a sign of crisis.

C.W.

And when there is crisis in those communities and institutions that have played a fundamental role in transmitting to younger generations our values and sensibility, our ways of life and our ways of struggle, we find ourselves distanced, not simply from our predecessors but from the critical project of black liberation. And so more and more we seem to have young black people who are very difficult to understand, because it seems as though they live in two very different worlds. We don't really understand their music. Black adults may not be listening to NWA (Niggers With Attitude) straight out of Compton, California. They may not understand why they are doing what Stetsasonic is doing, what Public Enemy is all about, because young people have been fundamentally shaped by the brutal side of American society. Their sense of reality is shaped on the one hand by a sense of coldness and callousness, and on the other hand by a sense of passion for justice, contradictory impulses which surface simultaneously. Mothers may find it difficult to understand their children. Grandparents may find it difficult to understand us—and it's this slow breakage that has to be restored.

b.h.

That sense of breakage, or rupture, is often tragically expressed in gender relations. When I told folks that Cornel West and I were talking about partnership between black women and men, they thought I meant romantic relationships. I replied that it was important for us to examine the multi-relationships between black women and men, how we deal with fathers, with brothers, with sons. We are talking about all our relationships across gender because it is not just the heterosexual love relationships between black women and men that are in trouble. Many of us can't communicate with parents, siblings, etc. I've talked with many of you and asked, "What is it you feel should be addressed?" And many of you responded that you wanted to talk about black men and how they need to "get it together."

Let's talk about why we see the struggle to assert agency—that is, the ability to act in one's best interest—as a male thing. I mean, black men are not the only ones among us who need to "get it together." And if black men collectively refuse to educate themselves for critical consciousness, to acquire the means to be self-determined, should our communities suffer, or should we not recognize that both black women and men must struggle for self-actualization, must learn to "get it together"? Since the culture we live in continues to equate blackness with maleness, black awareness of the extent to which our survival depends on mutual partnership between women and men is undermined. In renewed black liberation struggle, we recognize the position of black men and women, the tremendous role black women played in every freedom struggle.

Certainly Septima Clark's book *Ready from Within* is necessary reading for those of us who want to understand the historical development of sexual politics in black liberation struggle. Clark describes her father's insistence that she not fully engage herself in civil rights struggle because of her gender. Later, she found the source of her defiance in religion. It was the belief in spiritual community, that no difference must be made between the role of women and that of men, that enabled her to be "ready within." To Septima Clark, the call to participate in black liberation struggle was a call from God. Remembering and recovering the stories of how black women learned to assert historical agency in the struggle for self-determination in the context of community and collectivity is important for those of us who struggle to promote black liberation, a movement that has at its core a commitment to free our communities of sexist domination, exploitation, and oppression. We need to develop a political terminology that will enable black folks to talk deeply about what we mean when we urge black women and men to "get it together."

C.W.

I think again that we have to keep in mind the larger context of American society, which has historically expressed contempt for black men and black women. The very notion that black people are human beings is a new notion in western civilization and is still not widely accepted in practice. And one of the consequences of this pernicious idea is that it is very difficult for black men and women to remain attuned to each other's humanity, so when bell talks about black women's agency and some of the problems black men have when asked to acknowledge black women's humanity, it must be remembered that this refusal to acknowledge one another's humanity is a reflection of the way we are seen and treated in the larger society. And its certainly not true that white folks have a monopoly on human relationships. When we talk about a crisis in western civilization, black people are a part of that civilization even though we have been beneath it, our backs serving as a foundation for the building of that civilization, and we have to understand how it affects us so that we may remain attuned to each other's humanity, so that the partnership that bell talks about can take on real substance and content. I think partnerships between black men and black women can be made when we learn how to be supportive and think in terms of critical affirmation.

b.h.

Certainly black people have not talked enough about the importance of constructing patterns of interaction that strengthen our capacity to be affirming.

C.W.

We need to affirm one another, support one another, help, enable, equip, and empower one another to deal with the present crisis, but it can't be uncritical, because if it's uncritical then we are again refusing to acknowledge other people's humanity. If we are serious about acknowledging and affirming other people's humanity then we are committed to trusting and believing that they are forever in process. Growth, development, maturation happens in stages. People grow, develop, and mature along the lines in which they are taught. Disenabling critique and contemptuous feedback hinders.

b.h.

We need to examine the function of critique in traditional black communities. Often it does not serve as a constructive force. Like we have that popular slang word "dissin'" and we know that "dissin'" refers to a kind of disenabling contempt—when we "read" each other in ways that are so painful, so cruel, that the person can't get up from where you have knocked them down. Other destructive forces in our lives are envy and jealousy. These undermine our efforts to work for a collective good. Let me give a minor example. When I came in this morning I saw Cornel's latest book on the table. I immediately wondered why my book was not there and caught myself worrying about whether he was receiving some gesture of respect or recognition denied me. When he heard me say "where's my book?" he pointed to another table.

Often when people are suffering a legacy of deprivation, there is a sense that there are never any goodies to go around, so that we must viciously compete with one another. Again this spirit of competition creates conflict and divisiveness. In a larger social context, competition between black women and men has surfaced around the issue of whether black female writers are receiving more attention than black male writers. Rarely does anyone point to the reality that only a small minority of black women writers are receiving public accolades. Yet the myth that black women who succeed are taking something away from black men continues to permeate black psyches and inform how we as black women and men respond to one another. Since capitalism is rooted in unequal distribution of resources, it is not surprising that we as black women and men find ourselves in situations of competition and conflict.

C.W.

I think part of the problem is deep down in our psyche we recognize that we live in such a conservative society, a society of business elites, a society in which corporate power influences are assuring that a certain group of people do get up higher.

b.h.

Right, including some of you in this room.

C.W.

And this is true not only between male and female relations but also black and brown relations and black and Korean, and black and Asian relations. We are struggling over crumbs because we know that the bigger part of lower corporate America is already received. One half of one percent of America owns twenty-two percent of the wealth, one percent owns thirty-two percent, and the bottom forty-five percent of the population has twenty percent of the wealth. So, you end up with this kind of crabs-in-the-barrel mentality. When you see someone moving up you immediately think they'll get a bigger cut in big-loaf corporate America and you think that's something real because we're still shaped by the corporate ideology of the larger context.

b.h.

Here at Yale many of us are getting a slice of that mini-loaf and yet are despairing. It was discouraging when I came here to teach and found in many black people a quality of despair which is not unlike what we know is felt in "crack neighborhoods." I wanted to understand the connection between underclass black despair and that of black people here who have immediate and/or potential access to so much material privilege. This despair mirrors the spiritual crisis that is happening in our culture as a whole. Nihilism is everywhere. Some of this despair is rooted in a deep sense of loss. Many black folks who have made it or are making it undergo an identity crisis. This is especially true for individual black people working to assimilate into the "mainstream." Suddenly, they may feel panicked, alarmed by the knowledge that they do not understand their history, that life is without purpose and meaning. These feelings of alienation and estrangement create suffering. The suffering many black people experience today is linked to the suffering of the past, to "historical memory." Attempts by black people to understand that suffering, to come to terms with it, are the conditions which enable a work like Toni Morrison's *Beloved* to receive so much attention. To look back, not just to describe slavery but to try and reconstruct a psycho-social history of its impact has only recently been fully understood as a necessary stage in the process of collective black self-recovery.

C.W.

The spiritual crisis that has happened, especially among the well-to-do blacks, has taken the form of the quest for therapeutic release. So that you can get very thin, flat, and uni-dimensional forms of spirituality that are simply an attempt to sustain the well-to-do black folks as they engage in their consumerism and privatism. The kind of spirituality we're talking about is not the kind that remains superficial just physically but serves as an opium to help you justify and rationalize your own cynicism vis-à-vis the disadvantaged folk in our community. We could talk about churches and their present role in the crisis of America, religious faith as the American way of life, the gospel of health and wealth, helping the bruised psyches of the black middle class make it through America. That's not the form of spirituality that we're talking about. We're talking about something deeper—you used to call it conversion—so that notions of service and risk and sacrifice once again become fundamental. It's very important, for example, that those of you who remember the days in which black colleges were hegemonic among the black elite remember them critically but also acknowledge that there was something positive going on there. What was going on was that you were told every Sunday, with the important business of chapel, that you had to give service to the race. Now it may have been a petty bourgeois form, but it created a moment of accountability, and with the erosion of the service ethic the very possibility of putting the needs of others alongside of one's own diminishes. In this syndrome, me-ness, selfishness, and egocentricity become more and more prominent, creating a spiritual crisis where you need more psychic opium to get you over.

b.h.

We have experienced such a change in that communal ethic of service that was so necessary for survival in traditional black communities. That ethic of service has been altered by shifting class relations. And even those black folks who have little or no class mobility may buy into a bourgeois class sensibility; TV shows like *Dallas* and *Dynasty* teach ruling class ways of thinking and being to underclass poor people. A certain kind of bourgeois individualism of the mind prevails. It does not correspond to actual class reality or circumstances of deprivation. We need to remember the many economic structures and class politics that have led to a shift of priorities for "privileged" blacks. Many privileged black folks obsessed with living out a bourgeois dream of liberal individualistic success no longer feel as though they have any accountability in relation to the black poor and underclass.

C.W.

We're not talking about the narrow sense of guilt privileged black people can feel, because guilt usually paralyzes action. What we're talking about is how one uses one's time and energy. We're talking about the ways in which the black middle class, which is relatively privileged vis-à-vis the black working class, working poor, and underclass, needs to acknowledge that along with that privilege goes responsibility. Somewhere I read that for those to whom much is given, much is required. And the question becomes, "How do we exercise that responsibility given our privilege?" I don't think it's a credible notion to believe the black middle class will give up on its material toys. No, the black middle class will act like any other middle class in the human condition; it will attempt to maintain its privilege. There is something seductive about comfort and convenience. The black middle class will not return to the ghetto, especially given the territorial struggles going on with gangs and so forth. Yet, how can we use what power we do have to be sure more resources are available to those who are disadvantaged? So the question becomes "How do we use our responsibility and privilege?" Because, after all, black privilege is a result of black struggle.

I think the point to make here is that there is a new day in black America. It is the best of times and the worst of times in black America. Political consciousness is escalating in black America, among black students, among black workers, organized black workers and trade unions, increasingly we are seeing black leaders with vision. The black church is on the move, black popular music, political themes and motifs are on the move. So don't think in our critique we somehow ask you to succumb to a paralyzing pessimism. There are grounds for hope and when that corner is turned, and we don't know what particular catalytic event will serve as the take-off for it (just like we didn't know December 1955 would be the take-off), but when it occurs we have got to be ready. The privileged black folks can play a rather crucial role if we have a service ethic, if we want to get on board, if we want to be part of the progressive, prophetic bandwagon. And that is the question we will have to ask ourselves and each other.

b.h.

We also need to remember that there is a joy in struggle. Recently, I was speaking on a panel at a conference with another black woman from a privileged background. She mocked the notion of struggle. When she expressed, "I'm just tired of hearing about the importance of struggle; it doesn't interest me," the audience clapped. She saw struggle solely in negative terms, a perspective which led me to question whether she had ever taken part in any organized resistance movement. For if you have, you know that there is joy in struggle. Those of us who are old enough to remember segregated schools, the kind of political effort and sacrifice folks were making to ensure we would have full access to educational opportunities, surely remember the sense of fulfillment when goals that we struggled for were achieved. When we sang together "We shall overcome" there was a sense of victory, a sense of power that comes when we strive to be self-determining. When Malcolm X spoke about his journey to Mecca, the awareness he achieved, he gives expression to that joy that comes from struggling to grow. When Martin Luther King talked about having been to the mountain top, he was sharing with us that he arrived at a peak of critical awareness, and it gave him great joy. In our liberatory pedagogy we must teach young black folks to understand that struggle is process, that one moves from circumstances of difficulty and pain to awareness, joy, fulfillment. That the struggle to be critically conscious can be that movement which takes you to another level, that lifts you up, that makes you feel better. You feel good, you feel your life has meaning and purpose.

C.W.

A rich life is fundamentally a life of serving others, a life of trying to leave the world a little better than you found it. That rich life comes into being in human relationships. This is true at the personal level. Those of you who have been in love know what I am talking about. It is also true at the organizational and communal level. It's difficult to find joy by yourself even if you have all the right toys.

It's difficult. Just ask somebody who has got a lot of material possessions but doesn't have anybody to share them with. Now that's at the personal level. There is a political version of this. It has to do with what you see when you get up in the morning and look in the mirror and ask yourself whether you are simply wasting time on the planet or spending time in an enriching manner. We are talking fundamentally about the meaning of life and the place of struggle. bell talks about the significance of struggle and service. For those of us who are Christians there are certain theological foundations on which our commitment to serve is based. Christian life is understood to be a life of service. Even so, Christians have no monopoly on the joys that come from service and those of you who are part of secular culture can also enjoy this sense of enrichment. Islamic brothers and sisters share in a religious practice which also places emphasis on the importance of service. When we speak of commitment to a life of service we must also talk about the fact that such a commitment goes against the grain, especially the foundations of our society. To talk this way about service and struggle we must also talk about strategies that will enable us to sustain this sensibility, this commitment.

b.h.

When we talk about that which will sustain and nurture our spiritual growth as a people, we must once again talk about the importance of community. For one of the most vital ways we sustain ourselves is by building communities of resistance, places where we know we are not alone. In *Prophetic Fragments,* Cornel began his essay on Martin Luther King by quoting the lines of the spiritual, "He promised never to leave me, never to leave me alone." In black spiritual tradition the promise that we will not be alone cannot be heard as an affirmation of passivity. It does not mean we can sit around and wait for God to take care of business. We are not alone when we build community together. Certainly there is a great feeling of community in this room today. And yet when I was here at Yale I felt that my labor was not appreciated. It was not clear that my work was having meaningful impact. Yet I feel that impact today. When I walked into the room a black woman sister let me know how much my teaching and writing had helped her. There's more of the critical affirmation Cornel spoke of. That critical affirmation says, "Sister, what you're doing is uplifting me in some way." Often folks think that those folks who are spreading the message are so "together" that we do not need affirmation, critical dialogue about the impact of all that we teach and write about and how we live in the world.

C.W.

It is important to note the degree to which black people in particular, and progressive people in general, are alienated and estranged from communities that would sustain and support us. We are often homeless. Our struggles against a sense of nothingness and attempts to reduce us to nothing are ongoing. We confront regularly the question "Where can I find a sense of home?" That sense of home can only be found in our construction of those communities of resistance bell talks about and the solidarity we can experience within them. Renewal comes through participating in community. That is the reason so many folks continue to go to church. In religious experience they find a sense of renewal, a sense of home. In community one can feel that we are moving forward, that struggle can be sustained. As we go forward as black progressives, we must remember that community is not about homogeneity. Homogeneity is dogmatic imposition, pushing your way of life, your way of doing things onto somebody else. . . . [The] sense of home that we are talking about and searching for is a place where we can find compassion, recognition of difference, of the importance of diversity, of our individual uniqueness.

b.h.

When we evoke a sense of home as a place where we can renew ourselves, where we can know love and the sweet communion of shared spirit, I think it's important for us to remember that this location of well-being cannot exist in a context of sexist domination, in a setting where children are the objects of parental domination and abuse. On a fundamental level, when we talk about home, we must speak about the need to transform the African-American home, so that there, in that domestic space, we can experience the renewal of political commitment to the black liberation struggle. So that there in that domestic space we learn to serve and honor one another. If we look again at the civil rights, at the black power movement, folks organized so much in homes. They were the places where folks got together to educate themselves for critical consciousness. That sense of community, cultivated and developed in the home, extended outward into a larger more public context. As we talk about black power in the twenty-first century, about political partnership between black women and men, we must talk about transforming our notions of how and why we bond. In *Beloved,* Toni Morrison offers a paradigm for relationships between black men and women. Sixo describes his love for Thirty-Mile Woman, declaring, "She is a friend of mind. She gather me, man. The pieces I am, she gather them and give them back to me in all the right order. It's good, you know, when you got a woman who is a friend of your mind." In this passage Morrison evokes a notion of bonding that may be rooted in passion, desire, even romantic love, but the point of connection between black women and men is that space of recognition and understanding, where we know one another so well, our histories, that we can take the bits and pieces, the fragments of who we are, and put them back together, re-member them. It is this joy of intellectual bonding, or working together to create liberatory theory and analysis that black women and men can give one another, that Cornel and I give to each other. We are friends of one another's mind. We find a home with one another. It is that joy in community we celebrate and share with you this morning.

STUDY QUESTIONS

1. According to hooks and West, what is the crisis between black males and females, and how is the consolidation of corporate power related to it?
2. What role does Christian faith play in this selection? Specifically, what is the connection between religious faith in the black community and black power?
3. How, according to hooks and West, was the idea of service within the black community lost? How is the service ethic corroded by shifting class relations?
4. What are some of the specific factors that prevent black women and black men from establishing constructive partnerships? What can be done about these factors?

10

Gender in the Context of Community

David Kirp et al.

David Kirp and others are coeditors of the book *Gender Justice,* from which this selection is taken.

That both self-interest and *something else are satisfied by group life is the notion that is hardest for the hard-boiled—and half-baked—person to see.*

C. G. Homans, *The Human Group* (1950)

Individualism, if it can be purged of its defects and abuses, is the best safeguard of personal liberty in the sense that, compared with any other system, it greatly widens the field for the exercise of personal choice. It is also the best safeguard of the variety of life, which emerges precisely from this extended field of personal choice, and the loss of which is the greatest of all the losses of the homogeneous or totalitarian state. For this variety preserves the traditions which embody the most secure and successful choices of former generations; it colors the present with the diversification of its fancy. . . .

John Maynard Keynes, *The General Theory* (1936)

I

Our critique of the leftist feminists and naturalists centers on their shared assumption that individuals' lives are shaped by outside forces; we object to a view of human nature that rejects the proposition, key to liberalism, that women and men can shape their own lives. On the other side, critiques of liberalism often assail that approach for treating individuals as anomic and free-floating, with no connections to others. While we believe that individuals can and do make choices, neither do we deny that they are profoundly affected by the communities in which they live. Whether this realization should modify our conception of gender justice as grounded in individual choice is the question addressed in this chapter. Communities—clusterings bound by blood, propinquity, workplace, national identity, and interest—are viewed by some as meanly parochial and celebrated by others as the repository of civic virtue.[1] In either case, do they render choice illusory? Is there a form of community in which gender justice could flourish?

An ethic of individuality, taken to its logical extreme, looks alienating and frightening, as in Michael Walzer's bleak depiction of "individualism with a vengeance . . . a human being, thoroughly divorced, freed of parents, spouse, and children, watching pornographic performances in some dark theater, joining (it may be his only membership) this or that odd cult, which he will probably leave in a month or two for another still odder."[2] If individualism sustained only this sort of life, there would be little reason to advance it as the basis of a public philosophy. But upholding individualism does not necessarily undermine the value of at least some forms of community.[3]

The fact of community cannot be denied, for it is as potent as the families we are born into, the neighborhoods where we live, the countries to which we owe allegiance. No philosophical construct labelled "the human being" or "the individual" can undo the reality that we are in good measure what our relationships make us, that we are really, and not just incidentally, Chicagoans or Catholics or Chinese, husbands or sisters or uncles. Whether or not we choose to endow these facts with public significance, they remain facts. And even in an era that celebrates individualism, we still pity the orphan, extend charity to the homeless, work to find solutions for the problems of refugees. People do not participate in the drama of life as characters in some morality play, as Citizen or Consumer. They come with names, experiences, connections.[4]

If the reality of community in its many forms endures, the appearance of community has changed. When social and physical mobility were limited, people were joined in their quest for the necessities of life, coming together in the village, the church, and the guild. Now, however, with telephones and air travel sustaining connections across long distances and the possibilities of exiting from a class or social group having become more real, groups are more likely to be voluntarily embraced, not fixed at birth. This new form of community is harder to define than the traditional kind, of course, and some would deny that this is community at all. Still, at least one study of the contemporary experience of community finds that the new form is at least as vital as the old:

> The lowering of social and spacial barriers and the consequent increase in the freedom to choose social relationships have not led to less communal social ties. And it may just have led to the opposite. The disintegration of the monolithic community has perhaps led to the proliferation of many personal communities, each more compatible and more supportive to the individual than ascribed corporate groups.[5]

Although the rise of individualism undermines the traditional community, this may license individuals to embrace new types of association, new communities; these new ties may be more compelling because they are chosen. Drawing on his studies of both primitive and modern communities, anthropologist Oscar Lewis reports that "there are deeper, more mature human relations among cosmopolitan individuals who have chosen each other in friendship than are possible among . . . peasants who are thrown together because of kinship or residential proximity."[6] A network of associations, each affecting particular aspects of our lives, has largely supplemented the all-encompassing traditional communities.

To talk of freely chosen communities presumes that people *can* choose, that they are not so molded by the worlds into which they are born that choice is chimerical. Yet this assumption is open to challenge by those who advance the sociological equivalent of the determinist position. . . . Evidence of the all-powerful nature of communities, on the one hand, and of the snail's pace of social evolution, on the other, is marshalled to support the claim that individuals are not agents of their own destiny but merely the summing of their social influences. Concerning gender, the contention is that men and women are programmed to assume roles in precast forms of family and community.[7]

The critics have a case. It is hard to relate the concept of autonomy to the plight of poorly educated migrant workers who can hardly see beyond the next meal, for their realistic choices are pitifully few. It is similarly difficult to know what to make of the options actually open to children growing up in an Amish village, where heterodoxy is vigorously suppressed. These hard cases pose the most severe challenges to a conception of justice that is at once liberty-centered and hospitable to the claims of community.[8] The challenge of the sociological determinists, however, is not confined to the hard cases. They perceive all of us in the way we view Amish youngsters, as subjects and not agents. To believe otherwise, they contend, is to fall into the trap of false consciousness, in which the belief in our own volition is treated as a delusion fostered by the dominant social order.[9]

It would be foolish to deny that our life choices

are influenced by our upbringing or that our relationships shape our personalities. If persons are taught the values of Mormons or Jews, Democrats or Marxists, materialists or environmentalists, this will affect their future choices. Nor is that necessarily bad. The individual nurtured in a vacuum, free from the taint of social influence, is hardly the ideal. The influence of others—nurturers, guardians, role models, peers—is inevitable, because the young necessarily depend on others for their very survival. Usually it is also a benign inevitability, since without a clear starting point, a sense of who we are, it would be hard to know what we aspire to. The prospect of infinite choice unaccompanied by a compass that enables us to set a course invites only infinite confusion, not personal clarity; the metaphor of the tabula rasa ill fits human beings constructing their own identities out of materials partly given in advance.[10]

There is no Archimedean point from which an outsider can determine whether, for a given individual, a mode of community is stultifying and inescapable or supportive and freely chosen. Only the person involved can know whether his or her life decision represents mere acquiescence or thoughtful consideration. Some people may never evaluate the ways of life they grow up with; others have thought long and hard about their futures, and have consciously chosen a particular form of association.

The idea that people who live their lives in conventional communities are oppressed presumes that if people are given the chance to choose, they will necessarily do something different. Volition does not guarantee change, however; even the most self-conscious exercise of choice will not always bring on the revolution. Legal scholars John Coons and Stephen Sugarman make this point in another context:

> A large measure of institutional continuity is what one could expect; the race is not programmed for anarchy. Nevertheless freedom to select one's own way could have profound psychological significance, even if only the few employ it to alter their external experience in substantial respects. To choose what has previously been compelled is choosing nonetheless. Perhaps the difference is only a matter of human dignity and our view of one another. To us that seems enough.[11]

Psychological differences between men and women may contribute to the persistence of traditional community forms, even in an age in which choice is possible. Psychologist Carol Gilligan finds that women typically view moral dilemmas in terms of care and responsibility in relationships, rather than in the terms of rights and rules favored by men; women prefer an ethic of care to the formal logic of fairness.[12] If women are instinctively more committed to relationships than rules, they may continue to focus much of their energy on the personal and private realms, leaving the public sphere largely to men.

The plausibility of this extension of Gilligan's argument depends on the source of the psychological differences that the data reveal. Gilligan may just be reporting the impact of traditional socialization, which is itself subject to change. Or the differences may run deeper—we cannot know on the basis of the evidence at hand. In any event, Gilligan is not proferring a fixed rule. At most, she has identified a sexually linked tendency that limits the capacity of the social engineers to order our lives.

For both men and women, the fetters of community are weakening. In this society, what is held up as desirable is seldom imposed absolutely; few people are bound for the kitchen or the plow. Moreover, in a world of instantaneous communication and information overflow, ways of life unacceptable to the group cannot be hidden from view: radios are not unknown even among the Amish. Communities may bend the twig, but they seldom set identities in stone.

II

The leftist feminists read the evidence quite differently, identifying existing communities with oppression, seeing in political and economic structures a design to subordinate women by maintaining their peripheral status. For them, as the last chapter [in the original work] elaborates, a woman's identity as a woman precedes and necessarily forms part of her identity; thus she cannot have *chosen* her role. Since existing communities do not allow choice—and, by the feminist definition cannot, lest they destroy themselves—the only solution is to throw off the present and move to a wholly new future.

The one community that radical feminism can celebrate is a solidarity of sisterhood. In its extreme forms, that entity—variously known as the Amazon Nation, Lesbian Nation, or the Hag/ocracy—assumes its shape by the very fact of its exclusivity. It promises women freedom from oppression in a world from which men have been barred: "Lesbian or woman prime is *the* factor in advance of every projected solution for our embattled world. In her realization of herself both sensually polymorphously and genitally orgasmically she experiences her original self reproductive or parthenogenetic recreation of herself apart from the intruding and disturbing and subjugating male."[13]

This imaginary vision is described in prose that is designedly disjoint, even mystical, and devoid of particulars. Yet despite the poetic expression, the radical feminist view of *communitas* remains deeply dispiriting. To turn to the nunnery as a model for the new Atlantis betokens desperation, not inspiration—and even the nunnery is animated by a devotion to a common force that the abidingly secular radical feminists scorn. The community of exclusion signals not a new social form but a suicide pact among women so estranged from the present that an end to the species is preferable to intimate association with the antagonist, man; so prideful that they have arrogated all virtue to their sex, confusing sex with virtue; so self-centered as to dismiss the possibility that a succeeding generation might imagine a different way out of this predicament. Most charitably, the depiction is advanced as a metaphor to dramatize radical feminists' felt sense of hopelessness. Yet even appreciated metaphorically, the approach misfires, for the very idea of a world peopled entirely by a single sex remains morally obtuse.

Even those feminist proposals which accept that men cannot be banished entirely still assume that communities will look very different after the revolution, and that a revolution is required to alter them. For Marxist and socialist feminists alike, the realm of production will be transformed, and the family will also be recast.[14] In this view, women cannot break out of their roles as subservient wives and mothers on their own, and so must be prevented from taking on those roles.

The durability of particular forms of community gives rise to the leftist feminist lament that women are more shaped than shaping. But it is hard to accept their claim that male power is the only guiding force behind present institutions. The college-educated housewife depicted by Betty Friedan may have felt that there were roads not taken, that her role had been oversold, but the organization man of the same period was also subject to a socialization that, while different, nonetheless limited his options. There is nothing inherently oppressive about American families or neighborhoods or churches, nothing akin to such unambiguously imposed forms of association as slavery and apartheid. The demands of kith and kin, seen as oppressive and limiting by some, are comforting and fulfilling to others.

Leftist feminists believe that community is something that happens *to* women, not something chosen; that, as Friedan once wrote, the home is merely a "comfortable concentration camp." For this reason, nothing less than a revolution will do to bring about less oppressive forms of community. Yet while the fear of imposition may have been plausible when the revival of feminist thought began a few decades ago, it is less clear today. Our social milieu comes permeated by the values of the age, but the United States in the late twentieth century is not a totalitarian regime, nor is the conventional imposed by a state bureau. In a world where much change has already occurred, and where that change is trumpeted nightly on the evening news, can there be many women so brainwashed as to believe that only traditional roles are open? The fact that choice and change, while not universal, are upheld as possibilities and celebrated as good suggests that existing models of community are not so pervasive—or oppressive—as leftist feminism supposes.

III

At the other extreme, the naturalists described in the [original work's] last chapter, as well as those who long for the stable communities of the past, believe that choice is now too much in evidence, jeopardizing the community forms that ought properly exist. For their part, the naturalists regard the existence of gender-specific identities, clear and distinct understandings of masculinity and femininity, as a biological imperative that precedes and shapes social forms. We are what nature has programmed us to be, and those instincts cannot be wished away by social arrangement.[15] In the naturalists' world view, instinct should drive institutions.

The chorus of determinism about gender roles has recently been joined by the New Right. For them, the liberal acceptance of change and choice seems to have caused the deterioration of community, especially the breakdown of the conventional family. In the New Right's ideal world, men and women would live out their God-given roles, as specified in the Bible. In the form of family- and church-based community they propose, father knows best and mother and children know their places.[16] While that vision offers stability and comfort to the devout, any wife not herself a Christian Fundamentalist is unlikely to find a model for living in the injunction to treat her husband like Jesus.[17] The determinism of the New Right implies a notion of the good life as narrow as the forms imposed by the naturalist or leftist feminist paradigms.

Those who scour history rather than biology or the Bible for their conception of community have in mind an all-encompassing way of life, a secure haven against change, an island where lives are lived in preordained fashion. This backward-looking vision embraces an idea of community in its strongest sense: a congregation of the like-minded, animated by a single knowable conception of the good. Robert Nisbet describes what we would find in an earlier age: "Whether we are dealing with the family, the village, or the gild, we are in the presence of systems of authority and allegiance which were widely held to precede the individual in both origin and right. . . . The group was primary; it was the irreducible unit of the social system at large."[18] It is this strong form of community that Tönnies had in mind when contrasting *Gemeinschaft* with *Gesellschaft;* it recalls Durkheim's mechanical solidarity, Burke's organic community, the Utopian inventions of the Owenities, the subsistence society fondly contemplated in our day by Ivan Illich.[19]

The strong community does not deny the importance of individual freedom, but asserts that it can only be realized through integration into a cohesive collective force. In Rousseau's *moi commun,* for instance, there is no tension between self and society; instead, the particular pattern of social existence is assumed "to be immanent in man's reason and will, to constitute the fullest satisfaction of his true interest, and to be the guarantee of his freedom."[20] Without a stable society and unquestioned authority, the tight bonds of family, community, vocational group, and religious orders, the individual is said to feel lost; the strong community rescues people from this sorry state.

The fixed character of the social order in backward-looking communities does not always imply fixed roles for the sexes, but this is often the case. The strong community is usually based on a vision of the family which assumes that, whatever the roles that men and women take on, they will be given beforehand, not chosen by the individuals involved. This is the kind of community celebrated by Ivan Illich in *Gender.*[21] Illich regards the prevailing patterns of masculine oppression as resulting from the demise of "vernacular gender," a state of affairs that prevailed when men and women occupied complementary roles in a subsistence economy. Stability reigned when males and females had to rely on one another, when both had their proper places, with neither sex dominant over the other.

This simple household-centered society began to disappear in the twelfth century, however, and, in Illich's account, it was finished off by the industrial revolution, which separated work and family, substituting "consumption-dependent production." In the industrial era, men and women no longer consumed what they made, but became "economic neuters belonging to two biological sexes," paid a wage that allowed them to purchase what others produced. In this transformation, Illich reports, women have lost out. Where once "mutual dependence set limits to struggle, exploitation, defeat," women's responsibility for the unvalued "shadow work" of the industrial economy now dooms her to inferiority.[22]

Illich idealizes a moment in history, and would restore the values and practices of that epoch. Yet he is selective in his restoration, for he would keep innovations that are consistent with his idea of "convivial community." Concerning the many grimmer aspects of twelfth century life, Illich is silent. Nor does his harmonious vision take account of the oppressive use of political power in societies characterized by ancient family forms; feudalism was not exactly a peaceable era, nor one in which governance was especially providential. Why should women remain in a separate, "enigmatic and asymmetrical," complementary "space-time," when the functional reasons for such a separation have largely vanished with the demise of the self-sufficient household? "The oldest traditions" undergird a separation of male and female roles, Illich notes by way of justification for maintaining these patterns, but what moral claims do these traditions make? What of the emergence of individual identity, the painstaking attempts to craft a social order in which being a man or a woman does not define one's life?

It is not only male writers who would retreat from the choice-celebrating present to a more traditional past. Germaine Greer, one of the seminal figures of the modern feminist movement, has lately reconsidered her position that sexual freedom leads to liberation; we have become too materialistic, too much obsessed with recreational sex and too little concerned about producing children, she now asserts.[23] In her celebration of Third World practices, Greer implies that the modern way of life, to which her earlier work contributed, must be repudiated in the name of the collectivity. But why polygamy and natural birth control are better than freely chosen alternative arrangements goes unsaid, aside from attacks on the "consumer-oriented" Western way of life.

To retreat from the present, rather than respond to it, is the first instinct of the backward-looking communitarian, and therein lies the problem. Having glimpsed the future, there is no going back to the past, for we cannot deny what we are. Formed by the notion of individualism with which our institutions are suffused, we cannot take refuge in a vision that denies the revolution in thought that took place. The belief in the salutary effects of a distinct individual identity, determined not by economic or sexual status but largely by our own actions, is too deeply held for us to engage in some collective act of willed forgetfulness.

Whether given by God or Nature, or derived from adherence to an ideology that celebrates the past, the supposition of preordained gender roles results in forms of community where individual choice does not count for much. Even if these visions could realistically be effectuated, the strong community is fundamentally inconsistent with the idea of gender justice rooted in individual volition.

IV

One need not embrace the patterned orthodoxies of the strong community to find the idea of *communitas* attractive. Individually designed lives remain a cardinal value, but such lives are more fully lived, not in the isolation that a purist liberalism contemplates, but within a tracery of support and obligation. Not all those who have made community their subject have harkened to the past or assumed that sex roles were necessarily preordained. Philosopher Roberto Unger seeks to move beyond the constrictions of liberalism and socialism; social democrats Michael Walzer and Raymond Williams sketch a communal life that is designedly fit for our times; social scientists, among them Daniel Bell, Benjamin Barber, Philip Selznick, and Christopher Jencks, search in their very distinctive ways for a public philosophy that allows us to reconnect the individual and the society.[24] These thinkers comprehend what we term the *open community* in a range of related ways, but all look forward toward the unknown for their visions of new forms of community, and none assumes that men or women must be limited to particular roles.

In the literature of politics, the lineage of the open community is decidedly recent in vintage. Its roots can be located in Tocqueville's celebration, in *Democracy in America,* of local self-governance and voluntary associations as essential to a legitimate democratic state, as well as in Max Weber's anguished depiction of the tension between the looming world of organization and the choice-making individual, confronted with "ultimately possible attitudes towards life [that] are irreconcilable."[25]

Those who spell out the various meanings of the open community are less inclined to adopt Tocqueville's celebratory tone, instead taking as their starting point Weber's dilemma or the lament of Tocqueville's contemporary Benjamin Constant, who contrasted the citizen of the classical city, with "real influence" that gave rise to a "lively and continuous pleasure" in participation, and the denizen of the modern state, "lost in the multitude, [who] . . . rarely perceives the influence that he exercises." The modern citizen, Constant notes, occupies himself with "the peaceful enjoyment of private independence," opting out of civic life in a state where "individual existence has little embodiment in political existence."[26] How can the relationship among individual, association, and state be recast for our time, in a manner that eschews facile resolution of deep and abiding conflicts? And how does the capacity of individuals to determine for themselves the significance of gender relate to that reconceptualization?

The animating concerns of those attentive to the open community are familiar enough. They search for social forms to arrest anomie, the social disintegration that has seemed characteristic of our time, and to give intimacy and solidarity a meaning deeper than that usually evident in complex industrial society. This agenda invites the nostalgia of the naturalists and the backward-looking communitarians, but there is considerable resistance to revering or restoring the old among those who imagine new forms of association. The tendency of small groups to exclusivity of membership, parochialism in viewpoint, and destructive combativeness in relationships, does not go unacknowledged; what is envisioned is a departure from that tradition.

If the strong community locates the individual inside a defined and defining social setting, the open community is more attentive to the autonomous, choice-making individual. There is no one model to describe this new form of association; it promises no "single and exclusive truth in politics."[27] That seeming default of theory has an obvious explanation. It is easier for those anxious to give new meaning to the ancient norm of *civitas* or to reformulate an actively deliberating polity to specify why an unbounded individualism or a too-demanding communitarianism has failed than to draft a road map for the future. The lack of specificity has also to do with the fact that the open community is more a process of association than a defined social form; it is not utopia in twentieth century guise. Open community is not yet an entity, but the beginning of an idea. Thus Benjamin Barber argues that what is needed is "not a practical change in reform efforts but a change in attitude about the aims of reform"; not a program, but "a mood, a tone, an orientation, an ethos."[28]

The open community offers a complex way to think about the choosing self, a closer approximation to what we know ourselves to be than simplistic individualism. In this conception, the community itself partly constitutes a person's identity, and the desire to fulfill one's own life plan is intertwined with the claims of the group to which one belongs. This community has been variously depicted as a reinvigorated political life marked by "the rule of the people in their assemblies . . . arguing over every aspect of the common life";[29] a "strong democracy" where individuals are transformed into a society;[30] a collectivity building on the best of the British labor movement's social inventions during the past century;[31] and an organizational form that would allow the fullest development of complementary personalities, in the shadow of a God who has yet to reveal Himself. In any of these descriptions, "to join with others in a community of understandings and purposes increases rather than diminishes one's own individuality."[32] Individuals take into account their own needs and, having once committed themselves to the community, internalize its norms, in turn taking into account others' needs in calculating their own behavior.

Members of such communities are not "selfless," but rather identify some part of themselves with the welfare of the community. The task of the collectivity, whether it be a neighborhood association or a nation, is to find a language with which to articulate these moral sentiments and a politics of participation with which to develop them.[33] The open community promises a repoliticization of the decisions that shape our lives as citizens, for it is held that only through political discourse can individuals, motivated by self-interest, come to conceive of a common good. Concord does not derive solely from the force of tradition or the submergence of the individual will, but is also generated by the polity.[34]

Proponents of open community, in their acceptance of the rough-and-tumble of politics as a governing feature of the new vision, embrace conflict and change as a necessary part of the future. In this they differ from the backward-looking communitarians who long for a stable and static world. Their inability to specify their new vision thus becomes more fully understandable, because many values compete to govern the character of each particular community. This tension among values guarantees a multiplicity of forms of community to choose from, for there is no more reason to believe that one kind of communal life is right for all than to believe that individuals will all look the same.

The open community does not assume that those born there will remain or that those not born there can never enter. On the contrary, it posits that people grow and change, and need different forms of association at different points in their lives. Like the autonomous individual, it will not remain unaltered during its institutional life. The open community will be hospitable to new ideas, new ways of functioning; it will never be finished or complete. Raymond Williams describes how these two kinds of openness are related:

> The making of a community is always an exploration, for consciousness cannot precede creation, and there is no formula for unknown experience. A good community, a living culture, will, because of this, not only make room for but actively encourage all and any who can contribute to the advance in consciousness which is the common need. Wherever we have started from, we need to listen to others who

started from a different position. We need to consider every attachment, every value, with our whole attention; for we do not know the future, we can never be certain of what may enrich it; we can only, now, listen to and consider whatever may be offered and take up what we can.[35]

This is a somewhat precarious balancing point. The open community must strive to maintain itself as a coherent enterprise with institutionalized values, while at the same time it is susceptible to change, ready to give up the old in the light of new discoveries. That communities might develop the capacity to function in such a continuously evolving state demands a suspension of disbelief, for our experience with community is more likely to show us the closing of a circle of believers, ever suspicious of outsiders, tending toward militancy to maintain the apparent rightness of their position. Williams offers an image of what the open community must instead aspire to: "While the clenched fist is a necessary symbol, the clenching ought never to be such that the hand cannot open, and the fingers extend, to discover and give a shape to the newly forming reality."[36]

The hand that is both open and closed points to the intellectual paradox of the open community, the difficulty of prescribing a new synthesis when the available paradigms are opposites. Some new outlook is needed; that is why the open community is represented by an attitude rather than an agenda. But it is an appealing vision. It affirms the importance of individualism as well as the necessity for common life; it acknowledges that old forms will not work with new people, new times, new ideas. The partisans of the open community learn from history that big government and large institutions often do a worse job of giving meaning to the lives of the people within them than do small, flexible associations, which know their members' faces and lives, their triumphs and traumas.

Even in a world of open communities, central government would do more than mediate among the associations, because the complexity and heterogeneity of the contemporary world lies beyond the capacity of any single individual or group to comprehend; there remains a vital politics of the general constituency. In this sense, communities of choice necessarily depend on the larger society for survival, even as the larger society draws on small associations for shared values in mutually dependent relationships. A governance of the whole is also needed to protect the basic liberties of individuals. As philosopher John Rawls has written, "The basic liberties are not intended to keep persons in isolation from one another, or to persuade them to live private lives . . . but to secure the right of free movement between associations and smaller communities."[37]

To the proponent of liberty, the conception of the relevance of gender in the open community is far more palatable than that advanced by the partisans of the strong community. It is implicit in the various discussions of the open community that men and women are not expected to surrender their sense of themselves for the good of the whole, to prefer others' conceptions of masculinity or femininity to their own self-defined sexual identities. In the depictions of social virtue in the open community, the search for self-knowledge and the capacity to act on that knowledge are regarded as good. Men and women properly achieve their "particular good" by making choices, Roberto Unger writes, and this achievement "is one of the bases of the community of life."[38]

The strong individual has a central place in the conception of the open community, since such individuals are essential to the maintenance of political life. Yet the partisans of the open community cannot wish away the tension between the claims they advance on behalf of political association and the primacy of autonomy in making basic life choices. Although it is true that "when politics goes well, we can know a good in common that we cannot know alone,"[39] this political model carries within itself the danger of overwhelming any other value that might animate association. In certain of its versions, it assumes that all our ties are crafted in political debate; but some will be based on love or devotion, not rational discourse, for not everyone relishes a life of meetings.

The open community can thus excessively entangle the roles of person and citizen, the sphere of private and public. Jean Bethke Elshtain argues that women especially must avoid uncritically accepting the notion that only public life is worth living; instead, they should "keep alive a critical distance . . . between female self-identity and a social identity thoroughly tied to the ongoing public-political world revolving around the structures, institutions, values, and ends of the state."[40] This point of view could just as well be adopted by men, for public life is not the only sphere where men and women make important life choices. To see the domain of political discourse as prior diminishes the importance of private communities formed by families and friends, yet those enclaves encourage individuals to become more fully themselves.

While the model of the open community may overemphasize the public sphere, it offers the best alternative for those who would honor individual determinations of the social relevance of gender while still recognizing that life must be lived in common. Even if community is freely chosen, tensions between individualist and communitarian ideas of justice will endure; the demands of persons for self-realization will always war with the call of the community for solidarity. Because the open community celebrates choice and autonomy for both men and women rather than imposing some "best" form of association on individuals, it will have a better chance of successfully balancing these competing justice claims.

The open community is the form of community that will most further gender justice, but it remains true that the model will not be immediately embraced by most. Since individuals often carry on traditions, many communities will continue to look as they did in the past, and tolerance of communities of choice is important. Government cannot set out to change these private choices in the name of imposing a better kind of community. Rather, it is government's role to ensure that the public realm treats men and women as deserving of equal liberty. . .

NOTES

1. Compare Robert A. Nisbet, *The Quest for Community,* revised ed. (Oxford: Oxford University Press, 1969) with Grant McConnell, *Private Power and American Democracy* (New York: Random House, 1970).
2. Michael Walzer, *Radical Principles* (New York: Basic Books, 1980), 6.
3. Compare William M. Sullivan, *Reconstructing Public Philosophy* (Berkeley: University of California Press, 1981), which faults the liberal tradition on these grounds.
4. "What made liberalism endurable for all these years was the fact that the individualism it generated was imperfect, tempered by older constraints and loyalties, by stable patterns of local, ethnic, religious, and class relationships." Jean Bethke Elshtain, "Feminism, Family, and Community," *Dissent* (Fall 1982): 422, 446.
5. Claude S. Fischer, et al., *Networks and Places* (New York: Free Press, 1978), 202.
6. Quoted in Fischer, *Networks and Places,* supra note 5: 196.
7. This is the view of many of the radical feminists. . . . In the social sciences, it is implicit in the treatment of marriage and family in Judith Blake Davis, "The Changing Status of Women in Developed Countries" *Scientific American* 231 (September 1974): 144; Jessie Bernard, *Women and the Public Interest* (Chicago: Aldine-Atherton, 1971), 63–103; and Eli Zaretsky, *Capitalism, the Family, and Personal Life* (New York: Harper Colophon, 1976).
8. We do not deny that resource constraints may be powerful constraints on choice—in fact, they are likely to be more constraining than the socialization discussed in this [excerpt]. Resource constraints may also affect women more strongly, for two reasons: (1) women generally earn less than men; (2) women generally have more child care responsibilities, both in and out of marriage. . . .
9. The concept is developed in the writings of Jürgen Habermas. See, e.g., Thomas McCarthy, *The Critical Theory of Jürgen Habermas* (Cambridge: MIT Press, 1979); Raymond Geuss, *The Idea of a Critical Theory* (Cambridge: Cambridge University Press, 1981). See also Herbert Marcuse, *One-Dimensional Man* (Boston: Beacon Press, 1966).
10. See Janet Radcliffe Richards, *The Sceptical Feminist* (London: Routledge and Kegan Paul, 1980).
11. John E. Coons and Stephen D. Sugarman, "A Case for Choice," in *Parents, Teachers, and Children: Prospects for Choice in American Education* (San Francisco: Institute for Contemporary Studies, 1977), 129, 148.

12. Carol Gilligan, *In a Different Voice* (Cambridge: Harvard University Press, 1982).

13. Jill Johnston, *Lesbian Nation* (New York: Simon & Schuster, 1973), 174. See also Mary Daly, *Gyn/Ecology* (Boston: Beacon Press, 1977); Susan Griffin, *Woman and Nature: The Roaring Inside Her* (New York: Harper & Row, 1978).

14. See chapter 3 [of the original work].

15. See, e.g., Lionel Tiger and Robin Fox, *The Imperial Animal* (New York: Holt, Rinehart, and Winston, 1971), 146.

16. See generally Alan Crawford, *Thunder on the Right* (New York: Pantheon, 1980).

17. Marabel Morgan, *The Total Woman* (Old Tappan, New Jersey: F. H. Revell, 1973).

18. Nisbet, *Quest for Community,* supra note 1:81. Compare Alasdair MacIntyre, *After Virtue* (Notre Dame, Indiana: University of Notre Dame Press, 1981). The longing for traditional forms of community is shared by a group of social scientists who have been labelled neoconservatives. See generally Peter Steinfels, *The Neoconservatives* (New York: Simon & Schuster, 1979).

19. See generally Sheldon S. Wolin, *Politics and Vision* (Boston: Little, Brown, 1960); Lewis Coser, *Greedy Institutions* (New York: Free Press, 1974).

20. J. L. Talmon, *Political Messianism* (London: Martin Secker and Warburg, 1960), 20.

21. Ivan Illich, *Gender* (New York: Pantheon, 1982). See also his *Tools for Conviviality* (New York: Harper & Row, 1973) and *Shadow Work* (Salem, New Hampshire: Marion Boyars, 1981).

22. Christopher Lasch says much the same thing, in criticizing the new elite that "has torn away the veil of chivalry that once tempered the exploitation of women . . . [and] has expropriated the worker's knowledge and the mother's 'instinct'. . . ." *The Culture of Narcissism* (New York: Warner, 1979), 375.

23. Germaine Greer, *Sex and Destiny* (New York: Harper & Row, 1984). Compare her *The Female Eunuch* (New York: McGraw-Hill, 1971).

24. Roberto Mangabeira Unger, *Knowledge and Politics* (New York: Free Press, 1975); Michael Walzer, *Radical Principles,* supra note 2; Raymond Williams, *Culture and Society* (New York: Columbia University Press, 1960); Daniel Bell, *The Cultural Contradictions of Capitalism* (New York: Basic Books, 1976); Benjamin R. Barber, *Liberating Feminism* (New York: Delta, 1976); and *Strong Democracy* (Berkeley: University of California Press, 1984); Philip Selznick, *Law, Society, and Industrial Justice* (New York: Russell Sage, 1964); Christopher Jencks, "The Social Basis of Unselfishness," in Herbert J. Gans, et al., eds., *On the Making of Americans: Essays in Honor of David Riesman* (Philadelphia: University of Pennsylvania Press, 1979), 63.

25. Quoted in Wolin, *Politics and Vision,* supra note 19: 424.

26. Ibid., 281.

27. Talmon, *Political Messianism,* supra note 20: 20.

28. Barber, *Liberating Feminism,* supra note 24: 138–39. In his later work, Barber has proposed a program to rejuvenate politics, but it is so broad as to appear utopian. See his *Strong Democracy,* supra note 24: 261–311.

29. Walzer, *Radical Principles,* supra note 2: 35.

30. Barber, *Strong Democracy,* supra note 24.

31. Williams, *Culture and Society,* supra note 24.

32. Unger, *Knowledge and Politics,* supra note 24: 217.

33. See, e.g., Jencks, "Unselfishness," supra note 24: 69. See also Richard Titmuss, *The Gift Relationship* (New York: Pantheon, 1971). Titmuss argues that it is the capacity to nurture empathy that enabled Britain to secure blood from its citizens without promising money or blood in exchange.

34. See Barber, *Strong Democracy,* supra note 24.

35. Williams, *Culture and Society,* supra note 24: 334–35.

36. Ibid., 335.

37. John Rawls, "Fairness to Goodness," *Philosophical Review* 84 (1975): 536, 550.

38. Unger, *Knowledge and Politics,* supra note 24: 280.

39. Michael J. Sandel, *Liberalism and the Limits of Justice* (Cambridge: Cambridge University Press, 1982), 183.

40. Jean Bethke Elshtain, "Antigone's Daughters: Reflections on Female Identity and the State," in Irene Diamond, ed., *Families, Politics, and Public Policy* (New York: Longman, 1983), 300.

STUDY QUESTIONS

1. What do the authors mean by the "strong community"? How does this contrast with the "open community"?
2. What reasons do the authors give for the belief that the open community is the form of community that will most further gender justice?
3. Summarize the authors' criticisms of radical feminism, the New Right, and determinists. To what extent are these criticisms valid?
4. Formulate a response to these authors based on a careful reading of the essays by Gilligan and MacIntyre (in chapter one).

11

Useless Suffering

Emmanuel Levinas

Emmanuel Levinas is the author of a number of influential works in contemporary philosophy, including *Otherwise Than Being* and *Totality and Infinity,* from which this selection is taken.

PHENOMENOLOGY

Suffering is surely a *given* in consciousness, a certain 'psychological content', like the lived experience of colour, of sound, of contact, or like any sensation. But in this 'content' itself, it is in-spite-of-consciousness, unassumable. It is unassumable and 'unassumability'. 'Unassumability' does not result from the excessive intensity of a sensation, from some sort of quantitative 'too much', surpassing the measure of our sensibility and our means of grasping and holding. It results from an excess, a 'too much' which is inscribed in a sensorial content, penetrating as suffering the dimensions of meaning which seem to be opened and grafted on to it. For the Kantian 'I think'—which is capable of reuniting and embracing the most heterogeneous and disparate givens into order and meaning under its *a priori* forms—it is as if suffering were not only a *given* refractory to synthesis, but the *way* in which the refusal opposed to the assembling of givens into a meaningful whole is opposed to it: suffering is at once what disturbs order and this disturbance itself. It is not only the consciousness of rejection or a symptom of rejection, but this rejection itself: a backwards consciousness, 'operating' not as 'grasp' but as revulsion. It is a modality, or the categorial ambiguity of quality and modality. Taken as an 'experienced' content, the denial and refusal of meaning which is imposed as a sensible quality is the *way* in which the unbearable is precisely not borne by consciousness, the way this not-being-borne is, paradoxically, itself a sensation or a given. This is a quasi-contradictory structure, but a contradiction which is not formal like that of the dialectical tension between the affirmative and the negative which arises for the intellect; it is a contradiction by way of sensation: the plaintiveness of pain, hurt [*mal*].[1]

Suffering, in its hurt and its in-spite-of-consciousness, is passivity. Here, 'taking cognizance' is no longer, properly speaking, a taking; it is no longer *the performance of an act of consciousness,* but, in its adversity, a submission; and even a submission to the submitting, since the 'content' of which the aching consciousness is conscious is precisely this very adversity of suffering, its hurt. But, here again, this *passivity*—in the sense of a modality—signifies as a *quiddity,* and perhaps as the place where passivity signifies originally, independent of its conceptual opposition to activity. The latter is an abstraction made from its psycho-physical and psycho-physiological conditions; in its pure phenomenology, the passivity of suffering is in no way the reverse side of activity, as an effect would still be correlative to its cause, or as a sensorial receptivity would be correlative to the 'Obstance' of the object which affects and impresses it. The passivity of suffering is more profoundly passive than the receptivity of our senses, which is already the activity of welcome, and straight away becomes perception. In suffering sensibility is a vulnerability, more passive than receptivity; it is an ordeal more passive than experience. It is precisely an evil. It is not, to tell the truth, through passivity that evil is described, but through evil that suffering is understood. Suffering is a pure undergoing. It is not a matter of a passivity which would degrade man by striking a blow against his freedom. Pain would limit such freedom to the point of compromising self-consciousness, permitting man the identity of a thing only in the passivity of the submission. The evil which rends the humanity of the suffering person, overwhelms his humanity otherwise than non-freedom overwhelms it: violently and cruelly, more irremissibly than the negation which dominates or paralyzes the act in non-freedom. What counts in the non-freedom or the undergoing of suffering is the concreteness of the *not* looming as a hurt more negative than any apophantic *not*. This negativity of evil is, probably, the source or kernel of all apophantic negation. The *not* of evil is negative right up to non-sense. All evil refers to suffering. It is the *impasse* of life and being, their absurdity, where pain does not come, somehow innocently, 'to colour' consciousness with affectivity. The evil of pain, the harm itself, is the explosion and most profound articulation of absurdity.

Thus the least one can say about suffering is that in its own phenomenality, intrinsically, it is useless, 'for nothing'. Doubtlessly this basic sense-lessness that the analysis seems to suggest is confirmed by empirical situations of pain, where pain somehow remains undiluted and isolates itself in consciousness, or absorbs the rest of consciousness. It would suffice, for example, to extract from the medical journals certain cases of persistent or obstinate pain, the neuralgias and the intolerable lumbagos resulting from lesions of the peripheral nerves, and the tortures which are experienced by certain patients stricken with malignant tumours.[2] Pain can become the central phenomenon of the diseased state. These are the 'pain-illnesses' where the integration of other psychological states does not bring any relief but where, on the contrary, anxiety and distress add to the cruelty of the hurt. But one can go further—and doubtless thus arrive at the essential facts of pure pain—by evoking the 'pain-illnesses' of beings who are psychically deprived, backward, handicapped, in their relational life and in their relationships to the Other, relationships where suffering, without losing anything of its savage malignancy, no longer covers up the totality of the mental and comes across novel lights within new horizons. These horizons none the less remain closed to the mentally deficient, except that in their 'pure pain' they are projected into them to expose them *to me*, raising the fundamental ethical problem which pain poses 'for nothing': the inevitable and preemptory ethical problem of the medication which is my duty. Is not the evil of suffering—extreme passivity, impotence, abandonment and solitude—also the unassumable and thus the possibility of a half opening, and, more precisely, the possibility that wherever a moan, a cry, a groan or a sigh happen there is the original call for aid, for curative help, for help from the other[3] ego whose alterity, whose exteriority promises salvation? It is the original opening toward what is helpful, where the primordial, irreducible, and ethical, anthropological category of the medical comes to impose itself—across a demand for analgesia, more pressing, more urgent in the groan than a demand for consolation or a postponement of death. For pure suffering, which is intrinsically meaningless and condemned to itself without exit, a beyond takes shape in the inter-human.[4] It is starting from such situations—we say in passing—that medicine as technique, and consequently the general technology it presupposes, the technology so easily exposed to the attacks of 'right-thinking' rigour, does not merely originate in the so-called 'will to power'. This bad will is perhaps only the price which must sometimes be paid by the elevated thought of a civilization called to nourish persons and to lighten their sufferings.

This elevated thought is the honour of a still uncertain and blinking modernity coming at the end of a century of nameless sufferings, but in which the suffering of suffering, the suffering for the useless suffering of the other person, the just suffering in me for the unjustifiable suffering of the Other, opens upon suffering the ethical perspective of the inter-human. In this perspective a radical difference develops between *suffering in the Other,* which for *me* is unpardonable and solicits me and calls me, and suffering *in me,*[5] my own adventure of suffering, whose constitutional or congenital uselessness can take on a meaning, the only meaning to which suffering is susceptible, in becoming a suffering for the suffering—be it inexorable—of someone else. It is this attention to the Other which, across the cruelties of our century—despite these cruelties, because of these cruelties—can be affirmed as the very bond of human subjectivity, even to the point of being raised to a supreme ethical principle—the only one which it is not possible to contest—a principle which can go so far as to command the hopes and practical discipline of vast human groups. This attention and this action are so imperiously and directly incumbent on people—on their selves—that it makes waiting for the saving actions of an all-powerful God impossible without degradation. To be sure, consciousness of this inescapable obligation makes the idea of God more difficult, but it also makes it spiritually closer than confidence in any king of theodicy.

THEODICY

In the ambiguity of suffering which the above phenomenological essay brings out, its modality also shows the content or sensation that consciousness 'supports'. This adversity-to-all-harmony, as quiddity, enters into conjunction with other 'contents' which it disturbs, to be sure, but where it is given reasons or produces a reason. Already within an isolated consciousness, the pain of suffering can take on the meaning of a pain which merits and hopes for reward, and so lose, it seems, in diverse ways, its modality of uselessness. Is it not meaningful as a means with an end in view, when it tallies with the effort which leads to a work or in the fatigue which results from it? One can discover in it a biological finality: the role of an alarm signal manifesting itself for the preservation of life against the cunning dangers which menace life in illness. 'He that increaseth knowledge increaseth sorrow', says Ecclesiastes (1:18), where suffering appears at the very least as the price of reason and of spiritual refinement. It would also temper the individual's character. It would be necessary to the teleology of community life, where social unrest awakens a useful attention to the health of the collective body. The social utility of suffering is necessary to the pedagogic function of Power in education, discipline and repression. Is not fear of punishment the beginning of wisdom? Is it not believed that sufferings, submitted to as sanctions, regenerate the enemies of society and man? This political teleology is founded, to be sure, on the value of existence, on the perseverance of society and the individual in being, on their successful health as the supreme and ultimate end.

But the unpleasant and gratuitous non-sense of pain already pierces beneath the reasonable forms which the social 'uses' of suffering assume. These, in any case, do not make the torture which strikes the psychically handicapped and isolates them in their pain any less scandalous. But behind the rational administration of pain in sanctions distributed by human courts, immediately dressing up dubious appearances of repression, the arbitrary and strange failure of justice amidst wars, crimes and the oppression of the weak by the strong, rejoins, in a sort of fatality, the useless sufferings which spring from natural plagues as if effects of an ontological perversion. Beyond the fundamental malignity of suffering itself, revealed in its phenomenology, does not human experience in history attest to a malice and a bad will?

Western humanity has none the less sought for the meaning of this scandal by invoking the proper sense of a metaphysical order, an ethics, which is invisible in the immediate lessons of moral consciousness. This is a kingdom of transcendent ends, willed by a benevolent wisdom, by the absolute goodness of a God who is in some way defined by this super-natural goodness; or a widespread, invisible goodness in Nature and History, where it would command the paths which are, to be sure, painful, but which lead to the Good. Pain is henceforth meaningful, subordinated in one way or another to the metaphysical finality envisaged by faith or by a belief in progress. These beliefs are presupposed by theodicy! Such is the grand idea necessary to the inner peace of souls in our distressed world. It is called upon to make sufferings here below comprehensible. These will make sense by reference to an original fault or to the congenital finitude of human being. The evil which fills the earth would be explained in a 'plan of the whole'; it would be called upon to atone for a sin, or it would announce, to the ontologically limited consciousness, compensation or recompense at the end of time. These supra-sensible perspectives are invoked in order to envisage in a suffering which is essentially gratuitous and absurd, and apparently arbitrary, a signification and an order.

Certainly one may ask if theodicy, in the broad and narrow senses of the term, effectively succeeds in making God innocent, or in saving morality in the name of faith, or in making suffering—and this is the true intention of the thought which has recourse to theodicy—bearable. By underestimating its temptation one could, in any case, misunderstand the profundity of the empire which theodicy exerts over humankind, and the *epoch-making* character—or the *historical* character, as one says today—of its entry into thought. It has been, at least up to the trials of the twentieth century, a component of the self-consciousness of European humanity. It persisted in watered-down form at the core of atheist progressivism, which was confident, none the less, in the efficacy of the Good which is immanent to being, called to visible triumph by the simple play of the natural and historical laws of injustice, war, misery and illness. As providential, Nature and History furnished the eighteenth and nineteenth centuries with the norms of moral consciousness. They are associated with many essentials of the deism of the age of Enlightenment. But theodicy—ignoring the name that Leibniz gave to it in 1710—is as old as a certain reading of the Bible. It dominated the consciousness of the believer who explained his misfortunes by reference to the Sin, or at least by reference to his sins. In addition to the Christians' well-established reference to Original Sin, this theodicy is in a certain sense implicit in the Old Testament, where the drama of the Diaspora reflects the sins of Israel. The wicked conduct of ancestors, still non-expiated by the sufferings of exile, would explain to the exiles themselves the duration and the harshness of this exile.

THE END OF THEODICY

Perhaps the most revolutionary fact of our twentieth-century consciousness—but it is also an event in Sacred History—is that of the destruction of all balance between the explicit and implicit theodicy of Western thought and the forms which suffering and its evil take in the very unfolding of this century. This is the century that in thirty years has known two world wars, the totalitarianisms of right and left, Hitlerism and Stalinism, Hiroshima, the Gulag, and the genocides of Auschwitz and Cambodia. This is the century which is drawing to a close in the haunting memory of the return of everything signified by these barbaric names: suffering and evil are deliberately imposed, yet no reason sets limits to the exasperation of a reason become political and detached from all ethics.

Among these events the Holocaust of the Jewish people under the reign of Hitler seems to us the paradigm of gratuitous human suffering, where evil appears in its diabolical horror. This is perhaps not a subjective feeling. The disproportion between suffering and every theodicy was shown at Auschwitz with a glaring, obvious clarity. Its possibility puts into question the multi-millennial traditional faith. Did not the word of Nietzsche on the death of God take on, in the extermination camps, the signification of a quasi-empirical fact? Is it necessary to be surprised, then, that this drama of Sacred History has had among its principal actors a people which, since forever, has been associated with this history, whose collective soul and destiny would be wrongly understood as limited to any sort of nationalism, and whose *gesture,* in certain circumstances, still belongs to Revelation—be it as apocalypse—which 'provokes thought' from philosophers or which impedes them from thinking?[6]

Here I wish to evoke the analysis which the Canadian Jew, the philosopher Emil Fackenheim, of Toronto, has made of this catastrophe of the human and the divine, in his work, and notably in his book *God's Presence in History:*

> The Nazi Genocide of the Jewish people has no precedent within Jewish history. Nor . . . will one find a precedent outside Jewish history. . . . Even actual cases of genocide, however, still differ from the Nazi holocaust in at least two respects. Whole peoples have been killed for 'rational' (however horrifying) ends such as power, territory, wealth. . . . The Nazi murder . . . was annihilation for the sake of annihilation, murder for the sake of murder, evil for the sake of evil. Still more incontestably unique than the crime itself is the situation of the victims. The Albigensians died for their faith, believing unto death that God needs martyrs. Negro Christians have been murdered for their race, able to find comfort in a faith not at issue. The more than one million Jewish children murdered in the Nazi holocaust died neither because of their faith, nor despite their faith, nor for reasons unrelated to the Jewish faith [but] because of the Jewish faith of their great-grandparents [who brought] up Jewish children.[7]

The inhabitants of the Eastern European Jewish communities constituted the majority of the six million tortured and massacred; they represented the human beings least corrupted by the ambiguities of our world, and the million infants killed had the innocence of infants. Theirs is the death of martyrs, a death given in the torturers' unceasing destruction of the dignity which belongs to martyrs. The final act of this destruction is accomplished today in the posthumous denial of the very fact of martyrdom by the would-be 'revisers of history'. This would be pain in its undiluted malignity, suffering for nothing. It renders impossible and odious every proposal and every thought which would explain it by the sins of those who have suffered or are dead. But does not this end of theodicy, which obtrudes itself in the face of this century's inordinate distress, at the same time in a more general way reveal the unjustifiable character of suffering in the other person, the scandal which would occur by my justifying my neighbour's suffering? So that the very phenomenon of suffering in its uselessness is, in principle the pain of the Other. For an ethical sensibility—confirming itself, in the inhumanity of our time, against this inhumanity—the justification of the neighbour's pain is certainly the source of all immorality. Accusing oneself in suffering is undoubtedly the very turning back of the ego to itself. It is perhaps thus; and the for-the-other—the most upright relation to the Other—is the most profound adventure of subjectivity, its ultimate intimacy. But this intimacy can only be discreet. It could not be given as an example, or be narrated as an edifying discourse. It could not be made a predication without being perverted.

The philosophical problem, then, which is posed by the useless pain which appears in its fundamental malignancy across the events of the twentieth century, concerns the meaning that religiosity and the human morality of goodness can still retain after the end of theodicy. According to the philosopher we have just quoted, Auschwitz would paradoxically entail a revelation of the very God who nevertheless was silent at Auschwitz: a commandment of faithfulness. To renounce after Auschwitz this God absent from Auschwitz—no longer to assure the continuation of Israel—would amount to finishing the criminal enterprise of National-Socialism, which aimed at the annihilation of Israel and the forgetting of the ethical message of the Bible, which Judaism bears, and whose multi-millennial history is concretely prolonged by Israel's existence as a people. For if God was absent in the extermination camps, the devil was very obviously present in them. From whence, for Emil Fackenheim comes the obligation for Jews to live and to remain Jews, in order not to be made accomplices of a diabolical project. The Jew, after Auschwitz, is pledged to his faithfulness to Judaism and to the material and even political conditions of its existence.

This final reflection of the Toronto philosopher, formulated in terms which render it relative to the destiny of the Jewish people, can be given a universal signification. From Sarajevo to Cambodia humanity has witnessed a host of cruelties in the course of a century when Europe, in its 'human sciences', seemed to reach the end of its subject, the humanity which, during all these horrors, breathed—already or still—the fumes of the crematory ovens of the 'final solution' where theodicy abruptly appeared impossible. Is humanity, in its indifference, going to abandon the world to useless suffering, leaving it to the political fatality—or the drifting—of the blind forces which inflict misfortune on the weak and conquered, and which spare the conquerors, whom the wicked must join? Or, incapable of adhering to an order—or to a disorder—which it continues to think diabolic, must not humanity now, in a faith more difficult than ever, in a faith without theodicy, continue Sacred History; a history which now demands even more of the resources of the *self* in each one, and appeals to its suffering inspired by the suffering of the other person, to its compassion which is a non-useless suffering (or love), which is no longer suffering 'for nothing', and which straightaway has a meaning? At the end of the twentieth century and after the useless and unjustifiable pain which is exposed and displayed therein without any shadow of a consoling theodicy, are we not all pledged—like the Jewish people to their faithfulness—to the second term of this alternative?[8] This is a new modality in the faith of today, and also in our moral certainties, a modality quite essential to the modernity which is dawning.

THE INTER-HUMAN ORDER

To envisage suffering, as I have just attempted to do, in the inter-human perspective—that is, as meaningful in me, useless in the Other—does not consist in adopting a relative point of view on it, but in restoring it to the dimensions of meaning outside of which the immanent and savage concreteness of evil in a consciousness is but an abstraction. To think suffering in an inter-human perspective does not amount to seeing it in the coexistence of a multiplicity of consciousnesses, or in a social determinism, accompanied by the simple knowledge that people in society can have of their neighbourliness or of their common destiny. The inter-human perspective can subsist, but can also be lost, in the political order of the City where the Law establishes mutual obligations between citizens. Properly speaking, the inter-human lies in a non-indifference of one to another, in a responsibility of one for another. The inter-human is prior to the reciprocity of this responsibility, which inscribes itself in impersonal laws, and becomes superimposed on the pure altruism of this responsibility inscribed in the ethical position of the self as self. It is prior to every contact which would signify precisely the moment of reciprocity where it can, to be sure, continue, but where it can also attenuate or extinguish altruism and disinterestedness. The order of politics—post-ethical or pre-ethical—which inaugurates the 'social contract' is neither the sufficient condition nor the necessary outcome of ethics. In its ethical position, the self is distinct from the citizen born of the City, and from the individual who precedes all order in his natural egoism, from whom political philosophy, since Hobbes, tries to derive—or succeeds in deriving—the social or political order of the City.

The inter-human lies also in the recourse that people have to one another for help, before the marvellous alterity of the Other has been banalized or dimmed in a simple exchange of courtesies which become established as an 'inter-personal commerce' of customs. We have spoken of this in the first paragraph of this study. These are expressions of a properly ethical meaning, distinct from those which the *self* and *other* acquire in what one calls the state of Nature or civil society. It is in the inter-human perspective of *my* responsibility for the other person, without concern for reciprocity, in my call to help him gratuitously, in the asymmetry of the relation of *one* to the *other,* that we have tried to analyze the phenomenon of useless suffering.

'La Souffrance inutile' first appeared in *Giornale di Metafisica* 4 (1982), 13–26, and was reprinted in *Les Cahiers de la Nuit Surveillé, Numéro 3; Emmanuel Levinas,* edited by Jacques Rolland, Paris, Editions Verdief, pp. 329–38. It is translated here with the permission of the author.

NOTES

1. The French term '*mal*' means both 'hurt' and 'evil', and both words have been used to translate it.
2. See the article by Dr Escoffier-Lambiotte in *Le Monde,* 4 April 1981, entitled 'Le premier centre français de traitement de la douleur a été inauguré à l'hôpital Cochin' ['The First French Center for the Treatment of Pain has been Opened at the Cochin Hospital'].
3. With regard to this point we refer to Philippe Nemo's fine book, *Job et l'excess du Mal* [*Job and the Excess of Evil*] (Paris, Grasset, 1977): the very resistance of suffering to synthesis and order is interpreted as the rupture of pure immanence where, essentially, the psychism is enclosed, and as the event of transcendence, and even as an interpellation of God. Cf., also, our analysis of this book, 'Transcendance et mal' ['Transcendence and Evil'], reprinted in *De Dieu qui vient à l'idée,* Paris, J. Vrin, 1982, pp. 189–207.
4. There is a talmudic dialogue or apologue (tractate Berakhot of the *Babylonian Talmud,* 5b) which reflects the conception of the radical hurt of suffering, its intrinsic and uncompensated despair, its confinement and its recourse to the other person, to medication *exterior* to the immanent structure of hurt.

   Rav Hiya bar Abba falls ill and Rav Yohanan comes to visit him. He asks him: 'Are your sufferings fitted to you?' 'Neither them nor the compensations they promise.' 'Give me your hand', the visitor of the ill man then says. And the visitor lifts the ill man from his couch. But then Rav Yohanan himself falls ill and is visited by Rav Hanina. Same question: 'Are your sufferings fitted to you?' Same response: 'Neither them nor the compensations they promise.' 'Give me your hand', says Rav Hanina, and he lifts Rav Yohanan from his couch. Question: Could not Rav Yohanan lift himself by himself? Answer: The prisoner could not break free from his confinement by himself.
5. This suffering *in me* would be so radically mine that it could not become subject to a predication. It is as suffering *in me* and not as suffering in general, that *welcome* suffering, attested in the spiritual tradition of humanity, can signify a true idea: the expiatory suffering of the just suffering for others, the suffering that illuminates, the suffering that is sought after by Dostoevsky's characters. I think also of the Jewish religious tradition which is familiar to me, of the 'I am love-sick' of the *Song of Songs,* of the suffering about which certain talmudic texts speak and which they name 'Yessourine shel Ahava', sufferings through love, which is joined to the theme of expiation for others. This suffering is often described at the limit of 'its usefulness'. Cf. note 3, where, in the test of the just, suffering is also what 'does not fit me'—'Neither it, nor the "recompense" attached to it.'
6. Maurice Blanchot, who is known for his lucid and critical attention to literature and events, notes somewhere: 'How philosophize, how write in the memory of Auschwitz, of those who have said to us sometimes in notes buried near the crematories: "Know what has happened", "do not forget", and, at the same time, "You will never know"?' I think that all the dead of the Gulag and all the other places of torture in our political century are present when one speaks of Auschwitz. [Blanchot's words appear in his article 'Our Clandestine Companion', translated by David Allison, in *Face to Face with Levinas,* edited by Richard Cohen, Albany, State University of New York Press, 1986, p. 50: translator's addition.]
7. Emil Fackenheim, *God's Presence in History: Jewish Affirmations and Philosophical Reflections after Auschwitz,* New York, New York University Press, 1970, pp. 69–70. This work has been translated into French by M. Delmotte and B. Dupuy (Lagrasse, Veridier, 1980.): translator's note.

8. We said above that theodicy in the broad sense of the term is justified by a certain reading of the Bible. It is evident that another reading of it is possible, and that in a certain sense nothing of the spiritual experience of human history is foreign to the Scriptures. We are thinking here in particular of the book of Job which attests at once to Job's faithfulness to God (2:10) and to ethics (27:5 and 6), despite his sufferings without reason, and his opposition to the theodicy of his friends. He refuses theodicy right to the end and, in the last chapters of the text (42:7), is preferred to those who, hurrying to the safety of Heaven, would make God innocent before the suffering of the just. It is a little like the reading Kant makes of this book in his quite extraordinary short treatise of 1791, *Uber das Misslingen aller philosophischen Versuche in der Theodicee* ['On the Failure of All the Philosophical Attempts at a Theodicy'], where he demonstrates the theoretical weakness of the arguments in favour of theodicy. Here is the conclusion of his way of interpreting what 'this ancient book expresses allegorically': 'In this state of mind Job has proven that he did not found his morality on faith, but his faith on morality; in which case faith, however weak it may be, is nonetheless one of a pure and authentic kind, a kind which does not found a religion of solicited favours, but a well conducted life (*'welche eine Religion nicht der Gunstbewerbung, sondern des guten Lebenswandels grundet'*).

STUDY QUESTIONS

1. What does Levinas mean when he calls suffering passivity or "a submission to the submitting"?
2. Explain the "inter-human."
3. What duties do I have toward my suffering neighbors? What duties have they?
4. What are the implications of Levinas's thought for a philosophy of community life?

FOR FURTHER STUDY

Bellah, Robert, et al. *Habits of the Heart: Individualism and Commitment in American Life*. New York: HarperCollins, 1986.

Benhabib, Seyla, and Cornell, Drucilla. *Feminism as Critique: Essays on the Politics of Gender in Late-Capitalist Societies*. Minneapolis: University of Minnesota Press, 1987.

Benhabib, Seyla, and Dallmayr, Fred. *The Communicative Ethics Controversy.* Cambridge, Mass.: The MIT Press, 1990.

Cole, Eve Browning. *Explorations in Feminist Ethics: Theory and Practice*. Bloomington, Ind.: Indiana University Press, 1992.

Fitzgerald, Frances. *Cities on a Hill*. New York: Simon & Schuster, 1987.

Fraser, Nancy. "Toward a Discourse Ethic of Solidarity." *Praxis International* 5, no. 4 (January 1986).

Frye, Marilyn. *The Politics of Reality: Essays in Feminist Theory.* Freedom, Calif.: Crossing Press, 1983.

Lorde, Audre. *Sister Outsider: Essays and Speeches*. Freedom, Calif.: Crossing Press, 1984.

Young, Iris Marion. "The Ideal of Community and the Politics of Difference." In *Feminism/Postmodernism,* ed. Linda J. Nicholson. New York: Routledge, 1989.

Chapter Three

Ethics of Friendship, Love, and Caring

12

On Friendship

Henry David Thoreau

Henry David Thoreau (1817–62) is regarded as one of America's greatest naturalists. His best-known work, *Walden*, continues to influence many today with its call to simplicity and spiritual liberty.

. . . After years of vain familiarity, some distant gesture or unconscious behavior, which we remember, speaks to us with more emphasis than the wisest or kindest words. We are sometimes made aware of a kindness long passed, and realize that there have been times when our Friends' thoughts of us were of so pure and lofty a character that they passed over us like the winds of heaven unnoticed; when they treated us not as what we were, but as what we aspired to be. There has just reached us, it may be, the nobleness of some such silent behavior, not to be forgotten, not to be remembered, and we shudder to think how it fell on us cold, though in some true but tardy hour we endeavor to wipe off these scores. . . .

Friendship is evanescent in every man's experience, and remembered like heat lightning in past summers. Fair and flitting like a summer cloud—there is always some vapor in the air, no matter how long the drought; there are even April showers. Surely from time to time, for its vestiges never depart, it floats through our atmosphere. It takes place, like vegetation in so many materials, because there is such a law, but always without permanent form, though ancient and familiar as the sun and moon, and as sure to come again. The heart is forever inexperienced. They silently gather as by magic, these never failing, never quite deceiving visions, like the bright and fleecy clouds in the calmest and clearest days. The Friend is some fair floating isle of palms eluding the mariner in Pacific seas. Many are the dangers to be encountered, equinoctial gales and coral reefs, ere he may sail before the constant trades. But who would not sail through mutiny and storm, even over Atlantic waves, to reach the fabulous retreating shores of some continent man? . . .

No word is oftener on the lips of men than Friendship, and indeed no thought is more familiar to their aspirations. All men are dreaming of it, and its drama, which is always a tragedy, is enacted daily. It is the secret of the universe. You may thread the town, you may wander the country, and none shall ever speak of it, yet thought is everywhere busy about it, and the idea of what is possible in this respect affects our behavior toward all new men and women, and a great many old ones. Nevertheless, I can remember only two or three essays on this subject in all literature. No wonder that the mythology, and Arabian Nights, and Shakespeare, and Scott's novels entertain us—we are poets and fablers and dramatists and novelists ourselves. We are continually acting a part in a more interesting drama than any written. We are dreaming that our Friends are our *Friends*, and that we are our Friends' *Friends*. Our actual Friends are but distant relations of those to whom we are pledged. We never exchange more than three words with a Friend in our lives on that level to which our thoughts and feelings almost habitually rise. One goes forth prepared to say, "Sweet Friends!" and the salutation is, "Damn your eyes!"

But never mind; faint heart never won true Friend. O my Friend, may it come to pass once, that when you are my Friend I may be yours.

Of what use the friendliest dispositions even, if there are no hours given to Friendship, if it is forever postponed to unimportant duties and relations? Friendship is first, Friendship last. But it is equally impossible to forget our Friends, and to make them answer to our ideal. When they say farewell, then indeed we begin to keep them company. How often we find ourselves turning our backs on our actual Friends, that we may go and meet their ideal cousins. I would that I were worthy to be any man's Friend.

What is commonly honored with the name of Friendship is no very profound or powerful instinct. Men do not, after all, *love* their Friends greatly. I do not often see the farmers made seers and wise to the verge of insanity by their Friendship for one another. They are not often transfigured and translated by love in each other's presence. I do not observe them purified, refined, and elevated by the love of a man. If one abates a little the price of his wood, or gives a neighbor his vote at town meeting, or a barrel of apples, or lends him his wagon frequently, it is esteemed a rare instance of Friendship. Nor do the farmers' wives lead lives consecrated to Friendship. I do not see the pair of farmer Friends of either sex prepared to stand against the world. There are only two or three couples in history. To say that a man is your Friend means commonly no more than this, that he is not your enemy. Most contemplate only what would be the accidental and trifling advantages of Friendship, so that the Friend can assist in time of need, by his substance, or his influence, or his counsel; but he who foresees such advantages in this relation proves himself blind to its real advantage, or indeed wholly inexperienced in the relation itself. Such services are particular and menial, compared with the perpetual and all-embracing service which it is. Even the utmost good will and harmony and practical kindness are not sufficient for Friendship, for Friends do not live in harmony merely, as some say, but in melody. We do not wish for Friends to feed and clothe our bodies—neighbors are kind enough for that—but to do the like office to our spirits. For this few are rich enough, however well disposed they may be. For the most part we stupidly confound one man with another. The dull distinguish only races or nations, or at most classes, but the wise man, individuals. To his Friend a man's peculiar character appears in every feature and in every action, and it is thus drawn out and improved by him. . . .

All the abuses which are the object of reform with the philanthropist, the statesman, and the housekeeper are unconsciously amended in the intercourse of Friends. A Friend is one who incessantly pays us the compliment of expecting from us all the virtues, and who can appreciate them in us. It takes two to speak the truth—one to speak, and another to hear. How can one treat with magnanimity mere wood and stone? If we dealt only with the false and dishonest, we should at last forget how to speak truth. Only lovers know the value and magnanimity of truth, while traders prize a cheap honesty, and neighbors and acquaintances a cheap civility. In our daily intercourse with men, our nobler faculties are dormant and suffered to rust. None will pay us the compliment to expect nobleness from us. Though we have gold to give, they demand only copper. We ask our neighbor to suffer himself to be dealt with truly, sincerely, nobly; but he answers no by his deafness. He does not even hear this prayer. He says practically, I will be content if you treat me as "no better than I should be," as deceitful, mean, dishonest, and selfish. For the most part, we are contented so to deal and to be dealt with, and we do not think that for the mass of men there is any truer and nobler relation possible. A man may have *good* neighbors, so called, and acquaintances, and even companions, wife, parents, brothers, sisters, children, who meet himself and one another on this ground only. The State does not demand justice of its members, but thinks that it succeeds very well with the least degree of it, hardly more than rogues practice; and so do the neighborhood and the family. What is commonly called Friendship even is only a little more honor among rogues.

But sometimes we are said to *love* another, that is, to stand in a true relation to him, so that we give the best to, and receive the best from, him. Between whom there is hearty truth, there is love; and in proportion to our truthfulness and confidence in one another, our lives are divine and miraculous, and answer to our ideal. There are passages of affection in our intercourse with mortal men and women, such as no prophecy had taught us to expect, which transcend our earthly life, and anticipate Heaven for us. What is this Love that may come right into the middle of a prosaic Goffstown day, equal to any of the gods? that discovers a new world, fair and fresh and eternal, occupying the place of the old one, when to the common eye a dust has settled on the universe?—which world cannot else be reached, and does not exist. What other words, we may almost ask, are memorable and worthy to be repeated than those which love has inspired? . . .

. . . Friendship takes place between those who have an affinity for one another, and is a perfectly natural and inevitable result. No professions nor advances will avail. Even speech, at first, necessarily has nothing to do with it; but it follows after silence, as the buds in the graft do not put forth into leaves till long after the graft has taken. It is a drama in which the parties have no part to act. We are all Mussulmans and fatalists in this respect. Impatient and uncertain lovers think that they must say or do something kind whenever they meet; they must never be cold. But they who are Friends do not do what they *think* they must, but what they *must*. Even their Friendship is to some extent but a sublime phenomenon to them.

The true and not despairing Friend will address his Friend in some such terms as these. . . .

"You are the fact in a fiction, you are the truth more strange and admirable than fiction. Consent only to be what you are. I alone will never stand in your way. . . ."

The Friend asks no return but that his Friend will religiously accept and wear and not disgrace his apotheosis of him. They cherish each other's hopes. They are kind to each other's dreams.

Though the poet says, "'Tis the pre-eminence of Friendship to impute excellence," yet we can never praise our Friend, nor esteem him praiseworthy, nor let him think that he can please us by any *behavior*, or ever *treat* us well enough. That kindness which has so good a reputation elsewhere can least of all consist with this relation, and no such affront can be offered to a Friend, as a conscious goodwill, a friendliness which is not a necessity of the Friend's nature. . . .

Confucius said, "Never contract Friendship with a man who is no better than thyself." It is the merit and preservation of Friendship that it takes place on a level higher than the actual characters of the parties would seem to warrant. The rays of light come to us in such a curve that every man whom we meet appears to be taller than he actually is. Such foundation has civility. My Friend is that one whom I can associate with my choicest thought. . . .

. . . There are times when we have had enough even of our Friends, when we begin inevitably to profane one another, and must withdraw religiously into solitude and silence, the better to prepare ourselves for a loftier intimacy. Silence is the ambrosial night in the intercourse of Friends, in which their sincerity is recruited and takes deeper root.

Friendship is never established as an understood relation. Do you demand that I be less your Friend that you may know it? Yet what right have I to think that another cherishes so rare a sentiment for me? It is a miracle which requires constant proofs. It is an exercise of the purest imagination and the rarest faith. It says by a silent but eloquent behavior, "I will be so related to thee as thou canst imagine; even so thou mayest believe. I will spend truth, all my wealth on thee,"—and the Friend responds silently through his nature and life, and treats his Friend with the same divine courtesy. He knows us literally through thick and thin. He never asks for a sign of love, but can distinguish it by the features which it naturally wears. We never need to stand upon ceremony with him with regard to his visits. Wait not till I invite thee, but observe that I am glad to see thee when thou comest. It would be paying too dear for thy visit to ask for it. Where my Friend lives there are all riches and every attraction, and no slight obstacle can keep me from him. . . .

The language of Friendship is not words, but meanings. It is an intelligence above language. One imagines endless conversations with his Friend, in which the tongue shall be loosed, and thoughts be spoken without hesitancy or end; but the experience is commonly far otherwise. Acquaintances may come and go, and have a word ready for every occasion; but what puny word shall he utter whose very breath is thought and meaning? . . .

. . . Their relation implies such qualities as the warrior prizes; for it takes a valor to open the hearts of men as well as the gates of castles. It is not an idle sympathy and mutual consolation merely, but a heroic sympathy of aspiration and endeavor. . . .

. . . A base Friendship is of a narrowing and exclusive tendency, but a noble one is not exclusive; its very superfluity and dispersed love is the humanity which sweetens society, and sympathizes with foreign nations; for though its foundations are private, it is, in effect, a public affair and a public advantage, and the Friend, more than the father of a family, deserves well of the state.

The only danger in Friendship is that it will end. It is a delicate plant, though a native. The least unworthiness, even if it be unknown to one's self, vitiates it. Let the Friend know that those faults which he observes in his Friend his own faults attract. There is no rule more invariable than that we are paid for our suspicions by finding what we suspected. By our narrowness and prejudices we say, I will have so much and such of you, my Friend, no more. Perhaps there are none charitable, none disinterested, none wise, noble, and heroic enough, for a true and lasting Friendship.

I sometimes hear my Friends complain finely that I do not appreciate their fineness. I shall not tell them whether I do or not. As if they expected a vote of thanks for every fine thing which they uttered or did. Who knows but it was finely appreciated. It may be that your silence was the finest thing of the two. There are some things which a man never speaks of, which are much finer kept silent about. To the highest communications we only lend a silent ear. Our finest relations are not simply kept silent about, but buried under a positive depth of silence never to be revealed. It may be that we are not even yet acquainted. In human intercourse the tragedy begins, not when there is misunderstanding about words, but when silence is not understood. Then there can never be an explanation. What avails it that another loves you, if he does not understand you? Such love is a curse. What sort of companions are they who are presuming always that their silence is more expressive than yours? How foolish, and inconsiderate, and unjust, to conduct as if you were the only party aggrieved! Has not your Friend always equal ground of complaint? No doubt my Friends sometimes speak to me in vain, but they do not know what things I hear which they are not aware that they have spoken. I know that I have frequently disappointed them by not giving them words when they expected them, or such as they expected. Whenever I see my Friend I speak to him; but the expecter, the man with the ears, is not he. They will complain too that you are hard. O ye that would have the cocoanut wrong side outwards, when next I weep I will let you know. They ask for words and deeds, when a true relation is word and deed. If they know not of these things, how can they be informed? We often forbear to confess our feelings, not from pride, but for fear that we could not continue to love the one who required us to give such proof of our affection. . . .

For a companion, I require one who will make an equal demand on me with my own genius. Such a one will always be rightly tolerant. It is suicide, and corrupts good manners, to welcome any less than this. I value and trust those who love and praise my aspiration rather than my performance. If you would not stop to look at me, but look whither I am looking, and farther, then my education could not dispense with your company. . . .

Ignorance and bungling with love are better than wisdom and skill without. There may be courtesy, there may be even temper, and wit, and talent, and sparkling conversation, there may be good will even—and yet the humanest and divinest faculties pine for exercise. Our life without love is like coke and ashes. Men may be pure as alabaster and Parian marble, elegant as a Tuscan villa, sublime as Niagara, and yet if there is no milk mingled with the wine at their entertainments, better is the hospitality of Goths and Vandals.

My Friend is not of some other race or family of men, but flesh of my flesh, bone of my bone. He is my real brother. I see his nature groping yonder so like mine. We do not live far apart. Have not the fates associated us in many ways? It says, in the *Vishnu Purana:* "Seven paces together is sufficient for the friendship of the virtuous, but thou and I have dwelt together." Is it of no significance that we have so long partaken of the same loaf, drunk at the same fountain, breathed the same air summer and winter, felt the same heat and cold; that the same fruits have been pleased to refresh us both, and we have never had a thought of different fiber the one from the other! . . .

But all that can be said of Friendship is like botany to flowers. How can the understanding take account of its friendliness?

STUDY QUESTIONS

1. What is the danger in trying to force a friend into the Ideal one has molded for them?
2. Why does Thoreau think silence is so important to a true friendship? What can be communicated by silence that cannot be communicated with speech?
3. Why is it important for a friend to see us not as we are but as what we aspire to be? Are there ever times when such an attitude would be wrong?
4. How does Thoreau think friendship can keep an individual in the path of a moral life?

13

Throw the Emptiness out of Your Arms: Rilke's Doctrine of Nonpossessive Love

William H. Gass

William H. Gass is David May Distinguished University Professor in the Humanities at Washington University in Saint Louis. A novelist, literary critic, and philosopher, he is the author of *In the Heart of the Heart of the Country* and *Habitations of the Word.*

For a wide range of reasons, writing about love is a risky undertaking. It can't help but be revelatory. The point at which you begin, the assumptions you make, the elements you omit or ignore, emphasize or distort, the sorts of expository steps you take, the conclusions you draw: each choice will add a line to your portrait, as will the lyricism you display, your cynicism, scorn, or derision, whether you approach your subject as a psychologist, philosopher, or poet, and whether you adopt a scholar's scrupulosity, a theorist's elevation, the artist's ardency, or a politician's pose.

It is a word, furthermore, which the hypocrisies of society have corrupted. It has been suspiciously in the service of too many masters, the whole time wearing a most welcoming face, while want, desire, lust, need, pleasure even, reassurance, respect, admiration, friendship—as problematic as each is—concern, devotion, sacrifice, fidelity, passion, jealousy, and other states of character and feeling rise and fall in interest or estimation because everyone wants to hire love—of mother, country, God—to front for them, to do their business and support their cause.

One would suppose that love's opposite number would be hate, but this is rarely the case, although to love your country, at the very least, means to mistrust every other nation. More often death has the other star part, or sometimes loss does, or ennui.

Our language suggests that love is a wholly engrossing condition and can be expected to call upon the full range of our faculties, to demand our deepest and most continuous attention. Love absorbs the way the best paper towels are said to absorb. Love obsesses as if brought on by a whiff of seductive perfume. It cancels comradeship, replaces respect, absolves duty, supersedes every other inclination. The poet says that love feeds on itself like a fire, and must be fed its own flames, as if Prometheus were to dine on his own entrails instead of being pecked by the beaks of those vulturous birds. Is love then a punishment for the theft of a heart? Well, perhaps. It's also been argued that love's true opposite is justice.

Is there another state of soul that accepts the same class of modifiers, that demands a similar set of objects, that surrounds itself with prepositions of the same kind? Grammatically, being in love seems like being in pain. One is simply found there or thrown there like a cat in heat or a criminal in prison. But love's resemblance to pain is not perfect: I cannot have a love in my foot or a great pain for Jan Sibelius. Want and need might run on parallel syntactical tracks, but only for a time, because, although we fall in love as though it were an opening in the earth, and out of love as though it were a tree, want and need are simply too low down to fall from and too instinctive to fade. Sometimes it is sudden as a slap . . . the onset of love; sometimes we Alice into it, and fall through long parts of life as through a dream.

I can be peeved by you, and I can peeve you too, but I cannot be in peeve, only in a pet, in a state, in a snit, in a stew. I can find myself full of hate or I can run out of love as though both were a fuel; however, I can't make hate the way I make time, or make do, or make haste, or make love, as if hate or love were a hat. To make love is to "have" sex the way one might have a second helping of potatoes, but hate has no program to be fulfilled; there are no guidelines, no handbooks, for hate. And if sex didn't hide inside of love like a weevil in a biscuit, love and hate would be one of grammar's twins. However, hate is not a thing, like tracks, that can be made by putting a foot down. Hate has no space. Hate appears and disappears in us like a fever, whereas love is like a trap waiting to be sprung. Almost like a season, it has its time; almost like a climate, it has its place.

What more can usage tell us? That cupid has his bow, but only anger can be aimed. That "lovely" has no more to do with "love" than "like" with "likely." It's true that "like" is a love-like word, yet I can like Mike and still not do anything for the like of Mike. Certainly, joy is not its linguistic image, because joy is verbally passive; it's not jealousy, which is never a verb; it's not glee, which is never a noun; it's not envy, which can't be sent through the mail like a letter-bomb.

Some people claim that love resembles death because both involve the loss of self (our small deaths are the culminations of sex the way our one large and lasting death is the completion of life), whereas others will argue that our love of our neighbor is adulterous self-love in disguise and that the beloved is merely a mirror. Love is a form of flattery, of systematic overestimation. It is a power play, a ploy in the game of seduction. It is the parent we thought we wanted. Were we a grapefruit, it would be our other half. It is simply a hormonal imbalance and something we suffer at sixteen like acne, angst, and insecurity. It is the mutual adjustment of people to one another for their joint comfort. It is the highest condition of the soul. It is the desire to turn the other cheek as if spanking were a pleasure. It is a jangle of the genitals like a jingle of keys. It is one thing for women—tender and prolonged—another for men—brutal and brief. It is sacrificial and a state of devotion. It is a humiliating illness. It is union; it is takeover; it is buyout. Above all, it is big business. The commercialization of love has become so complete, it is now a word embarrassing to speak. Among teenagers, the term is reserved exclusively for french fries and phonograph records. It is uncool as can be.

Love wears out like a suit of clothes. Love comes and goes like the clouds. Love is the lie of the lover and the belief of the beloved. "To love" and "to believe" have the same etymological companions: "leman," or dear one, of course, and "lief" as in "leave" or permission to be absent.

Despite such roots, love is supposed to be a long-term proposition like loyalty, obedience, and trust, and therefore unlike lust, which is expected to be as brief as the flare of a match, and to be indelicate if prolonged beyond that. In addition, love is initially reserved for elevated objects: husbands, nations, gods, ideals; so that one's love of the Buick car is a case of commercial hyperbole; so that, of boating or broccoli, one is properly only fond; but, if the objects of love begin by being high and mighty—put on a pedestal like a poop spot for pigeons—they are not necessarily perfect, nor is their position permanent, because they will descend from their eminence in time; they will decline—indeed, they are this moment being seen through; they have, in fact, sagged like a slowing line of fast talk. To repeat an old saw: Familiarity seeds every intimacy with contempt. So the romantic realms of love grow unworthy like gardens overwhelmed with weeds. What then, about the so-called objects of love, is honestly lovable?

Among husbands, is it their bankrolls? Concerning boyfriends, is it their biceps, or the rumble-seats of their runabouts? And the pubic patch of the girl next door, is it not the real source of one's youthful wonder and despair?

I know of no more frequently cited word in *The Oxford Dictionary of Quotations* than "love," and the situation with *Bartlett's* is the same. Shouldn't this support the suspicion, along with rump-shaped hearts on bumper stickers, *billets-doux* and lying valentines, billboards, broadcasts, and inflammatory photos, that in our language there may be no more bankrupt a word? Still, these days, bankruptcy does not prevent one from continuing to do a very profitable business.

The poet Rainer Maria Rilke grew up surrounded by many examples of the fraudulent usage we are now accustomed to. Just because we're born, and even at the moment of our initial outcry, we are beloved: by God as a fresh soul to be saved; by the Nation as another mother or a future man-at-arms; by the Economy as an eventual customer; by each parent because they admire the miracle of their loins and because to do otherwise than love their child is unnatural; but also because a son will attest to his father's virility; he will carry on the family name and follow in his father's footsteps; because daughter will doubtless be beautiful, marry money, and care for papa in his gouty age, mama in her weeds; thus, in this way, the circle of beloving will widen to include every local aunt and uncle, grandthis and grandthat, peekaboo and kissing cousins, family chums and other seducers; since clearly the family comes first—it is the human nest—and whatever enlarges the family enlarges life, increases its clannish power, multiplies the number of hands for profitable labor.

What a fortunate child—to be bound by so many lines of love! lifted up by so many helping hands!

Rilke's parents had lost a daughter the year before they begot Renée, hoping for another daughter to replace her, and, until he was ready to enter school, his mother got him up girlishly, combed his curls, encouraged him to call his good self Sophie, and handled him like a china doll, cooing and cuddling his shiny porcelainities until such time as he was abruptly put away in a drawer. Later, with a recognition that resembled Gertrude Stein's, Rilke realized that someone else had had to die in order to provide him with a place in life.

His mother had aspired, when she married, to something grander than she got, though she poured cheap wine in better bottles and in other ways tried to keep up appearances. During his first year, Rilke's nurses came and went like hours of the day. His time as a toy continued. Affection, lit like a lamp, would be blown out by any sudden whim. As his parents drew away from one another like the trains his father oversaw, Rilke was more and more frequently farmed out by his mother, for whom a small boy was a social drag, to this or that carrier of concern. The child began to believe that love, like money, time, and food, was in limited supply and that what went into one life could not go into another.

> My mother spread her presents at the feet
> of those poor saints hewn of heart wood.
> Mute, unmoving, and amazed, they stood
> behind the pews, so straight and complete.
>
> They neglected to thank her, too,
> for her fervently offered gift.
> The little dark her candles lift
> was all of her faith they knew.
>
> Still my mother gave, in a paper roll,
> these flowers with their fragile blooms,
> which she took from a bowl in our modest rooms,
> in the sight and longing of my soul.*

His mother's religiosity was always on simmer, if not on boil, but its turbulence took place, Rilke increasingly felt, in a shallow pot. "I am horrified," he wrote Lou Salomé, "by her scatter-brained piety, by her pigheaded faith, by all those twisted and disfiguring things to which she has fastened

* The translations of Rilke are by the author.

herself, she who is as empty as a dress, ghostlike and terrible. And that I'm her child, that I came into the world through a scarcely perceptible hole in the paper of this faded wall. . . ."

This is love, we are told: Here are mother and father being nice to one another, exchanging gifts, loving their furniture, their cat, their child; here is a faintly smiling madonna, and there a stern saint, and now a priest, and then a nurse, a friend, a dog whose tail wags; but on top of what we are told, like a cold hand, soon lies what we see and feel and finally know: the mother who picks us up and puts us down like a hand of cards; the joyful union that parts, perhaps like wet paper, without a sound, in front of our fearful eyes; the cat who sings its sex in the night and runs away; those saints who swallow only candlesmoke and say nothing; the dog whose devotions knock us down; or the priest, with a forced warmth heating his polished face, who twists the arm of an unruly acolyte because the boy doesn't dare yelp during the service; the nurse who says "good night, sleep tight" over the closing latches of her traveling bags; and finally those friends . . . those friends who skip scornfully away to play with children who have called us dreadful names: which layer is the layer of love? Is it only made of words—that kiss called "lip service," that caress called "shake hands," that welcome that feels like "good-by"?

During childhood, contradiction paves every avenue of feeling, and we grow up in bewilderment like a bird in a ballroom, with all that space and none meant for flying, a wide, shining floor and nowhere to light. So out of the lies and confusions of every day the child constructs a way to cope, part of which will comprise a general manner of being in, and making, love. So from the contrast between the official language of love and the unofficial facts of life is born a dream of what this pain, this passion, this obsession, this belief, this relation, ought to be. Yes, love is some sort of ideal relation, but does it have a price and a payoff like that of husband and wife; ought it to resemble that of the master and the slave; is it the connection of con to conned, of the fanatic to his faith?

Rilke eventually learned what he thought it was, because, when he sought a mother in his mistress instead of a mistress, leaning, as one into the wind, on Lou Salomé's spirit, she finally sent him off into the world again—out of her schoolroom, bed, and maternal hug—she did so, she said, because of his increasing dependency, because of her need for freedom to develop, because of a similar hope on her part for himself and his art; and, although he did not realize it all at once, he would come to understand how we constantly endeavor to match the ideology of love we've learned with the reality of its practice; to harmonize our own mutilated methods with those we've dreamed. We seek to reconstitute an improved past in the present. Not only do we search for surrogate parents—parents who would neither intimidate nor disappoint—but we attempt to create an environment in which our reenactments will correct every error and put the world right. We regress to rework and repair, because, inside of each of us, for a long time, lives an ear which still trusts what it heard, and an eye which still wishes to see such things as have been said to be. Yet day by day that child disappears until we enter the end without our heartfelt and hoped for beginnings; not because we've grown out of our need for teddy bears, but because our spirit no longer has the strength for that kind of complete and innocent embrace.

Our enterprises meet defeat again and again. In order to repair the past we must recreate the essential conditions of its breakdown. Then the same face appears, saying the same cruel words, doing the same disenchanting things, and we helplessly repeat our response—Freud says compulsively—and in that way enrich another bad habit at the expense of our happiness.

Rilke sought solace in an art colony called Worpswede, which was located in the bog country not far from Bremen—a spare, flat land valued for its isolation and its light. There he met his future wife as well as the painter, Paula Becker, whom he fancied first. The rapidity with which these relations were secured can be accounted for, in part, by the cruise ship atmosphere such colonies often have, but mainly because Rilke simply threw himself in the air and cried "Catch!"

Carla Westhoff caught him; a cottage caught him; domesticity seemed to swaddle him and protect him with its warmth. Love is always dreamed before it is performed, and Rilke imagined himself in soft lamplight standing before his stove preparing a simple supper for his beloved—perhaps a vegetable, he writes her, perhaps a bit of porridge. He envisions a dish of honey gleaming on the table, butter pale as ivory, a long, narrow platter of Westphalian ham "larded with strips of white fat like an evening sky banded by clouds," and wheat-colored tea in glasses, too, all standing on a Russian cloth. Huge lemons, reddish tangerines, silver saucers are invited, and then long-stemmed roses, of course, to complete this picture of quiet, unanxious sensuality. We need not describe the layer of boring chores, the clutter of mismated china, sticky pots, and soiled silver, annoying habits and nervous tics, which will cloud the rich cloth when reality arrives; and the bellowing of the baby, her repeated poops, the sighs of reproach, the pure passages of self-pity which will violin from one small room to another before disappearing out the door—a poor smell seeking to improve itself by flight.

He possesses his wife. Her friends observe it: how he has enthralled her. Whereas she first encompasses and then possesses the child. On the other hand, when the couple appears in public, the large and robust Clara seems to have her little Rilke beneath her arm (a few wrote) like a pet pooch. Routines take over. How in the world can three live as one? In the same pout spot, the boudoir, in the same pantry? Clara concentrates on Rilke, and it compacts him. He feels himself growing hard, rindlike, remorseless.

Ich liebe dich. I love you. No sentence from a judge could be more threatening. It means that I am giving you a gift you may not want. I am making it very easy for you to injure me—if I am not making it inevitable—and in that way controlling your behavior. It means I want you as an adjunct to my life, or it means that I can survive like mistletoe or moss: only on the side of someone. It means that one way or other I intend to own you.

Will you be mine? Don't we ask that? Don't we desire that? Demand that? This breast, this thigh, this bankbook, this fine house, this princely carriage, this improved place in society. Don't we wait impatiently for the loved one's answer: I am yours? In *The Book of Hours* Rilke writes his first poem of possession, as reiterative as Pound's canto on usury and as fiercely full of invective. Mine, the verses chant. Mine: this land, this life, this wife, the stars. My dog? Mine, yes. My child? Mine, of course. Both the prince and the peasant are mine, as well as the flag of my country. What next? *Mein Gott.* From now on Rilke will wonder, when it comes to love, what it means, not to give, but to receive it—this onslaught; what it means to be hunted by loneliness and pursued by all the passions of possession.

Ownership is as awful as enslavement, for you shall see the marks of your fingers about wrists and ankles, the bruises of your angry eyes on cheeks and arms, the constriction of the chest, the terrible narrowing of a life to a whistle, to a whisper.

To take hold of someone is to be taken hold of. Isn't the hug a gesture of mutual envelopment? And so he tries to persuade his female admirers of the virtue of distance, and he sings to them through the safety of the posted page about the beauty of their adjacent solitudes and encourages them to stand on tiptoe (right where they are), the better to breathe the scent of their own society. When we hold on to one another, we do so only to go under together; we impoverish ourselves because no one person can become a world; to love this way is to live a surrogate life. "Throw the emptiness out of your arms," he will write in *The First Elegy*, "to broaden the spaces we breathe—

maybe the birds will feel the amplified air with an inner flight." Not holding on, then, but letting go, becomes, in love, its fullest expression.

Certainly there is sadness in change, but change is our condition. There is not a moment that isn't purely momentary. Arrival and departure share the same space, and have, in a sense, the same spelling.

> How I have felt it, that nameless state called
> parting,
> and how I feel it still: a dark, sharp, heartless
> Something that displays, holds out with unapparent
> hands,
> a perfect union to us, while tearing it in two.
>
> With what wide-open eyes I've watched whatever
> was, while calling to me, loosening its hold,
> remaining in the road behind as though all
> womankind,
> yet small and white and nothing more than this:
>
> a waving which has blown the hair beyond its
> brow,
> a slight, continuous flutter—scarcely now
> explicable: perhaps the tremor of a plum-tree
> and the bough a startled cuckoo has set free.

It is the poet's purpose to put the world in words, and, in that way, hold it steady for us. The poet can write of love, too, in a similarly immortalizing fashion. But love alters its lovers even as they love, so that their love is altered too, and the next kiss comes from a different mouth and is pressed to a different breast.

> Lovers, satisfied by one another, I am asking you
> about us. You embrace, but where's your proof?
> Look, sometimes it happens that my hands grow to
> know
> one another, or that my heavy head seeks their
> shelter.
> That yields me a slender sensation. But who wants
> to live just for that?
> You though, who, in one another's passion,
> grow until, near bursting, plead: "No more . . ."
> you, who, beneath one another's groping, swell
> with juice like the grapes of a vintage year;
> you, who may go like a bud into another's blossoming:
> I am asking you about us. I know
> you touch so blissfully because your touch survives
> such bliss,
> because the flesh you caress so tenderly stays flesh;
> because just below your fingertip you feel the tip of
> pure duration.
> So you expect eternity to entwine itself in your embrace.
> And yet, when you have endured the fear of that
> first look,
> the longing, later, at the window, and your first turn
> about the garden together: lovers, are you any
> longer what you were?
> When you lift yourselves up to one another's lips,
> and slip wine into wine like an added flavor: oh,
> how strangely
> soon is each drinker's disappearance from the ceremony.

Rilke and his wife set one another free, freeing their infant at the same time by leaving him, blanket and basket, in the rushes of a relative. In Paris, where Rilke goes to write on Rodin, he learns about another kind of love—that of the artist for his work, and about another kind of life—one in which women are only a relaxation; he learns of an existence utterly devoted to things—things observed, things made, things preserved; but what strikes him first are the streets and people of Paris itself, and his profound sense of estrangement from them—of disgust, loneliness, fear, despair; so that death is the topic which pursues his pen.

Love and death: a Germanic theme indeed. Just as going and coming are one, just as beginnings and endings overlap, so are loving and ceasing to love, living and ceasing to live, reciprocals, and as we mature our death matures too (for every teeter, there's a totter—that's the rule), the way one wave rolls up the beach while another wave recedes, and each roar of the surf is succeeded by a quiet hiss.

O Lord, grant each of us our own ripe death,
the dying fall that goes through life—
its love, significance, and need—like breath.

For we are nothing but the bark and burrs.
The great death we bear within ourselves
is the fruit which every growing serves.

For its sake young girls grow their charms,
as if a tree-like music issued from a lyre;
for its sake small boys long to shoulder arms,
and women lean on them to listen and inspire
these not yet men to share their heart's alarms.
For its sake all that's seen is seen sustained
by change itself, as if the frozen were the fire;
and the work of every artisan maintained
this myth and made a world out of this fruit,
brought frost to it, wind, sunlight, rain.
And into it life's warmth has followed suit,
heart's heat absorbed, the fever of the brain:
Yet when the angels swoop to pick us clean,
they shall find that all our fruits are green.

If the right kind of love releases all things to return to their natures, then dying is an equivalent letting go of life; it is a refusal, any longer, to possess it. This thought is old enough to have preceded Plato, but the renunciation involved here is only of ownership and assimilation, of conquest and compulsion, which is to be replaced by a respect for difference and an encouragement of freedom. Our obligation to life is to experience the qualities of things, to love otherness, and to stand guard over every solitude.

William James remarked that the greatest chasm we could encounter in nature was that between two minds, and it has always been the aim of romantic love to cross that abyss, to create a new creature made of mingled intimacies, to fill one soul with another, thus overcoming difference, which is always felt to be threatening, and replacing personal autonomy with the mutual dependencies of the loving couple. Rilke, one of the greatest and most extreme of romantic poets, does not subscribe to this Dionysian dream, however, but rather emphasizes the Apollonian denial of mergers and mixtures, and the superior functions of detachment. "A togetherness between two people is an impossibility," he writes; and when we realize that between one consciousness and another there is more distance than between the farthest stars, then a side-by-side life will become possible, like that of two monads whose worlds are distinct, complete, and unimpeachable, yet divinely harmonious.

I have thought it important to set down a few of the facts which can be lifted from Rilke's biography in order to insist (before being forced to admit) that his theory of love is an obvious rationalization and excuse for his own conduct. Rilke was unable to meet the demands of familial intimacy. He wanted to be, as a poet, always superior to the drudgeries of daily life; and if he encouraged us and himself to embrace the beauty and reality of all things, he was still not about to take hold of the household mop; nor could the spiritual self he aspired to survive being heard going to the bathroom, or observed picking its nose. This kind of quartered closeness—in which another person learns to accept us as we have learned to accept ourselves, thereby sanctioning that acceptance—was not possible for him. He was unable to forgive his stomach for growling, or lewdness for following him through his long bouts of solitude, or the moments, so untranscendental, when he allowed his longing to spring out of his pants.

Indeed, we never have enough of these petty, even puerile, details: precisely how he felt, as a child, hearing the conversations of visitors while screened by the simplest of thin partitions from the guests in the living room; or with what whitened face his first love, Valerie von David-Rhonfeld, read his practice letter of farewell: "Dear Vally, thank you for the gift of freedom . . . ," or the quality of his last visit to Lou's lips, or his reaction, each time, to Rodin's earthy pursuit of pleasure; because, of love, there is no *a priori* knowledge; because it is, I am convinced, only from the innumerable accumulations of these impressions that one's overall feeling about love arises: both one's understanding of what it is supposed to be (an overwhelming and permanent passion); one's perception of what it actually is (a whimsically exercised proprietory power); and one's picture of how it ought ideally to be (a devotion like that for painting and poetry); it is these leaves, little by little and layer after layer, which build up the floor of the forest, despite the occasional hard knocks and exceptional traumas, like storms, which disturb it, since even these primal scenes and secret shames are made of so many small discriminations—a leer, a wink, the flip of a skirt, an odor out of place, an overheard word, a sigh out of sight—which mysteriously play some part in the effect of the whole.

Rilke's intense feeling for the instability of things: of how many disappointments is that sense the sum? since it led him to protect himself by erasing relations as rapidly as they were inscribed; and into what unknown number of rented rooms did his need to justify the certainty that "all is fleeting" consequently drive him?

Caught in relationships which produced nothing but acute and constant embarrassment, it is not surprising that we find that word "freedom," in the form of a brutal cliché, in his first farewell, or that his model for a proper life was composed of Lou Salomé's struggle to achieve her independence (though tied to a husband who had snared her through an attempted suicide), as well as Auguste Rodin's success in creating freely despite the curse of custom; so it was freedom from family he sought, freedom from community, from country, from the local language, from the military and a militarized education, from the inanities of courtship, the mock-heroics of the husband and the manliness of the male, from the details of a daily life determined by the economic exercycle or measured in amounts of cash, from sentimental celebrations of all kinds and those lies which become the blackmail and the bribes we pay to existence; because we ordinarily cannot escape it: the fact that our feelings are so rarely really ours and spring from us as simply and directly as grass, for even the grass is mowed and fertilized and seeded, so our comparison has to be with the free, unwanted weed; in that guise the genuine appears—out of place, improper, gauche—because our feelings have been institutionalized like someone sick or mad, or they've been the "up" in our upbringing, what we've been taught to believe we can manage if we can earn enough to pay their price—so shall our tastes and temperament change through a successful life from tin lizzie to limousine, from canned peas to caviar and snails, from "wham bam, thank you, ma'am" to muff dives done according to Olympic regs and textbook standards.

We think we go to bed with our eager groom, our blushing bride, when we go to bed with the principles of the Republic and in the best interests of Chambers of Commerce and Bureaus of Better Business.

We are not only victims of our love and work life, we also need to defend our flights and seeming failures, to justify ourselves before our inner bench. We can do that by finding reasons for what we may have done dumbbellishly and in the dark, as if wisdom would have chosen the same path, gone for the same goals, served and celebrated the same ideals.

If love is the proper feeling to have for whatever is best, then we merely have to find whatever is best. If love is truly good for both lover and beloved, then acts of love ought to be honest acts of aid and comfort. Love ought to be an improvement and not an indulgence. Love ought to be given freely to any excellence and not mocked by being lavished on the unworthy. There is no higher service we can render our fellows than to increase their freedom; therefore our declarations of love ought also to be declarations of our loved one's independence. Weak as we are, we may not be able to be moral toward all men, but at least we ought to be able to treat those we claim we love as autonomous souls and ends-in-themselves.

But love says gimme; love says, "you play the slave and I'll play the master"; love says comfort me, flatter me, complete me, forgive me; love says reflect my weakness as a show of strength; so it seems notably hard-boiled to insist that love ought to seek out value and serve it, whether in others or in one's self, whether in persons or in things. But if I love the good in you, do I love you or just the good? And if I love your beauty, is it you or beauty I adore?

Rilke is too complete a poet to chase the philosopher's wisps. It is not the beauty of the landscape but the landscape that is real, just as the character you or I presumably have cannot be removed like an appendix or pulled out like a tooth but suffuses itself through the soul the way tea leaves steep in tea water.

It is true that I may be more devoted to a principle than to my spouse, motor car, or dog, but if I am treating you as an end rather than as a mere means out of obedience to a rule rather than from affection, the word that describes the case should rather be "justice" than "love."

If our reward for being loved is solitude preserved and freedom encouraged, we may pass right through it, like the tail of a distant comet, and never feel the wash, thus avoiding indebtedness and gratitude as well as love; but love, as we say, is strong stuff in any version of its nature and affects its object willy nilly. Perhaps, when we declare ourselves: "I love you!" it is best if we are never believed, because who knows what damage the knowledge of our love may do; how it may be taken; what weaknesses it may threaten with exposure; what acceptance it may encounter; what revulsion it may cause?

Under the circumstances (and following the advice of Spinoza), it is safer to love objects which can more easily withstand affection than we can; from whom no grateful response can be demanded; and whose freedom is not likely to tax our own generosity. That is, such a love as a musician has for music is normally purer than a spouse's for a spouse, or a daddy for his Sugar, and is probably not going to demean or enslave the soul of a single song. On the other hand, this displacement of love from person to thing is not in the spirit of Spinoza after all, since Spinoza recommended loving thingless objects, objects of intellect, objects of thought, acts of intelligence; whereas the poet wants his human consciousness (in which Spinoza's objects also, if not exclusively, exist) first of all improved past understanding into wonderment and then lodged intrinsically within the net and measure of the thing itself—how strongly? as strongly as a molecule holds its elements in thrall.

Freedom scarcely needs a poet's endorsement; but why is solitude its equal? Because freedom finally means the opportunity to pursue ourselves, not in the supermarket sense or in terms of stocks and bonds, but in terms of the great vast theater of our head, the space of our imagination, the place where, if we can, we create. What better thing can we do for this momentary and material world than bring it within and set it up in an inner and immaterial and invisible world where consciousness is king and queen, the whole court and the castle?

> Are we, perhaps, here just to utter: house,
> bridge, fountain, gate, jug, fruit tree, window—
> at most: column, tower . . . but to utter them, remember,
> to speak in a way which the named never dreamed
> they could be. Isn't it the hidden purpose
> of this cunning earth, in urging on lovers
> to remake itself in the forms of their feeling?

In innerworld space the wide-open world can rest in peace.

> These things whose life
> is a constant leaving, they know when you praise them.
> Transient, they trust us, the most unremaining, to come
> to their rescue; they wish us to alter them utterly,
> whatever's without our invisible hearts, into—so endlessly—us!
> Whoever we are.

There is one characteristic that is curiously absent from most philosophical accounts of virtue or the higher feelings—a characteristic I have already briefly touched on—and it concerns the way these qualities appear in the people who are supposed to have them, so that we are ready to say that they *are* theirs (whatever accounts for "the interesting man" in Ortega y Gasset's essay *On Love* or comprises "the great-souled one" in Aristotle); for there are some women, for instance, who seem to wear their beauty like a mask; there is no articulation of the spirit in their otherwise perfect faces; and other sorts in whom honesty resides like a guest who has come for a weekend visit, or what about that erotic passion which seems to have seized a soul as suddenly as a hiccup? A few people are so up-front about their virtues, they might be bearing sandwich boards, while others are discreet or even timid. There exist those who are scrupulous about money but careless with the truth. Some thieves will steal your change, others your time, others again will only Robin Hood, while still others have to filch knickknacks out of dime stores or swipe stamps from the office postage. Some are brazen, some are subtle, some are steady, others intermittent, and so on. In short, every vice and every virtue, every feeling, every gesture of the mind, has a manner, a style; and it is the style of many an errant knave which makes him charming to us, and the style of some saints which makes us wish they would go to the devil.

I suppose the popular word for this is "personality." Popular or not, one's personal style is real enough, and may be, after all—as in the case of the poet—what we fall in love with: a way of Being, a manner of moving, thinking, feeling: our presence (our *Dasein*) in the world.

We should speak more often of *how* one loves or is loved, when we speak of its nature, since it is there—in a style—that its nature really lies. Of course, we do talk of lovers making love well or badly, but in a technical sense more appropriate to putting up ladders or cleaning Venetian blinds; yet we rarely comment on how a person's manner of loving makes that love so elevating and vast, or how, in a different instance, it pains and poisons. Then such skills as are essential to the poet will come importantly into play: one's powers of observation, for instance, one's responsiveness, one's empathy and imagination, scrupulosity and care and respect for nuance, one's generosity and openness to experience, in short, one's general level of civilization: depth of desire, breadth of attention, degree of sensuality, sharpness of sight and range of feeling, an adventurous fancy and a noble high-mindedness of mind.

Are we surprised that the many women who loved the poet Rainer Maria Rilke loved first his lines and saw in them everywhere, like the breath you would need to pronounce them, these very deep and enduring qualities of spirit—not merely (to paraphrase Pope) the passion which lay behind them, but the art and character which shaped its expression (as in these words written by Rilke for his friend and lover, Lou Salomé):

> Put my eyes out: I can still see;
> slam my ears shut: I can still hear,
> walk without feet to where you were,
> and, tongueless, speak you into being.
> Snap off my arms: I'll hold you hard
> in my heart's longing like a fist;
> halt that, my brain will do its beating,
> and if you set this mind of mine aflame,
> then on my blood I'll carry you away.

STUDY QUESTIONS

1. What is "the commercialization of love"? How has *love* become a "bankrupt" word in modern culture?
2. "Love is always dreamed before it is performed." What does Gass mean by this in relation to Rilke? In relation to all people?
3. Describe Rilke's theory of possession and solitude. How does one love by "letting go"?

14

The Virtue of (Erotic) Love

Robert C. Solomon

Robert C. Solomon is a professor of philosophy at the University of Texas, Austin. He is the author of many books and articles, including *About Love* and *A Passion for Justice.*

In a famous—or infamous—passage, Kant offhandedly dismisses one of the most essential elements in ethics:

> Love out of inclination cannot be commanded; but kindness done from duty—although no inclination impels us, and even although natural and unconquerable disinclination stands in our way—is *Practical,* and not *Pathological* love, residing in the will and not of melting compassion.[1]

In the *Symposium,* on the other hand, Phaedrus offers us one of many contrasting comments by Plato in honor of *erōs*:

> That is why I say Love is the eldest of the gods and most honored and the most powerful for acquiring virtue and blessedness, for men both living and dead.[2]

This paper has two aims: to understand erotic (romantic, "pathological") love as itself a virtue, and to broaden our view of ethics.

ERŌS AND ETHICS

> *It (love) does not hesitate to intrude with its trash. . . . It knows how to slip its love-notes and ringlets even into ministerial portfolios and philosophical manuscripts. Every day it brews and hatches the worst and most perplexing quarrels and disputes, destroys the most valuable relationships and breaks the strongest bonds. . . . Why all this noise and fuss? . . . It is merely a question of every Jack finding his Jill. (The gracious reader should translate this phrase into precise Aristophanic language.) Why should such a trifle play so important a role?*[3]
>
> Arthur Schopenhauer

Love as a virtue? Well, hardly. Motherly love, certainly; patriotism, perhaps. The love of humanity, to be sure, but romantic love? Erotic love? The passion that makes fools of us all and has led to the demise of Anthony, Cleopatra, young Romeo, Juliet, and King Kong? Love is nice, but it is not a virtue. Maybe it is not even nice. Hesiod in the *Theogony* warned against *erōs* as a force contrary and antagonistic to reason. Sophocles and Euripides both denounced *erōs*, in *Antigone* and *Hippolytus* respectively, and even Virgil had his doubts. Schopenhauer, much more recently, thought all love to be sexual and damnable, and today we are much more likely to invoke the cynical wit of Oscar Wilde or Kingsley Amis than the saccharine pronouncements of our latter-day love pundits. Indeed, running through the history of ideas in the West one cannot but be struck by the ambivalence surrounding this central and celebrated concept. It is cursed as irrational and destructive and praised as the origin of everything. *Erōs* is famous for its foolishness and at the same time elevated and venerated as a god, albeit at first a rather minor one, but by the time of early Christianity, nothing less than God as such.

Today, we find ourselves torn between such mundane considerations as dependency and autonomy, security and the dubious freedom to remain "uncommitted." It is hard to remind ourselves, therefore, that the history of love is intellectual warfare between bestiality on one side and divinity on the other. The word "love" has so often functioned as a synonym for lust that it is hard to take it seriously as a virtue. It has just as long been raised to cosmological status, by Parmenides, Empedocles, and Plotinus, for example, and it therefore seems somewhat small-minded to reduce it to a mere source of human relationships. Most modern philosophers have, accordingly, ignored it, Schopenhauer here as elsewhere being a bit eccentric, while moralists have had a field day playing the one side (lust) against the other (divine grace, piety, and contempt for all bodily functions, but particularly those that are best when shared).

In any discussion of love as a virtue, it is necessary, if by now routine, to mention some different "kinds" of love. (The notion of "kinds" may already be question begging here, for the more difficult issue may be what links, rather than distinguishes, e.g., friendship, sexual love, and parental affection.) In particular, it is essential that we distinguish *erōs* and *agapé*, the former usually translated as sexual love, the latter as selfless and certainly sexless love for humanity. The distinction is often drawn crudely. For instance, *erōs* is taken to be purely erotic and reduced to sexual desire, which it surely is not. Or *agapé* is characterized as selfless giving, opposed by *erōs* which thus becomes selfish taking (or at least craving). *Agapé* is idealized to the point where it becomes an attitude possible only to God, thus rendering it virtually inapplicable to common human fellow-feelings. *Erōs* by contrast is degraded to the profanely secular and denied any hint of spirituality. To think of love as a virtue, therefore, is first of all to expand (once again) the domain of *erōs*. (Romantic love, I am presuming, is one historical variant of *erōs*.) One need not deny the desirability (or the possibility) of altruistic *agapé* to insist that erotic *erōs* shares at least some of its virtues.

Erōs, and what we now call "romantic love," should also be distinguished (carefully) from other forms of particular affection—for example, motherly, fatherly, brotherly, or sisterly love and friendship. I think that Schopenhauer was partly right when he suggested (with Freud following him) that all love is to some extent sexual. But to make this point one obviously needs a generously enlarged conception of sex and sexual desire, and I often fear that this insight is motivated as much by its titillating implications as by the impulse to clarify the nature of human bonding. A more modest thesis is that *erōs* (not sex) encompasses almost all intimate, personal affections. What characterizes *erōs* in general, we might then suggest, is an intense quasi-physical, even "grasping," affection for a particular person, a Buscaglian "urge to hug" if you will. (Plato often uses such desire-defined language in talking about *erōs*, even when he is reaching for the Forms.) In romantic love, sexual desire is undeniably a part of this affection, though it is not at all clear whether this is the source of the affection or rather its vehicle. *Erōs* differs from *agapé* in the prevalence of self-interested desire, but it is not thereby selfish and the desire is not just sexual. It also includes a much more general physical desire to "be with," such personal desires as "to be appreciated" and "to be happy together," such inspirational desires as "to be the best for you," and such "altruistic" desires as "to do anything I can for you." As La Rochefoucauld once put it, "in the soul . . . a thirst for mastery; in the mind sympathy; in the body, nothing but a delicately hidden desire to possess, after many mysteries."[4]

It is a common mistake to think of the other person in sex as a mere "object" of desire, which leads to the idea that *erōs* too is degrading and seeks only its own satisfaction. Consider Kant on the matter:

> Because sexuality is not an inclination which one human being has for another as such, but is an inclination for the sex of another, it is a principle of the degradation of human nature, in that it gives rise to the preference of one sex to the other, and to the dishonoring of that sex through the satisfaction of desire.[5]

But surely the question (as Plato raised it 2300 years earlier) is *what* one desires when one sexually desires another person. In the *Symposium,* Aristophanes suggested that one desires not sex but permanent (re-)unification with the other; Socrates insisted that one really wants the Forms. Even if we consider such goals too fantastic for *erōs*, it is clear that the Greeks—as opposed to Kant and many moderns—saw that sexual desire was much, much more than desire for sex and not at all opposed to virtuous desire. At the very least, it is clear that sexual desire is some sort of powerful desire *for* the other person *through* sex. The question is: a desire *for what*? And by no means should we assume from the outset that the answer to this question has anything to do with sexual *objects*. Indeed, taking our clue from Hegel and Sartre, we might suggest rather that it has everything to do with sexual *subject*, and subjects by their very nature cannot be wholly sexual.

The most obvious difference between erotic (romantic) and other particular forms of love is the centrality of sexual (do not read "genital") desire, but there are two other differences that, philosophically, are much more illuminating. The first, though quite controversial, is the prerequisite of *equality* between lovers. This may seem odd in the light of modern accusations against love as a vehicle for the degradation and oppression of women (Shulamith Firestone, Marilyn French), but in historical perspective it becomes clear that—however far we may be from real equality—romantic love emerges only with the relative liberation of women from traditional subservient social and economic roles. Romantic love emerges only when women begin to have more of a choice about their lives—and about their lovers and husbands in particular. One thinks of John Milton's Adam, created early in the era of romantic love, who specifically requested from God not a mere playmate or companion or a mirror image of himself but an *equal*, for "among unequals what society/Can sort, what harmony or true delight?"[6] Or, paraphrasing Stendhal, we might say that love tends to create equals even where it does not find them, for equality is as essential to romantic love as authority is to parenthood—whether or not this is adequately acknowledged or acted upon.

One other difference between *erōs* and other loves is that romantic love, unlike familial love, for example, is unprescribed and often spontaneous. ("Romantic friendships" are especially worth noting in this context.) Critical to erotic, romantic love is the sense of *choice*. Family love, in this sense, is always prescribed. The love between husband and wife, or what such authors as de Rougemont call "conjugal love," might be considered prescribed in this sense too, including its sexuality. This is emphatically not to say that married love cannot be romantic, or that romantic love is characterized only by its novelty or by the excitement and anxiety consequent to that novelty. It is a common mistake to take the exhilaration of love as love—without asking what that exhilaration is *about*. Love and marriage often begin together even if they do not always remain together, and to separate them is just to say that love can be unhitched just as horses can, while carriages sit unmoving.

What could be virtuous about *erōs*? One might rationalize sexual love as the slippery slope to marriage, but this faint praise only reinforces our image of romantic love as something in itself childish, foolish, and a kind of conspiracy of nature and society to trick self-consciously rebellious adolescents into maturity. One might celebrate *erōs* as the often unrecognized source of many of our most beautiful creations, from Dante's poetry to the Taj Mahal, but this too is to demean love as a virtue and see it merely as a means, as Freud once saw anal retention as a means to great art. But it seems to me that *erōs* is not considered a virtue for three general sorts of reasons:

(1) *Erōs* is reduced to mere sexuality, and philosophers, insofar as they deign to dirty their minds with sex at all (*qua* philosophers, of course), tend to see sexuality as vulgar and not even a candidate for virtue. Part of this is the common perception of sex as either a form of recreation or a means to procreation, but in any case a set of desires constrained by ethics but hardly of ethical value in themselves.

(2) Love is an emotion and emotions are thought to be irrational, beyond our control, merely episodic instead of an essential aspect of character, products of "instinct" and intractable in the face of all evidence and objective consideration. Even Aristotle, one of the few friends of the passions in the history of philosophy, insisted that only states of character, not passions, can count as virtues.

(3) *Erōs* even insofar as it is not just sexual is self-love and the self-indulgence of desire, while an essential characteristic of the virtues is, in Hume's phrase, their utility, their being pleasing to others and based on such sentiments as compassion and sympathy. Romantic love, far from being "pleasing to others," tends to be embarrassing and sometimes harmful to others and self-destructive. It tends to be possessive, jealous, obsessive, antisocial, even "mad." Such drama is not the stuff of which virtue is made.

I obviously believe that each of these objections to erotic love as a virtue is just plain wrong, but it will take most of this paper to spell out an alternative view. Simply, for now, let me state that these objections demean and misunderstand the nature of sexuality, the nature of emotions, and the nature of love in particular. So that I do not appear overly irrationalist and romantic here, let me draw Plato to my side. He clearly saw *erōs* as a virtue, and every one of the speakers in the *Symposium* agrees with this. Even Socrates, by far the most effete of the speakers, celebrates *erōs* not as the disinterested appreciation of beauty and wisdom (as many Oxford commentaries would make it seem) but rather as a "grasping" sensuality, perhaps of the mind rather than the body, but erotic none the less for that. (Why did he so distrust beauty in art but yet celebrate it in *erōs*?) In Plato's thinking, *erōs* was a virtue just because it was (in part) a passion, filled with desire and—in that peculiarly noble Socratic sense—self-obsessed as well.

ETHICS AND SUBJECTIVITY

> *One more word against Kant as a moralist. A virtue must be* our own *invention, our most necessary self-expression and self-defense; any other kind of virtue is a danger . . . "Virtue," "duty," the "good in itself," the good which is impersonal and universally valid—chimeras and expressions of decline, of the final exhaustion of life. . . . The fundamental laws of self-preservation and growth demand the opposite—that everyone invent* his own *virtue, his categorical imperative.*[7]
>
> Friedrich Nietzsche

A single paradigm of rationality has retained hegemony in ethics since the Enlightenment. In the shadow of this paradigm, there is less difference than similarity between Kant and the utilitarians: moral philosophy is nothing if not objective, rational, based on principles, and exclusive of particular self-reference and mere personal perspectives. What is shocking is what the paradigm leaves out: most emotions and love in particular (except insofar as these might motivate duty or serve "the greatest good for the greatest number"). The persistence of this paradigm (which I will call "Kantian") has turned the most exciting subject in philosophy—or so it would seem from novels, the newspapers, soap operas, and ordinary gossip—into the dry quasi-legal tedium that we find in some philosophy journals. And worse, it has proved to many people—including many philosophers—that ethics has little to do with the intricate realities of human behavior. The elegant observations of Hume are shunted aside in favor of *policy* decisions. The neglect of personal inclinations in favor of legalistic universal principles leaves out the substance of the ethical, which is not principles but feelings. Bernard Williams points out that it would be "insane" to prefer an act of kindness born of principle rather than personal affection, as Kant recommends.[8] When one thinks of the myriad delights, affections, and felt obligations in love, one cannot help but decide that, given a choice between insisting that love is amoral (at best) and retaining the Kantian paradigm, one's preference is quite clear. Kant's line that we quoted from the *Groundwork* about "pathological love," even on the most generous interpretation (as "pathos" rather than "diseased"), dismisses romantic affection as wholly irrelevant to moral worth, and with this eliminates most of what we—and most of Kant's more romantic colleagues—take to be the very heart of morality.

Richard Taylor once wrote that he found Kantian ethics basically offensive, so much so that he insisted that he would have the same attitude toward a true Kantian that he would toward a person who "regularly drowned children just to see them squirm."[9] This is extreme, and it ignores many recent attempts to "humanize" Kant,[10] but the Kantian position is offensive, and one of the reasons for this is its resistance, if not rejection, of any inclusion of personal, particular feelings in moral evaluation. We find similar resistance in many modern Kantians, for instance, in Bernard Gert's *The Moral Rules* where he dismisses feelings as morally worthless and insists instead that "feelings are morally important only insofar as they lead to morally good actions."[11] It seems to me, on the contrary, that nothing is more important to our evaluation of a person's moral character than feelings, and not just because of our reasonable expectation that actions generally follow feelings. The worth of our feelings is not parasitic on the desirability of our actions. In love, the worthiness of our actions depends on the feelings they express. Generous and even heroic actions may follow from love, but the virtue of love stands quite on its own, even without such consequences (Socrates' criticism of Phaedrus in the *Symposium*). We may think Othello foolish and tragic but we still admire the motive, while Victorian literature is filled with Kantian gentlemen acting on their principles who are utterly repulsive (for instance, Mr. Collins in Jane Austen's *Pride and Prejudice*). Not only is it desirable to love, but those who have not loved (if not lost), or fear they cannot, rightly worry not only about their character but about their completeness as human beings—quite apart from any questions about action or performance. Love itself is admirable, quite apart from its effect and consequences.

Why is the tradition so opposed to love and other feelings as essential, even primary ingredients, in morality? The opposition is all the more surprising given the heavy emphasis on love (though as *agapé*) as the supreme virtue in the New Testament—and it is just this oddity that Kant is trying to explain away in the passage quoted. There seem to be several reasons for Kant's antagonism to feelings in moral evaluation. First and foremost, he seems to believe that only that which can be "commanded" is morally obligatory, and love as a passion cannot be commanded. This particular claim has been admirably disputed in Ed Sankowski's . . . "Love and Moral Obligation," where, in particular, he argues that we at least hold people responsible for fostering or evading the conditions that breed love.[12] One might challenge as well the claim that only that which can be commanded is moral; much of what goes into "good character," while it can be cultivated, cannot be commanded. One might also argue—as I have often—that the emotions are far more voluntaristic and under our control than we normally believe, and not just in the sense that we can foster or avoid the conditions in which they typically emerge. This is not to say that an emotion such as love can simply be produced, by an act of will or volition, as one might now produce a thought or a movement of one's finger. There may be, in Danto-esque phrase, no "basic action" where love is concerned. But there are lots of intentional actions of both mind and body that are not basic, and to insist that love can be produced *de nihilo* by a volition is surely to place an unreasonable demand on its moral virtue.

Second, on the Kantian paradigm, it is always the universal that is in question, never the particular. Here Kant is once again in agreement with New Testament ethics, for *agapé* could be argued to be universal (or, one might also say, indiscriminate) love, and not love for any particular person. (It is worth noting that Christian psychology did hold people responsible for their feelings, did believe that love could be commanded, and, in just the phrase disputed by Kant, demanded it.) But on many interpretations Christian love, as love, is emphatically the love of particulars—even if of every particular and not just of the universal (God, humanity) as such. Love—especially erotic or romantic love—is wholly particular. It is the elevation of one otherwise ordinary person to extraordinary heights with extraordinary privileges. The idea of a categorical imperative in such instances is laughable. On the Kantian model, the particularity of love would seem to be a form of irrationality—comparable to our tendency to make "exceptions" of ourselves, in this case, making exceptions of persons close to us. In love the particular is everything. The virtue of love is and ought to be entirely preferential and personal. The lover who gives special preference to his love (though not, of course, in a bureaucratic or departmental position) is virtuous. A lover who insisted on treating everyone including his or her lover the same would strike us as utterly repulsive.

Third, because morality is a matter of reason, the irrationality of the emotions (in general) is good enough reason not to make them central to ethics. The alleged irrationality of emotions is something more than their supposed involuntariness and particularity. Kant thinks that emotions are irrational, Bernard Williams suggests, because they are capricious. One might add that they also seem to be intrusive, disruptive, stubborn, stupid, and pointless. These are very different accusations, but they are often levied together against emotions in general and love in particular. As "feelings," it is often said that emotions are *non*rational (not even smart enough to be *ir*rational). Or, granting emotions a modicum of aims and intelligence, it is insisted that emotions (*sui generis*) have limited ends and (at best) inefficient means. Against the "disruptive" view of emotions it should be argued that they do not always intrude or disrupt life but often (always?) define it and define the ultimate ends of rationality as well. Against the view that emotions are stupid, one could argue at length how emotional "intuition" is often more insightful and certainly more strategic than many of the ratiocinations of abstract moralizing, and against the view that emotions are aimless it should be said that all emotions have their aims, even if rather odd and sometimes limited. On the other hand, it should be commented that some emotions—among them love—have the most grandiose aims, far grander than the surely limited desire to be "reasonable." Consider Hegel:

> Love neither restricts nor is restricted; it is not finite at all . . . love completely destroys objectivity and thereby annuls and transcends reflection, deprives man's opposite of all foreign character, and discovers life itself without any further defect.[13]

The most common accusation against the emotions, and love in particular, is that they confuse or distort our experience (Leibniz called them "confused perceptions"). What is in question here is the infamous resistance of emotions to canons of consistency and evident facts, their alleged lack of "common sense" and tendency to bias perception and judgment, their apparent tolerance of contradiction (which Freud made one of the hallmarks of "the Unconscious"), their refusal to conform to obvious considerations of objectivity. In love, this is embarrassingly obvious. A homely lover looks longingly at his equally plain love and declares, "you are the most beautiful woman in the world." How are we to understand this? Self-deception? Insanity? Surely not "blindness" (which would be plain ignorance), for the problem is not that he cannot see. Indeed, he might well claim to see much *more* than we do, or more deeply. Impolitely pressed, our enraptured lover may resentfully concede the point, perhaps doing a phenomenological retreat to, "Well, she's the most beautiful woman in the world *to me*!" but we know how such qualifications are treated in philosophy—with proper epistemological disdain. In love one makes a claim, and it is a claim that is demonstrably false. Beauty is not in the eye of the beholder, perhaps, but is this an argument against love?

Consider in the same light the accusation of "intractability" that is thrown at the emotions as a charge, supposedly separating them from reason and rationality. (Amelie Rorty, for example, develops this charge at length in her "Explaining Emotions."[14]) It is worth noting that Kant rejected the emotions not because they were stubborn but because they were capricious, even though such a suggestion goes against the obvious—that emotions can be durable and devoted, even stubborn and intractable. In love, in particular, it is notoriously difficult, when one has been in love, to purge that emotion, even though it now has become an intolerable source of pain and not at all a source of pleasure. But is this an accusation against the emotions, or is it rather part of their virtue? It is passing fancy that we criticize, not unmovable devotion. It is sudden anger that we call irrational, not long-motivated and well-reasoned animosity (which is not to say, of course, that sudden anger is always improper or inappropriate, or that long-term outrage is not sometimes irrational and even insane). It is true that the emotions are stubborn and intractable, but this—as opposed to much less dependable action in accordance with principle—is what makes them so essential to ethics. Principles can be easily rationalized and reinterpreted. One trusts a person fighting in accordance with his passions far more than one fighting for abstract principles. (It is remarkable how principles can always admit convenient exceptions and emendations.) Intractability is a virtue of the emotions as rationalization is to reason a vice. Indeed we might even say that the "truth" of emotions is their intractability, their resistance to every attempt to change them.

Objectively, what love sees and thinks is mostly nonsense, and what it values is quite contrary to everything that philosophical ethics likes to emphasize—objectivity, impersonality, disinterestedness, universality, respect for evidence and arguments, and so on. And yet, it seems to me that such irrationality is among our most important and charming features. We care about each other prior to any evidence or arguments that we ought to. We find each other beautiful, charming, and desirable, seemingly without reference to common standards. We think less of a lover if his or her love alters when it alteration finds, or if one bends to the opinions of friends. Love *ought* to be intractable, we believe, even if this same stubbornness causes considerable pain once the love is over. We are thoroughly prejudiced, to use a jaundiced word, thoroughly unreasonable. "Why do you love *her*?!" is a question that need not be answered or even acknowledged. Indeed, we even think it admirable, if also foolish, to love someone totally undeserving (from someone else's point of view). Love itself is the virtue, a virtue so important that rationality itself pales in importance.

Ultimately, the charge against the emotions—and against love in particular—is that of "subjectivity." Subjectivity is a notoriously slippery notion in philosophy which is often opposed to contrastingly tidy concepts of rationality and objectivity. The charge of "subjectivity" typically turns into an accusation of bias and unreasonableness. But, on the other hand, there is a complementary charge against objectivity, against impersonal, merely abstract ratiocination. There is that sense of "objectivity"—pursued by Camus and Thomas Nagel, for example—in which we are all infinitesimal specks in the galaxy, our lives no more significant than the lives of trees or sea polyps, our bodies nothing but the stuff of physiology, our sex a dubious advancement of the reproduction of bacteria, our speech nothing but noise, our lives meaningless. It is what Nagel calls "the view from nowhere," and in its extreme forms it is as undesirable as it is impossible. But such a viewpoint tends to dominate ethics and value theory as well, if in a more humane or anthropocentric scope. Most of contemporary ethics is still framed not as personal but as policy—to be applied, one suspects, by some imagined philosopher-king. The emphasis is not on being a "good person" but rather a just and fair administrator (being a good person is presumably the same). The model, thinly disguised by the evasive logic of "universalizability," is the bureaucrat, who treats everyone the same and has no relevant personality of his or her own. Love is thus unethical, for against all principles of ethics it has the audacity to view one other person as someone very special and does not, as Mill insisted, count "everyone as one and only one" at all.

ON LOVE'S VIRTUES: PLATO'S *SYMPOSIUM* REVISITED

> *It is, in fact, just a love story. . . . Alcibiades, asked to speak about erōs, cannot describe the passion or its object in general terms, because his experience of love is an experience that happened to him only once, and in connection with an individual who is seen by him to be like nobody else in the world.*[15]
>
> Martha Nussbaum

The classical text on the virtue(s) of erotic love is, of course, Plato's *Symposium*, and Plato (not Socrates) provides us with a portrait of *erōs* as a virtue which is quite appropriate to our modern concept of romantic love. Let us begin by saying very quickly that the concept of *erōs* there discussed is not the same as our concept of romantic love, that Greek love is asymmetrical love between man and youth rather than our symmetrical romance between man and woman, that Plato is doing much in that dialogue which is by no means evident or easily comprehensible to the modern nonclassicist reader. That said, we can remind ourselves that the subject of the dialogue is the nature and the virtues of love. Each of the various speeches can be interpreted as a substantial theory. It is worth noting that Socrates objects to Phaedrus' speech, in particular, because he stresses only the virtues of love—we might say love's good social consequences—instead of the emotion itself, while Aristophanes would give us an account of the nature of love without giving us an adequate account of its virtues. I think that Socrates is right on both counts: virtues are not virtues by virtue of their consequences (against Hume, for example), and an analysis of love that does not tell us how important it is—not just why we are obsessed with it—is inadequate. But we might also note that the usual characterization of the dialogue is extremely misleading, that is, as a ladder of relatively forgettable speeches leading up to a culmination—the speech by Socrates that tells us exactly what love is. The usual assumption that Socrates acts here as the spokesman for Plato's own view seems utterly unsupportable. In this dialogue, even the minor speeches portray essential aspects of love. For example, the banal speech of Eryximachus the physician clumsily captures today's obsession with love as a physiological phenomenon with health as its virtue. Most important, however, is the fact that in this dialogue, Socrates does not have the last or the best word. Martha Nussbaum, Michael Gagarin, and others have shown, convincingly, I believe, that Alcibiades' tragi-comic description of Socrates at the end of the dialogue is essential, if not the key, to the *Symposium*.[16] Indeed, one might even make the case that Plato is partially opposed to Socrates and uses Alcibiades as his argument. Socrates' speech makes love virtuous but only by ignoring or denying most of its essential features—its sexual passion, its interpersonality, its particularity, and its apparent irrationality. *Erōs*, in short, becomes excitement about philosophy. It is impersonal, indifferent to any particular person, "above" bodily desire. In contrast, Alcibiades emphasizes the very personal, passionate, irrational, physical aspect of love, the love for a particular, incomparable human being, not a desexed universal. A similar foil for Socrates is the delightful story by Aristophanes, once he has gotten over his hiccups, in which we are all imagined to be the offspring of perfect (spherical) ancestral beings, split in two by Zeus, twisted around and now desperately looking for our other halves. This explains the "infinite longing" that every lover knows, which includes the longing for sexual union but by no means can be satisfied just with that. Aristophanes is about to continue his story near the end of the dialogue—perhaps completing the account by telling us about virtue—when he is interrupted by Alcibiades, wholly drunk, who launches into his paean for Socrates, contradicting everything Socrates has just been arguing. Socrates is sandwiched between Aristophanes and Alcibiades and it must be said that the conclusion of the debate is that Socrates is weird. Here, I think, is Plato's own voice, not as Socrates *via* Diotima, but as Alcibiades, presenting love as it is against the perhaps admirable but admittedly inhuman efforts of Socrates to say what it should be ideally. I think that this is important for our concern here, because the problem with understanding love as a virtue is not just its undervaluation as sex and emotion: it is also its excessive idealization as something more—or completely different from—sexuality and personal passion. If we think that the virtue of love is nothing less than the virtues of divinity itself, then love may be virtuous but it will have little to do with us and our petty particular affections. If love is a virtue in the sense that I want to defend here, it must apply to Alcibiades as well as Socrates. Socrates gives us a noble sense of the idealization that is part and parcel of *erōs* but I think that we can safely say that he goes too far in abandoning the eroticism of the particular.

THE HISTORY OF LOVE

> *Having said all this, we may now agree that the Western concept of love (in its heterosexual and humanistic aspects) was—if not "invented" or "discovered"—at least developed in the twelfth century as never before. Only at that late date was man able to begin thinking consecutively about ways of harmonizing sexual impulses with idealistic motives, of justifying amorous intimacy not as a means of preserving the race, or glorifying God, or attaining some ulterior metaphysical object but rather as an end in itself that made life worth living.*[17]
>
> Irving Singer

The virtues, according to Alasdair MacIntyre, are historical. They perform different functions in different societies, and one would not expect the virtues of a warrior in Homeric Greece to be similar to those of a gentleman in Jane Austen's England. Love as a virtue is also functional and historical. Sexuality "fits" into different societies in different ways, and conceptions of love and marriage vary accordingly. However "obvious" the universal function of uninterrupted and unhampered heterosexual intercourse may be in the preservation of every society, sexual desire is virtually never limited to this end, and the myriad courtship rituals, mores, and emotions invented by human cultures attest to the variety of ends to which this basic *ur-lust* can be employed. The virtues of love, accordingly, are the intrinsic ends which *erōs* serves, one of which may be, as Stendhal used to argue, its existence for its own sake.

Sexual desire may seem like something of a constant through history, but the objects of desire (obviously) and the source, nature, and vicissitudes of that desire vary as much as societies and their philosophies. Love is defined not primarily by sex or the libido but by ideas, and romantic love, which is a very modern (eighteenth century) concept, involves certain specific ideas about sex, gender, marriage, and the meaning of life as well as the perennial promptings of biology. Strictly speaking, there is nothing in the *Symposium* (or anywhere else before the seventeenth century) about romantic love. Romantic love is part and parcel of Romanticism, a distinctively modern movement. It presupposes an unusually strong conception of privacy and individual autonomy, a relatively novel celebration of the emotions for their own sake, and a dramatic metaphysics of unity—of which sexual unity in love is a particularly exciting and tangible example. (Compare Hegel, "In love the separate does still remain, but as something united and no longer as something separate," or Shelley, "one soul of interwoven flame.") The speakers in Plato's *Symposium* praised courage, education, and wisdom as the virtues of love, but they had little to say of the virtues of heterosexuality (apart, of course, from its function of producing more Athenians). Charity, devotion, and chastity were praised as virtues of Christian love, but there was too little to say about the joys of sexuality. (Consider the classic seventeenth-century preface: "Let virtue be rewarded, vice be punished, and chastity treated as it deserves.") Romantic love has among its virtues the metaphysical legitimization of sexual desire, the motivation for marriage, and the equalization of the sexes, surely no part of Greek love and doubtful in traditional Christian love. (Contemporary Christian concepts of love, of course, have adopted and incorporated much of the romantic ideology.) Romantic love has as its virtue the expansion of the self to include another, hardly necessary in societies in which citizenship and other memberships provided all of the shared identity one could possibly imagine. Romantic love has as a virtue the expression of what we opaquely call "the inner self," again not a virtue that would have been understood in less psychological and more socially minded societies. To put the matter bluntly (and without argument), romantic love came of age only when newly industrialized and increasingly anonymous societies fostered the economically independent and socially shrunken ("nuclear") family, when women as well as men were permitted considerable personal *choice* in their marriage partners, when romantic love novels spread the gospel to the multitude of women of the middle class (whereas courtly love had been the privilege of a few aristocratic heroines), and, philosophically most important, when the now many centuries old contrast between sacred and profane love had broken down and been synthesized in a secular mode (like so many ideas in the Enlightenment). Romantic love depended on what Robert Stone has called "affective individualism," an attitude to the individual and the importance of his or her emotions that did not and could not have arisen until modern times.

It is essential that we keep the historical character of love in mind so that we do not get seduced by an idea that might well be prompted by the seeming timelessness of the *Symposium* or the always familiar (and cynical) view that love is nothing but hormonal agitation coupled with the uncertainties and frustrations of courtship—or as Freud put it, "lust plus the ordeal of civility." This idea is that love is itself something timeless and universal, a singular phenomenon which varies only in its culturization and interpretation but is otherwise universally the same. In fact, even the *Symposium* provides us with no fewer than half-a-dozen conceptions of love, and it is not clear to what extent these are disagreements about the true nature of *erōs* or different kinds of *erōs*. Socrates, in particular, is certainly giving us a new conception, a "persuasive definition." Historically, we find these variations played out on a grand scale, with Socrates setting the stage for an ethereal concept of love that comes of age with Christian theology, Alcibiades displaying the "languor" and its imagery that would come to characterize late medieval courtly love, and Aristophanes anticipating modern romantic love. But paganism, even in Plato, cannot begin to capture the range and complexity of romantic conceptions of love in modern times. To understand erotic love as we know it, it is necessary to appreciate the power of the long, if often antagonistic, history of Christian conceptions of love.

The history of erotic love has been determined not only by the fact that Christian thought demeaned sexual love as such but also by the Christian emphasis on the "inner" individual soul and the importance of such emotions as faith and devotion. The genius of Christianity was that it coopted erotic love and turned it into something else, still the love of one's fellow man and even perhaps the love of one's wife or husband, but no longer particularly sexual, no longer personal, no longer merely human. In its positive presentation, love became a form of idealization, even worship, an attempt to transcend not only oneself and one's own self-interests but also the limited self-interests of an *égoisme-à-deux*. It did not have to deny the sexual or the personal so much as the Christian conception of love aimed always "higher," toward not just virtue or happiness but perfection itself. On the negative side, it must be said (and often has been) that the Christian conception of love was also brutal and inhuman, denying not only our "natural" impulses but even the conception of a loving marriage as such. Saint Paul's advice, "better to marry than to burn," was one of the more generous sentiments governing this revised concept of love. Tertullian was not alone in insisting that even to look on one's wife with lust was a sin. Aristophanes' thesis that lovers experience that "infinite longing" which manifests and only momentarily satisfies itself in sex would be lost here. Indeed all such desires become antithetical to love, not an expression of it. To Nietzsche's observation that Christianity is Platonism for the masses we might add that because of Christian psychology, we now have psychoanalysis.

Christian theology may have encouraged and revered love above all else, but it was not erotic love that flourished. Alternative names for love—"*caritas*" and "*agapé*"—may have clarified the scholarship but not the phenomenology of the emotion. When one looked lovingly at another, who could say whether the feeling was divine *caritas* or nasty *erōs*, except that one knew that one *should* feel the former. An entire literature grew up, from which some of our favorite first-date dialogues are derived, distinguishing loving from sexual desire as if these were not only always distinguishable but even opposed. By the fourteenth century, this confusion had become canonized as Platonic love, for which Plato (or at least Socrates) is indeed to blame. Platonic love dispensed with Agathon, Aristophanes, and the others, took Diotima (whose name means "honor the god") at her word, and substituted Christian faith for pagan wisdom. Love had become even more idealized than Socrates had urged, but what had been gained in spirituality was more than lost in the denial of the erotic passions and the importance of happy human relationships for their own sake.

It was in reaction to this insensitivity to human desires and affections that courtly love was directed in the twelfth century. Romantic love is often identified historically with courtly love—which is rightly recognized as its significant late medieval predecessor. But the two are quite distinct, as Irving Singer has argued in his *Nature of Love*.[18] The two are often conflated (e.g., by Denis de Rougemont, in his much celebrated but dubious study of the subject),[19] and courtly love, in particular, is often reduced to the ridiculous image of the horny troubadour singing pathetically before the (very tall) tower of some inevitably fair but also unavailable lady. The name "courtly love," it should be noted, was not employed by the participants themselves but rather was applied much later—in the romantic period—by Gaston Paris, who used it to refer to the hardly frustrated or separated couple of Lancelot and Guinevere. Indeed, the paradigm of courtly love began not as chaste and frustrated (if poetic) desire but as secret, adulterous, and all-embracing illicit love. (C. S. Lewis continues this paradigm well into this century.)

Socially, courtly love was a plaything of the upper class. It was as much talk (and crooning) as action, and, perhaps most important, it was wholly distinct from, even opposed to, marriage. (It is not surprising that the texts and theories of the male troubadours—Andreas Capellanus, especially—were typically drawn from the adulterous advice of Ovid. But their female counterparts—Eleanor of Aquitaine, for example—did not take love and marriage any more seriously, in part because they were almost always already married.) What is often said of courtly love—that it rarely resulted in consummation—is not true. Indeed, if anything, one might say that courtly love was *more* obsessed with sex than contemporary romantic love. The fact that consummation came slowly and after considerable effort does not eclipse the fact that consummation was the explicit and sometimes single end of the endeavor.

Much of the history of our changing conceptions of love has to do with the effort to bring together and synthesize the idealization suggested by Plato and Christian love with the very real demands and desires of a couple in love. The virtue of "courtly love" was its effort to carry out this synthesis and at the same time introduce some sexual and aesthetic satisfaction into a world of arranged marriages based wholly on social, political, and economic considerations (thus the separation—if not opposition—between courtly love and marriage). It is courtly love that also introduces the essential romantic conception of erotic love as good in itself, a conception that one does not find in the teleology of the *Symposium* and certainly does not find in Christian concepts of love. In his study, Singer formulates five general features of love that characterize the courtly: (1) that sexual love between men and women is *itself* an ideal worth striving for, (2) that love ennobles both lover and beloved, (3) that sexual love cannot be reduced to mere libidinal impulse, (4) that love has to do with courtship but not (necessarily) with marriage, and (5) that love involves a "holy oneness" between man and woman.[20] It should be clear, as Singer goes on to argue in great detail, how courtly love constituted an attempt to synthesize both pagan and Christian conceptions of love, incorporating both ethical ideals and sexual desire. The first feature signals a radical challenge to the traditional Christian view of love, while the third is a rebuke of the vulgar view that love is nothing but sexual desire. It is worth noting that the last feature listed is very much in tune with much of Christian theology, and indeed, the Aristophanic notion of love as a "union" would continue to be one of the central but most difficult (and therefore often "magical" or "mystical") themes of love through the romantic period. I shall try to develop this idea more literally in the following section.

The distinction between love and marriage is of particular interest in the history of love, and it is worth noting that these have not always been linked so essentially as "horse and carriage," as one popular song would have it. In Plato, for obvious reasons, the question of marriage did not even arise in considerations of *erōs* (at least, for that form of *erōs* that was worthy of philosophical consideration). Ovid considered love and marriage as opposites, although the marriage of one's intended did provide a challenging obstacle and thereby an additional source of excitement. The long history of marriage as a sacrament has little to say about sexual love and sometimes has much to say against it, and by the time of courtly love, courtship typically provided an alternative to loveless marriage rather than a prelude to marriage or—almost unheard of—the content of marriage itself. Gaston Paris and C. S. Lewis's paradigm of Lancelot and Guinevere may have represented excessive antagonism between love and all social and religious institutions and obligations, especially marriage, but courtly love cannot be conceived—whatever else it may have been—as a prelude to or a legitimate reason for marriage. Indeed, the idea that marriage is the culmination of love becomes popular only in the seventeenth century or so, as exemplified in Shakespeare's plays, especially in the comedies. And compared to the rigid ethos of Jane Austen's novels, for example, it must be said that our current understanding of love and marriage is quite in flux and confused.

Romantic love, we may now say, is the historical result of a long and painful synthesis between erotic pagan love and idealistic Christian love or, ahistorically, between Aristophanes and Alcibiades on the one hand and Socrates on the other. It is not just sexual, or even primarily sexual, but an idealistic up-dating of the pagan virtues of cultivation and sensuousness and Christian devotion and fidelity in the modern context of individual privacy, autonomy, and affectivity. To think that romantic love is without virtue is to grossly mistake romance with sexual recreation or unrealistic idealization and ignore the whole historical development that lies behind even the most ordinary love affair. But it is time to say something more about the nature of romantic love as such.

WHAT IS ROMANTIC LOVE?

> *Love is the expression of an ancient need, that human desire was originally one and we were whole, and the desire and the pursuit of the whole is called love.*[21]
>
> Aristophanes

Romantic love, we may need to remind ourselves, is an emotion—an ordinary and very common emotion, even if it is experienced by most of us but once or twice in a lifetime. It is not a "force" or a "mystery." Like all emotions, it is largely learned, typically obsessive, peculiar to certain kinds of cultures with certain brands of philosophy. I will not here rehearse once again my usual analysis of emotion as a complex of judgments, desires, and values. Let me just claim, without argument, the weaker thesis that every emotion presupposes, if it is not composed of, a set of specifiable concepts (e.g., anger as offense, sadness as loss, jealousy as the threat of loss) and more or less specific desires and values, such as revenge in anger, care in sadness, possessiveness in jealousy. Love, accordingly, can and must be analyzed in terms of such a set of concepts and desires, some of which are obvious, the more interesting perhaps not so. It is evident enough that one set of desires in romantic love is the desire to be with, the desire to touch, the desire to caress, and here we are immediately reminded of Aristophanes' lesson: that which manifests itself as a sexual urge in love is actually something much more, a desire to be reunited with, to be one with, one's love. From this, I want to suggest what I take to be the dominant conceptual ingredient in romantic love, which is just this urge for *shared identity*, a kind of *ontological dependency*. The challenge, however, is to get beyond this familiar idea (and its kindred characterizations as a "union," "a merger of souls," etc.) and explain exactly what "identity" could possibly mean in this context. Aristophanes' wonderful metaphor is still a metaphor, and whether or not we would want Hephaestus to weld the two of us together, body and soul, the image does not do our understanding much good. Aristophanes claims that we want the impossible, indeed the unimaginable; he does not give us any indication of how we might in fact share an identity, over and above brief and not always well-coordinated unifications of the flesh.

More to the point, one might well quote Cathy's climactic revelation in *Wuthering Heights*: "I *am* Heathcliff—he's always, always in my mind—not as a pleasure, anymore than I am always a pleasure to myself—but as my own being." Here we have more than a hint of what is involved in shared identity, not a mystical union nor a frustrated physicality but a sense of presence, always "in mind," defining one's sense of self to one's self. Love is just this shared identity, and the desires of love—including especially the strong nonphysiological desire for sexual intercourse—can best be understood with reference to this strange but not at all unfamiliar concept. I cannot do justice to this challenge here, but let me at least present the thesis: Shared identity is the intention of love, and the virtues of love are essentially the virtues of this intended identity. This is not to deny or neglect sex but to give it a context. Nor does this give away too much to marriage (which is a legal identity) but it does explain how romantic love and marriage have come so close together, the latter now considered to be the culmination of the former.

Before we say any more, however, let me express a Socratic caveat: I think that it is necessary to display love as it is by itself, without confusing it with all of the other Good Things we would like and expect to go with it—companionship, great sex, friendship, someone to travel with, someone who really cares, and, ultimately, marriage. Of course we want these things, and preferably all in the same package, but love can and must be understood apart from all of them. Without being depressing, let us remind ourselves that love often goes wrong, that love can be unrequited, that love can interfere with or at least it does not assure satisfying sex, that love and friendship are sometimes opposed, that love can be very lonely, that love can be not only obsessive but insane. Not that love must be or often is all of these, but it can be, and so let us look at the virtues of love itself, as Socrates insisted, not in terms of its consequences or its most desirable embellishments.

The nature of identity in love, briefly described, is this. (You will note, no doubt, a certain debt to Hegel and Sartre in what follows.) We define ourselves, not just in our own terms (as adolescent existentialists and pop-psychologists may argue) but in terms of each other. The virtues, in a society such as Aristotle's, are defined and assigned communally; the idea of "private" virtues would be incomprehensible. But we distinguish public and private with a vengeance, and we typically value our private, personal character more highly than our public persona, which is sometimes thought to be superficial, impersonal, "plastic," and merely manipulative, instrumental. A person's character is best determined by those who "really know him," and it is not odd to us that a person generally known as a bastard might be thought to be a good person just on the testimony of a wife, a husband, or a close friend. ("But if you knew Johnny as I do, you would see that. . . .") In a fragmented world so built on intimate privacies, love even more than family and friendship determines selfhood. Love is just this determining of selfhood. When we talk about "the real self" or "being true to ourselves," what we often mean is being true to the image of ourselves that we share with those we love most. We say, and are expected to say, that the self we display in public performance, the self we present on the job, the self we show to acquaintances, is not real. We sometimes take great pains to prove that the self we share with our family (a historical kind of love) is no longer the self that we consider real. Nor is it any surprise that the self we would like to think of as most real is the self that emerges in intimacy, and its virtues are the typically private virtues of honesty in feeling and expression, interpersonal passion, tenderness, and sensitivity.

The idea of an Aristophanic union—the reunification of two halves that already belong together—is charming and suggestive, but it is only half of the story. The other half starts with the fact of our differences and our stubbornness, and how we may ill fit together even after years of compromise and cohabitation. The freedom of choice that allows us virtually unrestricted range for our romantic intentions also raises the possibility—which was one of the suppositions of courtly love as well—that our choice will often be difficult, if not socially prohibited. (Who was the one girl in Verona that young Romeo should not have chosen? And the one woman wholly forbidden to Lancelot?) The process of mutual self-identification runs into conflict with one of its own presuppositions—the ideal of autonomous individualism. The selves that are to merge do not have the advantage of having adjusted to and complemented each other when the self was still flexible and only partially formed—as in societies where families arrange marriages between children who have grown up together. And whatever the nostalgic popularity of "first love" and the Romeo and Juliet paradigm, the truth is that most of us fall in love well advanced in our development, even into old age, when the self is full-formed and complementarity is more often an exercise in compromise. The development of love is consequently defined by a *dialectic*, often tender but sometimes ontologically vicious, in which each lover struggles for control over shared and reciprocal self-images, resists them, revises them, rejects them. For this reason, love—unlike many other emotions—takes time. It does not make sense to say of love, as it does of anger, that one was in love for fifteen minutes but then calmed down. But neither is this to say that there is no such thing as unrequited love, or that unrequited love is not love, for the dialectic, complete with resistance and conflict, can go on just as well in one soul as in two. Granted that the drama may be a bit impoverished, but as Stendhal often argued, the imagination may be enriched thereby. Or as Goethe once said, "If I love you, what business is that of yours?"

IN PURSUIT OF A PASSION (CONCLUSION)

> *True love, whatever is said of it, will always be honored by men; for although its transports lead us astray, although it does not exclude odious qualities from the heart that feels it—and even produces them—it nevertheless always presupposes estimable qualities without which one would not be in a condition to feel it.*[22]
>
> Jean-Jacques Rousseau

Love, briefly summarized, is a dialectical process of (mutually) reconceived selfhood with a long and varied history. As such, it is much more than a feeling and it need not be at all capricious or unintelligent or disruptive. But the idea that love is concerned with selfhood might suggest that love is essentially self-love, casting love in the role of a vice rather than a virtue. And the suggestion that love is essentially the reconception and determination of oneself through another looks dangerously similar to some familiar definitions of narcissism. But self-reference entails neither cynicism nor narcissism. Although one does see oneself through the other on this analysis, and although as in narcissism the idea of "separation of subject and object" is greatly obscured, love as mutual self-defining reflection does not encourage either vicious or clinical conclusions. Unlike narcissism, love takes the other as its standard, not just as its mirror, which is why the courtly lovers called it "devotion" (as in devoting oneself to God) and why Stendhal—himself an accomplished narcissist—called "passion-love" the one wholly unselfish experience. Love is not selfless but it is nevertheless the antithesis of selfishness. It embodies an expansion of self, modest, perhaps, but what it lacks in scope it more than makes up for in motivation.

The virtues of love can be understood in terms of this sense of this limited but passionate self-expansion. In a fragmented and mobile society, romantic love allows us to forge intensive ties to others, even to strangers. There is much talk in ethics today of "communitarian" as opposed to individualistic frameworks, but the fact is that passionately united community larger than a small circle of carefully chosen friends strikes most of us as oppressive if not dangerous. One may well lament the lack of public virtues or the priority of private virtues, but the fact is that the primacy of privacy is where we must now begin. Nor should one in Kantian enthusiasm for the universal ignore the dramatic importance of the modest move from caring only about oneself to caring about someone else. The expansion of selfhood in love may be modest but, in today's climate of personal greed and "self-fulfillment," it is for many successful citizens today one of the last virtues left standing.

Romantic love is a powerful emotional ally—far better than communal indignation and shared resentment—in breaking down the isolating individualism that has become the dubious heir of some of our favorite traditional values. But we remain staunch individualists, and the extent to which we will allow our virtues to be publicly determined remains limited indeed. But too many authors in recent years have simply dismissed such intimacies as love as not virtuous at all, when a more just judgment would seem to be that love is a particularly appropriate virtue in a society such as ours. With this it is essential to revise our concept of virtue. Some important virtues are not public, so we can no longer use Aristotle, nor even Hume, as our guide. Being virtuous does not mean for us "fitting into" the community; good character is rather privately determined by loving and being loved. This may make (some) virtues subjective, but subjectivity here does not mean capricious, incommensurable, eccentric, or "merely emotional"; it rather means private and personal. Our presumption is that a good person is not a public figure but a private one. Perhaps the accompanying assumption, no doubt false, is that a person who is loving in private will be a good person in public too.

There are other virtues of love, beyond this minimal self-expansion. We might, for instance, mention the sense of self-awareness that goes along with this dramatization of self and the often described sense of self-improvement that is its consequence, something argued by the early speakers in the *Symposium* and often propounded by some of the courtly troubadours. To love is to be intensely conscious of one's own "worth" and greatly concerned with one's virtues (not only charms) where being in love is already considered the first great step in the teleology of self-realization. ("Love me as I am" is not an expression or an instruction of love but rather a defensive reaction.) We might mention, too, the healthy and positive outlook on the world that often accompanies love, a form of generalized idealization that—while it might not take on the cosmic form suggested by Hegel in his early writings—nonetheless counters the cynicism and suspicion that have become the marks of wisdom in our society.

So too we might mention the fact that love is a remarkably inspirational and creative emotion—though one might somewhat cynically speculate that envy and resentment may be its betters in this regard. (It was not just Iago's intelligence that made him more than a match for Othello; he had his envy to motivate him.) The inspirational qualities of love and its impulse to creativity do not just refer, of course, to those who are particularly gifted, for we find at least attempts at poetic self-expression in even the most philistine lovers. Indeed, regardless of the quality of the products of such inspiration, one might argue—following Stendhal—that the exhilaration and inspiration of love is itself its greatest virtue, a virtue that is often ignored in the age-old over-appreciation for philosophical *apatheia*. I too would want to argue that romantic love is a virtue just because it is exciting. One rarely finds philosophers taking excitement as a virtue (Nietzsche being the most obvious exception), but I think many of us do in fact take energy, vitality, being "turned on" as virtuous, whatever might result and however exhausting. I think we ought to wonder about the frequent if implicit emphasis on dullness as a prominent feature of the virtues.

So too we might note the low esteem of sexuality in discussions of virtue. Romantic love is sexual love, and here too we can appreciate the resistance of traditionally modest moral philosophers. Sex, in the history of ethics, has been treated as a biological urge, a force (often an inhuman force) to be controlled. So treated, it is hard to see any virtue in it. Ethical questions about sex tend to focus on its restriction, and sexual love is offered at best as a legitimization of sex but still hardly a virtue. So too we should vehemently reject that picture of sex, evidently held by chaste Kant, which takes intercourse to be either a biological function (reproduction or, sanctioned by God, "procreation") or mere recreation—what Kant considered mutual masturbation. Either way, sex loses any status in ethics and, more mysteriously, loses its immediate connection with love (the conceptual problem that faced courtly love). But sex, I would argue, ought to be viewed not as an urge and neither as procreation nor recreation but rather as expression, defined neither by physiology nor by pleasure but rather circumscribed by ideas and what is expressed. In particular, sex is (or can be) an expression of love, though this is just part of the story (as Sartre in particular has gruesomely argued). But the point that should be made here is that love is a virtue in part because of and not despite its sexuality. My Nietzschean premise (though one can find a sublimated version of it in Spinoza) is that the virtues can be exhilarating, and this is (in part) what makes them virtues.

The foregoing points would be greatly misunderstood if they were taken to suggest that erotic love is some sort of "trump" virtue, more important than any others. Virtues can conflict, and any one virtue may be but a negligible exception in an otherwise wholly flawed or pathological character. To pretend that the private joys and obsessions of love raise no questions in terms of public engagement, to move from the objection that love has been neglected in ethics to the insistence that such personal emotions take the place of policy decisions in the public sphere, would be irresponsible. But the example of love makes it evident that the traditional objections to subjectivity in ethics, that appeal to emotions is whimsical, not serious and not subject to criticism, will not bear scrutiny. And against much of recent "virtue ethics," love seems to show that virtues should not be understood as traits (for no matter how "loving" one may be, the only virtue in love is actually loving), nor are all virtues instantiations of universal principles, as Frankena, for example, has argued.[23] It has too long been claimed without argument that subjectivity and emotion in ethics inevitably mean selfishness, prejudice, chaos, violence, and destruction, but the truth is that the nature of love, at least, is quite the opposite, not at all selfish, often tender, and creative. Indeed, against the obsessive emphasis on objectivity and impersonal equality in ethics, the aim of love is to *make* a single person extraordinary and to reconceptualize oneself in his or her terms, to *create* an escape from the anonymity of the Kantian moral world and thrive in a world *à deux* of one's own. Of course, to deny that love can go wrong—against the cumulative evidence of ten thousand romantic novels—would be absurd. It can destroy as well as conjoin relationships, and it can ruin as well as enhance a life. Yes, love can be dangerous, but why have we so long accepted the idea that the virtuous life is simple and uncomplicated rather than, as Nietzsche used to say, a work of romantic art? For love is a virtue as much of the imagination as of morals.

NOTES

1. I. Kant, *The Groundwork of the Metaphysics of Morals,* trans. H. J. Paton (New York: Harper & Row, 1964), p. 67 (p. 13 of the standard German edition).
2. Plato, *The Symposium,* trans. W. Hamilton (London: Penguin Classics, 1951), p. 43.
3. A. Schopenhauer, *The World as Will and Representation,* trans. E. Payne (New York, 1958), quoted in *Sexual Love and Western Morality,* ed. D. Verene (New York: Harper & Row, 1972), p. 175.
4. La Rochefoucauld, *Maxims,* trans. J. Heayd (Boston and New York: Houghton Mifflin, 1917), no. 68.
5. I. Kant, *Lectures on Ethics,* trans. L. Infield (Indianapolis, 1963), p. 164.
6. J. Milton, *Paradise Lost* (New York: Random House, 1969), bk. 8, lines 383–85.
7. F. Nietzsche, *The Antichrist,* trans. H. Kaufmann (New York, 1954), sect. 11.
8. Bernard Williams, "Morality and the Emotions," in *Problems of the Self* (Cambridge: Cambridge University Press, 1973).
9. Richard Taylor, *Good and Evil* (New York: Macmillan, 1970), p. xii.
10. Barbara Herman, "The Practice of Moral Judgment," *Journal of Philosophy* 82, no. 8 (1985).
11. Bernard Gert, *The Moral Rules* (New York: Harper & Row, 1973), p. 143.
12. Edward Sankowski, "Love and Moral Obligation" and "Responsibility of Persons for Their Emotions," *Canadian Journal of Philosophy* 7 (1977):829–40.
13. G. W. F. Hegel, *Early Theological Manuscripts,* trans. T. Knox (Philadelphia: University of Pennsylvania Press, 1971), p. 305.
14. Amelie Rorty, "Explaining Emotions," in *Explaining Emotions* (Berkeley: University of California Press, 1980).

15. M. Nussbaum, "The Speech of Alcibiades," *Philosophy and Literature* 3, no. 2 (1979).
16. Ibid., and Michael Gagarin, "Socrates' Hubris and Alcibiades' Failure," *Phoenix* 31 (1977).
17. I. Singer, *The Nature of Love,* vol. 2 (Chicago: University of Chicago Press, 1986), pp. 35–36.
18. Ibid.
19. Denis de Rougemont, *Love in the Western World* (New York: Harper & Row, 1974).
20. Singer, *Nature of Love,* pp. 22–23.
21. *Symposium,* 64.
22. J.-J. Rousseau, *Emile,* trans. A. Bloom (New York: Basic Books, 1979), p. 214.
23. William Frankena, *Ethics* (Englewood Cliffs, N.J.: Prentice-Hall, 1973), and in a recent newsletter to University of Michigan Philosophy Department alumni.

STUDY QUESTIONS

1. What are some virtues of romantic love, according to Solomon, and why are they important?
2. Are Solomon's arguments against the traditional objections to treating love as a virtue convincing? What about his objections to Kant?
3. What are the positive and negative roles Solomon believes Christianity has played in the development of the modern idea of romantic love? What is the role of courtly love?
4. How might love, according to Solomon, help determine self-hood? How is the self important, in an ethical sense?

15

An Ethics of Care

Nel Noddings

Nel Noddings is the author of *Women and Evil* and *Caring: A Feminine Approach to Ethics and Moral Education*, from which this selection is taken.

The main task in this chapter is a preliminary analysis of caring. I want to ask what it means to care and to lay down the lines along which analysis will proceed in chapters two and three [of the author's original work]. It seems obvious in an everyday sense why we should be interested in caring. Everywhere we hear the complaint "Nobody cares!" and our increasing immersion in bureaucratic procedures and regulations leads us to predict that the complaint will continue to be heard. As human beings we want to care and to be cared for. *Caring* is important in itself. It seems necessary, however, to motivate the sort of detailed analysis I propose; that is, it is reasonable in a philosophical context to ask: Why care about caring?

If we were starting out on a traditional investigation of what it means to be moral, we would almost certainly start with a discussion of moral judgment and moral reasoning. This approach has obvious advantages. It gives us something public and tangible to grapple with—the statements that describe our thinking on moral matters. But I shall argue that this is not the only—nor even the best—starting point. Starting the discussion of moral matters with principles, definitions, and demonstrations is rather like starting the solution of a mathematical problem formally. Sometimes we can and do proceed this way, but when the problematic situation is new, baffling, or especially complex, we cannot start this way. We have to operate in an intuitive or receptive mode that is somewhat mysterious, internal, and nonsequential. After the solution has been found by intuitive methods, we may proceed with the construction of a formal demonstration or proof. As the mathematician Gauss put it: "I have got my result but I do not know yet how to get (prove) it."[1]

A difficulty in mathematics teaching is that we too rarely share our fundamental mathematical thinking with our students. We present everything ready-made as it were, as though it springs from our foreheads in formal perfection. The same sort of difficulty arises when we approach the teaching of morality or ethical behavior from a rational-cognitive approach. We fail to share with each other the feelings, the conflicts, the hopes and ideas that influence our eventual choices. We share only the justification for our acts and not what motivates and touches us.

I think we are doubly mistaken when we approach moral matters in this mathematical way. First, of course, we miss sharing the heuristic processes in our ethical thinking just as we miss that sharing when we approach mathematics itself formally. But this difficulty could be remedied pedagogically. We would not have to change our approach to ethics but only to the teaching of ethical behavior or ethical thinking. Second, however, when we approach moral matters through the study of moral reasoning, we are led quite naturally to suppose that ethics is necessarily a subject that must be cast in the language of principle and demonstration. This, I shall argue, is a mistake.

Many persons who live moral lives do not approach moral problems formally. Women, in particular, seem to approach moral problems by placing themselves as nearly as possible in concrete situations and assuming personal responsibility for the choices to be made. They define themselves in terms of *caring* and work their way through moral problems from the position of one-caring.[2] This position or attitude of caring activates a complex structure of memories, feelings, and capacities. Further, the process of moral decision making that is founded on caring requires a process of concretization rather than one of abstraction. An ethic built on caring is, I think, characteristically and essentially feminine—which is not to say, of course, that it cannot be shared by men, any more than we should care to say that traditional moral systems cannot be embraced by women. But an ethic of caring arises, I believe, out of our experience as women, just as the traditional logical approach to ethical problems arises more obviously from masculine experience.

One reason, then, for conducting the comprehensive and appreciative investigation of caring to which we shall now turn is to capture conceptually a feminine—or simply an alternative—approach to matters of morality.

WHAT DOES IT MEAN TO CARE?

Our dictionaries tell us that "care" is a state of mental suffering or of engrossment: to care is to be in a burdened mental state, one of anxiety, fear, or solicitude about something or someone. Alternatively, one cares for something or someone if one has a regard for or inclination toward that something or someone. If I have an inclination toward mathematics, I may willingly spend some time with it, and if I have a regard for you, what you think, feel, and desire will matter to me. And, again, to care may mean to be charged with the protection, welfare, or maintenance of something or someone.

These definitions represent different uses of "care" but, in the deepest human sense, we shall see that elements of each of them are involved in caring. In one sense, I may equate "cares" with "burdens"; I have cares in certain matters (professional, personal, or public) if I have burdens or worries, if I fret over current and projected states of affairs. In another sense, I *care* for someone if I feel a stir of desire or inclination toward him. In a related sense, I *care* for someone if I have regard for his views and interests. In the third sense, I have the care of an elderly relative if I am charged with the responsibility for his physical welfare. But, clearly, in the deep human sense that will occupy us, I cannot claim to care for my relative if my caretaking is perfunctory or grudging.

We see that it will be necessary to give much of our attention to the one-caring in our analysis. Even though we sometimes judge caring from the outside, as third-persons, it is easy to see that the essential elements of caring are located in the relation between the one-caring and the cared-for. In a lovely little book, *On Caring*, Milton Mayeroff describes caring largely through the view of one-caring. He begins by saying: "To care for another person, in the most significant sense, is to help him grow and actualize himself."[3]

I want to approach the problem a bit differently, because I think emphasis on the actualization of the other may lead us to pass too rapidly over the description of what goes on in the one-caring. Further, problems arise in the discussion of reciprocity, and we shall feel a need to examine the role of the cared-for much more closely also. But Mayeroff has given us a significant start by pointing to the importance of constancy, guilt, reciprocation, and the limits of caring. All of these we shall consider in some detail.

Let's start looking at caring from the outside to discover the limitations of that approach. In the ordinary course of events, we expect some action from one who claims to care, even though action is not all we expect. How are we to determine whether Mr. Smith cares for his elderly mother, who is confined to a nursing home? It is not enough, surely, that Mr. Smith should say, "I care." (But the possibility of his saying this will lead us onto another path of analysis shortly. We shall have to examine caring from the inside.) We, as observers, must look for some action, some manifestation in Smith's behavior, that will allow us to agree that he cares. To care, we feel, requires some action in behalf of the cared-for. Thus, if Smith never visits his mother, nor writes to her, nor telephones her, we would be likely to say that, although he is charged formally with her care—he pays for her confinement—he does not really care. We point out that he seems to be lacking in regard, that he is not troubled enough to see for himself how his mother fares. There is no desire for her company, no inclination toward her. But notice that a criterion of action would not be easy to formulate from this case. Smith, after all, does perform some action in behalf of his mother: he pays for her physical maintenance. But we are looking for a qualitatively different sort of action.

Is direct, externally observable action necessary to caring? Can caring be present in the absence of action in behalf of the cared-for? Consider the problem of lovers who cannot marry because they are already committed to satisfactory and honorable marriages. The lover learns that his beloved is ill. All his instincts cry out for his presence at her bedside. Yet, if he fears for the trouble he may bring her, for the recriminations that may spring from his appearance, he may stay away from her. Surely, we would not say in such a case that the lover does not care. He is in a mental state of engrossment, even suffering; he feels the deepest regard and, charged by his love with the duty to protect, he denies his own need in order to spare her one form of pain. Thus, in caring, he chooses not to act directly and tenderly in response to the beloved's immediate physical pain. We see that, when we consider the action component of caring in depth, we shall have to look beyond observable action to acts of commitment, those acts that are seen only by the individual subject performing them.

In the case of the lover whose beloved has fallen ill, we might expect him to express himself when the crisis has passed. But even this might not happen. He might resolve never to contact her again, and his caring could then be known only to him as he renews his resolve again and again. We do not wish to deny that the lover cares, but clearly, something is missing in the relationship: caring is not completed in the cared-for. Or, consider the mother whose son, in young adulthood, leaves home in anger and rebellion. Should she act to bring about reconciliation? Perhaps. Are we sure that she does not care if she fails to act directly to bring him into loving contact with his family? She may, indeed, deliberately abstain from acting in the belief that her son must be allowed to work out his problem alone. Her regard for him may force her into anguished and carefully considered inaction. Like the lover, she may eventually express herself to her son—when the crisis has passed—but then again, she may not. After a period of, say, two years, the relationship may stabilize, and the mother's caring may resume its usual form. Shall we say, then, that she "cares again" and that for two years she "did not care"?

There are still further difficulties in trying to formulate an action criterion for caring. Suppose that I learn about a family in great need, and suppose that I decide to help them. I pay their back rent for them, buy food for them, and supply them with the necessities of life. I do all this cheerfully, willingly spending time with them. Can it be doubted that I care? This sort of case will raise problems also. Suppose both husband and wife in this family want to be independent, or at least have a latent longing in this direction. But my acts tend to suppress the urge toward independence. Am I helping or hindering?[4] Do I care or only seem to care? If it must be said that my relation to the needy family is not, properly, a caring relation, what has gone wrong?

Now, in this brief inspection of caring acts, we have already encountered problems. Others suggest themselves. What of indirect caring, for example? What shall we say about college students who engage in protests for the blacks of South Africa or the "boat people" of Indochina or the Jews of Russia? Under what conditions would we be willing to say that they care? Again, these may be questions that can be answered only by those claiming to care. We need to know, for example, what motivates the protest. Then, as we shall see, there is the recurring problem of "completion." How is the caring conveyed to the cared-for? What sort of meeting can there be between the one-caring and the cared-for?

We are not going to be able to answer all of these questions with certainty. Indeed, this essay is not aiming toward a systematic exposition of criteria for caring. Rather, I must show that such a systematic effort is, so far as the system is its goal, mistaken. We expend the effort as much to show what is not fruitful as what is. It is not my aim to be able to sort cases at the finish: A cares, B does not care, C cares but not about D, etc. If we can understand how complex and intricate, indeed how subjective, caring is, we shall perhaps be better equipped to meet the conflicts and pains it sometimes induces. Then, too, we may come to understand at least in part how it is that, in a country that spends billions on caretaking of various sorts, we hear everywhere the complaint, "Nobody cares."

In spite of the difficulties involved, we shall have to discuss behavioral indicators of caring in some depth, because we will be concerned about problems of entrusting care, of monitoring caretaking and assigning it. When we consider the possibility of institutional caring and what might be meant by the "caring school," we shall need to know what to look for. And so, even though the analysis will move us more and more toward first- and second-person views of caring, we shall examine caring acts and the "third-person" view also. In this initial analysis, we shall return to the third-person view after examining first- and second-person aspects.

So far, we have talked about the action component of caring, and we certainly have not arrived at a determinate set of criteria. Suppose, now, that we consider the engrossment we expect to find in the one-caring. When Mr. Smith, whose "caring" seems to us to be at best perfunctory, says, "I care," what can he mean? Now, clearly we can only guess, because Mr. Smith has to speak for himself on this. But he might mean: (1) I *do* care. I think of my mother often and worry about her. It is an awful burden. (2) I *do* care. I should see her more often, but I have so much to do—a houseful of kids, long working hours, a wife who needs my companionship. . . . (3) I *do* care. I pay the bills, don't I? I have sisters who could provide company. . . .

These suggested meanings do not exhaust Mr. Smith's possibilities, but they give us something to work with. In the first case, we might rightly conclude that Mr. Smith does not care for his mother as much as he does for himself as caretaker. He is burdened with cares, and the focus of his attention has shifted inward to himself and his worries. This, we shall see, is a risk of caring. There exists in all caring situations the risk that the one-caring will be overwhelmed by the responsibilities and duties of the task and that, as a result of being burdened, he or she will cease to care for the other and become instead the object of "caring." Now, here—and throughout our discussion on caring—we must try to avoid equivocation. There are, as we have noted, several common meanings of "to care," but no one of them yields the deep sense for which we are probing. When it is clear that "caring" refers to one of the restricted senses, or when we are not yet sure to what it refers, I shall enclose it in quotes. In the situation where Mr. Smith is *burdened with cares*, he is the object of "caring."

In the third case, also, we might justifiably conclude that Mr. Smith does not care. His interest is in equity. He wants to be credited with caring. By doing something, he hopes to find an acceptable substitute for genuine caring. We see similar behavior in the woman who professes to love animals and whisks every stray to the animal shelter. Most animals, once at the shelter, suffer death. Does one who cares choose swift and merciful death for the object of her care over precarious and perhaps painful life? Well, we might say, it depends. It depends on our caretaking capabilities, on traffic conditions where we live, on the physical condition of the animal. All this is exactly to the point. What we do depends not upon rules, or at least not wholly on rules—not upon a prior determination of what is fair or equitable—but upon a constellation of conditions that is viewed through both the eyes of the one-caring and the eyes of the cared-for. By and large, we do not say with any conviction that a person cares if that person acts routinely according to some fixed rule.

The second case is difficult. This Mr. Smith has a notion that caring involves a commitment of self, but he is finding it difficult to handle the commitments he has already made. He is in conflict over how he should spend himself. Undergoing conflict is another risk of caring, and we shall consider a variety of possible conflicts. Of special interest to us will be the question: When should I attempt to remove conflict, and when should I resolve simply to live with the conflict? Suppose, for example, that I care for both cats and birds. (I must use "care for" at this stage without attempting to justify its use completely.) Having particular cats of my own and *not* having particular birds of my own at the same time are indications of my concern for each. But there are wild birds in my garden, and they are in peril from the cats. I may give the matter considerable thought. I feed the cats well so that they will not hunt out of hunger. I hang small bells on their collars. I keep bird cages ready for victims I am able to rescue. I keep bird baths and feeders inaccessible to the cats. Beyond this, I live with the conflict. Others might have the cats declawed, but I will not do this. Now, the point here is not whether I care more for cats than birds, or whether Ms. Jones (who declaws her cats) cares more for birds than I do. The point lies in trying to discern the kinds of things I must think about when I am in a conflict of caring. When my caring is directed to living things, I must consider their natures, ways of life, needs, and desires. And, although I can never accomplish it entirely, I try to apprehend the reality of the other.

This is the fundamental aspect of caring from the inside. When I look at and think about how I am when I care, I realize that there is invariably this displacement of interest from my own reality to the reality of the other. (Our discussion now will be confined to caring for persons.) Kierkegaard has said that we apprehend another's reality as *possibility*.[5] To be touched, to have aroused in me something that will disturb my own ethical reality, I must see the other's reality as a possibility for my own. This is not to say that I cannot try to see the other's reality differently. Indeed, I can. I can look at it objectively by collecting factual data; I can look at it historically. If it is heroic, I can come to admire it. But this sort of looking does not touch my own ethical reality; it may even distract me from it. As Kierkegaard put it:

> Ethically speaking there is nothing so conductive to sound sleep as admiration of another person's ethical reality. And again ethically speaking, if there is anything that can stir and rouse a man, it is a possibility ideally requiring itself of a human being.[6]

But I am suggesting that we do not see only the direct possibilities for becoming better than we are when we struggle toward the reality of the other. We also have aroused in us the feeling, "I must do something." When we see the other's reality as a possibility for us, we must act to eliminate the intolerable, to reduce the pain, to fill the need, to actualize the dream. When I am in this sort of relationship with another, when the other's reality becomes a real possibility for me, I care. Whether the caring is sustained, whether it lasts long enough to be conveyed to the other, whether it becomes visible in the world, depends upon my sustaining the relationship or, at least, acting out of concern for my own ethicality as though it were sustained.

In this latter case, one in which something has slipped away from me or eluded me from the start but in which I strive to regain or to attain it, I experience a genuine caring for self. This caring for self, for the *ethical* self, can emerge only from a caring for others. But a sense of my physical self, a knowledge of what gives me pain and pleasure, precedes my caring for others. Otherwise, their realities as possibilities for my own reality would mean nothing to me. When we say of someone, "He cares only for himself," we mean that, in our deepest sense, he does not care at all. He has only a sense of that physical self—of what gives him pain and pleasure. Whatever he sees in others is pre-selected in relation to his own needs and desires. He does not see the reality of the other as a possibility for himself but only as an instance of what he has already determined as self or not-self. Thus, he is ethically both zero and finished. His only "becoming" is a physical becoming. It is clear, of course, that I must say more about what is meant by "ethical reality" and "ethical self," and I shall return to this question.

I need not, however, be a person who cares only for myself in order to behave occasionally as though I care only for myself. Sometimes I behave this way because I have not thought through things carefully enough and because the mode of the times pushes the thoughtless in its own direction. Suppose, for example, that I am a teacher who loves mathematics. I encounter a student who is doing poorly, and I decide to have a talk with him. He tells me that he hates mathematics. *Aha*, I think. *Here is the problem. I must help this poor boy to love mathematics, and then he will do better at it.* What am I doing when I proceed in this way? I am not trying to grasp the reality of the other as a possibility for myself. I have not even asked: *How would it feel to hate mathematics?* Instead, I project my own reality onto my student and say, *You will be just fine if only you learn to love mathematics.* And I have "data" to support me. There is evidence that intrinsic motivation is associated with higher achievement. (Did anyone ever doubt this?) So my student becomes an object of study and manipulation for me. Now, I have deliberately chosen an example that is not often associated with manipulation. Usually, we associate manipulation with trying to get our student to achieve some learning objective that we have devised and set for him. Bringing him to "love mathematics" is seen as a noble aim. And so it is, if it is held out to him as a possibility that he glimpses by observing me and others; but then I shall not be disappointed in him, or in myself, if he remains indifferent to mathematics. It is a possibility that may not be actualized. What matters to me, if I care, is that he find some reason, acceptable in his inner self, for learning the mathematics required of him or that he reject it boldly and honestly. How would it feel to hate mathematics? What reasons could I find for learning it? When I think this way, I refuse to cast about for rewards that might pull him along. He must find his rewards. I do not begin with dazzling performances designed to intrigue him or to change his attitude. I begin, as nearly as I can, with the view from his eyes: Mathematics is bleak, jumbled, scary, boring, boring, boring. . . . What in the world could induce me to engage in it? From that point on, we struggle together with it.

Apprehending the other's reality, feeling what he feels as nearly as possible, is the essential part of caring from the view of the one-caring. For if I take on the other's reality as possibility and begin to feel its reality, I feel, also, that I must act accordingly; that is, I am impelled to act as though in my own behalf, but in behalf of the other. Now, of course, this feeling that I must act may or may not be sustained. I must make a commitment to act. The commitment to act in behalf of the cared-for, a continued interest in his reality throughout the appropriate time span, and the continual renewal of commitment over this span of time are the essential elements of caring from the inner view. Mayeroff speaks of devotion and the promotion of growth in the cared-for. I wish to start with engrossment and motivational displacement. Both concepts will require elaboration.

PROBLEMS ARISING IN THE ANALYSIS OF ONE-CARING

As I think about how I feel when I care, about what my frame of mind is, I see that my caring is always characterized by a move away from self. Yet not all instances of caring are alike even from the view of one-caring. Conditions change, and the time spanned by caring varies. While I care for my children throughout our mutual lifetimes, I may care only momentarily for a stranger in need. The intensity varies. I care deeply for those in my inner circles and more lightly for those farther removed from my personal life. Even with those close to me, the intensity of caring varies; it may be calm and steady most of the time and desperately anxious in emergencies.

The acts performed out of caring vary with both situational conditions and type of relationship. It may bother me briefly, as a teacher, to learn that students in general are not doing well with the subject I teach, but I cannot really be said to care for each of the students having difficulty. And if I have not taken up a serious study of the difficulties themselves, I cannot be said to care about the problem qua problem. But if one of my own students is having difficulty, I may experience the engrossment and motivational displacement of caring. Does this caring spring out of the relationship I have formed with the student? Or, is it possible that I cared in some meaningful way before I even met the particular student?

The problems arising here involve time spans, intensity, and certain formal aspects of caring. Later, I shall explore the concept of chains of caring in which certain formal links to known cared-fors bind us to the possibility of caring. The construction of such formal chains places us in a state of readiness to care. Because my future students are related (formally, *as* students) to present, actual students for whom I do care, I am prepared to care for them also.

As we become aware of the problems involving time, intensity, and formal relationships, we may be led to reconsider the requirement of engrossment. We might instead describe caring of different sorts, on different levels and at varying degrees of intensity. Although I understand why several writers have chosen to speak of special kinds of caring appropriate to particular relationships, I shall claim that these efforts obscure the fundamental truth. At bottom, all caring involves engrossment. The engrossment need not be intense nor need it be pervasive in the life of the one-caring, but it must occur. This requirement does not force caring into the model of romantic love, as some critics fear,[7] for our engrossment may be latent for long periods. We may say of caring as Martin Buber says of love, "it endures, but only in the alternation of actuality and latency."[8] The difference that this approach makes is significant. Whatever roles I assume in life, I may be described in constant terms as one-caring. My first and unending obligation is to meet the other as one-caring. Formal constraints may be added to the fundamental requirement, but they do not replace or weaken it. When we discuss pedagogical caring, for example, we shall develop it from the analysis of caring itself and not from the formal requirements of teaching as a profession.[9]

Another problem arises when we consider situations in which we do not naturally care. Responding to my own child crying in the night may require a physical effort, but it does not usually require what might be called an ethical effort. I naturally want to relieve my child's distress. But receiving the other as he feels and trying to do so are qualitatively different modes. In the first, I am already "with" the other. My motivational energies are flowing toward him and, perhaps, toward his ends. In the second, I may dimly or dramatically perceive a reality that is a repugnant possibility for me. Dwelling in it may bring self-revulsion and disgust. Then I must withdraw. I do not "care" for this person. I may hate him, but I need not. If I do something in his behalf—defend his legal rights or confirm a statement he makes—it is because I care about my own ethical self. In caring for my ethical self, I grapple with the question: Must I try to care? When and for whom? A description of the ethical ideal and its construction will be essential in trying to answer these questions.

There are other limitations in caring. Not only are there those for whom I do not naturally care—situations in which engrossment brings revulsion and motivational displacement is unthinkable—but there are, also, many beyond the reach of my caring. I shall reject the notion of universal caring—that is, caring for everyone—on the grounds that it is impossible to actualize and leads us to substitute abstract problem solving and mere talk for genuine caring. Many of us think that it is not only possible to care for everyone but morally obligatory that we should do so. We can, in a sense that will need elaboration, "care about" everyone; that is, we can maintain an internal state of readiness to try to care for whoever crosses our path. But this is different from the caring-for to which we refer when we use the word "caring." If we are thoughtful persons, we know that the difference is great, and we may even deliberately restrict our contacts so that the caring-for of which we are capable does not deteriorate to mere verbal caring-about. I shall not try to maintain this linguistic distinction, because it seems somewhat unnatural, but we should keep in mind the real distinction we are pointing at: in one sense, "caring" refers to an actuality; in the other, it refers to a verbal commitment to the possibility of caring.

We may add both guilt and conflict to our growing list of problems in connection with the analysis of caring. Conflict arises when our engrossment is divided, and several cared-fors demand incompatible decisions from us. Another sort of conflict occurs when what the cared-for wants is not what we think would be best for him, and still another sort arises when we become overburdened and our caring turns into "cares and burdens." Any of these conflicts may induce guilt. Further, we may feel guilty when we fall short of doing what the cared-for wants us to do or when we bring about outcomes we ourselves did not intend to bring about. Conflict and guilt are inescapable risks of caring, and their consideration will suggest an exploration of courage.

The one-caring is, however, not alone in the caring relationship. Sometimes caring turns inward—as for Mr. Smith in his description of worries and burdens—because conditions are intolerable or because the cared-for is singularly difficult. Clearly, we need also to analyze the role of the cared-for.

THE CARED-FOR

We want to examine both the effects of caring on the cared-for and the special contributions that the cared-for makes to the caring relation. The first topic has received far more attention, and we shall start there also. We shall see that for (A, B) to be a caring relation, both A (the one-caring) and B (the cared-for) must contribute appropriately. Something from A must be received, completed, in B. Generally, we characterize this something as an attitude. B looks for something which tells him that A has regard for him, that he is not being treated perfunctorily.

Gabriel Marcel characterizes this attitude in terms of "disposability (disponibilité), the readiness to bestow and spend oneself and make oneself available, and its contrary, indisposability."[10] One who is disposable recognizes that she has a self to invest, to give. She does not identify herself with her objects and possessions. She is present to the cared-for. One who is indisposable, however, comes across even to one physically present as absent, as elsewhere. Marcel says: "When I am with someone who is indisposable, I am conscious of being with someone for whom I do not exist; I am thrown back on myself."[11]

The one-caring, in caring, is *present* in her acts of caring. Even in physical absence, acts at a distance bear the signs of presence: engrossment in the other, regard, desire for the other's well-being. Caring is largely reactive and responsive. Perhaps it is even better characterized as receptive. The one-caring is sufficiently engrossed in the other to listen to him and to take pleasure or pain in what he recounts. Whatever she does for the cared-for is embedded in a relationship that reveals itself as engrossment and in an attitude that warms and comforts the cared-for.

The caring attitude, this quality of disposability, pervades the situational time-space. So far as it is in my control, if we are conversing and if I care, I remain present to you throughout the conversation. Of course, if I care and you do not, then I may put my presence at a distance, thus freeing you to embrace the absence you have chosen. This is the way of dignity in such situations. To be treated as though one does not exist is a threatening experience, and one has to gather up one's self, one's presence, and place it in a safer, more welcome environment. And, of course, it is the way of generosity.

The one cared-for sees the concern, delight, or interest in the eyes of the one-caring and feels her warmth in both verbal and body language. To the cared-for no act in his behalf is quite as important or influential as the attitude of the one-caring. A major act done grudgingly may be accepted graciously on the surface but resented deeply inwardly, whereas a small act performed generously may be accepted nonchalantly but appreciated inwardly. When the attitude of the one-caring bespeaks caring, the cared-for glows, grows stronger, and feels not so much that he has been given something as that something has been added to him. And this "something" may be hard to specify. Indeed, for the one-caring and the cared-for in a relationship of genuine caring, there is no felt need on either part to specify what sort of transformation has taken place.

The intangible something that is added to the cared-for (and often, simultaneously, to the one-caring) will be an important consideration for us when we discuss caring in social institutions and, especially, in schools. It may be that much of what is most valuable in the teaching-learning relationship cannot be specified and certainly not prespecified. The attitude characteristic of caring comes through in acquaintance. When the student associates with the teacher, feeling free to initiate conversation and to suggest areas of interest, he or she is better able to detect the characteristic attitude even in formal, goal-oriented situations such as lectures. Then a brief contact of eyes may say, "I am still the one interested in you. All of this is of variable importance and significance, but you still matter more." It is no use saying that the teacher who "really cares" wants her students to learn the basic skills which are necessary to a comfortable life; I am not denying that, but the notion is impoverished on both ends. On the one extreme, it is not enough to want one's students to master basic skills. I would not want to choose, but if I had to choose whether my child would be a reader or a loving human being, I would choose the latter with alacrity. On the other extreme, it is by itself too much, for it suggests that I as a caring teacher should be willing to do almost anything to bring my students to mastery of the basic skills. And I am not. Among the intangibles that I would have my students carry away is the feeling that the subject we have struggled with is both fascinating and boring, significant and silly, fraught with meaning and nonsense, challenging and tedious, and that whatever attitude we take toward it, it will not diminish our regard for each other. The student is infinitely more important than the subject.

So far in this discussion of the cared-for, I have emphasized the attitude of the one-caring and how its reception affects the cared-for. But we are interested also in the unique contribution of the cared-for to the relation. In chapter three [of the original book], where we shall discuss the role of the cared-for in some detail, we shall encounter the problem of *reciprocity*. What exactly does the cared-for give to the relation, or does he simply receive? What responsibility does he have for the maintenance of the relation? Can he be blamed for ethical deterioration in the one-caring? How does he contribute to the construction of the ethical ideal in the one-caring?

AESTHETICAL CARING

I am going to use the expression "aesthetical caring" for caring about things and ideas, and I shall justify that use a bit later. Caring about things or ideas seems to be a qualitatively different form of caring. We do use "care about" and "care for" in relation to objects. We say, "Mr. Smith really cares about his lawn," and "Ms. Brown cares more for her kitchen than for her children." But we cannot mean by these expressions what we have been talking about in connection with caring for persons. We may be engrossed in our lawn or kitchen, but there is no "other" toward whom we move, no other subjective reality to grasp, and there is no second person to whom an attitude is conveyed. Such "caring" may be related to caring for persons other than ourselves and, of course, it is related to the ways in which we care for ourselves, but it may also distract us from caring about persons. We can become too busy "caring" for things to care about people.

We shall encounter challenging anomalies in this area of caring also. Most of us commonly take as pejorative, "He cares only about money"; but we have mixed feelings when we hear, "He cares only about mathematics," or "She cares only about music." In part, we react this way because we feel that a person who cares only about money is likely to hurt others in his pursuit of it, while one who cares only about mathematics is a harmless and, perhaps, admirable person who is denying himself the pleasures of life in his devotion to an esoteric object. But, again, our attitude may be partially conditioned by a traditional respect and regard for the intellectual and, especially, the aesthetic, here interpreted as a sort of passionate involvement with form and nonpersonal content. It will be a special problem for us to ask about the relation between the ethical and the aesthetic and how caring, which we shall take to be the very foundation of the ethical, may be enhanced, distorted, or even diminished by the aesthetic. From the writing of T. E. Lawrence on his Arabian adventures[12] to Kierkegaard's disinterested and skeptical "Mr. A,"[13] we see the loss of the ethical in a highly intellectualized aesthetic. To be always apart in human affairs, a critical and sensitive observer, to remain troubled but uncommitted, to be just so much affected or affected in just such a way, is to lose the ethical in the aesthetic.

And yet we feel, perhaps rightly, that the receptivity characteristic of aesthetic engagement is very like the receptivity of caring. Consciousness assumes a similar mode of being—one that attempts to grasp or to receive a reality rather than to impose it. Mozart spoke of hearing melodies in his head,[14] and the mathematician Gauss was "seized" by mathematics.[15] Similarly, one who cares for another is seized by the other's projects or plight and often "hears" without words having been spoken by the other. Further, the creative artist, in creating, is present to the work of art as it is forming: listening, watching, feeling, contributing. This exchange between artist and work, this sense of an apprehended or received reality that is nevertheless uniquely one's own, was attested to by Mozart when he asked: "Now, how does it happen that, while I am at work, my compositions assume the form or style which characterize Mozart and are not like anybody else's?"[16]

The sense of having something created through one and only incidentally *by* one is reported frequently by artists. In an interview celebrating his eighty-sixth birthday, Joan Miró tried to explain his creativity to questioning interviewers. He said such things as, "The paper has magnetism," "My hand is guided by a magnetic force," "It is like I am drunk."[17] Yet when we discuss creativity in schools our focus is almost invariably on the activity, the manipulation, the freedom. And, similarly, when we talk about caring, our emphasis is again on the action, on what might properly be called the caretaking. But the caring that gives meaning to the caretaking is too often dismissed as "sentiment." In part, our approaches to creativity and caring are induced by the dominating insistency on objective evaluation. How can we emphasize the receptivity that is at the core of both when we have no way of measuring it? Here we may ultimately decide that some things in life, and in education, must be undertaken and sustained by faith and not by objective evaluation.

Even though the receptivity characteristic of artistic creation resembles that of caring, we shall find important differences, and we are by no means convinced that artistic receptivity is correlated (in individual human beings) with the receptivity of caring. After all, we have known artistic monsters (Wagner comes to mind); men who have loved orchids and despised human life (Conan Doyle's fictional "Moriarty"); people such as some in the Nazi high command, who loved music and art and yet performed unbelievable cruelty on humans. And, of course, we are acquainted with those who care passionately for their families, tribes, or nations and tear the heads off enemies with gusto. We do not expect, then, to find a simple formula that will describe what our children should learn to care about in order to care meaningfully for persons. But we shall see, again, the great importance of the cared-for in contributing to caring relations. Perhaps some people find ideas and things more responsive than the humans they have tried to care for.

Finally, in our discussion of education, we shall be interested in aesthetical caring in its own right. Schools and teachers may, if they wish to do so, exercise some control over the nature and responsiveness of the potential "cared-fors" presented to students as subject matter, and there may be reasonable ways in which to give perceptive/creative modes an appropriate place alongside judgmental/evaluative modes.

CARING AND ACTING

Let's return briefly to the issue of action. Perhaps, with a better notion of what constitutes the first- and second-person aspects of caring, we can now say something more determinate about acts of caring. Our motivation in caring is directed toward the welfare, protection, or enhancement of the cared-for. When we care, we should, ideally, be able to present reasons for our action/inaction which would persuade a reasonable, disinterested observer that we have acted in behalf of the cared-for. This does not mean that all such observers have to agree that they would have behaved exactly as we did in a particular caring situation. They may, on the contrary, see preferred alternatives. They may experience the very conflicts that caused us anxiety and still suggest a different course of action; or they may proceed in a purely rational-objective way and suggest the same or a different course. But, frequently, and especially in the case of inaction, we are not willing to supply reasons to an actual observer; our ideal observer is, and remains, an abstraction. The reasons we would give, those we give to ourselves in honest subjective thinking, should be so well connected to the objective elements of the problem that our course of action clearly either stands a chance of succeeding in behalf of the cared-for, or can have been engaged in only with the hope of effecting something for the cared-for.

Caring involves stepping out of one's own personal frame of reference into the other's. When we care, we consider the other's point of view, his objective needs, and what he expects of us. Our attention, our mental engrossment is on the cared-for, not on ourselves. Our reasons for acting, then, have to do both with the other's wants and desires and with the objective elements of his problematic situation. If the stray cat is healthy and relatively safe, we do not whisk it off to the county shelter; instead, we provide food and water and encourage freedom. Why condemn it to death when it might enjoy a vagabond freedom? If our minds are on ourselves, however—if we have never really left our own a priori frame of reference—our reasons for acting point back at us and not outward to the cared-for. When we want to be thought of as caring, we often act routinely in a way that may easily secure that credit for us.

This gives us, as outsiders to the relation, a way, not infallible to be sure, to judge caretaking for signs of real caring. To care is to act not by fixed rule but by affection and regard. It seems likely, then, that the actions of one-caring will be varied rather than rule-bound; that is, her actions, while predictable in a global sense, will be unpredictable in detail. Variation is to be expected if the one claiming to care really cares, for her engrossment is in the variable and never fully understood other, in the particular other, in a particular set of circumstances. Rule-bound responses in the name of caring lead us to suspect that the claimant wants most to be credited with caring.

To act as one-caring, then, is to act with special regard for the particular person in a concrete situation. We act not to achieve for ourselves a commendation but to protect or enhance the welfare of the cared-for. Because we are inclined toward the cared-for, we want to act in a way that will please him. But we wish to please him for his sake and not for the promise of his grateful response to our generosity. Even this motivation—to act so that the happiness and pleasure of the cared-for will be enhanced—may not provide a sure external sign of caring. We are sometimes thrown into conflict over what the cared-for wants and what we think would be best for him. As caring parents, for example, we cannot always act in ways which bring immediate reactions of pleasure from our children, and to do so may bespeak a desire, again, to be credited with caring.

The one-caring desires the well-being of the cared-for and acts (or abstains from acting—makes an internal act of commitment) to promote that well-being. She is inclined to the other. An observer, however, cannot see the crucial motive and may misread the attitudinal signs. The observer, then, must judge caring, in part, by the following: First, the action (if there has been one) either brings about a favorable outcome for the cared-for or seems reasonably likely to do so; second, the one-caring displays a characteristic variability in her actions—she acts in a nonrule-bound fashion in behalf of the cared-for.

We shall have to spend some time and effort on the discussion of nonrule-bound, caring behavior. Clearly, I do not intend to advocate arbitrary and capricious behavior, but something more like the inconsistency advocated long ago by Ralph Waldo Emerson,[18] the sort of behavior that is conditioned not by a host of narrow and rigidly defined principles but by a broad and loosely defined ethic that molds itself in situations and has a proper regard for human affections, weaknesses, and anxieties. From such an ethic we do not receive prescriptions as to how we must behave under given conditions, but we are somewhat enlightened as to the kinds of questions we should raise (to ourselves and others) in various kinds of situations and the places we might look for appropriate answers. Such an ethic does not attempt to reduce the need for human judgment with a series of "Thou shalts" and "Thou shalt nots." Rather, it recognizes and calls forth human judgment across a wide range of fact and feeling, and it allows for situations and conditions in which judgment (in the impersonal, logical sense) may properly be put aside in favor of faith and commitment.

We establish funds, or institutions, or agencies in order to provide the caretaking we judge to be necessary. The original impulse is often the one associated with caring. It arises in individuals. But as groups of individuals discuss the perceived needs of another individual or group, the imperative changes from "I must do something" to "Something must be done." This change is accompanied by a shift from the nonrational and subjective to the rational and objective. What should be done? Who should do it? Why should the persons named do it? This sort of thinking is not in itself a mistake; it is needed. But it has buried within it the seed of major error. The danger is that caring, which is essentially nonrational in that it requires a constitutive engrossment and displacement of motivation, may gradually or abruptly be transformed into abstract problem solving. There is, then, a shift of focus from the cared-for to the "problem." Opportunities arise for self-interest, and persons entrusted with caring may lack the necessary engrossment in those to be cared-for. Rules are formulated and the characteristic variation in response to the needs of the cared-for may fade away. Those entrusted with caring may focus on satisfying the formulated requirements for caretaking and fail to be present in their interactions with the cared-for. Thus caring disappears and only its illusion remains.

It is clear, of course, that there is also danger in failing to think objectively and well in caring situations. We quite properly enter a rational-objective mode as we try to decide exactly what we will do in behalf of the cared-for. If I am ill informed, or if I make a mistake, or if I act impetuously, I may hurt rather than help the cared-for. But one may argue, here, that the failure is still at the level of engrossment and motivational displacement. Would I behave so carelessly in my own behalf?

It would seem, then, that one of the greatest dangers to caring may be premature switching to a rational-objective mode. It is not that objective thinking is of no use in problems where caring is required, but it is of limited and particular use, and we shall have to inquire deeply into what we shall call "turning points." If rational-objective thinking is to be put in the service of caring, we must at the right moments turn it away from the abstract toward which it tends and back to the concrete. At times we must suspend it in favor of subjective thinking and reflection, allowing time and space for *seeing* and *feeling*. The rational-objective mode must continually be re-established and redirected from a fresh base of commitment. Otherwise, we find ourselves deeply, perhaps inextricably, enmeshed in procedures that somehow serve only themselves; our thoughts are separated, completely detached, from the original objects of caring.

Now, before turning to a closer look at the one-caring, perhaps we should consider where we are headed through our analysis of caring.

ETHICS AND CARING

It is generally agreed that ethics is the philosophical study of morality, but we also speak of "professional ethics" and "a personal ethic." When we speak in the second way, we refer to something explicable—a set of rules, an ideal, a constellation of expressions—that guides and justifies our conduct. One can, obviously, behave ethically without engaging in ethics as a philosophical enterprise, and one can even put together an ethic of sorts—that is, a description of what it means to be moral—without seriously questioning what it means to be moral. Such an ethic, it seems to me, may or may not be a guide to moral behavior. It depends, in a fundamental way, on an assessment of the answer to the question: What does it mean to be moral? This question will be central to our investigation. I shall use "ethical" rather than "moral" in most of our discussions but, in doing so, I am assuming that to behave ethically is to behave under the guidance of an acceptable and justifiable account of what it means to be moral. To behave ethically is not to behave in conformity with just any description of morality, and I shall claim that ethical systems are not equivalent simply because they include rules concerning the same matters or categories.

In an argument for the possibility of an objective morality (against relativism), anthropologist Ralph Linton makes two major points that may serve to illuminate the path I am taking. In one argument, he seems to say that ethical relativism is false because it can be shown that all societies lay down rules of some sort for behavior in certain universal categories. All societies, for example, have rules governing sexual behavior. But Linton does not seem to recognize that the content of the rules, and not just their mere existence, is crucial to the discussion of ethicality. He says, for example: ". . . practically all societies recognize adultery as unethical and punish the offenders. The same man who will lend his wife to a friend or brother will be roused to fury if she goes to another man without his permission."[19] But, surely, we would like to know what conception of morality makes adultery "wrong" and the lending of one's wife "right." Just as surely, an ethical system that renders such decisions cannot be equivalent to one that finds adultery acceptable and wife lending unacceptable.

In his second claim, Linton is joined by a substantial number of anthropologists. Stated simply, the claim is that morality is based on common human characteristics and needs and that, hence, an objective morality is possible. That morality is rooted somehow in common human needs, feelings, and cognitions is agreed. But it is not clear to me that we can move easily or swiftly from that agreement to a claim that objective morality is possible. We may be able to describe the moral impulse as it arises in response to particular needs and feelings, and we may be able to describe the relation of thinking and acting in relation to that impulse; but as we tackle these tasks, we may move farther away from a notion of objective morality and closer to the conviction that an irremovable subjective core, a longing for goodness, provides what universality and stability there is in what it means to be moral.

I want to build an ethic on caring, and I shall claim that there is a form of caring natural and accessible to all human beings. Certain feelings, attitudes, and memories will be claimed as universal. But the ethic itself will not embody a set of universalizable moral judgments. Indeed, moral judgment will not be its central concern. It is very common among philosophers to move from the question: What is morality? to the seemingly more manageable question: What is a moral judgment? Fred Feldman, for example, makes this move early on. He suggests:

> Perhaps we can shed some light on the meaning of the noun "morality" by considering the adjective "moral." Proceeding in this way will enable us to deal with a less abstract concept, and we may thereby be more successful. So instead of asking "What is morality?" let us pick one of the most interesting of these uses of the adjective "moral" and ask instead, "What is a moral judgment?"[20]

Now, I am not arguing that this move is completely mistaken or that nothing can be gained through a consideration of moral judgments, but such a move is not the only possibility. We might choose another interesting use of the adjective and ask, instead, about the moral impulse or moral attitude. The choice is important. The long-standing emphasis on the study of moral judgments has led to a serious imbalance in moral discussion. In particular, it is well known that many women—perhaps most women—do not approach moral problems as problems of principle, reasoning, and judgment. I shall discuss this problem at length in chapter four [of the original work]. If a substantial segment of humankind approaches moral problems through a consideration of the concrete elements of situations and a regard for themselves as caring, then perhaps an attempt should be made to enlighten the study of morality in this alternative mode. Further, such a study has significant implications, beyond ethics, for education. If moral education, in a double sense, is guided only by the study of moral principles and judgments, not only are women made to feel inferior to men in the moral realm but also education itself may suffer from impoverished and one-sided moral guidance.

So building an ethic on caring seems both reasonable and important. One may well ask, at this point, whether an ethic so constructed will be a form of "situation ethics." It is not, certainly, that form of act-utilitarianism commonly labeled "situation ethics."[21] Its emphasis is not on the consequences of our acts, although these are not, of course, irrelevant. But an ethic of caring locates morality primarily in the pre-act consciousness of the one-caring. Yet it is not a form of agapism. There is no command to love nor, indeed, any God to make the commandment. Further, I shall reject the notion of universal love, finding it unattainable in any but the most abstract sense and thus a source of distraction. While much of what will be developed in the ethic of caring may be found, also, in Christian ethics, there will be major and irreconcilable differences. Human love, human caring, will be quite enough on which to found an ethic.

We must look even more closely at that love and caring.

NOTES

1. Gauss's remark is quoted by Morris Kline, *Why Johnny Can't Add* (New York: Vintage Books, 1974), p. 58.
2. See Carol Gilligan, "In a Different Voice: Women's Conception of the Self and of Morality," *Harvard Educational Review* 47 (1977), 481–517. Also, "Woman's Place in Man's Life Cycle," *Harvard Educational Review* 49 (1979), 431–446. Also, *In a Different Voice* (Cambridge, Mass.: Harvard University Press), 1982.
3. Milton Mayeroff, *On Caring* (New York: Harper and Row, 1971), p. 1.
4. See David Brandon, *Zen in the Art of Helping* (New York: Dell Publishing Co., 1978), chap. 3.
5. Søren Kierkegaard, *Concluding Unscientific Postscript,* trans. David F. Swenson and Walter Lowrie (Princeton: Princeton University Press, 1941).
6. Ibid., p. 322.
7. See Mary Anne Raywid, "Up from Agape: Response to 'Caring' by Nel Noddings," *Journal of Curriculum Theorizing* (1981), 152–156.
8. Martin Buber, *I and Thou,* trans. Walter Kaufmann (New York: Charles Scribner's Sons, 1970), p. 69.
9. See Richard E. Hult, Jr., "On Pedagogical Caring," *Educational Theory* 29 (1979), 237–244.
10. See H. J. Blackman, *Six Existentialist Thinkers* (New York: Harper and Row, 1959), p. 80.
11. Ibid., p. 80.
12. T. E. Lawrence, *Seven Pillars of Wisdom* (New York: Garden City Publishing Co., 1938), pp. 549, 562–566.
13. Søren Kierkegaard, *Either/Or,* I, trans. David F. Swenson and Lillian M. Swenson (Princeton: Princeton University Press, 1959).
14. See the account in Jacques Hadamard, *The Psychology of Invention in the Mathematical Field* (New York: Dover Publications, Inc., 1954), pp. 16–17.
15. See E. T. Bell, *Men of Mathematics* (New York: Simon and Schuster, 1965), p. 254.
16. Quoted in Hadamard, *The Psychology of Invention in the Mathematical Field,* pp. 16–17.
17. On NBC's *Prime Time Sunday* (July 8, 1979).
18. Ralph Waldo Emerson, "Self-Reliance," in *Essays,* First Series (Boston and New York: Houghton Mifflin Company, 1903), pp. 45–90.
19. Ralph Linton, "An Anthropologist's Approach to Ethical Principles," in *Understanding Moral Philosophy,* ed. James Rachels (Encino, Calif.: Dickenson Publishing Company, Inc., 1976), p. 8.
20. Fred Feldman, *Introductory Ethics* (Englewood Cliffs, N.J.: Prentice-Hall, Inc., 1978), p. 2.
21. See, for example, Joseph Fletcher, *Situation Ethics* (Philadelphia: The Westminster Press, 1966).

STUDY QUESTIONS

1. Is there tension between a system of care and a Kantian system of Categorical Imperatives?
2. How is trying to "apprehend the reality of the other" essential or important to honest care?
3. In caring for the other, my ethical sense will emerge. I want this to happen. Is it possible, then, that I am using the other merely as a means and not an end?
4. How does Noddings's approach compare with Carol Gilligan's (in chapter one)?
5. What is the difference between caretaking and caring?

16

Love and Women's Oppression *from* The Dialectic of Sex

Shulamith Firestone

Shulamith Firestone is a founder of Redstockings, a radical feminist group in New York, and the author of *The Dialectic of Sex*, from which this selection is taken.

LOVE

A book on radical feminism that did not deal with love would be a political failure. For love, perhaps even more than childbearing, is the pivot of women's oppression today. I realize this has frightening implications: Do we want to get rid of love?

The panic felt at any threat to love is a good clue to its political significance. Another sign that love is central to any analysis of women or sex psychology is its omission from culture itself, its relegation to "personal life." (And whoever heard of logic in the bedroom?) Yes, it is portrayed in novels, even metaphysics, but in them it is described, or better, recreated, not analyzed. Love has never been *understood*, though it may have been fully *experienced*, and that experience communicated.

There is reason for this absence of analysis: *Women and Love are underpinnings. Examine them and you threaten the very structure of culture.* The tired question "What were women doing while men created masterpieces?" deserves more than the obvious reply: Women were barred from culture, exploited in their role of mother. Or its reverse: Women had no need for paintings since they created children. Love is tied to culture in much deeper ways than that. Men were thinking, writing, and creating, because women were pouring their energy into those men; women are not creating culture because they are preoccupied with love.

That women live for love and men for work is a truism. Freud was the first to attempt to ground this dichotomy in the individual psyche: the male child, sexually rejected by the first person in his attention, his mother, "sublimates" his "libido"—his reservoir of sexual (life) energies—into long term projects, in the hope of gaining love in a more generalized form; thus he displaces his need for love into a need for recognition. This process does not occur as much in the female: most women never stop seeking direct warmth and approval.

There is also much truth in the clichés that "behind every man there is a woman," and that "women are the power behind [read: voltage in] the throne." (Male) culture was built on the love of women, and at their expense. Women provided the substance of those male masterpieces; and for millennia they have done the work, and suffered the costs, of one-way emotional relationships the benefits of which went to men and to the work of men. So if women are a parasitical class living off, and at the margins of, the male economy, the reverse too is true: *(Male) culture was (and is) parasitical, feeding on the emotional strength of women without reciprocity.*

Moreover, we tend to forget that this culture is not universal, but rather sectarian, presenting only half the spectrum. The very structure of culture itself, as we shall see, is saturated with the sexual polarity, as well as being in every degree run by, for, and in the interests of male society. But while the male half is termed all of culture, men have not forgotten there is a female "emotional" half: They live it on the sly. As the result of their battle to reject the female in themselves (the Oedipus Complex as we have explained it) they are unable to take love seriously as a cultural matter; but they can't do without it altogether. Love is the underbelly of (male) culture just as love is the weak spot of every man, bent on proving his virility in that large male world of "travel and adventure." Women have always known how men need love, and how they deny this need. Perhaps this explains the peculiar contempt women so universally feel for men ("men are so dumb"), for they can see their men are posturing in the outside world.

I

How does this phenomenon "love" operate? Contrary to popular opinion, love is not altruistic. The initial attraction is based on curious admiration (more often today, envy and resentment) for the self-possession, the integrated unity, of the other and a wish to become part of this Self in some way (today, read: intrude or take over), to become important to that psychic balance. The self-containment of the other creates desire (read: a challenge); admiration (envy) of the other becomes a wish to incorporate (possess) its qualities. A clash of selves follows in which the individual attempts to fight off the growing hold over him of the other. Love is the final opening up to (or, surrender to the dominion of) the other. The lover demonstrates to the beloved how he himself would like to be treated. ("I tried so hard to make him fall in love with me that I fell in love with him myself.") Thus love is the height of selfishness: the self attempts to enrich itself through the absorption of another being. Love is being psychically wide-open to another. It is a situation of total emotional vulnerability. Therefore it must be not only the incorporation of the other, but an *exchange* of selves. Anything short of a mutual exchange will hurt one or the other party.

There is nothing inherently destructive about this process. A little healthy selfishness would be a refreshing change. Love between two equals would be an enrichment, each enlarging himself through the other: instead of being one, locked in the cell of himself with only his own experience and view, he could participate in the existence of another—an extra window on the world. This accounts for the bliss that successful lovers experience: Lovers are temporarily freed from the burden of isolation that every individual bears.

But bliss in love is seldom the case: For every successful contemporary love experience, for every short period of enrichment, there are ten destructive love experiences, post-love "downs" of much longer duration—often resulting in the destruction of the individual, or at least an emotional cynicism that makes it difficult or impossible ever to love again. Why should this be so, if it is not actually inherent in the love process itself?

Let's talk about love in its destructive guise—and why it gets that way, referring . . . to the work of Theodor Reik. Reik's concrete observation brings him closer than many better minds to understanding the *process* of "falling in love," but he is off insofar as he confuses love as it exists in our present society with love itself. He notes that love is a reaction formation, a cycle of envy, hostility, and possessiveness: He sees that it is preceded by dissatisfaction with oneself, a yearning for something better, created by a discrepancy between the ego and the ego-ideal; That the bliss love produces is due to the resolution of this tension by the substitution, in place of one's own ego-ideal, of the other; And finally that love fades "because the other can't live up to your high ego-ideal any more than you could, and the judgment will be the harsher the higher are the claims on oneself." Thus in Reik's view love wears down just as it is wound up: Dissatisfaction with oneself (whoever heard of falling in love the week one is leaving for Europe?) leads to astonishment at the other person's self-containment; to envy; to hostility; to possessive love; and back again through exactly the same process. This is the love process *today.* But why must it be this way?

Many, for example, Denis de Rougemont in *Love in the Western World*, have tried to draw a distinction between romantic "falling in love" with its "false reciprocity which disguises a twin narcissism" (the Pagan Eros) and an unselfish love for the other person as the person really is (the Christian Agapé). De Rougemont attributes the morbid passion of Tristan and Iseult (romantic love) to a vulgarization of specific mystical and religious currents in Western civilization.

I submit that love is essentially a much simpler phenomenon—it becomes complicated, corrupted, or obstructed by *an unequal balance of power.* We have seen that love demands a mutual vulnerability or it turns destructive: the destructive effects of love occur only in a context of inequality. But because sexual inequality has remained a constant—however its *degree* may have varied—the corruption "romantic" love became characteristic of love between the sexes. (It remains for us only to explain why it has steadily increased in Western countries since the medieval period, which we shall attempt to do in the following chapter [of the original work].)

How does the sex class system based on the unequal power distribution of the biological family affect love between the sexes? In discussing Freudianism, we have gone into the psychic structuring of the individual within the family and how this organization of personality must be different for the male and the female because of their very different relationships to the mother. At present the insular interdependency of the mother/child relationship forces both male and female children into anxiety about losing the mother's love, on which they depend for physical survival. When later (Erich Fromm notwithstanding) the child learns that the mother's love is conditional, to be rewarded the child in return for approved behavior (that is, behavior in line with the mother's own values and personal ego-gratification—for she is free to mold the child's "creatively," however she happens to define that), the child's anxiety turns into desperation. This, coinciding with the sexual rejection of the male child by the mother, causes, as we have seen, a schizophrenia in the boy between the emotional and the physical, and in the girl, the mother's rejection, occurring for different reasons, produces an insecurity about her identity in general, creating a lifelong need for approval. (Later her lover replaces her father as a grantor of the necessary surrogate identity—she sees everything through his eyes.) Here originates the hunger for love that later sends both sexes searching in one person after the other for a state of ego security. But because of the early rejection, to the degree that it occurred, the male will be terrified of committing himself, of "opening up" and then being smashed. How this affects his sexuality we have seen: To the degree that a woman is like his mother, the incest taboo operates to restrain his total sexual/emotional commitment; for him to feel safely the kind of total response he first felt for his mother, which was rejected, he must degrade this woman so as to distinguish her from the mother. This behavior reproduced on a larger scale explains many cultural phenomena, including perhaps the ideal love-worship of chivalric times, the forerunner of modern romanticism.

Romantic idealization is partially responsible, at least on the part of men, for a peculiar characteristic of "falling" in love: the change takes place in the lover almost independently of the character of the love object. Occasionally the lover, though beside himself, sees with another rational part of his faculties that, objectively speaking, the one he loves isn't worth all this blind devotion; but he is helpless to act on this, "a slave to love." More often he fools himself entirely. But others can see what is happening ("How on earth he could love her is beyond me!"). This idealization occurs much less frequently on the part of women, as is borne out by Reik's clinical studies. A man must idealize one woman over the rest in order to justify his descent to a lower caste. Woman have no such reason to idealize men—in fact, when one's life depends on one's ability to "psych" men out, such idealization may actually be dangerous—though a fear of male power in general may carry over into relationships with individual men, appearing to be the same phenomenon. But though women know to be inauthentic this male "falling in love," all women, in one way or another, require proof of it from men before they can allow themselves to love (genuinely, in their case) in return. For this idealization process acts to artificially equalize the two parties, a minimum precondition for the development of an uncorrupted love—we have seen that love requires a mutual vulnerability that is impossible to achieve in an unequal power situation. *Thus "falling in love" is no more than the process of alteration of male vision—through idealization, mystification, glorification—that renders void the woman's class inferiority.*

However, the woman knows that this idealization, which she works so hard to produce, is a lie, and that it is only a matter of time before he "sees through her." Her life is a hell, vacillating between an all-consuming need for male love and approval to raise her from her class subjection, to persistent feelings of inauthenticity when she does achieve his love. Thus her whole identity hangs in the balance of her love life. She is allowed to love herself only if a man finds her worthy of love.

But if we could eliminate the political context of love between the sexes, would we not have some degree of idealization remaining in the love process itself? I think so. For the process occurs in the same manner whoever the love choice: the lover "opens up" to the other. Because of this fusion of egos, in which each sees and cares about the other as a new self, the beauty/character of the beloved, perhaps hidden to outsiders under layers of defenses, is revealed. "I wonder what she sees in him," then, means not only, "She is a fool, blinded with romanticism," but, "Her love has lent her x-ray vision. Perhaps we are missing something." (Note that this phrase is most commonly used about women. The equivalent phrase about *men's* slavery to love is more often something like, "She has him wrapped around her finger," she has him so "snowed" that he is the last one to see through her.) Increased sensitivity to the real, if hidden, values in the other, however, is not "blindness" or "idealization" but is, in fact, deeper vision. It is only the *false* idealization we have described above that is responsible for the destruction. Thus it is not the process of love itself that is at fault, but its *political*, i.e., unequal *power* context: the who, why, when and where of it is what makes it now such a holocaust.

II

Simone de Beauvoir said it: "The word love has by no means the same sense for both sexes, and this is one cause of the serious misunderstandings which divide them." Above I have illustrated some of the traditional differences between men and women in love that come up so frequently in parlor discussions of the "double standard," where it is generally agreed: That women are monogamous, better at loving, possessive, "clinging," more interested in (highly involved) "relationships" than in sex per se, and they confuse affection with sexual desire. That men are interested in nothing but a screw (Wham, bam, thank you M'am!), or else romanticize the woman ridiculously; that once sure of her, they become notorious philanderers, never satisfied; that they mistake sex for emotion. All this bears out what we have discussed—the difference in the psychosexual organizations of the two sexes, determined by the first relationship to the mother.

I draw three conclusions based on these differences:

1. That men can't love. (Male hormones?? Women traditionally expect and accept an emotional invalidism in men that they would find intolerable in a woman.)
2. That women's "clinging" behavior is necessitated by their objective social situation.
3. That this situation has not changed significantly from what it ever was.

Men can't love. We have seen why it is that men have difficulty loving and that while men may love, they usually "fall in love"—with their own projected image. Most often they are pounding down a woman's door one day, and thoroughly disillusioned with her the next; but it is rare for women to leave men, and then it is usually for more than ample reason.

It is dangerous to feel sorry for one's oppressor—women are especially prone to this failing—but I am tempted to do it in this case. Being unable to love is hell. This is the way it proceeds: as soon as the man feels any pressure from the other partner to commit himself, he panics and may react in one of several ways:

1. He may rush out and screw ten other women to prove that the first woman has no hold over him. If she accepts this, he may continue to see her on this basis. The other women verify his (false) freedom; periodic arguments about them keep his panic at bay. But the women are a paper tiger, for nothing very deep could be happening with them anyway: he is balancing them against each other so that none of them can get much of him. Many smart women, recognizing this to be only a safety valve on their man's anxiety, give him "a long leash." For the real issue under all the fights about other women is that the man is unable to commit himself.
2. He may consistently exhibit unpredictable behavior, standing her up frequently, being indefinite about the next date, telling her that "my work comes first," or offering a variety of other excuses. That is, though he senses her anxiety, he refuses to reassure her in any way, or even to recognize her anxiety as legitimate. For he *needs* her anxiety as a steady reminder that he is still free, that the door is not entirely closed.
3. When he *is* forced into (an uneasy) commitment, he makes her pay for it: by ogling other women in her presence, by comparing her unfavorably to past girlfriends or movie stars, by snide reminders in front of friends that she is his "ball and chain," by calling her a "nag," a "bitch," "a shrew," or by suggesting that if he were only a bachelor he would be a lot better off. His ambivalence about women's "inferiority" comes out: by being committed to one, he has somehow made the hated female identification, which he now must repeatedly deny if he is to maintain his self-respect in the (male) community. This steady derogation is not entirely put on: for in fact every other girl suddenly does look a lot better, he can't help feeling he has missed something—and, naturally, his woman is to blame. For he has never given up on the search for the ideal; she has forced him to resign from it. Probably he will go to his grave feeling cheated, never realizing that there isn't much difference between one woman and the other, that it is the loving that *creates* the difference.

There are many variations of straining at the bit. Many men go from one casual thing to another, getting out every time it begins to get hot. And yet to live without love in the end proves intolerable to men just as it does to women. The question that remains for every normal male is, then, *how do I get someone to love me without her demanding an equal commitment in return?*

Women's "clinging" behavior is required by the objective social situation. The female *response* to such a situation of male hysteria at any prospect of mutual commitment was the development of subtle methods of manipulation, to force as much commitment as *could* be forced from men. Over the centuries strategies have been devised, tested, and passed on from mother to daughter in secret tête-à-têtes, passed around at "kaffee-klatsches" ("I never understand what it is women spend so much time talking about!"), or, in recent times, via the telephone. These are not trivial gossip sessions at all (as women prefer men to believe), but desperate strategies for survival. More real brilliance goes into one one-hour coed telephone dialogue about men than into that same coed's four years of college study, or for that matter, than into most male political maneuvers. It is no wonder, then, that even the few women without "family obligations" always arrive exhausted at the starting line of any serious endeavor. It takes one's major energy for the best portion of one's creative years to "make a good catch," and a good part of the rest of one's life to "hold" that catch. ("To be in love can be a full-time job for a woman, like that of a profession for a man.") Women who choose to drop out of this race are choosing a life without love, something that, as we have seen, most *men* don't have the courage to do.

But unfortunately The Manhunt is characterized by an emotional urgency beyond this simple desire for return commitment. It is compounded by the very class reality that produced the male inability to love in the first place. In a male-run society that defines women as an inferior and parasitical class, a woman who does not achieve male approval in some form is doomed. To legitimate her existence, a woman must be *more* than woman, she must continually search for an out from her inferior definition; and men are the only ones in a position to bestow on her this state of grace. But because the woman is rarely allowed to realize herself through activity in the larger (male) society—and when she is, she is seldom granted the recognition she deserves—it becomes easier to try for the recognition of one man than of many; and in fact this is exactly the choice most women make. Thus once more the phenomenon of love, good in itself, is corrupted by its class context: women must have love not only for healthy reasons but actually to validate their existence.

In addition, the continued *economic* dependence of women makes a situation of healthy love between equals impossible. Women today still live under a system of patronage: With few exceptions, they have the choice, not between either freedom or marriage, but between being either public or private property. Women who merge with a member of the ruling class can at least hope that some of his privilege will, so to speak, rub off. But women without men are in the same situation as orphans: they are a helpless sub-class lacking the protection of the powerful. This is the antithesis of freedom when they are still (negatively) defined by a class situation: for now they are in a situation of *magnified* vulnerability. To participate in one's subjection by choosing one's master often gives the illusion of free choice; but in reality a woman is never free to choose love without external motivations. For her at the present time, the two things, love and status, must remain inextricably intertwined. . . .

Women of high ideals who believed emancipation possible, women who tried desperately to rid themselves of feminine "hangups," to cultivate what they believed to be the greater directness, honesty, and generosity of men, were badly fooled. They found that no one appreciated their intelligent conversation, their high aspirations, their great sacrifices to avoid developing the personalities of their mothers. For much as men were glad to enjoy their wit, their style, their sex, and their candlelight suppers, they always ended up marrying The Bitch, and then, to top it all off, came back to complain of what a horror she was. "Emancipated" women found out that the honesty, generosity, and camaraderie of men was a lie: men were all too glad to use them and then sell them out, in the name of *true* friendship. ("I respect and like you a great deal, but let's be reasonable. . . ." And then there are the men who take her out to discuss Simone de Beauvoir, leaving their wives at home with the diapers.) "Emancipated" women found out that men were far from "good guys" to be emulated; they found out that by imitating male sexual patterns (the roving eye, the search for the ideal, the emphasis on physical attraction, etc.), they were not only not achieving liberation, they were falling into something much worse than what they had given up. They were *imitating*. And they had inoculated themselves with a sickness that had not even sprung from their own psyches. They found that their new "cool" was shallow and meaningless, that their emotions were drying up behind it, that they were aging and becoming decadent: they feared they were losing their ability to love. They had gained nothing by imitating men: shallowness and callowness, and they were not so good at it either, because somewhere inside it still went against the grain.

Thus women who had decided not to marry because they were wise enough to look around and see where it led found that it was marry or nothing. Men gave their commitment only for a price: share (shoulder) his life, stand on his pedestal, become his appendage, or else. Or else—be consigned forever to that limbo of "chicks" who mean nothing or at least not what mother meant. Be the "other woman" for the rest of one's life, used to provoke his wife, prove his virility and/or his independence, discussed by his friends as his latest "interesting" conquest. (For even if she had given up those terms and what they stood for, no male had.) Yes, love means an entirely different thing to men than to women: it means ownership and control; it means jealousy, where he never exhibited it before—when she might have wanted him to (who cares if she is broke or raped until she officially belongs to him: then he is a raging dynamo, a veritable cyclone, because his property, his ego extension have been threatened); it means a growing lack of interest, coupled with a roving eye. Who needs it?

STUDY QUESTIONS

1. How does Firestone think love is used to silence and oppress women?
2. Can you think of examples of where this may have occurred, in your own experience or the experience of others?
3. How may the modern idea of romantic love affect a woman's self-perception? Is it the same or different for a man?

FOR FURTHER STUDY

Chodorow, Nancy. *The Reproduction of Mothering: Psychoanalysis and the Sociology of Gender.* Berkeley: University of California Press, 1978.

Manning, Rita C. *Speaking from the Heart: A Feminist Perspective on Ethics.* Lanham, Md.: Rowman & Littlefield, 1992.

Miller, Stuart. *Men and Friendship.* New York: Houghton-Mifflin, 1983.

Raymond, Janice. *A Passion for Female Friends.* Boston: Beacon Press, 1986.

de Rougemont, Denis. *Love in the Western World.* New York: Pantheon Books, 1940.

Solomon, Robert C., and Higgins, Kathleen M., eds. *The Philosophy of Erotic Love.* Lawrence, Kans.: University of Kansas Press, 1991.

Welty, Eudora, and Sharp, Ronald A., eds. *The Norton Book of Friendship.* New York: Norton, 1991.

Chapter Four

Ethics of Truth, Power, and Lying

17

The Evil of Lying

Charles Fried

Charles Fried teaches at the Harvard Law School. He has published extensively on law and ethics and is the author of *Right and Wrong,* from which this selection is taken.

The evil of lying is as hard to pin down as it is strongly felt. Is lying wrong or is it merely something bad? If it is bad, why is it bad—is it bad in itself or because of some tendency associated with it? Compare lying to physical harm. Harm is a state of the world and so it can only be classified as bad; the wrong I argued for was the *intentional doing* of harm. Lying, on the other hand, can be wrong, since it is an action. But the fact that lying is an action does not mean that it *must* be wrong rather than bad. It might be that the action of lying should be judged as just another state of the world—a time-extended state, to be sure, but there is no problem about that—and as such it would count as a negative element in any set of circumstances in which it occurred. Furthermore, if lying is judged to be bad it can be bad in itself, like something ugly or painful, or it can be bad only because of its tendency to produce results that are bad in themselves.

If lying were bad, not wrong, this would mean only that, other things being equal, we should avoid lies. And if lying were bad not in itself but merely because of its tendencies, we would have to avoid lies only when those tendencies were in fact likely to be realized. In either case lying would be permissible to produce a net benefit, including the prevention of more or worse lies. By contrast the categorical norm "Do not lie" does not evaluate states of affairs but is addressed to moral agents, forbidding lies. Now if lying is wrong it is also bad in itself, for the category of the intrinsically bad is weaker and more inclusive than the category of the wrong. And accordingly, many states of the world are intrinsically bad (such as destruction of valuable property) but intentional acts bringing them about are not necessarily wrong.

Bentham plainly believed that lying is neither wrong nor even intrinsically bad: "Falsehood, take it by itself, consider it as not being accompanied by any other material circumstances, nor therefore productive of any material effects, can never, upon the principle of utility, constitute any offense at all." By contrast, Kant and Augustine argued at length that lying is wrong. Indeed, they held that lying is not only wrong *unless* excused or justified in defined ways (which is my view) but that lying is always wrong. Augustine sees lying as a kind of defilement, the liar being tainted by the lie, quite apart from any consequences of the lie. Kant's views are more complex. He argues at one point that lying undermines confidence and trust among men generally: "Although by making a false statement I do no wrong to him who unjustly compels me to speak, yet I do wrong to men in general. . . . I cause that declarations in general find no credit, and hence all rights founded on contract should lose their force; and this is a wrong to mankind." This would seem to be a consequentialist argument, according to which lying is bad only insofar as it produces these bad results. But elsewhere he makes plain that he believes these bad consequences to be necessarily, perhaps even conceptually linked to lying. In this more rigoristic vein, he asserts that lying is a perversion of one's uniquely human capacities irrespective of any consequences of the lie, and thus lying is not only intrinsically bad but wrong.

Finally, a number of writers have taken what looks like an intermediate position: the evil of lying is indeed identified with its consequences, but the connection between lying and those consequences, while not a necessary connection, is close and persistent, and the consequences themselves are pervasive and profound. Consider this passage from a recent work by G. F. Warnock:

> I do not necessarily do you any harm at all by deed or word if I induce you to believe what is not in fact the case; I may even do you good, possibly by way, for example, of consolation or flattery. Nevertheless, though deception is not thus necessarily directly damaging it is easy to see how crucially important it is that the natural inclination to have recourse to it should be counteracted. It is, one might say, not the implanting of false beliefs that is damaging, but rather the generation of the suspicion that they may be being implanted. For this undermines trust; and, to the extent that trust is undermined, all cooperative undertakings, in which what one person can do or has reason to do is dependent on what others have done, are doing, or are going to do, must tend to break down. . . . There is no sense in my asking you for your opinion on some point, if I do not suppose that your answer will actually express your opinion (verbal communication is doubtless the most important of all our co-operative undertakings).

Warnock does not quite say that truth-telling is good in itself or that lying is wrong, yet the moral quality of truth-telling and lying is not so simply instrumental as it is, for instance, for Bentham. Rather, truth-telling seems to bear a fundamental, pervasive relation to the human enterprise, just by lying appears to be fundamentally subversive of that enterprise. What exactly is the nature of this relation? How does truth-telling bear to human goods a relation which is more than instrumental but less than necessary?

The very definition of lying makes plain that consequences are crucial, for lying is intentional and the intent is an intent to produce a consequence: false belief. But how can I then resist the consequentialist analysis of lying? Lying is an attempt to produce a certain effect on another, and if that effect (consequence) is not bad, how can lying be wrong? I shall have to argue, therefore, that to lie is to intend to produce an effect which always has something bad about it, an effect moreover of the special sort that it is wrong to produce it intentionally. To lay that groundwork for my argument about lying, I must consider first the moral value of truth.

TRUTH AND RATIONALITY

A statement is true when the world is the way the statement says it is. Utilitarians insist (as in the quotation from Bentham above) that truth, like everything else, has value just exactly as it produces value—pleasure, pain, the satisfaction or frustration of desire. And of course it is easy to show that truth (like keeping faith, not harming the innocent, respecting rights) does not always lead to the net satisfactions of desire, to the production of utility. It may *tend* to do so, but that tendency explains only why we should discriminate between occasions when truth does and when it does not have value—an old story. It is an old story, for truth—like justice, respect, and self-respect—has a value which consequentialist analyses (utilitarian or any other) do not capture. Truth, like respect, is a foundational value.

The morality of right and wrong does not count the satisfaction of desire as the overriding value.

Rather, the integrity of persons, as agents and as the objects of the intentional agency of others, has priority over the attainment of the goals which agents choose to attain. I have sought to show how respect for physical integrity is related to respect for the person. The person, I argued, is not just a locus of potential pleasure and pain but an entity with determinate characteristics. The person is, among other things, necessarily an incorporated, a physical, not an abstract entity. In relation to truth we touch another necessary aspect of moral personality: the capacity for judgment, and thus for choice. It is that aspect which Kant used to ground his moral theory, arguing that freedom and rationality are the basis for moral personality. John Rawls makes the same point, arguing that "moral personality and not the capacity for pleasure and pain . . . [is] the fundamental aspect of the self. . . . The essential unity of the self is . . . provided by the concept of right." The concept of the self is prior to the goods which the self chooses, and these goods gather their moral significance from the fact that they have been chosen by moral beings—beings capable of understanding and acting on moral principles.

In this view freedom and rationality are complementary capacities, or aspects of the same capacity, which is moral capacity. A man is free insofar as he is able to act on a judgment because he perceives it to be correct; he is free insofar as he may be moved to action by the judgments his reason offers to him. This is the very opposite of the Humean conception of reason as the slave of the passions. There is no slavery here. The man who follows the steps of a mathematical argument to its conclusion because he judges them to be correct is free indeed. To the extent that we choose our ends we are free; and as to objectively valuable ends which we choose because we see their value, we are still free.

Now, rational judgment is true judgment, and so the moral capacity for rational choice implies the capacity to recognize the matter on which choice is to act and to recognize the kind of result our choices will produce. This applies to judgments about other selves and to judgments in which one locates himself as a person among persons, a self among selves. These judgments are not just arbitrary suppositions: *they are judged to be true of the world.* For consider what the self would be like if these judgments were not supposed to be true. Maybe one might be content to be happy in the manner of the fool of Athens who believed all the ships in the harbor to be his. But what of our perceptions of other people? Would we be content to have those whom we love and trust the mere figments of our imaginations? The foundational values of freedom and rationality imply the foundational value of truth, for the rational man is the one who judges aright, that is, truly. Truth is not the same as judgment, as rationality; it is rather the proper subject of judgment. If we did not seek to judge truly, and if we did not believe we could judge truly, the act of judgment would not be what we know it to be at all.

Judgment and thus truth are *part* of a structure which as a whole makes up the concept of self. A person's relation to his body and the fact of being an incorporated self are another part of that structure. These two parts are related. The bodily senses provide matter for judgments of truth, and the body includes the physical organs of judgment.

THE WRONG OF LYING

So our capacity for judgment is foundational and truth is the proper object of that capacity, but how do we get to the badness of lying, much less its categorical wrongness? The crucial step to be supplied has to do not with the value of truth but with the evil of lying. We must show that to lie to someone is to injure him in a way that particularly touches his moral personality. From that, the passage is indeed easy to the conclusion that to inflict such injury intentionally (remember that all lying is by hypothesis intentional) is not only bad but wrong. It is this first, crucial step which is difficult. After all, a person's capacity for true judgment is not necessarily impaired by inducing in him a particular false belief. Nor would it seem that a person suffers a greater injury in respect to that capacity when he is induced to believe a falsity than when we intentionally prevent him from discovering the truth, yet only in the first case do we lie. Do we really do injury to a person's moral personality when we persuade him falsely that it rained yesterday in Bangkok—a fact in which he has no interest? And do we do him more injury than when we fail to answer his request for yesterday's football scores, in which he is mildly interested? Must we not calculate the injury by the *other* harm it does: disappointed expectations, lost property, missed opportunities, physical harm? In this view, lying would be a way of injuring a person in his various substantive interests—a way of stealing from him, hurting his feelings, perhaps poisoning him—but then the evil of lying would be purely instrumental, not wrong at all.

All truth, however irrelevant or trivial, has value, even though we may cheerfully ignore most truths, forget them, erase them as encumbrances from our memories. The value of every truth is shown just in the judgment that the only thing we must not do is falsify truth. Truths are like other people's property, which we can care nothing about but may not use for our own purposes. It is as if the truth were not ours (even truth we have discovered and which is known only to us), and so we may not exercise an unlimited dominion over it. Our relations to other people have a similar structure: we may perhaps have no duty to them, we may be free to put them out of our minds to make room for others whom we care about more, but we may not harm them. And so we may not falsify truth. But enough of metaphors—what does it mean to say that the truth is not ours?

The capacity for true judgment is the capacity to arrive at judgments which are in fact true of the world as it exists apart from our desires, our choices, our values. It is the world presented to us by true judgments—including true judgments about ourselves—which we then make the subject of our choices, our valuation. Now, if we treat the truth as our own, it must be according to desire or valuation. But for rational beings these activities are supposed to depend on truth; we are supposed to desire and choose according to the world as it is. To choose that something not be the case when it is in fact the case is very nearly self-contradictory—for choice is not *of* truth but *on the basis of* truth. To deliberate about whether to believe a truth (not whether it is indeed true—another story altogether) is like deciding whether to cheat at solitaire. All this is obvious. In fact I suppose one cannot even coherently talk about choosing to believe something one believes to be false. And this holds equally for all truths—big and little, useful, useless, and downright inconvenient. But we do and must calculate *about* (and not just *with*) truths all the time as we decide what truths to acquire, what to forget. We decide all the time not to pursue some inquiry because it is not worth it. Such calculations surely must go forward on the basis of what truths are useful, given one's plans and desires. Even when we pursue truth for its own sake, we distinguish between interesting and boring truths.

Considering what truth to acquire or retain differs, however, from deliberately acquiring false beliefs. All truths are acquired as propositions correctly (truly) corresponding to the world, and in this respect, all truths are equal. A lie, however, has the form and occupies the role of truth in that it too purports to be a proposition about the world; only the world does not correspond to it. So the choice of a lie is not like a choice among truths, for the choice of a lie is a choice to affirm as the basis for judgment a proposition which does not correspond to the world. So, when I say that truth is foundational, that truth precedes choice, what I mean is *not* that this or that truth is foundational but that judging according to the facts is foundational to judging at all. A scientist may deliberate about which subject to study and, having chosen his subject, about the data worth acquiring, but he cannot even deliberate as a scientist about whether to acquire false data. Clearly, then, there is something funny (wrong?) about lying to oneself, but how do we go from there to the proposition that it is wrong to lie to someone else? After all, much of the peculiarity about lying to oneself consists in the fact that it seems not so much bad as downright self-contradictory, logically impossible, but that does not support the judgment that it is wrong to lie to another. I cannot marry myself, but that hardly makes it wrong to marry someone else.

Let us imagine a case in which you come as close as you can to lying to yourself: You arrange some operation, some fiddling with your brain that has no effect other than to cause you to believe a proposition you know to be false and also to forget entirely the prior history of how you came to believe that proposition. It seems to me that you do indeed harm yourself in such an operation. This is because a free and rational person wishes to have a certain relation to reality: as nearly perfect as possible. He wishes to build his conception of himself and the world and his conception of the good on the basis of truth. Now if he affirms that the truth is available for fiddling in order to accommodate either his picture of the world or his conception of the good, then this affirms that reality is dependent on what one wants, rather than what one wants being fundamentally constrained by what there is. Rationality is the respect for this fundamental constraint of truth. This is just another way of saying that the truth is prior to our plans and prospects and must be respected whatever our plans might be. What if the truth we "destroy" by this operation is a very trivial and irrelevant truth—the state of the weather in Bangkok on some particular day? There is still an injury to self, because the fiddler must have some purpose in his fiddling. If it is a substantive purpose, then the truth is in fact relevant to that purpose, and my argument holds. If it is just to show it can be done, then he is only trying to show he can do violence to his rationality—a kind of moral blasphemy. Well, what if it is a very *little* truth? Why, then, it is a very little injury he does himself—but that does not undermine my point.

Now, when I lie to you, I do to you what you cannot actually do to yourself—brain-fiddling being only an approximation. The nature of the injury I would do to myself, if I could, explains why lying to you is to do you harm, indeed why it is wrong. The lie is an injury because it produces an effect (or seeks to) which a person as a moral agent should not wish to have produced in him, and thus it is as much an injury as any other effect which a moral agent would not wish to have produced upon his person. To be sure, some people may want to be lied to. That is a special problem; they are like people who want to suffer (not just are willing to risk) physical injury. In general, then, I do not want you to lie to me in the same way that as a rational man I would not lie to myself if I could. But why does this make lying wrong and not merely bad?

Lying is wrong because when I lie I set up a relation which is essentially exploitative. It violates the principle of respect, for I must affirm that the mind of another person is available to me in a way in which I cannot agree my mind would be available to him—for if I do so agree, then I would not expect my lie to be believed. When I lie, I am like a counterfeiter: I do not want the market flooded with counterfeit currency; I do not want to get back my own counterfeit bill. Moreover, in lying to you, I affirm such an unfairly unilateral principle in respect to an interest and capacity which is crucial, as crucial as physical integrity: your freedom and your rationality. When I do intentional physical harm, I say that your body, your person, is available for my purposes. When I lie, I lay claim to your mind.

Lying violates respect and is wrong, as is any breach of trust. Every lie is a broken promise, and the only reason this seems strained is that in lying the promise is made and broken at the same moment. Every lie necessarily implies—as does every assertion—an assurance, a warranty of its truth. The fact that the breach accompanies the making should, however, only strengthen the conclusion that this is wrong. If promise-breaking is wrong, then a lie must be wrong, since there cannot be the supervening factor of changed circumstances which may excuse breaches of promises to perform in the future.

The final one of the convergent strands that make up the wrong of lying is the shared, communal nature of language. This is what I think Kant had in mind when he argued that a lie does wrong "to men in general." If whether people stood behind their statements depended wholly on the particular circumstances of the utterance, then the whole point of communication would be undermined. For every utterance would simply be the occasion for an analysis of the total circumstances (speaker's and hearer's) in order to determine what, if anything, to make of the utterance. And though we do often wonder and calculate whether a person is telling the truth, we do so from a baseline, a presumption that people do stand behind their statements. After all, the speaker surely depends on such a baseline. He wants us to think he is telling the truth. Speech is a paradigm of communication, and all human relations are based on some form of communication. Our very ability to think, to conceptualize, is related to speech. Speech allows the social to penetrate the intimately personal. Perhaps that is why Kant's dicta seem to vacillate between two positions: lying as a social offense, and lying as an offense against oneself; the requirement of an intent to deceive another, and the insistence that the essence of the wrong is not injury to another but to humanity. Every lie violates the basic commitment to truth which stands behind the social fact of language.

I have already argued that bodily integrity bears a necessary relation to moral integrity, so that an attack upon bodily integrity is wrong, not just bad. The intimate *and* social nature of truth make the argument about lying stronger. For not only is the target aspect of the victim crucial to him as a moral agent but, by lying, we attack that target by a means which itself offends his moral nature; the means of attack are social means which can be said to belong as much to the victim as to his assailant. There is not only the attack at his moral vitals, but an attack with a weapon which belongs to him. Lying is, thus, a kind of treachery. (*Kind of* treachery? Why not treachery pure and simple?) It is as if we not only robbed a man of his treasure but in doing so used his own servants or family as our agents. That speech is our *common* property, that it belongs to the liar, his victim and all of us makes the matter if anything far worse.

So this is why lying is not only bad (a hurt), but wrong, why lying is wrong apart from or in addition to any other injury it does, and why lying seems at once an offense against the victim and against mankind in general, an offense against the liar himself, and against the abstract entity, truth. Whom do you injure when you pass a counterfeit bill?

What about little pointless lies? Do I really mean they are wrong? Well, yes, even a little lie is wrong, *if* it is a true piece of communication, an assertion of its own truth and not just a conventional way of asserting nothing at all or something else (as in the case of polite or diplomatic formulas). A little lie is a little wrong, but it is still something you must not do.

STUDY QUESTIONS

1. How is something that is bad different from something that is wrong, in the ethical sense?
2. Can lying be separated from the consequences of lying?
3. How does Fried connect truth to freedom and rationality?
4. Why is lying to another, even over something of very little consequence, a moral wrong?
5. If you lie, but not intentionally, are you still guilty of a moral wrong?

18

Power, Truth, and Right *from* Power/Knowledge

Michel Foucault

Michel Foucault (1926–84), one of the most influential thinkers in the contemporary world, was born in Poitiers, France. Before his untimely death of AIDS in 1984, he taught at the Collège de France. He is the author of many books, including *Madness and Civilization, The Order of Things,* and *Discipline and Punish: The Birth of the Prison.*

The course of study that I have been following until now . . . has been concerned with the *how* of power. I have tried, that is, to relate its mechanisms to two points of reference, two limits: on the one hand, to the rules of right that provide a formal delimitation of power; on the other, to the effects of truth that this power produces and transmits, and which in their turn reproduce this power. Hence we have a triangle: power, right, truth.

Schematically, we can formulate the traditional question of political philosophy in the following terms: how is the discourse of truth, or quite simply, philosophy as that discourse which *par excellence* is concerned with truth, able to fix limits to the rights of power? That is the traditional question. The one I would prefer to pose is rather different. Compared to the traditional, noble and philosophic question it is much more down to earth and concrete. My problem is rather this: what rules of right are implemented by the relations of power in the production of discourses of truth? Or alternatively, what type of power is susceptible of producing discourses of truth that in a society such as ours are endowed with such potent effects? What I mean is this: in a society such as ours, but basically in any society, there are manifold relations of power which permeate, characterise and constitute the social body, and these relations of power cannot themselves be established, consolidated nor implemented without the production, accumulation, circulation and functioning of a discourse. There can be no possible exercise of power without a certain economy of discourses of truth which operates through and on the basis of this association. (We are subjected to the production of truth through power and we cannot exercise power except through the production of truth.) This is the case for every society, but I believe that in ours the relationship between power, right and truth is organised in a highly specific fashion. If I were to characterise, not its mechanism itself, but its intensity and constancy, I would say that we are forced to produce the truth of power that our society demands, of which it has need, in order to function: we *must* speak the truth; we are constrained or condemned to confess or to discover the truth. Power never ceases its interrogation, its inquisition, its registration of truth: it institutionalises, professionalises and rewards its pursuit. In the last analysis, we must produce truth as we must produce wealth, indeed we must produce truth in order to produce wealth in the first place. In another way, we are also subjected to truth in the sense in which it is truth that makes the laws, that produces the true discourse which, at least partially, decides, transmits and itself extends upon the effects of power. In the end, we are judged, condemned, classified, determined in our undertakings, destined to a certain mode of living or dying, as a function of the true discourses which are the bearers of the specific effects of power.

So, it is the rules of right, the mechanisms of power, the effects of truth or if you like, the rules of power and the powers of true discourses, that can be said more or less to have formed the general terrain of my concern, even if, as I know full well, I have traversed it only partially and in a very zig-zag fashion. I should like to speak briefly about this course of research, about what I have considered as being its guiding principle and about the methodological imperatives and precautions which I have sought to adopt. As regards the general principle involved in a study of the relations between right and power, it seems to me that in Western societies since medieval times it has been royal power that has provided the essential focus around which legal thought has been elaborated. It is in response to the demands of royal power, for its profit and to serve as its instrument or justification, that the juridical edifice of our own society has been developed. Right in the West is the King's right. Naturally everyone is familiar with the famous, celebrated, repeatedly emphasised role of the jurists in the organisation of royal power. We must not forget that the re-vitalisation of Roman Law in the twelfth century was the major event around which, and on whose basis, the juridical edifice which had collapsed after the fall of the Roman Empire was reconstructed. This resurrection of Roman Law had in effect a technical and constitutive role to play in the establishment of the authoritarian, administrative, and, in the final analysis, absolute power of the monarchy. And when this legal edifice escapes in later centuries from the control of the monarch, when, more accurately, it is turned against that control, it is always the limits of this sovereign power that are put in question, its prerogatives that are challenged. In other words, I believe that the King remains the central personage in the whole legal edifice of the West. When it comes to the general organisation of the legal system in the West, it is essentially with the King, his rights, his power and its eventual limitations, that one is dealing. Whether the jurists were the King's henchmen or his adversaries, it is of royal power that we are speaking in every case when we speak of these grandiose edifices of legal thought and knowledge.

There are two ways in which we do so speak. Either we do so in order to show the nature of the juridical armoury that invested royal power, to reveal the monarch as the effective embodiment of sovereignty, to demonstrate that his power, for all that it was absolute, was exactly that which befitted his fundamental right. Or, by contrast, we do so in order to show the necessity of imposing limits upon this sovereign power, of submitting it to certain rules of right, within whose confines it had to be exercised in order for it to remain legitimate. The essential role of the theory of right, from medieval times onwards, was to fix the legitimacy of power; that is the major problem around which the whole theory of right and sovereignty is organised.

When we say that sovereignty is the central problem of right in Western societies, what we mean basically is that the essential function of the discourse and techniques of right has been to efface the domination intrinsic to power in order to present the latter at the level of appearance under two different aspects: on the one hand, as the legitimate rights of sovereignty, and on the other, as the legal obligation to obey it. The system of right is centered entirely upon the King, and it is therefore designed to eliminate the fact of domination and its consequences.

My general project over the past few years has been, in essence, to reverse the mode of analysis followed by the entire discourse of right from the time of the Middle Ages. My aim, therefore, was to invert it, to give due weight, that is, to the fact of domination, to expose both its latent nature and its brutality. I then wanted to show not only how right is, in a general way, the instrument of this domination—which scarcely needs saying—but also to show the extent to which, and the forms in which, right (not simply the laws but the whole complex of apparatuses, institutions and regulations responsible for their application) transmits and puts in motion relations that are not relations of sovereignty, but of domination. Moreover, in speaking of domination I do not have in mind that solid and global kind of domination that one person exercises over others, or one group over another, but the manifold forms of domination that can be exercised within society. Not the domination of the King in his central position, therefore, but that of his subjects in their mutual relations: not the uniform edifice of sovereignty, but the multiple forms of subjugation that have a place and function within the social organism.

The system of right, the domain of the law, are permanent agents of these relations of domination, these polymorphous techniques of subjugation. Right should be viewed, I believe, not in terms of a legitimacy to be established, but in terms of the methods of subjugation that it instigates.

The problem for me is how to avoid this question, central to the theme of right, regarding sovereignty and the obedience of individual subjects in order that I may substitute the problem of domination and subjugation for that of sovereignty and obedience. Given that this was to be the general line of my analysis, there were a certain number of methodological precautions that seemed requisite to its pursuit. In the very first place, it seemed important to accept that the analysis in question should not concern itself with the regulated and legitimate forms of power in their central locations, with the general mechanisms through which they operate, and the continual effects of these. On the contrary, it should be concerned with power at its extremities, in its ultimate destinations, with those points where it becomes capillary, that is, in its more regional and local forms and institutions. Its paramount concern, in fact, should be with the point where power surmounts the rules of right which organise and delimit it and extends itself beyond them, invests itself in institutions, becomes embodied in techniques, and equips itself with instruments and eventually even violent means of material intervention. To give an example: rather than try to discover where and how the right of punishment is founded on sovereignty, how it is presented in the theory of monarchical right or in that of democratic right, I have tried to see in what ways punishment and the power of punishment are effectively embodied in a certain number of local, regional, material institutions, which are concerned with torture or imprisonment, and to place these in the climate—at once institutional and physical, regulated and violent—of the effective apparatuses of punishment. In other words, one should try to locate power at the extreme points of its exercise, where it is always less legal in character.

A second methodological precaution urged that the analysis should not concern itself with power at the level of conscious intention or decision; that it should not attempt to consider power from its internal point of view and that it should refrain from posing the labyrinthine and unanswerable question: 'Who then has power and what has he in mind? What is the aim of someone who possesses power?' Instead, it is a case of studying power at the point where its intention, if it has one, is completely invested in its real and effective practices. What is needed is a study of power in its external visage, at the point where it is in direct and immediate relationship with that which we can provisionally call its object, its target, its field of application, there—that is to say—where it installs itself and produces its real effects.

Let us not, therefore, ask why certain people want to dominate, what they seek, what is their overall strategy. Let us ask, instead, how things work at the level of on-going subjugation, at the level of those continuous and uninterrupted processes which subject our bodies, govern our gestures, dictate our behaviours etc. In other words, rather than ask ourselves how the sovereign appears to us in his lofty isolation, we should try to discover how it is that subjects are gradually, progressively, really and materially constituted through a multiplicity of organisms, forces, energies, materials, desires, thoughts etc. We should try to grasp subjection in its material instance as a constitution of subjects. This would be the exact opposite of Hobbes' project in *Leviathan,* and of that, I believe, of all jurists for whom the problem is the distillation of a single will—or rather, the constitution of a unitary, singular body animated by the spirit of sovereignty—from the particular wills of a multiplicity of individuals. Think of the scheme of Leviathan: insofar as he is a fabricated man, Leviathan is no other than the amalgamation of a certain number of separate individualities, who find themselves reunited by the complex of elements that go to compose the State; but at the heart of the State, or rather, at its head, there exists something which constitutes it as such, and this is sovereignty, which Hobbes says is precisely the spirit of Leviathan. Well, rather than worry about the problem of the central spirit, I believe that we must attempt to study the myriad of bodies which are constituted as peripheral *subjects* as a result of the effects of power.

A third methodological precaution relates to the fact that power is not to be taken to be a phenomenon of one individual's consolidated and homogeneous domination over others, or that of one group or class over others. What, by contrast, should always be kept in mind is that power, if we do not take too distant a view of it, is not that which makes the difference between those who exclusively possess and retain it, and those who do not have it and submit to it. Power must be analysed as something which circulates, or rather as something which only functions in the form of a chain. It is never localised here or there, never in anybody's hands, never appropriated as a commodity or piece of wealth. Power is employed and exercised through a net-like organisation. And not only do individuals circulate between its threads; they are always in the position of simultaneously undergoing and exercising this power. They are not only its inert or consenting target; they are always also the elements of its articulation. In other words, individuals are the vehicles of power, not its points of application.

The individual is not to be conceived as a sort of elementary nucleus, a primitive atom, a multiple and inert material on which power comes to fasten or against which it happens to strike, and in so doing subdues or crushes individuals. In fact, it is already one of the prime effects of power that certain bodies, certain gestures, certain discourses, certain desires, come to be identified and constituted as individuals. The individual, that is, is not the *vis-à-vis* of power; it is, I believe, one of its prime effects. The individual is an effect of power, and at the same time, or precisely to the extent to which it is that effect, it is the element of its articulation. The individual which power has constituted is at the same time its vehicle.

The important thing here, I believe, is that truth isn't outside power, or lacking in power: contrary to a myth whose history and functions would repay further study, truth isn't the reward of free spirits, the child of protracted solitude, nor the privilege of those who have succeeded in liberating themselves. Truth is a thing of this world: it is produced only by virtue of multiple forms of constraint. And it induces regular effects of power. Each society has its regime of truth, its 'general politics' of truth: that is, the types of discourse which it accepts and makes function as true; the mechanisms and instances which enable one to distinguish true and false statements, the means by which each is sanctioned; the techniques and procedures accorded value in the acquisition of truth; the status of those who are charged with saying what counts as true.

In societies like ours, the 'political economy' of truth is characterised by five important traits. 'Truth' is centred on the form of scientific discourse and the institutions which produce it; it is subject to constant economic and political incitement (the demand for truth, as much for economic production as for political power), it is the object, under diverse forms, of immense diffusion and consumption (circulating through apparatuses of education and information whose extent is relatively broad in the social body, not withstanding certain strict limitations); it is produced and transmitted under the control, dominant if not exclusive, of a few great political and economic apparatuses (university, army, writing, media); lastly, it is the issue of a whole political debate and social confrontation ('ideological' struggles).

It seems to me that what must now be taken into account in the intellectual is not the 'bearer of universal values.' Rather, it's the person occupying a specific position—but whose specificity is linked, in a society like ours, to the general functioning of an apparatus of truth. In other words, the intellectual has a three-fold specificity: that of his class position (whether as petty-bourgeois in the service of capitalism or 'organic' intellectual of the proletariat); that of his conditions of life and work, linked to his condition as an intellectual (his field of research, his place in a laboratory, the political and economic demands to which he submits or against which he rebels, in the university, the hospital, etc.); lastly, the specificity of the politics of truth in our societies. And it's with this last factor that his position can take on a general significance and that his local, specific struggle can have effects and implications which are not simply professional or sectoral. The intellectual can operate and struggle at the general level of that régime of truth which is so essential to the structure and functioning of our society. There is a battle, 'for truth', or at least 'around truth'—it being understood once again that by truth I do not mean 'the ensemble of truths which are to be discovered and accepted', but rather 'the ensemble of rules according to which the true and the false are separated and specific effects of power attached to the true', it being understood also that it's not a matter of a battle 'on behalf' of the truth, but of a battle about the status of truth and the economic and political role it plays. It is necessary to think of the political problems of intellectuals not in terms of 'science' and 'ideology', but in terms of 'truth' and 'power'. And thus the question of the professionalisation of intellectuals and the division between intellectual and manual labour can be envisaged in a new way.

All this must seem very confused and uncertain. Uncertain indeed, and what I am saying here is above all to be taken as a hypothesis. In order for it to be a little less confused, however, I would like to put forward a few 'propositions'—not firm assertions, but simply suggestions to be further tested and evaluated.

'Truth' is to be understood as a system of ordered procedures for the production, regulation, distribution, circulation and operation of statements.

'Truth' is linked in a circular relation with systems of power which produce and sustain it, and to effects of power which it induces and which extend it. A 'régime' of truth.

This régime is not merely ideological or superstructural; it was a condition of the formation and development of capitalism. And it's this same régime which, subject to certain modifications, operates in the socialist countries. . . .

The essential political problem for the intellectual is not to criticise the ideological contents supposedly linked to science, or to ensure that his own scientific practice is accompanied by a correct ideology, but that of ascertaining the possibility of constituting a new politics of truth. The problem is not changing people's consciousnesses—or what's in their heads—but the political, economic, institutional régime of the production of truth.

It's not a matter of emancipating truth from every system of power (which would be a chimera, for truth is already power) but of detaching the power of truth from the forms of hegemony, social, economic and cultural, within which it operates at the present time.

The political question, to sum up, is not error, illusion, alienated consciousness or ideology; it is truth itself. Hence the importance of Nietzsche.

STUDY QUESTIONS

1. What does Foucault mean by a "régime of truth"?
2. Explain the roles of truth, power, and right in Foucault's triangle.
3. How would Foucault go about determining the rightness or wrongness of an action? Can he avoid the charge of relativism?

19

Living in Truth

Václav Havel

Václav Havel, a Czech playwright, was imprisoned in 1979 for his role in the Czech human rights movement's Charter 77, of which he was a founding spokesperson. The author of many influential essays on totalitarianism and dissent, he became his nation's president in December 1989.

The manager of a fruit and vegetable shop places in his window, among the onions and carrots, the slogan: 'Workers of the world, unite!' Why does he do it? What is he trying to communicate to the world? Is he genuinely enthusiastic about the idea of unity among the workers of the world? Is his enthusiasm so great that he feels an irrepressible impulse to acquaint the public with his ideals? Has he really given more than a moment's thought to how such a unification might occur and what it would mean?

I think it can safely be assumed that the overwhelming majority of shopkeepers never think about the slogans they put in their windows, nor do they use them to express their real opinions. That poster was delivered to our greengrocer from the enterprise headquarters along with the onions and carrots. He put them all into the window simply because it has been done that way for years, because everyone does it, and because that is the way it has to be. If he were to refuse, there could be trouble. He could be reproached for not having the proper 'decoration' in his window; someone might even accuse him of disloyalty. He does it because these things must be done if one is to get along in life. It is one of the thousands of details that guarantee him a relatively tranquil life 'in harmony with society', as they say.

Obviously the greengrocer is indifferent to the semantic content of the slogan on exhibit; he does not put the slogan in his window from any personal desire to acquaint the public with the ideal it expresses. This, of course, does not mean that his action has no motive or significance at all, or that the slogan communicates nothing to anyone. The slogan is really a *sign,* and as such it contains a subliminal but very definite message. Verbally, it might be expressed this way: 'I, the greengrocer XY, live here and I know what I must do. I behave in the manner expected of me. I can be depended upon and am beyond reproach. I am obedient and therefore I have the right to be left in peace.' This message, of course, has an addressee: it is directed above, to the greengrocer's superior, and at the same time it is a shield that protects the greengrocer from potential informers. The slogan's real meaning, therefore, is rooted firmly in the greengrocer's existence. It reflects his vital interests. But what are those vital interests?

Let us take note: if the greengrocer had been instructed to display the slogan, 'I am afraid and therefore unquestioningly obedient', he would not be nearly as indifferent to its semantics, even though the statement would reflect the truth. The greengrocer would be embarrassed and ashamed to put such an unequivocal statement of his own degradation in the shop window, and quite naturally so, for he is a human being and thus has a sense of his own dignity. To overcome this complication, his expression of loyalty must take the form of a sign which, at least on its textual surface, indicates a level of disinterested conviction. It must allow the greengrocer to say, 'What's wrong with the workers of the world uniting?' Thus the sign helps the greengrocer to conceal from himself the low foundations of his obedience, at the same time concealing the low foundations of power. It hides them behind the façade of something high. And that something is *ideology.*

Ideology is a specious way of relating to the world. It offers human beings the illusion of an identity, of dignity, and of morality while making it easier for them to *part* with them. As the repository of something 'supra-personal' and objective, it enables people to deceive their conscience and conceal their true position and their inglorious *modus vivendi,* both from the world and from themselves. It is a very pragmatic, but at the same time an apparently dignified, way of legitimizing what is above, below, and on either side. It is directed towards people and towards God. It is a veil behind which human beings can hide their own 'fallen existence', their trivialization, and their adaptation to the status quo. It is an excuse that everyone can use, from the greengrocer, who conceals his fear of losing his job behind an alleged interest in the unification of the workers of the world, to the highest functionary, whose interest in staying in power can be cloaked in phrases about service to the working class. The primary excusatory function of ideology, therefore, is to provide people, both as victims and pillars of the post-totalitarian system, with the illusion that the system is in harmony with the human order and the order of the universe.

The smaller a dictatorship and the less stratified by modernization the society under it, the more directly the will of the dictator can be exercised. In other words, the dictator can employ more or less naked discipline, avoiding the complex processes of relating to the world and of self-justification which ideology involves. But the more complex the mechanisms of power become, the larger and more stratified the society they embrace, and the longer they have operated historically, the more individuals must be connected to them from outside, and the greater the importance attached to the ideological excuse. It acts as a kind of bridge between the regime and the people, across which the regime approaches the people and the people approach the regime. This explains why ideology plays such an important role in the post-totalitarian system: that complex machinery of units, hierarchies, transmission belts, and indirect instruments of manipulation which ensure in countless ways the integrity of the regime, leaving nothing to chance, would be quite simply unthinkable without ideology acting as its all-embracing excuse and as the excuse for each of its parts.

Between the aims of the post-totalitarian system and the aims of life there is a yawning abyss: while life, in its essence, moves towards plurality, diversity, independent self-constitution and self-organization, in short, towards the fulfilment of its own freedom, the post-totalitarian system demands conformity, uniformity, and discipline. While life ever strives to create new and 'improbable' structures, the post-totalitarian system contrives to force life into its most probable states. The aims of the system reveal its most essential characteristic to be introversion, a movement towards being ever more completely and unreservedly *itself,* which means that the radius of its influence is continually widening as well. This system serves people only to the extent necessary to ensure that people will serve it. Anything beyond this, that is to say, anything which leads people to overstep their predetermined roles is regarded by the system as an attack upon itself. And in this respect it is correct: every instance of such transgression is a genuine denial of the system. It can be said, therefore, that the inner aim of the post-totalitarian system is not mere preservation of power in the hands of a ruling clique, as appears to be the case at first sight. Rather, the social phenomenon of self-preservation is subordinated to something higher, to a kind of blind *automatism* which drives the system. No matter what position individuals hold in the hierarchy of power, they are not considered by the system to be worth anything in themselves, but only as things intended to fuel and serve this automatism. For this reason, an individual's desire for power is admissible only in so far as its direction coincides with the direction of the automatism of the system.

Ideology, in creating a bridge of excuses between the system and the individual, spans the abyss between the aims of the system and the aims of life. It pretends that the requirements of the system derive from the requirements of life. It is a world of appearances trying to pass for reality.

The post-totalitarian system touches people at every step, but it does so with its ideological gloves on. This is why life in the system is so thoroughly permeated with hypocrisy and lies: government by bureaucracy is called popular government; the working class is enslaved in the name of the working class; the complete degradation of the individual is presented as his or her ultimate liberation; depriving people of information is called making it available; the use of power to manipulate is called the public control of power, and the arbitrary abuse of power is called observing the legal code; the repression of culture is called its development; the expansion of imperial influence is presented as support for the oppressed; the lack of free expression becomes the highest form of freedom; farcical elections become the highest form of democracy; banning independent thought becomes the most scientific of world views; military occupation becomes fraternal assistance. Because the regime is captive to its own lies, it must falsify everything. It falsifies the past. It falsifies the present, and it falsifies the future. It falsifies statistics. It pretends not to possess an omnipotent and unprincipled police apparatus. It pretends to respect human rights. It pretends to persecute no one. It pretends to fear nothing. It pretends to pretend nothing.

Individuals need not believe all these mystifications, but they must behave as though they did, or they must at least tolerate them in silence, or get along well with those who work with them. For this reason, however, they must *live within a lie*. They need not accept the lie. It is enough for them to have accepted their life with it and in it. For by this very fact, individuals confirm the system, fulfil the system, make the system, *are* the system.

We have seen that the real meaning of the greengrocer's slogan has nothing to do with what the text of the slogan actually says. Even so, this real meaning is quite clear and generally comprehensible because the code is so familiar: the greengrocer declares his loyalty (and he can do no other if his declaration is to be accepted) in the only way the regime is capable of hearing; that is, by accepting the prescribed *ritual*, by accepting appearances as reality, by accepting the given rules of the game. In doing so, however, he has himself become a player in the game, thus making it possible for the game to go on, for it to exist in the first place.

If ideology was originally a bridge between the system and the individual as an individual, then the moment he or she steps on to this bridge it becomes at the same time a bridge between the system and the individual as a component of the system. That is, if ideology originally facilitated (by acting outwardly) the constitution of power by serving as a psychological excuse, then from the moment that excuse is accepted, it constitutes power inwardly, becoming an active component of that power. It begins to function as the principal instrument of ritual communication *within* the system of power.

The whole power structure (and we have already discussed its physical articulation) could not exist at all if there were not a certain 'metaphysical' order binding all its components together, interconnecting them and subordinating them to a uniform method of accountability, supplying the combined operation of all these components with rules of the game, that is, with certain regulations, limitations, and legalities. This metaphysical order is fundamental to, and standard throughout, the entire power structure; it integrates its communication system and makes possible the internal exchange and transfer of information and instructions. It is rather like a collection of traffic signals and directional signs, giving the process shape and structure. This metaphysical order guarantees the inner coherence of the totalitarian power structure. It is the glue holding it together, its binding principle, the instrument of its discipline. Without this glue the structure as a totalitarian structure would vanish; it would disintegrate into individual atoms chaotically colliding with one another in their unregulated particular interests and inclinations. The entire pyramid of totalitarian power, deprived of the element that binds it together, would collapse in upon itself, as it were, in a kind of material implosion.

As the interpretation of reality by the power structure, ideology is always subordinated ultimately to the interests of the structure. Therefore, it has a natural tendency to disengage itself from reality, to create a world of appearances, to become ritual. In societies where there is public competition for power and therefore public control of that power, there also exists quite naturally public control of the way that power legitimates itself ideologically. Consequently, in such conditions there are always certain correctives that effectively prevent ideology from abandoning reality altogether. Under totalitarianism, however, these correctives disappear, and thus there is nothing to prevent ideology from becoming more and more removed from reality, gradually turning into what it has already become in the post-totalitarian system: a world of appearances, a mere ritual, a formalized language deprived of semantic contact with reality and transformed into a system of ritual signs that replace reality with pseudo-reality.

Yet, as we have seen, ideology becomes at the same time an increasingly important component of power, a pillar providing it with both excusatory legitimacy and an inner coherence. As this aspect grows in importance, and as it gradually loses touch with reality, it acquires a peculiar but very real strength. It becomes reality itself, albeit a reality altogether self-contained, one that on certain levels (chiefly inside the power structure) may have even greater weight than reality as such. Increasingly, the virtuosity of the ritual becomes more important than the reality hidden behind it. The significance of phenomena no longer derives from the phenomena themselves, but from their *locus* as concepts in the ideological context. Reality does not shape theory, but rather the reverse. Thus power gradually draws closer to ideology than it does to reality; it draws its strength from theory and becomes entirely dependent on it. This inevitably leads, of course, to a paradoxical result: rather than theory, or rather ideology, serving power, power begins to serve ideology. It is as though ideology had appropriated power from power, as though it had become dictator itself. It then appears that theory itself, ritual itself, ideology itself, makes decisions that affect people, and not the other way around.

Let us now imagine that one day something in our greengrocer snaps and he stops putting up the slogans merely to ingratiate himself. He stops voting in elections he knows are a farce. He begins to say what he really thinks at political meetings. And he even finds the strength in himself to express solidarity with those whom his conscience commands him to support. In this revolt the greengrocer steps out of living within the lie. He rejects the ritual and breaks the rules of the game. He discovers once more his suppressed identity and dignity. He gives his freedom a concrete significance. His revolt is an attempt to *live within the truth.*

The bill is not long in coming. He will be relieved of his post as manager of the shop and transferred to the warehouse. His pay will be reduced. His hopes for a holiday in Bulgaria will evaporate. His children's access to higher education will be threatened. His superiors will harass him and his fellow workers will wonder about him. Most of those who apply these sanctions, however, will not do so from any authentic inner conviction but simply under pressure from conditions, the same conditions that once pressured the greengrocer to display the official slogans. They will persecute the greengrocer either because it is expected of them, or to demonstrate their loyalty, or simply as part of the general panorama, to which belongs an awareness that this is how situations of this sort are dealt with, that this, in fact, is how things are always done, particularly if one is not to become suspect oneself. The executors, therefore, behave essentially like everyone else, to a greater or lesser degree: as components of the post-totalitarian system, as agents of its automatism, as petty instruments of the social auto-totality.

Thus the power structure, though the agency of those who carry out the sanctions, those anonymous components of the system, will spew the greengrocer from its mouth. The system, through its alienating presence in people, will punish him for his rebellion. It must do so because the logic of its automatism and self-defence dictate it. The greengrocer has not committed a simple, individual offence, isolated in its own uniqueness, but something incomparably more serious. By breaking the rules of the game, he has disrupted the game as such. He has exposed it as a mere game. He has shattered the world of appearances, the fundamental pillar of the system. He has upset the power structure by tearing apart what holds it together. He has demonstrated that living a lie is living a lie. He has broken through the exalted façade of the system and exposed the real, base foundations of power. He has said that the emperor is naked. And because the emperor is in fact naked, something extremely dangerous has happened: by his action, the greengrocer has addressed the world. He has enabled everyone to peer behind the curtain. He has shown everyone that it *is* possible to live within the truth. Living within the lie can constitute the system only if it is universal. The principle must embrace and permeate everything. There are no terms whatsoever on which it can coexist with living within the truth, and therefore everyone who steps out of line *denies it in principle and threatens it in its entirety*.

This is understandable: as long as appearance is not confronted with reality, it does not seem to be appearance. As long as living a lie is not confronted with living the truth, the perspective needed to expose its mendacity is lacking. As soon as the alternative appears, however, it threatens the very existence of appearance and living a lie in terms of what they are, both their essence and their all-inclusiveness. And at the same time, it is utterly unimportant how large a space this alternative occupies: its power does not consist in its physical attributes but in the light it casts on those pillars of the system and on its unstable foundations. After all, the greengrocer was a threat to the system not because of any physical or actual power he had, but because his action went beyond itself, because it illuminated its surroundings and, of course because of the incalculable consequences of that illumination. In the post-totalitarian system, therefore, living within the truth has more than a mere existential dimension (returning humanity to its inherent nature), or a noetic dimension (revealing reality as it is), or a moral dimension (setting an example for others). It also has an unambiguous *political* dimension. If the main pillar of the system is living a lie, then it is not surprising that the fundamental threat to it is living the truth. This is why it must be suppressed more severely than anything else.

In the post-totalitarian system, truth in the widest sense of the word has a very special import, one unknown in other contexts. In this system, truth plays a far greater (and above all, a far different) role as a factor of power, or as an outright political force. How does the power of truth operate? How does truth as a factor of power work? How can its power—as power—be realized?

Individuals can be alienated from themselves only because there is *something* in them to alienate. The terrain of this violation is their authentic existence. Living the truth is thus woven directly into the texture of living a lie. It is the repressed alternative, the authentic aim to which living a lie is an inauthentic response. Only against this background does living a lie make any sense: it exists *because* of that background. In its excusatory, chimerical rootedness in the human order, it is a response to nothing other than the human predisposition to truth. Under the orderly surface of the life of lies, therefore, there slumbers the hidden sphere of life in its real aims, of its hidden openness to truth.

The singular, explosive, incalculable political power of living within the truth resides in the fact that living openly within the truth has an ally, invisible to be sure, but omnipresent: this hidden sphere. It is from this sphere that life lived openly in the truth grows; it is to this sphere that it speaks, and in it that it finds understanding. This is where the potential for communication exists. But this place is hidden and therefore, from the perspective of power, very dangerous. The complex ferment that takes place within it goes on in semi-darkness, and by the time it finally surfaces into the light of day as an assortment of shocking surprises to the system, it is usually too late to cover them up in the usual fashion. Thus they create a situation in which the regime is confounded, invariably causing panic and driving it to react in inappropriate ways.

It seems that the primary breeding ground for what might, in the widest possible sense of the word, be understood as an opposition in the post-totalitarian system is living within the truth. The confrontation between these opposition forces and the powers that be, of course, will obviously take a form essentially different from that typical of an open society or a classical dictatorship. Initially, this confrontation does not take place on the level of real, institutionalized, quantifiable power which relies on the various instruments of power, but on a different level altogether: the level of human consciousness and conscience, the existential level. The effective range of this special power cannot be measured in terms of disciples, voters, or soldiers, because it lies spread out in the fifth column of social consciousness, in the hidden aims of life, in human beings' repressed longing for dignity and fundamental rights, for the realization of their real social and political interests. Its power, therefore, does not reside in the strength of definable political or social groups, but chiefly in the strength of a potential, which is hidden throughout the whole of society, including the official power structures of that society. Therefore this power does not rely on soldiers of its own, but on the soldiers of the enemy as it were—that is to say, on everyone who is living within the lie and who may be struck at any moment (in theory, at least) by the force of truth (or who, out of an instinctive desire to protect their position, may at least adapt to that force). It is a bacteriological weapon, so to speak, utilized when conditions are ripe by a single civilian to disarm an entire division. This power does not participate in any direct struggle for power; rather it makes its influence felt in the obscure arena of being itself. The hidden movements it gives rise to there, however, can issue forth (when, where, under what circumstances, and to what extent are difficult to predict) in something visible: a real political act or event, a social movement, a sudden explosion of civil unrest, a sharp conflict inside an apparently monolithic power structure, or simply an irrepressible transformation in the social and intellectual climate. And since all genuine problems and matters of critical importance are hidden beneath a thick crust of lies, it is never quite clear when the proverbial last straw will fall, or what that straw will be. This, too, is why the regime prosecutes, almost as a reflex action preventively, even the most modest attempts to live within the truth. . . .

When I speak of living within the truth, I naturally do not have in mind only products of conceptual thought, such as a protest or a letter written by a group of intellectuals. It can be any means by which a person or a group revolts against manipulation: anything from a letter by intellectuals to a workers' strike, from a rock concert to a student demonstration, from refusing to vote in the farcical elections, to making an open speech at some official congress, or even a hunger strike, for instance. If the suppression of the aims of life is a complex process, and if it is based on the multifaceted manipulation of all expressions of life then, by the same token, every free expression of life indirectly threatens the post-totalitarian system politically, including forms of expression to which, in other social systems, no one would attribute any potential political significance, not to mention explosive power. . . .

The profound crisis of human identity brought on by living within a lie, a crisis which in turn makes such a life possible, certainly possesses a moral dimension as well; it appears, among other things, as a *deep moral crisis in society.* A person who has been seduced by the consumer value system, whose identity is dissolved in an amalgam of the accoutrements of mass civilization, and who has no roots in the order of being, no sense of responsibility for anything higher than his or her own personal survival, is a *demoralized* person. The system depends on this demoralization, deepens it, is in fact a projection of it into society.

Living within the truth, as humanity's revolt against an enforced position, is, on the contrary, an attempt to regain control over one's own sense of responsibility. In other words, it is clearly a moral act, not only because one must pay so dearly for it, but principally because it is not self-serving: the risk may bring rewards in the form of a general amelioration in the situation, or it may not. In this regard, as I stated previously, it is an all-or-nothing gamble, and it is difficult to imagine a reasonable person embarking on such a course merely because he or she reckons that sacrifice today will bring rewards tomorrow, be it only in the form of general gratitude. . . .

If living within the truth in the post-totalitarian system becomes the chief breeding ground for independent, alternative political ideas, then all considerations about the nature and future prospects of these ideas must necessarily reflect this moral dimension as a political phenomenon. . . . The very special political significance of morality in the post-totalitarian system is a phenomenon that is at the very least unusual in modern political history, a phenomenon that might well have—as I shall soon attempt to show—far-reaching consequences. . . .

One concept that is a constant source of confusion chiefly because it has been imported into our circumstances from circumstances that are entirely different, is the concept of an opposition. What exactly is an opposition in the post-totalitarian system?

In democratic societies with a traditional parliamentary system of government, political opposition is understood as a political force on the level of actual power (most frequently a party or coalition of parties) which is not a part of the government. It offers an alternative political programme, it has ambitions to govern, and it is recognized and respected by the government in power as a natural element in the political life of the country. It seeks to spread its influence by political means, and competes for power on the basis of agreed-upon legal regulations.

In addition to this form of opposition, there exists the phenomenon of the 'extra-parliamentary opposition', which again consists of forces organized more or less on the level of actual power, but which operate outside the rules created by the system, and which employ different means than are usual within that framework.

In classical dictatorships, the term opposition is understood to mean the political forces which have also come out with an alternative political programme. They operate either legally or on the outer limits of legality, but in any case they cannot compete for power within the limits of some agreed-upon regulations. Or the term opposition may be applied to forces preparing for a violent confrontation with the ruling power, or who feel themselves to be in this state of confrontation already, such as various guerrilla groups or liberation movements.

An opposition in the post-totalitarian system does not exist in any of these senses. In what way, then, can the term be used?

1. Occasionally the term 'opposition' is applied, mainly by Western journalists, to persons or groups inside the power structure who find themselves in a state of *hidden* conflict with the highest authorities. The reasons for this conflict may be certain differences (not very sharp differences, naturally) of a conceptual nature, but more frequently it is quite simply a longing for power or a personal antipathy to others who represent that power.

2. Opposition here can also be understood as everything that does or can have an indirect political effect in the sense already mentioned, that is, everything the post-totalitarian system feels threatened by, which in fact means everything it *is* threatened by. In this sense, the opposition is every attempt to live within the truth, from the greengrocer's refusal to put the slogan in his window to a freely written poem; in other words, everything in which the genuine aims of life go beyond the limits placed on them by the aims of the system.

3. More frequently, however, the opposition is usually understood (again, largely by Western journalists) as groups of people who make public their nonconformist stances and crititical opinions, who make no secret of their independent thinking and who, to a greater or lesser degree, consider themselves a political force. In this sense, the notion of an 'opposition' more or less overlaps with the notion of 'dissent', although, of course, there are great differences in the degree to which that label is accepted or rejected. It depends not only on the extent to which these people understand their power as a directly political force, and on whether they have ambitions to participate in actual power, but also on how each of them understands the notion of an 'opposition'.

If the term 'opposition' has been imported from democratic societies into the post-totalitarian system without general agreement on what the word means in conditions that are so different, then the term 'dissident' was, on the contrary, chosen by Western journalists and is now generally accepted as the label for a phenomenon peculiar to the post-totalitarian system and almost never occurring—at least not in that form—in democratic societies.

Who are these 'dissidents'?

It seems that the term is applied primarily to citizens of the Soviet bloc who have decided to live within the truth and who, in addition, meet the following criteria:

1. They express their nonconformist positions and critical opinions publicly and systematically, within the very strict limits available to them, and because of this, they are known in the West.

2. Despite being unable to publish at home and despite every possible form of persecution by their governments, they have, by virtue of their attitudes, managed to win a certain esteem, both from the public and from their government, and thus they actually enjoy a very limited and very strange degree of indirect, actual power in their own milieu as well. This either protects them from the worst forms of persecution, or at least it ensures that if they are persecuted, it will mean certain political complications for their governments.

3. The horizon of their critical attention and their commitment reaches beyond the narrow context of their immediate surroundings or special

interests to embrace more general causes and, thus, their work becomes political in nature, although the degree to which they think of themselves as a directly political force may vary a great deal.

4. They are people who lean towards intellectual pursuits, that is, they are 'writing' people, people for whom the written word is the primary—and often the only—political medium they command, and that can gain them attention, particularly from abroad. Other ways in which they seek to live within the truth are either lost to the foreign observer in the elusive local milieu or—if they reach beyond this local framework—they appear to be only somewhat less visible complements to what they have written.
5. Regardless of their actual vocations, these people are talked about in the West more frequently in terms of their activities as committed citizens, or in terms of the critical, political aspects of their work, than in terms of the 'real' work they do in their own fields. From personal experience, I know that there is an invisible line you cross—without even wanting to or becoming aware of it—beyond which they cease to treat you as a writer who happens to be a concerned citizen and begin talking of you as a 'dissident' who almost incidentally (in his or her spare time, perhaps?) happens to write plays as well.

Unquestionably, there are people who meet all of these criteria. What is debatable is whether we should be using a special term for a group defined in such an essentially accidental way, and specifically, whether they should be called 'dissidents'. It does happen, however, and there is clearly nothing we can do about it. Sometimes, to facilitate communication, we even use the label ourselves, although it is done with distaste, rather ironically, and almost always in quotation marks.

Perhaps it is now appropriate to outline some of the reasons why 'dissidents' themselves are not very happy to be referred to in this way. In the first place, the word is problematic from an etymological point of view. A 'dissident', we are told in our press, means something like 'renegade' or 'backslider'. But dissidents do not consider themselves renegades for the simple reason that they are not primarily denying or rejecting anything. On the contrary, they have tried to affirm their own human identity, and if they reject anything at all, then it is merely what was false and alienating in their lives, that aspect of 'living within a lie'.

But that is not the most important thing. The term 'dissident' frequently implies a special profession, as if, along with the more normal vocations, there were another special one—grumbling about the state of things. In fact, a 'dissident' is simply a physicist, a sociologist, a worker, a poet, individuals who are merely doing what they feel they must and, consequently, who find themselves in open conflict with the regime. This conflict has not come about through any conscious intention on their part, but simply through the inner logic of their thinking, behaviour or work (often confronted with external circumstances more or less beyond their control). They have not, in other words, consciously decided to be professional malcontents, rather as one decides to be a tailor or a blacksmith.

In fact, of course, they do not usually discover they are 'dissidents' until long after they have actually become one. 'Dissent' springs from motivations far different from the desire for titles or fame. In short, they do not decide to become 'dissidents', and even if they were to devote twenty-four hours a day to it, it would still not be a profession, but primarily an existential attitude. Moreover, it is an attitude that is in no way the exclusive property of those who have earned themselves the title of 'dissident' just because they happen to fulfil those accidental external conditions already mentioned. There are thousands of nameless people who try to live within the truth and millions who want to but cannot, perhaps only because to do so in the circumstances in which they live, they would need ten times the courage of those who have already taken the first step. If several dozen are randomly chosen from among all these people and put into a special category, this can utterly distort the general picture. It does so in two different ways. Either it suggests that 'dissidents' are a group of prominent people, a 'protected species' who are permitted to do things others are not and whom the government may even be cultivating as living proof of its generosity; or it lends support to the illusion that since there is no more than a handful of malcontents to whom not very much is really being done, all the rest are therefore content, for were they not so, they would be 'dissidents' too.

But that is not all. This categorization also unintentionally supports the impression that the primary concern of these 'dissidents' is some vested interest that they share as a group, as though their entire argument with the government were no more than a rather abstruse conflict between two opposed groups, a conflict that leaves society out of it altogether. But such an impression profoundly contradicts the real importance of the 'dissident' attitude, which stands or falls on its interest in others, in what ails society as a whole, in other words, on an interest in all those who do not speak up. If 'dissidents' have any kind of authority at all and if they have not been exterminated long ago like exotic insects that have appeared where they have no business being, then this is not because the government holds this exclusive group and their exclusive ideas in such awe, but because it is perfectly aware of the potential political power of 'living within the truth' rooted in the hidden sphere, and well aware too of the kind of world 'dissent' grows out of and the world it addresses: the everyday human world, the world of daily tension between the aims of life and the aims of the system. . . .

Our greengrocer's attempt to live within the truth may be confined to not doing certain things. He decides not to put flags in his window when his only motive for putting them there in the first place would have been to avoid being reported by the house warden; he does not vote in elections that he considers false; he does not hide his opinions from his superiors. In other words, he may go no further than 'merely' refusing to comply with certain demands made on him by the system (which of course is not an insignificant step to take). This may, however, grow into something more. The greengrocer may begin to do something concrete, something that goes beyond an immediately personal self-defensive reaction against manipulation, something that will manifest his newfound sense of higher responsibility. He may, for example, organize his fellow greengrocers to act together in defence of their interests. He may write letters to various institutions, drawing their attention to instances of disorder and injustice around him. He may seek out unofficial literature, copy it and lend it to his friends.

If what I have called living within the truth is a basic existential (and of course potentially political) starting point for all those 'independent citizens' initiatives' and 'dissident' or 'opposition' movements . . . this does not mean that every attempt to live within the truth automatically belongs in this category. On the contrary, in its most original and broadest sense, living within the truth covers a vast territory whose outer limits are vague and difficult to map, a territory full of modest expressions of human volition, the vast majority of which will remain anonymous and whose political impact will probably never be felt or described any more concretely than simply as a part of a social climate or mood. Most of these expressions remain elementary revolts against manipulation: you simply straighten your backbone and live in greater dignity as an individual.

Here and there—thanks to the nature, the assumptions and the professions of some people, but also thanks to a number of accidental circumstances such as the specific nature of the local milieu, friends, and so on—a more coherent and visible initiative may emerge from this wide and anonymous hinterland, an initiative that transcends 'merely' individual revolt and is transformed into more conscious, structured and purposeful work. The point where living within the truth ceases to be a mere negation of living with a lie and becomes articulate in a particular way, is the point at which something is born that might be called the 'independent spiritual, social and political life of society'. This independent life is not separated from the rest of life ('dependent life') by some sharply defined line. Both types frequently coexist in the same people. Nevertheless, its most important focus is marked by a relatively high degree of inner emancipation. It sails upon the vast ocean of the manipulated life like little boats, tossed by the waves but always bobbing back as visible messengers of living within the truth, articulating the suppressed aims of life.

If the basic job of the 'dissident movements' is to serve truth, that is, to serve the real aims of life, and if that necessarily develops into a defence of the individual and his or her right to a free and truthful life (that is, a defence of human rights and a struggle to see the laws respected) then another stage of this approach, perhaps the most mature stage so far, is what Václav Benda has called the development of parallel structures.

When those who have decided to live within the truth have been denied any direct influence on the existing social structures, not to mention the opportunity to participate in them, and when these people begin to create what I have called the independent life of society, this independent life begins, of itself, to become structured in a certain way. Sometimes there are only very embryonic indications of this process of structuring; at other times, the structures are already quite well developed. Their genesis and evolution are inseparable from the phenomenon of 'dissent', even though they reach far beyond the arbitrarily defined area of activity usually indicated by that term.

What are these structures? Ivan Jirous was the first in Czechoslovakia to formulate and apply in practice the concept of a 'second culture'. Although at first he was thinking chiefly of nonconformist rock music and only certain literary, artistic or performance events close to the sensibilities of those nonconformist musical groups, the term 'second culture' very rapidly came to be used for the whole area of independent and repressed culture, that is, not only for art and its various currents but also for the humanities, the social sciences and philosophical thought. This 'second culture', quite naturally, has created elementary organizational forms: *samizdat* editions of books and magazines, private performances and concerts, seminars, exhibitions and so on. (In Poland all of this is vastly more developed: there are independent publishing houses and many more periodicals, even political periodicals; they have means of proliferation other than carbon copies, and so on. In the Soviet Union, *samizdat* has a longer tradition and clearly its forms are quite different.) Culture, therefore, is a sphere in which the 'parallel structures' can be observed in their most highly developed form. Benda, of course, gives thought to potential or embryonic forms of such structures in other spheres as well: from a parallel information network to parallel forms of education (private universities), parallel trade unions, parallel foreign contacts, to a kind of hypothesis on a parallel economy. On the basis of these parallel structures, he then develops the notion of a 'parallel *polis*' or state or, rather, he sees the rudiments of such a *polis* in these structures.

At a certain stage in its development, the independent life of society and the 'dissident movements' cannot avoid a certain amount of organization and institutionalization. This is a natural development and unless this independent life of society is somehow radically suppressed and eliminated, the tendency will grow. Along with it, a parallel political life will also necessarily evolve, and to a certain extent it exists already in Czechoslovakia. Various groupings of a more or less political nature will continue to define themselves politically, to act and confront each other.

These parallel structures, it may be said, represent the most articulated expressions so far of 'living within the truth'. One of the most important tasks the 'dissident movements' have set themselves is to support and develop them. Once again, it confirms the fact that all attempts by society to resist the pressure of the system have their essential beginnings in the pre-political area. For what else are parallel structures than an area where a different life can be lived, a life that is in harmony with its own aims and which in turn structures itself in harmony with those aims? What else are those initial attempts at social self-organization than the efforts of a certain part of society to live—as a society—within the truth, to rid itself of the self-sustaining aspects of totalitarianism and, thus, to extricate itself radically from its involvement in the post-totalitarian system? What else is it but a non-violent attempt by people to negate the system within themselves and to establish their lives on a new basis, that of their own proper identity? And does this tendency not confirm once more the principle of returning the focus to actual individuals? After all, the parallel structures do not grow a priori out of a theoretical vision of systemic changes (there are no political sects involved), but from the aims of life and the authentic needs of real people. In fact, all eventual changes in the system, changes we may observe here in their rudimentary forms, have come about as it were *de facto,* from 'below', because life compelled them to, not because they came before life, somehow directing it or forcing some change on it. . . .

Historical experience teaches us that any genuinely meaningful point of departure in an individual's life usually has an element of universality about it. In other words, it is not something partial, accessible only to a restricted community, and not transferable to any other. On the contrary, it must be potentially accessible to everyone; it must foreshadow a general solution and, thus, it is not just the expression of an introverted, self-contained responsibility that individuals have to and for themselves alone, but responsibility to and for the *world.* Thus it would be quite wrong to understand the parallel structures and the parallel *polis* as a retreat into a ghetto and as an act of isolation, addressing itself only to the welfare of those who had decided on such a course, and who are indifferent to the rest. It would be wrong, in short, to consider it an essentially group solution that has nothing to do with the general situation. Such a concept would, from the start, alienate the notion of living within the truth from its proper point of departure, which is concern for others, transforming it ultimately into just another more sophisticated version of 'living within a lie'. In doing so, of course, it would cease to be a genuine point of departure for individuals and groups and would recall the false notion of 'dissidents' as an exclusive group with exclusive interests, carrying on their own exclusive dialogue with the powers that be. In any case, even the most highly developed forms of life in the parallel structures, even that most mature form of the parallel *polis* can only exist—at least in post-totalitarian circumstances—when the individual is at the same time lodged in the 'first', official structure by a thousand different relationships, even though it may only be the fact that one buys what one needs in their stores, uses their money and obeys their laws. Certainly one can imagine life in its 'baser' aspects flourishing in the parallel *polis,* but would not such a life, lived deliberately that way, as a programme, be merely another version of the schizophrenic life 'within a lie' which everyone else must live in one way or another? Would it not just be further evidence that a point of departure that is not a 'model' solution, that is not applicable to others, cannot be meaningful for an individual either? Patočka used to say that the most interesting thing about responsibility is that we carry it with us everywhere. That means that responsibility is ours, that we must accept it and grasp it *here, now,* in this place in time and space where the Lord has set us down, and that we cannot lie our way out of it by moving somewhere else, whether it be to an Indian ashram or to a parallel *polis*. If Western young people so often discover that retreat to an Indian monastery fails them as an individual or group solution, then this is obviously because, and only because, it lacks that element of universality, since not everyone can retire to an ashram. Christianity is an example of an opposite way out: it is a point of departure for me here and now—but only because anyone, anywhere, at any time, may avail themselves of it.

In other words, the parallel *polis* points beyond itself and only makes sense as an act of deepening one's responsibility to and for the whole, as a way of discovering the most appropriate *locus* for this responsibility, not as an escape from it.

And now I may properly be asked the question: What then is to be done?

My scepticism towards alternative political models and the ability of systemic reforms or changes to redeem us does not, of course, mean that I am sceptical of political thought altogether. Nor does my emphasis on the importance of focusing concern on real human beings disqualify me from considering the possible structural consequences flowing from it. On the contrary, if A was said, then B should be said as well. Nevertheless, I will offer only a few very general remarks.

Above all, any existential revolution should provide hope of a moral reconstitution of society, which means a radical renewal of the relationship of human beings to what I have called the 'human order', which no political order can replace. A new experience of being, a renewed rootedness in the universe, a newly grasped sense of 'higher responsibility', a new-found inner relationship to other people and to the human community—these factors clearly indicate the direction in which we must go.

And the political consequences? Most probably they could be reflected in the constitution of structures that will derive from this 'new spirit', from human factors rather than from a particular formalization of political relationships and guarantees. In other words, the issue is the rehabilitation of values like trust, openness, responsibility, solidarity, love. I believe in structures that are not aimed at the 'technical' aspect of the execution of power, but at the significance of that execution in structures held together more by a commonly shared feeling of the importance of certain communities than by commonly shared expansionist ambitions directed 'outward'. There can and must be structures that are open, dynamic and small; beyond a certain point, human ties like personal trust and personal responsibility cannot work. There must be structures that in principle place no limits on the genesis of different structures. Any accumulation of power whatsoever (one of the characteristics of automatism) should be profoundly alien to it. They would be structures not in the sense of organizations or institutions, but like a community. Their authority certainly cannot be based on long-empty traditions, like the tradition of mass political parties, but rather on how, in concrete terms, they enter into a given situation. Rather than a strategic agglomeration of formalized organizations, it is better to have organizations springing up *ad hoc,* infused with enthusiasm for a particular purpose and disappearing when that purpose has been achieved. The leaders' authority ought to derive from their personalities and be personally tested in their particular surroundings, and not from their position in any *nomenklatura.* They should enjoy great personal confidence and even great lawmaking powers based on that confidence. This would appear to be the only way out of the classic impotence of traditional democratic organizations, which frequently seem founded more on mistrust than on mutual confidence, and more on collective irresponsibility than on responsibility. It is only with the full existential backing of every member of the community that a permanent bulwark against 'creeping totalitarianism' can be established. These structures should naturally arise from *below* as a consequence of authentic social 'self-organization'; they should derive vital energy from a living dialogue with the genuine needs from which they arise, and when these needs are gone, the structures should also disappear. The principles of their internal organization should be very diverse, with a minimum of external regulation. The decisive criterion of this 'self-constitution' should be the structure's actual significance, and not just a mere abstract norm.

Both political and economic life ought to be founded on the varied and versatile co-operation of such dynamically appearing and disappearing organizations. As far as the economic life of society goes, I believe in the principle of self-management, which is probably the only way of achieving what all the theorists of socialism have dreamed about, that is, the genuine (i.e. informal) participation of workers in economic decision-making, leading to a feeling of genuine responsibility for their collective work. The principles of control and discipline ought to be abandoned in favour of self-control and self-discipline.

As is perhaps clear from even so general an outline, the systemic consequences of an 'existential revolution' of this type go significantly beyond the framework of classical parliamentary democracy. Having introduced the term 'post-totalitarian' for the purposes of this discussion, perhaps I should refer to the notion I have just outlined—purely for the moment—as the prospects for a 'post-democratic' system.

Undoubtedly this notion could be developed further, but I think it would be a foolish undertaking, to say the least, because slowly but surely the whole idea would become alienated, separated from itself. After all, the essence of such a 'post-democracy' is also that it can only develop *via facti,* as a process deriving directly *from life,* from a new atmosphere and a new 'spirit' (political thought, of course, would play a role here, though not as a director, merely as a guide). It would be presumptuous, however, to try to foresee the structural expressions of this 'new spirit' without that spirit actually being present and without knowing its concrete physiognomy. . . .

I would probably have omitted the entire preceding section as a more suitable subject for private meditation were it not for a certain recurring sensation. It may seem rather presumptuous, and therefore I will present it as a question: Does not this vision of 'post-democratic' structures in some ways remind one of the 'dissident' groups or some of the independent citizens' initiatives as we already know them from our own surroundings? Do not these small communities, bound together by thousands of shared tribulations, give rise to some of those special 'humanly meaningful' political relationships and ties that we have been talking about? Are not these communities (and they *are* communities more than organizations)—motivated mainly by a common belief in the profound significance of what they are doing since they have no chance of direct, external success—joined together by precisely the kind of atmosphere in which the formalized and ritualized ties common in the official structures are supplanted by a living sense of solidarity and fraternity? Do not these 'post-democratic' relationships of immediate personal trust and the informal rights of individuals based on them come out of the background of all those commonly shared difficulties? Do not these groups emerge, live and disappear under pressure from concrete and authentic needs, unburdened by the ballast of hollow traditions? Is not their attempt to create an articulate form of 'living within the truth' and to renew the feeling of higher responsibility in an apathetic society really a sign of some kind of rudimentary moral reconstitution?

In other words, are not these informed, non-bureaucratic, dynamic and open communities that comprise the 'parallel *polis*' a kind of rudimentary prefiguration, a symbolic model of those more meaningful 'post-democratic' political structures that might become the foundation of a better society?

I know from thousands of personal experiences how the mere circumstance of having signed Charter 77 has immediately created a deeper and more open relationship and evoked sudden and powerful feelings of genuine community among people who were all but strangers before. This kind of thing happens only rarely, if at all, even among people who have worked together for long periods in some apathetic official structure. It is as though the mere awareness and acceptance of a common task and a shared experience were enough to transform people and the climate of their lives, as though it gave their public work a more human dimension that is seldom found elsewhere.

Perhaps all this is only the consequence of a common threat. Perhaps the moment the threat ends or eases, the mood it helped create will begin to dissipate as well. (The aim of those who threaten us, however, is precisely the opposite. Again and again, one is shocked by the energy they devote to contaminating, in various despicable ways, all the human relationships inside the threatened community.)

Yet even if that were so, it would change nothing in the question I have posed.

We do not know the way out of the marasmus of the world, and it would be an expression of unforgivable pride were we to see the little we do as a fundamental solution, or were we to present ourselves, our community and our solutions to vital problems as the only thing worth doing.

Even so, I think that given all these preceding thoughts on post-totalitarian conditions, and given the circumstances and the inner constitution of the developing efforts to defend human beings and their identity in such conditions, the questions I have posed are appropriate. If nothing else, they are an invitation to reflect concretely on our own experience and to give some thought to whether certain elements of that experience do not—without our really being aware of it—point somewhere further, beyond their apparent limits, and whether right here, in our everyday lives, certain challenges are not already encoded, quietly waiting for the moment when they will be read and grasped.

For the real question is whether the 'brighter future' is really always so distant. What if, on the contrary, it has been here for a long time already, and only our own blindness and weakness has prevented us from seeing it around us and within us, and kept us from developing it?

STUDY QUESTIONS

1. What is ideology? What role does it play in the post-totalitarian system?
2. What results, according to Havel, when power becomes subordinate to ideology?
3. What does it mean to "live within a lie"?
4. How is truth a political force, according to Havel?

20

Transcript from the Iran–Contra Affair

Oliver North

Lieutenant Colonel Oliver North worked in the National Security branch of the Reagan administration in the 1980s. He was a target of an extensive investigation by Special Prosecutor Lawrence Walsh for his role in the Iran–Contra scandal.

THURSDAY • JULY 9, 1987

Morning Session—9:00 A.M.

LT. COL. NORTH: As you all know by now, my name is Oliver North, Lieutenant Colonel, United States Marine Corps. My best friend is my wife Betsy, to whom I have been married for 19 years, and with whom I have had four wonderful children, aged 18, 16, 11 and 6. . . .

Since graduating from the Naval Academy in 1968, I have strived to be the best Marine officer that one can be. In combat, my goal was always to understand the objective, follow orders, accomplish the mission, and to keep alive the men who served under me. One of the good things that has come from the last seven months of worldwide notoriety has been the renewed contact that I've had with some of the finest people in the world—those with whom I served in Vietnam. Among the 50,000 or so messages of support that have arrived since I left the NSC are many from those who recount the horrors we lived through, and who now relate stories of their families and careers. After Vietnam, I worked with my fellow officers to train good Marines to be ready in case we were called upon elsewhere in the world, but at the same time to hope that we never were. I honestly believed that any soldier who has ever been to a war truly hopes he will never see one again.

My Marine Corps career was untracked in 1981, when I was detailed to the National Security Council. I was uneasy at the beginning, but I came to believe that it was important work, and as years passed and responsibilities grew, I got further from that which I loved, the Marine Corps and Marines.

During 1984, '85, and '86, there were periods of time when we worked two days in every one. My guess is that the average workday lasted at least 14 hours. To respond to various crises, the need for such was frequent, and we would often go without a night's sleep, hoping to recoup the next night or thereafter. If I had to estimate the number of meetings and discussions and phone calls over that five years, it would surely be in the tens of thousands. My only real regret is that I virtually abandoned my family for work during these years, and that work consisted of my first few years on the staff, as the project officer for a highly classified and compartmented National Security project, which is not a part of this inquiry.

I worked hard on the political military strategy for restoring and sustaining democracy in Central America, and in particular, El Salvador. We sought to achieve the democratic outcome in Nicaragua that this administration still supports, which involved keeping the contras together in both body and soul. We made efforts to open a new relationship with Iran, and recover our hostages. We worked on the development of a concerted policy regarding terrorists and terrorism and a capability for dealing in a concerted manner with that threat.

We worked on various crises, such as TWA 847, the capture of Achille Lauro, the rescue of American students in Grenada and the restoration of democracy on that small island, and the US raid in Libya in response to their terrorist attacks. And, as some may be willing to admit, there were efforts made to work with the Congress on legislative programs.

There were many problems. I believed that we worked as hard as we could to solve them, and sometimes we succeeded, and sometimes we failed, but at least we tried, and I want to tell you that I, for one, will never regret having tried.

I believe that this is a strange process that you are putting me and others through. Apparently, the President has chosen not to assert his prerogatives, and you have been permitted to make the rules. You called before you the officials of the Executive Branch. You put them under oath for what must be collectively thousands of hours of testimony. You dissect that testimony to find inconsistencies and declare some to be truthful and others to be liars. You make the rulings as to what is proper and what is not proper. You put the testimony which you think is helpful to your goals up before the people and leave others out. It's sort of like a baseball game in which you are both the player and the umpire. It's a game in which you call the balls and strikes and where you determine who is out and who is safe. And in the end you determine the score and declare yourselves the winner.

From where I sit, it is not the fairest process. One thing is, I think, for certain—that you will not investigate yourselves in this matter. There is not much chance that you will conclude at the end of these hearings that the Boland Amendments and the frequent policy changes therefore were unwise or that your restrictions should not have been imposed on the Executive Branch. You are not likely to conclude that the Administration acted properly by trying to sustain the freedom fighters in Nicaragua when they were abandoned, and you are not likely to conclude by commending the President of the United States who tried valiantly to recover our citizens and achieve an opening that is strategically vital—Iran. I would not be frank with you if I did not admit that the last several months have been difficult for me and my family. It has been difficult to be on the front pages of every newspaper in the land day after day, to be the lead story on national television day after day, to be photographed thousands of times by bands of photographers who chase us around since November just because my name arose at the hearings. It is difficult to be caught in the middle of a constitutional struggle between the Executive and legislative branches over who will formulate and direct the foreign policy of this nation. It is difficult to be vilified by people in and out of this body, some who have proclaimed that I am guilty of criminal conduct even before they heard me. Others have said that I would not tell the truth when I came here to testify, and one member asked a person testifying before this body whether he would believe me under oath. I asked when I got here—if you don't believe me, why call me at all? It has been difficult to see questions raised about my character and morality, my honesty, because only partial evidence was provided. And, as I indicated yesterday, I think it was insensitive of this Committee to place before the cameras my home address at a time when my family and I are under 24-hour armed guard by over a dozen government agents of the Naval Investigative Service because of fear that terrorists will seek revenge for my official acts and carry out their announced intentions to kill me.

It is also difficult to comprehend that my work at the NSC—all of which was approved and carried out in the best interests of our country—has led to two massive parallel investigations staffed by over 200 people. It is mind-boggling to me that one of those investigations is criminal and that some here have attempted to criminalize policy differences between co-equal branches of government and the Executive's conduct of foreign affairs.

I believe it is inevitable that the Congress will in the end blame the Executive Branch, but I suggest to you that it is the Congress which must accept at least some of the blame in the Nicaraguan freedom fighters' matter. Plain and simple, the Congress is to blame because of the fickle, vacillating, unpredictable, on-again off-again policy toward the Nicaraguan Democratic Resistance—the so-called Contras. I do not believe that the support of the Nicaraguan freedom fighters can be treated as the passage of a budget. I suppose that if the budget doesn't get passed on time again this year, it will be inevitably another extension of another month or two.

But, the contras, the Nicaraguan freedom fighters are people—living, breathing, young men and women who have had to suffer a desperate struggle for liberty with sporatic and confusing support from the United States of America.

Armies need food and consistent help. They need a flow of money, of arms, clothing and medical supplies. The Congress of the United States allowed the executive to encourage them, to do battle, and then abandoned them. The Congress of the United States left soldiers in the field unsupported and vulnerable to their communist enemies. When the executive branch did everything possible within the law to prevent them from being wiped out by Moscow's surrogates in Havana and Managua, you then had this investigation to blame the problem on the executive branch. It does not make sense to me.

In my opinion, these hearings have caused serious damage to our national interests. Our adversaries laugh at us, and our friends recoil in horror. I suppose it would be one thing if the intelligence committees wanted to hear all of this in private and thereafter pass laws which in the view of Congress make for better policies or better functioning government. But, to hold them publicly for the whole world to see strikes me as very harmful. Not only does it embarrass our friends and allies with whom we have worked, many of whom have helped us in various programs, but it must also make them very wary of helping us again.

I believe that these hearings, perhaps unintentionally so, have revealed matters of great secrecy in the operation of our government. And sources and methods of intelligence activities have clearly been revealed to the detriment of our security.

As a result of rumor and speculation and innuendo, I have been accused of almost every crime imaginable. Wild rumors have abounded. Some media reports have suggested that I was guilty of espionage for the way I handled US intelligence. Some have said that I was guilty of treason, and suggested in front of my 11-year-old daughter, that I should be given the death penalty. Some said I stole 10 million dollars. Some said I was second only in power to the President of the United States, and others that I condoned drug-trafficking to generate funds for the contras, or that I personally ordered assassinations, or that I was conducting my own foreign policy. It has even been suggested that I was the personal confidant of the President of the United States. These and many other stories are patently untrue.

I don't mind telling you that I'm angry that what some have attempted to do to me and my family. I believe that these committee hearings will show that you have struck some blows. But, I am going to walk from here with my head high and my shoulders straight because I am proud of what we accomplished. I am proud of the efforts that we made, and I am proud of the fight that we fought. I am proud of serving the administration of a great president. I am not ashamed of anything in my professional or personal conduct. As we go through this process I ask that you continue to please keep an open mind. Please be open minded, and able to admit that, perhaps, your preliminary conclusions about me were wrong. And please, also, do not mistake my attitude for lack of respect. I am in awe of this great institution just as I am in awe of the presidency. Both are equal branches of government with separate areas of responsibility under the constitution that I have taken an oath to support and defend, and I have done so, as many of you have. And although I do not agree with what you are doing, or the way that it is being done, I do understand your interest in obtaining the facts and I have taken an oath to tell the truth and helping you to do so. In closing, Mr. Chairman, and I thank you for this opportunity, I would just simply like to thank the tens of thousands of Americans who have communicated their support, encouragement and prayers for me and my family in this difficult time. Thank you, sir.

SEN. MITCHELL: . . . You've talked here often and eloquently about the need for a democratic outcome in Nicaragua. There's no disagreement on that. There is disagreement over how best to achieve that objective. Many Americans agreed with the President's policy. Many do not. Many patriotic Americans, strongly anti-Communist, believe there's a better way to contain the Sandinistas, to bring about a democratic outcome in Nicaragua and to bring peace to Central America. And many patriotic Americans are concerned that in the pursuit of democracy abroad we not compromise it in any way here at home. You and others have urged consistency in our policies. You've said repeatedly that if we are not consistent our allies and other nations will question our reliability. That's a real concern. But if it's bad to change policies, it's worse to have two different policies at the same time; one public policy and an opposite policy in private. It's difficult to conceive of a greater inconsistency than that. It's hard to imagine anything that would give our allies more cause to consider us unreliable, than that we say one thing in public and secretly do the opposite. And that's exactly what was done when arms were sold to Iran, and arms were swapped for hostages.

Now, you've talked a lot about patriotism and the love of our country. Most nations derive from a single tribe, a single race. They practice a single religion. Common racial, ethnic, religious heritages are the glue of nationhood for many.

The United States is different. We have all races, all religions. We have a limited common heritage. The glue of nationhood for us is the American ideal of individual liberty and equal justice. The rule of law is critical in our society. It's the great equalizer, because in America everybody is equal before the law.

We must never allow the end to justify the means, where the law is concerned, however important and noble an objective. And surely, democracy abroad is important, and is noble. It cannot be achieved at the expense of the rule of law in our country.

And our diversity is very broad. You talked about your background, and it was really very compelling; and is obviously one of the reasons why the American people are attracted to you. Let me tell you a story from my background.

Before I entered the Senate, I had the great honor of serving as a federal judge. In that position I had great power. The one I enjoyed exercising was the power to make people American citizens. From time to time I presided at what we call "naturalization" ceremonies. They're citizenship ceremonies.

These are people who came from all over the world, risked their lives, sometimes left their families and their fortunes behind, to come here. They'd gone through the required procedures, and I, in the final act, administered to them the oath of allegiance to the United States, and I made them American citizens. To this moment, to this moment, it was the most exciting thing I've ever done in my life. Ceremonies were always moving for me because my mother was an immigrant, my father, the orphan son of immigrants. Neither of them had any education, and they worked at very menial tasks in our society. But, because of the openness of America, because of "Equal Justice Under Law" in America, I sit here today, a United States Senator. And, after every one of these ceremonies, I made it a point to speak to these new Americans. I asked them why they came, how they came, and their stories, each of them, were inspiring.

I think you would be interested and moved by them, given the views you've expressed on this country. And, when I asked them why they came, they said several things, mostly two: The first is, they said, "We came because, here in America, everybody has a chance, opportunity." And, they also said, over and over again, particularly people from totalitarian societies who came here because here in America, you can criticize the government without looking over your shoulder. "Freedom to disagree with the government."

Now, you've addressed several pleas to this Committee, very eloquently, none more eloquent than last Friday, when in response to a question by Representative Cheney, you asked that Congress not cut off aid to the contras "For the love of God and for the love of country." I now address a plea to you. Of all the qualities which the American people find compelling about you, none is more impressing than your obvious deep devotion to this country. Please remember that others share that devotion, and recognize that it is possible for an American to disagree with you on aid to the contras and still love God and still love this country just as much as you do.

Although he's regularly asked to do so, God does not take sides in American politics, and in America disagreement with the policies of the government is not evidence of lack of patriotism. I want to repeat that. *In America, disagreement with the policies of the government is not evidence of lack of patriotism.* Indeed, it's the very fact that Americans can criticize their government openly and without fear of reprisal that is the essence of our freedom and that will keep us free.

Now, I have one final plea. Debate this issue forcefully and vigorously, as you have and as you surely will, but please do it in a way that respects the patriotism and the motives of those who disagree with you, as you would have them respect yours.

Thank you very much, Colonel. Mr. Chairman, I have no further questions.

CHAIRMAN HAMILTON: . . . Now Colonel North, let me join with others in expressing my appreciation to you for your testimony. And as the Chairman has indicated, I will use my time just to give you some of my impressions.

I recognize that a President and those carrying out his policies sometimes face agonizing choices, and you've had more than your share of them. I've never for a moment over the years that I have known you, doubted your good intentions to free hostages, to seek democracy in Nicaragua, to fight communism, and to advance the best interests of the nation. And for many in this country, I think the pursuit of such worthy objectives is enough in itself, or in themselves, and exonerate you and any others from all mistakes.

Yet what strikes me is that despite your very good intentions, you were a participant in actions which catapulted a President into the most serious crisis of his presidency, drove the Congress of the United States to launch an unprecedented investigation, and I think probably damaged the cause, or the causes that you sought to promote. It is not my task, and it is not the task of these Committees to judge you. As others have said, we're here to learn what went wrong, what caused the mistakes, and what we can do to correct them. And the appropriate standard for these Committees is whether we understand the facts better because of your testimony and I think we do, and we're grateful to you.

In your opening statement you said that these hearings have caused serious damage to our national interests. But I wonder whether the damage has been caused by these hearings or by the acts which prompted these hearings. I wonder whether you would have the Congress do nothing after it has been lied to and misled and ignored? Would we in the Congress then be true to our Constitutional responsibilities? Is it better under our system to ignore misdeeds or to investigate them behind closed doors, as some have suggested? Or is it better to bring them into the open and try to learn from them? I submit that we are truer to our Constitution if we chose the later course.

These Committees of course, build on the work of other committees, and I think that work is part of our Constitutional system of checks and balances. There are many parts of your testimony that I agree with. I agree with you that these Committees must be careful not to cripple the President. I agree with you that our government needs the capability to carry out covert actions. During my six years on the Intelligence Committee, over 90 percent of the covert actions that were recommended to us by the President were supported and approved. And only the large-scale paramilitary operations, which really could not be kept secret, were challenged. I agree with you, when you said in your opening statement, that you're caught in a struggle between the Congress and the President over the direction of American foreign policy, and that most certainly is not your fault. And I agree with you, that the Congress, whose record in all of this—is certainly not unblemished—also must be accountable for its actions.

Now let me tell you what bothers me. I want to talk about two things, first policy, and then, process. Chairman Inouye has correctly said, that the business of these Select Committees is not policy, and I agree with him, but you made such an eloquent and impassioned statement about policy, that I wanted to comment. I am very troubled by your defense of secret arms sales to Iran. There's no disagreement about the strategic importance of Iran or the desirability of an opening to Iran. My concern is with the means employed to achieve those objectives.

The President has acknowledged that his policy, as implemented, was an arms for hostage policy. And selling arms to Iran in secret, was, to put it simply, bad policy. The policy contradicted and undermined long-held, often articulated, widely supported public policies in the United States. It repudiated US policy to make no concessions to terrorists, to remain in the Gulf war, and to stop arms sales to Iran. We sold arms to a nation officially designated by our government, as a terrorist state. This secret policy of selling arms to Iran damaged US credibility.

A great power cannot base its policy on an untruth without a loss of credibility. Friendly governments were deceived about what we were doing. You spoke about the credibility of US policy in Central America, and you were right about that, but in the Middle East, mutual trust with some friends was damaged, even shattered. The policy of arms for hostages sent a clear message to the States of the Persian Gulf, and that message was, that the United States is helping Iran in its war effort, and making an accommodation with the Iranian revolution, and Iran's neighbors should do the same.

The policy provided the Soviets an opportunity they have now grasped, with which we are struggling to deal. The policy achieved none of the goals it sought. The Ayatollah got his arms, more Americans are held hostage today than when this policy began, subversion of US interests throughout the region by Iran continues. Moderates in Iran, if any there were, did not come forward.

And to those—today, those moderates are showing fidelity to the Iranian revolution by leading the charge against the United States in the Persian Gulf. In brief, the policy of selling arms to Iran, in my view at least, simply cannot be defended as in the interests of the United States. There were and there are other means to achieve that opening which should have been used.

Now let me comment on process as well, first with regard to covert actions. You and I agree that covert actions pose very special problems for a democracy. It is, as you said, a dangerous world, and we must be able to conduct covert actions, as every member of this panel has said. But it is contrary to all that we know about democracy to have no checks and balances on them.

We've established a lawful procedure to handle covert actions. It's not perfect by any means, but it works reasonably well. In this instance, those procedures were ignored. There was no presidential finding in one case, and a retroactive finding in another. The Intelligence Committees of the Congress were not informed, and they were lied to.

Foreign policies were created and carried out by a tiny circle of persons, apparently without the involvement of even some of the highest officials of our government. The administration tried to do secretly what the Congress sought to prevent it from doing. The administration did secretly what it claimed to all the world it was not doing. Covert action should always be used to supplement, not to contradict, our foreign policy. It should be consistent with our public policies. It should not be used to impose a foreign policy on the American people which they do not support.

Mr. McFarlane was right. He told these Committees it was clearly unwise to rely on covert action as the core of our policy. And as you noted in your testimony, and I agree with you, it would have been a better course to continue to seek contra funding through open debate. You have spoken with compelling eloquence about the Reagan Doctrine. And laudable as that doctrine may be, it will not succeed unless it has the support of the Congress and the American people.

Secondly, with regard to process, let me talk about accountability. What I find lacking about the events as you have described them is accountability. Who was responsible for these policies, for beginning them, for controlling them, for terminating them? You have said that you assumed you were acting on the authority of the President. I don't doubt your word, sir. But we have no evidence of his approval.

The President says he did not know that the National Security Council staff was helping the contras. You thought he knew. And you engaged in such activities with extraordinary energy. You do not recall what happened to the five documents on the diversion of funds to the contras. Those documents radically changed American policy. They are probably, I would think, the most important documents you have written. Yet you don't recall whether they were returned to you, and you don't recall whether they were destroyed, as I recall your testimony. There's no accountability for an $8 million account earned from the sale of US government property. There is no accountability for a quarter of a million dollars available to you.

You say you never took a penny. I believe you. But we have no records to support or to contradict what you say. Indeed, most of the important records concerning these events have been destroyed. Your testimony points up confusion throughout the foreign policy making process. You've testified that Director Casey sought to create an on-the-shelf, self-sustaining, stand-alone entity to carry out covert actions—apparently without the knowledge of other high officials in government. You've testified there was an unclear commitment to Israel concerning replenishment of missiles to Iran. You've testified that it's never been US policy not to negotiate with terrorists. Yet the President has said the opposite—that we will never negotiate with terrorists. You have testified that a lot of people were willing to go along with what we were doing, hoping against hope that it would succeed and willing to walk away when it failed. Now my guess is, that's a pretty accurate description of what happened. But it's not the way to run a government.

Secret operations should pass a sufficient test of accountability. And these secret operations did not pass that test. There was a lack of accountability for funds and for policy, and responsibility rests with the President. If he did not know of your highly significant activities done in his name, then he should have, and we'll obviously have to ask Admiral Poindexter some questions.

Now the next point with regard to process relates to your attitude toward the Congress. As you would expect, I'm bothered by your comments about the Congress. You show very little appreciation for its role in the foreign policy process. You acknowledge that you were "erroneous, misleading, evasive and wrong" in your testimony to the Congress. I appreciate, sir, that honesty can be hard in the conduct of government. But I am impressed that policy was driven by a series of lies—

lies to the Iranians, lies to the Central Intelligence Agency, lies to the Attorney General, lies to our friends and allies, lies to the Congress, and lies to the American people. So often during these hearings—not just during your testimony, but others as well, I have been reminded of President Thomas Jefferson's statement. "The whole art of government consists in the art of being honest."

Your experience has been in the Executive branch, and mine has been in the Congress. Inevitably our perspectives will differ. Nonetheless, if I may say so, you have an extraordinarily expansive view of presidential power. You would give the President free rein in foreign affairs.

You said on the first day of your testimony, and I quote, "I didn't want to show Congress a single word on this whole thing," end of quote. I do not see how your attitude can be reconciled with the Constitution of the United States. I often find in the Executive branch, in this administration as well as in others, a view that the Congress is not a partner, but an adversary. The Constitution grants foreign policy making powers to both the President and the Congress and our foreign policy cannot succeed unless they work together.

You blame the Congress as if the restrictions it approved were the cause of mistakes by the administration, yet congressional restrictions in the case of Nicaragua, if the polls are accurate, reflected the majority of the American people. In any case, I think you and I would agree that there is insufficient consensus on policy in Nicaragua. Public opinion is deeply divided.

And the task of leadership, it seems to me, is to build public support for policy. If that burden of leadership is not met, secret policies cannot succeed over the long term. The fourth point, with regard to process, relates to means and ends. As I understand your testimony, you did what you did because those were your orders and because you believed it was for a good cause. I cannot agree that the end has justified these means, that the threat in Central America was so great that we had to do something, even if it meant disregarding Constitutional processes, deceiving the Congress and the American people.

The means employed were a profound threat to the democratic process. A democratic government, as I understand it, is not a solution, but it's a way of seeking solutions. It's not a government devoted to a particular objective, but a form of government which specifies means and methods of achieving objectives. Methods and means are what this country are all about. We subvert our democratic process to bring about a desired end, no matter how strongly we may believe in that end. We've weakened our country and we have not strengthened it.

A few do not know what is better for Americans than Americans know themselves. If I understand our government correctly, no small group of people, no matter how important, no matter how well-intentioned they may be, should be trusted to determine policy. As President Madison said, "Trust should be placed not in a few, but in a number of hands."

Let me conclude. Your opening statement made the analogy to a baseball game. You said the playing field here was uneven and the Congress would declare itself the winner. I understand your sentiments, but may I suggest that we are not engaged in a game with winners and losers. That approach, if I may say so, is self-serving and ultimately self-defeating. We all lost. The interests of the United States have been damaged by what happened.

This country cannot be run effectively and major foreign policy—major foreign policies are formulated by only a few and are made and carried out in secret and when public officials lie to other nations and to each other. One purpose of these hearings is to change that. The self-cleansing process, the Tower Commission and these joint hearings and the report which will follow, are all part, we hope, of a process to reinvigorate and restore our system of government.

I don't have any doubt at all, Colonel North, that you are a patriot. There are many patriots, fortunately, and many forms of patriotism. For you, perhaps patriotism rested in the conduct of deeds, some requiring great personal courage, to free hostages and fight communism. And those of us who pursue public service with less risk to our physical well-being admire such courage.

But there's another form of patriotism, which is unique to democracy. It resides in those who have a deep respect for the rule of law and faith in America's democratic traditions. To uphold our Constitution requires not the exceptional efforts of the few, but the confidence and the trust and the work of the many.

Democracy has its frustrations. You've experienced some of them, but we, you and I, know of no better system of government. And when that democratic process is subverted, we risk all that we cherish. I thank you, sir, for your testimony, and I wish you and I wish your family well.

Thank you, Mr. Chairman.

CHAIRMAN INOUYE: . . . From the beginning of the history of mankind, organized societies, whether they be tribes or clans or nations, have nurtured and created heroes, because heroes are necessary, they serve as a cement to unite people, to bring unity in that nation. It provides glory to their history, it provides legends. We have many heroes. This hearing is being held in Washington, the city of heroes, the city of monuments. We have hundreds of monuments in this city. In the Capitol in Statuary Hall, each state has honored two of their heroes or heroines. The State of Hawaii honors King Kamehameha, the warrior king, and Father Damien, who is soon to become a saint.

And if you step on the west steps of the mall, and look down the majestic mall, you will see the monument of George Washington, very majestic. I remember as a child, long before I heard of the revolutionary war, that one day George Washington was confronted by his father, who asked "Who cut the cherry tree?" And little George answered, "Father, I cannot lie, I cut the cherry tree." It was an important lesson to all little children, and I believe it still is a very important lesson.

Then if you go further down you'll see the Lincoln Memorial where we honor a great President for the courage he demonstrated in upholding the brotherhood of men. It wasn't easy during those days. Then you have Arlington, a sacred place. Men you served with and men I served with used that as their final resting place, all heroes. Then you have Lee's mansion. This was the home of the great gentleman from Virginia. We honor him today for his great demonstration of loyalty and patriotism. And as we get back to the Lincoln Memorial nearby, we see this new and exciting monument—one to your fellow combat men, the Vietnam Memorial.

I believe during the past week we have participated in creating and developing very likely a new American hero. Like you, who has as one has felt the burning sting of bullet and shrapnel, and heard the unforgettable and frightening sounds of incoming shells, I salute you, sir, as a fellow combat man. And the rows of ribbons that you have on your chest will forever remind us of your courageous service and your willingness—your patriotic willingness to risk your life and your limb. I'm certain the life and the burdens of a hero will be difficult and heavy. And so, with all sincerity, I wish you well as you begin your journey into a new life. However, as an interested observer and as one who has participated in the making of this new American hero, I've found certain aspects of your testimony to be most troubling. Chairman Hamilton has most eloquently discussed them—because, as a result of your very gallant presence and your articulate statements, your life, I'm certain, will be emulated by many, many young Americans. I'm certain we will all of us receive an abundance of requests from young citizens throughout the land for entrance into the privileged ranks of cadets of the military services. These young citizens having been imbued with the passion of patriotism will do so. And to these young men and women, I wish to address a few words.

In 1964, when Col. North was a cadet, he took an oath of office, like all hundreds throughout the service academies. And he also said that he will abide with the regulations which set forth the cadet honor concept. The first honor concept—first, because it's so important, over and above all others, is a very simple one: a member of the brigade does not lie, cheat, or steal. And in this regulation of 1964, the word "lie" was defined as follows, quote: "A deliberate oral or written untruth, it may be an oral statement which is known to be false or a simple response to a question in which the answer is known to be false." End of quote. The words, "mislead" or "deceive," were defined as follows: "A deliberate misrepresentation of a true situation by being untruthful or withholding or omitting or subtly wording information in such a way, as to leave an erroneous or false impression of the known true situation."

And when the Colonel put on his uniform and the bars of a second lieutenant, he was well aware that he was subject to the Uniform Code of Military Justice. It's a special code of laws that apply to our men and women in uniform. It's a code that has been applicable to the conduct and activities of Colonel North throughout his military career, and even at this moment. And that code makes it abundantly clear, that orders of a superior officer must be obeyed by subordinate members—but it is lawful orders.

The Uniform Code makes it abundantly clear that it must be the lawful orders of a superior officer. In fact, it says, members of the military have an obligation to disobey unlawful orders. This principle was considered so important, that we—we, the government of the United States, proposed that it be internationally applied, in the Nuremberg trials. And so, in the Nuremberg trials, we said that the fact that the defendant—

MR. SULLIVAN:—Mr. Chairman. May I please register an objection.—

CHAIRMAN INOUYE:—May I continue my statement.—

MR. SULLIVAN:—I find this offensive! I find you engaging in a personal attack on Colonel North, and you're far removed from the issues of this case. To make reference to the Nuremberg trials, I find personally and professionally distasteful, and I can no longer sit here and listen to this.

CHAIRMAN INOUYE: You will have to sit there, if you want to listen.

MR. SULLIVAN: Mr. Chairman, please don't conclude these hearings on this unfair note. I have strong objections to many things in the hearings, and you up there speak about listening to the American people. Why don't you listen to the American people and what they've said as a result—(Chairman Inouye bangs the gavel)—of the last week. There are 20,000 telegrams in our room outside the corridor here that came in this morning. The American people—

CHAIRMAN INOUYE: I'm sure that there are.

MR. SULLIVAN: The American people have spoken and please stop this personal attack against Colonel North.

CHAIRMAN INOUYE: I have sat here, listened to the Colonel without interrupting. I hope you will accord me the courtesy of saying my piece.

MR. SULLIVAN: Sir, you may give speeches on the issues, it seems to me. You may ask questions, but you may not attack him personally. This has gone too far, in my opinion, with all due respect.

CHAIRMAN INOUYE: I'm not attacking him personally.

MR. SULLIVAN: That's the way I hear it, sir.

CHAIRMAN INOUYE: Colonel North, I'm certain it must have been painful for you, as you stated, to testify that you lied to senior officials of our government, that you lied and misled our Congress. And believe me, it was painful for all of us to sit here and listen to that testimony. It was painful. It was equally painful to learn from your testimony that you lied and misled because of what you believed to be a just cause—supporters of Nicaragua freedom fighters, the contras.

You have eloquently articulated your opposition to Marxism and communism and I believe that all of us—I'm certain that all of us on this panel are equally opposed to Marxism and communism. But should we, in the defense of democracy, adopt and embrace one of the most important tenets of communism and Marxism—the ends justify the means?

This is not one of the commandments of democracy. Our government is not a government of men. It is still a government of laws. And finally, to those thousands upon thousands of citizens who have called, sent telegrams, written letters, I wish to thank all of you most sincerely and commend you for your demonstrated interest in the well-being of our government, of our freedoms and our democracy. Your support or opposition of what is happening in this room is important—important because it dramatically demonstrates the strength of this democracy.

We Americans are confident in our strength to openly and without fear put into action one of the important teachings of our greatest Founding Fathers, Thomas Jefferson, who spoke of the right to dissent, the right to criticize the leaders of this government and he said, "The spirit of resistance to government is so valuable on certain occasions that I wish it to be always kept alive. It will often be exercised when wrong, but better so, than not be exercised at all."

Unlike communism, in a democracy such as ours, we are not afraid to wash our dirty linen in public. We're not afraid to let the world know that we do have failures and we do have shortcomings. I think all of us should recall the open invitation that we send to the press of the world to view the spaceflights, to record our successes and record our failures. We permit all to film and record our spaceflights. We don't, after the fact, let the world know only of our successes. And I think we should recall that we did not prohibit any member of the world press to film and record one of the bloodiest chapters of our domestic history, the demonstration and riots in the civil rights period. This was not easy to let the world know that we had police dogs and police officers with whips and clubs denying fellow citizens their rights. But I've always felt that, as long as we daily reaffirm our belief in and support of our Constitution and the great principles of freedom that was long ago enunciated by our Founding Fathers, we'll continue to prevail and flourish. . . .

STUDY QUESTIONS

1. What is the relation of ends to means in Col. North's position? Is North arguing a version of "the ends justify the means"? If a person's end (or goal) is just, must the means that he or she uses to attain that end be just as well?
2. North questions the propriety of the investigation. Do you find his argument satisfactory?
3. North admitted to using deception in the past, including lying to Congress. How relevant is this admission to the present testimony?

21

Lies for the Public Good

Sissela Bok

Sissela Bok was born in Sweden and educated in Switzerland, France, and the United States. She has taught at Brandeis, Harvard Medical School, and the John F. Kennedy School of Government. She is the author of *A Strategy for Peace* and *Secrets: On the Ethics of Concealment and Revelation*.

"How then," said I, "might we contrive one of those opportune falsehoods of which we were just now speaking, so as by one noble lie to persuade if possible the rulers themselves, but failing that the rest of the city?"

[. . .] "While all of you are brothers," we will say, "yet God in fashioning those of you who are fitted to hold rule mingled gold in their generation, for which reason they are most precious—but in their helpers silver and iron and brass in the farmers and other craftsmen."

[. . .] "Do you see any way of getting them to believe this tale?" "No, not these themselves," he said, "but I do, their sons and successors and the rest of mankind who come after." "Well," said I, "even that would have a good effect in making them more inclined to care for the state and one another."

—Plato, *The Republic*

HUGO *And do you think the living will agree to your schemes?*

HOEDERER *We'll get them to swallow them little by little.*

HUGO *By lying to them?*

HOEDERER *By lying to them sometimes.*

. . . .

HOEDERER *I'll lie when I must, and I have contempt for no one. I wasn't the one who invented lying. It grew out of a society divided into classes, and each one of us has inherited it from birth. We shall not abolish lying by refusing to tell lies, but by using every means at hand to abolish classes.*

—Jean-Paul Sartre, *Dirty Hands*

THE NOBLE LIE

In earlier chapters [of the original work] three circumstances have seemed to liars to provide the strongest excuse for their behavior—a crisis where overwhelming harm can be averted only through deceit; complete harmlessness and triviality to the point where it seems absurd to quibble about whether a lie has been told; and the duty to particular individuals to protect their secrets. I have shown how lies in times of crisis can expand into vast practices where the harm to be averted is less obvious and the crisis less and less immediate; how white lies can shade into equally vast practices no longer so harmless, with immense cumulative costs; and how lies to protect individuals and to cover up their secrets can be told for increasingly dubious purposes to the detriment of all.

When these three expanding streams flow together and mingle with yet another—a desire to advance the public good—they form the most dangerous body of deceit of all. These lies may not be justified by an immediate crisis nor by complete triviality nor by duty to any one person; rather, liars tend to consider them as right and unavoidable because of the altruism that motivates them. I want, in this chapter and the next [of the original work], to turn to this far-flung category.

Naturally, there will be large areas of overlap between these lies and those considered earlier. But the most characteristic defense for these lies is a separate one, based on the benefits they may confer and the long-range harm they can avoid. The intention may be broadly paternalistic, as when citizens are deceived "for their own good," or only a few may be lied to for the benefit of the community at large. Error and self-deception mingle with these altruistic purposes and blur them; the filters through which we must try to peer at lying are thicker and more distorting than ever in these practices. But I shall try to single out, among these lies, the elements that are consciously and purposely intended to benefit society.

A long tradition in political philosophy endorses some lies for the sake of the public. Plato, in the passage quoted at the head of this chapter, first used the expression "noble lie" for the fanciful story that might be told to people in order to persuade them to accept class distinctions and thereby safeguard social harmony. According to this story, God Himself mingled gold, silver, iron, and brass in fashioning rulers, auxiliaries, farmers, and craftsmen, intending these groups for separate tasks in a harmonious hierarchy.

The Greek adjective which Plato used to characterize this falsehood expresses a most important fact about lies by those in power: this adjective is "*gennaion,*" which means "noble" in the sense of both "high-minded" and "well-bred." The same assumption of nobility, good breeding, and superiority to those deceived is also present in Disraeli's statement that a gentleman is one who knows when to tell the truth and when not to. In other words, lying is excusable when undertaken for "noble" ends by those trained to discern these purposes.

Rulers, both temporal and spiritual, have seen their deceits in the benign light of such social purposes. They have propagated and maintained myths, played on the gullibility of the ignorant, and sought stability in shared beliefs. They have seen themselves as high-minded and well-bred—whether by birth or by training—and as superior to those they deceive. Some have gone so far as to claim that those who govern have a *right* to lie. The powerful tell lies believing that they have greater than ordinary understanding of what is at stake; very often, they regard their dupes as having inadequate judgment, or as likely to respond in the wrong way to truthful information.

At times, those who govern also regard particular circumstances as too uncomfortable, too painful, for most people to be able to cope with rationally. They may believe, for instance, that their country must prepare for long-term challenges of great importance, such as a war, an epidemic, or a belt-tightening in the face of future shortages. Yet they may fear that citizens will be able to respond only to short-range dangers. Deception at such times may seem to the government leaders as the only means of attaining the necessary results.

The perspective of the liar is paramount in all such decisions to tell "noble" lies. If the liar considers the responses of the deceived at all, he assumes that they will, once the deceit comes to light and its benefits are understood, be uncomplaining if not positively grateful. The lies are often seen as necessary merely at one *stage* in the education of the public. Thus Erasmus, in commenting on Plato's views, wrote:

> [. . .] [H]e sets forth deceitful fictions for the rabble, so that the people might not set fire to the magistracy, and similar falsifications by which the crass multitude is deceived in its own interest, in the same way that parents deceive children and doctors the sick.
>
> [. . .] Thus for the crass multitude there is need of temporary promises, figures, allegories, parables [. . .] so that little by little they might advance to loftier things.

Some experienced public officials are impatient with any effort to question the ethics of such deceptive practices (except actions obviously taken for private ends). They argue that vital objectives in the national interest require a measure of deception to succeed in the face of powerful obstacles. Negotiations must be carried on that are best left hidden from public view; bargains must be struck that simply cannot be comprehended by a politically unsophisticated electorate. A certain amount of illusion is needed in order for public servants to be effective. Every government, therefore, has to deceive people to some extent in order to lead them.

These officials view the public's concern for ethics as understandable but hardly realistic. Such "moralistic" concerns, put forth without any understanding of practical exigencies, may lead to the setting of impossible standards; these could seriously hamper work without actually changing the underlying practices. Government officials could then feel so beleaguered that some of them might quit their jobs; inefficiency and incompetence would then increasingly afflict the work of the rest.

If we assume the perspective of the deceived—those who experience the consequences of government deception—such arguments are not persuasive. We cannot take for granted either the altruism or the good judgment of those who lie to us, no matter how much they intend to benefit us. We have learned that much deceit for private gain masquerades as being in the public interest. We know how deception, even for the most unselfish motive, corrupts and spreads. And we have lived through the consequences of lies told for what were believed to be noble purposes.

Equally unpersuasive is the argument that there always has been government deception, and always will be, and that efforts to draw lines and set standards are therefore useless annoyances. It is certainly true that deception can never be completely absent from most human practices. But there are great differences among societies in the kinds of deceit that exist and the extent to which they are practiced, differences also among individuals in the same government and among successive governments within the same society. This strongly suggests that it is worthwhile trying to discover why such differences exist and to seek ways of raising the standards of truthfulness.

The argument that those who raise moral concerns are ignorant of political realities, finally, ought to lead, not to a dismissal of such inquiries, but to a more articulate description of what these realities are, so that a more careful and informed debate could begin. We have every reason to regard government as more profoundly injured by a dismissal of criticism and a failure to consider standards than by efforts to discuss them openly. If duplicity is to be allowed in exceptional cases, the criteria for these exceptions should themselves be openly debated and publicly chosen. Otherwise government leaders will have free rein to manipulate and distort the facts and thus escape accountability to the public.

The effort to question political deception cannot be ruled out so summarily. The disparagement of inquiries into such practices has to be seen as the defense of unwarranted power—power bypassing the consent of the governed. In the pages to come I shall take up just a few cases to illustrate both the clear breaches of trust that no group of citizens could desire, and circumstances where it is more difficult to render a judgment.

EXAMPLES OF POLITICAL DECEPTION

In September 1964, a State Department official, reflecting a growing administration consensus, wrote a memorandum advocating a momentous deceit of the American public. He outlined possible courses of action to cope with the deteriorating military situation in South Vietnam. These included a stepping up of American participation in the "pacification" in South Vietnam and a "crescendo" of military action against North Vietnam, involving heavy bombing by the United States. But an election campaign was going on; the President's Republican opponent, Senator Goldwater, was suspected by the electorate of favoring escalation of the war in Vietnam and of brandishing nuclear threats to the communist world. In keeping with President Johnson's efforts to portray Senator Goldwater as an irresponsible war hawk, the memorandum ended with a paragraph entitled "Special considerations during the next two months," holding that:

> During the next two months, because of the lack of "rebuttal time" before election to justify particular actions which may be distorted to the U.S. public, we must act with special care—signaling to . . . [the South Vietnamese] that we are behaving energetically despite the restraints of our political season, and to the U.S. public that we are behaving with good purpose and restraint.

As the campaign wore on, President Johnson increasingly professed to be the candidate of peace. He gave no indication of the growing pressure for escalation from high administrative officials who would remain in office should he win; no hint of the hard choice he knew he would face if reelected. Rather he repeated over and over again that:

> [T]he first responsibility, the only real issue in this campaign, the only thing you ought to be concerned about at all, is: Who can best keep the peace?

The stratagem succeeded; the election was won; the war escalated. Under the name of Operation Rolling Thunder, the United States launched massive bombing raids over North Vietnam early in 1965. In suppressing genuine debate about these plans during the election campaign and masquerading as the party of peace, government members privy to the maneuver believed that they knew what was best for the country and that history would vindicate them. They meant to benefit the nation and the world by keeping the danger of a communist victory at bay. If a sense of *crisis* was needed for added justification, the Domino Theory strained for it: one regime after another was seen as toppling should the first domino be pushed over.

But why the deceit, if the purposes were so altruistic? Why not espouse these purposes openly before the election? The reason must have been that the government could not count on popular support for the scheme. In the first place, the sense of crisis and threat from North Vietnam would have been far from universally shared. To be forthright about the likelihood of escalation might lose many votes; it certainly could not fit with the campaign to portray President Johnson as the candidate most likely to keep the peace. Second, the government feared that its explanations might be "distorted" in the election campaign, so that the voters would not have the correct information before them. Third, time was lacking for the government to make an effort at educating the people about all that was at issue. Finally, the plans were not definitive; changes were possible, and the Vietnamese situation itself very unstable. For all these reasons, it seemed best to campaign for negotiation and restraint and let the Republican opponent be the target for the fear of United States belligerence.

President Johnson thus denied the electorate any chance to give or to refuse consent to the escalation of the war in Vietnam. Believing they had voted for the candidate of peace, American citizens were, within months, deeply embroiled in one of the cruelest wars in their history. Deception of this kind strikes at the very essence of democratic government. It allows those in power to override or nullify the right vested in the people to cast an informed vote in critical elections. Deceiving the people for the sake of the people is a self-contradictory notion in a democracy, unless it can be shown that there has been genuine consent to deceit. The actions of President Johnson were therefore inconsistent with the most basic principle of our political system.

What if all governments felt similarly free to deceive provided they believed the deception genuinely necessary to achieve some important public end? The trouble is that those who make such calculations are always susceptible to bias. They overestimate the likelihood that the benefit will occur and that the harm will be averted; they underestimate the chances that the deceit will be discovered and ignore the effects of such a discovery on trust; they underrate the comprehension of the deceived citizens, as well as their ability and their right to make a reasoned choice. And, most important, such a benevolent self-righteousness disguises the many motives for political lying which could *not* serve as moral excuses: the need to cover up past mistakes; the vindictiveness; the desire to stay in power. These self-serving ends provide the impetus for countless lies that are rationalized as "necessary" for the public good.

As political leaders become accustomed to making such excuses, they grow insensitive to fairness and to veracity. Some come to believe that any lie can be told so long as they can convince themselves that people will be better off in the long run. From there, it is a short step to the conclusion that, even if people will not be better off from a particular lie, they will benefit by all maneuvers to keep the right people in office. Once public servants lose their bearings in this way, all the shabby deceits of Watergate—the fake telegrams, the erased tapes, the elaborate coverups, the bribing of witnesses to make them lie, the televised pleas for trust—become possible.

While Watergate may be unusual in its scope, most observers would agree that deception is part and parcel of many everyday decisions in government. Statistics may be presented in such a way as to diminish the gravity of embarrassing problems. Civil servants may lie to members of Congress in order to protect programs they judge important, or to guard secrets they have been ordered not to divulge. If asked, members of Congress who make deals with one another to vote for measures they would otherwise oppose deny having made such deals. False rumors may be leaked by subordinates who believe that unwise executive action is about to be taken. Or the leak may be correct, but falsely attributed in order to protect the source.

Consider the following situation and imagine all the variations on this theme being played in campaigns all over the United States, at the local, state, or federal level:

A big-city mayor is running for reelection. He has read a report recommending that he remove rent controls after his reelection. He intends to do so, but believes he will lose the election if his intention is known. When asked, at a news conference two days before his election, about the existence of such a report, he denies knowledge of it and reaffirms his strong support of rent control.

In the mayor's view, his reelection is very much in the public interest, and the lie concerns questions which he believes the voters are unable to evaluate properly, especially on such short notice. In all similar situations, the sizable bias resulting from the self-serving element (the desire to be elected, to stay in office, to exercise power) is often clearer to onlookers than to the liars themselves. This bias inflates the alleged justifications for the lie—the worthiness, superiority, altruism of the liar, the rightness of his cause, and the inability of those deceived to respond "appropriately" to hearing the truth.

These common lies are now so widely suspected that voters are at a loss to know when they can and cannot believe what a candidate says in campaigning. The damage to trust has been immense. I have already referred to the poll which found 69 percent of Americans agreeing, both in 1975 and 1976, that the country's leaders had consistently lied to the American people over the past ten years. Over 40 percent of the respondents also agreed that:

> Most politicians are so similar that it doesn't really make much difference who gets elected.

Many refuse to vote under such circumstances. Others look to appearance or to personality factors for clues as to which candidate might be more honest than the others. Voters and candidates alike are the losers when a political system has reached such a low level of trust. Once elected, officials find that their warnings and their calls to common sacrifice meet with disbelief and apathy, even when cooperation is most urgently needed. Law suits and investigations multiply. And the fact that candidates, should they win, are not expected to have meant what they said while campaigning, nor held accountable for discrepancies, only reinforces the incentives for them to bend the truth the next time, thus adding further to the distrust of the voters.

Political lies, so often assumed to be trivial by those who tell them, rarely are. They cannot be trivial when they affect so many people and when they are so peculiarly likely to be imitated, used to retaliate, and spread from a few to many. When political representatives or entire governments arrogate to themselves the right to lie, they take power from the public that would not have been given up voluntarily.

DECEPTION AND CONSENT

Can there be exceptions to the well-founded distrust of deception in public life? Are there times when the public itself might truly not care about possible lies, or might even prefer to be deceived? Are some white lies so trivial or so transparent that they can be ignored? And can we envisage public discussion of more seriously misleading government statements such that reasonable persons could consent to them in advance?

White lies, first of all, are as common to political and diplomatic affairs as they are to the private lives of most people. Feigning enjoyment of an embassy gathering or a political rally, toasting the longevity of a dubious regime or an unimpressive candidate for office—these are forms of politeness that mislead few. It is difficult to regard them as threats to either individuals or communities. As with all white lies, however, the problem is that they spread so easily, and that lines are very hard to draw. Is it still a white lie for a secretary of state to announce that he is going to one country when in reality he travels to another? Or for a president to issue a "cover story" to the effect that a cold is forcing him to return to the White House, when in reality an international crisis made him cancel the rest of his campaign trip? Is it a white lie to issue a letter of praise for a public servant one has just fired? Given the vulnerability of public trust, it is never more important than in public life to keep the deceptive element of white lies to an absolute minimum, and to hold down the danger of their turning into more widespread deceitful practices.

A great deal of deception believed not only innocent but highly justified by public figures concerns their private lives. Information about their marriages, their children, their opinions about others—information about their personal plans and about their motives for personal decisions—all are theirs to keep private if they wish to do so. Refusing to give information under these circumstances is justifiable—but the right to withhold information is not the right to lie about it. Lying under such circumstances bodes ill for conduct in other matters.

Certain additional forms of deception may be debated and authorized in advance by elected representatives of the public. The use of unmarked police cars to discourage speeding by drivers is an example of such a practice. Various forms of unannounced, sometimes covert, auditing of business and government operations are others. Whenever these practices are publicly regulated, they can be limited so that abuses are avoided. But they must be *openly* debated and agreed to in advance, with every precaution against abuses of privacy and the rights of individuals, and against the spread of such covert activities. It is not enough that a public official assumes that consent would be given to such practices.

Another type of deceit has no such consent in advance: the temporizing or the lie when truthful information at a particular *time* might do great damage. Say that a government is making careful plans for announcing the devaluation of its currency. If the news leaks out to some before it can be announced to all, unfair profits for speculators might result. Or take the decision to make sharp increases in taxes on imported goods in order to rescue a tottering economy. To announce the decision beforehand would lead to hoarding and to exactly the results that the taxes are meant to combat. Thus, government officials will typically seek to avoid any premature announcement and will refuse to comment if asked whether devaluation or higher taxes are imminent. At times, however, official spokesmen will go further and falsely deny that the actions in question will in fact take place.

Such lies may well be uttered in good faith in an effort to avoid harmful speculation and hoarding. Nevertheless, if false statements are made to the public only to be exposed as soon as the devaluation or the new tax is announced, great damage to trust will result. It is like telling a patient that an operation will be painless—the swifter the disproof, the more likely the loss of trust. In addition, these lies are subject to all the dangers of spread and mistake and deterioration of standards that accompany all deception.

For these reasons, it is far better to refuse comment than to lie in such situations. The objection may be made, however, that a refusal to comment will be interpreted by the press as tantamount to an admission that devaluation or higher taxes are very near. Such an objection has force only if a government has not already established credibility by letting it be known earlier that it would never comment on such matters, and by strictly adhering to this policy at all times. Since lies in these cases are so egregious, it is worth taking care to establish such credibility in advance, so that a refusal to comment is not taken as an invitation to monetary speculation.

Another form of deception takes place when the government regards the public as frightened, or hostile, and highly volatile. In order not to create a panic, information about early signs of an epidemic may be suppressed or distorted. And the lie to a mob seeking its victim is like lying to the murderer asking where the person he is pursuing has gone. It can be acknowledged and defended as soon as the threat is over. In such cases, one may at times be justified in withholding information; perhaps, on rare occasions, even in lying. But such cases are so rare that they hardly exist for practical purposes.

The fact that rare circumstances exist where the justification for government lying seems powerful creates a difficulty—these same excuses will often be made to serve a great many more purposes. For some governments or public officials, the information they wish to conceal is almost never of the requisite certainty, the time never the right one, and the public never sufficiently dispassionate. For these reasons, it is hard to see how a practice of lying to the public about devaluation or changes in taxation or epidemics could be consented to in advance, and therefore justified.

Are there any exceptionally dangerous circumstances where the state of crisis is such as to justify lies to the public for its own protection? We have already discussed lying to enemies in an acute crisis. Sometimes the domestic public is then also deceived, at least temporarily, as in the case of the U-2 incident. Wherever there is a threat—from a future enemy, as before World War II, or from a shortage of energy—the temptation to draw upon the excuses for deceiving citizens is very strong. The government may sincerely doubt that the electorate is capable of making the immediate sacrifices needed to confront the growing danger. (Or one branch of the government may lack confidence in another, for similar reasons, as when the administration mistrusts Congress.) The public may seem too emotional, the time not yet ripe for disclosure. Are there crises so exceptional that deceptive strategies are justifiable?

Compare, for instance, what was said and left unsaid by two United States Presidents confronted by a popular unwillingness to enter a war: President Lyndon Johnson, in escalating the war in Vietnam, and President Franklin D. Roosevelt, in moving the country closer to participating in

World War II, while making statements such as the following in his 1940 campaign to be reelected:

> I have said this before, but I shall say it again and again and again: Your boys are not going to be sent into any foreign wars.

By the standards set forth in this chapter, President Johnson's covert escalation and his failure to consult the electorate concerning the undeclared war in Vietnam was clearly unjustifiable. Consent was bypassed; there was no immediate danger to the nation which could even begin to excuse deceiving the public in a national election on grounds of an acute crisis.

The crisis looming before World War II, on the other hand, was doubtless much greater. Certainly this case is a difficult one, and one on which reasonable persons might not be able to agree. The threat was unprecedented; the need for preparations and for support of allies great; yet the difficulties of alerting the American public seemed insuperable. Would this crisis, then, justify proceeding through deceit?

To consent even to such deception would, I believe, be to take a frightening step. Do we want to live in a society where public officials can resort to deceit and manipulation whenever they decide that an exceptional crisis has arisen? Would we not, on balance, prefer to run the risk of failing to rise to a crisis honestly explained to us, from which the government might have saved us through manipulation? And what protection from abuse do we foresee should we surrender this choice?

In considering answers to these questions, we must take into account more than the short-run effects of government manipulation. President Roosevelt's manner of bringing the American people to accept first the possibility, then the likelihood, of war was used as an example by those who wanted to justify President Johnson's acts of dissimulation. And these acts in turn were pointed to by those who resorted to so many forms of duplicity in the Nixon administration. Secrecy and deceit grew at least in part because of existing precedents.

The consequences of spreading deception, alienation, and lack of trust could not have been documented for us more concretely than they have in the past decades. We have had a very vivid illustration of how lies undermine our political system. While deception under the circumstances confronting President Roosevelt may in hindsight be more excusable than much that followed, we could no more consent to it in advance than to all that came later.

Wherever lies to the public have become routine, then, very special safeguards should be required. The test of public justification of deceptive practices is more needed than ever. It will be a hard test to satisfy, the more so the more trust is invested in those who lie and the more power they wield. Those in government and other positions of trust should be held to the highest standards. Their lies are not ennobled by their positions; quite the contrary. Some lies—notably minor white lies and emergency lies rapidly acknowledged—may be more *excusable* than others, but only those deceptive practices which can be openly debated and consented to in advance are *justifiable* in a democracy.

STUDY QUESTIONS

1. Is a certain amount of deception, or rather opacity, necessary for a government to function smoothly?
2. Is political deceit unconstitutional?
3. Why might trust be important between a government and the governed in a democracy? What may be the result of a breach of this trust?
4. How can deceptive practices be openly discussed and consented to? Isn't this a contradiction?
5. Is it reasonable to assume that the general public has the information, resources, and emotional stability to deal with the truth of a difficult situation?

22

Women and Honor: Some Notes on Lying

Adrienne Rich

Adrienne Rich is one of America's finest poets. Her many poetry collections include *An Atlas of the Difficult World* and *The Dream of a Common Language*. She has also written *What Is Found There: Notebooks on Poetry and Politics*.

These notes were first read at the Hartwick Women Writers' Workshop, founded and directed by Beverly Tanenhaus, at Hartwick College, Oneonta, New York, in June 1975. They were published as a pamphlet by Motheroot Press in Pittsburgh, 1977; in Heresies: A Feminist Magazine of Art and Politics, *vol. 1, no. 1; and in a French translation by the Québecois feminist press, Les Editions du Remue-Ménage, 1979.*

It is clear that among women we need a new ethics; as women, a new morality. The problem of speech, of language, continues to be primary. For if in our speaking we are breaking silences long established, "liberating ourselves from our secrets" in the words of Beverly Tanenhaus, this is in itself a first kind of action. I wrote Women and Honor *in an effort to make myself more honest, and to understand the terrible negative power of the lie in relationships between women. Since it was published, other women have spoken and written of things I did not include: Michelle Cliff's "Notes on Speechlessness" in* Sinister Wisdom *no. 5 led Catherine Nicolson (in the same issue) to write of the power of "deafness," the frustration of our speech by those who do not want to hear what we have to say. Nelle Morton has written of the act of "hearing each other into speech." How do we listen? How do we make it possible for another to break her silence? These are some of the questions which follow on the ones I have raised here.*

(These notes are concerned with relationships between and among women. When "personal relationship" is referred to, I mean a relationship between two women. It will be clear in what follows when I am talking about women's relationships with men.)

1. The old, male idea of honor. A man's "word" sufficed—to other men—without guarantee.

2. "Our Land Free, Our Men Honest, Our Women Fruitful"—a popular colonial toast in America.

3. Male honor also having something to do with killing: *I could not love thee, Dear, so much/Lov'd I not Honour more.* ("To Lucasta, On Going to the Wars"). Male honor as something needing to be avenged: hence, the duel.

4. Women's honor, something altogether else: virginity, chastity, fidelity to a husband. Honesty in women has not been considered important. We have been depicted as generically whimsical, deceitful, subtle, vacillating. And we have been rewarded for lying.

5. Men have been expected to tell the truth about facts, not about feelings. They have not been expected to talk about feelings at all.

6. Yet even about facts they have continually lied.

7. We assume that politicians are without honor. We read their statements trying to crack the code. The scandals of their politics: not that men in high places lie, only that they do so with such indifference, so endlessly, still expecting to be believed. We are accustomed to the contempt inherent in the political lie.

8. To discover that one has been lied to in a personal relationship, however, leads one to feel a little crazy.

9. Lying is done with words, and also with silence.

10. The woman who tells lies in her personal relationships may or may not plan or invent her lying. She may not even think of what she is doing in a calculated way.

11. A subject is raised which the liar wishes buried. She has to go downstairs, her parking meter will have run out. Or, there is a telephone call she ought to have made an hour ago.

12. She is asked, point-blank, a question which may lead into painful talk: "How do you feel about what is happening between us?" Instead of trying to describe her feelings in their ambiguity and confusion, she asks, "How do *you* feel?" The other, because she is trying to establish a ground of openness and trust, begins describing her own feelings. Thus the liar learns more than she tells.

13. And she may also tell herself a lie: that she is concerned with the other's feelings, not with her own.

14. But the liar is concerned with her own feelings.

15. The liar lives in fear of losing control. She cannot even desire a relationship without manipulation, since to be vulnerable to another person means for her the loss of control.

16. The liar has many friends, and leads an existence of great loneliness.

17. The liar often suffers from amnesia. Amnesia is the silence of the unconscious.

18. To lie habitually, as a way of life, is to lose contact with the unconscious. It is like taking sleeping pills, which confer sleep but blot out dreaming. The unconscious wants truth. It ceases to speak to those who want something else more than truth.

19. In speaking of lies, we come inevitably to the subject of truth. There is nothing simple or easy about this idea. There is no "the truth," "a truth"—truth is not one thing, or even a system. It is an increasing complexity. The pattern of the carpet is a surface. When we look closely, or when we become weavers, we learn of the tiny multiple threads unseen in the overall pattern, the knots on the underside of the carpet.

20. This is why the effort to speak honestly is so important. Lies are usually attempts to make everything simpler—for the liar—than it really is, or ought to be.

21. In lying to others we end up lying to ourselves. We deny the importance of an event, or a person, and thus deprive ourselves of a part of our lives. Or we use one piece of the past or present to screen out another. Thus we lose faith with our own lives.

22. The unconscious wants truth, as the body does. The complexity and fecundity of dreams come from the complexity and fecundity of the unconscious struggling to fulfill that desire. The complexity and fecundity of poetry come from the same struggle.

23. An honorable human relationship—that is, one in which two people have the right to use the word "love"—is a process, delicate, violent, often terrifying to both persons involved, a process of refining the truths they can tell each other.

24. It is important to do this because it breaks down human self-delusion and isolation.

25. It is important to do this because in so doing we do justice to our own complexity.

26. It is important to do this because we can count on so few people to go that hard way with us.

27. I come back to the questions of women's honor. Truthfulness has not been considered important for women, as long as we have remained physically faithful to a man, or chaste.

28. We have been expected to lie with our bodies: to bleach, redden, unkink or curl our hair, pluck eyebrows, shave armpits, wear padding in various places or lace ourselves, take little steps, glaze finger and toe nails, wear clothes that emphasized our helplessness.

29. We have been required to tell different lies at different times, depending on what the men of the time needed to hear. The Victorian wife or the white southern lady, who were expected to have no sensuality, to "lie still"; the twentieth-century "free" woman who is expected to fake orgasms.

30. We have had the truth of our bodies withheld from us or distorted; we have been kept in ignorance of our most intimate places. Our instincts have been punished; clitoridectomies for "lustful" nuns or for "difficult" wives. It has been difficult, too, to know the lies of our complicity from the lies we believed.

31. The lie of the "happy marriage," of domesticity—we have been complicit, have acted out the fiction of a well-lived life, until the day we testify in court of rapes, beatings, psychic cruelties, public and private humiliations.

32. Patriarchal lying has manipulated women both through falsehood and through silence. Facts we needed have been withheld from us. False witness has been borne against us.

33. And so we must take seriously the question of truthfulness between women, truthfulness among women. As we cease to lie with our bodies, as we cease to take on faith what men have said about us, is a truly womanly idea of honor in the making?

34. Women have been forced to lie, for survival, to men. How to unlearn this among other women?

35. "Women have always lied to each other."

36. "Women have always whispered the truth to each other."

37. Both of these axioms are true.

38. "Women have always been divided against each other."

39. "Women have always been in secret collusion."

40. Both of these axioms are true.

41. In the struggle for survival we tell lies. To bosses, to prison guards, the police, men who have power over us, who legally own us and our children, lovers who need us as proof of their manhood.

42. There is a danger run by all powerless people: that we forget we are lying, or that lying becomes a weapon we carry over into relationships with people who do not have power over us.

43. I want to reiterate that when we talk about women and honor, or women and lying, we speak within the context of male lying, the lies of the powerful, the lie as false source of power.

44. Women have to think whether we want, in our relationships with each other, the kind of power that can be obtained through lying.

45. Women have been driven mad, "gaslighted," for centuries by the refutation of our experience and our instincts in a culture which validates only male experience. The truth of our bodies and our minds has been mystified to us. We therefore have a primary obligation to each other: not to undermine each other's sense of reality for the sake of expediency; not to gaslight each other.

46. Women have often felt insane when cleaving to the truth of our experience. Our future depends on the sanity of each of us, and we have a profound stake, beyond the personal, in the project of describing our reality as candidly and fully as we can to each other.

47. There are phrases which help us not to admit we are lying: "my privacy," "nobody's business but my own." The choices that underlie these phrases may indeed be justified; but we ought to think about the full meaning and consequences of such language.

48. Women's love for women has been represented almost entirely through silence and lies. The institution of heterosexuality has forced the lesbian to dissemble, or be labeled a pervert, a criminal, a sick or dangerous woman, etc. etc. The lesbian, then, has often been forced to lie, like the prostitute or the married woman.

49. Does a life "in the closet"—lying, perhaps of necessity, about ourselves to bosses, landlords, clients, colleagues, family, because the law and public opinion are founded on a lie—does this, can it, spread into private life, so that lying (described as *discretion*) becomes an easy way to avoid conflict or complication? Can it become a strategy so ingrained that it is used even with close friends and lovers?

50. Heterosexuality as an institution has also drowned in silence the erotic feelings between women. I myself lived half a lifetime in the lie of that denial. That silence makes us all, to some degree, into liars.

51. When a woman tells the truth she is creating the possibility for more truth around her.

52. The liar leads an existence of unutterable loneliness.

53. The liar is afraid.

54. But we are all afraid: without fear we become manic, hubristic, self-destructive. What is this particular fear that possesses the liar?

55. She is afraid that her own truths are not good enough.

56. She is afraid, not so much of prison guards or bosses, but of something unnamed within her.

57. The liar fears the void.

58. The void is not something created by patriarchy, or racism, or capitalism. It will not fade way with any of them. It is part of every woman.

59. "The dark core," Virginia Woolf named it, writing of her mother. The dark core. It is beyond personality; beyond who loves us or hates us.

60. We begin out of the void, out of darkness and emptiness. It is part of the cycle understood by the old pagan religions, that materialism denies. Out of death, rebirth; out of nothing, something.

61. The void is the creatrix, the matrix. It is not mere hollowness and anarchy. But in women it has been identified with lovelessness, barrenness, sterility. We have been urged to fill our "emptiness" with children. We are not supposed to go down into the darkness of the core.

62. Yet, if we can risk it, the something born of that nothing is the beginning of our truth.

63. The liar in her terror wants to fill up the void, with anything. Her lies are a denial of her fear; a way of maintaining control.

64. Why do we feel slightly crazy when we realize we have been lied to in a relationship?

65. We take so much of the universe on trust. You tell me: "In 1950 I lived on the north side of Beacon Street in Somerville." You tell me: "She and I were lovers, but for months now we have only been good friends." You tell me: "It is seventy degrees outside and the sun is shining." Because I love you, because there is not even a question of lying between us, I take these accounts of the universe on trust: your address twenty-five years ago, your relationship with someone I know only by sight, this morning's weather. I fling unconscious tendrils of belief, like slender green threads, across

statements such as these, statements made so unequivocally, which have no tone or shadow of tentativeness. I build them into the mosaic of my world. I allow my universe to change in minute, significant ways, on the basis of things you have said to me, of my trust in you.

66. I also have faith that you are telling me things it is important I should know; that you do not conceal facts from me in an effort to spare me, or yourself, pain.

67. Or, at the very least, that you will say, "There are things I am not telling you."

68. When we discover that someone we trusted can be trusted no longer, it forces us to reexamine the universe, to question the whole instinct and concept of trust. For awhile, we are thrust back onto some bleak, jutting ledge, in a dark pierced by sheets of fire, swept by sheets of rain, in a world before kinship, or naming, or tenderness exist; we are brought close to formlessness.

69. The liar may resist confrontation, denying that she lied. Or she may use other language: forgetfulness, privacy, the protection of someone else. Or, she may bravely declare herself a coward. This allows her to go on lying, since that is what cowards do. She does not say, *I was afraid,* since this would open the question of other ways of handling her fear. It would open the question of what is actually feared.

70. She may say, *I didn't want to cause pain.* What she really did not want is to have to deal with the other's pain. The lie is a short-cut through another's personality.

71. Truthfulness, honor, is not something which springs ablaze of itself; it has to be created between people.

72. This is true in political situations. The quality and depth of the politics evolving from a group depends in very large part on their understanding of honor.

73. Much of what is narrowly termed "politics" seems to rest on a longing for certainty even at the cost of honesty, for an analysis which, once given, need not be reexamined. Such is the deadendedness—for women—of Marxism in our time.

74. Truthfulness anywhere means a heightened complexity. But it is a movement into evolution. Women are only beginning to uncover our own truths; many of us would be grateful for some rest in that struggle, would be glad just to lie down with the shreds we have painfully unearthed, and be satisfied with those. Often I feel this like an exhaustion in my own body.

75. The politics worth having, the relationships worth having, demand that we delve still deeper.

76. The possibilities that exist between two people, or among a group of people, are a kind of alchemy. They are the most interesting thing in life. The liar is someone who keeps losing sight of these possibilities.

77. When relationships are determined by manipulation, by the need for control, they may possess a dreary, bickering kind of drama, but they cease to be interesting. They are repetitious; the shock of human possibilities has ceased to reverberate through them.

78. When someone tells me a piece of the truth which has been withheld from me, and which I needed in order to see my life more clearly, it may bring acute pain, but it can also flood me with a cold, sea-sharp wash of relief. Often such truths come by accident, or from strangers.

79. It isn't that to have an honorable relationship with you, I have to understand everything, or tell you everything at once, or that I can know, beforehand, everything I need to tell you.

80. It means that most of the time I am eager, longing for the possibility of telling you. That these possibilities may seem frightening, but not destructive, to me. That I feel strong enough to hear your tentative and groping words. That we both

know we are trying, all the time, to extend the possibilities of truth between us.

81. The possibility of life between us.

STUDY QUESTIONS

1. Why is truth especially important and why are lies especially destructive in the context of women's relationships with each other?
2. Read note 12. Why does Rich call that woman a liar? She has not falsified any fact.
3. How does Rich think that women have been complicit in the very lies that destroy them?
4. What is the "dark core" that women fear, and why do they fear it?
5. How does the word *honor* carry different connotations for women than for men?

FOR FURTHER STUDY

Arendt, Hannah. "Truth and Politics." In *Philosophy, Politics, and Society,* 3d series, ed. Peter Laslett and W. G. Runciman. New York: Barnes & Noble, 1967.

Aristotle. *Nicomachean Ethics.* Book 4, chap. 7.

Bok, Sissela. *Lying: Moral Choice in Public and Private Life.* New York: Pantheon Books, 1978.

———. *Secrets: On the Ethics of Concealment and Revelation.* New York: Pantheon Books, 1983.

Bonhoeffer, Dietrich. "What Is Meant by 'Telling the Truth.'" In *Ethics,* ed. Eberhard Bethge, 363–72. New York: Macmillan, 1965.

Foucault, Michel. *Power/Knowledge: Selected Interviews and Other Writings 1972–1977,* ed. Colin Gordon. New York: Pantheon Books, 1980.

Fried, Charles. *Right and Wrong.* Cambridge, Mass.: Harvard University Press, 1978.

Havel, Václav. *Living in Truth,* ed. Jan Vladislav. London: Faber & Faber, 1989.

Kant, Immanuel. "On a Supposed Right to Lie from Benevolent Motives." In *The Critique of Practical Reason and Other Writings in Moral Philosophy,* ed. and trans. Lewis White Beck, 346–50. Chicago: University of Chicago Press, 1949.

Chapter Five

Ethics of War, Violence, and Peace

23

Just-War Theory

William V. O'Brien

William V. O'Brien has served as a professor of international law and the chairman of the Institute of World Polity at Georgetown University. He has written extensively on international law.

The original just-war doctrine of St. Augustine, St. Thomas, and other Scholastics emphasized the conditions for permissible recourse to war—the *jus ad bellum*. To this doctrine was added another branch of prescriptions regulating the conduct of war, the *jus in bello*.

THE *JUS AD BELLUM*

The *jus ad bellum* lays down conditions that must be met in order to have permissible recourse to armed coercion. They are conditions that should be viewed in the light of the fundamental tenet of just-war doctrine: the presumption is always against war. The taking of human life is not permitted to man unless there are exceptional justifications. Just-war doctrine provides those justifications, but they are in the nature of special pleadings to overcome the presumption against killing. The decision to invoke the exceptional rights of war must be based on the following criteria: there must be competent authority to order the war for a public purpose; there must be a just cause (it may be self-defense or the protection of rights by offensive war) and the means must be proportionate to the just cause and all peaceful alternatives must have been exhausted; and there must be right intention on the part of the just belligerent. Let us examine these criteria.

Competent Authority

Insofar as large-scale, conventional war is concerned, the issue of competent authority is different in modern times than it was in the thirteenth century. The decentralized political system wherein public, private, and criminal violence overlapped, as well as the state of military art and science, permitted a variety of private wars. So it was important to insist that war—in which individuals would be called upon to take human lives—must be waged on the order of public authorities for public purposes. This is not a serious problem in most parts of the world today. Only states have the material capacity to wage large-scale, modern, conventional war. Two other problems do, however, exist in connection with the condition of competent authority. First, there may be disputes as to the constitutional competence of a particular official or organ of state to initiate war. Second, civil war and revolutionary terrorism are frequently initiated by persons and organizations claiming revolutionary rights.

Most states today, even totalitarian states, have specific constitutional provisions for the declaration and termination of war. If an official or state organ violates these provisions, there may not be a valid exercise of the sovereign right to declare and wage war. In such a case the first condition of the just war might not be met. This was the charge, implicitly or explicitly, against President Johnson in the Vietnam War. Johnson never requested a declaration of war from Congress with which he shared war-making powers. War critics asserted that the undeclared war was illegal. A sufficient answer to this charge is to be found in congressional cooperation in the war effort and in the refusal of the courts to declare the war unconstitutional.

In this connection a word should be said about declaring wars. Any examination of modern wars will show that the importance of a declaration of war has diminished greatly in international practice. Because of the split-second timing of modern war, it is often undesirable to warn the enemy by way of a formal declaration. Defense measures are geared to react to hostile behavior, not declarations. When war is declared it is often an announcement confirming a condition that has already been established. Nevertheless, if a particular state's constitution does require a formal declaration of war and one is not forthcoming, the issue of competence is raised. If a public official exceeds his authority in mobilizing the people and conducting war, there is a lack of competent authority.

The second problem, however, is by far the greatest. Today, rights of revolution are frequently invoked by organizations and individuals. They clearly do not have the authority and capacity to wage war in the conventional sense. However, they do wage revolutionary war, often on an international scale. Indeed, international terrorism is one of the most pervasive and difficult problems facing the international community.

All major ideologies and blocs or alignments of states in the international system recognize the right of revolution. Usually their interpretations will emphasize the rights of revolution against others, not themselves. Logically, there should be an elaborate *jus ad bellum* and *jus in bello* for revolutionary war, but development of such a doctrine has never been seriously attempted. As a result, the issues of revolutionary war tend to be treated on an ad hoc basis as special cases vaguely related to the regular categories of just war.

The differences between conventional war waged by states and revolutionary war waged by rebels against states are profound. Given the formidable power of most modern governments, particularly in regard to their comparative monopoly of armed force, revolutionary rights can be asserted mainly by covert organizations waging guerrilla warfare and terrorism. The option of organizing a portion of a state and fighting a conventional civil war in the manner of the American, Spanish, or Nigerian civil wars is seldom available.

The covert, secret character of modern revolutionary movements is such that it is often hard to judge their claims to qualify as the competent authority for oppressed people. There is a decided tendency to follow the Leninist model of revolutionary leadership wherein the self-selected revolutionary elite decides on the just revolutionary cause, the means, and the circumstances of taking the initiative, all done in the name of the people and revolutionary justice. As a revolution progresses, the task of certifying competent authority continues to be difficult. Support for the revolutionary leadership is often coerced or given under conditions where there is not popular acceptance of the revolutionary authority of that leadership or its ends and means. Recognition by foreign powers of belligerency—or even of putative governmental powers—is an unreliable guide given subjective, politicized recognition policies.

Two issues need to be resolved concerning revolutionary activity. First, insofar as treating revolutionaries as belligerents in a war and not as common criminals is concerned, the ultimate answer lies in the character, magnitude, and degree of success of the revolutionaries. If they can organize a government that carries on their war in a controlled fashion (assuming a magnitude requiring countermeasures that more resemble war than ordinary police operations), and if the conflict continues for an appreciable time, the revolutionaries may have won their right to be considered a competent authority for purposes of just war. Beyond this enumeration of criteria it seems unprofitable to generalize.

Second, concerning the authority of rebel leaders to mobilize the people by ordering or coercing individuals to fight for the revolutionary cause, the conscience of the individual takes precedence. Lacking any color of authority to govern, the rebels cannot of right compel participation in their cause.

Just Cause

Authorities vary in their presentation of just cause, but it seems to break down into four subdivisions: the substance of the just cause, the forms of pursuing just cause, the requirement of proportionality of ends and means, and the requirement of exhaustion of peaceful remedies.

The substance of the just cause must, in Childress's formulation, be sufficiently "serious and weighty" to overcome the presumption against killing in general and war in particular. In Childress's approach, with which I am in essential agreement, this means that there must be a "competing prima facie duty or obligation" to "the prima facie obligation not to injure and kill others."[1] Childress mentions as "serious and weighty" prima facie obligations the following: (1) "to protect the innocent from unjust attack," (2) "to restore rights wrongfully denied," (3) "to re-establish a just order."

This is an adequate basis, reflective of the older just-war literature, for discussing the substance of just cause. Indeed, Childress is more explicit than many modern commentators who simply state that there should be a just cause. Still, it is only a beginning. It is unfortunate that modern moralists have generally been so concerned with the issue of putatively disproportionate means in modern war that they have neglected the prior question of the ends for which these means might have to be used (that is, just cause). In practical terms, this task of evaluating the substance of just cause leads inescapably to a comparative analysis of the characteristics of the polities or political–social systems posed in warlike confrontation. Specifically, one must ask whether the political–social order of a country like the United States is sufficiently valuable to warrant its defense in a war against a country like the Soviet Union, which, if victorious, would impose its political–social order on the United States.

Even more difficult for those who would answer in the affirmative is the question whether the United States should intervene to protect a manifestly imperfect political–social order (South Korea, South Vietnam or, perhaps, that of a state such as Jordan, Saudi Arabia, or Pakistan) in order to prevent its conquest by a totalitarian communist state like the Soviet Union, North Korea, or North Vietnam; or even by a puppet state of the Soviet Union as Syria may turn out to be.

In brief, in our time the substance of the just-cause condition of just war has been essentially the issue of being either Red or dead. Whether the negative goal of not being Red is sufficient to justify a war that may leave many dead and still not ensure a political–social order of very high quality (a continuing probability in most of the Third World) is a most difficult question that has divided many men of goodwill in the post–World War II era. Any just-war analysis that does not face the question of the comparative justice and character of contending political–social orders is not offering responsible answers to the just-war ends/means dilemmas of the modern world.

By comparison, the substantive just causes of the older just-war literature are almost insignificant. In the modern world the just cause often has to do with the survival of a way of life. Claims that this is so can be false or exaggerated, but they are often all too legitimate. They must be taken seriously in assessing the substance of just cause in modern just-war analyses.[2]

However, passing the test of just cause is not solely a matter of positing an end that is convincingly just, although that is the indispensable starting point. It is also necessary to meet the tests posed by the other three subdivisions of just cause.

The forms of pursuing just cause are defensive and offensive wars. The justice of self-defense is generally considered to be axiomatic. Just-war doctrine, following Aristotle and St. Thomas as well as the later Scholastics, places great importance on the state as a natural institution essential for man's development. Defense of the state is prima facie defense of an essential social institution. So strong is the presumption in favor of the right of self-defense that the requirement of probable success, to be discussed under proportionality, is usually waived.

Offensive wars raise more complications. In classical just-war doctrine, offensive wars were permitted to protect vital rights unjustly threatened or injured. Moreover, in a form now archaic, offensive wars of vindictive justice against infidels and heretics were once permitted. Such wars disappeared with the decline of the religious, holy-war element as a cause of and rationale for wars. Thus, the forms of permissible wars today are twofold: wars of self-defense and offensive wars to enforce justice for oneself. [Moreover,] the second is now seemingly prohibited by positive international law. But in terms of basic just-war theory it remains an option. A war of vindictive justice wherein the belligerent fights against error and evil as a matter of principle and not of necessity is no longer condoned by just-war doctrine.

Turning from the forms of just war we come to the heart of just cause—proportionality between the just ends and the means. This concerns the relationship between *raison d'état* (the high interests of state) and the use of the military instrument in war as the means to achieve these interests. This concept of proportionality at the level of *raison d'état* is multidimensional. To begin with, the ends held out as the just cause must be sufficiently good and important to warrant the extreme means of war, the arbitrament of arms. Beyond that, a projection of the outcome of the war is required in which the probable good expected to result from success is weighed against the probable evil that the war will cause.

The process of weighing probable good against probable evil is extremely complex. The balance sheet of good and evil must be estimated for each belligerent. Additionally, there should be a balancing of effects on individual third parties and on the international common good. International interdependence means that international conflicts are difficult to contain and that their shock waves affect third parties in a manner that must be accounted for in the calculus of probable good and evil. Moreover, the international community as such has its international common good, which is necessarily affected by any war. Manifestly, the task of performing this calculus effectively is an awesome one. But even its successful completion does not fully satisfy the demands of the just-war condition of just cause. Probing even further, the doctrine requires a responsible judgment that there is a probability of success for the just party. All of these calculations must be concluded convincingly to meet the multidimensional requirement of just cause.

Moreover, the calculus of proportionality between probable good and evil in a war is a continuing one. It should be made before the decision to go to war. It must then be reviewed at critical points along the process of waging the war. The best informed estimates about wars are often in error. They may need revision or replacement by completely new estimates. The *jus ad bellum* requirement of proportionality, then, includes these requirements:

There must be a just cause of sufficient importance to warrant its defense by recourse to armed coercion.

The probable good to be achieved by successful recourse to armed coercion in pursuit of the just cause must outweigh the probable evil that the war will produce.

The calculation of proportionality between probable good and evil must be made with respect to all belligerents, affected neutrals, and the international community as a whole before initiating a war and periodically throughout a war to reevaluate the balance of good and evil that is actually produced by the war.

These calculations must be made in the light of realistic estimates of the probability of success.

There is an important qualification to the requirement of probability of success. A war of self-defense may be engaged in irrespective of the prospects for success, particularly if there is a great threat to continued existence and to fundamental values.

The last component of the condition of just cause is that war be employed only as a last resort after the exhaustion of peaceful alternatives. To have legitimate recourse to war, it must be the *ultima ratio,* the arbitrament of arms. This requirement has taken on added significance in the League of Nations–United Nations period. It was the intention of the nations that founded these international organizations to create the machinery for peace that would replace self-help in the form of recourse to war and limit the need for collective security enforcement action to extreme cases of defiance of international law and order. There are certainly adequate institutions of international negotiations, mediation, arbitration, and adjudication to accommodate any nation willing to submit its international disputes to peaceful settlement. Indeed, the existence of this machinery for peaceful settlement has prompted international lawyers and statesmen to adopt a rough rule of thumb: the state that fails to exhaust the peaceful remedies available before resorting to war is prima facie an aggressor.

Right Intention

Among the elements of the concept of right intention, several points may be distinguished. First, right intention limits the belligerent to the pursuit of the avowed just cause. That pursuit may not be turned into an excuse to pursue other causes that might not meet the conditions of just cause. Thus, if the just cause is to defend a nation's borders and protect them from future aggressions, but the fortunes of war place the just belligerent in the position to conquer the unjust nation, such a conquest might show a lack of right intention and change the just war into an unjust war. The just cause would have been realized by a war of limited objectives rather than a war of total conquest.

Second, right intention requires that the just belligerent have always in mind as the ultimate object of the war a just and lasting peace. There is an implicit requirement to prepare for reconciliation even as one wages war. This is a hard saying. It will often go against the grain of the belligerents' disposition, but pursuit of a just and lasting peace is an essential characteristic of the difference between just and unjust war. Accordingly, any belligerent acts that unnecessarily increase the destruction and bitterness of war and thereby endanger the prospects for true peace are liable to condemnation as violations of the condition of right intention.

Third, underlying the other requirements, right intention insists that charity and love exist even among enemies. Enemies must be treated as human beings with rights. The thrust of this requirement is twofold. Externally, belligerents must act with charity toward their enemies. Internally, belligerents must suppress natural animosity and hatred, which can be sinful and injurious to the moral and psychological health of those who fail in charity. Gratuitous cruelty may be as harmful to those who indulge in it as to their victims.

Right intention raises difficult moral and psychological problems. It may well be that its tenets set standards that will often be unattainable insofar as the thoughts and feelings of belligerents are concerned. War often treats individuals and nations so cruelly and unfairly that it is unrealistic to expect them to banish all hatred of those who have afflicted them. We can, however, more reasonably insist that just belligerents may not translate their strong feelings into behavior that is prohibited by the rule of right intention. A nation may feel tempted to impose a Carthaginian peace, but it may not exceed just cause by giving in to that temptation. A nation may have good reason for feeling that the enemy deserves the full force of all means available, but the requirement to build for a just and lasting peace prohibits this kind of vengeance. The enemy may have behaved abominably, engendering righteous indignation amounting to hatred, but the actions of the just belligerent must be based on charity.

Lest this appear to be so utterly idealistic as to warrant dismissal as irrelevant to the real world, let it be recalled that the greatest enemies of the modern era have often been brought around in the cyclical processes of international politics to become trusted allies against former friends who are now viewed with fear and distrust. If war is to be an instrument of policy and not, in St. Augustine's words, a "vendetta," right intention is a counsel of good policy as well as of morality. . . .

THE *JUS IN BELLO*

In the *jus in bello* that emerged rather late in the development of just-war doctrine, two basic limitations on the conduct of war were laid down. One was the principle of proportion requiring proportionality of military means to political and military ends. The other was the principle of discrimination prohibiting direct, intentional attacks on noncombatants and nonmilitary targets. These are the two categories of *jus in bello* limitations generally treated by modern works on just war.

The Principle of Proportion

In the preceding [discussion] the principle of proportion was discussed at the level of *raison d'état*. One of the criteria of just-war *jus ad bellum* requires that the good to be achieved by the realization of the war aims be proportionate to the evil resulting from the war. When the principle of proportion is again raised in the *jus in bello*, the question immediately arises as to the referent of proportionality in judging the means of war. Are the means to be judged in relation to the end of the war, the ends being formulated in the highest *raison d'état* terms? Or are intermediate political/military goals, referred to in the law-of-war literature as *raison de guerre*, the more appropriate referents in the calculus of proportionality as regards the conduct of a war?

There is no question that the ultimate justification for all means in war lies in the just cause that is a political purpose, *raison d'état*. But there are difficulties in making the ends of *raison d'état* the sole referent in the *jus in bello* calculus of proportionality. First, relation of all means to the highest ends of the war gives little rationale for or justification of discrete military means. If all means are simply lumped together as allegedly necessary for the war effort, one has to accept or reject them wholly in terms of the just cause, leaving no morality of means. The calculus of proportionality in just cause is the total good to be expected if the war is successful balanced against the total evil the war is likely to cause.

Second, it is evident that a discrete military means could, when viewed independently on the basis of its intermediary military end (*raison de guerre*), be proportionate or disproportionate to that military end for which it was used, irrespective of the ultimate end of the war at the level of *raison d'état*. If such a discrete military means were proportionate in terms of its military end, it would be a legitimate belligerent act. If it were disproportionate to the military end, it would be immoral and legally impermissible. Thus, an act could be proportionate or disproportionate to a legitimate military end regardless of the legitimacy of the just-cause end of *raison d'état*.

Third, there is the need to be realistic and fair in evaluating individual command responsibility for belligerent acts. The need to distinguish higher political ends from intermediate military ends was acute in the war-crimes trials after World War II. It is the law of Nuremberg, generally accepted in international law, that the *raison d'état* ends of Nazi Germany were illegal aggression. But the Nuremberg and other war-crimes tribunals rejected the argument that all military actions taken by the German armed forces were war crimes per se because they were carried out in pursuance of aggressive war.[3] The legitimacy of discrete acts of the German forces was judged, inter alia, in terms of their proportionality to intermediate military goals, *raison de guerre*. This was a matter of justice to military commanders accused of war crimes. It was also a reasonable way to evaluate the substance of the allegations that war crimes had occurred.

The distinction is equally important when applied to a just belligerent. Assuming that in World War II the Allied forces were fighting a just war, it is clear that some of the means they employed may have been unjust (for example, strategic bombing of cities and the two atomic bomb attacks). It is not difficult to assimilate these controversial means into the total Allied war effort and pronounce that total effort proportionate to the just cause of the war. It is much more difficult and quite a different calculation to justify these means as proportionate to discrete military ends. Even in the absence of war-crimes proceedings, a just belligerent ought to respect the *jus in bello* standards by meeting the requirement of proportionality of means to military ends.

It would appear that analyses of the proportionality of military means will have to take a twofold form. First, any military means must be proportionate to a discrete, legitimate military end. Second, military means proportionate to discrete, legitimate military ends must also be proportionate to the object of the war, the just cause. In judging the moral and legal responsibility of a military commander, emphasis should be placed on the proportionality of the means to a legitimate military end. In judging the ultimate normative permissibility, as well as the prudential advisability, of a means at the level of *raison d'état* the calculation should emphasize proportionality to the just cause.

The focus of normative analysis with respect to a means of war will depend on the place of the means in the total pattern of belligerent interaction. Means may be divided roughly according to the traditional distinction between tactical and strategic levels of war. Tactical means will normally be judged in terms of their proportionality to tactical military ends (for example, the tactics of attacking or defending a fortified population center will normally be judged in terms of their proportionality to the military end of taking or holding the center). Strategic means will normally be judged in terms of their proportionality to the political/military goals of the war.

It remains clear, however, that the two levels overlap. A number of tactical decisions regarding battles for population centers may produce an overall strategic pattern that ought to enter into the highest calculation of the proportionality of a just war. The strategic decisions, on the other hand, have necessary tactical implications (for example, strategic conventional and atomic bombing of Japan was an alternative to an amphibious invasion) the conduct of which is essentially a tactical matter. The potential costs of such a tactical invasion strongly influenced the strategic choice to seek Japan's defeat by strategic bombing rather than ground conquest.

Insofar as judgment of proportionality in terms of military ends is concerned, there is a central concept appearing in all normative analyses of human behavior—the norm of reasonableness. Reasonableness must always be defined in specific context. However, sometimes patterns of behavior recur so that there are typical situations for which common models of reasonable behavior may be prescribed. In domestic law this norm is concretized through the device of the hypothetically reasonable man whose conduct sets the standard to be emulated by law-abiding persons. The reasonable commander is the counterpart of the reasonable man in the law of war. The construct of the reasonable commander is based upon the experience of military men in dealing with basic military problems.

Formulation of this experience into the kinds of working guidelines that domestic law provides, notably in the field of torts, has not advanced very far. We do, however, have some instances in which this approach was followed. For example, the U.S. military tribunal in the *Hostage* case found that certain retaliatory means used by the German military in occupied Europe in World War II were reasonable in view of the threat to the belligerent occupant posed by guerrilla operations and their support by the civilian population. On the other hand, in the *Calley* case a court comprised of experienced combat officers found that Lieutenant Calley's response to the situation in My Lai was altogether unreasonable, below the standard of reasonableness expected in combat in Vietnam.

The difficulty with establishing the standards of reasonableness lies in the absence of authoritative decisions that can be widely disseminated for mandatory emulation. In a domestic public order such as the United States, the legislature and the courts set standards for reasonable behavior. While the standards have supporting rationales, their greatest strength lies in the fact that they are laid down by authority and must be obeyed. With the very rare exception of some of the post–World War II war-crimes cases, authoritative standards for belligerent conduct are found primarily in general conventional and customary international-law prescriptions.

The Principle of Discrimination

The principle of discrimination prohibits direct intentional attacks on noncombatants and nonmilitary targets. It holds out the potential for very great, specific limitations on the conduct of just war. Accordingly, debates over the meaning of the *principle of discrimination* have become increasingly complex and important as the character of war has become more total. It is in the nature of the principle of proportion to be elastic and to offer possibilities for justifications of means that are truly necessary for efficacious military action. However, it is in the nature of the principle of discrimination to remain rigidly opposed to various categories of means irrespective of their necessity to success in war. It is not surprising, then, that most debates about the morality of modern war have focused on the principle of discrimination.

Such debates are vastly complicated by the opportunities afforded in the definition of the principle of discrimination to expand or contract it by interpretations of its component elements. There are debates over the meaning of *direct intentional attack*, *noncombatants*, and *nonmilitary targets*.

In order to discuss the problem of interpreting the principle of discrimination, it is necessary to understand the origins of the principle. The most fundamental aspect of the principle of discrimination lies in its direct relation to the justification for killing in war. If the presumption against killing generally and war in particular is overcome (in the case of war by meeting the just-war conditions), the killing then permitted is limited to the enemy combatants, the aggressors. The exceptional right to take life in individual self-defense and in war is limited to the attacker in the individual case and the enemy's soldiers in the case of war. One may not attack innocent third parties as part of individual self-defense. In war the only permissible objects of direct attack are the enemy's soldiers. In both cases, the overriding moral prescription is that evil must not be done to obtain a good object. As will be seen, however, the literal application of the principle of discrimination tends to conflict with the characteristics of efficacious military action necessary to make the right of just war effective and meaningful.

However, it is important to recognize that the principle of discrimination did not find its historical origins solely or even primarily in the fundamental argument summarized above. As a matter of fact, the principle seems to have owed at least as much to codes of chivalry and to the subsequent development of positive customary laws of war. These chivalric codes and customary practices were grounded in the material characteristics of warfare during the medieval and Renaissance periods. During much of that time, the key to the conduct of war was combat between mounted knights and supporting infantry. Generally speaking, there was no military utility in attacking anyone other than the enemy knights and their armed retainers. Attacks on unarmed civilians, particularly women and children, would have been considered unchivalric, contrary to the customary law of war, and militarily gratuitous.

These multiple bases for noncombatant immunity were fortified by the growth of positive international law after the seventeenth century. In what came to be known as the Rousseau-Portalis Doctrine, war was conceived as being limited to what we could call today "counterforce warfare." Armies fought each other like athletic teams designated to represent national banners. The noncombatants were spectators to these struggles and, unless they had the bad fortune to find themselves directly on the battlefield, immune in principle from military attack. Attacks on noncombatants and nonmilitary targets were now prohibited by a rule of positive international law. Here again, the principle of discrimination was grounded in material facts, the state of the art of war and the limited nature of the conflicts, that continued to make possible its application. Moreover, the political philosophy of the time encouraged a separation of public armed forces and the populations they represented. All of these military and political supports for discrimination were to change with the advent of modern total war.

It is often contended that there is an absolute principle of discrimination prohibiting any use of means that kill noncombatants. It is further contended that this absolute principle constitutes the central limitation of just war and that it is based on an immutable moral imperative that may never be broken no matter how just the cause. This is the moral axiom mentioned above, that evil may never be done in order to produce a good result. In this formulation, killing noncombatants intentionally is always an inadmissible evil.

These contentions have produced two principal reactions. The first is pacifism. Pacifists rightly argue that war inevitably involves violation of the absolute principle of discrimination. If that principle is unconditionally binding, a just war is difficult if not impossible to envisage.[4] The second reaction to the claims of an absolute principle of discrimination is to modify the principle by some form of the principle of double effect whereby the counterforce component of a military means is held to represent the intent of the belligerent, whereas the countervalue, indiscriminate component of that means is explained as a tolerable, concomitant, unintended effect—collateral damage in contemporary strategic terms.

Paul Ramsey is unquestionably the most authoritative proponent of an absolute principle of discrimination as the cornerstone of just-war *jus in bello*. No one has tried more courageously to reconcile this absolute principle with the exigencies of modern war and deterrence. [But] neither Ramsey nor anyone else can reconcile the principle of discrimination in an absolute sense with the strategic countervalue nuclear warfare that is threatened in contemporary deterrence. It is possible that Ramsey's version of discrimination could survive the pressures of military necessity at levels below that of strategic nuclear deterrence and war. But the fate of Ramsey's effort to reconcile an absolute moral principle of discrimination with the characteristics of modern war should indicate the grave difficulties inherent in this effort.

It is my contention that the moral, just-war principle of discrimination is not an absolute limitation on belligerent conduct. Accordingly, I do not distinguish an absolute, moral, just-war principle of discrimination from a more flexible and variable international-law principle of discrimination. To be sure, the moral, just-war understanding of discrimination must remain independent of that of international law at any given time. But discrimination is best understood and most effectively applied in light of the interpretations of the principle in the practice of belligerents. This, after all, was the principal origin of this part of the *jus in bello*, and the need to check moral just-war formulations against contemporary international-law versions is perennial.

Such a position is in no sense a retreat from a position of maximizing normative limitations on the conduct of war. In the first place, as Ramsey's brave but ultimately unsuccessful efforts have demonstrated, attachment to an absolute principle of discrimination leads either to a finding that all war is immoral and the demise of the just-war doctrine or to tortured efforts to reconcile the irreconcilable. Neither serves the purposes of the *jus in bello*. Second, the rejection of an absolute principle of discrimination does not mean an abandonment of efforts to limit war on moral grounds. The principle of discrimination remains a critical source of both moral and legal limitations of belligerent behavior. As Tucker has observed, there are significant points of limitation between the position that no injury must ever be done to noncombatants and the position that there are no restraints on countervalue warfare. The interpretations that follow here will try to balance the need to protect noncombatants with the need to recognize the legitimate military necessities of modern forms of warfare. In this process one may err one way or the other, but at least some relevant, practical guidance may be offered belligerents. Adherence to an absolute principle of discrimination usually means irrelevance to the question of limiting the means of war or unconvincing casuistry.

In search of such practical guidance one may resume the examination of the principle of discrimination as interpreted both by moralists and international lawyers. Even before the principle of discrimination was challenged by the changing realities of total war, there were practical difficulties with the definition of *direct intentional attack, noncombatants,* and *nonmilitary targets*. It is useful, as a starting point for analysis, to recall a standard and authoritative exposition of the principle of discrimination by Fr. Richard McCormick.

> It is a fundamental moral principle [unanimously accepted by Catholic moralists] that it is immoral directly to take innocent human life except with divine authorization. "Direct" taking of human life implies that one performs a lethal action with the intention that death should result for himself or another. Death therefore is deliberately willed as the effect of one's action. "Indirect" killing refers to an action or omission that is designed and intended solely to achieve some other purpose(s) even though death is foreseen as a concomitant effect. Death therefore is not positively willed, but is reluctantly permitted as an unavoidable by-product.[5]

An example that is frequently used in connection with this question is the use of catapults in medieval sieges of castles. The intention—indeed, the purpose—of catapulting projectiles over the castle wall was to kill enemy defenders and perhaps to break down the defenses. If noncombatants—innocents as they were called then—were killed or injured, this constituted a "concomitant effect," an "undesired by-product."

The issues of intention, act, and multiple effects are often analyzed in terms of the principle of double effect, which Father McCormick's exposition employs without invoking the concept explicitly. After centuries of inconclusive efforts to apply the principle of double effect to the *jus in bello,* Michael Walzer has proposed his own version, which merits reflection and experimental application.

> The intention of the actor is good, that is, he aims narrowly at the acceptable effect; the evil effect is not one of his ends, nor is it a means to his ends, and, aware of the evil involved, he seeks to minimize it, accepting costs to himself.[6]

It is probably not possible to reconcile observance of the principle of discrimination with the exigencies of genuine military necessity without employing the principle of double effect in one form or another. However, this distinction between primary, desired effect and secondary, concomitant, undesired by-product is often difficult to accept.

It is not so hard to accept the distinction in a case where the concomitant undesired effect was accidental (for example, a case where the attacker did not know that noncombatants were present in the target area). There would still remain, in such a case, a question as to whether the attacker ought to have known that noncombatants might be present. Nor is it so hard to accept a double-effect justification in a situation where the attacker had reason to believe that there might be noncombatants present but that this was a remote possibility. If, however, the attacker knows that there are noncombatants intermingled with combatants to the point that any attack on the military target is highly likely to kill or injure noncombatants, then the death or injury to those noncombatants is certainly "intended" or "deliberately willed," in the common usage of those words.

Turning to the object of the protection of the principle of discrimination—the innocents or noncombatants—another critical question of interpretation arises. How does one define noncombatants? How does one define nonmilitary targets? The assumption of separability of military forces and the populations they represented, found in medieval theory and continued by the Rousseau-Portalis Doctrine, became increasingly less valid after the wars of the French Revolution.

As nations engaged in total mobilization, one society or system against another, it was no longer possible to distinguish sharply between the military forces and the home fronts that rightly held themselves out as critical to the war effort. By the American Civil War this modern phenomenon had assumed critical importance. The material means of supporting the Confederate war effort were attacked directly and intentionally by Union forces. War in the age of the Industrial Revolution was waged against the sources of war production. Moreover, the nature of the attacks on noncombatants was psychological as well as material. Military forces have always attempted to break the will of the opposing forces as well as to destroy or scatter them. It now became the avowed purpose of military forces to break the will of the home front as well as to destroy its resources for supporting the war. This, of course, was to become a major purpose of modern strategic aerial bombardment.

To be sure, attacks on the bases of military forces have historically often been an effective strategy. But in the simpler world before the Industrial Revolution, this was not such a prominent option. When the huge conscript armies began to fight for profound ideological causes with the means provided by modern industrial mobilization and technology, the home front and consequently the noncombatants became a critical target for direct intentional attack.

The question then arose whether a civilian could be a participant in the overall war effort to such a degree as to lose his previous noncombatant immunity. Likewise, it became harder to distinguish targets that were clearly military from targets, such as factories or railroad facilities, that were of sufficient military importance to justify their direct intentional attack. It is important to note that this issue arose before the great increase in the range, areas of impact, and destructive effects of modern weaponry, conventional and nuclear. What we may term *countervalue warfare* was carried out in the American Civil War not because it was dictated by the weapons systems but because the civilian population and war-related industries and activities were considered to be critical and legitimate targets to be attacked.

In World War I this kind of attack was carried out primarily by the belligerents with their maritime blockades. Above all, these blockades caused the apparent demise of the principle of noncombatant immunity in the positive international law of war. Other factors in this demise were developments that revealed potentials not fully realized until World War II (for example, aerial bombardment of population centers and unrestricted submarine warfare). In World War II aerial bombardment of population centers was preeminent as a source of attacks on traditional noncombatants and nonmilitary targets. By this time the concept of total mobilization had advanced so far that a plausible argument could be made that vast segments of belligerent populations and complexes of industry and housing had become so integral to the war effort as to lose their noncombatant immunity.

In summary, well before the advent of weapons systems that are usually employed in ways that do not discriminate between traditional combatants and noncombatants, military and nonmilitary targets, the distinction had eroded. The wall of separation between combatants and noncombatants had been broken down by the practice of total societal mobilization in modern total war and the resulting practice of attacking directly and intentionally that mobilization base. Given these developments, it was difficult to maintain that the principle of discrimination was still a meaningful limit on war. Those who clung to the principle tended to reject modern war altogether as inherently immoral because it inherently violates the principle. In the international law of war, distinguished publicists were reduced to stating that terror bombing of noncombatants with no conceivable proximate military utility was prohibited, but that the rights of noncombatants to protection otherwise were unclear.

NOTES

1. James F. Childress, "Just War Theories," *Theological Studies* Vol. 39 (1978), pp. 428–435.
2. A rare exception to the general tendency to avoid the "Red-or-dead" issue in evaluating just cause is provided in the work of Father Murray, whose writing on modern defense is based on his estimate of the nature of the communist threat to peace and justice. See, for example, Chapter 10, "Doctrine and Policy in Communist Imperialism," in John Courtney Murray, *We Hold These Truths* (New York: Sheed and Ward, 1960), pp. 221–247.
3. The position that all German belligerent acts were crimes per se because they served the illegal ends of aggression was advanced by one of the French prosecutors at Nuremberg, M. de Menthon. See Nuremberg International Military Tribunal, *Trial of the Major War Criminals before the International Military Tribunal, Nuremberg, 14 November 1945–1 October 1946* (Nuremberg: 1947–49), 5: 387–388. This argument was implicitly rejected by the Judgment of the Tribunal, which does not mention it.
4. See, for example, the pacifist views in Walter Stein, ed., *Nuclear Weapons and Christian Conscience* (London: Merlin, 1961); and Thomas Shannon, *War or Peace?* (Maryknoll, N.Y.: Orbis, 1980).
5. Richard McCormick, "Morality of War," *New Catholic Encyclopedia* 14 (1967), p. 805.
6. Michael Walzer, *Just and Unjust Wars* (New York: Basic Books, 1977), p. 155. Walzer's principal discussion of double effect is on pp. 151–159.

STUDY QUESTIONS

1. What difficulties does one face in applying just-war criteria to revolutionary activities?
2. Explain "proportionality," which O'Brien identifies as the heart of just cause.
3. How does the existence of the United Nations affect the "last resort" criteria? Was this criterion satisfied in the Persian Gulf War, in your estimation?
4. Explain the principle of discrimination.
5. What problems do adherents of an "absolute principle of discrimination" face (that is, those claiming that noncombatants must never be killed, under any circumstances)?

24

Self-Defense and Pacifism

Cheyney C. Ryan

Cheyney C. Ryan is a philosopher who has written on the ethics of war and social justice.

Pacifism has been construed by some as the view that all violence or coercion is wrong. This seems to be too broad, though undoubtedly some pacifists have held to this position. I shall focus here on the pacifist's opposition to killing, which stands at the heart of his opposition to war in any form.

In recent years, prompted largely by an article of Jan Narveson's, there has been a good deal of clucking about the "inconsistency" and "incoherence" of the pacifist position.[1] Narveson's argument, in a nutshell, is that, if the pacifist grants people the right not to be subjected to violence, or the right not to be killed in my reading, then by *logic* he must accord them the right to engage in any actions (hence, those involving killing) to protect that right. This argument fails for a number of reasons,[2] but the most interesting one involves the protective status of rights. Possession of a right generally entitles one to take some actions in defense of that right, but clearly there are limits to the actions one may take. To get back the washcloth which you have stolen from me, I cannot bludgeon you to death; even if this were the *only* way I had of securing my right to the washcloth, I could not do it. What the pacifist and the nonpacifist disagree about, then, are the limits to which one may go in defending one's right to life, or any other right. The "logic of rights" alone will not settle this disagreement, and such logic certainly does not render the pacifist's restrictions incoherent. That position might be incoherent, in Narveson's sense, if the pacifist allowed *no* actions in defense of the right to life, but this is not his position. The pacifist's position does seem to violate a fairly intuitive principle of proportionality, that in defense of one's rights one may take actions whose severity is equal to, though not greater than, the threat against one. This rules out the bludgeoning case but allows killing so as not to be killed. The pacifist can respond, though, that this principle becomes rather suspect as we move to more extreme actions. It is not *obviously* permissible to torture another so as not to be tortured or to rain nuclear holocaust on another country to prevent such a fate for oneself. Thus when the pacifist rejects the proportionality principle in cases of killing, insisting that such cases are themselves most extreme, the principle he thereby rejects hardly has the status of a self-evident truth.

I have touched on this issue not merely to point out the shallowness of some recent arguments against pacifism but because I believe that any argument pro or con which hinges on the issue of rights is likely to get us nowhere. . . .

George Orwell tells how early one morning [during the Spanish Civil War] he ventured out with another man to snipe at the fascists from the trenches outside their encampment. After having little success for several hours, they were suddenly alerted to the sound of Republican airplanes overhead. Orwell writes,

> At this moment a man, presumably carrying a message to an officer, jumped out of the trench

> and ran along the top of the parapet in full view. He was half-dressed and holding up his trousers with both hands as he ran. I refrained from shooting at him. It is true that I am a poor shot and unlikely to hit a running man at a hundred yards. Still, I did not shoot partly because of that detail about the trousers. I had come here to shoot "Fascists"; but a man who is holding up his trousers isn't a "Fascist," he is visibly a fellow creature, similar to yourself, and you don't feel like shooting him.[3]

Orwell was not a pacifist, but the problem he finds in this particular act of killing is akin to the problem which the pacifist finds in *all* acts of killing. That problem, the example suggests, takes the following form.

The problem with shooting the half-clothed man does not arise from the rights involved, nor is it dispensed with by showing that, yes indeed, you are justified (by your rights) in killing him. But this does not mean, as some have suggested to me, that the problem is therefore not a *moral* problem at all ("sheer sentimentality" was an objection raised by one philosopher ex-marine). Surely if Orwell had gleefully blasted away here, if he had not at least felt the tug of the other's "fellow-creaturehood," then this would have reflected badly, if not on his action, then on *him,* as a human being. The problem, in the Orwell case, is that the man's dishabille made inescapable the fact that he was a "fellow creature," and in so doing it stripped away the labels and denied the distance so necessary to murderous actions (it is not for nothing that armies give us stereotypes in thinking about the enemy). The problem, I am tempted to say, involves not so much the justification as the *possibility* of killing in such circumstances ("How could you *bring* yourself to do it?" is a natural response to one who felt no problem in such situations). And therein lies the clue to the pacifist impulse.

The pacifist's problem is that he cannot create, or does not wish to create, the necessary distance between himself and another to make the act of killing possible. Moreover, the fact that others obviously can create that distance is taken by the pacifist to reflect badly on them; they move about in the world insensitive to the half-clothed status which all humans, qua fellow creatures, share. This latter point is important to showing that the pacifist's position is indeed a moral position, and not just a personal idiosyncrasy. What should now be evident is the sense in which that moral position is motivated by a picture of the personal relationship and outlook one should maintain toward others, regardless of the actions they might take toward you. It is fitting in this regard that the debate over self-defense should come down to the personal relationship, the "negative bond" between Aggressor and Defender. For even if this negative bond renders killing in self-defense permissible, the pacifist will insist that the deeper bonds of fellow creaturehood should render it impossible.[4] That such an outlook will be branded by others as sheer sentimentality comes to the pacifist as no surprise.

I am aware that this characterization of the pacifist's outlook may strike many as obscure, but the difficulties in characterizing that outlook themselves reflect, I think, how truly fundamental the disagreement between the pacifist and the nonpacifist really is. That disagreement far transcends the familiar problems of justice and equity; it is no surprise that the familiar terms should fail us. As to the accuracy of this characterization, I would offer as indirect support the following example of the aesthetic of fascism, which I take to be at polar ends from that of pacifism, and so illustrative in contrast of the pacifist outlook: "War is beautiful because it establishes man's dominion over the subjugated machinery by means of gas masks, terrifying megaphones, flame throwers, and small tanks. War is beautiful because it initiates the dreamt-of metalization of the human body. War is beautiful because it enriches the flowering meadow with the fiery orchids of machine guns."[5] What the fascist rejoices in the pacifist rejects, in toto—the "metalization of the human body," the insensitivity to fellow creaturehood which the pacifist sees as the presupposition of killing.[6]

This account of the pacifist's position suggests some obvious avenues of criticism of the more traditional sort. One could naturally ask whether killing necessarily presupposes objectification and distance, as the pacifist feels it does. It seems to me though that the differences between the pacifist and the nonpacifist are substantial enough that neither side is likely to produce a simple "refutation" along such lines which the other conceivably could, or logically need, accept. If any criticism of pacifism is to be forthcoming which can make any real claim to the pacifist's attention, it will be one which questions the consistency of his conclusions with what I have described as his motivating impulse. Let me suggest how such a criticism might go.

If the pacifist's intent is to acknowledge through his attitudes and actions the other person's status as a fellow creature, the problem is that violence, and even killing, are at times a means of acknowledging this as well, a way of bridging the distance between oneself and another person, a way of acknowledging one's *own* status as a person. This is one of the underlying themes of Hegel's account of conflict in the master–slave dialectic, and the important truth it contains should not be lost in its seeming glorification of conflict. That the refusal to allow others to treat one as an object is an important step to defining one's own integrity is a point well understood by revolutionary theorists such as Fanon. It is a point apparently lost to pacifists like Gandhi, who suggested that the Jews in the Warsaw Ghetto would have made the superior moral statement by committing collective suicide, since their resistance proved futile anyway. What strikes us as positively bizarre in the pacifist's suggestion, for example, that we *not* defend our loved ones when attacked is not the fact that someone's rights might be abused by our refusal to so act. Our real concern is what the refusal to intervene would express about our relationships and ourselves, for one of the ways we acknowledge the importance of a relationship is through our willingness to take such actions, and that is why the problem in such cases is how we can bring ourselves *not* to intervene (how is passivity possible).

The willingness to commit violence is linked to our love and estimation for others, just as the capacity for jealousy is an integral part of affection. The pacifist may respond that this is just a sociological or psychological fact about how our community links violence and care, a questionable connection that expresses thousands of years of macho culture. But this connection is no *more* questionable than that which views acts of violence against an aggressor as expressing hatred, or indifference, or objectification. If the pacifist's problem is that he cannot consistently live out his initial impulse—the posture he wishes to assume toward others requires that he commit violence and that he not commit violence—does this reflect badly on his position? Well, if you find his goals attractive it may well reflect badly on the position—or *fix*—we are all in. Unraveling the pacifist's logic may lead us to see that our world of violence and killing is one in which regarding some as people requires we regard others as things and that this is not a fact that can be excused or absolved through the techniques of moral philosophy. If the pacifist's error arises from the desire to smooth this all over by hewing to one side of the dilemma, he is no worse than his opponent, whose "refutation" of pacifism serves to dismiss those very intractable problems of violence of which pacifism is the anxious expression. As long as this tragic element in violence persists, pacifism will remain with us as a response; we should not applaud its demise, for it may well mark that the dilemmas of violence have simply been forgotten.

Impatience will now ask: so do we kill or don't we? It should be clear that I do not have the sort of answer to this question that a philosopher, at least, might expect. One can attend to the problems involved in either choice, but the greatest problem is that the choice does not flow naturally from a desire to acknowledge in others and in ourselves their importance and weaknesses and worth.

NOTES

1. See Jan Narveson, "Pacifism: A Philosophical Analysis," in *Today's Moral Problems,* ed. Richard Wasserstrom (New York: Macmillan, 1976), pp. 450–463.
2. Narveson claims that the right to X entitles you to whatever is necessary to protect that right. It would follow that there can be no real problem about civil disobedience, since logic alone tells us that if the state infringes on our rights we can take whatever measures are required to protect them, including defying the state. But surely the problem is more complicated than this. Hence it is reasonable to reject the claim about the "logic" of rights which leads to such a facile conclusion.
3. George Orwell, "Looking Back on the Spanish Civil War," in *A Collection of Essays by George Orwell* (New York: Doubleday & Co., 1954), p. 199.
4. Stuart Hampshire discusses the notion of "moral impossibility" most perceptively in his essay "Morality and Pessimism," in *Public and Private Morality,* ed. Stuart Hampshire (Cambridge: Cambridge University Press, 1978), pp. 1–23. He employs the notion, which differs in his hands somewhat from mine, to point out inadequacies in the utilitarian approach to rights. I would employ it to criticize the language of rights as well, as inadequate for capturing certain features of our moral experience.
5. The quote is from Marinetti, a founder of Futurism, cited in Walter Benjamin's essay "The Work of Art in the Age of Mechanical Reproduction," *Illuminations* (New York: Schocken Books, 1969), p. 241.
6. This "insensitivity to fellow creaturehood" need not be a presupposition of mercy killing. Consider, e.g., the killing of the character played by Jane Fonda at the end of "They Shoot Horses, Don't They?" But the pacifist can grant this without rendering his position any less controversial.

STUDY QUESTIONS

1. Why does the propagation of a stereotype make it easier to do violence to or kill another?
2. How might Orwell's story of the half-clothed man parallel the story of Lady Macbeth's inability to kill Duncan as he slept? What does Ryan seem to think of this?
3. How might it be possible to acknowledge an individual's "fellow creaturehood" in acts of violence as well as in acts of nonviolence? What difficulties does this raise for the pacifist?
4. How might a person's relationship to another be mirrored in his or her willingness to defend that person? What problems does this pose for the pacifist who loves her husband, sister, father, or neighbor?

25

Violence, Power, and Bureaucracy

Hannah Arendt

Hannah Arendt (1906–1975) was born and educated in Germany. She fled the Nazis in 1933 and became a U.S. citizen in 1951. She wrote many books on social and political theory, including *The Origins of Totalitarianism* and *On Revolution*.

Power is indeed of the essence of all government, but violence is not. Violence is by nature instrumental; like all means, it always stands in need of guidance and justification through the end it pursues. And what needs justification by something else cannot be the essence of anything. The end of war—end taken in its twofold meaning—is peace or victory; but to the question And what is the end of peace? there is no answer. Peace is an absolute, even though in recorded history periods of warfare have nearly always outlasted periods of peace. Power is in the same category; it is, as they say, "an end in itself." (This, of course, is not to deny that governments pursue policies and employ their power to achieve prescribed goals. But the power structure itself precedes and outlasts all aims, so that power, far from being the means to an end, is actually the very condition enabling a group of people to think and act in terms of the means–end category.) And since government is essentially organized and institutionalized power, the current question What is the end of government? does not make much sense either. The answer will be either question-begging—to enable men to live together—or dangerously utopian—to promote happiness or to realize a classless society or some other nonpolitical ideal, which if tried out in earnest cannot but end in some kind of tyranny.

Power needs no justification, being inherent in the very existence of political communities; what it does need is legitimacy. The common treatment of these two words as synonyms is no less misleading and confusing than the current equation of obedience and support. Power springs up whenever people get together and act in concert, but it derives its legitimacy from the initial getting together rather than from any action that then may follow. Legitimacy, when challenged, bases itself on an appeal to the past, while justification relates to an end that lies in the future. Violence can be justifiable, but it never will be legitimate. Its justification loses in plausibility the farther its intended end recedes into the future. No one questions the use of violence in self-defense, because the danger is not only clear but also present, and the end justifying the means is immediate. . . .

In a head-on clash between violence and power, the outcome is hardly in doubt. If Gandhi's enormously powerful and successful strategy of nonviolent resistance had met with a different enemy—Stalin's Russia, Hitler's Germany, even prewar Japan, instead of England—the outcome would not have been decolonization, but massacre and submission. However, England in India and France in Algeria had good reasons for their restraint. Rule by sheer violence comes into play where power is being lost; it is precisely the shrinking power of the Russian government, internally and externally, that became manifest in its "solution" of the Czechoslovak problem—just as it was the shrinking power of European imperialism that became manifest in the alternative between decolonization and massacre. To substitute violence for power can bring victory, but the price is very high; for it is not only paid by the vanquished, it is also paid by the victor in terms of his own power. This is especially true when the victor happens to enjoy domestically the blessings of constitutional government. Henry Steele Commager is entirely right: "If we subvert world order and destroy world peace we must inevitably subvert and destroy our own political institutions first. . . ."

Politically speaking, the point is that loss of power becomes a temptation to substitute violence for power—in 1968 during the Democratic convention in Chicago we could watch this process on television—and that violence itself results in impotence. Where violence is no longer backed and restrained by power, the well-known reversal in reckoning with means and ends has taken place. The means, the means of destruction, now determine the end—with the consequence that the end will be the destruction of all power.

Nowhere is the self-defeating factor in the victory of violence over power more evident than in the use of terror to maintain domination, about whose weird successes and eventual failures we know perhaps more than any generation before us. Terror is not the same as violence; it is, rather, the form of government that comes into being when violence, having destroyed all power, does not abdicate but, on the contrary, remains in full control. It has often been noticed that the effectiveness of terror depends almost entirely on the degree of social atomization. Every kind of organized opposition must disappear before the full force of terror can be let loose. This atomization—an outrageously pale, academic word for the horror it implies—is maintained and intensified through the ubiquity of the informer, who can be literally omnipresent because he no longer is merely a professional agent in the pay of the police but potentially every person one comes into contact with. How such a fully developed police state is established and how it works—or rather, how nothing works where it holds sway—can now be learned in Aleksandr I. Solzhenitsyn's *The First Circle,* which will probably remain one of the masterpieces of twentieth-century literature and certainly contains the best documentation on Stalin's regime in existence. The decisive difference between totalitarian domination, based on terror, and tyrannies and dictatorships, established by violence, is that the former turns not only against its enemies but against its friends and supporters as well, being afraid of all power, even the power of its friends. The climax of terror is reached when the police state begins to devour its own children, when yesterday's executioner becomes today's victim. And this is also the moment when power disappears entirely. There exist now a great many plausible explanations for the de-Stalinization of Russia—none, I believe, so compelling as the realization by the Stalinist functionaries themselves that a continuation of the regime would lead, not to an insurrection, against which terror is indeed the best safeguard, but to paralysis of the whole country.

To sum up: politically speaking, it is insufficient to say that power and violence are not the same. Power and violence are opposites; where the one rules absolutely, the other is absent. Violence appears where power is in jeopardy, but left to its own course it ends in power's disappearance. This implies that it is not correct to think of the opposite of violence as nonviolence; to speak of nonviolent power is actually redundant. Violence can destroy power; it is utterly incapable of creating it. Hegel's and Marx's great trust in the dialectical "power of negation," by virtue of which opposites do not destroy but smoothly develop into each other because contradictions promote and do not paralyze development, rests on a much older philosophical prejudice: that evil is no more than a private *modus* of the good, that good can come out of evil; that, in short, evil is but a temporary manifestation of a still-hidden good. Such time-honored opinions have become dangerous. They are shared by many who have never heard of Hegel or Marx, for the simple reason that they inspire hope and dispel fear—a treacherous hope used to dispel legitimate fear. By this, I do not mean to equate violence with evil; I only want to stress that violence cannot be derived from its opposite, which is power, and that in order to understand it for what it is, we shall have to examine its roots and nature. . . .

Nothing, in my opinion, could be theoretically more dangerous than the tradition of organic thought in political matters by which power and violence are interpreted in biological terms. As these terms are understood today, life and life's alleged creativity are their common denominator, so that violence is justified on the ground of creativity. The organic metaphors with which our entire present discussion of these matters, especially of the riots, is permeated—the notion of a "sick society," of which riots are symptoms, as fever is a symptom of disease—can only promote violence in the end. Thus the debate between those who propose violent means to restore "law and order" and those who propose nonviolent reforms begins to sound ominously like a discussion between two physicians who debate the relative advantages of surgical as opposed to medical treatment of their patient. The sicker the patient is supposed to be, the more likely that the surgeon will have the last word. Moreover, so long as we talk in nonpolitical, biological terms, the glorifiers of violence can appeal to the undeniable fact that in the household of nature destruction and creation are but two sides of the natural process, so that collective violent action, quite apart from its inherent attraction, may appear as natural a prerequisite for the collective life of mankind as the struggle for survival and violent death for continuing life in the animal kingdom. . . .

Violence, being instrumental by nature, is rational to the extent that it is effective in reaching the end that must justify it. And since when we act we never know with any certainty the eventual consequences of what we are doing, violence can remain rational only if it pursues short-term goals. Violence does not promote causes, neither history nor revolution, neither progress nor reaction; but it can serve to dramatize grievances and bring them to public attention. As Conor Cruise O'Brien (in a debate on the legitimacy of violence in the Theatre of Ideas) once remarked, quoting William O'Brien, the nineteenth-century Irish agrarian and nationalist agitator: Sometimes "violence is the only way of ensuring a hearing for moderation." To ask the impossible in order to obtain the possible is not always counterproductive. And indeed, violence, contrary to what its prophets try to tell us, is more the weapon of reform than of revolution. France would not have received the most radical bill since Napoleon to change its antiquated education system if the French students had not rioted; if it had not been for the riots of the spring term, no one at Columbia University would have dreamed of accepting reforms; and it is probably quite true that in West Germany the existence of "dissenting minorities is not even noticed unless they engage in provocation." No doubt, "violence pays," but the trouble is that it pays indiscriminately, for "soul courses" and instruction in Swahili as well as for real reforms. And since the tactics of violence and disruption make sense only for short-term goals, it is even more likely, as was recently the case in the United States, that the established power will yield to nonsensical and obviously damaging demands—such as admitting students without the necessary qualifications and instructing them in nonexistent subjects—if only such "reforms" can be made with comparative ease, than that violence will be effective with respect to the relatively long-term objective of structural change. Moreover, the danger of violence, even if it moves consciously within a nonextremist framework of short-term goals, will always be that the means overwhelm to the end. If goals are not achieved rapidly, the result will be not merely defeat but the introduction of the practice of violence into the whole body politic. Action is irreversible, and a return to the *status quo* in case of defeat is always unlikely. The practice of violence, like all action, changes the world, but the most probable change is to a more violent world.

Finally . . . the greater the bureaucratization of public life, the greater will be the attraction of violence. In a fully developed bureaucracy there is nobody left with whom one can argue, to whom one can present grievances, on whom the pressures of power can be exerted. Bureaucracy is the form of government in which everybody is deprived of political freedom, of the power to act; for the rule by Nobody is not no-rule, and where all are equally powerless we have a tyranny without a tyrant. The crucial feature in the student rebellions around the world is that they are directed everywhere against the ruling bureaucracy. . . .

What makes man a political being is his faculty of action; it enables him to get together with his peers, to act in concert, and to reach out for goals and enterprises that would never enter his mind, let alone the desires of his heart, had he not been given this gift—to embark on something new. Philosophically speaking, to act is the human answer to the condition of natality. Since we all come into the world by virtue of birth, as newcomers and beginnings, we are able to start something new; without the fact of birth we would not even know what novelty is, all "action" would be either mere behavior or preservation. No other faculty except language, neither reason nor consciousness, distinguishes us so radically from all animal species. To act and to begin are not the same, but they are closely interconnected. . . .

Whatever the administrative advantages and disadvantages of centralization may be, its political result is always the same: monopolization of power causes the drying up or oozing away of all authentic power sources in the country. In the United States, based on a great plurality of powers and their mutual checks and balances, we are confronted not merely with the disintegration of power structures, but with power, seemingly still intact and free to manifest itself, losing its grip and becoming ineffective. To speak of the impotence of power is no longer a witty paradox. . . .

Again, we do not know where these developments will lead us, but we know, or should know, that every decrease in power is an open invitation to violence—if only because those who hold power and feel it slipping from their hands, be they the government or be they the governed, have always found it difficult to resist the temptation to substitute violence for it.

STUDY QUESTIONS

1. Arendt asserts that violence increases as power decreases. Is this always true?
2. What are some of the dangers of using violence as a means to an end? Is such action ever justifiable?
3. Why do people so often confuse violence and power? Why is this a problem?
4. What difference is there between justification and legitimacy? Why is power inherently justified, yet in need of legitimation?
5. How does centralization in a government cause a breakdown in power?

26

Kant on Peace

Sissela Bok

Sissela Bok was born in Sweden and educated in Switzerland, France, and the United States. She has taught at Brandeis, Harvard Medical School, and the John F. Kennedy School of Government. She is the author of *A Strategy for Peace* and *Secrets: On the Ethics of Concealment and Revelation.*

A WARNING AND A PLAN FOR LASTING PEACE

Immanuel Kant knew partisanship and the violence of war at close hand. Most of his life had been spent in one of the most militaristic nations in history: Frederick the Great's Prussia. All around him, Kant had heard ceaseless extolling of military courage, seen the young indoctrinated to accept death in battle, and witnessed war after war—now against one state, now against another, according to the changing patterns of alliances. He was scathing in his denunciation of rulers for siphoning off all available funds to pay for war, and he portrayed states as lawless protagonists displaying in their relations with one another "the depravity of human nature . . . without disguise."

When, in 1795, Kant finally published "Perpetual Peace," his passionate plea for a change in international relations, he was over seventy years old. In this essay, Kant presented a stark choice for governments: they must either make collective efforts to ensure survival or face joint self-destruction. To be sure, he argued, war had long served the function of motivating peoples to innovate and to exert themselves in order to prevail against their enemies. But unless nations could now reverse course, he warned, wars would grow increasingly violent and periods of peace would become more burdened by rearmament and by hostile policies that would lead to further conflict, ending in a final war of extermination.

Such a war of extermination, he wrote, "in which both parties and justice itself might all be simultaneously annihilated, would allow perpetual peace only on the vast graveyard of the human race." To the story so relentlessly retold through the centuries, of societies caught in a spiral of mutual distrust and injury that inflames partisanship on all sides, Kant could hint at an ending so final as to preclude any further reenactment. His conjecture that warring nations and justice itself might perish together speaks to us today in a more direct way than he could have anticipated. His own conclusion was firm: "A war [of extermination] and the employment of all means which might bring it about must thus be absolutely prohibited."

Kant proposed a plan, in his essay, for the nations of the world to break free from the destructive patterns of conduct that make such a war possible, by deciding to cooperate in bringing about a lasting peace. The plan involved a change, over time, to representative government in as many states as possible; and it called for their joining together in a federation of free states to keep the peace. Freedom and equality, he suggested, would be indispensable for citizens of such states and would enable them to resist being drawn into the new wars upon which their rulers were otherwise all too likely to embark. Federation would be most likely to promote justice within and between states, while preserving their unique characteristics and freedom vis-à-vis each other.

For this purpose, he called for autonomous states to join in submitting voluntarily to laws they had themselves authored. In speaking of "autonomy," Kant used a concept that the Greeks had applied primarily to states living under self-imposed laws; but he brought this notion of a law freely enacted and imposed upon oneself to bear on three levels of human conduct: on the conduct of individuals, of communities or nations in their internal affairs, and of a future federation of states. This self-imposed moral law would enjoin people, singly or collectively, to "act only according to that maxim whereby you can at the same time will that it should become a universal law." And such maxims could only be those which called for respecting all human beings in their own right, rather than treating them merely as means to other ends.

Only through autonomy, thus interpreted and applied, could governments achieve universal rather than partisan respect for human rights. First to go, for any person or group taking autonomy seriously, would be those policies of violence, deceit, and open or secret treachery which violate these rights and do most to increase distrust, exacerbate conflict, and endanger world peace. Such policies cannot be coherently framed as universal laws. If individuals could reject such policies in their own lives, and urge states to do so as well and to join with other states in diminishing their use internationally, they could help counteract the most debilitating aspects of partisanship. It would then be possible for people to strive for justice without blinding themselves to the humanity of others, without losing the capacity to reason adequately about their own predicament, and without succumbing to the patterns of bitterness and revenge that stand in the way of more reasonable approaches to conflicts.

For Kant to stress the need for attention to morality in order to reduce the threat of war was hardly new. But it was unusual to do so both with respect to individual and to government conduct, domestically and internationally. Those who have written on how to achieve a permanent peace before and after Kant have tended to focus, rather, on one single level of conduct—personal, societal, or international. Some, like the early Christian pacifists or Erasmus and Tolstoy, have written as if what is primarily needed is some fundamental change in human nature and in the thinking and conduct of individuals. Others, Marx, Lenin, and Mao among them, have trusted that changes in social structure that they believed historically determined would do away with the need or desire to go to war; thus Mao claimed that humanity, once it had destroyed capitalism, would "attain the era of eternal peace." Still others have proposed a world government or international order strong enough to prevent nations from going to war.

Kant, on the other hand, called for coordinated efforts at change on all three levels. Only in such a mutually supportive manner would it be possible to achieve the minimal trust without which no lasting peace can be established. Admittedly, there would be special difficulties in applying workable constraints at the international level. Kant fully agreed with the English thinker Thomas Hobbes that nations coexist in a "state of nature" in which they can call on no superior authority to impose justice among them. But unlike Hobbes, he nevertheless claimed that it was possible for them to bring about a condition of lasting peace, by freely choosing moral and political constraints and then abiding by them.

Of course Kant knew that despotism at home and lawlessness and intense distrust among nations stood in the way of bringing about such fundamental changes right away. He therefore proposed certain "preliminary articles" to help prepare the atmosphere for the larger institutional reforms and for lasting peace.* These articles must be preliminary, he suggested, for two reasons. They cannot solve the problems of nations or of a community of nations by themselves. Yet if they are not taken into account, there can be no lasting solutions whatsoever.

Some of these preliminary articles call for immediate implementation; others provide goals for more gradual change. It is from the former that I draw the four constraints most needed to achieve the climate in which the threat of war can be reduced. Three of these constraints—on violence, deceit, and breaches of trust—are common even in primitive human groups long before one can talk about states, much less an international community. They predate all debate about more complex principles such as those of equality, liberty, or justice; all discussion of rights and duties; and all philosophical systems. Kant also stresses a fourth constraint—on state secrecy—as a way of guarding against breaches of the first three within and between governments.

Although Kant does not set forth the four constraints as prominently in "Perpetual Peace" as in other works, he is the first, as far as I know, to have emphasized all four in the context of war and peace. He saw them as fundamental, however often breached, to the conduct of individuals and societies, no matter how different their forms of government. If they could be taken more seriously, not only at the individual but at the national and international levels, they could help establish the right climate for achieving widespread collaboration toward greater justice and a lasting peace.

*After the preliminary articles, Kant states three "definitive articles" of a perpetual peace between nations. They stipulate that the civil constitution of every state shall be republican in the sense of guaranteeing freedom for all members of a society, a common legislation for all, and legal equality for all; that the right of nations shall be based on a federation of free states; and that hospitality shall be extended even to strangers in at least the limited sense of not oppressing them, conquering them, or otherwise treating them with hostility. Kant acknowledges that the definitive articles will be attained gradually, if at all, and only on the basis of the trust made possible by first adhering to the preliminary articles. Yet only the definitive ones provide the conditions for lasting trust and thus for a lasting peace. Many nations have come closer to living up to the first article than in Kant's day, and we have much more experience with, and debate about, international federations (such as the UN) and the rights of strangers. While complexities far beyond what Kant envisaged have become apparent about the details of the institutions needed for a lasting peace, his three definitive articles point in the right direction. In this book, I focus primarily on the prerequisites for moving in that direction in a mixed world in which nonrepublics (in Kant's sense) still have great power.

MORAL CONSTRAINTS FREELY CHOSEN

I have nothing new to teach the world. Truth and nonviolence are as old as the hills.

Mohandas Gandhi

Kant would have agreed with Gandhi. There is nothing new either in stressing truth and nonviolence or in the corresponding constraints on deceit and violence, for these, too, are as old as the hills. Every major religion, every moral tradition, every society has recognized the need for at least some constraints on deceit and violence, since they are the two ways by which human beings deliberately injure one another. From the Buddhist Five Precepts that delineate "right action" to the Bible's Ten Commandments, from the five Jaina Great Vows to the maxims of Confucius and his followers or the dictates of the Roman Stoics, false speech and resort to violence are consistently rejected. These traditions differ when it comes to questions of religious belief, sexual conduct, and asceticism; but they speak in unison in condemning violence and lies.

To be sure, the various traditions do not agree in every detail even on these two counts. Some texts speak of violence in general, others of killing, still others of murder. Some groups condemn violence against any living organism down to the smallest gnat, as do the Jains; others intend most living beings; still others prohibit it only against human beings in particular or certain categories of people. Likewise, with respect to falsehood, some rule out all false speech, others all lies or, as in the biblical Commandment, the bearing of false witness against one's neighbors. All have found it necessary to debate just how to define and delimit the forms of violence and deceit that they reject and to consider the questions of scope and perspective raised in Chapter I [of the original work]. But in spite of differences of interpretation, the universal insistence on firm constraints on violence and on deceit speaks to the need for any community to keep them within bounds in its internal governance.

Toward outsiders on the other hand, the standards have often been more relaxed. Indeed, while restraining deceit and violence within the community, most cultures have at the same time gloried in certain outlets for such conduct, often carried out by particular gods, heroes, and occupational groups. This has often been a way to channel dangerous practices and thus, again, to constrain them—keeping the violence visited upon enemies, for instance, from breaking out among fellow tribesmen.

Kant, like Gandhi, links both constraints; like Gandhi, too, he sees them as required between all individuals and all nations, not merely within a community. Force and fraud, violence and cunning—no lasting peace will be possible, he argues, so long as nations continue to rely on these means of aggression. He proposes a strong and immediate prohibition of violence among nations, first of all, to prevent peace from degenerating into war, or war into mutual extermination. This is not to say that he was opposed to all use of force by a state; he concedes that the recourse to force is legitimate in defensive wars as a last resort. But even then, it must be limited to combatants; and forms of violence such as poisoning and assassination should be ruled out no matter what the provocation. He rejects the use of force to interfere in the governance of other nations and to colonize new territories. Like Simone Weil, Kant saw the capacity for violence brought by wars as intoxicating, corrupting, and debilitating to judgment. To him, war was "the destroyer of everything good."

Kant often denounced deceit with special vehemence. Even in his earliest lectures on ethics, he had singled it out as especially corrupting and as undermining the precarious trust on which human society is based. Though violence clearly represents the greatest immediate threat, deceit can disguise planned violence along with every other harm until it is too late to take precautions. Lying, for Kant, repudiates one's own human dignity just as it undercuts the communication that is the foundation of social intercourse. He therefore sees it as more hateful even than violence: it attacks "the very roots of our thinking," he wrote in a letter, "by casting doubt and suspicion on everything." In his emphasis on the effects of deceit on trust, Kant was at one with John Stuart Mill, who argued that every deviation from truth helps weaken that trustworthiness of human assertion which is the "principal support of all present social well-being."

To keep such practices of violence and deceit under control and cut them back, however, more than principles or commandments are usually needed. People have to undertake to respect them. Promises, vows, or covenants play a central role in most societies, as does the related virtue of trustworthiness, of holding to one's word, of being a person of honor. As a result, a third constraint is stressed in just about all moral traditions: that on betrayal, on going back on one's word. *Whatever* principle one has promised to uphold, fidelity to one's promise then becomes essential, and breaching it constitutes betrayal. (Indeed, keeping one's word is rarely more sacred than in criminal and other clandestine organizations, where members engage in violence and deceit directed against outsiders but need to guard against such tactics among themselves.)

The conflict between fidelity and betrayal is therefore as common in all societies as that between violence and nonviolence, or between deceit and truthfulness. It is no accident that the three lowest circles in Dante's *Inferno* are those devoted, precisely, to the sins of violence, deceit, and treachery. Nor is it hard to understand why those who personify evil as Satan or some other figure so often depict the character as a master tormentor, the "Father of Lies," and a traitor to all loyalties.

In his essay, Kant likewise emphasizes fidelity to promises and contracts. Breaches of trust, he argues, destroy not only the bonds between persons but also the far more fragile ones between nations. To undermine promises, contracts, and treaties is to invite further violence, further deceit, further betrayal. Elsewhere, he links the betrayal of promises with deceit and with the secrecy that conceals deceit. In his eyes, the "fawning, clandestine, deceitful enemy" was "far baser than the open one, even though the latter be violent. He who openly declares himself an enemy can be relied upon; but the treachery of secret malice, if it became universal, would mean the end of all confidence."

Needless to say, Kant did not hold that *all* promises are valid—in particular, not promises to do something unlawful or to infringe on human rights, as in conspiracies to rob or kill. But lawful promises between individuals should be honored at all costs; so should commitments between citizens and governments, and treaties between nations. On this score, Kant was in full agreement with Hugo Grotius, the Dutch scholar and diplomat, who had written a century and a half before that good faith is "not only the principal hold by which governments are bound together but the keystone by which the larger society of nations is united."

Kant broke new ground in stressing a fourth constraint, on excessive government secrecy. The functioning of the representative form of government that he advocated (the only stable example at the time being that of the United States) depended crucially on citizens having access to accurate information on which to base their decisions. Both at the beginning and at the end of his essay, Kant insisted on the need to curtail official secrecy. When states sign a peace agreement, they should not make secret reservations enabling them to fight a future war. And between rulers and their subjects, matters of public concern should be openly debated. Secret police, star-chamber proceedings, and the rigid political and religious censorship that prevailed in so many nations offended justice and allowed corruption and abuses of every kind to flourish. It was the citizens' right, however rarely honored, to be openly consulted about whether or not their nation should go to war. This, too, would serve the cause of peace; since citizens had to bear the brunt of the suffering that wars bring, they would be much more cautious than kings and chancellors about agreeing to such ventures.

But the warning against state secrecy had to be carefully worded, since secrecy can also protect what is legitimately private. Secrecy differs from violence, deceit, and breaches of faith in that there can be no general presumption against it. While it is to be feared when it conceals wrongdoing, it can also protect individuals and groups from unjustified intrusions and all other harm. With respect to individuals, in particular, the presumption must be in favor of their retaining control over secrecy and openness regarding personal matters; the burden of proof is on those who would deny the individual citizen such control. But this burden shifts for governments. They must justify *all* recourse to secrecy, since their vast power to do harm and to disregard the rights of citizens is magnified to the extent that they can do so in a clandestine way.

The constraint on secrecy serves a double function in Kant's essay. In the first place, it is meant to limit the degree to which governments actually engage in secret policies that cannot stand the light of day. And second, the publicity that it calls for can serve as a test of wrongful policies. "All actions affecting the rights of others are wrong if their maxim is not compatible with their being made public." Secret government practices, unless they can be publicly and persuasively justified (as in the case of confidential employee records, ongoing diplomatic negotiations, and certain matters of military security), are dangerous in the extreme. The test of publicity can also be applied to forms of secrecy themselves. Citizens may well be able to accept secrecy with respect to employee records, for instance, if reasons thought to justify it are carefully explained; but they will judge very differently efforts to defend secrecy regarding the theft of public funds or other violations of the law.

Secretive regimes in Kant's time and our own demonstrate the mismanagement and oppression that accompany unrestrained state secrecy. But the Spycatcher scandal in Great Britain and the Iran-Contra schemes of the Reagan government offer a reminder, if any were needed, that democratic nations are anything but immune to the plague of excessive state secrecy. The events in both cases have shown once again how secret practices permit abuses to grow, with corrupting effects on those who are empowered to deceive and to manipulate others undetected. These practices of secrecy tend to spread precisely because they are so tempting and because of the power they confer; they add to the danger of acts of violence, deceit, and betrayal by concealing plans for such acts from normal legislative and judicial checks until it is too late.

Just as Kant saw all four constraints as necessary and as reinforcing one another, so he saw the breach of any one of them as facilitating breaches of the others. This was one of the reasons why he ruled out secret schemes of violence against enemies—of poisoning or assassination, for example—even in a war of self-defense. As for widespread deceit and betrayal through breaches of treaties or the secret instigation of treason within enemy ranks, such activities should also be ruled out, even in times of war. For a state to ask subjects to engage in any of them not only risks corrupting those who are thus made to go against their principles but also damages the integrity of the state in the eyes of outsiders. This undermines any chance of a lasting peace, for it "would make mutual confidence impossible during a future time of peace."

The more governments disregard these fundamental moral constraints in wartime by sponsoring such practices, the easier it will be to do so in peacetime as well, whether to forestall attacks or prepare for new wars. At that point, they will have forfeited their own integrity and the capacity to inspire even the minimal trust that genuine negotiations and lasting peace require.

For Kant, some degree of trust is therefore a starting point in the development of fully viable international coexistence. By this he does not mean the naive trust that would invite aggression but, rather, the minimum of mutual and verifiable trust blended with commonsense caution without which the end of a war would lead to what he called "a mere truce."* This would be just a suspension of hostilities rather than a true peace—a cold war. A truce between countries armed to the teeth and caught up in that atmosphere of mutual distrust which stems from long-standing policies of hostility, deceit, and treachery could hardly end in anything but another war.

ADDRESSING MACHIAVELLI

So far, no prince has contributed one iota to the betterment of mankind . . . ; all of them look ever and only to the prosperity of their own countries, making that their chief concern. A proper educa-

*Compare the function of trust among nations for Kant and in the lives of individuals for Erik Erikson. Both see it as a foundation. For Kant trust is indispensable if nations are to control violence enough to achieve a genuine peace; for Erikson it is necessary from early childhood on if individuals are to be able to live at peace with themselves and with others. Erikson speaks of trust as an individual's attitude toward the world as well as toward the self—one that involves perceiving others and oneself as worthy of trust. Kant similarly stresses the respect for others and for oneself that should preclude treating anyone unjustly. Neither writer claims that the requisite trust should go beyond prudence or call for some impossible moral perfection in others; rather, it operates together with the rational distrust discussed in Chapter I [of the original work], and relies on certain minimal mutual expectations. And both Erikson and Kant recognize that such attitudes of even minimal trust are more difficult for nations to achieve and to maintain than for children, who do not generally experience the iniquity, treachery, and constant risk of assault that states have to guard against as a matter of common precaution.

tion would teach them so to frame their minds as to promote conciliation.

Immanuel Kant, *Lectures on Ethics*

From Kant's earliest lectures and writings on political issues to his last, he addresses what he knows to be the most compelling challenge to views such as his: do they work in practice or are they suited only to saints ready to suffer martyrdom for the sake of their principles? In so doing, he aims his remarks, as in the above quotation, at Niccolò Machiavelli, the most forceful proponent of such a challenge. In *The Prince,* his influential book of advice to rulers, Machiavelli argues that while it is all very well and good to preach moral constraints, following them simply does not work. Leaders foolish enough to insist on honoring their promises and to recoil from killing the innocent will end up tricked and defeated by those who lack such scruples.

Writing from his vantage point in sixteenth-century Italy, with its feuding city-states the pawns in a power struggle between the papacy, Germany, France, and Spain, Machiavelli has little patience with those well-meaning leaders who jeopardize the security of their states through excessive concern for piety and morality. He urges a prince eager to stay in power and to secure his state against attacks to disregard at will all fundamental moral constraints that stand in his way. Force and fraud, in particular, are indispensable, Machiavelli argues: almost all who have achieved great riches or power have attained them by such means.

A prince, Machiavelli suggests, must therefore learn "not to be good." He must learn to make use of force and of fraud by imitating both the fox and the lion, "for the lion cannot protect himself from traps and the fox cannot defend himself from wolves." When acting as a lion the prince has recourse to violence; and in his capacity as a fox he breaks his word when it suits his interest, and lies if he needs false excuses. But because such actions are likely to be misunderstood, Machiavelli advises a prince to proceed with all necessary secrecy and to be "a great feigner and a dissembler," in order to get away with actions that would otherwise be held against him.

Machiavelli saw Cesare Borgia, with his ruthless recourse to force and fraud to consolidate his bloody reign, as a model for a prince striving to achieve greater power. "Cesare Borgia was considered cruel, but his cruelty had brought order to the Romagna, united it, and reduced it to peace and fealty," Machiavelli writes; whereas others allow bloodshed and rapine to arise from "excess of tenderness." The threat of force can often accomplish as much as actual violence; in relations with other states, fraud is less costly than force and therefore preferable as a means to achieving one's ends.

Kant knows that if he wants to be persuasive in addressing this challenge, he has to use not merely the language of morality but also that of strategy: he has to speak of what works to promote the interests of a leader or a state. Consequently, "Perpetual Peace" stresses the shortsightedness and naiveté of imagining that violations of fundamental moral standards have no deleterious effect on those leaders responsible for them or on their nations. He points to the corruption and the evils that attend such violations and to the inevitable distrust they arouse; and he warns that the cumulative effects of such actions will be to undermine the negotiated collaboration that alone can avert a final war of extermination. He shows how narrow self-interest on the part of leaders, given such practical realities, will achieve short-term gains, if at all, at the cost of far greater long-term damage even to their own states. And though Kant agrees with Machiavelli that it is essential that leaders receive training more in line with the realities of governing, he insists that these very realities call for greater attention to an extended and deepened perspective on human affairs and to the moral constraints without which they will go from bad to worse.

In the four centuries since Machiavelli advised the judicious recourse to force and fraud, betrayal and secrecy, these practices have found new expression. The technology that has permitted such extraordinary escalation in the violence at the disposal of rulers as well as insurgent groups, has also brought great sophistication to the techniques of deceit, cheating, and betrayal. Wars to end all wars have been followed by still more destructive ones; violent revolutions and coups have too often merely replaced one brutal regime with another.

. . . In our century, we have witnessed the growth of movements that rely on nonviolent and open means of resistance to uphold human rights, bring about social change, and create the conditions for peace. Like Kant, their members address the challenge voiced so eloquently by Machiavelli. By now, their successes provide a telling answer to the charge that their methods won't work. . . .

Gandhi's leadership of the independence movement in India is a case in point. The central element in his efforts at personal and social change was nonviolence, or *ahimsa*. It was meant to be forceful and therefore different from the passive acceptance of evil that had traditionally been associated with the concept of nonviolence. For someone insufficiently prepared to practice such resistance against an aggressor, Gandhi acknowledged that it might be better to use violence in self-defense rather than to give up in cowardice. And he insisted from the outset that nonviolence by itself cannot render a cause just. It can be coercive, harmful, unfair, untrue—as in nonviolent slander campaigns or bureaucratic harassment. Nonviolence had, therefore, to be part of a framework of moral principles, or "observances," as he called them.*

*There were eleven of these observances. Among the others were ones also quite common in different traditions, such as courage and nonstealing. Some, such as celibacy, the cultivation of detachment, and work with the body, are found in different religions but far from all; and a few, such as the home production of goods and the disposition to touch everyone, including India's so-called untouchables, were linked to the particular circumstances in which Gandhi carried on his struggle.

Along with nonviolence, the most important observance for Gandhi was a concern for truthfulness and truth. And fidelity—to his vows in their own right, to his ideals and thus to himself, to his obligations to others—was for him what held all the observances together and bound him to them in turn. Through making and holding such vows, he trained himself to become someone who could trust himself and who could be trusted by others. Finally, Gandhi rejected secrecy in his dealings with supporters as with those who opposed him. He regularly sent his policy statements and plans to those who might oppose him, to give them an opportunity to respond in the search for a just solution. He also disseminated these plans and articles on his movement as broadly as possible in the press. This allowed him to build up a much wider following at home and abroad than might otherwise have been possible, and helped prevent some of the worst forms of repression that could otherwise have been deployed against him. Secrecy in political work, moreover, would have exposed him to government spies and agents provocateurs, with all the smears and scandal they can generate.* . . .

DRAWBACKS IN PRACTICE?

It had taken courage for Kant to publish his essay on perpetual peace under the narrowly chauvinistic and doctrinaire King Frederick William II of Prussia, the successor, in 1786, of Frederick the Great. Only six months earlier, the king had ac-

*Gandhi has been justly criticized for rushing to advocate an open campaign of nonviolent resistance by Jews in Nazi Germany without adequately understanding their predicament. In the . . . years since he made suggestions to that effect, those who undertake or study nonviolent resistance have been able to exchange information and to learn from one another in ways denied to pioneers like Gandhi. One can hardly accuse those who have taken part in such resistance in the Philippines or Guatemala or Poland of ignoring the realities posed by a government far more repressive than that of the British in India.

cused Kant of debasing Christianity through his writings and insisted that he promise never to write or lecture on religion again. Otherwise, "unpleasant consequences" would ensue. Yet in this, his very next published work, Kant denounced despotism and the barbarism of warring states like Prussia and dared to link the observance of human rights to the prospects for world peace.

It is perhaps no wonder that he begins his essay by poking fun at philosophers who "blissfully dream of perpetual peace." Practical politicians, he hints, need not imagine that the abstract ideas of mere academics can endanger the state, which after all must be founded on experience: "it thus seems safe to let him fire off his whole broadside, and the worldly-wise politician need not turn a hair." Having said as much, Kant claims that he will consider himself "expressly safeguarded, in correct and proper style, against all malicious interpretation."

In the remainder of the essay, he could not be farther from jesting or from dismissing the ideas he was setting forth. He is especially concerned to disprove the notion that his views might be impractical—that what seems simple in theory is bound to encounter obstacles and perhaps fail altogether in practice. He intends his plan for a lasting peace to be more practical by far than the run-of-the-mill rationalizations of war on grounds of greater realism. As a result, he explores the practical aspects of achieving a "cosmopolitan"—or world citizen—perspective, of having moral principles guide political action, and of taking part in a program of gradual reforms within and among states.

Both from a theoretical and a practical point of view, Kant's plan represents a considerable improvement over all prior writings on perpetual peace. Previous authors had been farsighted and often eloquent, but their solutions had tended to be simplistic. Some had advocated a change of heart among citizens and rulers, others rudimentary leagues or federations of nations, still others a delicate international system whereby a balance of power would keep war from getting out of control. In his essay, Kant responds to their writings and to other works on war and peace, drawing on the moral, religious, and political debates of his and earlier periods and on his own writings. The result is a forceful and subtle defense of the role that morality should play in human affairs and a persuasive insistence that it be allowed to do so while there is still time. In considering the moral foundation of a strategy for peace, I have found no other work that comes close to his in scope, in depth, and in relevance for our own period.

Nevertheless, Kant's essay has drawbacks from the point of view of the practical application of his views to present needs. He offers a strategy for peace in the most abstract sense of the word only. Much of what he says in his essay about the role of morality and about political changes such as bringing about a federation of states is too compressed to be practically applicable, say, by government leaders sincerely wishing to further the cause of peace. And while he gives advice about how a national and foreign policy that stresses human rights will further this cause, he does not address the question of how peoples and civic organizations might resist unjust governments or threats of invasions from abroad. It would be difficult, therefore, to derive the specifics of a strategy for peace from his essay.

The obliqueness and abstraction of Kant's essay stem in part from his background. Although he followed political and diplomatic events closely, he never had to make day-to-day choices affecting them. Diplomats, military strategists, public officials, members of resistance movements, and the many others who have to do so—all need more to go on than he offers. Even if they agree with his views on an expanded perspective and on morality, they may wish to qualify some of his judgments. For instance, they may disagree with his view that rules out as "dishonorable" all spying. Intelligence-gathering is at present indispensable for defensive purposes. It can shorten some wars and prevent erroneous information from unleashing others. Kant himself might, faced with today's many forms of intelligence activities, evaluate codebreaking and satellite surveillance differently from, say, covert acts of deceit and violence that clearly breach basic moral constraints.

Those involved daily in practical decisions having to do with war and peace might find another aspect of Kant's position unacceptable: his all-or-nothing attitude toward what he regarded as right and wrong. Though he despised political or religious zealotry, he had an intransigence all his own with respect to morality. There could, he declared, be no exception to moral prohibitions. Unlawful recourses to force, as well as all lying and all breaches of valid promises, in particular, were out of the question, no matter how catastrophic the consequences at stake. He ruled out a lie even to save the life of a friend being stalked by a murderer. To be truthful, he held, is "a sacred and absolutely commanding decree of reason, limited by no expediency." On this subject, most people have disagreed with him. A lie may offer the only way to avert disaster in exceptional circumstances; why should we accept the use of force in an emergency to defend ourselves or our fellow citizens but reject deception under the same circumstances?*

It is clear from "Perpetual Peace" that Kant meant to uphold absolute moral intransigence in international affairs as vigorously as in relations between individuals. Not even national security or self-defense in extreme danger could give reasons, in his view, for breaching moral principles. "Do what is right though the world should perish" was for him no idle rhetoric. Here is yet a third aspect of Kant's impracticality: in spite of his own warnings about a possible end to human existence, he refused to believe that it might come about as a result of someone following such a motto.† He defended the motto against all comers, holding that though it might sound inflated it was nevertheless true: it was a "sound principle that blocked up all the devious paths followed by cunning or violence." The world would not in fact come to an end if governments took such a motto literally, he argued, since moral evil is inherently self-destructive and "makes way for the moral principle of goodness, even if such progress is slow."

In Kant's defense, it must be said that though he could imagine a final war of extermination, neither he nor anyone else in the eighteenth century could possibly envisage what we now know to be true: that such a war might be sudden, brief, and single-handedly brought about by the decision of just a few individuals. Moreover, he clung to the belief that Providence had a plan for mankind that included the achievement of permanent peace *on earth* rather than in some future existence, no matter how horrendous the events that would lead up to it. According to this belief, the world could in fact not perish if one did what was just.

I say that Kant "clung" to this belief, for all his late essays show extraordinary anguish about it. In his earlier writings, he was still imbued with the optimism about peace and human progress so common to Enlightenment thinkers. But as he grew older without witnessing the slightest sign that the human propensity for war was abating, his writings show increasing ambivalence in this re-

* Indeed it is possible to use Kant's own criterion of publicity in order to show that a maxim of lying in defending oneself or another person from direct and imminent assault is as legitimate as the recourse to violence at such a time. A maxim allowing both forms of self-defense is perfectly compatible with its being public; indeed, most people would surely prefer forms of self-defense that endangered no one's life.

† Kant undoubtedly realized that the consequentialist challenge to his position has special force here. What is at issue is not only "the vast graveyard of the human race" but also the end of "justice itself". . . . In this context, his unsupported claims that this fate won't come about if uncompromising morality guides political choice—because moral evil is self-destructive and because Providence may have a different plan for humanity—are not adequate to meet the consequentialist challenge. On the contrary, it is Kant's appeal to the disastrous *consequences* for humanity if nations do not take moral considerations into account that are most persuasive; and such an appeal need not be linked with his particular view of the uncompromising nature of these considerations.

gard. In "Perpetual Peace" he alternately suggests and then doubts the possibility of a peace that could stave off a final war of extermination. He had to hope, he wrote, that Providence had planned something nobler and better for human beings and aimed to teach them—if need be, through the very horrors of war—to turn to peace.

Yet he also held that human beings will progress only by their own efforts—Providence won't do it for them; and he feared that, although it would be best for governments to recognize right away the peril in which they were placing humanity, the world might have to go through ever more horrendous wars until one final war of extermination would be staring everyone in the face. The prospect of such a war could then *force* the shift of perspective and implement the moral constraints that all should have acknowledged long before.

Kant's warning that nations would face a war of extermination unless they could establish a lasting peace speaks to us more directly than ever. We can draw on his essay in working out a perspective and a set of constraints capable of guiding a strategy to deal with this threat. In so doing, however, we need to look elsewhere for ways to overcome in practice the three drawbacks of his proposals: their generality and abstraction, their absolutism, and their reliance on Providence to still any doubts about the consequences of acting on such absolutist views.

For a century and a half after his death, Kant's warning sounded too alarmist by far. It was ridiculed by many who proclaimed the virtues of war, from Joseph de Maistre to Hegel and Mussolini. Their voices ring hollow now as we hear them extolling war's cleansing nature, its nurturing of manliness, and its capacity to stir peoples to great and noble deeds. But the strongest of their taunts remains troubling. It questions the practicality of Kant's entire approach by rejecting as sheer, unrealistic folly any effort to do away with so elemental and abiding an aspect of the human condition as war.

STUDY QUESTIONS

1. Describe in your own words Kant's plan for a lasting peace among nations.
2. What obstacles to his plan did Kant foresee?
3. Where is Kant in agreement with Gandhi and Grotius?
4. What was Kant's thinking about state secrecy?
5. What drawbacks to Kant's plan does Bok identify?

27

On Satyagraha

Mohandas K. Gandhi

Mohandas Karamchand Gandhi (1869–1948) (known by the honorific title "Mahatma"), born in India, experienced racial discrimination in his travels to South Africa and subsequently became a committed social activist. When he was fifty he organized a satyagraha (a "holding fast to the truth"); eventually, his efforts led to the independence of India in 1947.

Before one can be fit for the practice of civil disobedience one must have rendered a willing and respectful obedience to the State laws. For the most part we obey such laws for fear of the penalty for their breach, and this holds good particularly in respect of such laws as do not involve a moral principle. For instance, an honest, respectable man will not suddenly take to stealing whether there is a law against stealing or not, but this very man will not feel any remorse for failure to observe the rule about carrying headlights on bicycles after dark. Indeed, it is doubtful whether he would even accept advice kindly about being more careful in this respect. But he would observe any obligatory rule of this kind, if only to escape the inconvenience of facing a prosecution for a breach of the rule. Such compliance is not, however, the willing and spontaneous obedience that is required of a Satyagrahi. A Satyagrahi obeys the laws of society intelligently and of his own free will, because he considers it to be his sacred duty to do so. It is only when a person has thus obeyed the laws of society scrupulously that he is in a position to judge as to which particular rules are good and just and which unjust and iniquitous. Only then does the right accrue to him of the civil disobedience of certain laws in well-defined circumstances.

SOUL-FORCE AND *TAPASYA*

[About 2 September 1917]

The force denoted by the term "passive resistance" and translated into Hindi as *nishkriya pratirodha* is not very accurately described either by the original English phrase or by its Hindi rendering. Its correct description is "*satyagraha.*" *Satyagraha* was born in South Africa in 1908. There was no word in any Indian language denoting the power which our countrymen in South Africa invoked for the redress of their grievances. There was an English equivalent, namely, "passive resistance," and we carried on with it. However, the need for a word to describe this unique power came to be increasingly felt, and it was decided to award a prize to anyone who could think of an appropriate term. A Gujarati-speaking gentleman submitted the word "*satyagraha,*" and it was adjudged the best.

"Passive resistance" conveyed the idea of the Suffragette Movement in England. Burning of houses by these women was called "passive resistance" and so also their fasting in prison. All such acts might very well be "passive resistance" but they were not "*satyagraha.*" It is said of "passive resistance" that it is the weapon of the weak, but the power which is the subject of this article can be used only by the strong. This power is not "passive" resistance; indeed it calls for intense activity. The movement in South Africa was not passive but active. The Indians of South Africa believed that Truth was their object, that Truth ever triumphs, and with this definiteness of purpose they persistently held on to Truth. They put up with all the suffering that this persistence implied. With the conviction that Truth is not to be renounced even unto death, they shed the fear of death. In the cause of Truth, the prison was a palace to them and its doors the gateway to freedom.

Satyagraha is not physical force. A *satyagrahi* does not inflict pain on the adversary; he does not seek his destruction. A *satyagrahi* never resorts to firearms. In the use of *satyagraha,* there is no ill-will whatever.

Satyagraha is pure soul-force. Truth is the very substance of the soul. That is why this force is called *satyagraha.* The soul is informed with knowledge. In it burns the flame of love. If someone gives us pain through ignorance, we shall win him through love. "Non-violence is the supreme *dharma*" [*Ahimsa paramo Dharma*] is the proof of this power of love. Non-violence is a dormant state. In the waking state, it is love. Ruled by love, the world goes on. In English there is a saying, "Might is Right." Then there is the doctrine of the survival of the fittest. Both these ideas are contradictory to the above principle. Neither is wholly true. If ill-will were the chief motive-force, the world would have been destroyed long ago; and neither would I have had the opportunity to write this article nor would the hopes of the readers be fulfilled. We are alive solely because of love. We are all ourselves the proof of this. Deluded by modern western civilization, we have forgotten our ancient civilization and worship the might of arms.

We forget the principle of non-violence, which is the essence of all religions. The doctrine of arms stands for irreligion. It is due to the sway of that doctrine that a sanguinary war is raging in Europe.

In India also we find worship of arms. We see it even in that great work of Tulsidas. But it is seen in all the books that soul-force is the supreme power.

Rama stands for the soul and Ravan for the non-soul. The immense physical might of Ravana is as nothing compared to the soul-force of Rama. Ravana's ten heads are as straw to Rama. Rama is a *yogi,* he has conquered self and pride. He is "placid equally in affluence and adversity," he has "neither attachment, nor greed nor the intoxication of status." This represents the ultimate in *satyagraha.* The banner of *satyagraha* can again fly in the Indian sky and it is our duty to raise it. If we take recourse to *satyagraha,* we can conquer our conquerors the English, make them bow before our tremendous soul-force, and the issue will be of benefit to the whole world.

It is certain that India cannot rival Britain or Europe in force of arms. The British worship the war-god and they can all of them become, as they are becoming, bearers of arms. The hundreds of millions in India can never carry arms. They have made the religion of non-violence their own. It is impossible for the *varnashrama* system to disappear from India.

The way of *varnashrama* is a necessary law of nature. India, by making a judicious use of it, derives much benefit. Even the Muslims and the English in India observe this system to some extent. Outside of India, too, people follow it without being aware of it. So long as this institution of *varnashrama* exists in India, everyone cannot bear arms here. The highest place in India is assigned to the *brahmana dharma*—which is soul-force. Even the armed warrior does obeisance to the *Brahmin.* So long as this custom prevails, it is vain for us to aspire for equality with the West in force of arms.

It is our Kamadhenu. It brings good both to the *satyagrahi* and his adversary. It is ever victorious. For instance, Harishchandra was a *satyagrahi,* Prahlad was a *satyagrahi,* Mirabai was a *satyagrahi.* Daniel, Socrates and those Arabs who hurled themselves on the fire of the French artillery were all *satyagrahis.* We see from these examples that a *satyagrahi* does not fear for his body, he does not give up what he thinks is Truth; the word "defeat" is not to be found in his dictionary, he does not wish for the destruction of his antagonist, he does not vent anger on him; but has only compassion for him.

A *satyagrahi* does not wait for others, but throws himself into the fray, relying entirely on his own resources. He trusts that when the time comes, others will do likewise. His practice is his precept. Like air, *satyagraha* is all-pervading. It is infectious, which means that all people—big and small, men and women—can become *satyagrahis*. No one is kept out from the army of *satyagrahis*. A *satyagrahi* cannot perpetrate tyranny on anyone; he is not subdued through application of physical force; he does not strike at anyone. Just as anyone can resort to *satyagraha*, it can be resorted to in almost any situation.

People demand historical evidence in support of *satyagraha*. History is for the most part a record of armed activities. Natural activities find very little mention in it. Only uncommon activities strike us with wonder. *Satyagraha* has been used always and in all situations. The father and the son, the man and the wife are perpetually resorting to *satyagraha*, one towards the other. When a father gets angry and punishes the son, the son does not hit back with a weapon, he conquers his father's anger by submitting to him. The son refuses to be subdued by the unjust rule of his father but he puts up with the punishment that he may incur through disobeying the unjust father. We can similarly free ourselves of the unjust rule of the Government by defying the unjust rule and accepting the punishments that go with it. We do not bear malice towards the Government. When we set its fears at rest, when we do not desire to make armed assaults on the administrators, nor to unseat them from power, but only to get rid of their injustice, they will at once be subdued to our will.

The question is asked why we should call any rule unjust. In saying so, we ourselves assume the function of a judge. It is true. But in this world, we always have to act as judges for ourselves. That is why the *satyagrahi* does not strike his adversary with arms. If he has Truth on his side, he will win, and if his thought is faulty, he will suffer the consequences of his fault.

What is the good, they ask, of only one person opposing injustice; for he will be punished and destroyed, he will languish in prison or meet an untimely end through hanging. The objection is not valid. History shows that all reforms have begun with one person. Fruit is hard to come by without *tapasya*. The suffering that has to be undergone in *satyagraha* is *tapasya* in its purest form. Only when the *tapasya* is capable of bearing fruit do we have the fruit. This establishes the fact that when there is insufficient *tapasya*, the fruit is delayed. The *tapasya* of Jesus Christ, boundless though it was, was not sufficient for Europe's need. Europe has disapproved Christ. Through ignorance, it has disregarded Christ's pure way of life. Many Christs will have to offer themselves as sacrifice at the terrible altar of Europe, and only then will realization dawn on that continent. But Jesus will always be the first among these. He has been the sower of the seed and his will therefore be the credit for raising the harvest. . . .

NON-VIOLENCE AND NON-RETALIATION

Mansehra,
[8 November 1938]

It has become the fashion these days to say that society cannot be organized or run on non-violent lines. I join issue on that point. In a family, when a father slaps his delinquent child, the latter does not think of retaliating. He obeys his father not because of the deterrent effect of the slap but because of the offended love which he senses behind it. That in my opinion is an epitome of the way in which society is or should be governed. What is true of family must be true of society which is but a larger family. It is man's imagination that divides the world into warring groups of enemies and friends. In the ultimate resort it is the power of love that acts even in the midst of the clash and sustains the world. . . .

NON-VIOLENCE OF THE STRONG AND OF THE WEAK

Hence I ask you, is our non-violence the non-violence of the coward, the weak, the helpless, the timid? In that case, it is of no value. A weakling is a born saint. A weak person is obliged to become a saint. But we are soldiers of non-violence, who, if the occasion demands, will lay down their lives for it. Our non-violence is not a mere policy of the coward. But I doubt this. I am afraid that the non-violence we boast of might really be only a policy. It is true that, to some extent, non-violence works even in the hands of the weak. And, in this manner, this weapon has been useful to us. But, if one makes use of non-violence in order to disguise one's weakness or through helplessness, it makes a coward of one. Such a person is defeated on both the fronts. Such a one cannot live like a man and the Devil he surely cannot become. It is a thousand times better that we die trying to acquire the strength of the arm. Using physical force with courage is far superior to cowardice. At least we would have attempted to act like men. That was the way of our forefathers. That is because some people hold the view that the ancestors of the human race were animals. I do not wish to enter into the controversy whether Darwin's theory is tenable or not. However, from one standpoint we must all have originally been animals. And I am ready to believe that we are evolved from the animal into the human state. That is why physical strength is called brute force.

We are born with such strength, hence if we used it we could be, to say the least, courageous. But we are born as human beings in order that we may realize God who dwells within our hearts. This is the basic distinction between us and the beasts. . . .

Man is by nature non-violent. But he does not owe his origin to non-violence. We fulfil our human life when we see the *atman,* and when we do so we pass the test. Now is the time for our test. God-realization means seeing Him in all beings. Or, in other words, we should learn to become one with every creature. This is man's privilege and that distinguishes him from the beasts. This can happen only when we voluntarily give up the use of physical force and when we develop the non-violence which lies dormant in our hearts. It can be awakened only through real strength. . . .

Non-violence is an active principle of the highest order. It is soul-force or the power of the godhead within us. Imperfect man cannot grasp the whole of that Essence—he would not be able to bear its full blaze—but even an infinitesimal fraction of it, when it becomes active within us, can work wonders. The sun in the heavens fills the whole universe with its life-giving warmth. But if one went too near it, it would consume him to ashes. Even so is it with godhead. We become godlike to the extent we realize non-violence; but we can never become wholly God. Non-violence is like radium in its action. An infinitesimal quantity of it imbedded in a malignant growth acts continuously, silently, and ceaselessly till it has transformed the whole mass of the diseased tissue into a healthy one. Similarly, even a tiny grain of true non-violence acts in a silent, subtle, unseen way and leavens the whole society.

It is self-acting. The soul persists even after death, its existence does not depend on the physical body. Similarly, non-violence or soul-force too, does not need physical aids for its propagation or effect. It acts independently of them. It transcends time and space.

It follows, therefore, that if non-violence becomes successfully established in one place, its influence will spread everywhere. So long as a single dacoity takes place in Utmanzai, I will say that our non-violence is not genuine.

The basic principle on which the practice of non-violence rests is that what holds good in respect of yourself holds good equally in respect of the whole universe. All mankind in essence are alike. . . .

NON-VIOLENCE AND BRAVERY

Just as one must learn the art of killing in the training for violence, so one must learn the art of dying in the training for non-violence. Violence does not mean emancipation from fear, but discovering the means of combating the cause of fear. Non-violence, on the other hand, has no cause for fear. The votary of non-violence has to cultivate the capacity for sacrifice of the highest type in order to be free from fear. He recks not if he should lose his land, his wealth, his life. He who has not overcome all fear cannot practise *ahimsa* to perfection. The votary of *ahimsa* has only one fear, that is of God. He who seeks refuge in God ought to have a glimpse of the *atman* that transcends the body; and the moment one has a glimpse of the Imperishable *atman* one sheds the love of the perishable body. Training in non-violence is thus diametrically opposed to training in violence. Violence is needed for the protection of things external, non-violence is needed for the protection of the *atman,* for the protection of one's honour.

This non-violence cannot be learnt by staying at home. It needs enterprise. In order to test ourselves we should learn to dare danger and death, mortify the flesh and acquire the capacity to endure all manner of hardships. He who trembles or takes to his heels the moment he sees two people fighting is not non-violent, but a coward. A non-violent person will lay down his life in preventing such quarrels. The bravery of the non-violent is vastly superior to that of the violent. The badge of the violent is his weapon—spear, or sword, or rifle. God is the shield of the non-violent.

This is not a course of training for one intending to learn non-violence. But it is easy to evolve one from the principles I have laid down.

It will be evident from the foregoing that there is no comparison between the two types of bravery. The one is limited, the other is limitless. There is no such thing as out-daring or out-fighting non-violence. Non-violence is invincible. There need be no doubt that this non-violence can be achieved. . . .

THE ACID TEST

Indeed the acid test of non-violence is that one thinks, speaks and acts non-violently, even when there is the gravest provocation to be violent. There is no merit in being non-violent to the good and the gentle. Non-violence is the mightiest force in the world capable of resisting the greatest imaginable temptation. Jesus knew "the generation of vipers," minced no words in describing them, but pleaded for mercy for them before the Judgment Throne, "for they knew not what they were doing."

I gave the company chapter and verse in support of the statements I made. I regard myself as a friend of the missionaries. I enjoy happy relations with many of them. But my friendships have never been blind to the limitations of my friends or the systems or methods they have supported.

False notions of propriety or fear of wounding susceptibilities often deter people from saying what they mean and ultimately land them on the shores of hypocrisy. But if non-violence of thought is to be evolved in individuals or societies or nations, truth has to be told, however harsh or unpopular it may appear to be for the moment. And mere non-violent action without the thought behind it is of little value. It can never be infectious. It is almost like a whited sepulchre. Thought is the power and the life behind it. We hardly know that thought is infinitely greater than action or words. When there is correspondence between thought, word and deed, either is a limitation of the first. And the third is a limitation of the second.

Needless to say that here I am referring to the living thought which awaits translation into speech and action. Thoughts without potency are airy nothings and end in smoke. . . .

The way of peace is the way of truth. Truthfulness is even more important than peacefulness. Indeed, lying is the mother of violence. A truthful man cannot long remain violent. He will perceive in the course of his search that he has no need to be violent and he will further discover that so long as there is the slightest trace of violence in him, he will fail to find the truth he is searching.

There is no half way between truth and non-violence on the one hand and untruth and violence on the other. We may never be strong enough to be entirely non-violent in thought, word and deed. But we must keep non-violence as our goal and make steady progress towards it. The attainment of freedom, whether for a man, a nation or the world, must be in exact proportion to the attainment of non-violence by each. Let those, therefore, who believe in non-violence as the only method of achieving real freedom, keep the lamp of non-violence burning bright in the midst of the present impenetrable gloom. The truth of a few will count, the untruth of millions will vanish even like chaff before a whiff of wind.

STUDY QUESTIONS

1. Gandhi says, "Lying is the mother of violence." What, then, is the connection between truth and nonviolence?
2. Bravery and strength are very often defined and made visible by acts of violence. How does Gandhi define bravery and strength?
3. Gandhi states that nonviolence is love in a dormant state. What is meant by this? Is he correct? He also states that nonviolence is active. Is this a contradiction?
4. What reason might an individual have for choosing nonviolence as a form of social protest?

FOR FURTHER STUDY

Bok, Sissela. *A Strategy for Peace: Human Values and the Threat of War.* New York: Vintage Books, 1990.

Boserup, Anders, and Mack, Andrew. *War without Weapons: Non-Violence in National Defense.* New York, 1975.

Brown, Seyom. *The Causes and Prevention of War.* New York: St. Martin's Press, 1987.

Clausewitz, Carl von. *On War,* ed. and trans. Michael Howard and Peter Paret. Princeton, N.J.: Princeton University Press, 1976.

Gandhi, Mohandas K. *Autobiography: Experiments with Truth.* Boston: Beacon Press, 1977.

Hardin, Russell, et al., eds. *Nuclear Deterrence: Ethics and Strategy.* Chicago: University of Chicago Press, 1985.

Holmes, Arthur, ed. *War and Christian Ethics.* Grand Rapids, Mich.: Baker Book House, 1975.

Jonas, Hans. *The Imperative of Responsibility: In Search of an Ethics for the Technological Age.* Chicago: University of Chicago Press, 1984.

Kant, Immanuel. "Perpetual Peace: A Philosophical Sketch." In *Kant's Political Writings,* ed. Hans Reiss. Cambridge: Cambridge University Press, 1970.

Ruddick, Sara. *Maternal Thinking: Toward a Politics of Peace.* Boston: Beacon Press, 1989.

Walzer, Michael. *Just and Unjust Wars: A Moral Argument with Historical Illustrations.* New York: Basic Books, 1992.

Chapter Six

Ethics of Hunger, Welfare, and Homelessness

28

The Kingdom of God

Jesus of Nazareth

Jesus of Nazareth was a Jewish religious leader whose teachings founded Christianity. He was executed by crucifixion around A.D. 29.

---

31 When the Son of man shall come in his glory, and all the holy angels with him, then shall he sit upon the throne of his glory:

32 And before him shall be gathered all nations: and he shall separate them one from another, as a shepherd divideth *his* sheep from the goats:

33 And he shall set the sheep on his right hand, but the goats on the left.

34 Then shall the King say unto them on his right hand, Come, ye blessed of my Father, inherit the kingdom prepared for you from the foundation of the world:

35 For I was an hungred, and ye gave me meat: I was thirsty, and ye gave me drink: I was a stranger, and ye took me in:

36 Naked, and ye clothed me: I was sick, and ye visited me: I was in prison, and ye came unto me.

37 Then shall the righteous answer him, saying, Lord, when saw we thee an hungred, and fed *thee?* or thirsty, and gave *thee* drink?

38 When saw we thee a stranger, and took *thee* in? or naked, and clothed *thee?*

39 Or when saw we thee sick, or in prison, and came unto thee?

40 And the King shall answer and say unto them, Verily I say unto you, Inasmuch as ye have done *it* unto one of the least of these my brethren, ye have done *it* unto me.

41 Then shall he say also unto them on the left hand, Depart from me, ye cursed, into everlasting fire, prepared for the devil and his angels:

42 For I was an hungred, and ye gave me no meat: I was thirsty, and ye gave me no drink:

43 I was a stranger, and ye took me not in: naked, and ye clothed me not: sick, and in prison, and ye visited me not.

44 Then shall they also answer him, saying, Lord, when saw we thee an hungred, or athirst, or a stranger, or naked, or sick, or in prison, and did not minister unto thee?

45 Then shall he answer them, saying, Verily I say unto you, Inasmuch as ye did *it* not to one of the least of these, ye did *it* not to me.

46 And these shall go away into everlasting punishment: but the righteous into life eternal.

STUDY QUESTIONS

1. Who, according to Jesus, is righteous in the eyes of God?
2. Who are "the least of these"?
3. Why, according to Jesus, are the needy near to God?

29

Famine, Affluence, and Morality

Peter Singer

Peter Singer is a professor of philosophy and the director of the Center for Human Bioethics at Monash University in Australia. He is the author of many books and articles on animals and the nonhuman environment, including *Animal Liberation* and *Practical Ethics*.

As I write this, in November 1971, people are dying in East Bengal from lack of food, shelter, and medical care. The suffering and death that are occurring there now are not inevitable, not unavoidable in any fatalistic sense of the term. Constant poverty, a cyclone, and a civil war have turned at least nine million people into destitute refugees; nevertheless, it is not beyond the capacity of the richer nations to give enough assistance to reduce any further suffering to very small proportions. The decisions and actions of human beings can prevent this kind of suffering. Unfortunately, human beings have not made the necessary decisions. At the individual level, people have, with very few exceptions, not responded to the situation in any significant way. Generally speaking, people have not given large sums to relief funds; they have not written to their parliamentary representatives demanding increased government assistance; they have not demonstrated in the streets, held symbolic fasts, or done anything else directed toward providing the refugees with the means to satisfy their essential needs. At the government level, no government has given the sort of massive aid that would enable the refugees to survive for more than a few days. Britain, for instance, has given rather more than most countries. It has, to date, given £14,750,000. For comparative purposes, Britain's share of the nonrecoverable development costs of the Anglo-French Concorde project is already in excess of £275,000,000, and on present estimates will reach £440,000,000. The implication is that the British government values a supersonic transport more than thirty times as highly as it values the lives of the nine million refugees. Australia is another country which, on a per capita basis, is well up in the "aid to Bengal" table. Australia's aid, however, amounts to less than one-twelfth of the cost of Sydney's new opera house. The total amount given, from all sources, now stands at about £65,000,000. The estimated cost of keeping the refugees alive for one year is £464,000,000. Most of the refugees have now been in the camps for more than six months. The World Bank has said that India needs a minimum of £300,000,000 in assistance from other countries before the end of the year. It seems obvious that assistance on this scale will not be forthcoming. India will be forced to choose between letting the refugees starve or diverting funds from her own development program, which will mean that more of her own people will starve in the future.[1]

These are the essential facts about the present situation in Bengal. So far as it concerns us here, there is nothing unique about this situation except its magnitude. The Bengal emergency is just the latest and most acute of a series of major emergencies in various parts of the world, arising both from natural and from man-made causes. There are also many parts of the world in which people die from malnutrition and lack of food independent of any special emergency. I take Bengal as my example only because it is the present concern, and because the size of the problem has ensured that it has been given adequate publicity. Neither individuals nor governments can claim to be unaware of what is happening there.

What are the moral implications of a situation like this? In what follows, I shall argue that the way people in relatively affluent countries react to a situation like that in Bengal cannot be justified; indeed, the whole way we look at moral issues—our moral conceptual scheme—needs to be altered, and with it, the way of life that has come to be taken for granted in our society.

In arguing for this conclusion I will not, of course, claim to be morally neutral. I shall, however, try to argue for the moral position that I take, so that anyone who accepts certain assumptions, to be made explicit, will, I hope, accept my conclusion.

I begin with the assumption that suffering and death from lack of food, shelter, and medical care are bad. I think most people will agree about this, although one may reach the same view by different routes. I shall not argue for this view. People can hold all sorts of eccentric positions, and perhaps from some of them it would not follow that death by starvation is in itself bad. It is difficult, perhaps impossible, to refute such positions, and so for brevity I will henceforth take this assumption as accepted. Those who disagree need read no further.

My next point is this: if it is in our power to prevent something bad from happening, without thereby sacrificing anything of comparable moral importance, we ought, morally, to do it. By "without sacrificing anything of comparable moral importance" I mean without causing anything else comparably bad to happen, or doing something that is wrong in itself, or failing to promote some moral good, comparable in significance to the bad thing that we can prevent. This principle seems almost as uncontroversial as the last one. It requires us only to prevent what is bad, and not to promote what is good, and it requires this of us only when we can do it without sacrificing anything that is, from the moral point of view, comparably important. I could even, as far as the application of my argument to the Bengal emergency is concerned, qualify the point so as to make it: if it is in our power to prevent something very bad from happening, without thereby sacrificing anything morally significant, we ought, morally, to do it. An application of this principle would be as follows: if I am walking past a shallow pond and see a child drowning in it, I ought to wade in and pull the child out. This will mean getting my clothes muddy, but this is insignificant, while the death of the child would presumably be a very bad thing.

The uncontroversial appearance of the principle just stated is deceptive. If it were acted upon, even in its qualified form, our lives, our society, and our world would be fundamentally changed. For the principle takes, firstly, no account of proximity or distance. It makes no moral difference whether the person I can help is a neighbor's child ten yards from me or a Bengali whose name I shall never know, ten thousand miles away. Secondly, the principle makes no distinction between cases in which I am the only person who could possibly do anything and cases in which I am just one among millions in the same position.

I do not think I need to say much in defense of the refusal to take proximity and distance into account. The fact that a person is physically near to us, so that we have personal contact with him, may make it more likely that we *shall* assist him, but this does not show that we *ought* to help him rather than another who happens to be further away. If we accept any principle of impartiality, universalizability, equality, or whatever, we cannot discriminate against someone merely because he is far away from us (or we are far away from him). Admittedly, it is possible that we are in a better position to judge what needs to be done to help a person near to us than one far away, and perhaps also to provide the assistance we judge to be necessary. If this were the case, it would be a reason for helping those near to us first. This may once have been a justification for being more concerned with the poor in one's own town than with famine victims in India. Unfortunately for those who like to keep their moral responsibilities limited, instant communication and swift transportation have changed the situation. From the moral point of view, the development of the world into a "global village" has made an important, though still unrecognized, difference to our moral situation. Expert observers and supervisors, sent out by famine relief organizations or permanently stationed in famine-prone areas, can direct our aid to a refugee in Bengal almost as effectively as we could get it to someone in our own block. There would seem, therefore, to be no possible justification for discriminating on geographical grounds.

There may be a greater need to defend the second implication of my principle—that the fact that there are millions of other people in the same position, in respect to the Bengali refugees, as I am, does not make the situation significantly different from a situation in which I am the only person who can prevent something very bad from occurring. Again, of course, I admit that there is a psychological difference between the cases; one feels less guilty about doing nothing if one can point to others, similarly placed, who have also done nothing. Yet this can make no real difference to our moral obligations.[2] Should I consider that I am less obliged to pull the drowning child out of the pond if on looking around I see other people, no further away than I am, who have also noticed the child but are doing nothing? One has only to ask this question to see the absurdity of the view that numbers lessen obligation. It is a view that is an ideal excuse for inactivity; unfortunately most of the major evils—poverty, overpopulation, pollution—are problems in which everyone is almost equally involved.

The view that numbers do make a difference can be made plausible if stated in this way: if everyone in circumstances like mine gave £5 to the Bengal Relief Fund, there would be enough to provide food, shelter, and medical care for the refugees; there is no reason why I should give more than anyone else in the same circumstances as I am; therefore I have no obligation to give more than £5. Each premise in this argument is true, and the argument looks sound. It may convince us, unless we notice that it is based on a hypothetical premise, although the conclusion is not stated hypothetically. The argument would be sound if the conclusion were: if everyone in circumstances like mine were to give £5, I would have no obligation to give more than £5. If the conclusion were so stated, however, it would be obvious that the argument has no bearing on a situation in which it is not the case that everyone else gives £5. This, of course, is the actual situation. It is more or less certain that not everyone in circumstances like mine will give £5. So there will not be enough to provide the needed food, shelter, and medical care. Therefore by giving more than £5 I will prevent more suffering than I would if I gave just £5.

It might be thought that this argument has an absurd consequence. Since the situation appears to be that very few people are likely to give substantial amounts, it follows that I and everyone else in similar circumstances ought to give as much as possible, that is, at least up to the point at which by giving more one would begin to cause serious suffering for oneself and one's dependents—perhaps even beyond this point to the point of marginal utility, at which by giving more one would cause oneself and one's dependents as much suffering as one would prevent in Bengal. If everyone does this, however, there will be more than can be used for the benefit of the refugees, and some of the sacrifice will have been unnecessary. Thus, if everyone does what he ought to do, the result will not be as good as it would be if everyone did a little less than he ought to do, or if only some do all that they ought to do.

The paradox here arises only if we assume that the actions in question—sending money to the relief funds—are performed more or less simultaneously, and are also unexpected. For if it is to be expected that everyone is going to contribute something, then clearly each is not obliged to give as much as he would have been obliged to had others not been giving too. And if everyone is not acting more or less simultaneously, then those giving later will know how much more is needed, and will have no obligation to give more than is necessary to reach this amount. To say this is not to deny the principle that people in the same circumstances have the same obligations, but to point out that the fact that others have given, or may be expected to give, is a relevant circumstance: those giving after it has become known that many others are giving and those giving before are not in the same circumstances. So the seemingly absurd consequence of the principle I have put forward can occur only if people are in error about the actual circumstances—that is, if they think they are giving when others are not, but in fact they are giving when others are. The result of everyone doing what he really ought to do cannot be worse than the result of everyone doing less than he ought to do, although the result of everyone doing what he reasonably believes he ought to do could be.

If my argument so far has been sound, neither our distance from a preventable evil nor the number of other people who, in respect to that evil, are in the same situation as we are, lessens our obligation to mitigate or prevent that evil. I shall therefore take as established the principle I asserted earlier. As I have already said, I need to assert it only in its qualified form: if it is in our power to prevent something very bad from happening, without thereby sacrificing anything else morally significant, we ought, morally, to do it.

The outcome of this argument is that our traditional moral categories are upset. The traditional distinction between duty and charity cannot be drawn, or at least, not in the place we normally draw it. Giving money to the Bengal Relief Fund is regarded as an act of charity in our society. The bodies which collect money are known as "charities." These organizations see themselves in this way—if you send them a check, you will be thanked for your "generosity." Because giving money is regarded as an act of charity, it is not thought that there is anything wrong with not giving. The charitable man may be praised, but the man who is not charitable is not condemned. People do not feel in any way ashamed or guilty about spending money on new clothes or a new car instead of giving it to famine relief. (Indeed, the alternative does not occur to them.) This way of looking at the matter cannot be justified. When we buy new clothes not to keep ourselves warm but to look "well-dressed" we are not providing for any important need. We would not be sacrificing anything significant if we were to continue to wear our old clothes, and give the money to famine relief. By doing so, we would be preventing another person from starving. It follows from what I have said earlier that we ought to give money away, rather than spend it on clothes which we do not need to keep us warm. To do so is not charitable, or generous. Nor is it the kind of act which philosophers and theologians have called "supererogatory"—an act which it would be good to do, but not wrong not to do. On the contrary, we ought to give the money away, and it is wrong not to do so.

I am not maintaining that there are no acts which are charitable, or that there are no acts which it would be good to do but not wrong not to do. It may be possible to redraw the distinction between duty and charity in some other place. All I am arguing here is that the present way of drawing the distinction, which makes it an act of charity for a man living at the level of affluence which most people in the "developed nations" enjoy to give money to save someone else from starvation, cannot be supported. It is beyond the scope of my argument to consider whether the distinction should be redrawn or abolished altogether. There would be many other possible ways of drawing the distinction—for instance, one might decide that it is good to make other people as happy as possible, but not wrong not to do so.

Despite the limited nature of the revision in our moral conceptual scheme which I am proposing, the revision would, given the extent of both affluence and famine in the world today, have radical implications. These implications may lead to further objections, distinct from those I have already considered. I shall discuss two of these.

One objection to the position I have taken might be simply that it is too drastic a revision of our moral scheme. People do not ordinarily judge in the way I have suggested they should. Most people reserve their moral condemnation for those who violate some moral norm, such as the norm against taking another person's property. They do not condemn those who indulge in luxury instead of giving to famine relief. But given that I did not set out to present a morally neutral description of the way people make moral judgments, the way people do in fact judge has nothing to do with the validity of my conclusion. My conclusion follows from the principle which I advanced earlier, and unless that principle is rejected, or the arguments shown to be unsound, I think the conclusion must stand, however strange it appears.

It might, nevertheless, be interesting to consider why our society, and most other societies, do judge differently from the way I have suggested they should. In a well-known article, J. O. Urmson suggests that the imperatives of duty, which tell us what we must do, as distinct from what it would be good to do but not wrong not to do, function so as to prohibit behavior that is intolerable if men are to live together in society.[3] This may explain the origin and continued existence of the present division between acts of duty and acts of charity. Moral attitudes are shaped by the needs of society, and no doubt society needs people who will observe the rules that make social existence tolerable. From the point of view of a particular society, it is essential to prevent violations of norms against killing, stealing, and so on. It is quite inessential, however, to help people outside one's own society.

If this is an explanation of our common distinction between duty and supererogation, however, it is not a justification of it. The moral point of view requires us to look beyond the interests of our own society. Previously, as I have already mentioned, this may hardly have been feasible, but it is quite feasible now. From the moral point of view, the prevention of the starvation of millions of people outside our society must be considered at least as pressing as the upholding of property norms within our society.

It has been argued by some writers, among them Sidgwick and Urmson, that we need to have a basic moral code which is not too far beyond the capacities of the ordinary man, for otherwise there will be a general breakdown of compliance with the moral code. Crudely stated, this argument suggests that if we tell people that they ought to refrain from murder and give everything they do not really need to famine relief, they will do neither, whereas if we tell them that they ought to refrain from murder and that it is good to give to famine relief but not wrong not to do so, they will at least refrain from murder. The issue here is: Where should we drawn the line between conduct that is required and conduct that is good although not required, so as to get the best possible result? This would seem to be an empirical question, although a very difficult one. One objection to the Sidgwick–Urmson line of argument is that it takes insufficient account of the effect that moral standards can have on the decisions we make. Given a society in which a wealthy man who gives five percent of his income to famine relief is regarded as most generous, it is not surprising that a proposal that we all ought to give away half our incomes will be thought to be absurdly unrealistic. In a society which held that no man should have more than enough while others have less than they need, such a proposal might seem narrow-minded. What it is possible for a man to do and what he is likely to do are both, I think, very greatly influenced by what people around him are doing and expecting him to do. In any case, the possibility that by spreading the idea that we ought to be doing very much more than we are to relieve famine we shall bring about a general breakdown of moral behavior seems remote. If the stakes are an end to widespread starvation, it is worth the risk. Finally, it should be emphasized that these considerations are relevant only to the issue of what we should require from others, and not to what we ourselves ought to do.

The second objection to my attack on the present distinction between duty and charity is one which has from time to time been made against utilitarianism. It follows from some forms of utilitarian theory that we all ought, morally, to be working full time to increase the balance of happiness over misery. The position I have taken here would not lead to this conclusion in all circumstances, for if there were no bad occurrences that we could prevent without sacrificing something of comparable moral importance, my argument would have no application. Given the present conditions in many parts of the world, however, it does follow from my argument that we ought, morally, to be working full time to relieve great suffering of the sort that occurs as a result of famine or other disasters. Of course, mitigating circumstances can be adduced—for instance, that if we wear ourselves out through overwork, we shall be less effective than we would otherwise have been. Nevertheless, when all considerations of this sort have been taken into account, the conclusion remains: we ought to be preventing as much suffering as we can without sacrificing something else of comparable moral importance. This conclusion is one which we may be reluctant to face. I cannot see, though, why it should be regarded as a criticism of the position for which I have argued, rather than a criticism of our ordinary standards of behavior. Since most people are self-interested to some degree, very few of us are likely to do everything that we ought to do. It would, however, hardly be honest to take this as evidence that it is not the case that we ought to do it.

It may still be thought that my conclusions are so wildly out of line with what everyone else thinks and has always thought that there must be something wrong with the argument somewhere. In order to show that my conclusions, while certainly contrary to contemporary Western moral standards, would not have seemed so extraordinary at other times and in other places, I would like to quote a passage from a writer not normally thought of as a way-out radical, Thomas Aquinas.

> Now, according to the natural order instituted by divine providence, material goods are provided for the satisfaction of human needs. Therefore the division and appropriation of property, which proceeds from human law, must not hinder the satisfaction of man's necessity from such goods. Equally, whatever a man has in superabundance is owed, of natural right, to the poor for their sustenance. So Ambrosius says, and it is also to be found in the *Decretum Gratiani:* "The bread which you withhold belongs to the hungry; the clothing you shut away, to the naked; and the money you bury in the earth is the redemption and freedom of the penniless."[4]

I now want to consider a number of points, more practical than philosophical, which are relevant to the application of the moral conclusion we have reached. These points challenge not the idea that we ought to be doing all we can to prevent starvation, but the idea that giving away a great deal of money is the best means to this end.

It is sometimes said that overseas aid should be a government responsibility, and that therefore one ought not to give to privately run charities. Giving privately, it is said, allows the government and the noncontributing members of society to escape their responsibilities.

This argument seems to assume that the more people there are who give to privately organized famine relief funds, the less likely it is that the government will take over full responsibility for such aid. This assumption is unsupported, and does not strike me as at all plausible. The opposite view—that if no one gives voluntarily, a government will assume that its citizens are uninterested in famine relief and would not wish to be forced into giving aid—seems more plausible. In any case, unless there were a definite probability that by refusing to give one would be helping to bring about massive government assistance, people who do refuse to make voluntary contributions are refusing to prevent a certain amount of suffering without being able to point to any tangible beneficial consequence of their refusal. So the onus of showing how their refusal will bring about government action is on those who refuse to give.

I do not, of course, want to dispute the contention that governments of affluent nations should be giving many times the amount of genuine, no-strings-attached aid that they are giving now. I agree, too, that giving privately is not enough, and that we ought to be campaigning actively for entirely new standards for both public and private contributions to famine relief. Indeed, I would sympathize with someone who thought that campaigning was more important than giving oneself, although I doubt whether preaching what one does not practice would be very effective. Unfortunately, for many people the idea that "it's the government's responsibility" is a reason for not giving which does not appear to entail any political action either.

Another, more serious reason for not giving to famine relief funds is that until there is effective population control, relieving famine merely postpones starvation. If we save the Bengal refugees now, others, perhaps the children of these refugees, will face starvation in a few years' time. In support of this, one may cite the now well-known facts about the population explosion and the relatively limited scope for expanded production.

This point, like the previous one, is an argument against relieving suffering that is happening now, because of a belief about what might happen in the future; it is unlike the previous point in that very good evidence can be adduced in support of this belief about the future. I will not go into the evidence here. I accept that the earth cannot support indefinitely a population rising at the present rate. This certainly poses a problem for anyone who thinks it important to prevent famine. Again, however, one could accept the argument without drawing the conclusion that it absolves one from any obligation to do anything to prevent famine. The conclusion that should be drawn is that the best means of preventing famine, in the long run, is population control. It would then follow from the position reached earlier that one ought to be doing all one can to promote population control (unless one held that all forms of population control were wrong in themselves, or would have significantly bad consequences). Since there are organizations working specifically for population control, one would then support them rather than more orthodox methods of preventing famine.

A third point raised by the conclusion reached earlier relates to the question of just how much we all ought to be giving away. One possibility, which has already been mentioned, is that we ought to give until we reach the level of marginal utility—that is, the level at which, by giving more, I would cause as much suffering to myself or my dependents as I would relieve by my gift. This would mean, of course, that one would reduce oneself to very near the material circumstances of a Bengali refugee. It will be recalled that earlier I put forward both a strong and a moderate version of the principle of preventing bad occurrences. The strong version, which required us to prevent bad things from happening unless in doing so we would be sacrificing something of comparable moral significance, does seem to require reducing ourselves to the level of marginal utility. I should also say that the strong version seems to me to be the correct one. I proposed the more moderate version—that we should prevent bad occurrences unless, to do so, we had to sacrifice something morally significant—only in order to show that even on this surely undeniable principle a great change in our way of life is required. On the more moderate principle, it may not follow that we ought to reduce ourselves to the level of marginal utility, for one might hold that to reduce oneself and one's family to this level is to cause something significantly bad to happen. Whether this is so I shall not discuss, since, as I have said, I can see no good reason for holding the moderate version of the principle rather than the strong version. Even if we accepted the principle only in its moderate form, however, it should be clear that we would have to give away enough to ensure that the consumer society, dependent as it is on people spending on trivia rather than giving to famine relief, would slow down and perhaps disappear entirely. There are several reasons why this would be desirable in itself. The value and necessity of economic growth are now being questioned not only by conservationists, but by economists as well.[5] There is no doubt, too, that the consumer society has had a distorting effect on the goals and purposes of its members. Yet looking at the matter purely from the point of view of overseas aid, there must be a limit to the extent to which we should deliberately slow down our economy; for it might be the case that if we gave away, say, forty percent of our Gross National Product, we would slow down the economy so much that in absolute terms we would be giving less than if we gave twenty-five percent of the much larger GNP than we would have if we limited our contribution to this smaller percentage.

I mention this only as an indication of the sort of factor that one would have to take into account in working out an ideal. Since Western societies generally consider one percent of the GNP an acceptable level for overseas aid, the matter is entirely academic. Nor does it affect the question of how much an individual should give in a society in which very few are giving substantial amounts.

It is sometimes said, though less often now than it used to be, that philosophers have no special role to play in public affairs, since most public issues depend primarily on an assessment of facts. On questions of fact, it is said, philosophers as such have no special expertise, and so it has been possible to engage in philosophy without committing oneself to any position on major public issues. No doubt there are some issues of social policy and foreign policy about which it can truly be said that a really expert assessment of the facts is required before taking sides or acting, but the issue of famine is surely not one of these. The facts about the existence of suffering are beyond dispute. Nor, I think, is it disputed that we can do something about it, either through orthodox methods of famine relief or through population control or both. This is therefore an issue on which philosophers are competent to take a position. The issue is one which faces everyone who has more money than he needs to support himself and his dependents, or who is in a position to take some sort of political action. These categories must include practically every teacher and student of philosophy in the universities of the Western world. If philosophy is to deal with matters that are relevant to both teachers and students, this is an issue that philosophers should discuss.

Discussion, though, is not enough. What is the point of relating philosophy to public (and personal) affairs if we do not take our conclusions seriously? In this instance, taking our conclusion seriously means acting upon it. The philosopher will not find it any easier than anyone else to alter his attitudes and way of life to the extent that, if I am right, is involved in doing everything that we ought to be doing. At the very least, though, one can make a start. The philosopher who does so will have to sacrifice some of the benefits of the consumer society, but he can find compensation in the satisfaction of a way of life in which theory and practice, if not yet in harmony, are at least coming together.

NOTES

1. There was also a third possibility: that India would go to war to enable the refugees to return to their lands. Since I wrote this paper, India has taken this way out. The situation is no longer that described above, but this does not affect my argument, as the next paragraph indicates.

2. In view of the special sense philosophers often give to the term, I should say that I use "obligation" simply as the abstract noun derived from "ought," so that "I have an obligation to" means no more, and no less, than "I ought to." This usage is in accordance with the definition of "ought" given by the *Shorter Oxford English Dictionary:* "the general verb to express duty or obligation." I do not think any issue of substance hangs on the way the term is used; sentences in which I use "obligation" could all be rewritten, although somewhat clumsily, as sentences in which a clause containing "ought" replaces the term "obligation."
3. J. O. Urmson, "Saints and Heroes," in *Essays in Moral Philosophy,* ed. Abraham I. Melden (Seattle and London, 1958), p. 214. For a related but significantly different view see also Henry Sidgwick, *The Methods of Ethics,* 7th edn. (London, 1907), pp. 220–221, 492–493.
4. *Summa Theologica,* II–II, Question 66, Article 7, in *Aquinas, Selected Political Writings,* ed. A. P. d'Entreves, trans. J. G. Dawson (Oxford, 1948), p. 171.
5. See, for instance, John Kenneth Galbraith, *The New Industrial State* (Boston, 1967); and E. J. Mishan, *The Costs of Economic Growth* (London, 1967).

STUDY QUESTIONS

1. How have technological advances increased the duties of the modern affluent individual?
2. What similarities are there between Singer and Jesus, in terms of helping those in need? What differences?
3. How did the universal need to financially help others, which Singer considers a duty, get relegated to the category of "charity"?
4. What might a world operating on Singer's principles look like? Is it a possibility?

30

Lifeboat Ethics: The Case against Helping the Poor

Garrett Hardin

Garrett Hardin is a professor emeritus of human ecology at the University of California at Santa Barbara. He has published widely on human ecology and evolution.

Environmentalists use the metaphor of the earth as a "spaceship" in trying to persuade countries, industries and people to stop wasting and polluting our natural resources. Since we all share life on this planet, they argue, no single person or institution has the right to destroy, waste, or use more than a fair share of its resources.

But does everyone on earth have an equal right to an equal share of its resources? The spaceship metaphor can be dangerous when used by misguided idealists to justify suicidal policies for sharing our resources through uncontrolled immigration and foreign aid. In their enthusiastic but unrealistic generosity, they confuse the ethics of a spaceship with those of a lifeboat.

A true spaceship would have to be under the control of a captain, since no ship could possibly survive if its course were determined by committee. Spaceship Earth certainly has no captain; the United Nations is merely a toothless tiger, with little power to enforce any policy upon its bickering members.

If we divide the world crudely into rich nations and poor nations, two thirds of them are desperately poor, and only one third comparatively rich, with the United States the wealthiest of all. Metaphorically each rich nation can be seen as a lifeboat full of comparatively rich people. In the ocean outside each lifeboat swim the poor of the world, who would like to get in, or at least to share some of the wealth. What should the lifeboat passengers do?

First, we must recognize the limited capacity of any lifeboat. For example, a nation's land has a limited capacity to support a population and as the current energy crisis has shown us, in some ways we have already exceeded the carrying capacity of our land.

ADRIFT IN A MORAL SEA

So here we sit, say fifty people in our lifeboat. To be generous, let us assume it has room for ten more, making a total capacity of sixty. Suppose the fifty of us in the lifeboat see 100 others swimming in the water outside, begging for admission to our boat or for handouts. We have several options: we may be tempted to live by the Christian ideal of being "our brother's keeper," or by the Marxist ideal of "to each according to his needs." Since the needs of all in the water are the same, and since they can all be seen as "our brothers," we could take them all into our boat, making a total of 150 in a boat designed for sixty. The boat swamps, everyone drowns. Complete justice, complete catastrophe.

Since the boat has an unused excess capacity of ten more passengers, we could admit just ten more to it. But which ten do we let in? How do we choose? Do we pick the best ten, the neediest ten, "first come, first served"? And what do we say to the ninety we exclude? If we do let an extra ten into our lifeboat, we will have lost our "safety factor," an engineering principle of critical importance. For example, if we don't leave room for excess capacity as a safety factor in our country's agriculture, a new plant disease or a bad change in the weather could have disastrous consequences.

Suppose we decide to preserve our small safety factor and admit no more to the lifeboat. Our survival is then possible, although we shall have to be constantly on guard against boarding parties.

While this last solution clearly offers the only means of our survival, it is morally abhorrent to many people. Some say they feel guilty about their good luck. My reply is simple: "Get out and yield your place to others." This may solve the problem of the guilt-ridden person's conscience, but it does not change the ethics of the lifeboat. The needy person to whom the guilt-ridden person yields his place will not himself feel guilty about his good luck. If he did, he would not climb aboard. The net result of conscience-stricken people giving up their unjustly held seats is the elimination of that sort of conscience from the lifeboat.

This is the basic metaphor within which we must work out our solutions. Let us now enrich the image, step by step, with substantive additions from the real world, a world that must solve real and pressing problems of overpopulation and hunger.

The harsh ethics of the lifeboat become even harsher when we consider the reproductive differences between the rich nations and the poor nations. The people inside the lifeboats are doubling in numbers every eighty-seven years; those swimming around outside are doubling, on the average, every thirty-five years, more than twice as fast as the rich. And since the world's resources are dwindling, the difference in prosperity between the rich and the poor can only increase.

As of 1973, the U.S. had a population of 210 million people, who were increasing by 0.8 percent per year. Outside our lifeboat, let us imagine another 210 million people (say the combined populations of Colombia, Ecuador, Venezuela, Morocco, Pakistan, Thailand and the Philippines) who are increasing at a rate of 3.3 percent per year. Put differently, the doubling time for this aggregate population is twenty-one years, compared to eighty-seven years of the U.S.

MULTIPLYING THE RICH AND THE POOR

Now suppose the U.S. agreed to pool its resources with those seven countries, with everyone receiving an equal share. Initially the ratio of Americans to non-Americans in this model would be one-to-one. But consider what the ratio would be after eighty-seven years, by which time the Americans would have doubled to a population of 420 million. By then, doubling every twenty-one years, the other group would have swollen to 354 billion. Each American would have to share the available resources with more than eight people.

But, one could argue, this discussion assumes that current population trends will continue, and they may not. Quite so. Most likely the rate of population increase will decline much faster in the U.S. than it will in the other countries and there does not seem to be much we can do about it. In sharing with "each according to his needs," we must recognize that needs are determined by population size, which is determined by the rate of reproduction, which at present is regarded as a sovereign right of every nation, poor or not. This being so, the philanthropic load created by the sharing ethic of the spaceship can only increase.

THE TRAGEDY OF THE COMMONS

The fundamental error of spaceship ethics, and the sharing it requires, is that it leads to what I call "the tragedy of the commons." Under a system of private property, the men who own property recognize their responsibility to care for it, for if they don't they will eventually suffer. A farmer, for instance, will allow no more cattle in a pasture than its carrying capacity justifies. If he overloads it, erosion sets in, weeds take over, and he loses the use of the pasture.

If a pasture becomes a commons open to all, the right of each to use it may not be matched by a corresponding responsibility to protect it. Asking everyone to use it with discretion will hardly do, for the considerate herdsman who refrains from overloading the commons suffers more than a selfish one who says his needs are greater. If everyone would restrain himself, all would be well; but it takes only one less than everyone to ruin a system of voluntary restraint. In a crowded world of less than perfect human beings, mutual ruin is inevitable if there are no controls. This is the tragedy of the commons.

One of the major tasks of education today should be the creation of such an acute awareness of the dangers of the commons that people will recognize its many varieties. For example, the air and water have become polluted because they are treated as commons. Further growth in the population or per capita conversion of natural resources into pollutants will only make the problem worse. The same holds true for the fish of the oceans. Fishing fleets have nearly disappeared in many parts of the world, technological improvements in the art of fishing are hastening the day of complete ruin. Only the replacement of the system of the commons with a responsible system of control will save the land, air, water and oceanic fisheries.

THE WORLD FOOD BANK

In recent years there has been a push to create a new commons called a World Food Bank, an international depository of food reserves to which nations would contribute according to their abilities and from which they would draw according to their needs. This humanitarian proposal has received support from many liberal international groups, and from such prominent citizens as Margaret Mead, U.N. Secretary General Kurt Waldheim, and senators Edward Kennedy and George McGovern.

A world food bank appeals powerfully to our humanitarian impulses. But before we rush ahead with such a plan, let us recognize where the greatest political push comes from, lest we be disillusioned later. Our experience with the "Food for Peace program," or Public Law 480, gives us the answer. This program moved billions of dollars worth of U.S. surplus grain to food-short, population-long countries during the past two decades. But when P.L. 480 first became law, a headline in the business magazine *Forbes* revealed the real power behind it: "Feeding the World's Hungry Millions: How It Will Mean Billions for U.S. Business."

And indeed it did. In the years 1960 to 1970, U.S. taxpayers spent a total of $7.9 billion on the Food for Peace program. Between 1948 and 1970, they also paid an additional $50 billion for other economic-aid programs, some of which went for food and food-producing machinery and technology. Though all U.S. taxpayers were forced to contribute to the cost of P.L. 480, certain special interest groups gained handsomely under the program. Farmers did not have to contribute the grain; the Government, or rather the taxpayers, bought it from them at full market prices. The increased demand raised prices of farm products generally. The manufacturers of farm machinery, fertilizers and pesticides benefited by the farmers' extra efforts to grow more food. Grain elevators profited from storing the surplus until it could be shipped. Railroads made money hauling it to ports, and shipping lines profited from carrying it overseas. The implementation of P.L. 480 required the creation of a vast Government bureaucracy, which then acquired its own vested interest in continuing the program regardless of its merits.

EXTRACTING DOLLARS

Those who proposed and defended the Food for Peace program in public rarely mentioned its importance to any of these special interests. The public emphasis was always on its humanitarian effects. The combination of silent selfish interests and highly humanitarian apologists made a powerful and successful lobby for extracting money from taxpayers. We can expect the same lobby to push now for the creation of a World Food Bank.

However great the potential benefit to selfish interests, it should not be a decisive argument against a truly humanitarian program. We must ask if such a program would actually do more good than harm, not only momentarily but also in the long run. Those who propose the food bank usually refer to a current "emergency" or "crisis" in terms of world food supply. But what is an emergency? Although they may be infrequent and sudden, everyone knows that emergencies will occur from time to time. A well-run family, company, organization or country prepares for the likelihood of accidents and emergencies. It expects them, it budgets for them, it saves for them.

LEARNING THE HARD WAY

What happens if some organizations or countries budget for accidents and others do not? If each country is solely responsible for its own well-being, poorly managed ones will suffer. But they can learn from experience. They may mend their ways, and learn to budget for infrequent but certain emergencies. For example, the weather varies from year to year, and periodic crop failures are certain. A wise and competent government saves out of the production of the good years in anticipation of bad years to come. Joseph taught this policy to Pharaoh in Egypt more than 2,000 years ago. Yet the great majority of the governments in the world today do not follow such a policy. They lack either the wisdom or the competence, or both. Should those nations that do manage to put something aside be forced to come to the rescue each time an emergency occurs among the poor nations?

"But it isn't their fault!" some kindhearted liberals argue. "How can we blame the poor people who are caught in an emergency? Why must they suffer for the sins of their governments?" The concept of blame is simply not relevant here. The real question is, what are the operational consequences of establishing a world food bank? If it is open to every country every time a need develops, slovenly rulers will not be motivated to take Joseph's advice. Someone will always come to their aid. Some countries will deposit food in the world food bank, and others will withdraw it. There will be almost no overlap. As a result of such solutions to food shortage emergencies, the poor countries will not learn to mend their ways, and will suffer progressively greater emergencies as their populations grow.

POPULATION CONTROL THE CRUDE WAY

On the average, poor countries undergo a 2.5 percent increase in population each year; rich countries, about 0.8 percent. Only rich countries have anything in the way of food reserves set aside, and even they do not have as much as they should. Poor countries have none. If poor countries received no food from the outside, the rate of their population growth would be periodically checked by crop failures and famines. But if they can always draw on a world food bank in time of need, their population can continue to grow unchecked, and so will their "need" for aid. In the short run, a world food bank may diminish that need, but in the long run it actually increases the need without limit.

Without some system of worldwide food sharing, the proportion of people in the rich and poor nations might eventually stabilize. The overpopulated poor countries would decrease in numbers, while the rich countries that had room for more people would increase. But with a well-meaning system of sharing, such as a world food bank, the growth differential between the rich and the poor countries will not only persist, it will increase. Because of the higher rate of population growth in the poor countries of the world, 88 percent of today's children are born poor, and only 12 percent rich. Year by year the ratio becomes worse, as the fast-reproducing poor outnumber the slow-reproducing rich.

A world food bank is thus a commons in disguise. People will have more motivation to draw from it than to add to any common store. The less provident and less able will multiply at the expense of the abler and more provident, bringing eventual ruin upon all who share in the commons. Besides, any system of "sharing" that amounts to foreign aid from the rich nations to the poor nations will carry the taint of charity, which will contribute little to the world peace so devoutly desired by those who support the idea of a world food bank.

As past U.S. foreign-aid programs have amply and depressingly demonstrated, international charity frequently inspires mistrust and antagonism rather than gratitude on the part of the recipient nation.

CHINESE FISH AND MIRACLE RICE

The modern approach to foreign aid stresses the export of technology and advice, rather than money and food. As an ancient Chinese proverb goes: "Give a man a fish and he will eat for a day; teach him how to fish and he will eat for the rest of his days." Acting on this advice, the Rockefeller and Ford Foundations have financed a number of programs for improving agriculture in the hungry nations. Known as the "Green Revolution," these programs have led to the development of "miracle rice" and "miracle wheat," new strains that offer bigger harvests and greater resistance to crop damage. Norman Borlaug, the Nobel Prize winning agronomist who, supported by the Rockefeller Foundation, developed "miracle wheat," is one of the most prominent advocates of a world food bank.

Whether or not the Green Revolution can increase food production as much as its champions claim is a debatable but possibly irrelevant point. Those who support this well-intended humanitarian effort should first consider some of the fundamentals of human ecology. Ironically, one man who did was the late Alan Gregg, a vice president of the Rockfeller Foundation. Two decades ago he expressed strong doubts about the wisdom of such attempts to increase food production. He likened the growth and spread of humanity over the surface of the earth to the spread of cancer in the human body, remarking that "cancerous growths demand food; but, as far as I know, they have never been cured by getting it."

OVERLOADING THE ENVIRONMENT

Every human born constitutes a draft on all aspects of the environment: food, air, water, forests, beaches, wildlife, scenery and solitude. Food can, perhaps, be significantly increased to meet a growing demand. But what about clean beaches, unspoiled forests, and solitude? If we satisfy a growing population's need for food, we necessarily decrease its per capita supply of the other resources needed by men.

India, for example, now has a population of 600 million, which increases by 15 million each year. This population already puts a huge load on a relatively impoverished environment. The country's forests are now only a small fraction of what they were three centuries ago, and floods and erosion continually destroy the insufficient farmland that remains. Every one of the 15 million new lives added to India's population puts an additional burden on the environment, and increases the economic and social costs of crowding. However humanitarian our intent, every Indian life saved through medical or nutritional assistance from abroad diminishes the quality of life for those who remain, and for subsequent generations. If rich countries make it possible, through foreign aid, for 600 million Indians to swell to 1.2 billion in a mere twenty-eight years, as their current growth rate threatens, will future generations of Indians thank us for hastening the destruction of their environment? Will our good intentions be sufficient excuse for the consequences of our actions?

My final example of a commons in action is one for which the public has the least desire for rational discussion—immigration. Anyone who publicly questions the wisdom of current U.S. immigration policy is promptly charged with bigotry, prejudice, ethnocentrism, chauvinism, isolationism or selfishness. Rather than encounter such accusations, one would rather talk about other matters, leaving immigration policy to wallow in the crosscurrents of special interests that take no account of the good of the whole, or the interests of posterity.

Perhaps we still feel guilty about things we said in the past. Two generations ago the popular press frequently referred to Dagos, Wops, Polacks, Chinks and Krauts, in articles about how America was being "overrun" by foreigners of supposedly inferior genetic stock. But because the implied inferiority of foreigners was used then as justification for keeping them out, people now assume that restrictive policies could only be based on such misguided notions. There are other grounds.

A NATION OF IMMIGRANTS

Just consider the numbers involved. Our Government acknowledges a net inflow of 400,000 immigrants a year. While we have no hard data on the extent of illegal entries, educated guesses put the figure at about 600,000 a year. Since the natural increase (excess of births over deaths) of the resident population now runs about 1.7 million per year, the yearly gain from immigration amounts to at least 19 percent of the total annual increase, and may be as much as 37 percent if we include the estimate for illegal immigrants. Considering the growing use of birth control devices, the potential effect of educational campaigns by such organizations as Planned Parenthood Federation of America and Zero Population Growth, and the influence of inflation and the housing shortage, the fertility rate of American women may decline so much that immigration could account for all the yearly increase in population. Should we not at least ask if that is what we want?

For the sake of those who worry about whether the "quality" of the average immigrant compares favorably with the quality of the average resident, let us assume that immigrants and nativeborn citizens are of exactly equal quality, however one defines that term. We will focus here only on quantity; and since our conclusions will depend on nothing else, all charges of bigotry and chauvinism become irrelevant.

IMMIGRATION VS. FOOD SUPPLY

World food banks *move food to the people,* hastening the exhaustion of the environment of the poor countries. Unrestricted immigration, on the other hand, *moves people to the food,* thus speeding up the destruction of the environment of the rich countries. We can easily understand why poor people should want to make this latter transfer, but why should rich hosts encourage it?

As in the case of foreign-aid programs, immigration receives support from selfish interests and humanitarian impulses. The primary selfish interest in unimpeded immigration is the desire of employers for cheap labor, particularly in industries and trades that offer degrading work. In the past, one wave of foreigners after another was brought into the U.S. to work at wretched jobs for wretched wages. In recent years the Cubans,

Puerto Ricans and Mexicans have had this dubious honor. The interests of the employers of cheap labor mesh well with the guilty silence of the country's liberal intelligentsia. White Anglo-Saxon Protestants are particularly reluctant to call for a closing of the doors to immigration for fear of being called bigots.

But not all countries have such reluctant leadership. Most educated Hawaiians, for example, are keenly aware of the limits of their environment, particularly in terms of population growth. There is only so much room on the islands, and the islanders know it. To Hawaiians, immigrants from the other forty-nine states present as great a threat as those from other nations. At a recent meeting of Hawaiian government officials in Honolulu, I had the ironic delight of hearing a speaker, who like most of his audience was of Japanese ancestry, ask how the country might practically and constitutionally close its doors to further immigration. One member of the audience countered: "How can we shut the doors now? We have many friends and relatives in Japan we'd like to bring here some day so that they can enjoy Hawaii too." The Japanese-American speaker smiled sympathetically and answered; "Yes, but we have children now, and someday we'll have grandchildren too. We can bring people here from Japan only by giving away some of the land that we hope to pass on to our grandchildren some day. What right do we have to do that?"

At this point, I can hear U.S. liberals asking: "How can you justify slamming the door once you're inside? You say that immigrants should be kept out. But aren't we all immigrants, or the descendants of immigrants? If we insist on staying, must we not admit all others?" Our craving for intellectual order leads us to seek and prefer symmetrical rules and morals: a single rule for me and everybody else; the same rule yesterday, today, and tomorrow. Justice, we feel, should not change with time and place.

We Americans of non-Indian ancestry can look upon ourselves as the descendants of thieves who are guilty morally, if not legally, of stealing this land from its Indian owners. Should we then give back the land to the now living American descendants of those Indians? However morally or logically sound this proposal may be, I, for one, am unwilling to live by it and I know no one else who is. Besides, the logical consequence would be absurd. Suppose that, intoxicated with a sense of pure justice, we should decide to turn our land over to the Indians. Since all our wealth has also been derived from the land, wouldn't we be morally obliged to give that back to the Indians too?

PURE JUSTICE VS. REALITY

Clearly, the concept of pure justice produces an infinite regression to absurdity. Centuries ago, wise men invented statutes of limitations to justify the rejection of such pure justice, in the interest of preventing continual disorder. The law zealously defends property rights, but only relatively recent property rights. Drawing a line after an arbitrary time has elapsed may be unjust, but the alternatives are worse.

We are all the descendants of thieves, and the world's resources are inequitably distributed. But we must begin the journey to tomorrow from the point where we are today. We cannot remake the past. We cannot safely divide the wealth equitably among all peoples so long as people reproduce at different rates. To do so would guarantee that our grandchildren, and everyone else's grandchildren, would have only a ruined world to inhabit.

To be generous with one's own possessions is quite different from being generous with those of posterity. We should call this point to the attention of those who, from a commendable love of justice and equality, would institute a system of the commons, either in the form of a world food bank, or of unrestricted immigration. We must convince them if we wish to save at least some parts of the world from environmental ruin.

Without a true world government to control reproduction and the use of available resources, the sharing ethic of the spaceship is impossible. For the foreseeable future, our survival demands that we govern our actions by the ethics of a lifeboat, harsh though they may be. Posterity will be satisfied with nothing less.

STUDY QUESTIONS

1. Does Hardin's lifeboat analogy break down?
2. What is the tragedy of the commons?
3. What are Hardin's reasons for restricting immigration? Do you agree?

31

Helping and Hating the Homeless

Peter Marin

Peter Marin is a contributing editor at *Harper's*.

The trouble begins with the word "homeless." It has become such an abstraction, and is applied to so many different kinds of people, with so many different histories and problems, that it is almost meaningless.

Homelessness, in itself, is nothing more than a condition visited upon men and women (and, increasingly, children) as the final stage of a variety of problems about which the word "homelessness" tells us almost nothing. Or, to put it another way, it is a catch basin into which pour all of the people disenfranchised or marginalized or scared off by processes beyond their control, those which lie close to the heart of American life. Here are the groups packed into the single category of "the homeless":

- Veterans, mainly from the war in Vietnam. In many American cities, vets make up close to 50 percent of all homeless males.
- The mentally ill. In some parts of the country, roughly a quarter of the homeless would, a couple of decades ago, have been institutionalized.
- The physically disabled or chronically ill, who do not receive any benefits or whose benefits do not enable them to afford permanent shelter.
- The elderly on fixed incomes whose funds are no longer sufficient for their needs.
- Men, women, and whole families pauperized by the loss of a job.
- Single parents, usually women, without the resources or skills to establish new lives.
- Runaway children, many of whom have been abused.
- Alcoholics and those in trouble with drugs (whose troubles often begin with one of the other conditions listed here).
- Immigrants, both legal and illegal, who often are not counted among the homeless because they constitute a "problem" in their own right.
- Traditional tramps, hobos, and transients, who have taken to the road or the streets for a variety of reasons and who prefer to be there.

You can quickly learn two things about the homeless from this list. First, you can learn that many of the homeless, before they were homeless, were people more or less like ourselves: members of the working or middle class. And you can learn that the world of the homeless has its roots in various policies, events, and ways of life for which some of us are responsible and from which some of us actually prosper.

We decide, as a people, to go to war, we ask our children to kill and to die, and the result, years later, is grown men homeless on the street.

We change, with the best intentions, the laws pertaining to the mentally ill and then, without intention, neglect to provide them with services; and the result, in our streets, drives some of us crazy with rage.

We cut taxes and prune budgets, we modernize industry and shift the balance of trade, and the result of all these actions and errors can be read, sleeping form by sleeping form, on our city streets.

The liberals cannot blame the conservatives. The conservatives cannot blame the liberals. Homelessness is the *sum total* of our dreams, policies, intentions, errors, omissions, cruelties, kindnesses, all of it recorded, in flesh, in the life of the streets.

You can also learn from this list one of the most important things there is to know about the homeless—that they can be roughly divided into two groups: those who have had homelessness forced upon them and want nothing more than to escape it; and those who have at least in part *chosen* it for themselves, and now accept, or in some cases, embrace it.

I understand how dangerous it is to introduce the idea of choice into a discussion of homelessness. It can all too easily be used to justify indifference or brutality toward the homeless, or to argue that they are only getting what they "deserve." And yet it seems to me that it is only by taking choice into account, in all of the intricacies of its various forms and expressions, that one can really understand certain kinds of homelessness.

The fact is, many of the homeless are not only hapless victims but voluntary exiles, "domestic refugees," people who have turned not against life itself but against *us,* our life, American life. Look for a moment at the vets. The price of returning to America was to forget what they had seen or learned in Vietnam, to "put it behind them." But some could not do that, and the stress of trying showed up as alcoholism, broken marriages, drug addiction, crime. And it showed up too as life on the street, which was for some vets a desperate choice made in the name of life—the best they could manage. It was a way of avoiding what might have occurred had they stayed where they were: suicide, or violence done to others.

We must learn to accept that there may indeed be people, and not only vets, who have seen so much of our world, or seen it so clearly, that to live in it becomes impossible. Here, for example, is the story of Alice, a homeless middle-aged woman in Los Angeles, where there are, perhaps, 50,000 homeless people. It was set down a few months ago by one of my students at the University of California, Santa Barbara, where I taught for a semester. I had encouraged them to go find the homeless and listen to their stories. And so, one day, when this student saw Alice foraging in a dumpster outside a McDonald's, he stopped and talked to her:

> She told me she had led a pretty normal life as she grew up and eventually went to college. From there she went on to Chicago to teach school. She was single and lived in a small apartment.
>
> One night, after she got off the train after school, a man began to follow her to her apartment building. When she got to her door she saw a knife and the man hovering behind her. She had no choice but to let him in. The man raped her.
>
> After that, things got steadily worse. She had a nervous breakdown. She went to a mental institution for three months, and when she went back to her apartment she found her belongings gone. The landlord had sold them to cover the rent she hadn't paid.
>
> She had no place to go and no job because the school had terminated her employment. She slipped into depression. She lived with friends until she could muster enough money for a ticket to Los Angeles. She said she no longer wanted to burden her friends, and that if she had to live outside, at least Los Angeles was warmer than Chicago.
>
> It is as if she began back then to take on the mentality of a street person. She resolved herself to homelessness. She's been out West since 1980, without a home or job. She seems happy, with her best friend being her cat. But the scars of memories still haunt her, and she is running from them, or should I say *him.*

This is, in essence, the same story one hears over and over again on the street. You begin with an ordinary life; then an event occurs—traumatic, catastrophic; smaller events follow, each one deepening the original wound; finally, homelessness becomes inevitable, or begins to *seem* inevitable to the person involved—the only way out of an intolerable situation. You are struck continually, hearing these stories, by something seemingly unique in American life, the absolute isolation involved. In what other culture would there be such an absence or failure of support from familial, social, or institutional sources? Even more disturbing is the fact that it is often our supposed sources of support—family, friends, government organizations—that have caused the problem in the first place.

Everything that happened to Alice—the rape, the loss of job and apartment, the breakdown—was part and parcel of a world gone radically wrong, a world, for Alice, no longer to be counted on, no longer worth living in. Her homelessness can be seen as flight, as failure of will or nerve, even, perhaps, as *disease*. But it can also be seen as a mute, furious refusal, a self-imposed exile far less appealing to the rest of us than ordinary life, but *better,* in Alice's terms.

We like to think, in America, that everything is redeemable, that everything broken can be magically made whole again, and that what has been "dirtied" can be cleansed. Recently I saw on television that one of the soaps had introduced the character of a homeless old woman. A woman in her thirties discovers that her long-lost mother has appeared in town, on the streets. After much searching the mother is located and identified and embraced; and then she is scrubbed and dressed in style, restored in a matter of days to her former upper-class habits and role.

A triumph—but one more likely to occur on television than in real life. Yes, many of those on the streets could be transformed, rehabilitated. But there are others whose lives have been irrevocably changed, damaged beyond repair, and who no longer want help, who no longer recognize the *need* for help, and whose experience in our world has made them want only to be left alone. How, for instance, would one restore Alice's life, or reshape it in a way that would satisfy *our* notion of what a life should be? What would it take to return her to the fold? How to erase the four years of homelessness, which have become as familiar to her, and as much a home, as her "normal" life once was? Whatever we think of the way in which she has resolved her difficulties, it constitutes a sad peace made with the world. Intruding ourselves upon it in the name of redemption is by no means as simple a task—or as justifiable a task—as one might think.

It is important to understand too that however disorderly and dirty and unmanageable the world of homeless men and women like Alice appears to us, it is not without its significance, and its rules and rituals. The homeless in our cities mark out for themselves particular neighborhoods, blocks, buildings, doorways. They impose on themselves often obsessively strict routines. They reduce their world to a small area, and thereby protect themselves from a world that might otherwise be too much to bear.

Pavlov, the Russian psychologist, once theorized that the two most fundamental reflexes in all animals, including humans, are those involving freedom and orientation. Grab any animal, he said, and it will immediately struggle to accomplish two things: to break free and to orient itself. And this is what one sees in so many of the homeless. Having been stripped of all other forms of connection, and of most kinds of social identity, they are left only with this: the raw stuff of nature, something encoded in the cells—the desire to be free, the need for familiar space. Perhaps this is why so many of them struggle so vehemently against us when we offer them aid. They are clinging to their freedom and their space, and they do not believe that this is what we, with our programs and our shelters, mean to allow them. . . .

It is important to . . . recognize the immensity of the changes that have occurred in the marginal world in the past twenty years. Whole sections of many cities—the Bowery in New York, the Tenderloin in San Francisco—were once ceded to the transient. In every skid-row area in America you could find what you needed to survive: hash houses, saloons offering free lunches, pawnshops, surplus-clothing stores, and, most important of all, cheap hotels and flophouses and two-bit employment agencies specializing in the kinds of labor (seasonal, shape-up) transients have always done.

It was by no means a wonderful world. But it *was* a world. Its rituals were spelled out in ways most of the participants understood. In hobo jungles up and down the tracks, whatever there was to eat went into a common pot and was divided equally. Late at night, in empties criss-crossing the country, men would speak with a certain anonymous openness, as if the shared condition of transience created among them a kind of civility.

What most people in that world wanted was simply to be left alone. Some of them had been on the road for years, itinerant workers. Others were recuperating from wounds they could never quite explain. There were young men and a few women with nothing better to do, and older men who had no families or had lost their jobs or wives, or for whom the rigor and pressure of life had proved too demanding. The marginal world offered them a respite from the other world, a world grown too much for them.

But things have changed. There began to pour into the marginal world—slowly in the sixties, a bit faster in the seventies, and then faster still in the eighties—more and more people who neither belonged nor knew how to survive there. The sixties brought the counterculture and drugs; the streets filled with young dropouts. Changes in the law loosed upon the streets mentally ill men and women. Inflation took its toll, then recession. Working-class and even middle-class men and women—entire families—began to fall into a world they did not understand.

At the same time the transient world was being inundated by new inhabitants, its landscape, its economy, was shrinking radically. Jobs became harder to find. Modernization had something to do with it; machines took the place of men and women. And the influx of workers from Mexico and points farther south created a class of semi-permanent workers who took the place of casual transient labor. More important, perhaps, was the fact that the forgotten parts of many cities began to attract attention. Downtown areas were redeveloped, reclaimed. The skid-row sections of smaller cities were turned into "old townes." The old hotels that once catered to transients were upgraded or torn down or became warehouses for welfare families—an arrangement far more profitable to the owners. The price of housing increased; evictions increased. The mentally ill, who once could afford to house themselves in cheap rooms, the alcoholics, who once would drink themselves to sleep at night in their cheap hotels, were out on the street—exposed to the weather and to danger, and also in plain and public view: "problems" to be dealt with.

Nor was it only cheap shelter that disappeared. It was also those "open" spaces that had once been available to those without other shelter. As property rose in value, the nooks and crannies in which the homeless had been able to hide became more visible. Doorways, alleys, abandoned buildings, vacant lots—these "holes" in the cityscape, these gaps in public consciousness, became *real estate.* The homeless, who had been there all the time, were overtaken by economic progress, and they became intruders.

You cannot help thinking, as you watch this process, of what happened in parts of Europe in the eighteenth and nineteenth centuries: the effects of the enclosure laws, which eliminated the "commons" in the countryside and drove the rural poor, now homeless, into the cities. The centuries-old tradition of common access and usage was swept away by the beginning of industrialism; land became *privatized* as a commodity. At the same time something occurred in the cultural psyche. The world itself, space itself, was subtly altered. It was no longer merely to be lived in; it was now to be owned. What was enclosed was not only the land. It was also *the flesh itself;* it was cut off from, denied access to, the physical world.

And one thinks too, when thinking of the homeless, of the American past, the settlement of the "new" world which occurred at precisely the same time that the commons disappeared. The dream of freedom and equality that brought men and women here had something to do with *space,* as if the wilderness itself conferred upon those arriving here a new beginning: the Eden that had been lost. Once God had sent Christ to redeem men; now he provided a new world. Men discovered, or believed, that this world, and perhaps time itself, had no edge, no limit. Space was a sign of God's magnanimity. It was a kind of grace.

Somehow, it is all this that is folded into the sad shapes of the homeless. In their mute presence one can sense, however faintly, the dreams of a world gone aglimmering, and the presence of our failed hopes. A kind of claim is made, silently, an ethic is proffered, or, if you will, a whole cosmology, one older than our own ideas of privilege and property. It is as if flesh itself were seeking, this one last time, the home in the world it has been denied.

Daily the city eddies around the homeless. The crowds flowing past leave a few feet, a gap. We do not touch the homeless world. Perhaps we cannot touch it. It remains separate even as the city surrounds it.

The homeless, simply because they are homeless, are strangers, alien—and therefore a threat. Their presence, in itself, comes to constitute a kind of violence; it deprives us of our sense of safety. Let me use myself as an example. I know, and respect, many of those now homeless on the streets of Santa Barbara. Twenty years ago, some of them would have been my companions and friends. And yet, these days, if I walk through the park near my home and see strangers bedding down for the night, my first reaction, if not fear, is a sense of annoyance and intrusion, of worry and alarm. I think of my teenage daughter, who often walks through the park, and then of my house, a hundred yards away, and I am tempted—only tempted, but tempted, still—to call the "proper" authorities to have the strangers moved on. Out of sight, out of mind.

Notice: I do not bring them food. I do not offer them shelter or a shower in the morning. I do not even stop to talk. Instead, I think: my daughter, my house, my privacy. What moves me is not the threat of *danger*—nothing as animal as that. Instead there pops up inside of me, neatly in a row, a set of anxieties, ones you might arrange in a dollhouse living room and label: Family of bourgeois fears. The point is this: our response to the homeless is fed by a complex set of cultural attitudes, habits of thought, and fantasies and fears so familiar to us, so common, that they have become a *second* nature and might as well be instinctive, for all the control we have over them. And it is by no means easy to untangle this snarl of responses. What does seem clear is that the homeless embody all that bourgeois culture has for centuries tried to eradicate and destroy.

If you look to the history of Europe you find that homelessness first appears (or is first acknowledged) at the very same moment that bourgeois culture begins to appear. The same processes produced them both: the breakup of feudalism, the rise of commerce and cities, the combined triumphs of capitalism, industrialism, and individualism. The historian Fernand Braudel, in *The Wheels of Commerce,* describes, for instance, the armies of impoverished men and women who began to haunt Europe as far back as the eleventh century. And the makeup of these masses? Essentially the same then as it is now: the unfortunates, the throwaways, the misfits, the deviants. . . .

It is in the nineteenth century, in the Victorian era, that you can find the beginnings of our modern strategies for dealing with the homeless: the notion that they should be controlled and perhaps eliminated through "help." With the Victorians we begin to see the entangling of self-protection with social obligation, the strategy of masking self-interest and the urge to control as *moral duty.* Michel Foucault has spelled this out in his books on madness and punishment: the zeal with which the overseers of early bourgeois culture tried to purge, improve, and purify all of urban civilization—whether through schools and prisons, or, quite literally, with public baths and massive new water and sewage systems. Order, ordure—this is, in essence, the tension at the heart of bourgeois culture, and it was the singular genius of the Victorians to make it the main component of their medical, aesthetic, *and* moral systems. It was not a sense of justice or even empathy which called for charity or new attitudes toward the poor; it was *hygiene.* The very same attitudes appear in nineteenth-century America. Charles Loring Brace, in an essay on homeless and vagrant children written in 1876, described the treatment of delinquents in this way: "Many of their vices drop from them like the old and verminous clothing they left behind. . . . The entire change of circumstances seems to cleanse them of bad habits." Here you have it all: *vices, verminous clothing, cleansing them of bad habits*—the triple association of poverty with vice with dirt, an equation in which each term comes to stand for all of them.

These attitudes are with us still; that is the point. In our own century the person who has written most revealingly about such things is George Orwell, who tried to analyze his own middle-class attitudes toward the poor. . . .

To put it as bluntly as I can, for many of us the homeless are *shit.* And our policies toward them, our spontaneous sense of disgust and horror, our wish to be rid of them—all of this has hidden in it, close to its heart, our feelings about excrement. Even Marx, that most bourgeois of revolutionaries, described the deviant *lumpen* in *The Eighteenth Brumaire of Louis Bonaparte* as "scum, offal, refuse of all classes." These days, in puritanical Marxist nations, they are called "parasites"—a word, perhaps not incidentally, one always associates with human waste.

What I am getting at here is the *nature* of the desire to help the homeless—what is hidden behind it and why it so often does harm. Every government program, almost every private project, is geared as much to the needs of those giving help as it is to the needs of the homeless. Go to any government agency, or, for that matter, to most private charities, and you will find yourself enmeshed, at once, in a bureaucracy so tangled and oppressive, and confronted with so much moral arrogance and contempt, that you will be driven back out into the streets for relief.

Santa Barbara, where I live, is as good an example as any. There are three main shelters in the city—all of them private. Between them they provide fewer than a hundred beds a night for the homeless. Two of the three shelters are religious in nature: the Rescue Mission and the Salvation Army. In the mission, as in many places in the country, there are elaborate and stringent rules. Beds go first to those who have not been there for two months, and you can stay for only two nights in any two-month period. No shelter is given to those who are not sober. Even if you go to the mission only for a meal, you are required to listen to sermons and participate in prayer, and you are regularly proselytized—sometimes overtly, sometimes subtly. There are obligatory, regimented showers. You go to bed precisely at ten: lights out, no reading, no talking. After the lights go out you will find fifteen men in a room with double-decker bunks. As the night progresses the room grows stuffier and hotter. Men toss, turn, cough, and moan. In the morning you are awakened precisely at five forty-five. Then breakfast. At seven-thirty you are back on the street.

The town's newest shelter was opened almost a year ago by a consortium of local churches. Families and those who are employed have first call on the beds—a policy which excludes the congenitally homeless. Alcohol is not simply forbidden *in* the shelter; those with a history of alcoholism must sign a "contract" pledging to remain sober and chemical-free. Finally, in a paroxysm of therapeutic bullying, the shelter has added a new wrinkle: if you stay more than two days you are required to fill out and then discuss with a social worker a complex form listing what you perceive as your personal failings, goals, and strategies—all of this for men and women who simply want a place to lie down out of the rain!

It is these attitudes, in various forms and permutations, that you find repeated endlessly in America. We are moved either to "redeem" the homeless or to punish them. Perhaps there is nothing consciously hostile about it. Perhaps it is simply that as the machinery of bureaucracy cranks itself up to deal with these problems, attitudes assert themselves automatically. But whatever the case, the fact remains that almost every one of our strategies for helping the homeless is simply an attempt to rearrange the world *cosmetically,* in terms of how it looks and smells to *us*. Compassion is little more than the passion for control.

The central question emerging from all this is, What does a society owe to its members in trouble, and *how* is that debt to be paid? It is a question which must be answered in two parts: first, in relation to the men and women who have been marginalized against their will, and then, in a slightly different way, in relation to those who have chosen (or accept or even prize) their marginality.

As for those who have been marginalized against their wills, I think the general answer is obvious: A society owes its members whatever it takes for them to regain their places in the social order. And when it comes to specific remedies, one need only read backward the various processes which have created homelessness and then figure out where help is likely to do the most good. But the real point here is not the specific remedies required—affordable housing, say—but the basis upon which they must be offered, the necessary underlying ethical notion we seem in this nation unable to grasp that those who are the inevitable casualties of modern industrial capitalism and the free-market system are entitled, *by right,* and by the simple virtue of their participation in that system, to whatever help they need. They are entitled to help to find and hold their places in the society whose social contract they have, in effect, signed and observed.

Look at that for just a moment: the notion of a contract. The majority of homeless Americans have kept, insofar as they could, to the terms of that contract. In any shelter these days you can find men and women who have worked ten, twenty, forty years, and whose lives have nonetheless come to nothing. These are people who cannot afford a place in the world they helped create. And in return? Is it life on the street they have earned? Or the cruel charity we so grudgingly grant them?

But those marginalized against their will are only half the problem. There remains, still, the question of whether we owe anything to those who are voluntarily marginal. What about them: the street people, the rebels, and the recalcitrants, those who have torn up their social contracts or returned them unsigned?

I was in Las Vegas last fall, and I went out to the Rescue Mission at the lower end of town, on the edge of the black ghetto, where I first stayed years ago on my way west. It was twilight, still hot; in the vacant lot next door to the mission 200 men were lining up for supper. A warm wind blew along the street lined with small houses and salvage yards, and in the distance I could see the desert's edge and the smudge of low hills in the fading light. There were elderly alcoholics in line, and derelicts, but mainly the men were the same sort I had seen here years ago: youngish, out of work, restless and talkative, the drifters and wanderers for whom the word "wanderlust" was invented.

At supper—long communal tables, thin gruel, stale sweet rolls, ice water—a huge black man in his twenties, fierce and muscular, sat across from me. "I'm from the Coast, man," he said. "Never been away from home before. Ain't sure I like it. Sure don't like *this* place. But I lost my job back home a couple of weeks ago and figured, why wait around for another. I thought I'd come out here, see me something of the world."

After supper, a squat Portuguese man in his mid-thirties, hunkered down against the mission wall, offered me a smoke and told me: "Been sleeping in my car, up the street, for a week. Had my own business back in Omaha. But I got bored, man. Sold everything, got a little dough, came out here. Thought I'd work construction. Let me tell you, this is one tough town."

In a world better than ours, I suppose men (or women) like this might not exist. Conservatives seem to have no trouble imagining a society so well disciplined and moral that deviance of this kind would disappear. And leftists envision a world so just, so generous, that deviance would vanish along with inequity. But I suspect that there will always be some thing at work in some men and women to make them restless with the systems others devise for them, and to move them outward toward the edges of the world where life is always riskier, less organized, and easier going.

Do we owe anything to these men and women, who reject our company and what we offer and yet nonetheless seem to demand *something* from us?

We owe them, I think, at least a place to exist, a way to exist. That may not be a *moral* obligation, in the sense that our obligation to the involuntarily marginal is clearly a moral one, but it is an obligation nevertheless, one you might call an existential obligation.

Of course, it may be that I think we owe these men something because I have liked men like them, and because I want their world to be there always, as a place to hide or rest. But there is more to it than that. I think we as a society need men like these. A society needs its margins as much as it needs art and literature; it needs holes and gaps, *breathing space,* let us say, into which men and women can escape and live, when necessary, in ways otherwise denied them. Margins guarantee to society a flexibility, an elasticity, and allow it to accommodate itself to the natures and needs of its members. When margins vanish, society becomes too rigid, too oppressive by far, and therefore inimical to life.

It is for such reasons that, in cultures like our own, marginal men and women take on a special significance. They are all we have left to remind us of the narrowness of the received truths we take for granted. "Beyond the pale," they somehow redefine the pale, or remind us, at least, that *something* is still out there, beyond the pale. They preserve, perhaps unconsciously, a dream that would otherwise cease to exist, the dream of having a place in the world, and of being *left alone.*

Quixotic? Infantile? Perhaps. But remember Pavlov and his reflexes coded in the flesh: animal, and therefore as if given by God. What we are talking about here is *freedom,* and with it, perhaps, an echo of the dream men brought, long ago, to wilderness America. I use the word "freedom" gingerly, in relation to lives like these: skewed, crippled, emptied of everything we associate with a full, or realized, freedom. But perhaps this is the condition into which freedom has fallen among us. Art has been "appreciated" out of existence; literature has become an extension of the university, replete with tenure and pensions; and as for politics, the ideologies which ring us round seem too silly or shrill by far to speak for life. What is left, then, is this mute and intransigent independence, this "waste" of life which refuses even interpretation, and which cannot be assimilated to any ideology, and which therefore can be put to no one's use. In its crippled innocence and the perfection of its superfluity it amounts, almost, to a rebellion against history, and that is no small thing.

Let me put it as simply as I can: what we see on the streets of our cities are two dramas, both of which cut to the troubled heart of the culture and demand from us a response we may not be able to make. There is the drama of those struggling to survive by regaining their place in the social order. And there is the drama of those struggling to survive outside of it.

The resolution of both struggles depends on a third drama occurring at the heart of the culture: the tension and contention between the magnanimity we owe to life and the darker tendings of the human psyche: our fear of strangeness, our hatred of deviance, our love of order and control. How we mediate by default or design between those contrary forces will determine not only the destinies of the homeless but also something crucial about the nation, and perhaps—let me say it—about our own souls.

STUDY QUESTIONS

1. How has American society, according to Marin, failed the homeless?
2. How has the "marginal world" changed, and what are the factors that caused this change?
3. What is the "typical" attitude toward the homeless?
4. What reasons does the middle class have for helping the homeless?
5. What about those who "choose" homelessness, for whatever reason? Does society still have obligations to them?

32

The Racialization of Poverty

Margaret B. Wilkerson and Jewell Handy Gresham

Margaret B. Wilkerson and Jewell Handy Gresham have contributed to a special theme issue of *The Nation,* "Scapegoating the Black Family" (July 24, 1989), from which this selection is taken.

> *American policymakers have an uncanny ability to obfuscate and compartmentalize social problems—to recognize on the one hand that the United States has an unacceptably high level of unemployment, particularly among specific groups, and to recognize that we also have an incredibly high number of female-headed families, particularly within the same groups, but to avoid the cause-and-effect relationship between the two phenomena.*
>
> Ruth Sidel, *Women and Children Last*

The term "feminization of poverty," which was devised to describe the significant numbers of women and children living in poverty, is a distortion that negates the role played by racial barriers to black employment, particularly among males. The feminization of poverty is real, but the *racialization* of poverty is at its heart. To discuss one without the other is to play a mirror game with reality.

In *Women and Children Last: The Plight of Poor Women in Affluent America,* sociologist Ruth Sidel observes that in contemporary America, "welfare" has become a euphemism for Aid to Families with Dependent Children (A.F.D.C.). More, the term is now used to mask, barely, negative images of teeming black female fecundity—particularly among teen-agers—and of feckless black males who abandon their children. The fact that it is specifically black unwed mothers who evoke this atavistic response shows that race, not gender, is the source of revulsion.

Currently, the most critical problem relating to the plight of black unwed mothers is the massive unemployment of the males who would otherwise be potential mates for them. Sidel ties her discussion of black male unemployment to a survey of black versus white incomes. In 1981, for example, 47 percent of black college graduates earned $20,000 to $40,000 a year, the income spread for the majority of white *high school* graduates. This is only one of many facts evidencing the degree of discrimination against blacks in the workplace.

Although the number of black men holding professional, technical, managerial and sales jobs has increased significantly, the number who are unemployed is "astronomical," Sidel observed. "It is estimated that approximately 45 percent of black men do not have jobs, including not only those officially classified by the Census Bureau but also those who are counted as 'discouraged and no longer looking for work.'" In addition, she wrote,

> according to a statistician with the Children's Defense Fund, approximately 15–29 percent of black men aged twenty to forty *could not be found by the Bureau in 1980.* They are presumed to have neither permanent residences nor jobs. If they are added to the number of unemployed, the number of black men without jobs can be estimated to be well over 50 percent. [Emphasis added.]

This level of unemployment is more than double the figure for all workers at the height of the Great Depression. William Julius Wilson, author of *The Truly Disadvantaged,* states that in one of the Chicago ghetto neighborhoods he studied, the ratio of employed black males to their impoverished female counterparts was 18 to 100.

Such a "shockingly high rate of male unemployment," Sidel points out, "has had a direct bearing on the dramatic rise in black female-headed families." Yet we still look for "the 'causes' of the rise in black-female families, debate whether the welfare system encourages their proliferation, blame the mothers for having babies outside of marriage—but largely ignore the impact of male unemployment on family life."

One of the most pernicious aspects of the white patriarchal definition of an acceptable household (one headed by a male who is able to provide for his family) is that the masses of black youth and men who are excluded from the opportunities and rewards of the economic system cannot possibly meet this requirement. Then both males and females of the subjugated class are castigated as being morally unfit because they have not held their reproductive functions in abeyance.

At the same time, there is the insidious notion that households headed by black women are *destined* for poverty, not because of the absence of economic means but because of the absence of the male. (Unwed mothers who happen to be affluent are sometimes dubbed "bachelor mothers" to distinguish them from this group.) Feminists who omit race and racism as a possible decisive variable in any analysis of American poverty—and most particularly the poverty of black women—unwittingly contribute to this notion. When sociologist Diana Pearce coined the term "feminization of poverty" in 1978, she had in mind "two characteristics of women's poverty that distinguish it from the poverty experienced by men: children and labor market discrimination."

But in view of the astronomical levels of black males who are excluded from the labor market, the plight of black children must be examined in light of the circumstances of both their mothers and fathers, even though the mothers are usually left with the responsibility of caring for the children after the fathers depart under economic duress.

"ALL THEY'LL DO IS HAVE MORE CHILDREN"

In her recent book *Regulating the Lives of Women: Social Welfare Policy from Colonial Times to the Present,* Mimi Abramovitz provides a comprehensive account of the welfare policies of this society from their beginnings in 1935, when the Social Security Act legitimized the idea of social insurance. The immediate predecessor of the act was a pension to widows with young children, limited almost entirely to white women. In the 1930s, Aid to Dependent Children (A.D.C.) was born in the provisions for a "means-tested" public assistance program for the impoverished elderly, blind adults and poor children with absent fathers.

With the passage of this program, Abramovitz notes, the state took direct responsibility for reproduction in female-headed households under certain conditions, foremost among them that the mothers stay at home to rear their children. While that patriarchal model was set up for some women, however, an opening was left to insure that an ample supply of low-paid female domestic and casual labor reached the market through provisions denying aid to "undeserving" women.

By race, black women fell collectively into the category of "the undeserving." By class, so did large numbers of white women. Some states drew up, Abramovitz noted, "employable mother" rules that disqualified able-bodied women with school-age children, especially black women, on the ground that they should work. In the late 1930s, one Southern public assistance field supervisor reported the following:

> The number of Negro cases is few due to the unanimous feeling on the part of the staff and board that there are more work opportunities for Negro women and to their intense desire not to interfere with local labor conditions. The attitude that they have always gotten along, and that "all they'll do is have more children" is definite. . . . There is hesitancy on the part of lay boards to advance too rapidly over the thinking of their own communities, which see no reason why the employable Negro mother should not continue her usual sketchy seasonal labor or indefinite domestic service rather than receive a public assistance grant.

This commonplace form of discrimination is only one example of the vicissitudes of the marketplace to which black women and children, like black men, have historically been subjected.

The A.D.C. program, which grew from 372,000 families in 1940 to 803,000 in 1960, declined temporarily during World War II and the Korean War. In 1962, it became Aid to Families with Dependent Children. In the face of its rapid expansion and a shift in the composition of the caseload from white widows to unwed mothers and women of color, A.D.C. was attacked for faltering in the task of regulating the lives of poor women by excluding the undeserving. With the entry of significant numbers of black women into the program, the attacks upon it became widespread and systematically racist.

The black women who are caught in oppressive circumstances can articulate better than anyone else the flavor of their predicament. Abramovitz quotes Johnnie Tillmon, welfare mother and a leader of the National Welfare Rights Organization in the 1960s and 1970s, who calls the relationship between A.F.D.C. mothers and the system a "super-sexist marriage." Tillmon explains:

> You trade in "a" man for "The" man. But you can't divorce him if he treats you bad. He can divorce you of course, cut you off anytime he wants. But in that case "he" keeps the kids, not you. "The" man runs everything. In ordinary marriage, sex is supposed to be for your husband. On AFDC you're not supposed to have any sex at all. You give up control over your body. It's a condition of aid. . . . "The" man, the welfare system, controls your money. He tells you what to buy and what not to buy, where to buy it, and how much things cost. If things—rent, for instance—really cost more than he says they do, it's too bad for you.

Clearly, the impact of race, class and gender cannot be adequately examined by focusing on the status of women alone; it must also be viewed in the context of prescribed black and white women's roles in the labor marketplace vis-à-vis those of privileged males. It is interesting, for instance, to reflect on the significance of the polar extremes to which women, by race and class, are currently assigned. Felice Schwartz's article on "Management Women and the New Facts of Life," which caused such a furor when it appeared in the January–February issue of the *Harvard Business Review,* has little relevance to black women, whose presence in corporate management positions is negligible.

Schwartz recommended that a double-track system be set up to permit part-time work by women who wanted to spend time with their children (the so-called Mommy track) and full-time employment for "career primary" women who can be "worked like men." The corporate world's enthusiastic response to this proposal raises a question: Did it do so because the proposal offered desirable adjustments relating to the reproductive roles of women, or because it would lessen the economic competition coming from women of the corporate class and provide highly skilled female labor at a lower cost? Whatever the case, the issues affect only upper-class women, who can choose whether they work full- or part-time.

THE MOYNIHAN-ARMSTRONG "REFORM"

It is instructive to contrast Schwartz's plan with the welfare reform legislation enacted last fall for which New York Democratic Senator Daniel Patrick Moynihan and Republican Senator William Armstrong of Colorado took major public credit. Under this program, A.F.D.C. mothers, in keeping with Tillmon's description, will *not* be the ones making the decision as to whether they should remain at home with their children. Those who have children older than 3 *must* go forth as cheaply paid laborers unless they are under 19, in which case they are required to seek educational advancement, assuming the states chip in to fund such programs.

When one considers that a single Chicago housing project may hold as many as 20,000 largely jobless people packed into high-rise buildings of thirty or more stories, just how this program's proponents intend to insure adequate child care services for the poor mothers forced to leave their children is not clear, especially when day care facilities and personnel are unavailable even to large numbers of middle-class and upper-class mothers. And what means of transportation will these poor (and frequently inexperienced) mothers use when they pack themselves and their children off to baby-sitters? One wonders how many of the men who sit in the halls of Congress have ever played a parenting role in which they had the opportunity to engage in such tasks for even, let us say, one week.

For tens of thousands of the urban poor in housing projects, the length of time it takes for the elevators in their buildings merely to rise to their floors and descend again—assuming they work at all—can present a crisis. How far a mother and her child or children must travel after that—and by what means—before the youngsters can be deposited and mothers continue on their way may represent another; what arrangements can be made with the employer when the children are ill, yet another. What surcease will be available for the women themselves if they are ill, or harried, or weary beyond bearing? How can they summon up sufficient energy to help their school-age children with homework, assuming they have sufficient education to do so? And so on, endlessly.

Ponder just a fraction of the problems in populations in which babies, children, youth and adults die off at unconscionably high ratios from preventable or manageable diseases and conditions (and whose mothers, and fathers when they are present, must be particularly vigilant to guard their children against becoming casualties of the pervasive scourge of drugs, in psychologically and physically violent neighborhoods) and it becomes apparent why some "experts" and officials take refuge in abstract solutions, or none at all.

When one further reflects on where any jobs will come from, and—in the case of teen-age mothers ordered to finish high school—what miraculous educational services are contemplated, the picture for those deprived by race *and* class appears not brighter but potentially even more retrogressive.

In a chapter of her book entitled "Welfare," Sidel provides a picture of the intolerable treatment systematically accorded the nation's poor when applying for or receiving A.F.D.C. aid. In spite of the attempts of many caseworkers to preserve a sense of personal compassion, the weight of the system overwhelms them.

More than any other single factor, women on welfare report that the most damaging traumas they suffer are the humiliations daily meted out in welfare offices all over the country, which are designed to demean and punish them for being in need. Besides a barrage of examples drawn from

A.F.D.C. mothers, Sidel quotes from an analysis of the working class, *The Hidden Injuries of Class*, by Richard Sennett and Jonathan Cobb.

"Dignity is as compelling a human need as food or sex," these men wrote, "and yet here is a society which casts the mass of its people into limbo, never satisfying their hunger for dignity." In describing the "plight of blue-collar workers who feel shamed and demeaned by their position in American society," the authors point out that these workers survive by keeping

> a certain distance from the problems of class and class consciousness, by separating themselves from their feelings when they are interacting with the world the same way as the poor attempt to protect themselves from the not-so-hidden injuries of poverty. They try to deal with the welfare bureaucracies with resignation and deadened emotions. They leave "the real me" somewhere else when they must cope with the intrusive questions, the unspoken (and all-too-often spoken) criticisms, the disregard for their humanness.

White blue-collar workers humiliated in such fashion may be able, in general, to hide behind a blanket of public anonymity, but black welfare recipients are seldom permitted even this refuge. Sidel quotes a black social worker in Atlanta, who describes the county offices that administer A.F.D.C. as "little nations" and the client population as "very fearful":

> They will use all of their resources rather than go to welfare. They're not going to take that ugliness, that humiliation. . . . Georgia will not give welfare to a two-parent family. These people are treated so badly that they would rather sell dope and steal instead.

The director of Family and Children Services in DeKalb County, Georgia, reports a dramatic increase over the past years in requests for emergency aid arising out of the state's "trimming the rolls." County workers may give emergency aid only once to a family. "When asked what a family did if it had received emergency aid once and was in dire need again, one worker replied dryly, 'Pray a lot.' "

Sidel recounts numerous tales of fortitude among welfare recipients, such as that of the mother of two children who took two buses to get her children to her grandmother's every day so that she could attend a community college. When she completed her work and, with the help of scholarships, went on to a four-year school, she could not tell her caseworker—because A.F.D.C. did not support students in four-year programs, only two-year or vocational schools. In such blatant fashion is revealed A.F.D.C.'s policy of keeping the poor poor.

The role of racism in the system is the traditional one of making racial and class exploitation easier. Dangerous precedents that will be harmful to the welfare of major segments of the society can be established by first applying them only to blacks. One can gain some idea of how this works by examining the way the national political leadership treats the masses. An example is the targeting of black adolescents by top "centrist" echelons of the Democratic Party. On the one hand, teenage mothers are projected as carriers of a particular strain of pathology against which drastic measures must be taken. (Only recently, Moynihan ascribed malignancy to the black "matriarchy"!) Concomitantly, black male teen-agers are propelled to the forefront of black criminality, which must be destroyed. This may be the first time in history that a nation has singled out a specific race of youths against whom to direct its frustration and fury.

SAM NUNN'S "NATIONAL SERVICE" SOLUTION

Writing in *The New York Times* on May 30, 1987, Frances Fox Piven and Barbara Ehrenreich argued that the welfare reform act will accomplish little more than creating a new form of "mass peonage." Some idea of what is in store for youthful black males and females bound into a single package for manipulation may be glimpsed in the legislation currently sponsored in the Senate by Sam Nunn. The ill-conceived proposal would eliminate all forms of Federal educational grants for higher education to poor students and replace them with a "Citizenship and National Service Act," which is, in effect, a "workfare" program. For two years of labor, young people would receive a stipend of $10,000 annually at the conclusion of their "service." If they volunteered for the military, their reward would be $12,000 per year. Virtually the only way that most of the poor could get into college would be through this "national service."

In combination, the two programs—welfare and national service—would create bureaucratic machinery for manipulating black young people. It would channel a pool of cheap black female labor, composed of welfare mothers, into the work force and harness the energies of their male counterparts through the national service plan. Disproportionate numbers of young black males would be drawn to the military by the added stipend, and thereby rendered disproportionately vulnerable to wartime death. (America has always found it easier to propel its black youths toward death than to educate them.)

One might also ask whether the stipends will help many deprived young people to enter college. Not very much in the way of higher education can be purchased for $10,000 or $12,000, and the temptation would be great for black and white families of limited means to spend the money on a dozen needs having higher priority.

In the case of A.F.D.C. mothers, former Secretary of Labor Ray Marshall points out that 86 percent of all social welfare spending since the 1960s has gone to America's elderly, and only a small proportion to A.F.D.C. mothers or their offspring. The result has been that poverty among the elderly has declined almost by half, from more than 25 percent at the beginning of the War on Poverty to 14 percent in 1983. Just the opposite is true with regard to America's children, primarily blacks and others of color whose parents are poor. In a 1986 article in *Southern Changes* titled "The War Against the Poor," Robert Greenstein, director of the Washington-based Center on Budget and Policy Priorities, wrote:

> If you look at the statistics of American poverty today, one set—the figures for children's poverty—hits you over the head. Fifteen years ago the child poverty rate was between thirteen and fourteen percent. Last year it was over twenty-one percent. . . . And, while there has been a very slight recent reduction in the overall poverty rate during the past year, and in the overall child poverty rate, all the reduction in child poverty has occurred among white children. None of it has occurred among black or Hispanic children.
>
> The poverty rate for black children under the age of six now has reached just over fifty-one percent.

If one out of every two black children in this country is born poor, and the national leadership regards black adolescents as exemplars of pathology instead of promise, what must black Americans do? What must society do?

For one thing, we might begin by reviewing the attitudes of officials of the national government—of the Bush Administration and members of Congress of both political parties—toward the well-being of *all* members of the society. In particular, we should make certain that the political conditions are created and sustained that will encourage those who serve in positions of leadership to do so not by ignoring race, gender and class as determining variables affecting the lives of the people, but by developing infinitely more sophisticated means to address and redress what is wrong. And we, who are most directly affected by race, class and gender, should advance our own knowledge accordingly.

Even, for example, if we were concerned simply with the reproductive roles, functions and rights of women, it would still be necessary to develop a keener awareness of the interrelated roles of race, gender and class oppression—including the institutionalized white-male-over-black-male oppression, which in this patriarchal (not matriarchal) society underpins everything else.

Black women must address the enormous problems within the black community, including black male sexism and rage, particularly the violence and, yes, the pathology of anger and frustration that is taken out against them and other members of the community. But we cannot turn our attention to any condition besetting black people without consideration of the terrible toll of the white racism and sexism which undergird and perpetuate an oppressive system.

Barbara Ommolade, a single-mother college counselor, activist and writer who has been on welfare, neatly and eloquently summed up the picture in "It's a Family Affair: The Real Lives of Black Single Mothers" (*Village Voice,* July 15, 1986):

> Today, the context of the struggle to have a black family is legal desegregation and superficial political gains for black people, along with high unemployment among black men, depressed wages for black women, and public denigration of poor people. The concept of a pathological underclass has become the rationale for continued racism and economic injustice; in attempting to separate racial from economic inequality and [in] blaming family pathology for black people's condition, current ideology obscures the system's inability to provide jobs, decent wages, and adequate public services for the black poor. And in a racist-patriarchal society, the effects of the system's weaknesses fall most heavily on black women and children. Just as black family life has always been a barometer of racial and economic injustice and at the same time a means of transcending and surviving those injustices, black families headed by women reflect the strength and the difficulty of black life in the 80's.

Black women know the critical problems of our communities, but we also know their strengths. We have to call on those strengths collectively from blacks now, but we also call on more. It is the obligation of all concerned Americans to join forces in seeking to remove the stigma from government assistance to citizens in need. And to make certain that channels exist for people who are temporarily down to recover their footing, thankful that a nurturing society exists for them and conscious of their responsibility to be nurturing too.

STUDY QUESTIONS

1. What is the relationship between the high rate of black male unemployment and the number of single black mothers on welfare?
2. In what ways does the welfare system degrade and oppress black women?
3. How does the welfare system keep single mothers in poverty? Is this intentional? Does it matter?
4. How do the children caught in this cycle suffer? What would have to happen before they could be freed from this cycle?

FOR FURTHER STUDY

Amott, Teresa L., and Mattaei, Julie A. *Race, Gender, and Work: A Multicultural Economic History of Women in the United States*. Boston: South End Press, 1991.

Dreze, Jean, and Sen, Amartya. *Hunger and Public Action*. Oxford: Clarendon Press, 1989.

Goodin, Robert. *Protecting the Vulnerable: A Reanalysis of Our Social Responsibilities*. Chicago: University of Chicago Press, 1985.

Harvard School of Public Health. *Hunger in America: The Growing Epidemic*. Cambridge, Mass.: Harvard University Press, 1985.

Kozol, Jonathon. *Rachel and Her Children: Homeless Families in America*. New York: Fawcett, 1988.

Lappé, Frances Moore. *World Hunger: Twelve Myths*. New York: Grove Press, 1986.

O'Neill, Onora. "Ending World Hunger." In *Matters of Life and Death,* 3d edition, ed. Tom Regan. New York: McGraw-Hill, 1993.

Shue, Henry. *Basic Rights*. Princeton, N.J.: Princeton University Press, 1980.

Timberlake, Lloyd. *Africa in Crisis*. London: Earthscan Publications, 1988.

World Bank. *The Challenge of Hunger: A Call to Action*. Washington, D.C.: World Bank, 1988.

Chapter Seven

Ethics of Race and Power

33

Race Matters

Cornel West

Cornel West is a professor of religion and the director of Afro-American studies at Princeton University. He is the author of *The American Evasion of Philosophy* and *Race Matters*.

Since the beginning of the nation, white Americans have suffered from a deep inner uncertainty as to who they really are. One of the ways that has been used to simplify the answer has been to seize upon the presence of black Americans and use them as a marker, a symbol of limits, a metaphor for the "outsider." Many whites could look at the social position of blacks and feel that color formed an easy and reliable gauge for determining to what extent one was or was not American. Perhaps that is why one of the first epithets that many European immigrants learned when they got off the boat was the term "nigger"—it made them feel instantly American. But this is tricky magic. Despite his racial difference and social status, something indisputably American about Negroes not only raised doubts about the white man's value system but aroused the troubling suspicion that whatever else the true American is, he is also somehow black.

Ralph Ellison, "What America Would Be Like Without Blacks" (1970)

What happened in Los Angeles in April of 1992 was neither a race riot nor a class rebellion. Rather, this monumental upheaval was a multiracial, trans-class, and largely male display of justified social rage. For all its ugly, xenophobic resentment, its air of adolescent carnival, and its downright barbaric behavior, it signified the sense of powerlessness in American society. Glib attempts to reduce its meaning to the pathologies of the black underclass, the criminal actions of hoodlums, or the political revolt of the oppressed urban masses miss the mark. Of those arrested, only 36 percent were black, more than a third had full-time jobs, and most claimed to shun political affiliation. What we witnessed in Los Angeles was the consequence of a lethal linkage of economic decline, cultural decay, and political lethargy in American life. Race was the visible catalyst, not the underlying cause.

The meaning of the earthshaking events in Los Angeles is difficult to grasp because most of us remain trapped in the narrow framework of the dominant liberal and conservative views of race in America, which with its worn-out vocabulary leaves us intellectually debilitated, morally disempowered, and personally depressed. The astonishing disappearance of the event from public dialogue is testimony to just how painful and distressing a serious engagement with race is. Our truncated public discussions of race suppress the best of who and what we are as a people because they fail to confront the complexity of the issue in a candid and critical manner. The predictable pitting of liberals against conservatives, Great Society Democrats against self-help Republicans, reinforces intellectual parochialism and political paralysis.

The liberal notion that more government programs can solve racial problems is simplistic—precisely because it focuses *solely* on the economic dimension. And the conservative idea that what is needed is a change in the moral behavior of poor black urban dwellers (especially poor black men, who, they say, should stay married, support their children, and stop committing so much crime) highlights immoral actions while ignoring public responsibility for the immoral circumstances that haunt our fellow citizens.

The common denominator of these views of race is that each still sees black people as a "problem people," in the words of Dorothy I. Height, president of the National Council of Negro Women, rather than as fellow American citizens with problems. Her words echo the poignant "unasked question" of W. E. B. Du Bois, who, in *The Souls of Black Folk* (1903), wrote:

> They approach me in a half-hesitant sort of way, eye me curiously or compassionately, and then instead of saying directly, How does it feel to be a problem? they say, I know an excellent colored man in my town. . . . Do not these Southern outrages make your blood boil? At these I smile, or am interested, or reduce the boiling to a simmer, as the occasion may require. To the real question, How does it feel to be a problem? I answer seldom a word.

Nearly a century later, we confine discussions about race in America to the "problems" black people pose for whites rather than consider what this way of viewing black people reveals about us as a nation.

This paralyzing framework encourages liberals to relieve their guilty consciences by supporting public funds directed at "the problems"; but at the same time, reluctant to exercise principled criticism of black people, liberals deny them the freedom to err. Similarly, conservatives blame the "problems" on black people themselves—and thereby render black social misery invisible or unworthy of public attention.

Hence, for liberals, black people are to be "included" and "integrated" into "our" society and culture, while for conservatives they are to be "well behaved" and "worthy of acceptance" by "our" way of life. Both fail to see that the presence and predicaments of black people are neither additions to nor defections from American life, but rather *constitutive elements of that life*.

To engage in a serious discussion of race in America, we must begin not with the problems of black people but with the flaws of American society—flaws rooted in historic inequalities and longstanding cultural stereotypes. How we set up the terms for discussing racial issues shapes our perception and response to these issues. As long as black people are viewed as a "them," the burden falls on blacks to do all the "cultural" and "moral" work necessary for healthy race relations. The implication is that only certain Americans can define what it means to be American—and the rest must simply "fit in."

The emergence of strong black-nationalist sentiments among blacks, especially among young people, is a revolt against this sense of having to "fit in." The variety of black-nationalist ideologies, from the moderate views of Supreme Court Justice Clarence Thomas in his youth to those of Louis Farrakhan today, rest upon a fundamental truth: white America has been historically weak-willed in ensuring racial justice and has continued to resist fully accepting the humanity of blacks. As long as double standards and differential treatment abound—as long as the rap performer Ice-T is harshly condemned while former Los Angeles Police Chief Daryl F. Gates's antiblack comments are received in polite silence, as long as Dr. Leonard Jeffries's anti-Semitic statements are met with vitriolic outrage while presidential candidate Patrick J. Buchanan's anti-Semitism receives a genteel response—black nationalisms will thrive.

Afrocentrism, a contemporary species of black nationalism, is a gallant yet misguided attempt to define an African identity in a white society perceived to be hostile. It is gallant because it puts black doings and sufferings, not white anxieties and fears, at the center of discussion. It is misguided because—out of fear of cultural hybridization and through silence on the issue of class, retrograde views on black women, gay men, and lesbians, and a reluctance to link race to the common good—it reinforces the narrow discussions about race.

To establish a new framework, we need to begin with a frank acknowledgment of the basic humanness and Americanness of each of us. And we must acknowledge that as a people—*E Pluribus Unum*—we are on a slippery slope toward economic strife, social turmoil, and cultural chaos. If we go down, we go down together. The Los Angeles upheaval forced us to see not only that we are not connected in ways we would like to be but also, in a more profound sense, that this failure to connect binds us even more tightly together. The paradox of race in America is that our common destiny is more pronounced and imperiled precisely when our divisions are deeper. The Civil War and its legacy speak loudly here. And our divisions are growing deeper. Today, eighty-six percent of white suburban Americans live in neighborhoods that are less than 1 percent black, meaning that the prospects for the country depend largely on how its cities fare in the hands of a suburban electorate. There is no escape from our interracial interdependence, yet enforced racial hierarchy dooms us as a nation to collective paranoia and hysteria—the unmaking of any democratic order.

The verdict in the Rodney King case which sparked the incidents in Los Angeles was perceived to be wrong by the vast majority of Americans. But whites have often failed to acknowledge the widespread mistreatment of black people, especially black men, by law enforcement agencies, which helped ignite the spark. The verdict was merely the occasion for deep-seated rage to come to the surface. This rage is fed by the "silent" depression ravaging the country—in which real weekly wages of all American workers since 1973 have declined nearly 20 percent, while at the same time wealth has been upwardly distributed.

The exodus of stable industrial jobs from urban centers to cheaper labor markets here and abroad, housing policies that have created "chocolate cities and vanilla suburbs" (to use the popular musical artist George Clinton's memorable phrase), white fear of black crime, and the urban influx of poor Spanish-speaking and Asian immigrants—all have helped erode the tax base of American cities just as the federal government has cut its supports and programs. The result is unemployment, hunger, homelessness, and sickness for millions.

And a pervasive spiritual impoverishment grows. The collapse of meaning in life—the eclipse of hope and absence of love of self and others, the breakdown of family and neighborhood bonds—leads to the social deracination and cultural denudement of urban dwellers, especially children. We have created rootless, dangling people with little link to the supportive networks—family, friends, school—that sustain some sense of purpose in life. We have witnessed the collapse of the spiritual communities that in the past helped Americans face despair, disease, and death and that transmit through the generations dignity and decency, excellence and elegance.

The result is lives of what we might call "random nows," of fortuitous and fleeting moments preoccupied with "getting over"—with acquiring pleasure, property, and power by any means necessary. (This is not what Malcolm X meant by this famous phrase.) Post-modern culture is more and more a market culture dominated by gangster mentalities and self-destructive wantonness. This culture engulfs all of us—yet its impact on the disadvantaged is devastating, resulting in extreme violence in everyday life. Sexual violence against women and homicidal assaults by young black men on one another are only the most obvious signs of this empty quest for pleasure, property, and power.

Last, this rage is fueled by a political atmosphere in which images, not ideas, dominate, where politicians spend more time raising money than debating issues. The functions of parties have been displaced by public polls, and politicians behave less as thermostats that determine the climate of opinion than as thermometers registering the public mood. American polities has been rocked by an unleashing of greed among opportunistic public officials—who have followed the lead of their counterparts in the private sphere, where, as of 1989, 1 percent of the population owned 37 percent of the wealth and 10 percent of the population owned 86 percent of the wealth—leading to a profound cynicism and pessimism among the citizenry.

And given the way in which the Republican Party since 1968 has appealed to popular xenophobic images—playing the black, female, and homophobic cards to realign the electorate along race, sex, and sexual-orientation lines—it is no surprise that the notion that we are all part of one garment of destiny is discredited. Appeals to special interests rather than to public interests reinforce this polarization. The Los Angeles upheaval was an expression of utter fragmentation by a powerless citizenry that includes not just the poor but all of us.

What is to be done? How do we capture a new spirit and vision to meet the challenges of the post-industrial city, post-modern culture, and post-party politics?

First, we must admit that the most valuable sources for help, hope, and power consist of ourselves and our common history. As in the ages of Lincoln, Roosevelt, and King, we must look to new frameworks and languages to understand our multilayered crisis and overcome our deep malaise.

Second, we must focus our attention on the public square—the common good that undergirds our national and global destinies. The vitality of any public square ultimately depends on how much we *care* about the quality of our lives together. The neglect of our public infrastructure, for example—our water and sewage systems, bridges, tunnels, highways, subways, and streets—reflects not only our myopic economic policies, which impede productivity, but also the low priority we place on our common life.

The tragic plight of our children clearly reveals our deep disregard for public well-being. About one out of every five children in this country lives in poverty, including one out of every two black children and two out of every five Hispanic children. Most of our children—neglected by overburdened parents and bombarded by the market values of profit-hungry corporations—are ill-equipped to live lives of spiritual and cultural quality. Faced with these facts, how do we expect ever to constitute a vibrant society?

One essential step is some form of large-scale public intervention to ensure access to basic social goods—housing, food, health care, education, child care, and jobs. We must invigorate the common good with a mixture of government, business, and labor that does not follow any existing blueprint. After a period in which the private sphere has been sacralized and the public square gutted, the temptation is to make a fetish of the public square. We need to resist such dogmatic swings.

Last, the major challenge is to meet the need to generate new leadership. The paucity of courageous leaders—so apparent in the response to the events in Los Angeles—requires that we look beyond the same elites and voices that recycle the older frameworks. We need leaders—neither saints nor sparkling television personalities—who can situate themselves within a larger historical narrative of this country and our world, who can grasp the complex dynamics of our peoplehood and imagine a future grounded in the best of our past, yet who are attuned to the frightening obstacles that now perplex us. Our ideals of freedom, democracy, and equality must be invoked to invigorate all of us, especially the landless, propertyless, and luckless. Only a visionary leadership that can motivate "the better angels of our nature," as Lincoln said, and activate possibilities for a freer, more efficient, and stable America—only that leadership deserves cultivation and support.

This new leadership must be grounded in grassroots organizing that highlights democratic accountability. Whoever *our* leaders will be as we approach the twenty-first century, their challenge will be to help Americans determine whether a genuine multiracial democracy can be created and sustained in an era of global economy and a moment of xenophobic frenzy.

Let us hope and pray that the vast intelligence, imagination, humor, and courage of Americans will not fail us. Either we learn a new language of empathy and compassion, or the fire this time will consume us all.

STUDY QUESTIONS

1. What does it mean to be an American? Who can be considered an American, in practice as well as in theory?
2. How do liberal as well as conservative attitudes toward "problem" blacks drive the wedge between races even further? Does black nationalism help or harm this situation?
3. Is unity, or a focus on the public good, possible in America? What would be required of us, as a people, to accomplish this?
4. Who is it that determines how a person must look, behave, and think to "fit in"? Why does rebellion against this classification cause fear?
5. Who needs to take the first step toward a "unification" of American society? Does this require a "putting away" of race, religion, and all differences?

34

I'm Black, You're White, Who's Innocent?

Shelby Steele

Shelby Steele teaches history at San Jose State University in California. He is the author of *The Content of Our Character*, from which this selection is taken.

It is a warm, windless California evening, and the dying light that covers the redbrick patio is tinted pale orange by the day's smog. Eight of us, not close friends, sit in lawn chairs sipping chardonnay. A black engineer and I (we had never met before) integrate the group. A psychologist is also among us, and her presence encourages a surprising openness. But not until well after the lovely twilight dinner has been served, when the sky has turned to deep black and the drinks have long since changed to scotch, does the subject of race spring awkwardly upon us. Out of nowhere the engineer announces, with a coloring of accusation in his voice, that it bothers him to send his daughter to a school where she is one of only three black children. "I didn't realize my ambition to get ahead would pull me into a world where my daughter would lose touch with her blackness," he says.

Over the course of the evening we have talked about money, infidelity, past and present addictions, child abuse, even politics. Intimacies have been revealed, fears named. But this subject, race, sinks us into one of those shaming silences where eye contact terrorizes. Our host looks for something in the bottom of his glass. Two women stare into the black sky as if to locate the Big Dipper and point it out to us. Finally, the psychologist seems to gather herself for a challenge, but it is too late. "Oh, I'm sure she'll be just fine," says our hostess, rising from her chair. When she excuses herself to get the coffee, the two sky gazers offer to help.

With three of us now gone, I am surprised to see the engineer still silently holding his ground. There is a willfulness in his eyes, an inner pride. He knows he has said something awkward, but he is determined not to give a damn. His unwavering eyes intimidate me. At last the host's head snaps erect. He has an idea. "The hell with coffee," he says. "How about some of the smoothest brandy you ever tasted?" An idea made exciting by the escape it offers. Gratefully we follow him back into the house, quickly drink his brandy, and say our good-byes.

An autopsy of this party might read: death induced by an abrupt and lethal injection of the American race issue. An accurate if superficial assessment. Since it has been my fate to live a rather integrated life, I have often witnessed sudden deaths like this. The threat of them, if not the reality, is a part of the texture of integration. In the late 1960s, when I was just out of college, I took a delinquent's delight in playing the engineer's role, and actually developed a small reputation for playing it well. Those were the days of flagellatory white guilt; it was such great fun to pinion some professor or housewife or, best of all, a large group of remorseful whites, with the knowledge of both their racism and their denial of it. The adolescent impulse to sneer at convention, to startle the middle-aged with doubt, could be indulged under the guise of racial indignation. And how could I lose? My victims—earnest liberals for the most part—

could no more crawl out from under my accusations than Joseph K. in Kafka's *Trial* could escape the amorphous charges brought against him. At this odd moment in history the world was aligned to facilitate my immaturity.

About a year of this was enough: the guilt that follows most cheap thrills caught up to me, and I put myself in check. But the impulse to do it faded more slowly. It was one of those petty talents that is tied to vanity, and when there were ebbs in my self-esteem the impulse to use it would come alive again. In integrated situations I can still feel the faint itch. But then there are many youthful impulses that still itch, and now, just inside the door of mid-life, this one is least precious to me.

In the literature classes I teach, I often see how the presence of whites all but seduces some black students into provocation. When we come to a novel by a black writer, say Toni Morrison, the white students can easily discuss the human motivations of the black characters. But, inevitably, a black student, as if by reflex, will begin to set in relief the various racial problems that are the background of these characters' lives. This student's tone will carry a reprimand: the class is afraid to confront the reality of racism. Classes cannot be allowed to die like dinner parties, however. My latest strategy is to thank that student for his or her moral vigilance, and then appoint the young man or woman as the class's official racism monitor. But even if I get a laugh—I usually do, but sometimes the student is particularly indignant, and it gets uncomfortable—the strategy never quite works. Our racial division is suddenly drawn in neon. Over-caution spreads like spilled paint. And, in fact, the black student who started it all does become a kind of monitor. The very presence of this student imposes a new accountability on the class.

I think those who provoke this sort of awkwardness are operating out of a black identity that obliges them to badger white people about race almost on principle. Content hardly matters. (For example, it made no sense for the engineer to expect white people to sympathize with his anguish over sending his daughter to school with *white* children.) Race indeed remains a source of white shame; the goal of these provocations is to put whites, no matter how indirectly, in touch with this collective guilt. In other words, these provocations I speak of are *power* moves, little shows of power that try to freeze the "enemy" in self-consciousness. They gratify and inflate the provocateur. They are the underdog's bite. And whites, far more secure in their power, respond with a self-contained and tolerant silence that is, itself, a show of power. What greater power than that of non-response, the power to let a small enemy sizzle in his own juices, to even feel a little sad at his frustration just as one is also complimented by it. Black anger always, in a way, flatters white power. In America, to know that one is not black is to feel an extra grace, a little boost of impunity.

I think the real trouble between the races in America is that the races are not just races but competing power groups—a fact that is easily minimized perhaps because it is so obvious. What is not so obvious is that this is true quite apart from the issue of class. Even the well-situated middle-class (or wealthy) black is never completely immune to that peculiar contest of power that his skin color subjects him to. Race is a separate reality in American society, an entity that carries its own potential for power, a mark of fate that class can soften considerably but not eradicate.

The distinction of race has always been used in American life to sanction each race's pursuit of power in relation to the other. The allure of race as a human delineation is the very shallowness of the delineation it makes. Onto this shallowness—mere skin and hair—men can project a false depth, a system of dismal attributions, a series of malevolent or ignoble stereotypes that skin and hair lack the substance to contradict. These dark projections then rationalize the pursuit of power. Your difference from me makes you bad, and your badness justifies, even demands, my pursuit of power over you—the oldest formula for aggression known to man. Whenever much importance is given to race, power is the primary motive.

But the human animal almost never pursues power without first convincing himself that he is *entitled* to it. And this feeling of entitlement has its own precondition: to be entitled one must first believe in one's innocence, at least in the area where one wishes to be entitled. By innocence I mean a feeling of essential goodness in relation to others and, therefore, superiority to others. Our innocence always inflates us and deflates those we seek power over. Once inflated we are entitled; we are in fact licensed to go after the power our innocence tells us we deserve. In this sense, *innocence is power*. Of course, innocence need not be genuine or real in any objective sense, as the Nazis demonstrated not long ago. Its only test is whether or not we can convince ourselves of it.

I think the racial struggle in America has always been primarily a struggle for innocence. White racism from the beginning has been a claim of white innocence and, therefore, of white entitlement to subjugate blacks. And in the '60s, as went innocence so went power. Blacks used the innocence that grew out of their long subjugation to seize more power, while whites lost some of their innocence and so lost a degree of power over blacks. Both races instinctively understand that to lose innocence is to lose power (in relation to each other). Now to be innocent someone else must be guilty, a natural law that leads the races to forge their innocence on each other's backs. The inferiority of the black always makes the white man superior; the evil might of whites makes blacks good. This pattern means that both races have a hidden investment in racism and racial disharmony, despite their good intentions to the contrary. Power defines their relations, and power requires innocence, which, in turn, requires racism and racial division.

I believe it was this hidden investment that the engineer was protecting when he made his remark—the white "evil" he saw in a white school "depriving" his daughter of her black heritage confirmed his innocence. Only the logic of power explained this—he bent reality to show that he was once again a victim of the white world and, as a victim, innocent. His determined eyes insisted on this. And the whites, in their silence, no doubt protected their innocence by seeing him as an ungracious troublemaker—his bad behavior underscoring their goodness. I can only guess how he was talked about after the party. But it isn't hard to imagine that his blunder gave everyone a lift. What none of us saw was the underlying game of power and innocence we were trapped in, or how much we needed a racial impasse to play that game.

When I was a boy of about twelve, a white friend of mine told me one day that his uncle, who would be arriving the next day for a visit, was a racist. Excited by the prospect of seeing such a man, I spent the following afternoon hanging around the alley behind my friend's house, watching from a distance as this uncle worked on the engine of his Buick. Yes, here was evil and I was compelled to look upon it. And I saw evil in the sharp angle of his elbow as he pumped his wrench to tighten nuts, I saw it in the blade-sharp crease of his chinos, in the pack of Lucky Strikes that threatened to slip from his shirt pocket as he bent, and in the way his concentration seemed to shut out the human world. He worked neatly and efficiently, wiping his hands constantly, and I decided that evil worked like this.

I felt a compulsion to have this man look upon me so that I could see evil—so that I could see the face of it. But when he noticed me standing beside his toolbox, he said only, "If you're looking for Bobby, I think he went up to the school to play baseball." He smiled nicely and went back to work. I was stunned for a moment, but then I realized that evil could be sly as well, could smile when it wanted to trick you.

Need, especially hidden need, puts a strong pressure on perception, and my need to have this man embody white evil was stronger than any contravening evidence. As a black person you always hear about racists but never meet any. And I needed to incarnate this odious category of humanity, those people who hated Martin Luther King Jr. and thought blacks should "go slow" or not at all. So, in my mental dictionary, behind the term "white racist," I inserted this man's likeness. I would think of him and say to myself, "There is no reason for him to hate black people. Only evil explains unmotivated hatred." And this thought soothed me; I felt innocent. If I hated white people, which I did not, at least I had a reason. His evil commanded me to assert in the world the goodness he made me confident of in myself.

In looking at this man I was *seeing for innocence*—a form of seeing that has more to do with one's hidden need for innocence (and power) than with the person or group one is looking at. It is quite possible, for example, that the man I saw that day was not a racist. He did absolutely nothing in my presence to indicate that he was. I invested an entire afternoon in seeing not the man but in seeing my innocence through the man. *Seeing for innocence* is, in this way, the essence of racism—the use of others as a means to our own goodness and superiority.

Black Americans have always had to find a way to handle white society's presumption of racial innocence whenever they have sought to enter the American mainstream. Louis Armstrong's exaggerated smile honored the presumed innocence of white society—I will not bring you your racial guilt if you will let me play my music. Ralph Ellison calls this "masking"; I call it bargaining. But whatever it's called, it points to the power of white society to enforce its innocence. I believe this power is greatly diminished today. Society has reformed and transformed—Miles Davis never smiles. Nevertheless, this power has not faded altogether; blacks must still contend with it.

Historically, blacks have handled white society's presumption of innocence in two ways: they have bargained with it, granting white society its innocence in exchange for entry into the mainstream; or they have challenged it, holding that innocence hostage until their demand for entry (or other concessions) was met. A bargainer says, I a*lready believe you are innocent (good, fair-minded) and have faith that you will prove it.* A challenger says, *If you are innocent, then prove it.* Bargainers *give* in hope of receiving; challengers *withhold* until they receive. Of course, there is risk in both approaches, but in each case the black is negotiating his own self-interest against the presumed racial innocence of the larger society. . . .

"Innocence is ignorance," Kierkegaard says, and if this is so, the claim of innocence amounts to an insistence on ignorance, a refusal to know. In their assertions of innocence both races carve out very functional areas of ignorance for themselves—territories of blindness that license a misguided pursuit of power. Whites gain superiority by *not* knowing blacks; blacks gain entitlement by *not* seeing their own responsibility for bettering themselves. The power each race seeks in relation to the other is grounded in a double-edged ignorance, ignorance of the self as well as the other.

The original sin that brought us to an impasse at the dinner party I mentioned at the outset occurred centuries ago, when it was first decided to exploit racial difference as a means to power. It was the determinism that flowed karmically from this sin that dropped over us like a net that night. What bothered me most was our helplessness. Even the engineer did not know how to go forward. His challenge hadn't worked, and he'd lost the option to bargain. The marriage of race and power depersonalized us, changed us from eight people to six whites and two blacks. The easiest thing was to let silence blanket our situation, our impasse.

I think the civil rights movement in its early and middle years offered the best way out of America's racial impasse: in this society, race must not be a source of advantage or disadvantage for anyone. This is fundamentally a *moral* position, one that seeks to breach the corrupt union of race and power with principles of fairness and human equality: if all men are created equal, then racial difference cannot sanction power. The civil rights movement was conceived for no other reason than to redress that corrupt union, and its guiding insight was that only a moral power based on enduring principles of justice, equality, and freedom could offset the lower impulse in man to exploit race as a means to power. Three hundred years of suffering had driven the point home, and in Montgomery, Little Rock, and Selma, racial power was the enemy and moral power the weapon.

An important difference between genuine and presumed innocence, I believe, is that the former must be earned through sacrifice, while the latter is unearned and only veils the quest for privilege. And there was much sacrifice in the early civil rights movement. The Gandhian principle of non-violent resistance that gave the movement a spiritual center as well as a method of protest demanded sacrifice, a passive offering of the self in the name of justice. A price was paid in terror and lost life, and from this sacrifice came a hard-earned innocence and a credible moral power.

Non-violent passive resistance is a bargainer's strategy. It assumes the power that is the object of the protest has the genuine innocence to morally respond, and puts the protesters at the mercy of that innocence. I think this movement won so many concessions precisely because of its belief in the capacity of whites to be moral. It did not so much demand that whites change as offer them relentlessly the opportunity to live by their own morality—to attain a true innocence based on the sacrifice of their racial privilege, rather than a false innocence based on presumed racial superiority. Blacks always bargain with or challenge the larger society; but I believe that in the early civil rights years, these forms of negotiation achieved a degree of integrity and genuineness never seen before or since.

In the mid-'60s all this changed. Suddenly a sharp *racial* consciousness emerged to compete with the moral consciousness that had defined the movement to that point. Whites were no longer welcome in the movement, and a vocal "black power" minority gained dramatic visibility. Increasingly, the movement began to seek racial as well as moral power, and thus it fell into a fundamental contradiction that plagues it to this day. Moral power precludes racial power by denouncing race as a means to power. Now suddenly the movement itself was using race as a means to power, and thereby affirming the very union of race and power it was born to redress. In the end, black power can claim no higher moral standing than white power.

It makes no sense to say this shouldn't have happened. The sacrifices that moral power demands are difficult to sustain, and it was inevitable that blacks would tire of these sacrifices and seek a more earthly power. Nevertheless, a loss of genuine innocence and moral power followed. The movement, splintered by a burst of racial militancy in the late '60s, lost its hold on the American conscience and descended more and more to the level of secular, interest-group politics. Bargaining and challenging once again became racial rather than moral negotiations.

You hear it asked, why are there no Martin Luther Kings around today? I think one reason is that there are no black leaders willing to resist the seductions of racial power, or to make the sacrifices moral power requires. King understood that racial power subverts moral power, and he pushed the principles of fairness and equality rather than black power because he believed these principles would bring blacks their most complete liberation. He sacrificed race for morality, and his innocence was made genuine by that sacrifice. What made King the most powerful and extraordinary black leader of this century was not his race but his morality.

Black power is a challenge. It grants whites no innocence; it denies their moral capacity and then demands that they be moral. No power can long insist on itself without evoking an opposing power. Doesn't an insistence on black power call up white power? (And could this have something to do with what many are now calling a resurgence of white racism?) I believe that what divided the races at the dinner party I attended, and what divides them in the nation, can only be bridged by an adherence to those moral principles that disallow race as a source of power, privilege, status, or entitlement of any kind. In our age, principles like fairness and equality are ill-defined and all but drowned in relativity. But this is the fault of people, not principles. We keep them muddied because they are the greatest threat to our presumed innocence and our selective ignorance. Moral principles, even when somewhat ambiguous, have the power to assign responsibility and therefore to provide us with knowledge. At the dinner party we were afraid of so severe an accountability.

What both black and white Americans fear are the sacrifices and risks that true racial harmony demands. This fear is the measure of our racial chasm. And though fear always seeks a thousand justifications, none is ever good enough, and the problems we run from only remain to haunt us. It would be right to suggest courage as an antidote to fear, but the glory of the word might only intimidate us into more fear. I prefer the word effort—relentless effort, moral effort. What I like most about this word are its connotations of everydayness, earnestness, and practical sacrifice. No matter how badly it might have gone for us that warm summer night, we should have talked. We should have made the effort.

STUDY QUESTIONS

1. Why are racism and race relations in general such an awkward and uncomfortable subject to most Americans?
2. How does power rely on innocence, or at least the perception of innocence? Why is perception of such great importance?
3. What is "seeing for innocence"? How does this state destroy the reality of the person you are seeing and promote racism?
4. What is the relationship between racial power and moral power?

35

On Racism and Sexism

Richard A. Wasserstrom

Richard A. Wasserstrom teaches philosophy at the University of California, in Santa Cruz.

INTRODUCTION

Racism and sexism are two central issues that engage the attention of many persons living within the United States today. But while there is relatively little disagreement about their importance as topics, there is substantial, vehement, and apparently intractable disagreement about what individuals, practices, ideas, and institutions are either racist or sexist—and for what reasons. In dispute are a number of related questions concerning how individuals ought to regard and respond to matters relating to race or sex.

There are, I think, a number of important similarities between issues of racism and issues of sexism, but there are also some significant differences. More specifically, while the same general method of analysis can usefully be employed to examine a number of the issues that arise in respect to either, the particular topics of controversy often turn out to be rather different. What I want to do in this essay is first propose a general way of looking at issues of racism and sexism, then look at several of the respects in which racism and sexism are alike and different, and then, finally, examine one somewhat neglected but fundamental issue; namely that of what a genuinely nonracist or nonsexist society might look like.

There are, I think, at least four questions that anyone interested in issues of racism and sexism ought to see as both distinct and worth asking. The first is what I call the question of the social realities. That question is concerned with rendering a correct description of the existing social arrangements, including the existing institutional structures, practices, attitudes and ideology. The second is devoted to the question of explanation. Given a correct understanding of what the existing social reality is, there can be a variety of theories to explain how things got that way and by what mechanisms they tend to be perpetuated. Much of the feminist literature, for example, is concerned with the problem of explanation. Complex and sophisticated accounts have been developed which utilize the theories of Freud, Lévi-Strauss, and Marx to explain the oppression of women. Other, equally complex accounts have insisted on the non-reductionist character of the nature and causes of the present sexual arrangements. Although important in their own right, as well as for the solution of other problems, I will have virtually nothing else to say about these explanatory issues in this essay.

The third question, and one that I will concentrate upon, is what I term the question of ideals. I see it as concerned with asking: If we had the good society, if we could change the social reality so that it conformed to some vision of what a nonracist or nonsexist society would be like, what would that society's institutions, practices, and ideology be in respect to matters of racial or sexual differentiation? Here, what I find especially interesting is the question of whether anything like the ideal that is commonly accepted as a very plausible one for a nonracist society can be as plausibly proposed for a conception of a nonsexist society.

The fourth and final question is that of instrumentalities. Once one has developed the correct account of the social realities, and the most defensible conception of what the good society would look like, and the most comprehensive theory of how the social realities came about and are maintained, then the remaining question is the instrumental one of social change: How, given all of this, does one most effectively and fairly move from the social realities to a closer approximation of the ideal. This, too, is a question with which I will not be concerned in what follows, although it is, for instance, within this context and this perspective that, it seems to me, all of the significant questions concerning the justifiability of programs of preferential treatment arise. That is to say, the way to decide whether such programs are justifiable is to determine whether they are appropriate means by which to bring about a particular, independently justifiable end.

These, then, are four central questions which any inquiry into sexism, racism or any other comparable phenomenon must distinguish and examine. I turn first to an examination of this question of the social realities and then to a consideration of ideals and the nature of a nonracist or a nonsexist society.

SOCIAL REALITIES

The Position of Blacks and Women

Methodologically, the first thing it is important to note is that to talk about social realities is to talk about a particular social and cultural context. And in our particular social and cultural context race and sex are socially very important categories. They are so in virtue of the fact that we live in a culture which has, throughout its existence, made race and sex extremely important characteristics of and for all the people living in the culture.

It is surely possible to imagine a culture in which race would be an unimportant, insignificant characteristic of individuals. In such a culture race would be largely if not exclusively a matter of superficial physiology; a matter, we might say, simply of the way one looked. And if it were, then any analysis of race and racism would necessarily assume very different dimensions from what they do in our society. In such a culture, the meaning of the term "race" would itself have to change substantially. This can be seen by the fact that in such a culture it would literally make no sense to say of a person that he or she was "passing." This is something that can be said and understood in our own culture and it shows at least that to talk of race is to talk of more than the way one looks.

Sometimes when people talk about what is wrong with affirmative action programs, or programs of preferential hiring, they say that what is wrong with such programs is that they take a thing as superficial as an individual's race and turn it into something important. They say that a person's race doesn't matter; other things do, such as qualifications. Whatever else may be said of statements such as these, as descriptions of the social realities they seem to be simply false. One complex but true empirical fact about our society is that the race of an individual is much more than a fact of superficial physiology. It is, instead, one of the dominant characteristics that affects both the way the individual looks at the world and the way the world looks at the individual. As I have said, that need not be the case. It may in fact be very important that we work toward a society in which that would not be the case, but it is the case now and it must be understood in any adequate and complete discussion of racism. That is why, too, it does not make much sense when people sometimes say, in talking about the fact that they are not racists, that they would not care if an individual were green and came from Mars, they would treat that individual the same way they treat people exactly like themselves. For part of *our* social and cultural history is to treat people of certain races in a certain way, and we do not have a social or cultural history of treating green people from Mars in any particular way. To put it simply, it is to misunderstand the social realities of race and racism to think of them simply as questions of how some people respond to other people whose skins are of different hues, irrespective of the social context.

I can put the point another way: Race does not function in our culture as does eye color. Eye color is an irrelevant category; nobody cares what color people's eyes are; it is not an important cultural fact; nothing turns on what eye color you have. It is important to see that race is not like that at all. And this truth affects what will and will not count as cases of racism. In our culture to be nonwhite—especially to be black—is to be treated and seen to be a member of a group that is different from and inferior to the group of standard, fully developed persons, the adult white males. To be black is to be a member of what was a despised minority and what is still a disliked and oppressed one. That is simply part of the awful truth of our cultural and social history, and a significant feature of the social reality of our culture today.

We can see fairly easily that the two sexual categories, like the racial ones, are themselves in important respects products of the society. Like one's race, one's sex is not merely or even primarily a matter of physiology. To see this we need only realize that we can understand the idea of a transsexual. A transsexual is someone who would describe himself or herself as a person who is essentially a female but through some accident of nature is trapped in a male body, or a person who is essentially a male but through some accident of nature is trapped in the body of a female. His (or her) description is some kind of a shorthand way of saying that he (or she) is more comfortable with the role allocated by the culture to people who are physiologically of the opposite sex. The fact that we regard this assertion of the transsexual as intelligible seems to me to show how deep the notion of sexual identity is in our culture and how little it has to do with physiological differences between males and females. Because people do pass in the context of race and because we can understand what passing means; because people are transsexuals and because we can understand what transsexuality means, we can see that the existing social categories of both race and sex are in this sense creations of the culture.

It is even clearer in the case of sex than in the case of race that one's sexual identity is a centrally important, crucially relevant category within our culture. I think, in fact, that it is more important and more fundamental than one's race. It is evident that there are substantially different role expectations and role assignments to persons in accordance with their sexual physiology, and that the positions of the two sexes in the culture are distinct. We do have a patriarchal society in which it matters enormously whether one is a male or a female. By almost all important measures it is more advantageous to be a male rather than a female.

Women and men are socialized differently. We learn very early and forcefully that we are either males or females and that much turns upon which sex we are. The evidence seems to be overwhelming and well-documented that sex roles play a fundamental role in the way persons think of themselves and the world—to say nothing of the way the world thinks of them. Men and women are taught to see men as independent, capable, and powerful; men and women are taught to see women as dependent, limited in abilities, and passive. A woman's success or failure in life is defined largely in terms of her activities within the family. It is important for her that she marry, and when she does she is expected to take responsibility for the wifely tasks: the housework, the child care, and the general emotional welfare of the husband and children. Her status in society is determined in substantial measure by the vocation and success of her husband. Economically, women are substantially worse off than men. They do not receive any pay for the work that is done in the home. As members of the labor force their wages are significantly lower than those paid to men, even when they are engaged in similar work and have similar educational backgrounds. The higher the prestige or the salary of the job, the less present women are in the labor force. And, of course, women are conspicuously absent from most positions of authority and power in the major economic and political institutions of our society.

As is true for race, it is also a significant social fact that to be a female is to be an entity or creature viewed as different from the standard, fully developed person who is male as well as white. But to be female, as opposed to being black, is not to be conceived of as simply a creature of less worth. That is one important thing that differentiates sexism from racism: The ideology of sex, as opposed to the ideology of race, is a good deal more complex and confusing. Women are both put on a pedestal and deemed not fully developed persons. They are idealized; their approval and admiration is sought; and they are at the same time regarded as less competent than men and less able to live fully developed, fully human lives—for that is what men do. At best, they are viewed and treated as having properties and attributes that are valuable and admirable for humans of this type. For example, they may be viewed as especially empathetic, intuitive, loving, and nurturing. At best, these qualities are viewed as good properties for women to have, and, provided they are properly muted, are sometimes valued within the more well-rounded male. Because the sexual ideology is complex, confusing, and variable, it does not unambiguously proclaim the lesser value attached to being female rather than being male, nor does it unambiguously correspond to the existing social realities. For these, among other reasons, sexism could plausibly be regarded as a deeper phenomenon than racism. It is more deeply embedded in the culture, and thus less visible. Being harder to detect, it is harder to eradicate. Moreover, it is less unequivocally regarded as unjust and unjustifiable. That is to say, there is less agreement within the dominant ideology that sexism even implies an unjustifiable practice or attitude. Hence, many persons announce, without regret or embarrassment, that they are sexists or male chauvinists; very few announce openly that they are racists. For all of these reasons sexism may be a more insidious evil than racism, but there is little merit in trying to decide between two seriously objectionable practices which one is worse.

While I do not think that I have made very controversial claims about either our cultural history or our present-day culture, I am aware of the fact that they have been stated very imprecisely and that I have offered little evidence to substantiate them. In a crude way we ought to be able both to understand the claims and to see that they are correct if we reflect seriously and critically upon our own cultural institutions, attitudes, and practices. But in a more refined, theoretical way, I am imagining that a more precise and correct description of the social reality in respect to race and sex would be derivable from a composite, descriptive account of our society which utilized the relevant social sciences to examine such things as the society's institutions, practices, attitudes and ideology—if the social sciences could be value-free and unaffected in outlook or approach by the fact that they, themselves, are largely composed of persons who are white and male.

Viewed from the perspective of social reality it should be clear, too, that racism and sexism should not be thought of as phenomena that consist simply in taking a person's race or sex into account, or even simply in taking a person's race or sex into account in an arbitrary way. Instead, racism and sexism consist in taking race and sex into account in a certain way, in the context of a specific set of institutional arrangements and a specific ideology which together create and maintain a specific *system* of institutions, role assignments, beliefs and attitudes. That system is one, and has been one, in which political, economic, and social power and advantage is concentrated in the hands of those who are white and male.

The evils of such systems are, however, not all of a piece. For instance, sometimes people say that what was wrong with the system of racial discrimination in the South was that it took an irrelevant characteristic, namely race, and used it systematically to allocate social benefits and burdens of various sorts. The defect was the irrelevance of the characteristic used, i.e., race, for that meant that individuals ended up being treated in a manner that was arbitrary and capricious.

I do not think that was the central flaw at all—at least of much of the system. Take, for instance, the most hideous of the practices, human slavery. The primary thing that was wrong with the institution was not that the particular individuals who were assigned the place of slaves were assigned there arbitrarily because the assignment was made in virtue of an irrelevant characteristic, i.e., their race. Rather, it seems to me clear that the primary thing that was and is wrong with slavery is the practice itself—the fact of some individuals being able to own other individuals and all that goes with that practice. It would not matter by what criterion individuals were assigned; human slavery would still be wrong. And the same can be said for many of the other discrete practices and institutions that comprised the system of racial discrimination even after human slavery was abolished. The practices were unjustifiable—they were oppressive—and they would have been so no matter how the assignment of victims had been made. What made it worse, still, was that the institutions and ideology all interlocked to create a system of human oppression whose effects on those living under it were as devastating as they were unjustifiable.

Some features of the system of sexual oppression are like this and others are different. For example, if it is true that women are socialized to play the role of servers of men and if they are in general assigned that position in the society, what is objectionable about that practice is the practice itself. It is not that women are being arbitrarily or capriciously assigned the social role of server, but rather that such a role is at least *prima facie* unjustifiable as a role in a decent society. As a result, the assignment on any basis of individuals to such a role is objectionable.

The assignment of women to primary responsibility for child rearing and household maintenance may be different; it may be objectionable on grounds of unfairness of another sort. That is to say, if we assume that these are important but undesirable aspects of social existence—if we assume that they are, relatively speaking, unsatisfying and unfulfilling ways to spend one's time, then the objection is that women are unduly and unfairly allocated a disproportionate share of unpleasant, unrewarding work. Here the objection, if it is proper, is to the degree to which the necessary burden is placed to a greater degree than is fair on women, rather than shared equally by persons of both sexes.

Even here, though, it is important to see that the essential feature of both racism and sexism consists in the fact that race or sex is taken into account in the context of a specific set of arrangements and a specific ideology which is systemic and which treats and regards persons who are nonwhite or female in a comprehensive, systemic way. Whether it would be capricious to take either a person's race or a person's sex into account in the good society, because race and sex were genuinely irrelevant characteristics is a question that can only be answered after we have a clearer idea of what the good society would look like in respect either to race or sex. . . .

Types of Racism or Sexism

Another recurring question that can profitably be examined within the perspective of social realities is whether the legal system is racist or sexist. Indeed, it seems to me essential that the social realities of the relationships and ideologies concerning race and sex be kept in mind whenever one is trying to assess claims that are made about the racism or sexism of important institutions such as the legal system. It is also of considerable importance in assessing such claims to understand that even within the perspective of social reality, racism or sexism can manifest itself, or be understood, in different ways. That these are both important points can be seen through a brief examination of the different, distinctive ways in which our own legal system might plausibly be understood to be racist. The mode of analysis I propose serves as well, I believe, for an analogous analysis of the sexism of the legal system, although I do not undertake the latter analysis in this paper.

The first type of racism is the simplest and the least controversial. It is the case of overt racism, in which a law or a legal institution expressly takes into account the race of individuals in order to assign benefits and burdens in such a way as to bestow an unjustified benefit upon a member or members of the racially dominant group or an unjustified burden upon members of the racial groups that are oppressed. We no longer have many, if any, cases of overt racism in our legal system today, although we certainly had a number in the past. Indeed, the historical system of formal, racial segregation was both buttressed by, and constituted of, a number of overtly racist laws and practices. At different times in our history, racism included laws and practices which dealt with such things as the exclusion of nonwhites from the franchise, from decent primary and secondary schools and most professional schools, and the prohibition against interracial marriages.

The second type of racism is very similar to overt racism. It is covert, but intentional, racism, in which a law or a legal institution has as its purpose the allocation of benefits and burdens in order to support the power of the dominant race, but does not use race specifically as a basis for allocating these benefits and burdens. One particularly good historical example involves the use of grandfather clauses which were inserted in statutes governing voter registration in a number of states after passage of the Fifteenth Amendment.

Covert racism within the law is not entirely a thing of the past. Many instances of de facto school segregation in the North and West are cases of covert racism. At times certain school boards—virtually all of which are overwhelmingly white in composition—quite consciously try to maintain exclusively or predominantly white schools within a school district. The classifications such school boards use are not ostensibly racial, but are based upon the places of residence of the affected students. These categories provide the opportunity for covert racism in engineering the racial composition of individual schools within the board's jurisdiction. . . .

There are at least two kinds of institutional racism. The first is the racism of sub-institutions within the legal system such as the jury, or the racism of practices built upon or countenanced by the law. These institutions and practices very often, if not always, reflect in important and serious ways a variety of dominant values in the operation of what is apparently a neutral legal mechanism. The result is the maintenance and reenforcement of a system in which whites dominate over nonwhites. One relatively uninteresting (because familiar) example is the case of de facto school segregation. As observed above, some cases of de facto segregation are examples of covert racism. But even in school districts where there is no intention to divide pupils on grounds of race so as to maintain existing power relationships along racial lines, school attendance zones are utilized which are based on the geographical location of the pupil. Because it is a fact in our culture that there is racial discrimination against black people in respect to housing, it is also a fact that any geographical allocation of pupils—unless one pays a lot of attention to housing patterns—will have the effect of continuing to segregate minority pupils very largely on grounds of race. It is perfectly appropriate to regard this effect as a case of racism in public education.

A less familiar, and hence perhaps more instructive, example concerns the question of the importance of having blacks on juries, especially in cases in which blacks are criminal defendants. The orthodox view within the law is that it is unfair to try a black defendant before an all-white jury if blacks were overtly or covertly excluded from the jury rolls used to provide the jury panel, but not otherwise. One reason that is often given is that the systematic exclusion of blacks increases too greatly the chance of racial prejudice operating against the black defendant. The problem with this way of thinking about things is that it does not make much sense. If whites are apt to be prejudiced against blacks, then an all-white jury is just as apt to be prejudiced against a black defendant, irrespective of whether blacks were systematically excluded from the jury rolls. I suspect that the rule has developed in the way it has because the courts think that many, if not most, whites are not prejudiced against blacks, unless, perhaps, they happen to live in an area where there is systematic exclusion of blacks from the jury rolls. Hence prejudice is the chief worry, and a sectional, if not historical, one at that.

White prejudice against blacks is, I think, a problem, and not just a sectional one. However, the existence or nonexistence of prejudice against blacks does not go to the heart of the matter. It is a worry, but it is not the chief worry. A black person may not be able to get a fair trial from an all-white jury even though the jurors are disposed to be fair and impartial, because the whites may unknowingly bring into the jury box a view about a variety of matters which affects in very fundamental respects the way they will look at and assess the facts. Thus, for example, it is not, I suspect, part of the experience of most white persons who serve on juries that police often lie in their dealings with people and the courts. Indeed, it is probably not part of their experience that persons lie about serious matters except on rare occasions. And they themselves tend to take truth telling very seriously. As a result, white persons for whom these facts about police and lying are a part of their social reality will have very great difficulty taking seriously the possibility that the inculpatory testimony of a police witness is a deliberate untruth. However, it may also be a part of the social reality that many black persons, just because they are black, have had encounters with the police in which the police were at best indifferent to whether they, the police, were speaking the truth. And even more black persons may have known a friend or a relative who has had such an experience. As a result, a black juror would be more likely than his or her white counterpart to approach skeptically the testimony of ostensibly neutral, reliable witnesses such as police officers. The point is not that all police officers lie; nor is the point that all whites always believe everything police say, and blacks never do. The point is that because the world we live in is the way it is, it is likely that whites and blacks will on the whole be disposed to view the credibility of police officers very differently. If so, the legal system's election to ignore this reality, and to regard as fair and above reproach the common occurrence of all-white juries (and white judges) passing on the guilt or innocence of black defendants is a decision in fact to permit and to perpetuate a kind of institutional racism within the law.

The second type of institutional racism is what I will call "conceptual" institutional racism. We have a variety of ways of thinking about the legal system, and we have a variety of ways of thinking within the legal system about certain problems. We use concepts. Quite often without realizing it, the concepts used take for granted certain objectionable aspects of racist ideology without our being aware of it. The second *Brown* case (*Brown II*) provides an example. There was a second *Brown* case because, having decided that the existing system of racially segregated public education was unconstitutional (*Brown I*), the Supreme Court gave legitimacy to a second issue—the nature of the relief to be granted—by treating it as a distinct question to be considered and decided separately. That in itself was striking because in most cases, once the Supreme Court has found unconstitutionality, there has been no problem about relief (apart from questions of retroactivity): The unconstitutional practices and acts are to cease. As is well known, the Court in *Brown II* concluded that the desegregation of public education had to proceed "with all deliberate speed." The Court said that there were "complexities arising from the transition to a system of public education freed from racial discrimination." More specifically, time might be necessary to carry out the ruling because of

> problems related to administration, arising from the physical condition of the school plant, the school transportation system personnel, revision of school districts and attendance areas into compact units to achieve a system of determining admission to the public school on a non-racial basis, and revision of local laws and regulations which may be necessary in solving the foregoing problems.

Now, I do not know whether the Court believed what it said in this passage, but it is a fantastic bit of nonsense that is, for my purposes, most instructive. Why? Because there was nothing complicated about most of the dual school systems of the southern states. Many counties, especially the rural ones, had one high school, typically called either "Booker T. Washington High School" or "George Washington Carver High School," where all the black children in the county went; another school, often called "Sidney Lanier High School" or "Robert E. Lee High School," was attended by all the white children in the county. There was nothing difficult about deciding that—as of the day after the decision—half of the children in the county, say all those who lived in the southern part of the county, would go to Robert E. Lee High School, and all those who lived in the northern half would go to Booker T. Washington High School. *Brown I* could have been implemented the day after the Court reached its decision. But it was also true that the black schools throughout the South were utterly wretched when compared to the white schools. There never had been any system of separate but equal education. In almost every measurable respect, the black schools were inferior. One possibility is that, without being explicitly aware of it, the members of the Supreme Court made use of some assumptions that were a significant feature of the dominant racist ideology. If the assumptions had been made explicit, the reasoning would have gone something like this: Those black schools are wretched. We cannot order white children to go to those schools, especially when they have gone to better schools in the past. So while it is unfair to deprive blacks, to make them go to these awful, segregated schools, they will have to wait until the black schools either are eliminated or are sufficiently improved so that there are good schools for everybody to attend.

What seems to me to be most objectionable, and racist, about *Brown II* is the uncritical acceptance of the idea that during this process of change, black schoolchildren would have to suffer by continuing to attend inadequate schools. The Supreme Court's solution assumed that the correct way to deal with this problem was to continue to have the black children go to their schools until the black schools were brought up to par or eliminated. That is a kind of conceptual racism in which the legal system accepts the dominant racist ideology, which holds that the claims of black children are worth less than the claims of white children in those cases in which conflict is inevitable. It seems to me that any minimally fair solution would have required that during the interim process, if anybody had to go to an inadequate school, it would have been the white children, since they were the ones who had previously had the benefit of the good schools. But this is simply not the way racial matters are thought about within the dominant ideology.

A study of *Brown II* is instructive because it is a good illustration of conceptual racism within the legal system. It also reflects another kind of conceptual racism—conceptual racism about the system. *Brown I* and *II* typically are thought of by our culture, and especially by our educational institutions, as representing one of the high points in the legal system's fight against racism. The dominant way of thinking about the desegregation cases is that the legal system was functioning at its very best. Yet, as I have indicated, there are important respects in which the legal system's response to the then existing system of racially segregated education was defective and hence should hardly be taken as a model of the just, institutional way of dealing with this problem of racial oppression. But the fact that we have, as well as inculcate, these attitudes of effusive praise toward *Brown I* and *II* and its progeny reveals a kind of persistent conceptual racism in talk about the character of the legal system, and what constitutes the right way to have dealt with the social reality of American racial oppression of black people.

In theory, the foregoing analytic scheme can be applied as readily to the social realities of sexual oppression as to racism. Given an understanding of the social realities in respect to sex—the ways in which the system of patriarchy inequitably distributes important benefits and burdens for the benefit of males, and the ideology which is a part of that patriarchal system and supportive of it—one can examine the different types of sexism that exist within the legal system. In practice the task is more difficult because we are inclined to take as appropriate even overt instances of sexist laws, e.g., that it is appropriately a part of the definition of rape that a man cannot rape his wife. The task is also more difficult because sexism is, as I have suggested, a "deeper" phenomenon than racism. As a result, there is less awareness of the significance of much of the social reality, e.g., that the language we use to talk about the world and ourselves has embedded within it ideological assumptions and preferences that support the existing patriarchal system. Cases of institutional sexism will therefore be systematically harder to detect. But these difficulties to one side, the mode of analysis seems to me to be in principle equally applicable to sexism, although, as I indicate in the next section on ideals, a complete account of the sexism of the legal system necessarily awaits a determination of what is the correct picture of the good society in respect to sexual differences.

IDEALS

The second perspective, described at the outset, which is also important for an understanding and analysis of racism and sexism, is the perspective of the ideal. Just as we can and must ask what is involved today in our culture in being of one race or of one sex rather than the other, and how individuals are in fact viewed and treated, we can also ask different questions: namely, what would the good or just society make of race and sex, and to what degree, if at all, would racial and sexual distinctions ever be taken into account? Indeed, it could plausibly be argued that we could not have an adequate idea of whether a society was racist or sexist unless we had some conception of what a thoroughly nonracist or nonsexist society would look like. This perspective is an extremely instructive as well as an often neglected one. Comparatively little theoretical literature that deals with either racism or sexism has concerned itself in a systematic way with this perspective.

In order to ask more precisely what some of the possible ideals are of desirable racial or sexual differentiation, it is necessary to see that we must ask: "In respect to what?" And one way to do this is to distinguish in a crude way among three levels or areas of social and political arrangements and activities. These correspond very roughly to the matters of status, role, and temperament identified earlier. First, there is the area of basic political rights and obligations, including the rights to vote and to travel, and the obligation to pay income taxes. Second, there is the area of important, nongovernmental institutional benefits and burdens. Examples are access to and employment in the significant economic markets, the opportunity to acquire and enjoy housing in the setting of one's choice, the right of persons who want to marry each other to do so, and the duties (nonlegal as well as legal) that persons acquire in getting married. And third, there is the area of individual, social interaction, including such matters as whom one will have as friends, and what aesthetic preferences one will cultivate and enjoy.

As to each of these three areas we can ask, for example, whether in a nonracist society it would be thought appropriate ever to take the race of the individuals into account. Thus, one picture of a nonracist society is that which is captured by what I call the assimilationist ideal: a nonracist society would be one in which the race of an individual would be the functional equivalent of the eye color of individuals in our society today. In our society no basic political rights and obligations are determined on the basis of eye color. No important institutional benefits and burdens are connected with eye color. Indeed, except for the mildest sort of aesthetic preferences, a person would be thought odd who even made private, social decisions by taking eye color into account. And for reasons that we could fairly readily state we could explain why it would be wrong to permit anything but the mildest, most trivial aesthetic preference to turn on eye color. The reasons would concern the irrelevance of eye color for any political or social institution, practice or arrangement. According to the assimilationist ideal, a nonracist society would be one in which an individual's race was of no more significance in any of these three areas than is eye color today.

The assimilationist ideal in respect to sex does not seem to be as readily plausible and obviously attractive here as it is in the case of race. In fact, many persons invoke the possible realization of the assimilationist ideal as a reason for rejecting the Equal Rights Amendment and indeed the idea of women's liberation itself. My own view is that the assimilationist ideal may be just as good and just as important an ideal in respect to sex as it is in respect to race. But many persons think there are good reasons why an assimilationist society in respect to sex would not be desirable.

To be sure, to make the assimilationist ideal a reality in respect to sex would involve more profound and fundamental revisions of our institutions and our attitudes than would be the case in respect to race. On the institutional level we would have to alter radically our practices concerning the family and marriage. If a nonsexist society is a society in which one's sex is no more significant than eye color in our society today, then laws that require the persons who are getting married to be of different sexes would clearly be sexist laws.

And on the attitudinal and conceptual level, the assimilationist ideal would require the eradication of all sex-role differentiation. It would never teach about the inevitable or essential attributes of masculinity or feminity; it would never encourage or discourage the ideas of sisterhood or brotherhood; and it would be unintelligible to talk about the virtues as well as disabilities of being a woman or a man. Were sex like eye color, these things would make no sense. Just as the normal, typical adult is virtually oblivious to the eye color of other persons for all major interpersonal relationships, so the normal, typical adult in this kind of nonsexist society would be indifferent to the sexual, physiological differences of other persons for all interpersonal relationships.

To acknowledge that things would be very different is, of course, hardly to concede that they would be undesirable. But still, perhaps the problem is with the assimilationist ideal. And the assimilationist ideal is certainly not the only possible, plausible ideal.

There are, for instance, two others that are closely related, but distinguishable. One I call the ideal of diversity; the other, the ideal of tolerance. Both can be understood by considering how religion, rather than eye color, tends to be thought about in our culture. According to the ideal of diversity, heterodoxy in respect to religious belief and practice is regarded as a positive good. On this view there would be a loss—it would be a worse society—were everyone to be a member of the same religion. According to the other view, the ideal of tolerance, heterodoxy in respect to religious belief and practice would be seen more as a necessary, lesser evil. On this view there is nothing intrinsically better about diversity in respect to religion, but the evils of achieving anything like homogeneity far outweigh the possible benefits.

Now, whatever differences there might be between the ideals of diversity and tolerance, the similarities are more striking. Under neither ideal would it be thought that the allocation of basic political rights and duties should take an individual's religion into account. And we would want equalitarianism even in respect to most important institutional benefits and burdens—for example, access to employment in the desirable vocations. Nonetheless, on both views it would be deemed appropriate to have some institutions (typically those that are connected in an intimate way with these religions) that do in a variety of ways take the religion of members of the society into account. For example, it might be thought permissible and appropriate for members of a religious group to join together in collective associations which have religious, educational and social dimensions. And on the individual, interpersonal level, it might be thought unobjectionable, or on the diversity view, even admirable, were persons to select their associates, friends, and mates on the basis of their religious orientation. So there are two possible and plausible ideals of what the good society would look like in respect to religion in which religious differences would be to some degree maintained because the diversity of religions was seen either as an admirable, valuable feature of the society, or as one to be tolerated. The picture is a more complex, less easily describable one than that of the assimilationist ideal.

It may be that in respect to sex (and conceivably, even in respect to race) something more like either of these ideals in respect to religion is the right one. But one problem then—and it is a very substantial one—is to specify with a good deal of precision and care what that ideal really comes to. Which legal, institutional and personal differentiations are permissible and which are not? Which attitudes and beliefs concerning sexual identification and differences are properly introduced and maintained and which are not? Part, but by no means all, of the attractiveness of the assimilationist ideal is its clarity and simplicity. In the good society of the assimilationist sort we would be able to tell easily and unequivocally whether any law, practice, or attitude was in any respect either racist or sexist. Part, but by no means all, of the unattractiveness of any pluralistic ideal is that it makes the question of what is racist or sexist a much more difficult and complicated one to answer. But although simplicity and lack of ambiguity may be virtues, they are not the only virtues to be taken into account in deciding among competing ideals. We quite appropriately take other considerations to be relevant to an assessment of the value and worth of alternative nonracist and nonsexist societies.

Nor do I even mean to suggest that all persons who reject the assimilationist ideal in respect to sex would necessarily embrace either something like the ideal of tolerance or the ideal of diversity. Some persons might think the right ideal was one in which substantially greater sexual differentiation and sex-role identification was retained than would be the case under either of these conceptions. Thus, someone might believe that the good society was, perhaps, essentially like the one they think we now have in respect to sex: equality of political rights, such as the right to vote, but all of the sexual differentiation in both legal and nonlegal institutions that is characteristic of the way in which our society has been and still is ordered. And someone might also believe that the usual ideological justifications for these arrangements are the correct and appropriate ones.

This could, of course, be regarded as a version of the ideal of diversity, with the emphasis upon the extensive character of the institutional and personal difference connected with sexual identity. Whether it is a kind of ideal of diversity or a different ideal altogether turns, I think, upon two things: First, however pervasive the sexual differentiation is, second, whether the ideal contains a conception of the appropriateness of significant institutional and interpersonal inequality, e.g., that the woman's job is in large measure to serve and be dominated by the male. The more this latter feature is present, the clearer the case for regarding this as ideal, distinctively different from any of those described by me so far.

The next question, of course, is that of how a choice is rationally to be made among these different, possible ideals. One place to begin is with the empirical world. For the question of whether something is a plausible and attractive ideal does turn in part on the nature of the empirical world. If it is true, for example, that any particular characteristic, such as sex, is not only a socially significant category in our culture but that it is largely a socially created one as well, then many ostensible objections to the assimilationist ideal appear immediately to disappear.

What I mean is this: It is obvious that we could formulate and use some sort of a crude, incredibly imprecise physiological concept of race. In this sense we could even say that race is a naturally occurring rather than a socially created feature of the world. There are diverse skin colors and related physiological characteristics distributed among human beings. But the fact is that except for skin hue and the related physiological characteristics, race is a socially created category. And skin hue, as I have shown, is neither a necessary nor a sufficient condition for being classified as black in our culture. Race as a naturally occurring characteristic is also a socially irrelevant category. There do not in fact appear to be any characteristics that are part of this natural concept of race and that are in any plausible way even relevant to the appropriate distribution of any political, institutional, or interpersonal concerns in the good society. Because in this sense race is like eye color, there is no plausible case to be made on this ground against the assimilationist ideal.

There is, of course, the social reality of race. In creating and tolerating a society in which race matters, we must recognize that we have created a vastly more complex concept of race which includes what might be called the idea of ethnicity as well—a set of attitudes, traditions, beliefs, etc., which the society has made part of what it means to be of a race. It may be, therefore, that one could argue that a form of the pluralist ideal ought to be preserved in respect to race, in the socially created sense, for reasons similar to those that might be offered in support of the desirability of some version of the pluralist ideal in respect to religion. As I have indicated, I am skeptical, but for the purposes of this essay it can well be left an open question.

Despite appearances, the case of sex is more like that of race than is often thought. What opponents of assimilationism seize upon is that sexual difference appears to be a naturally occurring category of obvious and inevitable social relevance in a way, or to a degree, which race is not. The problems with this way of thinking are twofold. To begin with, an analysis of the social realities reveals that it is the socially created sexual differences which tend in fact to matter the most. It is sex-role differentiation, not gender per se, that makes men and women as different as they are from each other, and it is sex-role differences which are invoked to justify most sexual differentiation at any of the levels of society.

More importantly, even if naturally occurring sexual differences were of such a nature that they were of obvious prima facie social relevance, this would by no means settle the question of whether in the good society sex should or should not be as minimally significant as eye color. Even though there are biological differences between men and women in nature, this fact does not determine the question of what the good society can and should make of these differences. I have difficulty understanding why so many persons seem to think that it does settle the question adversely to anything like the assimilationist ideal. They might think it does settle the question for two different reasons. In the first place, they might think the differences are of such a character that they substantially affect what would be possible within a good society of human persons. Just as the fact that humans are mortal necessarily limits the features of any possible good society, so, they might argue, the fact that males and females are physiologically different limits the features of any possible good society.

In the second place, they might think the differences are of such a character that they are relevant to the question of what would be desirable in the good society. That is to say, they might not think that the differences *determine* to a substantial degree what is possible, but that the differences ought to be taken into account in any rational construction of an ideal social existence.

The second reason seems to me to be a good deal more plausible than the first. For there appear to be very few, if any, respects in which the ineradicable, naturally occurring differences between males and females *must* be taken into account. The industrial revolution has certainly made any of the general differences in strength between the sexes capable of being ignored by the good society in virtually all activities. And it is sex-role acculturation, not biology, that mistakenly leads many persons to the view that women are both naturally and necessarily better suited than men to be assigned the primary responsibilities of child rearing. Indeed, the only fact that seems required to be taken into account is the fact that reproduction of the human species requires that the fetus develop *in utero* for a period of months. Sexual intercourse is not necessary, for artificial insemination is available. Neither marriage nor the family is required for conception or child rearing. Given the present state of medical knowledge and the natural realities of female pregnancy, it is difficult to see why any important institutional or interpersonal arrangements *must* take the existing gender difference of *in utero* pregnancy into account.

But, as I have said, this is still to leave it a wholly open question to what degree the good society *ought* to build upon any ineradicable gender differences to construct institutions which would maintain a substantial degree of sexual differentiation. The arguments are typically far less persuasive for doing so than appears upon the initial statement of this possibility. Someone might argue that the fact of menstruation, for instance, could be used as a premise upon which to predicate different social roles for females than for males. But this could only plausibly be proposed if two things were true: first, that menstruation would be debilitating to women and hence relevant to social role even in a culture which did not teach women to view menstruation as a sign of uncleanliness or as a curse; and second, that the way in which menstruation necessarily affected some or all women was in fact related in an important way to the role in question. But even if both of these were true, it would still be an open question whether any sexual differentiation ought to be built upon these facts. The society could still elect to develop institutions that would nullify the effect of the natural differences. And suppose, for example, what seems implausible—that some or all women will not be able to perform a particular task while menstruating, e.g., guard a border. It would be easy enough, if the society wanted to, to arrange for substitute guards for the women who were incapacitated. We know that persons are not good guards when they are sleepy, and we make arrangements so that persons alternate guard duty to avoid fatigue. The same could be done for menstruating women, even given these implausibly strong assumptions about menstruation. At the risk of belaboring the obvious, what I think it important to see is that the case against the assimilationist ideal—if it is to be a good one—must rest on arguments concerned to show why some other ideal would be preferable; it cannot plausibly rest on the claim that it is either necessary or inevitable.

There is, however, at least one more argument based upon nature, or at least the "natural," that is worth mentioning. Someone might argue that significant sex-role differentiation is natural not in the sense that it is biologically determined but only in the sense that it is a virtually universal phenomenon in human culture. By itself, this claim of virtual universality, even if accurate, does not directly establish anything about the desirability or undesirability of any particular ideal. But it can be made into an argument by the addition of the proposition that where there is a virtually universal social practice, there is probably some good or important purpose served by the practice. Hence, given the fact of sex-role differentiation in all, or almost all, cultures, we have some reason to think that substantial sex-role differentiation serves some important purpose for and in human society.

This is an argument, but I see no reason to be impressed by it. The premise which turns the fact of sex-role differentiation into any kind of a strong reason for sex-role differentiation is the premise of conservatism. And it is no more convincing here than elsewhere. There are any number of practices that are typical and yet upon reflection seem without significant social purpose. Slavery was once such a practice; war perhaps, still is.

More to the point, perhaps, the concept of "purpose" is ambiguous. It can mean in a descriptive sense "plays some role" or "is causally relevant." Or it can mean in a prescriptive sense "does something desirable" or "has some useful function." If "purpose" is used descriptively in the conservative premise, then the argument says nothing about the continued desirability of sex-role differentiation or the assimilationist ideal. If "purpose" is used prescriptively in the conservative premise, then there is no reason to think that premise is true.

To put it another way, the question is whether it is desirable to have a society in which sex-role differences are to be retained at all. The straightforward way to think about that question is to ask what would be good and what would be bad about a society in which sex functioned like eye color does in our society. We can imagine what such a society would look like and how it would work. It is hard to see how our thinking is substantially advanced by reference to what has typically or always been the case. If it is true, as I think it is, that the sex-role differentiated societies we have had so far have tended to concentrate power in the hands of males, have developed institutions and ideologies that have perpetuated that concentration and have restricted and prevented women from living the kinds of lives that persons ought to be able to live for themselves, then this says far more about what may be wrong with any nonassimilationist ideal than does the conservative premise say what may be right about any nonassimilationist ideal.

Nor is this all that can be said in favor of the assimilationist ideal. For it seems to me that the strongest affirmative moral argument on its behalf is that it provides for a kind of individual autonomy that a nonassimilationist society cannot attain. Any nonassimilationist society will have sex roles. Any nonassimilationist society will have some institutions that distinguish between individuals in virtue of their gender, and any such society will necessarily teach the desirability of doing so. Any substantially nonassimilationist society will make one's sexual identity an important characteristic, so that there are substantial psychological, role, and status differences between persons who are males and those who are females. Even if these could be attained without systemic dominance of one sex over the other, they would, I think, be objectionable on the ground that they necessarily impaired an individual's ability to develop his or her own characteristics, talents and capacities to the fullest extent to which he or she might desire. Sex roles, and all that accompany them, necessarily impose limits—restrictions on what one can do, be or become. As such, they are, I think, at least prima facie wrong.

To some degree, all role-differentiated living is restrictive in this sense. Perhaps, therefore, all role-differentiation in society is to some degree troublesome, and perhaps all strongly role-differentiated societies are objectionable. But the case against sexual differentiation need not rest upon this more controversial point. For one thing that distinguishes sex roles from many other roles is that they are wholly involuntarily assumed. One has no choice whatsoever about whether one shall be born a male or female. And if it is a consequence of one's being born a male or a female that one's subsequent emotional, intellectual, and material development will be substantially controlled by this fact, then substantial, permanent, and involuntarily assumed restraints have been imposed on the most central factors concerning the way one will shape and live one's life. The point to be emphasized is that this would necessarily be the case, even in the unlikely event that substantial sexual differentiation could be maintained without one sex or the other becoming dominant and developing institutions and an ideology to support that dominance.

I do not believe that all I have said in this section shows in any conclusive fashion the desirability of the assimilationist ideal in respect to sex. I have tried to show why some typical arguments against the assimilationist ideal are not persuasive, and why some of the central ones in support of that ideal are persuasive. But I have not provided a complete account, or a complete analysis. At a minimum, what I have shown is how thinking about this topic ought to proceed, and what kinds of arguments need to be marshalled and considered before a serious and informed discussion of alternative conceptions of a nonsexist society can even take place. Once assembled, these arguments need to be individually and carefully assessed before any final, reflective choice among the competing ideals can be made. There does, however, seem to me to be a strong presumptive case for something very close to, if not identical with, the assimilationist ideal.

STUDY QUESTIONS

1. In what ways is sexism, according to Wasserstrom, perhaps more deeply embedded in American culture and institutions than racism? Do you agree?
2. What are some of the similarities between racism and sexism? What are some differences?
3. What does assimilation mean in the context of race? In the context of sex?
4. What problems would assimilation pose in the context of sex that would not be problems in the context of race?

36

Theories of Race and Gender: The Erasure of Black Women

Elizabeth V. Spelman

Elizabeth V. Spelman teaches philosophy at Smith College. She is the author of *Inessential Woman: Problems of Exclusion in Feminist Thought*.

Recent feminist theory has not totally ignored white racism, though white feminists have paid much less attention to it than have black feminists. Nor have white feminists explicitly enunciated and espoused positions of white superiority. Yet much of feminist theory has reflected and contributed to what Adrienne Rich has called "white solipsism":

> to think, imagine, and speak as if whiteness described the world.
>
> not the consciously held *belief* that one race is inherently superior to all others, but a tunnel-vision which simply does not see nonwhite experience or existence as precious or significant, unless in spasmodic, impotent guilt-reflexes, which have little or no long-term, continuing momentum or political usefulness.

In this essay, I shall focus on what I take to be instances and sustaining sources of such solipsism in recent theoretical works by, or of interest to, feminists—in particular, certain ways of comparing sexism and racism, and some well-ingrained habits of thought about the source of women's oppression and the possibility of our liberation. . . . To begin, I will examine some recent prominent claims to the effect that sexism is more fundamental than racism. . . . Before turning to the evidence that has been given in behalf of that claim, we need to ask what it means to say that sexism is more fundamental than racism. It has meant or might mean several different though related things:

- It is harder to eradicate sexism than it is to eradicate racism.
- There might be sexism without racism but not racism without sexism: any social and political changes which eradicate sexism will have eradicated racism, but social and political changes which eradicate racism will not have eradicated sexism.
- Sexism is the first form of oppression learned by children.
- Sexism is historically prior to racism.
- Sexism is the cause of racism.
- Sexism is used to justify racism.

In the process of comparing racism and sexism, Richard Wasserstrom describes ways in which women and blacks have been stereotypically conceived of as less fully developed than white men. "Men and women are taught to see men as independent, capable, and powerful; men and women are taught to see women as dependent, limited in abilities, and passive. . . ." But who is taught to see black men as "independent, capable, and powerful," and by whom are they taught? Are black men taught that? Black women? White men? White women? Similarly, who is taught to see black women as "dependent, limited in abilities, and passive"? If this stereotype is so prevalent, why then have black women had to defend themselves against the images of matriarch and whore?

Wasserstrom continues:

> As is true for race, it is also a significant social fact that to be a female is to be an entity or creature viewed as different from the standard, fully developed person who is male as well as white. *But to be female, as opposed to being black*, is not to be conceived of as simply a creature of less worth. That is one important thing that differentiates sexism from racism: the ideology of sex, as opposed to the ideology of race, is a good deal more complex and confusing. *Women are both put on a pedestal* and deemed not fully developed persons. (emphasis mine)

In this brief for the view that sexism is a "deeper phenomenon" than racism, Wasserstrom leaves no room for the black woman. For a black woman cannot be "female, as opposed to being black"; she is female *and* black. Since Wasserstrom's argument proceeds from the assumption that one is either female or black, it cannot be an argument that applies to black women. Moreover, we cannot generate a composite image of the black women from the above, since the description of women as being put on a pedestal, or being dependent, never generally applied to black women in the United States and was never meant to apply to them.

Wasserstrom's argument about the priority of sexism over racism has an odd result, which stems from the erasure of black women in his analysis. He wishes to claim that in this society sex is a more fundamental fact about people than race. Yet his description of woman does not apply to the black woman, which implies that being black is a more fundamental fact about her than being a woman. I am not saying that Wasserstrom actually believes this is true, but that paradoxically the terms of his theory force him into that position. . . .

ADDITIVE ANALYSES

Sexism and racism do not have different "objects" in the case of black women. Moreover, it is highly misleading to say, without further explanation, that black women experience sexism and racism. For to say *merely* that suggests that black women experience one form of oppression, *as blacks*—the same thing black men experience—and that they experience another form of oppression, *as women*—the same thing white women experience. But this way of describing and analyzing black women's experience seems to me to be inadequate. For while it is true that images and institutions that are described as sexist affect both black and white women, they are affected in different ways, depending upon the extent to which they are affected by other forms of oppression.

For example, . . . it will not do to say that women are oppressed by the image of the "feminine" woman as fair, delicate, and in need of support and protection by men. While all women are oppressed by the use of that image, we are not oppressed in the same ways. As Linda Brent puts it so succinctly, "That which commands admiration in the white woman only hastens the degradation of the female slave." More specifically, as Angela Davis reminds us, "the alleged benefits of the ideology of femininity did not accrue" to the black female slave—she was expected to toil in the fields for just as long and hard as the black male was.

Reflection on the experience of black women also shows that it is not as if one form of oppression is merely piled upon another. As Barbara Smith has remarked, the effect of multiple oppression "is not merely arithmetic." Such an "additive" analysis informs, for example, Gerda Lerner's remark about the nature of the oppression of black women under slavery: "Their work and duties were the same as that of the men, while childbearing and rearing fell upon them as an added burden." But, as Angela Davis has pointed out, the mother/housewife role (even the words seem inappropriate) doesn't have the same *meaning* for women who experience racism as it does for those who are not so oppressed:

> . . . . In the infinite anguish of ministering to the needs of the men and children around her (who were not necessarily members of her immediate family), she was performing the *only* labor of the slave community which could not be directly and immediately claimed by the oppressor. . . . Even as she was suffering from her unique oppression as female, she was thrust by the force of circumstances into the center of the slave community.

The meaning and the oppressive nature of the "housewife" role has to be understood in relation to the roles against which it is contrasted. The work of mate/mother/nurturer has a different meaning depending on whether it is contrasted to work which has high social value and ensures economic independence, or to labor which is forced, degrading and unpaid. All of these factors are left out in a simple additive analysis. How one form of oppression (e.g., sexism) is experienced, is influenced by and influences how another form (i.e., racism) is experienced. So it would be quite misleading to say simply that black women and white women both are oppressed *as women*, and that a black woman's oppression as a black is thus separable from her oppression as a woman because she shares the latter but not the former with the white woman. An additive analysis treats the oppression of a black woman in a sexist and racist society as if it were a *further* burden than her oppression in a sexist but non-racist society, when, in fact, it is a *different* burden. As the article by Davis, among others, shows, to ignore the difference is to deny or obscure the particular reality of the black woman's experience.

If sexism and racism must be seen as interlocking, and not as piled upon each other, serious problems arise for the claim that one of them is more fundamental than the other. As we saw, one meaning of the claim that sexism is more fundamental than racism is that sexism causes racism: racism would not exist if sexism did not, while sexism could and would continue to exist even in the absence of racism. In this connection, racism is sometimes seen as something which is both derivative from sexism and in the service of it: racism keeps women from uniting in alliance against sexism. This view has been articulated by Mary Daly in *Beyond God the Father*. According to Daly, sexism is "root and paradigm" of other forms of oppression such as racism. Racism is a "deformity *within* patriarchy. . . . It is most unlikely that racism will be eradicated as long as sexism prevails."

Daly's theory relies on an additive analysis, and we can see again why such an analysis fails to describe adequately black women's experience. Daly's analysis makes it look simply as if both black and white women experience sexism, while black women also experience racism. Black women should realize, Daly says, that they must see what they have in common with white women—shared sexist oppression—and see that black and white women are "pawns in the racial struggle, which is basically not the struggle that will set them free as *women*." The additive analysis obscures the differences between black and white women's struggles. Insofar as she is oppressed by racism in a sexist context and sexism in a racist context, the black woman's struggle cannot be compartmentalized into two struggles—one *as a black* and one *as a woman*. But that way of speaking about her struggle is required by a theory which insists not only that sexism and racism are distinct but that one might be eradicated before the other. Daly rightly points out that the black woman's struggle can easily be, and has usually been, subordinated to the black man's struggle in anti-racist organizations. But she does not point out that the black woman's struggle can easily be, and usually has been, subordinated to the white woman's struggle in anti-sexist organizations.

Daly's line of thought also promotes the idea that, were it not for racism, there would be no important differences between black and white women. Since sexism is the fundamental form of oppression, and racism works in its service, the only significant differences between black and white women are differences which men have created and which are the source of antagonism between women. What is really crucial about us is our sex; racial distinctions are one of the many products of sexism, of patriarchy's attempt to keep women from uniting. It is through our shared sexual identity that we are oppressed together; it is through our shared sexual identity that we shall be liberated together.

A serious problem in thinking or speaking this way, however, is that it seems to deny or ignore the positive aspects of "racial" identities. It ignores the fact that being black is a source of pride, as well as an occasion for being oppressed. It suggests that once racism is eliminated (!), black women no longer need be concerned about or interested in their blackness—as if the only reason for paying attention to one's blackness is that it is the source of pain and sorrow and agony. But that is racism pure and simple, if it assumes that there is nothing positive about having a black history and identity. . . .

RACISM AND SOMATOPHOBIA

Feminist theorists as politically diverse as Simone de Beauvoir, Betty Friedan and Shulamith Firestone have described the conditions of women's liberation in terms which suggest that the identification of woman with her body has been the source of our oppression, and that, hence, the source of our liberation lies in sundering that connection. For example, de Beauvoir introduces *The Second Sex* with the comment that woman has been regarded as "womb"; woman is thought of as planted firmly in the world of "immanence," that is, the physical world of nature, her life defined by the dictates of her "biologic fate." In contrast, men live in the world of "transcendence," actively using their minds to create "values, mores, religions," the world of culture as opposed to the world of nature. Among Friedan's central messages is that women should be allowed and encouraged to be "culturally" as well as "biologically" creative, because the former activities, which are "mental," are of "highest value to society" in comparison to childbearing and rearing—"mastering the secrets of atoms, or the stars, composing symphonies, pioneering a new concept in government or society." . . .

I bring up the presence of somatophobia in the work of Firestone and others because I think it is a force that contributes to white solopsism in feminist thought, in at least three related ways.

First, insofar as feminists do not examine somatophobia, but actually accept it and embrace it in prescriptions for women's liberation, we will not be examining what often has been an important element in racist thinking. For the superiority of men to women is not the only hierarchical relationship that has been linked to the superiority of the mind to the body. Certain kinds, or "races," of people have been held to be more body-like than others, and this has been meant as more animal-like and less god-like.

For example, in *The White Man's Burden*, Winthrop Jordan describes ways in which white Englishmen portrayed black Africans as beastly, dirty, highly sexed beings. Lillian Smith tells us in *Killers of the Dream* how closely run together were her lessons about the evil of the body and the evil of blacks.

Derogatory stereotypes of blacks versus whites (as well as of manual workers versus intellectuals) have been very similar to the derogatory stereotypes of women versus men. Indeed, the grounds on which Plato ridiculed women were so similar to those on which he ridiculed slaves, beasts and children that he typically ridiculed them in one breath. He also thought it sufficient ridicule of one such group to accuse it of being like another (women are like slaves, slaves are like children, etc.). Aristotle's defense of his claim about the inferiority of women to men in the *Politics* is almost the same as his defense of the view that some people are meant to be slaves. (Aristotle did not identify what he called the natural class of slaves by skin color, but he says that identifying that class would be much easier if there were readily available physical characteristics by which one could do that.) Neither in women nor in slaves does the rational element work the way it ought to. Hence women and slaves are, though in different ways, to attend to the physical needs of the men/masters/intellectuals. . . .

So we need to examine and understand somatophobia and look for it in our own thinking, for the idea that the work of the body and for the body has no part in real human dignity has been part of racist as well as sexist ideology. That is, oppressive stereotypes of "inferior races" and of women have typically involved images of their lives as determined by basic bodily functions (sex, reproduction, appetite, secretions and excretions) and as given over to attending to the bodily functions of others (feeding, washing, cleaning, doing the "dirty work"). Superior groups, we have been told from Plato on down, have better things to do with their lives. As Hannah Arendt has pointed out, the position of women and slaves has been directly tied to the notion that their lives are to be devoted to taking care of bodily functions. It certainly does not follow from the presence of somatophobia in a person's writings that she or he is a racist or a sexist. But somatophobia historically has been symptomatic of sexist and racist (as well as classist) attitudes.

Human groups know that the work of the body and for the body is necessary for human existence, and they make provisions for that fact. And so even when a group views its liberation in terms of being free of association with, or responsibility for, bodily tasks, explicitly or implicitly, its own liberation may be predicated on the oppression of other groups—those assigned to do the body work. For example, if feminists decide that women are not going to be relegated to doing such work, who do we think is going to do it? Have we attended to the role that racism (and classism) historically has played in settling that question?

Finally, if one thinks—as de Beauvoir, Friedan and Firestone do—that the liberation of women requires abstracting the notion of woman from the notion of woman's body, then one perhaps also will think that the liberation of blacks requires abstracting the notion of a black person from the notion of a black body. Since the body is thought to be the culprit (or anyway certain aspects of the body are thought to be the culprits), the solution may seem to be: keep the person and leave the occasion for oppression behind. Keep the woman, somehow, but leave behind her woman's body; keep the black person but leave the blackness behind. . . .

Once the concept of woman is divorced from the concept of woman's body, conceptual room is made for the idea of a woman who is no particular historical woman—she has no color, no accent, no particular characteristics that require having a body. She is somehow all and only woman; that is her only identifying feature. And so it will seem inappropriate or beside the point to think of women in terms of any physical characteristics, especially if it has been in the name of such characteristics that oppression has been rationalized. . . .

RICH ON EMBODIMENT

Adrienne Rich is perhaps the only well-known white feminist to have noted "white solipsism" in feminist theorizing and activity. I think it is no coincidence that she also noticed and attended to the strong strain of somatophobia in feminist theory. . . .

Both de Beauvoir and Firestone wanted to break it by insisting that women need be no more connected—in thought or deed—with the body than men have been. De Beauvoir and Firestone more or less are in agreement, with the patriarchal cultural history they otherwise question, that embodiment is a drag. Rich, however, insists that the negative connection between woman and body be broken along other lines. She asks us to think about whether what she calls "flesh-loathing" is the only attitude it is possible to have toward our bodies. Just as she explicitly distinguishes between motherhood as experience and motherhood as institution, so she implicitly asks us to distinguish between embodiment as experience and embodiment as institution. Flesh-loathing is part of the well-entrenched beliefs, habits and practices epitomized in the treatment of pregnancy as a disease. But we need not experience our flesh, our body, as loathsome. . . .

I think it is not a psychological or historical accident that having reflected so thoroughly on flesh-loathing, Rich focused on the failure of white women to see black women's experiences as different from their own. For looking at embodiment is one way (though not the only one) of coming to note and understand the *particularity* of experience. Without bodies we could not have personal histories, for without them we would not live at a particular time nor in a particular place. Moreover, without them we could not be identified as woman or man, black or white. This is not to say that reference to publicly observable bodily characteristics settles the question of whether someone is woman or man, black or white; nor is it to say that being woman or man, black or white, just means having certain bodily characteristics. But different meanings are attached to having those characteristics, in different places and at different times and by different people, and those differences make a huge difference in the kinds of lives we lead or experiences we have. Women's oppression has been linked to the meanings assigned to having a woman's body by male oppressors. Blacks' oppression has been linked to the meanings assigned to having a black body by white oppressors. We cannot hope to understand the meaning of a person's experiences, including her experiences of oppression, without first thinking of her as embodied, and second thinking about the particular meanings assigned to that embodiment. If, because of somatophobia, we think and write as if we are not embodied, or as if we would be better off if we were not embodied, we are likely to ignore the ways in which different forms of embodiment are correlated with different kinds of experience. . . .

Rich does not run away from the fact that women have bodies, nor does she wish that women's bodies were not so different from men's. That healthy regard for the ground of our differences from men is logically connected—though of course does not ensure—to a healthy regard for the ground of the differences between black women and white women.

STUDY QUESTIONS

1. What is meant by "white solipsism"?
2. Where does Spelman criticize Wasserstrom? Are her criticisms valid?
3. How does "additive analysis" obscure the particular reality of black women's experience?
4. How is the "fear of the body" (somatophobia) a symptom of sexist, racist, and classist attitudes, according to Spelman?
5. What corrective to somatophobia does Spelman find in the work of Adrienne Rich?

37

Reverse Discrimination as Unjustified

Lisa Newton

Lisa Newton is a professor of philosophy at Fairfield University.

I have heard it argued that "simple justice" requires that we favor women and blacks in employment and educational opportunities, since women and blacks were "unjustly" excluded from such opportunities for so many years in the not so distant past. It is a strange argument, an example of a possible implication of a true proposition advanced to dispute the proposition itself, like an octopus absentmindedly slicing off his head with a stray tentacle. A fatal confusion underlies this argument, a confusion fundamentally relevant to our understanding of the notion of the rule of law.

Two senses of justice and equality are involved in this confusion. The root notion of justice, progenitor of the other, is the one that Aristotle (*Nicomachean Ethics* 5.6; *Politics* 1.2; 3.1) assumes to be the foundation and proper virtue of the political association. It is the conclusion which free men establish among themselves when they "share a common life in order that their association bring them self-sufficiency"—the regulation of their relationship by law, and the establishment, by law, of equality before the law. Rule of law is the name and pattern of this justice; its equality stands against the inequalities—of wealth, talent, etc.—otherwise obtaining among its participants, who by virtue of that equality are called "citizens." It is an achievement—complete, or, more frequently, partial—of certain people in certain concrete situations. It is fragile and easily disrupted by powerful individuals who discover that the blind equality of rule of law is inconvenient for their interests. Despite its obvious instability, Aristotle assumed that the establishment of justice in this sense, the creation of citizenship, was a permanent possibility for men and that the resultant association of citizens was the natural home of the species. At levels below the political association, this rule-governed equality is easily found; it is exemplified by any group of children agreeing together to play a game. At the level of the political association, the attainment of this justice is more difficult, simply because the stakes are so much higher for each participant. The equality of citizenship is not something that happens of its own accord, and without the expenditure of a fair amount of effort it will collapse into the rule of a powerful few over an apathetic many. But at least it has been achieved, at some times in some places; it is always worth trying to achieve, and eminently worth trying to maintain, wherever and to whatever degree it has been brought into being.

Aristotle's parochialism is notorious; he really did not imagine that persons other than Greeks could associate freely in justice, and the only form of association he had in mind was the Greek *polis*. With the decline of the *polis* and the shift in the center of political thought, his notion of justice underwent a sea change. To be exact, it ceased to represent a political type and became a moral ideal: the ideal of equality as we know it. This ideal demands that all men be included in citizenship—that one Law govern all equally, that all men regard all other men as fellow citizens, with the same guarantees, rights, and protections. Briefly, it demands that the circle of citizenship achieved by any group be extended to include the entire human race. Properly understood, its effect on our associations can be excellent: It congratulates us on our achievement of rule of law as a process of government but refuses to let us remain complacent until we have expanded the associations to include others within the ambit of the rules, as often and as far as possible. While one man is a slave, none of us may feel truly free. We are constantly prodded by this ideal to look for possible unjustifiable discrimination, for inequalities not absolutely required for the functioning of the society and advantageous to all. And after twenty centuries of pressure, not at all constant, from this ideal, it might be said that some progress has been made. To take the cases in point for this problem, we are now prepared to assert, as Aristotle would never have been, the equality of sexes and of persons of different colors. The ambit of American citizenship, once restricted to white males of property, has been extended to include all adult free men, then all adult males including ex-slaves, then all women. The process of acquisition of full citizenship was for these groups a sporadic trail of half-measures, even now not complete; the steps on the road to full equality are marked by legislation and judicial decisions which are only recently concluded and still often not enforced. But the fact that we can now discuss the possibility of favoring such groups in hiring shows that over the area that concerns us, at least, full equality is presupposed as a basis for discussion. To that extent, they are full citizens, fully protected by the law of the land.

It is important for my argument that the moral ideal of equality be recognized as logically distinct from the condition (or virtue) of justice in the political sense. Justice in this sense exists *among* a citizenry, irrespective of the number of the populace included in that citizenry. Further, the moral ideal is parasitic upon the political virtue, for "equality" is unspecified—it means nothing until we are told in what respect that equality is to be realized. In a political context, "equality" is specified as "equal rights"—equal access to the public realm, public goods and offices, equal treatment under the law—in brief, the equality of citizenship. If citizenship is not a possibility, political equality is unintelligible. The ideal emerges as a generalization of the real condition and refers back to that condition for its content.

Now, if justice (Aristotle's justice in the political sense) is equal treatment under law for all citizens, what is injustice? Clearly, injustice is the violation of that equality, discrimination for or against a group of citizens, favoring them with special immunities and privileges or depriving them of those guaranteed to the others. When the southern employer refuses to hire blacks in white-collar jobs, when Wall Street will only hire women as secretaries with new titles, when Mississippi high schools routinely flunk all the black boys above ninth grade, we have examples of injustice, and we work to restore the equality of the public realm by ensuring that equal opportunity will be provided in such cases in the future. But of course, when the employers and the schools *favor* women and blacks, the same injustice is done. Just as the previous discrimination did, this reverse discrimination violates the public equality which defines citizenship and destroys the rule of law for the areas in which these favors are granted. To the extent that we adopt a program of discrimination, reverse or otherwise, justice in the political sense is destroyed, and none of us, specifically affected or not, is a citizen, a bearer of rights—we are all petitioners for favors. And to the same extent, the ideal of equality is undermined, for it has content only where justice obtains, and by destroying justice we render the ideal meaningless. It is, then, an ironic paradox, if not a contradiction in terms, to assert that the ideal of equality justifies the violation of justice; it is as if one should argue, with William Buckley, that an ideal of humanity can justify the destruction of the human race.

Logically, the conclusion is simple enough: All discrimination is wrong *prima facie* because it violates justice, and that goes for reverse discrimination too. No violation of justice among the citizens may be justified (may overcome the *prima facie* objection) by appeal to the ideal of equality, for that ideal is logically dependent upon the notion of justice. Reverse discrimination, then, which attempts no other justification than an appeal to equality, is wrong. But let us try to make the conclusion more plausible by suggesting some of the implications of the suggested practice of reverse discrimination in employment and education. My argument will be that the problems raised there are insoluble, not only in practice but in principle.

We may argue, if we like, about what "discrimination" consists of. Do I discriminate against blacks if I admit none to my school when none of the black applicants are qualified by the tests I always give? How far must I go to root out cultural bias from my application forms and tests before I can say that I have not discriminated against those of different cultures? Can I assume that women are not strong enough to be roughnecks on my oil rigs, or must I test them individually? But this controversy, the most popular and well-argued aspect of the issue, is not as fatal as two others which cannot be avoided: If we are regarding the blacks as a "minority" victimized by discrimination, what is a "minority"? And for any group—blacks, women, whatever—that has been discriminated against, what amount of reverse discrimination wipes out the initial discrimination? Let us grant as true that women and blacks were discriminated against, even where laws forbade such discrimination, and grant for the sake of argument that a history of discrimination must be wiped out by reverse discrimination. What follows?

First, are there other groups which have been discriminated against? For they should have the same right of restitution. What about American Indians, Chicanos, Appalachian Mountain whites, Puerto Ricans, Jews, Cajuns, and Orientals? And if these are to be included, the principle according to which we specify a "minority" is simply the criterion of "ethnic (sub) group," and we're stuck with every hyphenated American in the lower middle class clamoring for special privileges for *his* group—and with equal justification. For be it noted, when we run down the Harvard roster, we find not only a scarcity of blacks (in comparison with the proportion in the population) but an even more striking scarcity of those second-, third-, and fourth-generation ethnics who make up the loudest voice of Middle America. Shouldn't they demand *their* share? And eventually, the WASPs will have to form their own lobby; for they too are a minority. The point is simply this: There is no "majority" in America who will not mind giving up just a bit of their rights to make room for a favored minority. There are only other minorities, each of which is discriminated against by the favoring. The initial injustice is then repeated dozens of times, and if each minority is granted the same right of restitution as the others, an entire area of rule governance is dissolved into a pushing and shoving match between self-interested groups. Each works to catch the public eye and political popularity by whatever means of advertising and power politics lend themselves to the effort, to capitalize as much as possible on temporary popularity until the restless mob picks another group to feel sorry for. Hardly an edifying spectacle, and in the long run no one can benefit: The pie is no larger—it's just that instead of setting up and enforcing rules for getting a piece, we've turned the contest into a free-for-all, requiring much more effort for no larger a reward. It would be in the interests of all the participants to reestablish an objective rule to govern the process, carefully enforced and the same for all.

Second, supposing that we do manage to agree in general that women and blacks (and all the others) have some right of restitution, some right to a privileged place in the structure of opportunities for a while, how will we know when that while is up? How much privilege is enough? When will the guilt be gone, the price paid, the balance restored? What recompense is right for centuries of exclusion? What criterion tells us when we are done? Our experience with the Civil Rights movement shows us that agreement on these terms cannot be presupposed: A process that appears to some to be going at a mad gallop into a black takeover appears to the rest of us to be at a standstill. Should a practice of reverse discrimination be adopted, we may safely predict that just as some of us begin to see "a satisfactory start toward righting the balance," others of us will see that we "have already gone too far in the other direction" and will suggest that the discrimination ought to be reversed again. And such disagreement is inevitable, for the point is that we could not *possibly* have any criteria for evaluating the kind of recompense we have in mind. The context presumed by any discussion of restitution is the context of the rule of law: Law sets the rights of men and simultaneously sets the method for remedying the violation of those rights. You may exact suffering from others and/or damage payments for yourself if and only if the others have violated your rights; the suffering you have endured is not sufficient reason for them to suffer. And remedial rights exist only where there is law: Primary human rights are useful guides to legislation but cannot stand as reasons for awarding remedies for injuries sustained. But then, the context presupposed by any discussion of restitution is the context of preexistent full citizenship. No remedial rights could exist for the excluded; neither in law nor in logic does there exist a right to *sue* for a standing to sue.

From these two considerations, then, the difficulties with reverse discrimination become evident. Restitution for a disadvantaged group whose rights under the law have been violated is possible by legal means, but restitution for a disadvantaged group whose grievance is that there was no law to protect them simply is not. First, outside of the area of justice defined by the law, no sense can be made of "the group's rights," for no law recognizes that group or the individuals in it, qua members, as bearers of rights (hence *any* group can constitute itself as a disadvantaged minority in some sense and demand similar restitution). Second, outside of the area of protection of law, no sense can be made of the violation of rights (hence the amount of the recompense cannot be decided by any objective criterion). For both reasons, the practice of reverse discrimination undermines the foundation of the very ideal in whose name it is advocated; it destroys justice, law, equality, and citizenship itself, and replaces them with power struggles and popularity contests.

STUDY QUESTIONS

1. What is the root notion of justice, according to Newton?
2. How is the ideal of equality logically distinct from the political sense of justice? How does justice in this political sense relate to equality?
3. What is injustice, according to Newton?
4. Do you think that Newton's arguments against reverse discrimination are valid? Why or why not?
5. Is it true that some injustice is done when employers favor blacks? Can this practice be justified? If so, how?

38

Beyond Affirmative Action

Cornel West

Cornel West is a professor of religion and the director of Afro-American studies at Princeton University. He is the author of *The American Evasion of Philosophy* and *Race Matters.*

> *Institutionalized rejection of* difference *is an absolute necessity in a profit economy which needs outsiders as surplus people. As members of such an economy, we have* all *been programmed to respond to the human differences between us with fear and loathing and to handle that difference in one of three ways: ignore it, and if that is not possible, copy it if we think it is dominant, or destroy it if we think it is subordinate. But we have no patterns for relating across our human differences as equals. As a result, those differences have been misnamed and misused in the service of separation and confusion.*
>
> Audre Lorde, *Sister Outsider* (1984)

The fundamental crisis in black America is twofold: too much poverty and too little self-love. The urgent problem of black poverty is primarily due to the distribution of wealth, power, and income—a distribution influenced by the racial caste system that denied opportunities to most "qualified" black people until two decades ago.

The historic role of American progressives is to promote redistributive measures that enhance the standard of living and quality of life for the have-nots and have-too-littles. Affirmative action was one such redistributive measure that surfaced in the heat of battle in the 1960s among those fighting for racial equality. Like earlier *de facto* affirmative action measures in the American past—contracts, jobs, and loans to select immigrants granted by political machines; subsidies to certain farmers; FHA mortgage loans to specific home buyers; or GI Bill benefits to particular courageous Americans—recent efforts to broaden access to America's prosperity have been based upon preferential policies. Unfortunately, these policies always benefit middle-class Americans disproportionately. The political power of big business in big government circumscribes redistributive measures and thereby tilts these measures away from the have-nots and have-too-littles.

Every redistributive measure is a compromise with and concession from the caretakers of American prosperity—that is, big business and big government. Affirmative action was one such compromise and concession achieved after the protracted struggle of American progressives and liberals in the courts and in the streets. Visionary progressives always push for substantive redistributive measures that make opportunities available to the have-nots and have-too-littles, such as more federal support to small farmers, or more FHA mortgage loans to urban dwellers as well as suburban home buyers. Yet in the American political system, where the powers that be turn a skeptical eye toward any program aimed at economic redistribution, progressives must secure whatever redistributive measures they can, ensure their enforcement, then extend their benefits if possible.

If I had been old enough to join the fight for racial equality in the courts, the legislatures, and the board rooms in the 1960s (I *was* old enough to be in the streets), I would have favored—as I do now—a class-based affirmative action in principle. Yet in the heat of battle in American politics, a redistributive measure in principle with no power and pressure behind it means no redistributive measure at all. The prevailing discriminatory practices during the sixties, whose targets were working people, women, and people of color, were atrocious. Thus, an *enforceable* race-based—and later gender-based—affirmative action policy was the best possible compromise and concession.

Progressives should view affirmative action as neither a major solution to poverty nor a sufficient means to equality. We should see it as primarily playing a negative role—namely, to ensure that discriminatory practices against women and people of color are abated. Given the history of this country, it is a virtual certainty that without affirmative action racial and sexual discrimination would return with a vengeance. Even if affirmative action fails significantly to reduce black poverty or contributes to the persistence of racist perceptions in the workplace, without affirmative action black access to America's prosperity would be even more difficult to obtain and racism in the workplace would persist anyway.

This claim is not based on any cynicism toward my white fellow citizens; rather, it rests upon America's historically weak will toward racial justice and substantive redistributive measures. This is why an attack on affirmative action is an attack on redistributive efforts by progressives unless there is a real possibility of enacting and enforcing a more wide-reaching class-based affirmative action policy.

In American politics, progressives must not only cling to redistributive ideals, but must also fight for those policies that—out of compromise and concession—imperfectly conform to those ideals. Liberals who give only lip service to these ideals, trash the policies in the name of *realpolitik*, or reject the policies as they perceive a shift in the racial bellwether give up precious ground too easily. And they do so even as the sand is disappearing under our feet on such issues as regressive taxation, layoffs or takebacks from workers, and cutbacks in health and child care.

Affirmative action is not the most important issue for black progress in America, but it is part of a redistributive chain that must be strengthened if we are to confront and eliminate black poverty. If there were social democratic redistributive measures that wiped out black poverty, and if racial and sexual discrimination could be abated through the good will and meritorious judgments of those in power, affirmative action would be unnecessary. Although many of my liberal and progressive citizens view affirmative action as a redistributive measure whose time is over or whose life is no longer worth preserving, I question their view because of the persistence of discriminatory practices that increase black social misery, and the warranted suspicion that good will and fair judgment among the powerful does not loom as large toward women and people of color.

If the elimination of black poverty is a necessary condition of substantive black progress, then the affirmation of black humanity, especially among black people themselves, is a sufficient condition of such progress. Such affirmation speaks to the existential issues of what it means to be a degraded African (man, woman, gay, lesbian, child) in a racist society. How does one affirm oneself without reenacting negative black stereotypes or overreacting to white supremacist ideals?

The difficult and delicate quest for black identity is integral to any talk about racial equality. Yet it is not solely a political or economic matter. The quest for black identity involves self-respect and self-regard, realms inseparable from, yet not identical to, political power and economic status. The flagrant self-loathing among black middle-class professionals bears witness to this painful process. Unfortunately, black conservatives focus on the issue of self-respect as if it were the one key that would open all doors to black progress. They illustrate the fallacy of trying to open all doors with one key: they wind up closing their eyes to all doors except the one the key fits.

Progressives, for our part, must take seriously the quest for self-respect, even as we train our eye on the institutional causes of black social misery. The issues of black identity—both black self-love and self-contempt—sit alongside black poverty as realities to confront and transform. The uncritical acceptance of self-degrading ideals, that call into question black intelligence, possibility, and beauty not only compounds black social misery but also paralyzes black middle-class efforts to defend broad redistributive measures.

This paralysis takes two forms: black bourgeois preoccupation with white peer approval and black nationalist obsession with white racism.

The first form of paralysis tends to yield a navel-gazing posture that conflates the identity crisis of the black middle class with the state of siege raging in black working-poor and very poor communities. That unidimensional view obscures the need for redistributive measures that significantly affect the majority of blacks, who are working people on the edge of poverty.

The second form of paralysis precludes any meaningful coalition with white progressives because of an undeniable white racist legacy of the modern Western world. The anger this truth engenders impedes any effective way of responding to the crisis in black America. Broad redistributive measures require principled coalitions, including multiracial alliances. Without such measures, black America's sufferings deepen. White racism indeed contributes to this suffering. Yet an obsession with white racism often comes at the expense of more broadly based alliances to affect social change and borders on a tribal mentality. The more xenophobic versions of this viewpoint simply mirror the white supremacist ideals we are opposing and preclude any movement toward redistributive goals.

How one defines oneself influences what analytical weight one gives to black poverty. Any progressive discussion about the future of racial equality must speak to black poverty and black identity. My views on the necessity and limits of affirmative action in the present moment are informed by how substantive redistributive measures and human affirmative efforts can be best defended and expanded.

STUDY QUESTIONS

1. Why does West believe that affirmative action remains necessary in our society?
2. What two forms of "paralysis" does West identify around this issue?
3. What is "class-based" affirmative action, and why does West think this kind is superior to race-based or gender-based affirmative action? Do you agree? Why or why not?

FOR FURTHER STUDY

Beauchamp, Tom. "The Justification of Reverse Discrimination." In *Social Justice and Preferential Treatment*, ed. William T. Blackstone and Robert Heslep. Athens, Ga.: University of Georgia Press, 1976.

Carter, Steven. *Reflections of an Affirmative Action Baby*. New York: Basic Books, 1992.

Collins, Patricia Hill. *Black Feminist Thought: Knowledge, Consciousness, and the Politics of Empowerment*. London: HarperCollins, 1990.

hooks, bell. *Black Looks: Race and Representation*. Boston: South End Press, 1992.

hooks, bell, and West, Cornel. *Breaking Bread*. Boston: South End Press, 1991.

Lorde, Audre. *Sister Outsider: Essays and Speeches*. Freedom, Calif.: Crossing Press, 1984.

Morrison, Toni, et al. *Race-ing Justice, Engendering Power*. New York: Pantheon, 1992.

Steele, Shelby. *The Content of Our Character*. New York: St. Martin's Press, 1990.

West, Cornel. *Race Matters*. Boston: Beacon Press, 1993.

Chapter Eight

Ethics of Sex and Power

39

Declaration on Sexual Ethics

The Vatican

1. According to contemporary scientific research, the human person is so profoundly affected by sexuality that it must be considered as one of the factors which give to each individual's life the principal traits that distinguish it. In fact it is from sex that the human person receives the characteristics which, on the biological, psychological and spiritual levels, make that person a man or a woman, and thereby largely condition his or her progress towards maturity and insertion into society. Hence sexual matters, as is obvious to everyone, today constitute a theme frequently and openly dealt with in books, reviews, magazines, and other means of social communication.

In the present period, the corruption of morals has increased, and one of the most serious indications of this corruption is the unbridled exaltation of sex. Moreover, through the means of social communication and through public entertainment this corruption has reached the point of invading the field of education and of infecting the general mentality.

In this context certain educators, teachers, and moralists have been able to contribute to a better understanding and integration into life of the values proper to each of the sexes; on the other hand there are those who have put forward concepts and modes of behavior which are contrary to the true moral exigencies of the human person. Some members of the latter group have even gone so far as to favor a licentious hedonism.

As a result, in the course of a few years, teachings, moral criteria, and modes of living hitherto faithfully preserved have been very much unsettled, even among Christians. There are many people today who, being confronted with so many widespread opinions opposed to the teachings which they received from the Church, have come to wonder what they must still hold as true.

2. The Church cannot remain indifferent to this confusion of minds and relaxation of morals. It is a question, in fact, of a matter which is of the utmost importance both for the personal lives of Christians and for the social life of our time.[1]

The Bishops are daily led to note the growing difficulties experienced by the faithful in obtaining knowledge of wholesome moral teaching, especially in sexual matters, and of the growing difficulties experienced by pastors in expounding this teaching effectively. The Bishops know that by their pastoral charge they are called upon to meet the needs of their faithful in this very serious matter, and important documents dealing with it have already been published by some of them or by Episcopal Conferences. Nevertheless, since the erroneous opinions and resulting deviations are continuing to spread everywhere, the Sacred Congregation for the Doctrine of the Faith, by virtue of its function in the universal Church[2] and by a mandate of the Supreme Pontiff, has judged it necessary to publish the present Declaration.

3. The people of our time are more and more convinced that the human person's dignity and vocation demand that they should discover, by the light of their own intelligence, the values innate in their nature, that they should ceaselessly develop these values and realize them in their lives, in order to achieve an ever greater development.

In moral matters man cannot make value judgments according to his personal whim: "In the depths of his conscience, man detects a law which he does not impose on himself, but which holds him to obedience. . . . For man has in his heart a law written by God. To obey it is the very dignity of man; according to it he will be judged."[3]

Moreover, through his revelation God has made known to us Christians his plan of salvation, and he has held up to us Christ, the Saviour and Sanctifier, in his teaching and example, as the supreme and immutable law of life: "I am the light of the world; anyone who follows me will not be walking in the dark, he will have the light of life."[4]

Therefore there can be no true promotion of man's dignity unless the essential order of his nature is respected. Of course, in the history of civilization many of the concrete conditions and needs of human life have changed and will continue to change. But all evolution of morals and every type of life must be kept within the limits imposed by the immutable principles based upon every human person's constitutive elements and essential relations—elements and relations which transcend historical contingency.

These fundamental principles, which can be grasped by reason, are contained in "the divine law—eternal, objective, and universal—whereby God orders, directs, and governs the entire universe and all the ways of the human community, by a plan conceived in wisdom and love. Man has been made by God to participate in this law, with the result that, under the gentle disposition of divine Providence, he can come to perceive ever increasingly the unchanging truth."[5] This divine law is accessible to our minds.

4. Hence, those many people are in error who today assert that one can find neither in human nature nor in the revealed law any absolute and immutable norm to serve for particular actions other than the one which expresses itself in the general law of charity and respect for human dignity. As a proof of their assertion they put forward the view that so-called norms of the natural law or precepts of Sacred Scripture are to be regarded only as given expressions of a form of particular culture at a certain moment of history.

But in fact, divine Revelation and, in its own proper order, philosophical wisdom, emphasize the authentic exigencies of human nature. They thereby necessarily manifest the existence of immutable laws inscribed in the constitutive elements of human nature and which are revealed to be identical in all beings endowed with reason.

Furthermore, Christ instituted his Church as "the pillar and bulwark of truth."[6] With the Holy Spirit's assistance, she ceaselessly preserves and transmits without error the truths of the moral order, and she authentically interprets not only the revealed positive law but "also . . . those principles of the moral order which have their origin in human nature itself"[7] and which concern man's full development and sanctification. Now in fact the Church throughout her history has always considered a certain number of precepts of the natural law as having an absolute and immutable value, and in their transgression she has seen a contradiction of the teaching and spirit of the Gospel.

5. Since sexual ethics concern certain fundamental values of human and Christian life, this general teaching equally applies to sexual ethics. In this domain there exist principles and norms which the Church has always unhesitatingly transmitted as part of her teaching, however much the opinions and morals of the world may have been opposed to them. These principles and norms in no way owe their origin to a certain type of culture, but rather to knowledge of the divine law and of human nature. They therefore cannot be considered as having become out of date or doubtful under the pretext that a new cultural situation has arisen.

It is these principles which inspired the exhortations and directives given by the Second Vatican Council for an education and an organization of social life taking account of the equal dignity of man and woman while respecting their difference.[8]

Speaking of "the sexual nature of man and the human faculty of procreation," the Council noted that they "wonderfully exceed the dispositions of lower forms of life."[9] It then took particular care to expound the principles and criteria which concern human sexuality in marriage, and which are based upon the finality of the specific function of sexuality.

In this regard the Council declares that the moral goodness of the acts proper to conjungal life, acts which are ordered according to true human dignity, "does not depend solely on sincere intentions or on an evaluation of motives. It must be determined by objective standards. These, based on the nature of the human person and his acts, preserve the full sense of mutual self-giving and human procreation in the context of true love."[10]

These final words briefly sum up the Council's teaching—more fully expounded in an earlier part of the same Constitution[11]—on the finality of the sexual act and on the principal criterion of its morality: it is respect for its finality that ensures the moral goodness of this act.

This same principle, which the Church holds from divine Revelation and from her authentic interpretation of the natural law, is also the basis of her traditional doctrine, which states that the use of the sexual function has its true meaning and moral rectitude only in true marriage.[12]

6. It is not the purpose of the present declaration to deal with all the abuses of the sexual faculty, nor with all the elements involved in the practice of chastity. Its object is rather to repeat the Church's doctrine on certain particular points, in view of the urgent need to oppose serious errors and widespread aberrant modes of behavior.

7. Today there are many who vindicate the right to sexual union before marriage, at least in those cases where a firm intention to marry and an affection which is already in some way conjugal in the psychology of the subjects require this completion, which they judge to be connatural. This is especially the case when the celebration of the marriage is impeded by circumstances or when this intimate relationship seems necessary in order for love to be preserved.

This opinion is contrary to Christian doctrine, which states that every genital act must be within the framework of marriage. However firm the intention of those who practice such premature sexual relations may be, the fact remains that these relations cannot ensure, in sincerity and fidelity, the interpersonal relationship between a man and a woman, nor especially can they protect this relationship from whims and caprices. Now it is a stable union that Jesus willed, and he restored its original requirement, beginning with the sexual difference. "Have you not read that the creator from the beginning made them male and female and that he said: This is why a man must leave father and mother, and cling to his wife, and the two become one body? They are no longer two, therefore, but one body. So then, what God has united, man must not divide."[13] Saint Paul will be even more explicit when he shows that if unmarried people or widows cannot live chastely they have no other alternative than the stable union of marriage: ". . . it is better to marry than to be aflame with passion."[14] Through marriage, in fact, the love of married people is taken up into that love which Christ irrevocably has for the Church,[15] while dissolute sexual union[16] defiles the temple of the Holy Spirit which the Christian has become. Sexual union therefore is only legitimate if a definitive community of life has been established between the man and the woman.

This is what the Church has always understood and taught,[17] and she finds a profound agreement with her doctrine in men's reflection and in the lessons of history.

Experience teaches us that love must find its safeguard in the stability of marriage, if sexual intercourse is truly to respond to the requirements of its own finality and to those of human dignity. These requirements call for a conjugal contract sanctioned and guaranteed by society—a contract which establishes a state of life of capital importance both for the exclusive union of the man and the woman and for the good of their family and of the human community. Most often, in fact, premarital relations exclude the possibility of children. What is represented to be conjugal love is not able, as it absolutely should be, to develop into paternal and maternal love. Or, if it does happen to do so, this will be to the detriment of the children, who will be deprived of the stable environment in which they ought to develop in order to find in it the way and the means of their insertion into society as a whole.

The consent given by people who wish to be united in marriage must therefore be manifested externally and in a manner which makes it valid in the eyes of society. As far as the faithful are concerned, their consent to the setting up of a community of conjugal life must be expressed according to the laws of the Church. It is a consent which makes their marriage a Sacrament of Christ.

8. At the present time there are those who, basing themselves on observations in the psychological order, have begun to judge indulgently, and even to excuse completely, homosexual relations between certain people. This they do in opposition to the constant teaching of the Magisterium and to the moral sense of the Christian people.

A distinction is drawn, and it seems with some reason, between homosexuals whose tendency comes from a false education, from a lack of normal sexual development, from habit, from bad example, or from other similar causes, and is transitory or at least not incurable; and homosexuals who are definitively such because of some kind of innate instinct or a pathological constitution judged to be incurable.

In regard to this second category of subjects, some people conclude that their tendency is so natural that it justifies in their case homosexual relations within a sincere communion of life and love analogous to marriage insofar as such homosexuals feel incapable of enduring a solitary life.

In the pastoral field, these homosexuals must certainly be treated with understanding and sustained in the hope of overcoming their personal difficulties and their inability to fit into society. Their culpability will be judged with prudence. But no pastoral method can be employed which would give moral justification to these acts on the grounds that they would be consonant with the condition of such people. For according to the objective moral order, homosexual relations are acts which lack an essential and indispensable finality. In Sacred Scripture they are condemned as a serious depravity and even presented as the sad consequence of rejecting God.[18] This judgment of Scripture does not of course permit us to conclude that all those who suffer from this anomaly are personally responsible for it, but it does attest to the fact that homosexual acts are intrinsically disordered and can in no case be approved.

9. The traditional Catholic doctrine that masturbation constitutes a grave moral disorder is often called into doubt or expressly denied today. It is said that psychology and sociology show that it is a normal phenomenon of sexual development, especially among the young. It is stated that there is real and serious fault only in the measure that the subject deliberately indulges in solitary pleasure closed in on self ("ipsation"), because in this case the act would indeed be radically opposed to the loving communion between persons of different sex which some hold is what is principally sought in the use of the sexual faculty.

This opinion is contradictory to the teaching and pastoral practice of the Catholic Church. Whatever the force of certain arguments of a biological and philosophical nature, which have sometimes been used by theologians, in fact both the Magisterium of the Church—in the course of a constant tradition—and the moral sense of the faithful have declared without hesitation that masturbation is an intrinsically and seriously disordered act.[19] The main reason is that, whatever the motive for acting in this way, the deliberate use of the sexual faculty outside normal conjugal relations essentially contradicts the finality of the faculty. For it lacks the sexual relationship called for by the moral order, namely the relationship which realizes "the full sense of mutual self-giving and human procreation in the context of true love."[20] All deliberate exercise of sexuality must be reserved to this regular relationship. Even if it cannot be proved that Scripture condemns this sin by name, the tradition of the Church has rightly understood it to be condemned in the New Testament when the latter speaks of "impurity," "unchasteness," and other vices contrary to chastity and continence.

Sociological surveys are able to show the frequency of this disorder according to the places, populations, or circumstances studied. In this way facts are discovered, but facts do not constitute a criterion for judging the moral value of human acts.[21] The frequency of the phenomenon in question is certainly to be linked with man's innate weakness following original sin; but it is also to be linked with the loss of a sense of God, with the corruption of morals engendered by the commercialization of vice, with the unrestrained licentiousness of so many public entertainments and publications, as well as with the neglect of modesty, which is the guardian of chastity.

On the subject of masturbation modern psychology provides much valid and useful information for formulating a more equitable judgment on moral responsibility and for orienting pastoral action. Psychology helps one to see how the immaturity of adolescence (which can sometimes persist after that age), psychological imbalance, or habit can influence behavior, diminishing the deliberate character of the act and bringing about a situation whereby subjectively there may not always be serious fault. But in general, the absence of serious responsibility must not be presumed; this would be to misunderstand people's moral capacity.

In the pastoral ministry, in order to form an adequate judgment in concrete cases, the habitual behavior of people will be considered in its totality, not only with regard to the individual's practice of charity and of justice but also with regard to the individual's care in observing the particular precepts of chastity. In particular, one will have to examine whether the individual is using the necessary means, both natural and supernatural, which Christian asceticism from its long experience recommends for overcoming the passions and progressing in virtue. . . .

NOTES

1. See Vatican II, *Pastoral Constitution on the Church in the World of Today,* no. 47: *Acta Apostolicae Sedis* 58 (1966) 1067 [*The Pope Speaks* XI, 289–290].
2. See the Apostolic Constitution *Regimini Ecclesiae universae* (August 15, 1967), no. 29: *AAS* 59 (1967) 897 [*TPS* XII, 401–402].
3. *Pastoral Constitution on the Church in the World of Today,* no. 16: *AAS* 58 (1966) 1037 [*TPS* XI, 268].
4. *Jn* 8, 12.
5. *Declaration on Religious Freedom,* no. 3: *AAS* 58 (1966) 931 [*TPS* XI, 86].
6. 1 *Tm* 3, 15.
7. *Declaration on Religious Freedom,* no. 14: *AAS* 58 (1966) 940 [*TPS* XI, 93]. See also Pius XI, Encyclical *Casti Connubii* (December 31, 1930): *AAS* 22 (1930) 579–580; Pius XII, Address of November 2, 1954 *AAS* 46 (1954) 671–672 [*TPS* I 380–381]; John XXIII, Encyclical *Mater et Magistra* (May 25, 1961), no. 239: *AAS* 53 (1961) 457 [*TPS* VII, 388]; Paul VI, Encyclical *Humanae Vitae* (July 25, 1968), no. 4: *AAS* 60 (1968) 483 [*TPS* XIII, 331–332].
8. See Vatican II, *Declaration on Christian Education,* nos. 1 and 8: *AAS* 58 (1966) 729–730, 734–736 [*TPS* XI, 201–202, 206–207]; *Pastoral Constitution on the Church in the World of Today,* nos. 29, 60, 67: *AAS* 58 (1966)

1048–1049, 1080–1081, 1088–1089 [*TPS* XI, 276–277, 299–300, 304–305].

9. *Pastoral Constitution on the Church in the World of Today,* no. 51: *AAS* 58 (1966) 1072 [*TPS* XI, 293].

10. *Loc. cit.;* see also no. 49: *AAS* 58 (1966) 1069–1070 [*TPS* XI, 291–292].

11. See *Pastoral Constitution on the Church in the World of Today,* nos. 49–50: *AAS* 58 (1966) 1069–1072 [*TPS* XI, 291–293].

12. The present Declaration does not review all the moral norms for the use of sex, since they have already been set forth in the encyclicals *Casti Connubii* and *Humanae Vitae.*

13. *Mt* 19, 4–6.

14. 1 *Cor* 7, 9.

15. See *Eph* 5, 25–32.

16. Extramarital intercourse is expressly condemned in *1 Cor* 5, 1; 6, 9; 7, 2; 10, 8; *Eph* 5, 5–7; *1 Tm* 1, 10; *Heb* 13, 4; there are explicit arguments given in *1 Cor* 6, 12–20.

17. See Innocent IV, Letter *Sub Catholicae professione* (March 6, 1254) (*DS* 835); Pius II, Letter *Cum sicut accepimus* (November 14, 1459) (*DS* 1367); Decrees of the Holy Office on September 24, 1665 (*DS* 2045) and March 2, 1679 (*DS* 2148); Pius XI, Encyclical *Casti Connubii* (December 31, 1930): *AAS* 22 (1930) 538–539.

18. *Rom* 1:24–27: "In consequence, God delivered them up in their lusts to unclean practices; they engaged in the mutual degradation of their bodies, these men who exchanged the truth of God for a lie and worshiped and served the creature rather than the Creator—blessed be he forever, amen! God therefore delivered them to disgraceful passions. Their women exchanged natural intercourse for unnatural, and the men gave up natural intercourse with women and burned with lust for one another. Men did shameful things with men, and thus received in their own persons the penalty for their perversity." See also what St. Paul says of sodomy in *1 Cor* 6, 9; *1 Tm* 1, 10.

19. See Leo IX, Letter *Ad splendidum nitentes* (1054) (*DS* 687–688); Decree of the Holy Office on March 2, 1679 (*DS* 2149); Pius XII, Addresses of October 8, 1953: *AAS* 45 (1953) 677–678, and May 19, 1956: *AAS* 48 (1956) 472–473.

20. *Pastoral Constitution on the Church in the World of Today,* no. 51: *AAS* 58 (1966) 1072 [*TPS* XI, 293].

21. See Paul VI, Apostolic Exhortation *Quinque iam anni* (December 8, 1970): *AAS* 63 (1971) 102 [*TPS* XV, 329]: "If sociological surveys are useful for better discovering the thought patterns of the people of a particular place, the anxieties and needs of those to whom we proclaim the word of God, and also the oppositions made to it by modern reasoning through the widespread notion that outside science there exists no legitimate form of knowledge, still the conclusions drawn from such surveys could not of themselves constitute a determining criterion of truth."

STUDY QUESTIONS

1. What is the traditional Christian teaching about sex, according to the Vatican declaration?
2. Why is sexuality so important to the spiritual life of an individual, according to the declaration?
3. Why is premarital sex immoral, according to the declaration?
4. Why are homosexual practices immoral, according to the declaration?
5. Does the Roman Catholic Church have the right to regulate the sexual practices of those outside the Church? Those within? Why or why not?
6. Do you think that contraception is wrong? Is procreation the only natural purpose of sex? Defend your answers to these questions.

40

Foucault, Femininity, and the Modernization of Patriarchal Power

Sandra Bartky

Sandra Bartky is the author of *Philosophy and Feminism* and *Originative Thought in the Later Philosophy of Heidegger.*

I

In a striking critique of modern society, Michel Foucault has argued that the rise of parliamentary institutions and of new conceptions of political liberty was accompanied by a darker counter-movement, by the emergence of a new and unprecedented discipline directed against the body. More is required of the body now than mere political allegiance or the appropriation of the products of its labor: The new discipline invades the body and seeks to regulate its very forces and operations, the economy and efficiency of its movements.

The disciplinary practices Foucault describes are tied to peculiarly modern forms of the army, the school, the hospital, the prison, and the manufactory; the aim of these disciplines is to increase the utility of the body, to augment its forces:

> What was then being formed was a policy of coercions that act upon the body, a calculated manipulation of its elements, its gestures, its behaviour. The human body was entering a machinery of power that explores it, breaks it down and rearranges it. A 'political anatomy', which was also a 'mechanics of power', was being born; it defined how one may have a hold over others' bodies, not only so that they may do what one wishes, but so that they may operate as one wishes, with the techniques, the speed and the efficiency that one determines. Thus, discipline produces subjected and practiced bodies, 'docile' bodies.

The production of "docile bodies" requires that an uninterrupted coercion be directed to the very processes of bodily activity, not just their result; this "micro-physics of power" fragments and partitions the body's time, its space, and its movements.

The student, then, is enclosed within a classroom and assigned to a desk he cannot leave; his ranking in the class can be read off the position of his desk in the serially ordered and segmented space of the classroom itself. Foucault tells us that "Jean-Baptiste de la Salle dreamt of a classroom in which the spatial distribution might provide a whole series of distinctions at once, according to the pupil's progress, worth, character, application, cleanliness, and parents' fortune." The student must sit upright, feet upon the floor, head erect; he may not slouch or fidget; his animate body is brought into a fixed correlation with the inanimate desk.

The minute breakdown of gestures and movements required of soldiers at drill is far more relentless:

> Bring the weapon forward. In three stages. Raise the rifle with the right hand, bringing it close to the body so as to hold it perpendicular

> with the right knee, the end of the barrel at eye level, grasping it by striking it with the right hand, the arm held close to the body at waist height. At the second stage, bring the rifle in front of you with the left hand, the barrel in the middle between the two eyes, vertical, the right hand grasping it at the small of the butt, the arm outstretched, the triggerguard resting on the first finger, the left hand at the height of the notch, the thumb lying along the barrel against the moulding. At the third stage. . . .

These "body-object articulations" of the soldier and his weapon, the student and his desk, effect a "coercive link with the apparatus of production." We are far indeed from older forms of control that "demanded of the body only signs or products, forms of expression or the result of labour."

The body's time, in these regimes of power, is as rigidly controlled as its space: The factory whistle and the school bell mark a division of time into discrete and segmented units that regulate the various activities of the day. The following timetable, similar in spirit to the ordering of my grammar school classroom, was suggested for French "écoles mutuelles" of the early nineteenth century:

> 8:45 entrance of the monitor, 8:52 the monitor's summons, 8:56 entrance of the children and prayer, 9:00 the children go to their benches, 9:04 first slate, 9:08 end of dictation, 9:12 second slate, etc.

Control this rigid and precise cannot be maintained without a minute and relentless surveillance.

Jeremy Bentham's design for the Panopticon, a model prison, captures for Foucault the essence of the disciplinary society. At the periphery of the Panopticon, a circular structure; at the center, a tower with wide windows that opens onto the inner side of the ring. The structure on the periphery is divided into cells, each with two windows, one facing the windows of the tower, the other facing the outside, allowing an effect of backlighting to make any figure visible within the cell. "All that is needed, then, is to place a supervisor in a central tower and to shut up in each cell a madman, a patient, a condemned man, a worker or a schoolboy." Each inmate is alone, shut off from effective communication with his fellows, but constantly visible from the tower. The effect of this is "to induce in the inmate a state of conscious and permanent visibility that assures the automatic functioning of power"; each becomes to himself his own jailer. This "state of conscious and permanent visibility" is a sign that the tight, disciplinary control of the body has gotten a hold on the mind as well. In the perpetual self-surveillance of the inmate lies the genesis of the celebrated "individualism" and heightened self-consciousness which are hallmarks of modern times. For Foucault, the structure and effects of the Panopticon resonate throughout society: Is it surprising that "prisons resemble factories, schools, barracks, hospitals, which all resemble prisons?"

Foucault's account in *Discipline and Punish* of the disciplinary practices that produce the "docile bodies" of modernity is a genuine *tour de force*, incorporating a rich theoretical account of the ways in which instrumental reason takes hold of the body with a mass of historical detail. But Foucault treats the body throughout as if it were one, as if the bodily experiences of men and women did not differ and as if men and women bore the same relationship to the characteristic institutions of modern life. Where is the account of the disciplinary practices that engender the "docile bodies" of women, bodies more docile than the bodies of men? Women, like men, are subject to many of the same disciplinary practices Foucault describes. But he is blind to those disciplines that produce a modality of embodiment that is peculiarly feminine. To overlook the forms of subjection that engender the feminine body is to perpetuate the silence and powerlessness of those upon whom these disciplines have been imposed. Hence, even though a liberatory note is sounded in Foucault's critique of power, his analysis as a whole reproduces that sexism which is endemic throughout Western political theory.

We are born male or female, but not masculine or feminine. Femininity is an artifice, an achievement, "a mode of enacting and reenacting received gender norms which surface as so many styles of the flesh." In what follows, I shall examine those disciplinary practices that produce a body which in gesture and appearance is recognizably feminine. I consider three categories of such practices: those that aim to produce a body of a certain size and general configuration; those that bring forth from this body a specific repertoire of gestures, postures, and movements; and those directed toward the display of this body as an ornamented surface. I shall examine the nature of these disciplines, how they are imposed and by whom. I shall probe the effects of the imposition of such discipline on female identity and subjectivity. In the final section I shall argue that these disciplinary practices must be understood in the light of the modernization of patriarchal domination, a modernization that unfolds historically according to the general pattern described by Foucault.

II

Styles of the female figure vary over time and across cultures: they reflect cultural obsessions and preoccupations in ways that are still poorly understood. Today, massiveness, power, or abundance in a woman's body is met with distaste. The current body of fashion is taut, small-breasted, narrow-hipped, and of a slimness bordering on emaciation; it is a silhouette that seems more appropriate to an adolescent boy or a newly pubescent girl than to an adult woman. Since ordinary women have normally quite different dimensions, they must of course diet.

Mass-circulation women's magazines run articles on dieting in virtually every issue. The *Ladies' Home Journal* of February 1986 carries a "Fat-Burning Exercise Guide," while *Mademoiselle* offers to "Help Stamp Out Cellulite" with "Six Sleek-Down Strategies." After the diet-busting Christmas holidays and later, before summer bikini season, the titles of these features become shriller and more arresting. The reader is now addressed in the imperative mode: Jump into shape for summer! Shed ugly winter fat with the all-new Grapefruit Diet! More women than men visit diet doctors, while women greatly outnumber men in self-help groups such as Weight Watchers and Overeaters Anonymous—in the case of the latter, by well over 90 percent.

Dieting disciplines the body's hungers: Appetite must be monitored at all times and governed by an iron will. Since the innocent need of the organism for food will not be denied, the body becomes one's enemy, an alien being bent on thwarting the disciplinary project. Anorexia nervosa, which has now assumed epidemic proportions, is to women of the late twentieth century what hysteria was to women of an earlier day: the crystallization in a pathological mode of a widespread cultural obsession. A survey taken recently at UCLA is astounding: Of 260 students interviewed, 27.3 percent of the women but only 5.8 percent of men said they were "terrified" of getting fat: 28.7 percent of women and only 7.5 percent of men said they were obsessed or "totally preoccupied" with food. The body images of women and men are strikingly different as well: 35 percent of women but only 12.5 percent of men said they felt fat though other people told them they were thin. Women in the survey wanted to weigh ten pounds less than their average weight; men felt they were within a pound of their ideal weight. A total of 5.9 percent of women and no men met the psychiatric criteria for anorexia or bulimia.

Dieting is one discipline imposed upon a body subject to the "tyranny of slenderness"; exercise is another. Since men as well as women exercise, it is not always easy in the case of women to distinguish what is done for the sake of physical fitness from what is done in obedience to the requirements of femininity. Men as well as women lift weights, do yoga, calisthenics, and aerobics, though "jazzercise" is a largely female pursuit. Men and women alike engage themselves with a variety of machines, each designed to call forth from the body a different exertion: There are Nautilus machines, rowing machines, ordinary and motorized exercycles, portable hip and leg cycles, belt massagers, trampolines; treadmills, arm and leg pulleys. However, given the widespread female obsession with weight, one suspects that many women are working out with these apparatuses in the health club or at the gym with a different aim in mind and in quite a different spirit than the men.

But there are classes of exercises meant for women alone, these designed not to firm or to reduce the body's size overall, but to resculpture its various parts on the current model. M. J. Saffon, "international beauty expert," assures us that his twelve basic facial exercises can erase frown lines, smooth the forehead, raise hollow cheeks, banish crow's feet, and tighten the muscles under the chin. There are exercises to build the breasts and exercises to banish "cellulite," said by "figure consultants" to be a special type of female fat. There is "spot-reducing," an umbrella term that covers dozens of punishing exercises designed to reduce "problem areas" like thick ankles or "saddlebag" thighs. The very idea of "spot-reducing" is both scientifically unsound and cruel, for it raises expectations in women that can never be realized: The pattern in which fat is deposited or removed is known to be genetically determined.

It is not only her natural appetite or unreconstructed contours that pose a danger to women: The very expressions of her face can subvert the disciplinary project of bodily perfection. An expressive face lines and creases more readily than an inexpressive one. Hence, if women are unable to suppress strong emotions, they can at least learn to inhibit the tendency of the face to register them. Sophia Loren recommends a unique solution to this problem: A piece of tape applied to the forehead or between the brows will tug at the skin when one frowns and act as a reminder to relax the face. The tape is to be worn whenever a woman is home alone.

III

There are significant gender differences in gesture, posture, movement, and general bodily comportment: Women are far more restricted than men in their manner of movement and in their lived spatiality. In her classic paper on the subject, Iris Young observes that a space seems to surround women in imagination which they are hesitant to move beyond: This manifests itself both in a reluctance to reach, stretch, and extend the body to meet resistances of matter in motion—as in sport or in the performance of physical tasks—and in a typically constricted posture and general style of movement. Woman's space is not a field in which her bodily intentionality can be freely realized but an enclosure in which she feels herself positioned and by which she is confined. The "loose woman" violates these norms: Her looseness is manifest not only in her morals, but in her manner of speech, and quite literally in the free and easy way she moves.

In an extraordinary series of over two thousand photographs, many candid shots taken in the street, the German photographer Marianne Wex has documented differences in typical masculine and feminine body posture. Women sit waiting for trains with arms close to the body, hands folded together in their laps, toes pointing straight ahead or turned inward, and legs pressed together. The women in these photographs make themselves small and narrow, harmless; they seem tense; they take up little space. Men, on the other hand, expand into the available space; they sit with legs far apart and arms flung out at some distance from the body. Most common in these sitting male figures is what Wex calls the "proferring position": the men sit with legs thrown wide apart, crotch visible, feet pointing outward, often with an arm and casually dangling hand resting comfortably on an open, spread thigh.

In proportion to total body size, a man's stride is longer than a woman's. The man has more spring and rhythm to his step; he walks with toes pointed outward, holds his arms at a greater distance from his body, and swings them farther; he tends to point the whole hand in the direction he is moving. The woman holds her arms closer to her body, palms against her sides; her walk is circumspect. If she has subjected herself to the additional constraint of high-heeled shoes, her body is thrown forward and off-balance: The struggle to walk under these conditions shortens her stride still more.

But women's movement is subjected to a still finer discipline. Feminine faces, as well as bodies, are trained to the expression of deference. Under male scrutiny, women will avert their eyes or cast them downward; the female gaze is trained to abandon its claim to the sovereign status of seer. The "nice" girl learns to avoid the bold and unfettered staring of the "loose" woman who looks at whatever and whomever she pleases. Women are trained to smile more than men, too. In the economy of smiles, as elsewhere, there is evidence that women are exploited, for they give more than they receive in return; in a smile elicitation study, one researcher found that the rate of smile return by women was 93 percent, by men only 67 percent. In many typical women's jobs, graciousness, deference, and the readiness to serve are part of the work; this requires the worker to fix a smile on her face for a good part of the working day, whatever her inner state. The economy of touching is out of balance, too: men touch women more often and on more parts of the body than women touch men: female secretaries, factory workers, and waitresses report that such liberties are taken routinely with their bodies.

Feminine movement, gesture, and posture must exhibit not only constriction, but grace as well, and a certain eroticism restrained by modesty: all three. Here is field for the operation for a whole new training: A woman must stand with stomach pulled in, shoulders thrown slightly back, and chest out, this to display her bosom to maximum advantage. While she must walk in the confined fashion appropriate to women, her movements must, at the same time, be combined with a subtle but provocative hip-roll. But too much display is taboo: Women in short, low-cut dresses are told to avoid bending over at all, but if they must, great care must be taken to avoid an unseemly display of breast or rump. From time to time, fashion magazines offer quite precise instructions on the proper way of getting in and out of cars. These instructions combine all three imperatives of women's movement: A woman must not allow her arms and legs to flail about in all directions; she must try to manage her movements with the appearance of grace—no small accomplishment when one is climbing out of the back seat of a Fiat—and she is well advised to use the opportunity for a certain display of leg.

All the movements we have described so far are self-movements; they arise from within the woman's own body. But in a way that normally goes unnoticed, males in couples may literally steer a woman everywhere she goes: down the street, around corners, into elevators, through doorways, into her chair at the dinner table, around the dance-floor. The man's movement "is not necessarily heavy and pushy or physical in an ugly way; it is light and gentle but firm in the way of the most confident equestrians with the best trained horses."

IV

We have examined some of the disciplinary practices a woman must master in pursuit of a body of the right size and shape that also displays the proper styles of feminine motility. But woman's body is an ornamented surface too, and there is much discipline involved in this production as well. Here, especially in the application of make-up and the selection of clothes, art and discipline converge, though, as I shall argue, there is less art involved than one might suppose.

A woman's skin must be soft, supple, hairless, and smooth; ideally, it should betray no sign of wear, experience, age, or deep thought. Hair must be removed not only from the face but from large surfaces of the body as well, from legs and thighs, an operation accomplished by shaving, buffing with fine sandpaper, or foul-smelling depilatories. With the new high-leg bathing suits and leotards, a substantial amount of pubic hair must be removed too. The removal of facial hair can be more specialized. Eyebrows are plucked out by the roots with a tweezer. Hot wax is sometimes poured onto the mustache and cheeks and then ripped away when it cools. The woman who wants a more permanent result may try electrolysis: This involves the killing of a hair root by the passage of an electric current down a needle which has been inserted into its base. The procedure is painful and expensive.

The development of what one "beauty expert" calls "good skin-care habits" requires not only attention to health, the avoidance of strong facial expressions, and the performance of facial exercises, but the regular use of skin-care preparations, many to be applied oftener than once a day: cleansing lotions (ordinary soap and water "upsets the skin's acid and alkaline balance"), wash-off cleansers (milder than cleansing lotions), astringents, toners, make-up removers, night creams, nourishing creams, eye creams, moisturizers, skin balancers, body lotions, hand creams, lip pomades, suntan lotions, sun screens, facial masks. Provision of the proper facial mask is complex: There are sulfur masks for pimples; hot or oil masks for dry areas; also cold masks for dry areas; tightening masks; conditioning masks; peeling masks; cleansing masks made of herbs, cornmeal, or almonds; mud packs. Black women may wish to use "fade creams" to "even skin tone." Skin-care preparations are never just sloshed onto the skin, but applied according to precise rules: Eye cream is dabbed on gently in movements toward, never away from, the nose; cleansing cream is applied in outward directions only, straight across the forehead, the upper lip, and the chin, never up but straight down the nose and up and out on the cheeks.

The normalizing discourse of modern medicine is enlisted by the cosmetics industry to gain credibility for its claims. Dr. Christiaan Barnard lends his enormous prestige to the Glycel line of "cellular treatment activators"; these contain "glycosphingolipids" that can "make older skin behave and look like younger skin." The Clinique computer at any Clinique counter will select a combination of preparations just right for you. Ultima II contains "procollagen" in its anti-aging eye cream that "provides hydration" to "demoralizing lines." "Biotherm" eye cream dramatically improves the "biomechanical properties of the skin." The Park Avenue clinic of Dr. Zizmor, "chief of dermatology at one of New York's leading hospitals," offers not only medical treatment such as dermabrasion and chemical peeling but "total deep skin cleansing" as well.

Really good skin-care habits require the use of a variety of aids and devices: facial steamers; faucet filters to collect impurities in the water; borax to soften it; a humidifier for the bedroom; electric massagers; backbrushes; complexion brushes; loofahs; pumice stones; blackhead removers. I will not detail the implements or techniques involved in the manicure or pedicure.

The ordinary circumstances of life as well as a wide variety of activities cause a crisis in skin-care and require a stepping up of the regimen as well as an additional laying on of preparations. Skin-care discipline requires a specialized knowledge: A woman must know what to do if she has been skiing, taking medication, doing vigorous exercise, boating, or swimming in chlorinated pools; if she has been exposed to pollution, heated rooms, cold, sun, harsh weather, the pressurized cabins on airplanes, saunas or steam rooms, fatigue or stress. Like the schoolchild or prisoner, the woman mastering good skin-care habits is put on a timetable:

Georgette Klinger requires that a shorter or longer period of attention be paid to the complexion at least four times a day. Hair-care, like skin-care, requires a similar investment of time, the use of a wide variety of preparations, the mastery of a set of techniques and again, the acquisition of a specialized knowledge.

The crown and pinnacle of good hair care and skin care is, of course, the arrangement of the hair and the application of cosmetics. Here the regimen of hair care, skin care, manicure, and pedicure is recapitulated in another mode. A woman must learn the proper manipulation of a large number of devices—the blow dryer, styling brush, curling iron, hot curlers, wire curlers, eye-liner, lipliner, lipstick brush, eyelash curler, mascara brush—and the correct manner of application of a wide variety of products—foundation, toner, covering stick, mascara, eye shadow, eye gloss, blusher, lipstick, rouge, lip gloss, hair dye, hair rinse, hair lightener, hair "relaxer," etc.

In the language of fashion magazines and cosmetic ads, making up is typically portrayed as an aesthetic activity in which a woman can express her individuality. In reality, while cosmetic styles change every decade or so and while some variation in make-up is permitted depending on the occasion, making up the face is, in fact, a highly stylized activity that gives little rein to self-expression. Painting the face is not like painting a picture; at best, it might be described as painting the same picture over and over again with minor variations. Little latitude is permitted in what is considered appropriate make-up for the office and for most social occasions; indeed, the woman who uses cosmetics in a genuinely novel and imaginative way is liable to be seen not as an artist but as an eccentric. Furthermore, since a properly made-up face is, if not a card of entrée, at least a badge of acceptability in most social and professional contexts, the woman who chooses not to wear cosmetics at all faces sanctions of a sort which will never be applied to someone who chooses not to paint a watercolor.

V

Are we dealing in all this merely with sexual *difference?* Scarcely. The disciplinary practices I have described are part of the process by which the ideal body of femininity—and hence the feminine body-subject—is constructed; in doing this, they produce a "practiced and subjected" body, i.e., a body on which an inferior status has been inscribed. A woman's face must be made up, that is to say, made over, and so must her body: she is ten pounds overweight; her lips must be made more kissable; her complexion dewier; her eyes more mysterious. The "art" of make-up is the art of disguise, but this presupposes that a woman's face, unpainted, is defective. Soap and water, a shave, and routine attention to hygiene may be enough for *him*; for *her* they are not. The strategy of much beauty-related advertising is to suggest to women that their bodies are deficient, but even without such more or less explicit teaching, the media images of perfect female beauty which bombard us daily leave no doubt in the minds of most women that they fail to measure up. The technologies of femininity are taken up and practiced by women against the background of a pervasive sense of bodily deficiency: This accounts for what is often their compulsive or even ritualistic character.

The disciplinary project of femininity is a "set-up": It requires such radical and extensive measures of bodily transformation that virtually every woman who gives herself to it is destined in some degree to fail. Thus, a measure of shame is added to a woman's sense that the body she inhabits is deficient: she ought to take better care of herself; she might after all have jogged that last mile. Many women are without the time or resources to provide themselves with even the minimum of what such a regimen requires, e.g., a decent diet. Here is an additional source of shame for poor women who must bear what our society regards as the more general shame of poverty. The burdens poor women bear in this regard are not merely psychological, since conformity to the prevailing standards of bodily acceptability is a known factor in economic mobility.

The larger disciplines that construct a "feminine" body out of a female one are by no means race- or class-specific. There is little evidence that women of color or working-class women are in general less committed to the incarnation of an ideal femininity than their more privileged sisters. This is not to deny the many ways in which factors of race, class, locality, ethnicity, or personal taste can be expressed within the kinds of practices I have described. The rising young corporate executive may buy her cosmetics at Bergdorf-Goodman while the counter-server at McDonald's gets hers at the K-Mart; the one may join an expensive "upscale" health club, while the other may have to make do with the $9.49 GFX Body-Flex II Home-Gym advertised in the *National Enquirer*: Both are aiming at the same general result.

In the regime of institutionalized heterosexuality woman must make herself "object and prey" for the man: It is for him that these eyes are limpid pools, this cheek baby-smooth. In contemporary patriarchal culture, a panoptical male connoisseur resides within the consciousness of most women: They stand perpetually before his gaze and under his judgment. Woman lives her body as seen by another, by an anonymous patriarchal Other. We are often told that "women dress for other women." There is some truth in this: Who but someone engaged in a project similar to my own can appreciate the panache with which I bring it off? But women know for whom this game is played: They know that a pretty young woman is likelier to become a flight attendant than a plain one and that a well-preserved older woman has a better chance of holding onto her husband than one who has "let herself go."

Here it might be objected that performance for another in no way signals the inferiority of the performer to the one for whom the performance is intended: The actor, for example, depends on his audience but is in no way inferior to it; he is not demeaned by his dependency. While femininity is surely something enacted, the analogy to theater breaks down in a number of ways. First, as I argued earlier, the self-determination we think of as requisite to an artistic career is lacking here: Femininity as spectacle is something in which virtually every woman is required to participate. Second, the precise nature of the criteria by which women are judged, not only the inescapability of judgment itself, reflects gross imbalances in the social power of the sexes that do not mark the relationship of artists and their audiences. An aesthetic of femininity, for example, that mandates fragility and a lack of muscular strength produces female bodies that can offer little resistance to physical abuse, and the physical abuse of women by men, as we know, is widespread. It is true that the current fitness movement has permitted women to develop more muscular strength and endurance than was heretofore allowed; indeed, images of women have begun to appear in the mass media that seem to eroticize this new muscularity. But a woman may by no means develop more muscular strength than her partner; the bride who would tenderly carry her groom across the threshold is a figure of comedy, not romance.

Under the current "tyranny of slenderness" women are forbidden to become large or massive; they must take up as little space as possible. The very contours a woman's body takes on as she matures—the fuller breasts and rounded hips—have become distasteful. The body by which a woman feels herself judged and which by rigorous discipline she must try to assume is the body of early adolescence, slight and unformed, a body lacking flesh or substance, a body in whose very contours the image of immaturity has been inscribed. The requirement that a woman maintain a smooth and hairless skin carries further the theme of inexperience, for an infantilized face must accompany her infantilized body, a face that never ages or furrows its brow in thought. The face of the ideally feminine woman must never display the marks of character, wisdom, and experience that we so admire in men.

To succeed in the provision of a beautiful or sexy body gains a woman attention and some admiration but little real respect and rarely any social power. A woman's effort to master feminine body discipline will lack importance just because she does it: Her activity partakes of the general depreciation of everything female. In spite of unrelenting pressure to "make the most of what they have," women are ridiculed and dismissed for the triviality of their interest in such "trivial" things as clothes and make-up. Further, the narrow identification of woman with sexuality and the body in a society that has for centuries displayed profound suspicion toward both does little to raise her status. Even the most adored female bodies complain routinely of their situation in ways that reveal an implicit understanding that there is something demeaning in the kind of attention they receive. Marilyn Monroe, Elizabeth Taylor, and Farrah Fawcett have all wanted passionately to become actresses-artists and not just "sex objects."

But it is perhaps in their more restricted motility and comportment that the inferiorization of women's bodies is most evident: Women's typical body language, a language of relative tension and constriction, is understood to be a language of subordination when it is enacted by men in male status hierarchies. In groups of men, those with higher status typically assume looser and more relaxed postures: The boss lounges comfortably behind the desk while the applicant sits tense and rigid on the edge of his seat. Higher-status individuals may touch their subordinates more than they themselves get touched; they initiate more eye contact and are smiled at by their inferiors more than they are observed to smile in return. What is announced in the comportment of superiors is confidence and ease, especially ease of access to the Other. Female constraint in posture and movement is no doubt over-determined: The fact that women tend to sit and stand with legs, feet, and knees close or touching may well be a coded declaration of sexual circumspection in a society that still maintains a double standard, or an effort, albeit unconscious, to guard the genital area. In the latter case, a woman's tight and constricted posture must be seen as the expression of her need to ward off real or symbolic sexual attack. Whatever proportions must be assigned in the final display to fear or deference, one thing is clear: Woman's body language speaks eloquently, though silently, of her subordinate status in a hierarchy of gender.

VI

If what we have described is a genuine discipline—a "system of micropower that is essentially non-egalitarian and asymmetrical"—who then are the disciplinarians? Who is the top sergeant in the disciplinary regime of femininity? Historically, the law has had some responsibility for enforcement: In times gone by, for example, individuals who appeared in public in the clothes of the other sex could be arrested. While cross-dressers are still liable to some harassment, the kind of discipline we are considering is not the business of the police or the courts. Parents and teachers, of course, have extensive influence, admonishing girls to be demure and ladylike, to "smile pretty," to sit with their legs together. The influence of the media is pervasive, too, constructing as it does an image of the female body as spectacle, nor can we ignore the role played by "beauty experts" or by emblematic public personages such as Jane Fonda and Lynn Redgrave.

But none of these individuals—the skin-care consultant, the parent, the policeman—does in fact wield the kind of authority that is typically invested in those who manage more straightforward disciplinary institutions. The disciplinary power that inscribes femininity in the female body is everywhere and it is nowhere; the disciplinarian is everyone and yet no one in particular. Women regarded as overweight, for example, report that they are regularly admonished to diet, sometimes by people they scarcely know. These intrusions are often softened by reference to the natural prettiness just waiting to emerge: "People have always said that I had a beautiful face and 'if you'd only lose weight you'd be really beautiful.'" Here, "people"—friends and casual acquaintances alike—act to enforce prevailing standards of body size.

Foucault tends to identify the imposition of discipline upon the body with the operation of specific institutions, e.g., the school, the factory, the prison. To do this, however, is to overlook the extent to which discipline can be institutionally *unbound* as well as institutionally bound. The anonymity of disciplinary power and its wide dispersion have consequences which are crucial to a proper understanding of the subordination of women. The absence of a formal institutional structure and of authorities invested with the power to carry out institutional directives creates the impression that the production of femininity is either entirely voluntary or natural. The several senses of "discipline" are instructive here. On the one hand, discipline is something imposed on subjects of an "essentially inegalitarian and asymmetrical" system of authority. Schoolchildren, convicts, and draftees are subject to discipline in this sense. But discipline can be sought voluntarily as well, as, for example, when an individual seeks initiation into the spiritual discipline of Zen Buddhism. Discipline can, of course, be both at once: The volunteer may seek the physical and occupational training offered by the army without the army's ceasing in any way to be the instrument by which he and other members of his class are kept in disciplined subjection. Feminine bodily discipline has this dual character: On the one hand, no one is marched off for electrolysis at the end of a rifle, nor can we fail to appreciate the initiative and ingenuity displayed by countless women in an attempt to master the rituals of beauty. Nevertheless, insofar as the disciplinary practices of femininity produce a "subjected and practiced," an inferiorized, body, they must be understood as aspects of a far larger discipline, an oppressive and inegalitarian system of sexual subordination. This system aims at turning women into the docile and compliant companions of men just as surely as the army aims to turn its raw recruits into soldiers.

Now the transformation of oneself into a properly feminine body may be any or all of the following: a rite of passage into adulthood; the adoption and celebration of a particular aesthetic; a way of announcing one's economic level and social status; a way to triumph over other women in the competition for men or jobs; or an opportunity for massive narcissistic indulgence. The social construction of the feminine body is all these things, but it is at base discipline, too, and discipline of the inegalitarian sort. The absence of formally identifiable disciplinarians and of a public schedule of sanctions serves only to disguise the extent to which the imperative to be "feminine" serves the interest of domination. This is a lie in which all concur: Making up is merely artful play; one's first pair of high-heeled shoes is an innocent part of growing up and not the modern equivalent of foot-binding.

Why aren't all women feminists? In modern industrial societies, women are not kept in line by fear of retaliatory male violence; their victimization is not that of the South African black. Nor will it suffice to say that a false consciousness engendered in women by patriarchal ideology is at the basis of female subordination. This is not to deny the fact that women are often subject to gross male violence or that women and men alike are ideologically mystified by the dominant gender arrangements. What I wish to suggest instead is that an adequate understanding of women's oppression will require an appreciation of the extent to which not only women's lives but their very subjectivities are structured within an ensemble of systematically duplicitous practices. The feminine discipline of the body is a case in point: The practices which construct this body have an overt aim and character far removed, indeed radically distinct, from their covert function. In this regard, the system of gender subordination, like the wage-bargain under capitalism, illustrates in its own way the ancient tension between what is and what appears: The phenomenal forms in which it is manifested are often quite different from the real relations which form its deeper structure.

VII

The lack of formal public sanctions does not mean that a woman who is unable or unwilling to submit herself to the appropriate body discipline will face no sanctions at all. On the contrary, she faces a very severe sanction indeed in a world dominated by men: the refusal of male patronage. For the heterosexual woman, this may mean the loss of a badly needed intimacy; for both heterosexual women and lesbians, it may well mean the refusal of a decent livelihood.

As noted earlier, women punish themselves too for the failure to conform. The growing literature on women's body size is filled with wrenching confessions of shame from the overweight:

> I felt clumsy and huge. I felt that I would knock over furniture, bump into things, tip over chairs, not fit into VW's, especially when people were trying to crowd into the back seat. I felt like I was taking over the whole room. . . . I felt disgusting and like a slob. In the summer I felt hot and sweaty and I knew people saw my sweat as evidence that I was too fat.

> I feel so terrible about the way I look that I cut off connection with my body. I operate from the neck up. I do not look in mirrors. I do not want to spend time buying clothes. I do not want to spend time with make-up because it's painful for me to look at myself.

> I can no longer bear to look at myself. Whenever I have to stand in front of a mirror to comb my hair I tie a large towel around my neck. Even at night I slip my nightgown on before I take off my blouse and pants. But all this has only made it worse and worse. It's been so long since I've really looked at my body.

The depth of these women's shame is a measure of the extent to which all women have internalized patriarchal standards of bodily acceptability. A fuller examination of what is meant here by "internalization" may shed light on a question posed earlier: Why isn't every woman a feminist?

Something is "internalized" when it gets incorporated into the structure of the self. By "structure of the self" I refer to those modes of perception and of self-perception which allow a self to distinguish itself both from other selves and from things which are not selves. I have described elsewhere how a generalized male witness comes to structure woman's consciousness of herself as a bodily being. This, then, is one meaning of "internalization." The sense of oneself as a distinct and valuable individual is tied not only to the sense of how one is perceived, but also to what one knows, especially to what one knows how to do; this is a second sense of "internalization." Whatever its ultimate effect, discipline can provide the individual upon whom it is imposed with a sense of mastery as well as a secure sense of identity. There is a certain contradiction here: While its imposition may promote a larger disempowerment, discipline may bring with it a certain development of a person's powers. Women, then, like other skilled individuals, have a stake in the perpetuation of their skills, whatever it may have cost to acquire them and quite apart from the question whether, as a gender, they would have been better off had they never had to acquire them in the first place. Hence, feminism, especially a genuinely radical feminism that questions the patriarchal construction of the female body, threatens women with a certain deskilling, something people normally resist: Beyond this, it calls into question that aspect of personal identity which is tied to the development of a sense of competence.

Resistance from this source may be joined by a reluctance to part with the rewards of compliance;

further, many women will resist the abandonment of an aesthetic that defines what they take to be beautiful. But there is still another source of resistance, one more subtle perhaps, but tied once again to questions of identity and internalization. To have a body felt to be "feminine"—a body socially constructed through the appropriate practices—is in most cases crucial to a woman's sense of herself as female and, since persons currently can *be* only as male or female, to her sense of herself as an existing individual. To possess such a body may also be essential to her sense of herself as a sexually desiring and desirable subject. Hence, any political project which aims to dismantle the machinery that turns a female body into a feminine one may well be apprehended by a woman as something that threatens her with desexualization, if not outright annihilation.

The categories of masculinity and femininity do more than assist in the construction of personal identities; they are critical elements in our informal social ontology. This may account to some degree for the otherwise puzzling phenomenon of homophobia and for the revulsion felt by many at the sight of female bodybuilders; neither the homosexual nor the muscular woman can be assimilated easily into the categories that structure everyday life. The radical feminist critique of femininity, then, may pose a threat not only to a woman's sense of her own identity and desirability but to the very structure of her social universe.

Of course, many women *are* feminists, favoring a program of political and economic reform in the struggle to gain equality with men. But many "reform" or liberal feminists, indeed, many orthodox Marxists, are committed to the idea that the preservation of a woman's femininity is quite compatible with her struggle for liberation. These thinkers have rejected a normative femininity based upon the notion of "separate spheres" and the traditional sexual division of labor while accepting at the same time conventional standards of feminine body display. If my analysis is correct, such a feminism is incoherent. Foucault has argued that modern bourgeois democracy is deeply flawed in that it seeks political rights for individuals constituted as unfree by a variety of disciplinary micropowers that lie beyond the realm of what is ordinarily defined as the "political." "The man described for us whom we are invited to free," he says, "is already in himself the effect of a subjection much more profound than himself." If, as I have argued, female subjectivity is constituted in any significant measure in and through the disciplinary practices that construct the feminine body, what Foucault says here of "man" is perhaps even truer of "woman." Marxists have maintained from the first the inadequacy of a purely liberal feminism: We have reached the same conclusion through a different route, casting doubt at the same time on the adequacy of traditional Marxist prescriptions for women's liberation as well. Liberals call for equal rights for women, traditional Marxists for the entry of women into production on an equal footing with men, the socialization of housework and proletarian revolution; neither calls for the deconstruction of the categories of masculinity and femininity. Femininity as a certain "style of the flesh" will have to be surpassed in the direction of something quite different, not masculinity, which is in many ways only its mirror opposite, but a radical and as yet unimagined transformation of the female body.

VIII

Foucault has argued that the transition from traditional to modern societies has been characterized by a profound transformation in the exercise of power, by what he calls "a reversal of the political axis of individualization." In older authoritarian systems, power was embodied in the person of the monarch and exercised upon a largely anonymous body of subjects; violation of the law was seen as an insult to the royal individual. While the methods employed to enforce compliance in the past were often quite brutal, involving gross assaults against the body, power in such a system operated in a haphazard and discontinuous fashion; much in the social totality lay beyond its reach.

By contrast, modern society has seen the emergence of increasingly invasive apparatuses of power: These exercise a far more restrictive social and psychological control than was heretofore possible. In modern societies, effects of power "circulate through progressively finer channels, gaining access to individuals themselves, to their bodies, their gestures and all their daily actions." Power now seeks to transform the minds of those individuals who might be tempted to resist it, not merely to punish or imprison their bodies. This requires two things: a finer control of the body's time and its movements—a control that cannot be achieved without ceaseless surveillance and a better understanding of the specific person, of the genesis and nature of his "case." The power these new apparatuses seek to exercise requires a new knowledge of the individual: Modern psychology and sociology are born. Whether the new modes of control have charge of correction, production, education, or the provision of welfare, they resemble one another; they exercise power in a bureaucratic mode—faceless, centralized, and pervasive. A reversal has occurred: Power has now become anonymous, while the project of control has brought into being a new individuality. In fact, Foucault believes that the operation of power constitutes the very subjectivity of the subject. Here, the image of the Panopticon returns: Knowing that he may be observed from the tower at any time, the inmate takes over the job of policing himself. The gaze which is inscribed in the very structure of the disciplinary institution is internalized by the inmate: Modern technologies of behavior are thus oriented toward the production of isolated and self-policing subjects.

Women have their own experience of the modernization of power, one which begins later but follows in many respects the course outlined by Foucault. In important ways, a woman's behavior is less regulated now than it was in the past. She has more mobility and is less confined to domestic space. She enjoys what to previous generations would have been an unimaginable sexual liberty. Divorce, access to paid work outside the home, and the increasing secularization of modern life have loosened the hold over her of the traditional family and, in spite of the current fundamentalist revival, of the church. Power in these institutions was wielded by individuals known to her. Husbands and fathers enforced patriarchal authority in the family. As in the *ancien régime*, a woman's body was subject to sanctions if she disobeyed. Not Foucault's royal individual but the Divine Individual decreed that her desire be always "unto her husband," while the person of the priest made known to her God's more specific intentions concerning her place and duties. In the days when civil and ecclesiastical authority were still conjoined, individuals formally invested with power were charged with the correction of recalcitrant women whom the family had somehow failed to constrain.

By contrast, the disciplinary power that is increasingly charged with the production of a properly embodied femininity is dispersed and anonymous; there are no individuals formally empowered to wield it; it is, as we have seen, invested in everyone and in no one in particular. This disciplinary power is peculiarly modern: It does not rely upon violent or public sanctions, nor does it seek to restrain the freedom of the female body to move from place to place. For all that, its invasion of the body is well-nigh total: The female body enters "a machinery of power that explores it, breaks it down and rearranges it." The disciplinary techniques through which the "docile bodies" of women are constructed aim at a regulation which is perpetual and exhaustive—a regulation of the body's size and contours, its appetite, posture, gestures, and general comportment in space and the appearance of each of its visible parts.

As modern industrial societies change and as women themselves offer resistance to patriarchy, older forms of domination are eroded. But new forms arise, spread, and become consolidated. Women are no longer required to be chaste or modest, to restrict their sphere of activity to the home, or even to realize their properly feminine destiny in maternity: Normative femininity is coming more and more to be centered on woman's body—not its duties and obligations or even its capacity to bear children, but its sexuality, more precisely, its presumed heterosexuality and its appearance. There is, of course, nothing new in women's preoccupation with youth and beauty. What is new is the growing power of the image in a society increasingly oriented toward the visual media. Images of normative femininity, it might be ventured, have replaced the religiously oriented tracts of the past. New too is the spread of this discipline to all classes of women and its deployment throughout the life-cycle. What was formerly the specialty of the aristocrat or courtesan is now the routine obligation of every woman, be she a grandmother or a barely pubescent girl.

To subject oneself to the new disciplinary power is to be up-to-date, to be "with-it"; as I have argued, it is presented to us in ways that are regularly disguised. It is fully compatible with the current need for women's wage labor, the cult of youth and fitness, and the need of advanced capitalism to maintain high levels of consumption. Further, it represents a saving in the economy of enforcement: Since it is women themselves who practice this discipline on and against their own bodies, men get off scot-free.

The woman who checks her make-up half a dozen times a day to see if her foundation has caked or her mascara run, who worries that the wind or rain may spoil her hairdo, who looks frequently to see if her stockings have bagged at the ankle, or who, feeling fat, monitors everything she eats, has become, just as surely as the inmate of Panopticon, a self-policing subject, a self committed to a relentless self-surveillance. This self-surveillance is a form of obedience to patriarchy. It is also the reflection in woman's consciousness of the fact that *she* is under surveillance in ways that *he* is not, that whatever else she may become, she is importantly a body designed to please or to excite. There has been induced in many women, then, in Foucault's words, "a state of conscious and permanent visibility that assures the automatic functioning of power." Since the standards of female bodily acceptability are impossible fully to realize, requiring as they do a virtual transcendence of nature, a woman may live much of her life with a pervasive feeling of bodily deficiency. Hence, a tighter control of the body has gained a new kind of hold over the mind.

Foucault often writes as if power constitutes the very individuals upon whom it operates:

> The individual is not to be conceived as a sort of elementary nucleus, a primitive atom, a multiple and inert material on which power comes to fasten or against which it happens to strike. . . . In fact, it is already one of the prime effects of power that certain bodies, certain gestures, certain discourses, certain desires, come to be identified and constituted as individuals.

Nevertheless, if individuals were wholly constituted by the power/knowledge regime Foucault describes, it would make no sense to speak of resistance to discipline at all. Foucault seems sometimes on the verge of depriving us of a vocabulary in which to conceptualize the nature and meaning of those periodic refusals of control which, just as much as the imposition of control, mark the course of human history.

Peter Dews accuses Foucault of lacking a theory of the "libidinal body," i.e., the body upon which discipline is imposed and whose bedrock impulse toward spontaneity and pleasure might perhaps become the locus of resistance. Do women's "libidinal" bodies, then, not rebel against the pain, constriction, tedium, semi-starvation, and constant self-surveillance to which they are currently condemned? Certainly they do, but the rebellion is put down every time a woman picks up her eyebrow tweezers or embarks upon a new diet. The harshness of a regimen alone does not guarantee its rejection, for hardships can be endured if they are thought to be necessary or inevitable.

While "nature," in the form of a "libidinal" body, may not be the origin of a revolt against "culture," domination and the discipline it requires are never imposed without some cost. Historically, the forms and occasions of resistance are manifold. Sometimes, instances of resistance appear to spring from the introduction of new and conflicting factors into the lives of the dominated: The juxtaposition of old and new and the resulting incoherence or "contradiction" may make submission to the old ways seem increasingly unnecessary. In the present instance, what may be a major factor in the relentless and escalating objectification of women's bodies—namely, women's growing independence—produces in many women a sense of incoherence that calls into question the meaning and necessity of the current discipline. As women (albeit a small minority of women) begin to realize an unprecedented political, economic, and sexual self-determination, they fall ever more completely under the dominating gaze of patriarchy. It is this paradox, not the "libidinal body," that produces, here and there, pockets of resistance.

In the current political climate, there is no reason to anticipate either widespread resistance to currently fashionable modes of feminine embodiment or joyous experimentation with new "styles of the flesh"; moreover, such novelties would face profound opposition from material and psychological sources identified earlier in this essay (see Section VII). In spite of this, a number of oppositional discourses and practices have appeared in recent years. An increasing number of women are "pumping iron," a few with little concern for the limits of body development imposed by current canons of femininity. Women in radical lesbian communities have also rejected hegemonic images of femininity and are struggling to develop a new female aesthetic. A striking feature of such communities is the extent to which they have overcome the oppressive identification of female beauty and desirability with youth: Here, the physical features of aging—"character" lines and greying hair—not only do not diminish a woman's attractiveness, they may even enhance it. A popular literature of resistance is growing, some of it analytical and reflective, like Kim Chernin's *The Obsession*, some oriented toward practical self-help, like Marcia Hutchinson's recent *Transforming Body Image: Learning to Love the Body You Have*. This literature reflects a mood akin in some ways to that other and earlier mood of quiet desperation to which Betty Friedan gave voice in *The Feminine Mystique*. Nor should we forget that a mass-based women's movement is in place in this country which has begun a critical questioning of the meaning of femininity, if not yet in this, then in other domains of life. We women cannot begin the re-vision of our own bodies until we learn to read the cultural messages we inscribe upon them daily and until we come to see that even when the mastery of the disciplines of femininity produce a triumphant result, we are still only women.

STUDY QUESTIONS

1. What does Foucault mean by a "micro-physics of power"?
2. What social practices construct femininity as an achievement and an artifice?
3. What, according to Bartky, is the relationship between modern forms of surveillance and women's "internalization" of patriarchal oppression?
4. Why does Bartky assert that modern disciplinary practices that construct femininity also cause shame?
5. What are some ways in which the disciplinary practices of femininity differ according to race, class, or regional specificity?
6. What are the elements in the modernization of patriarchal power that make resistance difficult? What are some forms of resistance?

41

Philosophers Against the Family

Christina Sommers

Christina Sommers teaches philosophy at Clark University in Worcester, Massachusetts. She is the author of a number of articles on moral philosophy and the director of the New England Society for Philosophy and Public Affairs.

Much of what commonly counts as personal morality is measured by how well we behave within family relationships. We live our moral lives as son or daughter to this mother and that father, as brother or sister to this sister or brother, as father or mother, grandfather, granddaughter to this boy or girl or that man or woman. These relationships and the moral duties defined by them were once popular topics of moral casuistry; but when we turn to the literature of recent moral philosophy, we find little discussion of what it means to be a good son or daughter, a good mother or father, a good husband or wife, a good brother or sister.

Modern ethical theory concentrates on more general topics. Perhaps the majority of us who involve ourselves with ethics accept some version of Kantianism or Utilitarianism, yet these mainstream doctrines are better designed for telling us about what we should do as persons in general than about our special duties as parents or children or siblings. We believe, perhaps, that such universal theories can account fully for the morality of special relations. In any case, modern ethics is singularly silent on the bread and butter issues of personal morality in everyday life. However, silence is only part of it. With the exception of marriage itself, family relationships are a biological given. The contemporary philosopher is, on the whole, actively unsympathetic to the idea that we have *any* duties defined by relationships into which we have not voluntarily entered. We do not, after all, choose our parents or siblings. And even if we do choose to have children, this is not the same as choosing, say, our friends. Because the special relationships that constitute the family as a social arrangement are, in this sense, not voluntarily assumed, many moralists feel bound in principle to dismiss them altogether. The practical result is that philosophers are to be found among those who are contributing to an ongoing disintegration of the traditional family. In what follows I shall expose some of the philosophical roots of the current hostility to family morality. My own view that the ethical theses underlying this hostility are bad philosophy will be made evident throughout the discussion.

THE MORAL VANTAGE

Social criticism is a heady pastime to which philosophers are professionally addicted. One approach, Aristotelian in method and temperament, is antiradical, though it may be liberal, and approaches the task of needed reform with a prima facie respect for the norms of established morality. It is conservationist and cautious in its recommendations for change. It is, therefore, not given to such proposals as abolishing the family or abolishing private property and, indeed, does not look kindly on such proposals from other philosophers. The antiradicals I am concerned about are not those who would be called Burkean. I shall call them liberal but this use of "liberal" is somewhat perverse since, in my stipulative use of the term, a liberal is a philosopher who advocates social reform but always in a conservative spirit. My liberals share with Aristotle the conviction that the traditional arrangements have great moral weight and that common opinion is a primary source of moral truth. A good modern example is Henry Sidgwick with his constant appeal to Common Sense. But philosophers like John Stuart Mill, William James, and Bertrand Russell also can be cited. On the other hand, because no radical can be called a liberal in my sense, many so-called liberals could be excluded perversely. Thus when John Rawls toys with the possibility of abolishing the family because kinship bias is a force inimical to equality of opportunity, he is no liberal.

The more exciting genre of social criticism is not liberal-Aristotelian but radical and Platonist in spirit. Its vantage is external or even supernal to the social institutions it has placed under moral scrutiny. Plato was as aware as anyone could be that what he called the cave was social reality. One reason for calling it a cave was to emphasize the need, as he saw it, for an external, objective perspective on established morality. Another consideration in calling it a cave was his conviction that common opinion was benighted, and that reform could not be accomplished except by substantial "consciousness raising" and enlightened social engineering. Plato's supernal vantage made it possible for him to look on social reality in somewhat the way the Army Corps of Engineers looks upon a river that must have its course changed and its waywardness tamed. In our own day much social criticism of a Marxist variety has taken this radical approach to social change. And, of course, much contemporary feminist philosophy is radical.

Some philosophers are easily classifiable as radical or liberal. John Locke is clearly a liberal, Leon Trotsky is clearly a radical. I remarked a moment ago that there is a radical strain in Rawls. But it is a strain only: Rawls' attitude to social reality is not, finally, condescending. On the other hand, much contemporary social criticism is radical in temper. In particular, I shall suggest that the prevailing attitude toward the family is radical and not liberal. And the inability of mainstream ethical theory to come to grips with the special obligations that family members bear to one another contributes to the current disregard of the commonsense morality of the family cave. We find, indeed, that family obligations are criticized and discounted precisely because they do not fit the standard theories of obligation. If I am right, contemporary ethics is at a loss when it comes to dealing with parochial morality; but few have acknowledged this as a defect to be repaired. Instead the common reaction has been: if the family does not fit my model of autonomy, rights, or obligations, then so much the worse for the family.

To illustrate this, I cite without comment recent views on some aspects of family morality.

1. Michael Slote[1] maintains that any child capable of supporting itself is "morally free to opt out of the family situation." To those who say that the child should be expected to help his needy parents for a year or two out of reciprocity or fair play, Slote responds:

   > The duty of fair play presumably exists only where past benefits are voluntarily accepted . . . and we can hardly suppose that a child has voluntarily accepted his role in family . . . life.[2]

2. Virginia Held[3] wants traditional family roles to be abolished and she recommends that husbands and wives think of themselves as roommates of the same sex in assigning household and parental tasks. (She calls this the "Roommate Test.") To the objection that such a restructuring might injure family life, she replies that similar objections were made when factory workers demanded overtime pay.

3. The late Jane English[4] defended the view that adult children owe their parents no more than they owe their good friends. "[A]fter friendship ends, the duties of friendship end." John Simmons[5] and Jeffrey Blustein[6] also look with suspicion upon the idea that there is a debt of gratitude to the parents for what, in any case, they were duty bound to do.
4. Where Slote argues for the older child's right to leave, Howard Cohen[7] argues for granting that right to young children who still need parental care. He proposes that every child be assigned a "trusted advisor" or agent. If the child wants to leave his parents, his agent will be charged with finding alternative caretakers for him.

The philosophers I have cited are not atypical in their dismissive attitude to commonsense morality or in their readiness to replace the parochial norms of the family cave with practices that would better approximate the ideals of human rights and equality. A theory of rights and obligations that applies generally to moral agents is, in this way, applied to the family with the predictable results that the family system of special relations and non-contractual special obligations is judged to be grossly unfair to its members.

FEMINISM AND THE FAMILY

I have said that the morality of the family has been relatively neglected. The glaring exception to this is, of course, the feminist movement. Although the movement is complex, I am confined primarily to its moral philosophers, of whom the most influential is Simone de Beauvoir. For de Beauvoir, a social arrangement that does not allow all its participants full autonomy is to be condemned. De Beauvoir criticizes the family as an unacceptable arrangement since, for women, marriage and childbearing are essentially incompatible with their subjectivity and freedom:

> The tragedy of marriage is not that it fails to assure woman the promised happiness . . . but that it mutilates her; it dooms her to repetition and routine. . . . At twenty or thereabouts mistress of a home, bound permanently to a man, a child in her arms, she stands with her life virtually finished forever.[8]

For de Beauvoir the tragedy goes deeper than marriage. The loss of subjectivity is unavoidable as long as human reproduction requires the woman's womb. De Beauvoir starkly describes the pregnant woman who ought to be a "free individual" as a "stockpile of colloids, an incubator, an egg."[9] And as recently as 1977 she compared childbearing and nurturing to slavery.[10]

It would be a mistake to say that de Beauvoir's criticism of the family is outside the mainstream of Anglo-American philosophy. Her criterion of moral adequacy may be formulated in continental existentialist terms, but its central contention is generally accepted: who would deny that an arrangement that systematically thwarts the freedom and autonomy of the individual is *eo ipso* defective? What is perhaps a bit odd to Anglo-American ears is that de Beauvoir makes such scant appeal to ideals of fairness and equality. For her, it is the loss of autonomy that is decisive.

De Beauvoir is more pessimistic than most feminists she has influenced about the prospects for technological and social solutions. But implicit in her critique is the ideal of a society in which sexual differences are minimal or nonexistent. This ideal is shared by many contemporary feminist philosophers. The views of Richard Wasserstrom, Ann Ferguson, Carol Gould, and Alison Jaggar are representative.

Wasserstrom's approach to social criticism is Platonist in its hypothetical use of a good society. The ideal society is nonsexist and "assimilationist."[11] Social reality is scrutinized for its approximation to this ideal and criticism is directed against all existing norms. Take the custom of having sexually segregated bathrooms: whether this is right or wrong "depends on what the good society would look like in respect to sexual differentiation." The key question in evaluating any law or arrangement in which sex difference figures is: "What would the good or just society make of [it]?"[12]

Thus the supernal light shines on the cave, revealing its moral defects. *There*, in the ideal society, gender in the choice of lover or spouse would be of no more significance than eye color. *There* the family would consist of adults but not necessarily of different sexes and not necessarily in pairs. *There* we find equality ensured by a kind of affirmative action which compensates for disabilities. If women are somewhat weaker than men, or if they are subject to lunar disabilities, then this must be compensated for. (Wasserstrom compares women to persons with congenital defects for whom the good society makes special arrangements.) Such male-dominated sports as wrestling and football will there be eliminated and marriage, as we know it, will not exist. "Bisexuality, not heterosexuality or homosexuality, would be the typical intimate, sexual relationship in the ideal society that was assimilationist in respect to sex."[13]

Other feminist philosophers are equally confident about the need for sweeping change. Ann Ferguson wants a "radical reorganization of child rearing." She recommends communal living and a deemphasis on biological parenting. In the ideal society "[l]ove relationships, and the sexual relationships developing out of them, would be based on the individual meshing-together of androgynous human beings."[14] Carol Gould argues for androgyny and for abolishing legal marriage. She favors single parenting, co-parenting and communal parenting. The only arrangement she opposes emphatically is the traditional one where the mother provides primary care for the children.[15] Alison Jaggar, arguing for a "socialist feminism," wants a society that is both classless and genderless. She looks to the day of a possible transformation of such biological functions as insemination, lactation, and gestation "so that one woman could inseminate another . . . and . . . fertilized ova could be transplanted into women's or even men's bodies." This idea is partly illustrated in a science fiction story that Jaggar praises in which "neither sex bears children, but both sexes, through hormone treatments, suckle them . . ."[16] To those of us who find this bizarre, Jaggar replies that this betrays the depth of our prejudice in favor of the "natural" family.

Though they differ in detail, the radical feminists hold to a common social ideal that is broadly assimilationist in character and inimical to the traditional family. Sometimes it seems as if the radical feminist simply takes the classical Marxist eschatology of the Communist Manifesto and substitutes "gender" for "class." Indeed, the feminist and the old-fashioned Marxist do have much in common. Both see their caves as politically divided into two warring factions: one oppressing, the other oppressed. Both see the need of raising the consciousness of the oppressed group to its predicament and to the possibility of removing its shackles. Both look forward to the day of a classless or genderless society. Both deny the value and naturalness of tradition. Both believe that people and the institutions they inhabit are as malleable as Silly Putty. And both groups are zealots, paying little attention to the tragic personal costs to be paid for the revolution they wish to bring about. The feminists tell us little about that side of things. To begin with, how will the benighted myriads in the cave who do not wish to "mesh together" with other androgynous beings be reeducated? And how are children to be brought up in the genderless society? Plato took great pains to explain his methods: would the new methods be as thoroughgoing? Unless these questions can be given plausible answers, the supernal attack on the family must always be irresponsible. The appeal to the just society justifies nothing until it can be shown that the radical proposals do not have monstrous consequences. That has not been shown. Indeed, given the perenially dubious state of the social sciences, it is precisely what *cannot* be shown.

Any social arrangement that falls short of the assimilationist ideal is labeled "sexist." It should be noted that this characteristically feminist use of the term "sexist" differs significantly from its popular or literal sense. Literally, and popularly, "sexism" connotes unfair discrimination. But in its extended philosophical use it connotes discrimination, period. Wasserstrom and many feminists trade on the popular pejorative connotations of sexism when they invite us to be antisexist. Most liberals are antisexist in the popular sense. But to be antisexist in the technical, radical philosophical sense is not merely to be opposed to discrimination against women; it is to be *for* what Wasserstrom calls the assimilationist ideal. The antisexist philosopher opposes any social policy that is nonandrogynous, objecting, for example, to legislation that allows for maternity leave. As Alison Jaggar remarks: "We do not, after all, elevate 'prostate leave' into a special right of men."[17] From being liberally opposed to sexism, one may in this way be led insensibly to a radical critique of the family whose ideal is assimilationist and androgynous. For it is very clear that the realization of the androgynous ideal is incompatible with the survival of the family as we know it.

The neological extension of such labels as "sexism," "slavery," and "prostitution" is a feature of radical discourse. The liberal too sometimes calls for radical solutions to social problems. Some institutions are essentially unjust. To "reform" slavery or a totalitarian system of government is to eliminate them. Radicals trade on these extreme practices in characterizing other practices. They may, for example, characterize low wages as "slave" wages and the workers who are paid them as "slave" laborers. Taking these descriptions seriously may start one on the way to treating a free-labor market system as a "slave system" that, in simple justice, must be overthrown and replaced by an alternative system of production. The radical feminist typically explains that, "existentially," women, being treated by men as sex objects, are especially prone to bad faith and false consciousness. Marxist feminists see them as part of an unawakened and oppressed economic class. Clearly we cannot call on a deluded woman to cast off her bonds before we have made her aware of her bondage. So the first task of freeing the slave woman is dispelling the thrall of a false and deceptive consciousness. One must "raise" her consciousness to the "reality" of her situation. (Some feminists acknowledge that it may in fact be too late for many of the women who have fallen too far into the delusions of marriage and motherhood. But the educative process can save many from falling into the marriage and baby trap.)

In this sort of rhetorical climate nothing is what it seems. Prostitution is another term that has been subjected to a radical enlargement. Alison Jaggar believes that a feminist interpretation of the term "prostitution" is badly needed and asks for a "philosophical theory of prostitution." Observing that the average woman dresses for men, marries a man for protection, and so forth, she says: "For contemporary radical feminists, prostitution is the archetypal relationship of women to men."[18]

Of course, the housewife Jaggar has in mind might be offended at the suggestion that she herself is a prostitute, albeit less well paid and less aware of it than the professional street prostitute. To this the radical feminist reply is (quoting Jaggar):

> [I]ndividuals' intentions do not necessarily indicate the true nature of what is going on. Both man and woman might be outraged at the description of their candlelit dinner as prostitution, but the radical feminist argues this outrage is due simply to the participants' failure or refusal to perceive the social context in which their dinner date occurs.[19]

Apparently, this failure or refusal to perceive affects most women. Thus we may even suppose that the majority of women who have been treated to a candlelit dinner by a man prefer it to other dining alternatives they have experienced. To say that these preferences are misguided is a hard and condescending doctrine. It would seem that most feminist philosophers are not overly impressed with Mill's principle that there can be no appeal from a majority verdict of those who have experienced two alternatives.

The dismissive feminist attitude to the widespread preferences of women takes its human toll. Most women, for example, prefer to have children and those who have them rarely regret having them. It is no more than sensible, from a utilitarian standpoint, to take note of such widespread preferences and to take it seriously in planning one's own life. But a significant number of women discount this general verdict as benighted, taking more seriously the idea that the reported joys of motherhood are exaggerated and fleeting, if not altogether illusory. These women tell themselves and others that having babies is a trap to be avoided. But for many women childlessness has become a trap of its own, somewhat lonelier than the more conventional traps of marriage and babies. Some come to find their childlessness regrettable; this sort of regret is common to those who flout Mill's reasonable maxim by putting the verdict of ideology over the verdict of human experience.

FEMINISTS AGAINST FEMININITY

It is a serious defect of American feminism that it concentrates its zeal on impugning femininity and feminine culture at the expense of the grass roots fight against economic and social injustices to which women are subjected. As we have seen, the radical feminist attitude to the woman who enjoys her femininity is condescending or even contemptuous. Indeed, the contempt for femininity reminds one of misogynist biases in such philosophers as Kant, Rousseau, and Schopenhauer, who believed that femininity was charming but incompatible with full personhood and reasonableness. The feminists deny the charm, but they too accept the verdict that femininity is weakness. It goes without saying that an essential connection between femininity and powerlessness has not been established by *either* party.

By denigrating conventional feminine roles and holding to an assimilationist ideal in social policy, the feminist movement has lost its natural constituency. The actual concerns, beliefs, and aspirations of the majority of women are not taken seriously *except* as illustrations of bad faith, false consciousness, and successful brainwashing. What women actually want is discounted and reinterpreted as to what they (have been led to) *think* they want ("a man," "children"). What most women *enjoy* (male gallantry, candlelit dinners, sexy clothes, makeup) is treated as an obscenity (prostitution).

As the British feminist Janet Radcliffe Richards says:

> Most women still dream about beauty, dress, weddings, dashing lovers, domesticity and babies . . . but if feminists seem (as they do) to want to eliminate nearly all of these things—beauty, sex conventions, families and all—for most people that simply means the removal of everything in life which is worth living for.[20]

Radical feminism creates a false dichotomy between sexism and assimilation, as if there were nothing in between. This view ignores completely the middle ground in which a woman can be free of oppression and nevertheless feminine in the sense abhorred by many feminists. For women are simply not waiting to be freed from the particular chains the radical feminists are trying to sunder. The average woman enjoys her femininity. She wants a man, not a roommate. She wants children and the time to care for them. When she enters the work force, she wants fair opportunity and equal treatment. These are the goals that women actually have, and they are not easily attainable. But they will never be furthered by an elitist radical movement that views the actual aspirations of women as the product of a false consciousness. There is room for a liberal feminism that would work for reforms that would give women equal opportunity in the workplace and in politics, but would leave unimpugned the basic institutions that women want and support, i.e., marriage and motherhood. Such a feminism is already in operation in some European countries. But it has been obstructed here in the United States by the ideologues who now hold the seat of power in the feminist movement.[21]

In characterizing and criticizing American feminism, I have not taken into account the latest revisions and qualifications of a lively and variegated movement. There is a kind of "Feminism of the Week" that one cannot hope to keep abreast of short of divorcing all other concerns. The best one can do for present purposes is attend to central theses and arguments that bear on the feminist treatment of the family. Nevertheless, even for this limited purpose it would be wrong to omit discussion of an important turn taken by feminism in the past few years. I have in mind the recent literature on the theme that there is a specific female ethic that differs from the male ethic in being more "concrete," less rule oriented, more empathic and "caring," and more attentive to the demands of a particular context.[22] The kind of feminism that accepts the idea that women differ from men in approaching ethical dilemmas and social problems from a "care perspective" is not oriented to androgyny as a positive ideal. Rather it seeks to develop a special female ethic and to give it greater practical scope.

The stress on context might lead one to think that these feminists are more sympathetic to the family as the social arrangement that shapes the moral development of women since the family is the context for many of the moral dilemmas that women actually face. However, one sees as yet no attention being paid to the fact that feminism itself is a force working against the preservation of the family. Psychologists like Carol Gilligan and philosophers like Lawrence Blum concentrate their attention on the moral quality of caring relationships, yet these relationships themselves are not viewed in their concrete embedment in any formal social or institutional arrangement.

It should also be said that some feminists are moving away from the earlier hostility to motherhood.[23] Here, too, one sees the weakening of the positive assimilationist ideal in the acknowledgment of a primary gender role. However, childrearing is not seen primarily within the context of the family but as a special relationship between mother and daughter or (more awkwardly) between mother and son, a relationship that effectively excludes the male parent. And the new celebration of motherhood remains largely hostile to traditional familial arrangements.

It is too early to say whether a new style of nonassimilationist feminism will lead to a mitigation of the feminist assault on the family or even on femininity. In any case, the recognition of a female ethic of care and responsibility is hardly inconsistent with a social ethic that values the family as a vital (perhaps indispensable) institution. And the recognition that women have their own moral style may well be followed by a more accepting attitude toward the kind of femininity that some feminists currently reject. One may even hope to see the "holier than thou" aspects of feminism fade into a relaxed recognition that both sexes have their distinctive graces and virtues. Such a feminism would not be radical but liberal.

THE INDIRECT ATTACK

The philosophers I shall now discuss do not criticize the family directly; in some cases they do not even mention the family. However, each one holds a view that subverts, ignores, or denies the special moral relations that characterize the family and are responsible for its functioning. And if they are right, family morality is a vacuous subject.

Judith Thomson maintains that an abortion may be permissible even if the fetus is deemed a person from the moment of conception,[24] for in that case being pregnant would be like having an adult surgically attached to one's body. And it is arguable that if one finds oneself attached to another person, one has the right to free oneself even if such freedom is obtained at the price of the other person's death by, say, kidney failure. I shall, for purposes of this discussion, refer to the fetus as a prenatal child. I myself do not think the fetus is a person from the moment of conception. Nor does Thomson. But here we are interested in her argument for the proposition that abortion of a prenatal child/person should be permissible.

Many have been repelled by Thomson's comparison of pregnancy to arbitrary attachment. Thomson herself is well aware that the comparison may be bizarre. She says:

> It may be said that what is important is not merely the fact that the fetus is a person, but that it is a person for whom the woman has a special kind of responsibility issuing from the fact that she is its mother.[25]

To this Thomson replies: "Surely we do not have any such 'special responsibility' for a person unless we have assumed it, explicitly or implicitly." If the mother does not try to prevent pregnancy, does not obtain an abortion, but instead gives birth to it and takes it home with her, then, at least implicitly, she has assumed responsibility for it.

One might object that although pregnancy is a state into which many women do not enter voluntarily, it is nevertheless a state in which one has some responsibility to care for the prenatal child. Many pregnant women do feel such a prenatal responsibility, and take measures to assure the prenatal child's survival and future health. But here one must be grateful to Professor Thomson for her clarity. A mother who has not sought pregnancy deliberately bears *no* special responsibility to her prenatal child. For she has neither implicitly nor explicitly taken on the responsibility of caring for it. For example, the act of taking the infant home from the hospital implies voluntary acceptance of such responsibility. By choosing to take it with her, the mother undertakes to care for the infant and no longer has the right to free herself of the burden of motherhood at the cost of the child's life.

The assumption, then, is that there are no noncontractual obligations or special duties defined by the kinship of mother to child. As for social expectations, none are legitimate in the morally binding sense unless they are underpinned by an implicit or explicit contract freely entered into. If this assumption is correct, sociological arrangements and norms have no moral force unless they are voluntarily accepted by the moral agent who is bound by them. I shall call this the "volunteer theory of moral obligation." It is a thesis that is so widely accepted today that Thomson saw no need to argue for it.

Michael Tooley's arguments in defense of infanticide provide another solid example of how a contemporary philosopher sidetracks and ultimately subverts the special relations that bind the family.[26] Tooley holds that being sentient confers the prima facie right not to be treated cruelly, and that possession of those characteristics that make one a person confers the *additional* right to life. Tooley then argues that infants lack these characteristics and so may be painlessly killed. In reaching this conclusion, Tooley's sole consideration is whether the infant intrinsically possesses the relevant "right-to-life-making characteristic" of personality—a consideration that abstracts from any right to care and protection that the infant's relation to its parents confers on it causally and institutionally. For Tooley, as for Thomson, the relations of family or motherhood are morally irrelevant. So it is perhaps not surprising that one finds nothing in the index under "family," "mother," or "father" in Tooley's book on abortion and infanticide.

Howard Cohen is concerned strictly with the rights of persons irrespective of the special relations they may bear to others.[27] Just as Thomson holds that the mother's right to the free unencumbered use of her body is not qualified by any special obligations to her child, so Cohen holds that the child's right to a no-fault divorce from its parents cannot be diminished because of the special relation it bears to them. Where Thomson is concerned with the overriding right of the mother, Cohen is concerned with the right of the child. Yet all three philosophers agree that the right of a child is not less strong than the right of any adult. Indeed, Thomson compares the unborn child to a fully grown adult and Tooley holds that any person—be it child, adult, or sapient nonhuman—is equal in rights.

Our three philosophers are typical in holding that any moral requirement is either a general duty incumbent on everyone or else a specific obligation voluntarily assumed. Let us call a requirement a *duty* if it devolves on the moral agents whether or not they have voluntarily assumed it. (It is, for example, a duty to refrain from murder.) And let us call a requirement an *obligation* only if it devolves on certain moral agents but not necessarily on all moral agents. (One is, for example, morally obligated to keep a promise.) According to our three philosophers, all duties are general in the sense of being requirements on all moral agents. Any moral requirement that is *specific* to a given moral agent must be grounded in his or her voluntary commitment. Thus, there is no room for any special requirement on a moral agent that has not been assumed voluntarily by that agent. In other words, *there are no special duties*. This is what I am calling the volunteer theory of obligation. According to the voluntaristic thesis, all duties are general and only those who volunteer for them have any obligations toward them.

This thesis underlies Cohen's view that the child can divorce its parents. For it is unnecessary to consider whether the child has any special duties to the parents that could conflict with the exercise of its right to leave them. It underlies Thomson's view that the woman who had not sought pregnancy has no special responsibility to her unborn child and that any such responsibility that she may later have is assumed implicitly by her voluntary act of taking it home with her. It underlies Tooley's psychobiological method for answering the moral question of infanticide by determining the right-making characteristics of personhood: all we need to know about the neonate is whether or not it possesses the psychological characteristics of personhood. If it does, then it has a right to life. If it does not, then it is not a person and thus may be killed painlessly. It is unnecessary to consider the question of whether the child has a special relation to anyone who may have a "special responsibility" to see to the child's survival.

What I am calling the volunteer thesis is a confidently held thesis of many contemporary Anglo-American philosophers. It is easy to see that the thesis is contrary to what Sidgwick called Common Sense. For it means that there is no such thing as filial duty per se, no such thing as the special duty of mother to child, and generally no such thing as a morality of special family or kinship relations. All of which is contrary to what people think. For most people think that we do own special debts to our parents even though we have not voluntarily assumed our obligations to them. Most people think that what we owe to our own children does not have its origin in any voluntary undertaking, explicit or implicit, that we have made to them. And, "preanalytically," many people believe that we owe special consideration to our siblings even at times when we may not *feel* very friendly to them. But if there are no special duties, then most of these prima facie requirements are misplaced and without moral force, and should be looked upon as archaic survivals to be ignored in assessing our moral obligations.

The idea that to be committed to an individual is to have made a voluntarily implicit or explicit commitment to that individual is generally fatal to family morality. For it looks upon the network of felt obligation and expectation that binds family members as a sociological phenomenon that is without presumptive moral force. The social critics who hold this view of family obligation usually are aware that promoting it in public policy must further the disintegration of the traditional family as an institution. But whether they deplore the disintegration or welcome it, they are bound in principle to abet it.

It may be that so many philosophers have accepted the voluntaristic dogma because of an uncritical use of the model of promises as the paradigm for obligations. If all obligations are like the obligation to keep a promise, then indeed they could not be incumbent on anyone who did not undertake to perform in a specified way. But there is no reason to take promises as paradigmatic of obligation. Indeed, the moral force of the norm of promise-keeping must itself be grounded in a theory of obligations that moral philosophers have yet to work out.

A better defense of the special duties would require considerably more space than I can give it here.[28] However, I believe the defense of special duties is far more plausible than rival theories that reject special duties. My primary objective has been to raise the strong suspicion that the volunteer theory of obligation is a dogma that is very probably wrong and misconceived, a view that is certainly at odds with common opinion.

Once we reject the doctrine that a voluntary act by the person concerned is a necessary condition of special obligation, we are free to respect the commonsense views that attribute moral force to many obligations associated with kinship and other family relationships. We may then accept the family as an institution that defines many special duties but that is nevertheless imperfect in numerous respects. Nevertheless, we still face the choice of how, as social philosophers, we are to deal with these imperfections. That is, we have the choice of being liberal or conservative in our attitude toward reform.

Burkean conservatives would change little or nothing, believing that the historical development of an institution has its own wisdom. They oppose utopian social engineering, considering it altogether immoral in the profound sense of destroying the very foundations of the special duties. But Burkeans also oppose what Karl Popper called "piecemeal social engineering," which seeks to remedy unjust practices without destroying the institution that harbors them. For Burkeans believe, on empirical grounds, that reform is always dangerous: that reform usually has unforeseen consequences worse than the original injustices sought to be eliminated. Thus, conservatives are much like environmental conservationists in their attitude toward an ecological system: their general advice is extreme caution or hands off.

Liberals are more optimistic about the consequences of reform. Like conservatives, they believe that the norms of any tradition or institution not essentially unjust have prima facie moral force. All of which means we can rely on our commonsense beliefs that the system of expectations within the family is legitimate and should be respected. The liberal will acknowledge that a brother has the right to expect more help from a brother than from a stranger and not just because of what he has done for him lately. And the case is the same for all traditional expectations that characterize family members. On the other hand, there may be practices within the family that are systematically discriminatory and unfair to certain members. Unlike conservatives, liberals are prepared to do some piecemeal social engineering to eliminate injustice in the family.

It should be said that the appeal to common sense or common opinion is not final. For common sense often delivers conflicting verdicts on behavior. But a commonsense verdict is strongly presumptive. For example, there is the common belief that biological mothers have a special responsibility to care for their children, even their unwanted children. One *takes* this as presumptive evidence of an *objective* moral responsibility on the part of the mother. Note that the "verdict" of common sense is not really a verdict at all. Rather, it is evidence of a moral consideration that *must* enter into the final verdict on what to do and how to behave. Thomson ignores common sense when she asserts that the mother of a child, born or unborn, has no special responsibility to it unless she has in some way voluntarily assumed responsibility for it. Now, to say that a pregnant woman may have a moral responsibility to her unborn child does not entail that abortion is impermissible. For there are other commonsense considerations that enter here and other responsibilities that the mother may have (to her other children, to herself) that may conflict and override the responsibility to the fetus. So common sense is often not decisive. One may say that a commonsense opinion is symptomatic of a prima facie duty or liberty, as the case may be. Yet it still remains for the casuist to determine the *weight* of the duty in relation to other moral considerations that also may have the support of common sense. Politically and morally, lack of respect for common sense fosters illiberalism and elitism. Here we have the radical temper that often advocates actions and policies wildly at odds with common opinion—from infanticide to male lactation, from no-fault divorce on demand for children to the "roommate test" for marital relationships.

THE BROKEN FAMILY

In the final section we look at certain of the social consequences of applying radical theory to family obligation. I have suggested that, insofar as moral philosophers have any influence on the course of social history, their influence has recently been in aid of institutional disintegration. I shall now give some indication of how the principled philosophical disrespect for common sense in the area of family morality has weakened the family and how this affects the happiness of its members. Although much of what I say here is fairly well known, it is useful to say it in the context of an essay critical of the radical way of approaching moral philosophy. For there are periods in history when the radical way has great influence. And it is worth seeing what happens when Plato succeeds in Syracuse.

The most dramatic evidence of the progressive weakening of the family is found in the statistics on divorce. Almost all divorce is painful and most divorce affects children. Although divorce does not end but merely disrupts the life of a child, the life it disrupts is uncontroversially the life of a person who can be wronged directly by the actions of a moral agent. One might, therefore, expect that philosophers who carefully examine the morality of abortion also would carefully examine the moral ground for divorce. But here, too, the contemporary reluctance of philosophers to deal with the special casuistry of family relations is evidenced. For example, there are more articles on euthanasia or on recombinant DNA research than on divorce.

Each year there are another million and a quarter divorces in the United States affecting over one million children. The mother is granted custody in ninety percent of the cases, although legally it is no longer a matter of course. There is very persuasive evidence that children of divorced parents are affected seriously and adversely. Compared with children from intact families, they are referred more often to school psychologists, are more likely to have lower IQ and achievement test scores, are arrested more often, and need more remedial classes.[29] Moreover, these effects show little correlation to economic class. Children in the so-called latency period (between six and twelve) are the most seriously affected. In one study of children in this age group, one-half the subjects showed evidence of a "consolidation into troubled and conflicted depressive behavior patterns."[30] Their behavior patterns included "continuing depression and low self-esteem, combined with frequent school and peer difficulties."

One major cause for the difference between children from broken and intact families is the effective loss of the father. In the *majority* of cases the child has not seen the father within the past year. Only one child in six has seen his or her father in the past week; only 16 percent have seen their fathers in the past month; 15 percent see them once a year; the remaining 52 percent have had no contact at all for the past year. Although 57 percent of college educated fathers see their children at least once a month, their weekly contact is the same as for all other groups (one in six).[31]

It would be difficult to demonstrate that the dismissive attitude of most contemporary moral philosophers to the moral force of kinship ties and conventional family roles has been a serious factor in contributing to the growth in the divorce rate. But that is only because it is so difficult in general to demonstrate how much bread is baked by the dissemination of philosophical ideas. It is surely fair to say that the emphasis on autonomy and equality, when combined with the philosophical denigration of family ties, may have helped to make divorce both easy and respectable, thereby facilitating the rapid change from fault-based to no-fault divorce. If contemporary moralists have not caused the tide of family disintegration, they are avidly riding it. On the other side, it is not difficult to demonstrate that there is very little in recent moral philosophy that could be cited as possibly contributing to *stemming* the tide.

In the past two decades there has been a celebrated resurgence of interest in applied or practical ethics. It would appear, however, that the new enthusiasm for getting down to normative cases does not extend to topics of personal morality defined by family relationships. Accordingly, the children who are being victimized by the breakdown of the family have not benefited from this. Indeed, we find far more concern about the effect of divorce on children from philosophers a generation or two ago when divorce was relatively rare than we find today. Thus, Bertrand Russell writes:

> [H]usband and wife, if they have any love for their children, will so regulate their conduct as to give their children the best chance of a happy and healthy development. This may involve, at times, very considerable self-repression. And it certainly requires that both should realize the superiority of the claims of children to the claims of their own romantic emotions.[32]

And while Russell is not opposed to divorce, he believes that children place great constraints on it.

> . . . parents who divorce each other, except for grave cause, appear to me to be failing their parental duty.[33]

Discerning and sensitive observers of a generation ago did not need masses of statistics to alert them to the effects of divorce on children. Nor did it take a professional philosopher (citing statistics gathered by a professional sociologist) to see that acting to dissolve a family must be evaluated morally primarily in terms of what such action means for the children.

Writing in the *London Daily Express* in 1930, Rebecca West says:

> The divorce of married people with children is nearly always an unspeakable calamity. It is only just being understood . . . how much a child depends for its healthy growth on the presence in the home of both its parents. . . . The point is that if a child is deprived of either its father or its mother it feels that it has been cheated out of a right.[34]

West describes the harmful effects of divorce on children as effects of "a radiating kind, likely to travel down and down through the generations, such as few would care to have on their consciences."

I have quoted West in some fullness because her remarks contrast sharply with what one typically finds in contemporary college texts. In a book called *Living Issues in Ethics*, the authors discuss unhappy parents and the moral questions they face in contemplating divorce.

> We believe that staying together for the sake of the children is worse than the feelings and adjustment of separation and divorce.[35]

Further on the authors give what they feel to be a decisive reason for this policy:

> Remaining together in an irreconcilable relationship violates the norm of interpersonal love.

One of the very few philosophers to discuss the question of divorce and its consequences for children is Jeffrey Blustein in his book, *Parents and Children.* Blustein looks with equanimity on the priority of personal commitment to parental responsibility, pointing out that

> The traditional view . . . that the central duties of husband and wife are the . . . duties of parenthood is giving way to a conception of marriage as essentially involving a serious commitment between two individuals as individuals.[36]

Blustein also tells us (without telling us how he knows it) that children whose parents are unhappily married are worse off than if their parents were divorced.

> Indeed it could be argued that precisely on account of the children the parents' unhappy marriage should be dissolved. . . .[37]

The suggestion that parents who are unhappy should get a divorce "for the sake of the children" is *very* contemporary.

To my knowledge, no reliable study has yet been made that compares children of divorced parents to children from intact families whose parents do not get on well together. So I have no way of knowing whether the claims of these authors are true or not. Moreover, because any such study would be compromised by certain arbitrary measures of parental incompatibility, one should probably place little reliance on them. It is, therefore, easy to see that contemporary philosophers are anxious to jump to conclusions that do not render implausible the interesting view that the overriding question in considering divorce is the compatibility of the parents, and that marital ties should be dissolved when they threaten or thwart the personal fulfillment of one or both the marital partners.

These philosophers set aside special duties and replace them with an emphasis on friendship, compatibility, and interpersonal love among family members. However, this has a disintegrative effect. That is to say, if what one owes to members of one's family is largely to be understood in terms of feelings of personal commitment, definite limits are placed on what one owes. For as feelings change, so may one's commitments. The result is a structure of responsibility within the family that is permanently unstable.

I have, in this final section, illustrated the indifference of contemporary philosophers to the family by dwelling on their indifference to the children affected by divorce. Nevertheless, I hope it is clear that nothing I have said is meant to convey that I oppose divorce. I do not. Neither Russell nor West nor any of the sane and compassionate liberal thinkers of the recent past opposed divorce. They simply did not play fast and loose with family mores, did not encourage divorce, and pointed out that moralists must insist that the system of family obligations is only partially severed by a divorce that cuts the marital tie. Morally, as well as legally, the obligations to the children remain as before. Legally, this is still recognized. But in a moral climate where the system of family obligation is given no more weight than can be justified in terms of popular theories of deontic volunteerism, the obligatory ties are too fragile to survive the personal estrangements that result from divorce. It is, therefore, to be expected that parents (especially fathers) will be off and away doing their own thing. And the law is largely helpless.

I have no special solutions to the tragedy of economic impoverishment and social deprivation that results from the weakening of family ties. I believe in the right of divorce and do not even oppose no-fault divorce. I do not know how to get back to the good old days when moral philosophers had the common sense to acknowledge the moral weight of special ties and the courage to condemn those who failed in them—the days when, in consequence, the *climate* of moral approval and disapproval was quite different from what it is today. I do not know how to make fathers ashamed of their neglect and inadvertent cruelty. What I do know is that moral philosophers should be paying far more attention to the social consequences of their views than they are. It is as concrete as taking care that what one says will not affect adversely the students whom one is addressing. If what students learn from us encourages social disintegration, then we are responsible for the effects this may have on their lives and on the lives of their children. This then is a grave responsibility, even graver than the responsibility we take in being for or against something as serious as euthanasia or capital punishment—since most of our students will never face these questions in a practical way.

I believe then that responsible moral philosophers are liberal or conservative but not radical. They respect human relationships and traditions and the social environment in which they live as much as they respect the natural environment and its ecology. They respect the family. William James saw the rejection of radicalism as central to the pragmatist way of confronting moral questions.

> [Experience] has proved that the laws and usages of the land are what yield the maximum of satisfaction. . . . The presumption in cases of conflict must always be in favor of the conventionally recognized good. The philosopher must be a conservative, and in the construction of his casuistic scale must put things most in accordance with the customs of the community on top.[38]

A moral philosophy that does not give proper weight to the customs and opinions of the community is presumptuous in its attitude and pernicious in its consequences. In an important sense it is not a moral philosophy at all. For it is humanly irrelevant.

NOTES

1. Michael Slote, "Obedience and Illusions," in Onora O'Neill and William Ruddick, eds., *Having Children* (New York: Oxford, 1979), p. 320.
2. Slote, p. 230.
3. Virginia Held, "The Obligations of Mothers and Fathers," in Joyce Trebilcot, ed., *Mothering: Essays in Feminist Theory* (Totowa, NJ: Rowman and Allanheld, 1984), pp. 7–20.
4. Jane English, "What Do Grown Children Owe Their Parents?" in O'Neill and Ruddick, *op. cit.*, pp. 351–56.
5. John Simmons, *Moral Principles and Political Obligation* (Princeton, NJ: Princeton University Press, 1979), p. 162.
6. Jeffrey Blustein, *Parents and Children: The Ethics of the Family* (New York: Oxford, 1982), p. 182.
7. Howard Cohen, *Equal Rights for Children* (Totowa, NJ: Rowman and Littlefield, 1980), p. 66.
8. Simone de Beauvoir, *The Second Sex*, tr. H. M. Parshley (New York: Random House, 1952), p. 534.
9. De Beauvoir, p. 553.
10. De Beauvoir, "Talking to De Beauvoir," *Spare Rib* (March 1977), p. 2.
11. Richard Wasserstrom, *Philosophy and Social Issues* (Notre Dame, IN: University of Notre Dame Press, 1980), p. 26.
12. Wasserstrom, p. 23.
13. Wasserstrom, p. 26.
14. Ann Ferguson, "Androgyny as an Ideal for Human Development," in *Feminism and Philosophy*, eds. M. Vetterling-Braggin, F. Elliston and J. English (Totowa, NJ: Rowman and Littlefield, 1977), pp. 45–69.
15. Carol Gould, "Private Rights and Public Virtues: Woman, the Family and Democracy," in *Beyond Domination*, ed. Carol Gould (Totowa, NJ: Rowman and Allanheld, 1983), pp. 3–18.
16. Alison Jaggar, "Human Biology in Feminist Theory: Sexual Equality Reconsidered," in Gould, *op. cit.*, p. 41. Jaggar is serious about the possibility and desirability of what she calls the "transformation of sexuality," which is elaborated in her book *Feminist Politics and Human Nature* (Totowa, NJ: Rowman and Allanheld, 1983), p. 132.
17. Alison Jaggar, "On Sex Equality," in *Sex Equality*, ed. Jane English (Englewood Cliffs, NJ: Prentice-Hall, 1977), p. 102.
18. Alison Jaggar, "Prostitution," in Marilyn Pearsell, ed., *Women and Values: Reading in Recent Feminist Philosophy* (Belmont, CA: Wadsworth, 1986), pp. 108–121.
19. Jaggar, "Prostitution," p. 117.
20. Janet Radcliffe Richards, *The Skeptical Feminist* (Middlesex, England: Penguin Books, 1980), pp. 341–42.
21. See Sylvia Ann Hewlett, *A Lesser Life: The Myth of Woman's Liberation in America* (New York: William Morrow, 1986).

22. See, for example, Carol Gilligan, *In a Different Voice* (Cambridge, MA: Harvard University Press, 1982); Eva Kittay and Diana Meyers, eds., *Women and Moral Theory* (Totowa, NJ: Rowman and Littlefield, 1987); Lawrence Blum, *Friendship, Altruism and Morality* (London: Routledge & Kegan Paul, 1980); Jean Grimshaw, *Philosophy and Feminist Thinking* (Minneapolis, MN: University of Minnesota Press, 1986); Nel Noddings, *Caring: A Feminine Approach to Ethics and Moral Education* (Berkeley, CA: University of California Press, 1984).
23. See, for example, Joyce Trebilcot, ed., *Mothering: Essays in Feminist Theory* (Totowa, NJ: Rowman and Allanheld, 1984).
24. Judith Thomson, "A Defense of Abortion," in *Philosophy and Public Affairs,* vol. 1, no. 1, 1972.
25. Thomson, p. 64.
26. Michael Tooley, "Abortion and Infanticide," in *Philosophy and Public Affairs,* vol. 2, no. 1, 1972.
27. Howard Cohen, *Equal Rights for Children,* chs. V and VI.
28. For a defense of the special duties not assumed voluntarily, see Christina Sommers, "Filial Morality," *The Journal of Philosophy,* no. 8, August 1986.
29. Lenore Weitzman, *The Divorce Revolution: The Unexpected Social and Economic Consequences for Women and Children in America* (New York: The Free Press, 1985).
30. A. Skolnick and J. Skolnick, eds., *Family in Transition* (Boston: Little Brown, 1929), p. 452.
31. Weitzman, p. 259.
32. Bertrand Russell, *Marriage and Morals* (New York: Liveright, 1929), p. 236.
33. Russell, p. 238.
34. Rebecca West, *London Daily Express,* 1930.
35. R. Nolan and F. Kirkpatrick, eds., *Living Issues in Ethics* (Belmont, CA: Wadsworth, 1983), p. 147.
36. Blustein, *Parents and Children,* p. 230.
37. Blustein, p. 232.
38. William James, "The Moral Philosopher and the Moral Life," in *Essays in Pragmatism* (New York: Hafner, 1948), p. 80.

STUDY QUESTIONS

1. What bearing does Sommers's distinction between Aristotelian and Platonic social criticism have on the feminist debate?
2. Sommers suggests that radical feminists are unsympathetic to "femininity." What is femininity, and do you agree with her analysis?
3. What evidence does Sommers offer in support of her claim that moral philosophers have indirectly attacked the family? Do you agree with her analysis?
4. Do you accept or reject the "volunteerist" theory, as the author describes it?

42

Rapist Ethics

John Stoltenberg

John Stoltenberg is the author of *The End of Manhood: A Book for Men of Conscience* and *Refusing to Be a Man: Essays on Sex and Justice.*

Stories have beginnings, middles, and endings. Ideas do not. Stories can be told and understood in terms of who did what and what happened to whom, what happened next, and what happened after that. Ideas do not exist in time and space that way, yet it is only through our apprehension of certain ideas that historical reality makes any sense at all. We interpret all the data of our senses—including characters, actions, consequences, even our so-called selves—according to ideas, concepts, or mental structures, some of which we understand, some of which we just believe.

Sexual identity is an idea. Sexual identity—the belief that there is maleness and femaleness and that one is either male or female—is among the most fundamental ideas with which we interpret our experience. Not only do we "know" and "believe in" the idea of sexual identity, but the idea of sexual identity largely determines how and what we know. With the idea of sexual identity in our head, we see things and feel things and learn things in terms of it. Like a sketch artist who looks at a still life or figure and sees lines to be drawn where in fact there are contours and surfaces that wrap around out of sight, we observe human beings about us and distinguish appearances and behaviors belonging to a male sexual identity or a female sexual identity. We say to ourselves, "There goes a man," "There goes a woman." Like the sketch artist, we draw lines at the edges beyond which we cannot see.

The idea of sexual identity, in fact, has a claim on us that our actual experience does not; for if our experience "contradicts" it, we will bend our experience so that it will make sense in terms of the idea. Other ideas—such as our belief that there is an up and a down and that objects will tend to fall toward earth—are supportable with much less mental effort. Gravity is a sturdy, reliable category into which most of our everyday experience fits without much fiddling. No one need worry their head that gravity will somehow cease if too many people abandon faith in it. Nor need we contend with the occasional exceptions that could nag us and cause us anxiety about whether, say, a dropped object will truly fall. The force of gravity would be with us even without our idea of it. Gravity just is; we don't have to make it be. Not so the idea of sexual identity. Sexual identity is a political idea. Its force derives entirely from the human effort required to sustain it, and it requires the lifelong, nearly full-time exertion of everybody for its maintenance and verification. Though everyone, to some extent, plays their part in keeping the idea of sexual identity real, some people, it should be noted, work at this project with more fervor than do others.

We are remarkably resistant to recognizing the idea of sexual identity as having solely a political meaning. We very much prefer to believe, instead, that it has a metaphysical existence. For instance, we want to think that the idea of sexual identity "exists" the way that the idea of a chair does. The idea of a chair can have an actual existence in the form of a real chair. There can be many different kinds of chairs, but we can know one when we see one, because we have the idea of a chair in our head. And every actual chair has a degree of permanence to its chairness; we can look at it and sit in it today and tomorrow and the day after that and know it solidly as a chair. We believe the idea of sexual identity can have such a continuity and permanence too, in the form of a real man or a real woman. We believe that though people's appearances and behaviors differ greatly, we can know a real man or a real woman when we see one, because we have the ideas of maleness and femaleness in our head. We think that when we perceive this maleness or femaleness in another person, that person's sexual identity has a durability, a constancy, a certainty—to themselves as well as to us. We think that it is truly possible for us ourselves to be a real man or a real woman with the same certainty that we see in others. We think the idea of sexual identity is an idea like the idea of a chair, yet we can be dimly aware at moments that the idea of one's sexual identity is sometimes in doubt, is never fully realized, never settled, never really "there" for any dependable length of time. We can observe that, oddly, the idea of one's own sexual identity must be re-created, over and over again, in action and sensation—in doing things that make one feel really male or really female and in not doing things that leave room for doubt. To each person's own self, the idea of a fixed and certain sexual identity can seem "out there" somewhere, elusive, always more fully realized in someone else. Almost everyone thinks someone else's sexual identity is more real than one's own, and almost everyone measures themselves against other people who are perceived to be more male or more female. At the same time, almost everyone's own sexual identity feels certain and real to themselves only fleetingly, with troublesome interruptions. Chairs do not seem to have the same problem, and we do not have the same problem with chairs.

Many attempts have been made to locate a basis in material reality for our belief in sexual identity. For instance, it is claimed quite scientifically that people think and behave as they do, in a male way or in a female way, because of certain molecules called hormones, which with rather circular logic are designated male or female. It is said, quite scientifically, that the prenatal presence or absence of these hormones produces male brains or female brains—brains predisposed to think gender-typed thoughts and to act out gender-typed behaviors. In fetuses becoming male, it is said, allegedly male hormones called androgens "masculinize" the brain cells by, among other things, chemically connecting the brainwave pathways for sex and aggression, so that eroticism and terrorism will ever after be mental neighbors. It is also said that in fetuses becoming female those androgens are absent, so those two circuits do not fuse. The scientists who study and document such phenomena (most of whom, of course, believe their brains to be quite male) claim to have determined that some female fetuses receive an abnormal overdose of androgens in the womb, an accident that explains, they say, why tomboy girls climb trees and why uppity women want careers. The gist of such theories—and there are many others that are similar—is that behavior follows sexual identity, rather than the other way around.

If it is true that behavior follows sexual identity, then the rightness or wrongness of any human action can justifiably be judged differently depending on whether it was done by a male or a female, on grounds such as biology, the natural order, or human nature. The cross-cultural indisposition of able-bodied males to do dishes, to pick up after themselves, or to handle child-care responsibilities, for example, can be said to derive from their hormonal constitutions, which were engineered for stalking mastodons and which have not evolved for doing the laundry.

Nearly all people believe deeply and unshakably that some things are wrong for a woman to do while right for a man and that other things are wrong for a man to do while right for a woman. This faith, like most, is blind; but unlike most, it does not perceive itself as a faith. It is, in fact, an ethic without an epistemology—a particular system of attaching values to conduct without the slightest comprehension of how or why people believe that the system is true. It is a creed whose articles never really require articulation, because its believers rarely encounter anyone who does not already believe it, silently and by heart. The valuation of human actions according to the gender of the one who acts is a notion so unremarkable, so unremittingly commonplace, and so self-evident to so many that its having come under any scrutiny whatsoever is a major miracle in the history of human consciousness.

Oddly, at the same time, many people cherish a delusion that their ethical judgments are really gender-neutral. In popular psychobabble, for instance, one hears the words "give and take" in countless conversations about interpersonal relationships between men and women. The catchphrase evokes both the ideal and the practical possibility of a perfectly reciprocal dyadic relationship, in harmony and equilibrium, exchanging back and forth, like a blissfully unbiased teeter-totter. Men and women alike will swear by it, extolling giving and taking as if it were a first principle of socio-sexual interaction. The actual reality beneath "give and take" may be quite different: for her, swallowed pride and self-effacing forgiveness; from him, punishing emotional withdrawal and egomaniacal defensiveness. Or perhaps they will trade off tears for temporary reforms, capitulation for a moment's tranquillity, her subordination in exchange for an end to his threats of force. They will speak of this drama, embittering and brutalizing, as "give and take," the only form they can imagine for a love across the chasm that keeps male distinct from female. They may grieve over their failed communication, yet they will defend to the teeth their tacit sex-specific ethics—by which men and women are held accountable to two different systems of valuing conduct—and they will not, ever, comprehend what has gone wrong.

In no arena of human activity are people more loyal to that sex-specific ethics than in transactions involving overt genital stimulation. When people have sex, make love, or screw, they act as a rule in conformity with two separate systems of behavior valuation, one male and one female, as if their identities or lives depended on it. For males, generally, it tends to be their identities; for females, often, it is more a matter of their lives. Behaving within the ethical limits of what is wrong or right for their sexual identities becomes so critical, in fact, that physicalized anxiety about whether one is "male enough" or "female enough" is virtually indistinguishable from most bodily sensations that are regarded as "erotic." For a male, the boundaries of what he wants to make happen in a sexual encounter with a partner—when and for how long, and to whom he wants it to happen—are rarely unrelated to this pivotal consideration: what is necessary in order "to be the man there," in order to experience the functioning of his own body "as a male," and in order to be regarded by his partner as having no tactile, visual, behavioral, or emotional resemblance to a *not*-male, a female. The anxiety he feels—fearing he may not be able to make that happen and striving to inhabit his body so that it *will* happen—is a component of the sexual tension he feels. For many females, deference to a male partner's overriding identity anxiety can know no bounds; for her, the fear is that his precariously rigged sexual-arousal mechanism will go awry, haywire, and that he will hold her responsible and punish her somehow for turning him off (Or is it for turning him on to begin with? That part is never clear). To avoid that fate, that can of hysterical worms, no sacrifice no matter how demeaning can be too great. In such ways as these are most people's experiences of sexual tension due in large measure to their anxiety about whether they are behaving within the ethical parameters of what is wrong or right conduct for their putative sexual identities. The sexual tension and the gender anxiety are so closely associated within everyone's body and brain that the anxiety predictably triggers the tension and the release of the tension can be expected to absolve the anxiety—at least until next time.

This, then, is the nexus of eroticism and ethics—the hookup between the eroticism we feel and the ethics of our acts, between sensation and action, between feeling and doing. It is a connection at the core of both our selves and our culture. It is the point at which gender-specific sexuality emerges from behavioral choices, not from anatomy. It is the point at which our erotic feelings make manifest the fear with which we conform to the structure of right and wrong for either gender, a structure mined on all sides by every peril we dare imagine. This is the point at which we might recognize that our very sexual identities are artifices and illusions, the result of a lifetime of striving to do the right male thing not the right female thing, or the right female thing not the right male thing. This is the point, too, at which we can see that we are not dealing with anything so superficial as roles, images, or stereotypes, but that in fact we have come face to face with an aspect of our identities even more basic than our corporeality—namely, our faith that there are two sexes and our secret and public desperation to belong to one not the other.

The fiction of a sexual identity becomes clearer upon examining more closely the case of male sexual identity. What exactly is the set of behaviors that are prescribed as right for it and proscribed as wrong? How does someone learn to know the difference? What is the difference between the male right and wrong and the female right and wrong? And how is it possible that someone who has successfully attained a male sexual identity can feel so right in doing an action—for instance, rape—that to someone else, someone female, is so totally wrong?

That last question reduces, approximately, to Why do men rape? As a preliminary answer, I propose an analogy to the craft of acting in the theater:

There is a theory of acting, quite common today, that to achieve recognizable naturalism, an actor must play a character as if everything that character does is completely justifiable; so, for instance, an actor playing a villain ought not "play" villainousness, or the evilness of that character. Only an untrained or amateur actor would ever try to portray the quality of maliciousness in a character who does morally decrepit things (the roles of Shakespeare's Richard the Third and Büchner's Woyzeck come to mind). Rather, according to this theory, the actor must believe at all times that what the character is doing is right, no matter what the audience or the other characters onstage may think of the goodness or badness of that character's actions. The actor playing the part must pursue the character's objectives in each scene, wholly believing that there is absolutely nothing wrong with doing so. Although in the eyes of observers the character might commit the most heinous crimes, the actor playing the character must have prepared for the role by adopting a belief system in which it makes moral sense to do those acts.

The problem of portraying character in the theater is one that Aristotle dissected in his classic fifth century B.C. text *Poetics*. His points are still central to acting theory as it is practiced today:

> With regard to . . . characters, there are four things to be aimed at. First, and most important, they must be good. Now any speech or action that manifests some kind of moral purpose will be expressive of character: the character will be good if the purpose is good. The goodness is possible in every class of persons. Even a woman may be good, and also a slave, though the one is liable to be an inferior being, and the other quite worthless. The second thing to aim at is appropriateness. There is a type of manly valor, but manliness in a woman, or unscrupulous cleverness, is inappropriate. Thirdly, a character must be true to life: which is something quite different from goodness and appropriateness, as here described. The fourth point

is consistency: for even though the person being imitated . . . is inconsistent, still he must be consistently inconsistent.

The impersonation of male sexual identity in life bears several striking resemblances to the techniques by which an actor portrays character. Paraphrasing Aristotle's admonitions from twenty-five centuries ago, one can generalize that to act out convincingly a male sexual identity requires:

- An unfailing belief in one's own goodness and the moral rightness of one's purposes, regardless of how others may value what one does;
- A rigorous adherence to the set of behaviors, characteristics, and idiosyncrasies that are appropriately male (and therefore inappropriate for a female);
- An unquestioning belief in one's own consistency, notwithstanding any evidence to the contrary—a consistency rooted, for all practical purposes, in the relentlessness of one's will and in the fact that, being superior by social definition, one can want whatever one wants and one can expect to get it.

This much, we can assume, Aristotle meant by "true to life," for in fact in life this is how male sexual identity is acted out, and this is how "maleness" is inferred and assessed—as, fundamentally, a characterological phenomenon. Most people, whether as spectators of real life or staged life, regard as credible and laudable someone's convictions about the rightness of what that one is doing—no matter what, at no matter what cost—when that someone is a male, operating within the behavioral choices of male sexual identity. A "he," being a he, can get away with murder—figuratively, and sometimes even literally—simply by virtue of the fact that he dissembles so sincerely, or he uses up someone's life with such single-minded purpose, or he betrays someone's trust with such resolute passion, or he abandons commitments with such panache. When men are held to account for what they do in their lives to women—which happens relatively rarely—their tunnel vision, their obliviousness to consequences, their egotism, their willfulness, all tend to excuse, rather than compound, their most horrific interpersonal offenses. Someone female, however, is regarded very differently. What is expected of her is hesitancy, qualms, uncertainty that what she is doing is right—even while doing something right. She should, as Aristotle might have put it, play her part as if in perpetual stage fright, a comely quality befitting one as inferior as she. And when she is called to account—which happens relatively often—not only is there never an excuse, but her lack of appropriate faintheartedness may be grounds for yet more blame.

Blame, of course, figures prominently in what happens when a man rapes a woman: The man commits the rape, then the woman gets blamed for it. If rape was a transaction where gender-specific ethics were not operative, that assessment of responsibility would be regarded as the *non sequitur* it is. But in rape that illogic is believed to explain what happened and why: If a man rapes a woman, the woman is responsible; therefore the rape is not a rape. What is the meaning of that nonsensical blaming? And how does it illuminate the structure of sex-specific ethics?

According to the tacit ethics of male sexual identity, one who would act out the character of "a man, not a woman" will necessarily believe that the series of actions appropriate to that character is right and that there is absolutely nothing wrong with doing anything in pursuit of the character's objectives. Rape is, of course, such an action in that it is committed almost exclusively by those who are acting out the character of "a man, not a woman." Rape is not the only action that is congruent with the tacit ethics of male sexual identity. Wife beating, for instance, is another. So, for that matter, are any number of things men do every day that are faithless, heedless, irresponsible, or humiliating in relation to women—things men do with impunity and women suffer silently because "that's just how men are." If ever a woman decides not to suffer such an offense silently—if, for instance, she decides not to tolerate being treated as if she is less of a person than he—and if she decides to confront him on terms that come close to exposing the gender-specific ethics in what he has done ("You acted just like a man. You treated me as if I completely didn't matter just because I'm a woman"), she will likely experience his vengeful defensiveness at gale force; and he will likely try to blow her away. That sorry scenario is also consistent with the tacit ethics by which male sexual identity is played out. Sex-specific ethics are tacit and they must remain tacit, otherwise the jig would be up.

The series of actions that are appropriate to the character of "a man, not a woman" is profoundly influenced by the presence of rape among them. This series of acts is not like a dissonance composed of random, unharmonious notes. It is, rather, a chord in which the root or fundament colors every pitch above it, its overtones enhancing every note that is struck. Rape is like the fundamental tone; played sometimes fortissimo, sometimes pianissimo, sometimes a mere echo, it determines the harmonics of the whole chord. "Sometimes," "just a little," "now and then," "only rarely"—however much one may wish to qualify the salient feature of the series, the act of prevailing upon another to admit of penetration without full and knowledgeable assent so sets the standard in the repertoire of male-defining behaviors that it is not at all inaccurate to suggest that the ethics of male sexual identity are essentially rapist.

Rapist ethics is a definitive and internally consistent system for attaching value to conduct: The concepts of both right and wrong exist within rapist ethics; it is not an ethic in which blame and moral condemnation go unreckoned or unremarked. There is also in rapist ethics a structural view of personal responsibility for acts, but it views the one *to whom* the act is done as being responsible for the act. It is a little like the driver of a car believing that the tree beside the road caused the car to collide with it. For example, one victim of a rape told an interviewer:

> There he was, a man who had the physical power to lock me up and rape me, without any real threat of societal punishment, telling me that I was oppressive because I was a woman! Then he started telling me he could understand how men sometimes go out and rape women. . . . He looked at me and said, "Don't make me hurt you," as though I was, by not giving in to him, forcing him to rape me. That's how he justified the whole thing. He kept saying women were forcing him to rape them by not being there when he needed them.

This reversal of moral accountability is not an isolated instance; it is a characteristic of nearly all acts that are committed within the ethic of male sexual identity. It is a type of projection, of seeing one's "wrong" in the person one is wronging, which is the same as saying that one has done no wrong. Social scientists who have surveyed the attitudes of prisoners report that "[s]ex offenders are twice as likely to insist on their own innocence as the general offenders" and that "they frequently see in their victims aggressive, offensive persons who force them into abnormal acts."

And a psychiatrist who has worked extensively with admitted rapists reports, "It is becoming increasingly more difficult for these men to see their actions as criminal, as being anything more than the normal male response to a female."

In the twisted logic of rapist ethics, the victim is ultimately culpable; the victim is the culprit; the victim did the wrong. Absurdly, the most obvious and absolute facts about the act—who did what to whom—become totally obfuscated because responsibility is imputed to the victim for an act that someone else committed. Myths that promulgate this ethic abound: Women want to be raped, women deserve to be raped, women provoke rape, women need to be raped, and women *enjoy* being raped. The societal force of these myths is so great that many rape victims fear to reveal to anyone what has happened to them, believing themselves to be the cause of what happened. Several years after she was gang-raped at the age of fourteen, for instance, a woman recalled:

> I felt like I'd brought out the worst in these men just by being an available female body on the road. I felt like if I hadn't been on the road, these men would have continued in their good upstanding ways, and that it was my fault that they'd been lowered to rape me.

Also, she remembered:

> I forgave them immediately. I felt like it was all my fault that I'd been raped. I said, well, they're men. They just can't help themselves. That's the way men are.

Implicit in this victim's recollected feelings are the twin tenets of rapist ethics: It is right to rape; it is wrong to be raped. That translates more often than not into a precept even more appalling yet probably closer to the raw insides of male-supremacist eroticism: It is right to be male; it is wrong to be female. Or, in the words of a character who has just raped, beaten, and forcibly sodomized his wife in the pornographic novel *Juliette* by the Marquis de Sade:

> There are two sides to every passion . . . : seen from the side of the victim upon whom the pressure is brought to bear, the passion appears unjust; whereas . . . to him who applies the pressure, his passion is the justest thing imaginable.

It is right to be male; it is wrong to be female; therefore anything done against a woman to the purpose of one's passion—realizing male sexual identity—is justifiable and good within the frame of rapist ethics.

In rape, in addition to the physical act, a transaction occurs that can be understood as the obliteration of the victim's moral identity. In an act of rape, the ethical structure of male right and wrong jams or destroys the victim's sense of herself as someone who is responsible for her own acts; rapist ethics disintegrates her accumulated knowledge of acts and consequences and of the relation between herself and her own acts. She regards herself as "at fault" for the assault, perhaps "forgiving" of her assailant at the same time, taking upon herself all the blame there is to be had, because the most basic connection has been severed—the connection between her identity and her own real deeds. The obliteration can result in a near total eclipse of her sense of herself as a being with integrity, as ever actually having had the capacity for moral deciding, rational thought, and conscientious action. The one who rapes, on the other hand, experiences himself as reintegrated, miraculously made whole again, more vital and more real. Rapists often report that they felt "bad" before they raped—and that's why they set out to rape—but that they felt "better" afterward, that the rape itself was stimulating, exciting, enjoyable, and fun. The disintegration of the victim's sense of self is, one might say, a prerequisite for the integration of the rapist's sense of self—a dynamic that is replicated whenever anyone acts within the ethical structure of male sexual identity. As one man said, succinctly stating the modern and ancient male dilemma: "A man gotta have a woman or he don't know he's a man."

Some actions congruent with rapist ethics are committed with what appears to be a "conscience" that is not quite clear. It would seem that while committing the act with complete conviction, the actor who does it experiences some remorse as well. This familiar show of contrition is apparent in the following, a story told by a woman about her twenty-four-year-old husband:

> He didn't only hit me. He bit me and tore my hair. I have a scar on my arm from where he bit a hole out of it one time. The only way to end the beating situation was to become submissive, so it could go on for hours and hours and

> hours until I couldn't take it any longer, and I'd end up on the floor a sobbing heap, and then he would continue kicking at me for a while. Then he would pick me up and brush the tears away and tell me how sorry he was. And he'd ask me to stay in so that people wouldn't see the black eye and bruises. Another trip he laid on me was how heavy it was for him to deal with his guilt about beating me.

On the face of the matter, remorse, regret, or guilt would seem to contradict the unequivocal conviction with which a man acts out rapist ethics, since all responsibility for "wrongdoing" has been imputed to the victim, the female, the one to whom the act was done. Perplexingly, there does sometimes occur a kind of ritual dance of repentance after certain acts, especially brutal ones, through which men realize male sexual identity. It is as if one can hear the man murmuring some lyrical longing for atonement and propitiation: "I'm sorry, forgive me, I didn't mean to, I apologize; I promise I will never do it again." The refrain about refraining.

What is the erotic substructure of that swift transition from violence and brutality to pangs of remorse? How are we to understand what happens once a man has teased (perhaps) or toyed with, or betrayed or humiliated, or attacked or terrorized a woman and then he turns suddenly repentant, and just as suddenly he indicates that what he wants to do now is fuck her? And what are we to make of his entreaties for forgiveness, for another chance, for reconciliation? his protestations of self-reproach? the woebegone look in his eyes? Is there, after all, such a thing in rapist ethics as a genuine moral consciousness of the true consequences of one's acts to other actual human beings?

The answer, I think, is no.

I believe that for those who strive toward male sexual identity, there is always the critical problem of how to manage one's affairs so that one always has available a supply of sustenance in the form of feminine deference and submission—someone female to whom to do the things that will adequately realize one's maleness. The sustenance must be personal, from one or more particular females who are in personal relation to oneself. The appeal for "forgiveness" within any such relationship functions to trap and lock in any female who may have been considering withdrawing her sustenance from him. The forgiveness asked—though it is almost always demanded, because even here pressure is applied—is a form of insistence that she remain in relation to him. One who lives by rapist ethics, after all, constantly risks alienating the objects of his pressures and passions—and with good reason. But forgiveness elicited at those critical moments seduces the woman back into victimization. Without that relation, male sexual identity withers. As one man put it: "When women are losing their will to be women . . . how can men be men? What the hell have we got to be male about any more?" The unforgiving woman is the judging woman, the angry woman, the withdrawing woman; she has lost her will to be a woman as men define it. Forgiveness from a woman represents her continued commitment to be present for him, to stay in relationship to him, enabling him to remain by contrast male. Her charity, her mercy, her grace (not for nothing have men personified all those abstractions as female in legend and art!) are in fact the emblems of female subordination to rapist ethics.

STUDY QUESTIONS

1. Is Stoltenberg saying that all men have "rapist" ethics? Or is he saying something else?
2. Why are gender-specific ethics dangerous, not just for women but also for men?
3. What risks are there in giving up gender-specific ethics?
4. How does a woman victimized by rape become the one who is seen as culpable? Why does the victim herself often believe this to be true?
5. Is Stoltenberg suggesting that sex roles be abandoned or, rather, reconstructed?

43

Sex and Violence

Catharine MacKinnon

Catharine MacKinnon is a noted feminist legal scholar. She teaches law at the University of Michigan and is the author of *Feminism Unmodified: Discourse on Life and Law, Toward a Feminist Theory of the State,* and *Only Words.*

I want to raise some questions about the concept of this panel's title, "Violence against Women," as a concept that may coopt us as we attempt to formulate our own truths. I want to speak specifically about four issues: rape, sexual harassment, pornography, and battery. I think one of the reasons we say that each of these issues is an example of violence against women is to reunify them. To say that aggression against women has this unity is to criticize the divisions that have been imposed on that aggression by the legal system. What I see to be the danger of the analysis, what makes it potentially cooptive, is formulating it—and it is formulated this way—these are issues of violence, *not* sex: rape is a crime of violence, not sexuality; sexual harassment is an abuse of power, not sexuality; pornography is violence against women, it is not erotic. Although battering is not categorized so explicitly, it is usually treated as though there is nothing sexual about a man beating up a woman so long as it is with his fist. I'd like to raise some questions about that as well.

I hear in the formulation that these issues are violence against women, not sex, that we are in the shadow of Freud, intimidated at being called repressive Victorians. We're saying we're *op*pressed and they say we're *re*pressed. That is, when we say we're against rape, the immediate response is, "Does that mean you're against sex?" "Are you attempting to impose neo-Victorian prudery on sexual expression?" This comes up with sexual harassment as well. When we say we're against sexual harassment, the first thing people want to know is, "What's the difference between that and ordinary male-to-female sexual initiation?" That's a good question. . . . The same is also true of criticizing pornography. "You can't be against erotica?" It's the latest version of the accusation that feminists are antimale. To distinguish ourselves from this, and in reaction to it, we call these abuses violence. The attempt is to avoid the critique—we're not against sex—and at the same time retain our criticism of these practices. So we rename as violent those abuses that have been seen to be sexual, without saying that we have a very different perspective on violence and on sexuality and their relationship. I also think a reason we call these experiences violence is to avoid being called lesbians, which for some reason is equated with being against sex. In order to avoid that, yet retain our opposition to sexual violation, we put this neutral, objective, abstract word *violence* on it all.

To me this is an attempt to have our own perspective on these outrages without owning up to having one. To have our point of view but present it as *not* a particular point of view. Our problem has been to label something as rape, as sexual harassment, as pornography in the face of a suspicion that it might be intercourse, it might be ordinary sexual initiation, it might be erotic. To say that these purportedly sexual events violate us, to be against them, we call them not sexual. But the attempt to be objective and neutral avoids owning up to the fact that women do have a specific point of view on these events. It avoids saying that from women's point of view, intercourse, sex roles, and eroticism can be and at times are violent to us as women.

My approach would claim our perspective; we are not attempting to be objective about it, we're attempting to represent the point of view of women. The point of view of men up to this time, called objective, has been to distinguish sharply between rape on the one hand and intercourse on the other; sexual harassment on the one hand and normal, ordinary sexual initiation on the other; pornography or obscenity on the one hand and eroticism on the other. The male point of view defines them by distinction. What women experience does not so clearly distinguish the normal, everyday things from those abuses from which they have been defined by distinction. Not just "Now we're going to take what *you* say is rape and call it violence"; "Now we're going to take what *you* say is sexual harassment and call it violence"; "Now we're going to take what *you* say is pornography and call it violence." We have a deeper critique of what has been done to women's sexuality and who controls access to it. What we are saying is that sexuality in exactly these normal forms often *does* violate us. So long as we say those things are abuses of violence, not sex, we fail to criticize what has been made of *sex*, what has been done to us *through* sex, because we leave the line between rape and intercourse, sexual harassment and sex roles, pornography and eroticism, right where it is.

I think it is useful to inquire how women and men (I don't use the term *persons*, I guess, because I haven't seen many lately) live through the meaning of their experience with these issues. When we ask whether rape, sexual harassment, and pornography are questions of violence or questions of sexuality, it helps to ask, to whom? What is the perspective of those who are involved, whose experience it is—to rape or to have been raped, to consume pornography or to be consumed through it. As to what these things *mean* socially, it is important whether they are about sexuality to women and men or whether they are instead about "violence"—or whether violence and sexuality can be distinguished in that way, as they are lived out.

The crime of rape—this is a legal and observed, not a subjective, individual, or feminist definition—is defined around penetration. That seems to me a very male point of view on what it means to be sexually violated. And it is exactly what heterosexuality as a social institution is fixated around, the penetration of the penis into the vagina. Rape is defined according to what men think violates women, and that is the same as what they think of as the *sine qua non* of sex. What women experience as degrading and defiling when we are raped includes as much that is distinctive to us as is our experience of sex. Someone once termed penetration a "peculiarly resented aspect" of rape—I don't know whether that meant it was peculiar that it was resented or that it was resented with heightened peculiarity. Women who have been raped often do resent having been penetrated. But that is not all there is to what was intrusive or expropriative of a woman's sexual wholeness.

I do think the crime of rape focuses more centrally on what men define as sexuality than on women's experience of our sexual being, hence its violation. A common experience of rape victims is to be unable to feel good about anything heterosexual thereafter—or anything sexual at all, or men at all. The minute they start to have sexual feelings or feel sexually touched by a man, or even a woman, they start to relive the rape. I had a client who came in with her husband. She was a rape victim, a woman we had represented as a witness. Her husband sat the whole time and sobbed. They couldn't have sex anymore because every time he started to touch her, she would flash to the rape scene and see his face change into the face of the man who had raped her. That, to me, is sexual.

When a woman has been raped, and it is sex that she then cannot experience without connecting it to that, it was her sexuality that was violated.

Similarly, men who are in prison for rape think it's the dumbest thing that ever happened. . . . It isn't just a miscarriage of justice; they were put in jail for something very little different from what most men do most of the time and call it sex. The only difference is they got caught. That view is nonremorseful and not rehabilitative. It may also be true. It seems to me we have here a convergence between the rapist's view of what he has done and the victim's perspective on what was done to her. That is, for both, their ordinary experiences of heterosexual intercourse and the act of rape have something in common. Now this gets us into intense trouble, because that's exactly how judges and juries see it who refuse to convict men accused of rape. A rape victim has to prove that it was not intercourse. She has to show that there was force and she resisted, because if there was sex, consent is inferred. Finders of fact look for "more force than usual during the preliminaries." Rape is defined by distinction from intercourse—not nonviolence, intercourse. They ask, does this event look more like fucking or like rape? But what is their standard for sex, and is this question asked from the *woman's point of view*? The level of force is not adjudicated at her point of violation; it is adjudicated at the standard of the normal level of force. Who sets this standard?

In the criminal law, we can't put everybody in jail who does an ordinary act, right? Crime is supposed to be deviant, not normal. Women continue not to report rape, and a reason is that they believe, and they are right, that the legal system will not see it from their point of view. We get very low conviction rates for rape. We also get many women who believe they have never been raped, although a lot of force was involved. They mean that they were not raped in a way that is legally provable. In other words, in all these situations, there was not *enough* violence against them to take it beyond the category of "sex"; they were not coerced enough. Maybe they were forced-fucked for years and put up with it, maybe they tried to get it over with, maybe they were coerced by something other than battery, something like economics, maybe even something like love.

What I am saying is that unless you make the point that there is much violence in intercourse, as a usual matter, none of that is changed. Also we continue to stigmatize the women who claim rape as having experienced a deviant violation and allow the rest of us to go through life feeling violated but thinking we've never been raped, when there were a great many times when we, too, have had sex and didn't want it. What this critique does that is different from the "violence, not sex" critique is ask a series of questions about normal, heterosexual intercourse and attempt to move the line between heterosexuality on the one hand—intercourse—and rape on the other, rather than allow it to stay where it is.

Having done that so extensively with rape, I can consider sexual harassment more briefly. The way the analysis of sexual harassment is sometimes expressed now (and it bothers me) is that it is an abuse of power, not sexuality. That does not allow us to pursue whether sexuality, as socially constructed in our society through gender roles, is *itself* a power structure. If you look at sexual harassment as power, not sex, what is power supposed to be? Power is employer / employee, not because courts are marxist but because this is a recognized hierarchy. Among men. Power is teacher/ student, because courts recognize a hierarchy there. Power is on one side and sexuality on the other. Sexuality is ordinary affection, everyday flirtation. Only when ordinary, everyday affection and flirtation and "I was just trying to be friendly" come into the context of *another* hierarchy is it considered potentially an abuse of power. What is not considered to be a hierarchy is women and men—men on top and women on the bottom. That is not considered to be a question of power or social hierarchy, legally or politically. A feminist perspective suggests that it is.

When we have examples of coequal sexual harassment (within these other hierarchies), worker to worker on the same level, involving women and men, we have a lot of very interesting, difficult questions about sex discrimination, which is supposed to be about gender difference, but does not conceive of gender as a social hierarchy. I think that implicit in race discrimination cases for a brief moment of light was the notion that there is a social hierarchy between Blacks and whites. So that presumptively it's an exercise of power for a white person to do something egregious to a Black person or for a white institution to do something egregious systematically to many Black people. Situations of coequal power—among coworkers or students or teachers—are difficult to see as examples of sexual harassment unless you have a notion of male power. I think we lie to women when we call it not power when a woman is come onto by a man who is not her employer, not her teacher. What do we labor under, what do we feel, when a man—any man—comes and hits on us? I think we require women to feel fine about turning down male-initiated sex so long as the man doesn't have some *other* form of power over us. Whenever—every and any time—a woman feels conflicted and wonders what's wrong with her that she can't decline although she has no inclination, and she feels open to male accusations, whether they come from women or men, of "why didn't you just tell him to buzz off?" we have sold her out, not named her experience. We are taught that we exist for men. We should be flattered or at least act as if we are—be careful about a man's ego because you never know what he can do to you. To flat out say to him, "You?" or "I don't want to" is not *in* most women's sex-role learning. To say it is, is bravado. And that's because he's a man, not just because you never know what he can do to you because he's your boss (that's two things—he's a man and he's the boss) or your teacher or in some other hierarchy. It seems to me that we haven't talked very much about gender *as* a hierarchy, as a division of power, in the way that's expressed and acted out, primarily I think sexually. And therefore we haven't expanded the definition according to women's experience of sexuality, including our own sexual intimidation, of what things are sexual in this world. So men have also defined what can be called sexual about us. They say, "I was just trying to be affectionate, flirtatious and friendly," and we were just all felt up. We criticize the idea that rape comes down to her word against his—but it really *is* her perspective against his perspective, and the law has been written from *his* perspective. If he didn't mean to be sexual, it's not sexual. If he didn't see it as forced, it wasn't forced. Which is to say, only male sexual violations, that is, only male ideas of what sexually violates us as women are illegal. We buy into this when we say our sexual violations are abuses of power, not sex.

Just as rape is supposed to have nothing against intercourse, just as sexual harassment is supposed to have nothing against normal sexual initiation (men initiate, women consent—that's mutual?), the idea that pornography is violence against women, not sex, seems to distinguish artistic creation on the one hand from what is degrading to women on the other. It is candid and true but not enough to say of pornography, as Justice Stewart said, "I know it when I see it." *He* knows what he thinks it is when he sees it—but is that what *I* know? Is that the same "it"? Is he going to know what I know when I see it? I think pretty much not, given what's on the newsstand, given what is not considered hard-core pornography. Sometimes I think what is obscene is what does *not* turn on the Supreme Court—or what revolts them more. Which is uncommon, since revulsion is eroticized. We have to admit that pornography turns men on; it is therefore erotic. It is a lie to say that pornography is not erotic. When we say it is violence, not sex, we are saying, there is this degrading to women, over here, and this erotic, over there, without saying to whom. It is overwhelmingly disproportionately men to whom pornography is erotic. It is women, on the whole, to whom it is violent, among other things. And this is not just a matter of perspective, but a matter of reality.

Pornography turns primarily men on. Certainly they are getting something out of it. They pay incredible amounts of money for it; it's one of the largest industries in the country. If women got as much out of it as men do, we would buy it instead of cosmetics. It's a massive industry, cosmetics. We are poor but we have *some* money; we are some market. We spend our money to set ourselves up as the objects that emulate those images that are sold as erotic to men. What pornography says about us is that we enjoy degradation, that we are sexually turned on by being degraded. For me that obliterates the line, as a line at all, between pornography on one hand and erotica on the other, if what turns men on, what men find beautiful, is what degrades women. It is pervasively present in art, also, and advertising. But it is definitely present in eroticism, if that is what it is. It makes me think that women's sexuality as such is a stigma. We also sometimes have an experience of sexuality authentic somehow in all this. We are not allowed to have it; we are not allowed to talk about it; we are not allowed to speak of it or image it as from our own point of view. And, to the extent we try to assert that we are beings equal with men, we have to be either asexual or virgins.

To worry about cooptation is to realize that lies make bad politics. It is ironic that cooptation often results from an attempt to be "credible," to be strategically smart, to be "effective" on existing terms. Sometimes you become what you're fighting. Thinking about issues of sexual violation as issues of violence not sex could, if pursued legally, lead to opposing sexual harassment and pornography through morals legislation and obscenity laws. It is actually interesting that this theoretical stance has been widely embraced but these legal strategies have not been. Perhaps women realize that these legal approaches would not address the subordination of women to men, specifically and substantively. These approaches are legally as abstract as the "violence not sex" critique is politically abstract. They are both not enough and too much of the wrong thing. They deflect us from criticizing everyday behavior that is pervasive and normal and concrete and fuses sexuality with gender in violation and is not amenable to existing legal approaches. I think we need to think more radically in our legal work here.

Battering is called violence, rather than something sex-specific: this is done to women. I also think it is sexually done to women. Not only in where it is done—over half of the incidents are in the bedroom. Or the surrounding events—precipitating sexual jealousy. But when violence against women is eroticized as it is in this culture, it is very difficult to say that there is a major distinction in the level of sex involved between being assaulted by a penis and being assaulted by a fist, especially when the perpetrator is a man. If women as gender female are defined as sexual beings, and violence is eroticized, then men violating women has a sexual component. I think men rape women because they get off on it in a way that fuses dominance with sexuality. (This is different in emphasis from what Susan Brownmiller says.) I think that when men sexually harass women it expresses male control over sexual access to us. It doesn't mean they all want to fuck us, they just want to hurt us, dominate us, and control us, and that *is* fucking us. They want to be able to have that and to be able to say when they can have it, to *know* that. That is in itself erotic. The idea that opposing battering is about saving the family is, similarly, abstracted, gender-neutral. There are gender-neutral formulations of all these issues: law and order as opposed to derepression, Victorian morality as opposed to permissiveness, obscenity as opposed to art and freedom of expression. Gender-neutral, objective formulations like these avoid asking *whose* expression, from whose point of view? Whose law and whose order? It's not just a question of who is free to express ourselves; it's not just that there is almost no, if any, self-respecting women's eroticism. The fact is that what we do see, what we are allowed to experience, even in our own suffering, even in what we are allowed to complain about, is overwhelmingly constructed from the male point of view. Laws against sexual violation express what men see and do when they engage in sex with women; laws against obscenity center on the display of women's bodies in ways that men are turned on by viewing. To me, it not only makes us cooptable to define such abuses in gender-neutral terms like violence; when we fail to assert that we are fighting for the affirmative definition and control of our own sexuality, of our own lives as women, and that these experiences violate *that*, we have already been bought.

STUDY QUESTIONS

1. Why does MacKinnon think women have placed specifically sexual violations against women under the generic genderless heading of "violence"? What are women protecting themselves against by doing this? What is lost in the process?
2. Why is there a fear of allowing sexuality into the discussion of rape, sexual harassment, pornography, and battery, according to MacKinnon?
3. Who has defined what rape is, and why it is wrong? What are the consequences of this?
4. Is MacKinnon saying or suggesting that all sex is inherently violent toward women?
5. What is the difference between pornography and erotica, according to MacKinnon?

FOR FURTHER STUDY

Baker, Robert, and Elliston, Frederick, eds. *Philosophy and Sex*. Buffalo, N.Y.: Prometheus Books, 1984.

Barry, Kathleen. *Female Sexual Slavery*. Englewood Cliffs, N.J.: Prentice-Hall, 1979.

Bartky, Sandra Lee. *Femininity and Domination: Studies in the Phenomenology of Oppression*. New York: Routledge, 1990.

Belenkey, Mary Field, et al. *Women's Ways of Knowing: The Development of Self, Voice, and Mind*. New York: Basic Books, 1986.

Brownmiller, Susan. *Against Our Will: Men, Women, and Rape*. New York: Simon & Schuster, 1975.

Enloe, Cynthia. *Bananas, Beaches, and Bases: Making Feminist Sense of International Politics*. Berkeley: University of California Press, 1990.

Kimmel, Michael. *Men Confront Pornography*. New York: Crown, 1990.

Lederer, Laura. *Take Back the Night: Women on Pornography*. New York: Morrow, 1980.

MacKinnon, Catharine A. *Sexual Harassment of Working Women: A Case of Sex Discrimination*. New Haven, Conn.: Yale University Press, 1979.

———. *Toward a Feminist Theory of the State*. Cambridge, Mass.: Harvard University Press, 1989.

Mohr, Richard D. *Gays/Justice: A Study of Ethics, Society and Law*. New York: Columbia University Press, 1989.

Pierce, Christine, and VanDeVeer, Donald, eds. *AIDS: Ethics and Public Policy*. Belmont, Calif.: Wadsworth, 1987.

Rhode, Deborah L. *Theoretical Perspectives on Sex Difference*. New Haven, Conn.: Yale University Press, 1990.

Soble, Alan, ed. *The Philosophy of Sex*. Totowa, N.J.: Littlefield, Adams, 1980.

Chapter Nine

Ethics of Abortion

44

Excerpts from *Roe* v. *Wade* (1973)

The Supreme Court

MAJORITY OPINION

A recent review of the common law precedents argues . . . that even post-quickening abortion was never established as a common law crime. This is of some importance because while most American courts ruled, in holding or dictum, that abortion of an unquickened fetus was not criminal under their received common law, others followed Coke in stating that abortion of a quick fetus was a "misprison," a term they translated to mean "misdemeanor." That their reliance on Coke on this aspect of the law was uncritical and, apparently in all the reported cases, dictum (due probably to the paucity of common law prosecutions for post-quickening abortion), makes it now appear doubtful that abortion was ever firmly established as a common law crime even with respect to the destruction of a quick fetus. . . .

It is thus apparent that at common law, at the time of the adoption of our Constitution, and throughout the major portion of the 19th century, abortion was viewed with less disfavor than under most American statutes currently in effect. Phrasing it another way, a woman enjoyed a substantially broader right to terminate a pregnancy than she does in most States today. At least with respect to the early stage of pregnancy, and very possibly without such a limitation, the opportunity to make this choice was present in this country well into the 19th century. Even later, the law continued for some time to treat less punitively an abortion procured in early pregnancy. . . .

Three reasons have been advanced to explain historically the enactment of criminal abortion laws in the 19th century and to justify their continued existence.

It has been argued occasionally that these laws were the product of a Victorian social concern to discourage illicit sexual conduct. Texas, however, does not advance this justification in the present case, and it appears that no court or commentator has taken the argument seriously. . . .

A second reason is concerned with abortion as a medical procedure. When most criminal abortion laws were first enacted, the procedure was a hazardous one for the woman. This was particularly true prior to the development of antisepsis. Antiseptic techniques, of course, were based on discoveries by Lister, Pasteur, and others first announced in 1867, but were not generally accepted and employed until about the turn of the century. Abortion mortality was high. Even after 1900, and perhaps until as late as the development of antibiotics in the 1940s, standard modern techniques such as dilation and curettage were not nearly so safe as they are today. Thus it has been argued that a State's real concern in enacting a criminal abortion law was to protect the pregnant woman, that is, to restrain her from submitting to a procedure that placed her life in serious jeopardy.

Modern medical techniques have altered this situation. Appellants and various *amici* refer to medical data indicating that abortion in early pregnancy, that is, prior to the end of first trimester, although not without its risk, is now relatively safe. Mortality rates for women undergoing early abortions, where the procedure is legal, appear to be as low as or lower than the rates for normal childbirth. Consequently, any interest of the State in protecting the woman from an inherently hazardous procedure, except when it would be equally dangerous for her to forgo it, has largely disappeared. Of course, important state interests in the area of health and medical standards do remain. The State has a legitimate interest in seeing to it that abortion, like any other medical procedure, is performed under circumstances that insure maximum safety for the patient. This interest obviously extends at least to the performing physician and his staff, to the facilities involved, to the availability of aftercare, and to adequate provision for any complication or emergency that might arise. The prevalence of high mortality rates at illegal "abortion mills" strengthens, rather than weakens, the State's interest in regulating the conditions under which abortions are performed. Moreover, the risk to the woman increases as her pregnancy continues. Thus the State retains a definite interest in protecting the woman's own health and safety when an abortion is performed at a late stage of pregnancy.

The third reason is the State's interest—some phrase it in terms of duty—in protecting prenatal life. Some of the argument for this justification rests on the theory that a new human life is present from the moment of conception. . . .

Parties challenging state abortion laws have sharply disputed in some courts the contention that a purpose of these laws, when enacted, was to protect prenatal life. Pointing to the absence of legislative history to support the contention, they claim that most state laws were designed solely to protect the woman. Because medical advances have lessened this concern, at least with respect to abortion in early pregnancy, they argue that with respect to such abortions the laws can no longer be justified by any state interest. There is some scholarly support for this view of original purpose. The few state courts called upon to interpret their laws in the late 19th and early 20th centuries did focus on the State's interest in protecting the woman's health rather than in preserving embryo and fetus. . . .

The Constitution does not explicitly mention any right of privacy. In a line of decisions, however, going back perhaps as far as *Union Pacific R. Co.* v. *Botsford*, 141 U.S. 250, 251 (1891), the Court has recognized that a right of personal privacy, or a guarantee of certain areas or zones of privacy, does exist under the Constitution. In varying contexts the Court or individual Justices have indeed found at least the roots of that right in the First Amendment, . . . in the Fourth and Fifth Amendments . . . in the penumbras of the Bill of Rights . . . in the Ninth Amendment . . . or in the concept of liberty guaranteed by the first section of the Fourteenth Amendment. . . . These decisions make it clear that only personal rights that can be deemed "fundamental" or "implicit in the concept of ordered liberty," . . . are included in this guarantee of personal privacy. They also make it clear that the right has some extension to activities relating to marriage, . . . procreation, . . . contraception, . . . family relationships, . . . and child rearing and education. . . .

This right of privacy, whether it be founded in the Fourteenth Amendment's concept of personal liberty and restrictions upon state action, as we feel it is or, as the District Court determined, in the Ninth Amendment's reservation of rights to the people, is broad enough to encompass a woman's decision whether or not to terminate her pregnancy. . . .

. . . Appellants and some *amici* argue that the woman's right is absolute and that she is entitled to terminate her pregnancy at whatever time, in whatever way, and for whatever reason she alone chooses. With this we do not agree. Appellants' arguments that Texas either has no valid interest at all in regulating the abortion decision, or no interest strong enough to support any limitation upon the woman's sole determination, is unpersuasive. The Court's decisions recognizing a right of privacy also acknowledge that some state regulation in areas protected by that right is appropriate. As noted above, a state may properly assert important interests in safeguarding health, in maintaining medical standards, and in protecting potential life. At some point in pregnancy, these respective interests become sufficiently compelling to sustain regulation of the factors that govern the abortion decision. The privacy right involved, therefore, cannot be said to be absolute. . . .

We therefore conclude that the right of personal privacy includes the abortion decision, but that this right is not unqualified and must be considered against important state interests in regulation.

We note that those federal and state courts that have recently considered abortion law challenges have reached the same conclusion. . . .

Although the results are divided, most of these courts have agreed that the right of privacy, however based, is broad enough to cover the abortion decision; that the right, nonetheless, is not absolute and is subject to some limitations; and that at some point the state interests as to protection of health, medical standards, and prenatal life, become dominant. We agree with this approach.

The appellee and certain *amici* argue that the fetus is a "person" within the language and meaning of the Fourteenth Amendment. In support of this they outline at length and in detail the well-known facts of fetal development. If this suggestion of personhood is established, the appellant's case, of course, collapses, for the fetus' right to life is then guaranteed specifically by the Amendment. The appellant conceded as much on reargument. On the other hand, the appellee conceded on reargument that no case could be cited that holds that a fetus is a person within the meaning of the Fourteenth Amendment.

All this, together with our observation, supra, that throughout the major portion of the 19th century prevailing legal abortion practices were far freer than they are today, persuades us that the word "person," as used in the Fourteenth Amendment, does not include the unborn. . . . Indeed, our decision in *United States* v. *Vuitch*, 402 U.S. 62 (1971), inferentially is to the same effect, for we there would not have indulged in statutory interpretation favorable to abortion in specified circumstances if the necessary consequence was the termination of life entitled to Fourteenth Amendment protection.

. . . As we have intimated above, it is reasonable and appropriate for a State to decide that at some point in time another interest, that of health of the mother or that of potential human life, becomes significantly involved. The woman's privacy is no longer sole and any right of privacy she possesses must be measured accordingly.

. . . We need not resolve the difficult question of when life begins. When those trained in the respective disciplines of medicine, philosophy, and theology are unable to arrive at any consensus, the judiciary, at this point in the development of man's knowledge, is not in a position to speculate as to the answer.

It should be sufficient to note briefly the wide divergence of thinking on this most sensitive and difficult question. There has always been strong support for the view that life does not begin until live birth. This was the belief of the Stoics. It appears to be the predominant, though not the unanimous, attitude of the Jewish faith. It may be taken to represent also the position of a large segment of the Protestant community, insofar as that can be ascertained; organized groups that have taken a formal position on the abortion issue have generally regarded abortion as a matter for the conscience of the individual and her family. As we have noted, the common law found greater significance in quickening. Physicians and their scientific colleagues have regarded that event with less interest and have tended to focus either upon conception or upon live birth or upon the interim point at which the fetus becomes "viable," that is, potentially able to live outside the mother's womb, albeit with artificial aid. Viability is usually placed at about seven months (28 weeks) but may occur earlier, even at 24 weeks. . . .

In areas other than criminal abortion the law has been reluctant to endorse any theory that life, as we recognize it, begins before live birth or to accord legal rights to the unborn except in narrowly defined situations and except when the rights are contingent upon live birth. . . . In short, the unborn have never been recognized in the law as persons in the whole sense.

In view of all this, we do not agree that, by adopting one theory of life, Texas may override the rights of the pregnant woman that are at stake. We repeat, however, that the State does have an important and legitimate interest in preserving and protecting the health of the pregnant woman, whether she be a resident of the State or a nonresident who seeks medical consultation and treatment there, and that it has still *another* important and legitimate interest in protecting the potentiality of human life. These interests are separate and distinct. Each grows in substantiality as the woman approaches term and, at a point during pregnancy, each becomes "compelling."

With respect to the State's important and legitimate interest in the health of the mother, the "compelling" point, in the light of present medical knowledge, is at approximately the end of the first trimester. This is so because of the now established medical fact . . . that until the end of the first trimester mortality in abortion is less than mortality in normal childbirth. It follows that, from and after this point, a State may regulate the abortion procedure to the extent that the regulation reasonably relates to the preservation and protection of maternal health. Examples of permissible state regulation in this area are requirements as to the qualifications of the person who is to perform the abortion; as to the licensure of that person; as to the facility in which the procedure is to be performed, that is, whether it must be a hospital or may be a clinic or some other place of less-than-hospital status; as to the licensing of the facility; and the like.

This means, on the other hand, that, for the period of pregnancy prior to this "compelling" point, the attending physician, in consultation with his patient, is free to determine, without regulation by the State, that in his medical judgment the patient's pregnancy should be terminated. If that decision is reached, the judgment may be effectuated by an abortion free of interference by the State.

With respect to the State's important and legitimate interest in potential life, the "compelling" point is at viability. . . . State regulation protective of fetal life after viability thus has both logical and biological justifications. If the State is interested in protecting fetal life after viability, it may go so far as to proscribe abortion during that period except when it is necessary to preserve the life or health of the mother. . . .

To summarize and repeat:

1. A state criminal abortion statute of the current Texas type, that excepts from criminality only a *life-saving* procedure on behalf of the mother, without regard to pregnancy stage and without recognition of the other interests involved, is violative of the Due Process Clause of the Fourteenth Amendment.
   (a) For the stage prior to approximately the end of the first trimester, the abortion decision and its effectuation must be left to the medical judgment of the pregnant woman's attending physician.
   (b) For the stage subsequent to approximately the end of the first trimester, the State, in promoting its interest in the health of the mother, may, if it chooses, regulate the abortion procedure in ways that are reasonably related to maternal health.
   (c) For the stage subsequent to viability the State, in promoting its interest in the potentiality of human life, may, if it chooses, regulate, and even proscribe, abortion except where it is necessary, in appropriate medical judgment, for the preservation of the life or health of the mother.

2. The State may define the term "physician," as it has been employed in the preceding numbered paragraphs of this Part XI of this opinion, to mean only a physician currently licensed by

the State, and may proscribe any abortion by a person who is not a physician as so defined.

. . . The decision leaves the State free to place increasing restrictions on abortion as the period of pregnancy lengthens, so long as those restrictions are tailored to the recognized state interests. The decision vindicates the right of the physician to administer medical treatment according to his professional judgment up to the points where important state interests provide compelling justifications for intervention. Up to those points the abortion decision in all its aspects is inherently, and primarily, a medical decision, and basic responsibility for it must rest with the physician. If an individual practitioner abuses the privilege of exercising proper medical judgment, the usual remedies, judicial and intraprofessional, are available. . . .

DISSENT

At the heart of the controversy in these cases are those recurring pregnancies that pose no danger whatsoever to the life or health of the mother but are nevertheless unwanted for any one or more of a variety of reasons—convenience, family planning, economics, dislike of children, the embarrassment of illegitimacy, etc. The common claim before us is that for any one of such reasons, or for no reason at all, and without asserting or claiming any threat to life or health, any woman is entitled to an abortion at her request if she is able to find a medical advisor willing to undertake the procedure.

The Court for the most part sustains this position: During the period prior to the time the fetus becomes viable, the Constitution of the United States values the convenience, whim or caprice of the putative mother more than the life or potential life of the fetus; the Constitution, therefore, guarantees the right to an abortion as against any state law or policy seeking to protect the fetus from an abortion not prompted by more compelling reasons of the mother.

With all due respect, I dissent. I find nothing in the language or history of the Constitution to support the Court's judgment. . . . As an exercise of raw judicial power, the Court perhaps has authority to do what it does today; but in my view its judgment is an improvident and extravagant exercise of the power of judicial review which the Constitution extends to this Court.

The Court apparently values the convenience of the pregnant mother more than the continued existence and development of the life or potential life which she carries. . . .

It is my view, therefore, that the Texas statute is not constitutionally infirm because it denies abortions to those who seek to serve only their convenience rather than to protect their life or health. . . .

STUDY QUESTIONS

1. Where does the Constitution guarantee a "right to privacy," according to the majority opinion?
2. Is a fetus a person in the legal sense of the term?
3. When does the state have a "compelling" interest in the health of the mother? When does the state have a compelling interest in potential life, according to Justice Blackmun (writing for the majority of the Court)?
4. Does the fetus have any legal rights? Moral rights? Defend your answer.
5. What are Justice White's objections (in the dissent) to Justice Blackmun's conclusions?
6. Do you think that abortion should remain legal under the limitations placed by *Roe* v. *Wade*? Why or why not?

45

An Almost Absolute Value in History

John T. Noonan Jr.

John T. Noonan Jr. is professor of law at the University of California, Berkeley. He is the author of *Contraception: A History of Its Treatment by the Catholic Theologians and Canonists* and of *Persons and Masks of the Law*.

The most fundamental question involved in the long history of thought on abortion is: How do you determine the humanity of a being? To phrase the question that way is to put in comprehensive humanistic terms what the theologians either dealt with as an explicitly theological question under the heading of "ensoulment" or dealt with implicitly in their treatment of abortion. The Christian position as it originated did not depend on a narrow theological or philosophical concept. It had no relation to theories of infant baptism.[1] It appealed to no special theory of instantaneous ensoulment. It took the world's view on ensoulment as that view changed from Aristotle to Zacchia. There was, indeed, theological influence affecting the theory of ensoulment finally adopted, and, of course, ensoulment itself was a theological concept, so that the position was always explained in theological terms. But the theological notion of ensoulment could easily be translated into humanistic language by substituting "human" for "rational soul"; the problem of knowing when a man is a man is common to theology and humanism.

If one steps outside the specific categories used by the theologians, the answer they gave can be analyzed as a refusal to discriminate among human beings on the basis of their varying potentialities. Once conceived, the being was recognized as man because he had man's potential. The criterion for humanity, thus, was simple and all-embracing: if you are conceived by human parents, you are human.

The strength of this position may be tested by a review of some of the other distinctions offered in the contemporary controversy over legalizing abortion. Perhaps the most popular distinction is in terms of viability. Before an age of so many months, the fetus is not viable, that is, it cannot be removed from the mother's womb and live apart from her. To that extent, the life of the fetus is absolutely dependent on the life of the mother. This dependence is made the basis of denying recognition to its humanity.

There are difficulties with this distinction. One is that the perfection of artificial incubation may make the fetus viable at any time: it may be removed and artificially sustained. Experiments with animals already show that such a procedure is possible. This hypothetical extreme case relates to an actual difficulty: there is considerable elasticity to the idea of viability. Mere length of life is not an exact measure. The viability of the fetus depends on the extent of its anatomical and functional development. The weight and length of the fetus are better guides to the state of its development than age, but weight and length vary. Moreover, different racial groups have different ages at which their fetuses are viable. Some evidence, for example, suggests that Negro fetuses mature more quickly than white fetuses. If viability is the norm, the standard would vary with race and with many individual circumstances.

The most important objection to this approach is that dependence is not ended by viability. The fetus is still absolutely dependent on someone's care in order to continue existence; indeed a child of one or three or even five years of age is absolutely dependent on another's care for existence; uncared for, the older fetus or the younger child will die as surely as the early fetus detached from the mother. The unsubstantial lessening in dependence at viability does not seem to signify any special acquisition of humanity.

A second distinction has been attempted in terms of experience. A being who has had experience, has lived and suffered, who possesses memories, is more human than one who has not. Humanity depends on formation by experience. The fetus is thus "unformed" in the most basic human sense.

This distinction is not serviceable for the embryo which is already experiencing and reacting. The embryo is responsive to touch after eight weeks and at least at that point is experiencing. At an earlier stage the zygote is certainly alive and responding to its environment. The distinction may also be challenged by the rare case where aphasia has erased adult memory: has it erased humanity? More fundamentally, this distinction leaves even the older fetus or the younger child to be treated as an unformed inhuman thing. Finally, it is not clear why experience as such confers humanity. It could be argued that certain central experiences, such as loving or learning, are necessary to make a man human. But then human beings who have failed to love or to learn might be excluded from the class called man.

A third distinction is made by appeal to the sentiments of adults. If a fetus dies, the grief of the parents is not the grief they would have for a living child. The fetus is an unnamed "it" till birth, and is not perceived as personality until at least the fourth month of existence when movements in the womb manifest a vigorous presence demanding joyful recognition by the parents.

Yet feeling is notoriously an unsure guide to the humanity of others. Many groups of humans have had difficulty in feeling that persons of another tongue, color, religion, sex, are as human as they. Apart from reactions to alien groups, we mourn the loss of a ten-year-old boy more than the loss of his one-day-old brother or his 90-year-old grandfather. The difference felt and the grief expressed vary with the potentialities extinguished, or the experience wiped out; they do not seem to point to any substantial difference in the humanity of baby, boy, or grandfather.

Distinctions are also made in terms of sensation by the parents. The embryo is felt within the womb only after about the fourth month. The embryo is seen only at birth. What can be neither seen nor felt is different from what is tangible. If the fetus cannot be seen or touched at all, it cannot be perceived as man.

Yet experience shows that sight is even more untrustworthy than feeling in determining humanity. By sight, color became an appropriate index for saying who was a man, and the evil of racial discrimination was given foundation. Nor can touch provide the test; a being confined by sickness, "out of touch" with others, does not thereby seem to lose his humanity. To the extent that touch still has appeal as a criterion, it appears to be a survival of the old English idea of "quickening"—a possible mistranslation of the Latin *animatus* used in the canon law. To that extent touch as a criterion seems to be dependent on the Aristotelian notion of ensoulment, and to fall when this notion is discarded.

Finally, a distinction is sought in social visibility. The fetus is not socially perceived as human. It cannot communicate with others. Thus, both subjectively and objectively, it is not a member of society. As moral rules are rules for the behavior of members of society to each other, they cannot be made for behavior toward what is not yet a member. Excluded from the society of men, the fetus is excluded from the humanity of men.[2]

By force of the argument from the consequences, this distinction is to be rejected. It is more subtle than that founded on an appeal to physical sensation, but it is equally dangerous in its implications. If humanity depends on social recognition, individuals or whole groups may be dehumanized by being denied any status in their society. Such a fate is fictionally portrayed in *1984* and has actually been the lot of many men in many societies. In the Roman empire, for example, condemnation to slavery meant the practical denial of most human rights; in the Chinese Communist world, landlords have been classified as enemies of the people and so treated as nonpersons by the state. Humanity does not depend on social recognition, though often the failure of society to recognize the prisoner, the alien, the heterodox as human has led to the destruction of human beings. Anyone conceived by a man and a woman is human. Recognition of this condition by society follows a real event in the objective order, however imperfect and halting the recognition. Any attempt to limit humanity to exclude some group runs the risk of furnishing authority and precedent for excluding other groups in the name of the consciousness or perception of the controlling group in the society.

A philosopher may reject the appeal to the humanity of the fetus because he views "humanity" as a secular view of the soul and because he doubts the existence of anything real and objective which can be identified as humanity. One answer to such a philosopher is to ask how he reasons about moral questions without supposing that there is a sense in which he and the others of whom he speaks are human. Whatever group is taken as the society which determines who may be killed is thereby taken as human. A second answer is to ask if he does not believe that there is a right and wrong way of deciding moral questions. If there is such a difference, experience may be appealed to: to decide who is human on the basis of the sentiment of a given society has led to consequences which rational men would characterize as monstrous.

The rejection of the attempted distinctions based on viability and visibility, experience and feeling, may be buttressed by the following considerations: Moral judgments often rest on distinctions, but if the distinctions are not to appear arbitrary *fiat*, they should relate to some real difference in probabilities. There is a kind of continuity in all life, but the earlier stages of the elements of human life possess tiny probabilities of development. Consider, for example, the spermatozoa in any normal ejaculate: There are about 200,000,000 in any single ejaculate, of which one has a chance of developing into a zygote. Consider the oocytes which may become ova: there are 100,000 to 1,000,000 oocytes in a female infant, of which a maximum of 390 are ovulated. But once spermatozoon and ovum meet and the conceptus is formed, such studies as have been made show that roughly in only 20 percent of the cases will spontaneous abortion occur. In other words, the chances are about 4 out of 5 that this new being will develop. At this stage in the life of the being there is a sharp shift in probabilities, an immense jump in potentialities. To make a distinction between the rights of spermatozoa and the rights of the fertilized ovum is to respond to an enormous shift in possibilities. For about twenty days after conception the egg may split to form twins or combine with another egg to form a chimera, but the probability of either event happening is very small.

It may be asked, What does a change in biological probabilities have to do with establishing humanity? The argument from probabilities is not aimed at establishing humanity but at establishing an objective discontinuity which may be taken into account in moral discourse. As life itself is a matter of probabilities, as most moral reasoning is an estimate of probabilities, so it seems in accord with the structure of reality and the nature of moral thought to found a moral judgment on the change in probabilities at conception. The appeal to probabilities is the most commonsensical of arguments; to a greater or smaller degree all of us base our actions on probabilities, and in morals, as in law, prudence and negligence are often measured by the account one has taken of the probabilities. If the chance is 200,000,000 to 1 that the movement in the bushes into which you shoot is a man's, I doubt if many persons would hold you careless in shooting; but if the chances are 4 out of 5 that the movement is a human being's, few would acquit you of blame. Would the argument be different if only one out of ten children conceived came to term? Of course this argument would be different. This argument is an appeal to probabilities that actually exist, not to any and all states of affairs which may be imagined.

The probabilities as they do exist do not show the humanity of the embryo in the sense of a demonstration in logic any more than the probabilities of the movement in the bush being a man demonstrate beyond all doubt that the being is a man. The appeal is a "buttressing" consideration, showing the plausibility of the standard adopted. The argument focuses on the decisional factor in any moral judgment and assumes that part of the business of a moralist is drawing lines. One evidence of the nonarbitrary character of the line drawn is the difference of probabilities on either side of it. If a spermatozoon is destroyed, one destroys a being which had a chance of far less than 1 in 200 million of developing into a reasoning being, possessed of the genetic code, a heart and other organs, and capable of pain. If a fetus is destroyed, one destroys a being already possessed of the genetic code, organs, and sensitivity to pain, and one which had an 80 percent chance of developing further into a baby outside the womb who, in time, would reason.

The positive argument for conception as the decisive moment of humanization is that at conception the new being receives the genetic code. It is this genetic information which determines his characteristics, which is the biological carrier of the possibility of human wisdom, which makes him a self-evolving being. A being with a human genetic code is man.

This review of current controversy over the humanity of the fetus emphasizes what a fundamental question the theologians resolved in asserting the inviolability of the fetus. To regard the fetus as possessed of equal rights with other humans was not, however, to decide every case where abortion might be employed. It did decide the case where the argument was that the fetus should be aborted for its own good. To say a being was human was to say it had a destiny to decide for itself which could not be taken from it by another man's decision. But human beings with equal rights often come in conflict with each other, and some decision must be made as to whose claims are to prevail. Cases of conflict involving the fetus are different only in two respects: the total inability of the fetus to speak for itself and the fact that the right of the fetus regularly at stake is the right to life itself.

The approach taken by the theologians to these conflicts was articulated in terms of "direct" and "indirect." Again, to look at what they were doing from outside their categories, they may be said to have been drawing lines or "balancing values." "Direct" and "indirect" are spatial metaphors; "line-drawing" is another. "To weigh" or "to balance" values is a metaphor of a more complicated mathematical sort hinting at the process which goes on in moral judgments. All the metaphors suggest that, in the moral judgments made, comparisons were necessary, that no value completely controlled. The principle of double effect was no doctrine fallen from heaven, but a method of analysis appropriate where two relative values were being compared. In Catholic moral theology, as it developed, life even of the innocent was not taken as an absolute. Judgments on acts affecting life issued from a process of weighing. In the weighing, the fetus was always given a value greater than zero, always a value separate and independent from its parents. This valuation was crucial and fundamental in all Christian thought on the subject and marked it off from any approach which considered that only the parents' interests needed to be considered.

Even with the fetus weighed as human, one interest could be weighed as equal or superior: that of the mother in her own life. The casuists between 1450 and 1895 were willing to weigh this interest as superior. Since 1895, that interest was given decisive weight only in the two special cases of the cancerous uterus and the ectopic pregnancy. In both of these cases the fetus itself had little chance of survival even if the abortion were not performed. As the balance was once struck in favor of the mother whenever her life was endangered, it could be so struck again. The balance reached between 1895 and 1930 attempted prudentially and pastorally to forestall a multitude of exceptions for interests less than life.

The perception of the humanity of the fetus and the weighing of fetal rights against other human rights constituted the work of the moral analysts. But what spirit animated their abstract judgments? For the Christian community it was the injunction of Scripture to love your neighbor as yourself. The fetus as human was a neighbor; his life had parity with one's own. The commandment gave life to what otherwise would have been only rational calculation.

The commandment could be put in humanistic as well as theological terms: Do not injure your fellow man without reason. In these terms, once the humanity of the fetus is perceived, abortion is never right except in self-defense. When life must be taken to save life, reason alone cannot say that a mother must prefer a child's life to her own. With this exception, now of great rarity, abortion violates the rational humanist tenet of the equality of human lives.

For Christians the commandment to love had received a special imprint in that the exemplar proposed of love was the love of the Lord for his disciples. In the light given by this example, self-sacrifice carried to the point of death seemed in the extreme situations not without meaning. In the less extreme cases, preference for one's own interests to the life of another seemed to express cruelty or selfishness irreconcilable with the demands of love.

NOTES

1. According to Glanville Williams . . . "The historical reason for the Catholic objection to abortion is the same as for the Christian Church's historical opposition to infanticide: the horror of bringing about the death of an unbaptized child." This statement is made without any citation of evidence. As has been seen, desire to administer baptism could, in the Middle Ages, even be urged as a reason for procuring an abortion. It is highly regrettable that the American Law Institute was apparently misled by Williams' account and repeated after him the same baseless statement. See American Law Institute, *Model Penal Code: Tentative Draft No. 9* (1959), p. 148, n. 12.
2. . . . Thomas Aquinas gave an analogous reason against baptizing a fetus in the womb: "As long as it exists in the womb of the mother, it cannot be subject to the operation of the ministers of the Church as it is not known to men" (*In sententias Petri Lombardi* 4.6 1.1.2).

STUDY QUESTIONS

1. Explain Noonan's critique of the five distinctions used by defenders of abortion.
2. What argument does Noonan offer for his position that conception is the "decisive moment of humanization"? Do you agree?
3. What are the necessary and sufficient conditions of humanness, according to Noonan?
4. How do Christian theologians resolve the conflict of rights between innocents, that is, the mother's right to life and the fetus's right to life?
5. Are there cases, in Noonan's view, where the fetus's right to life may override the mother's right to life?

46

A Defense of Abortion

Judith Jarvis Thomson

Judith Jarvis Thomson is a professor of philosophy at the Massachusetts Institute of Technology. She has written extensively in the field of ethics and is coeditor of an anthology entitled *Ethics*. Many of her important articles are collected in a volume entitled *Rights, Restitution, and Risk*.

Most opposition to abortion relies on the premise that the fetus is a human being, a person, from the moment of conception. The premise is argued for, but, as I think, not well. Take, for example, the most common argument. We are asked to notice that the development of a human being from conception through birth into childhood is continuous; then it is said that to draw a line, to choose a point in this development and say "before this point the thing is not a person, after this point it is a person" is to make an arbitrary choice, a choice for which in the nature of things no good reason can be given. It is concluded that the fetus is, or anyway that we had better say it is, a person from the moment of conception. But this conclusion does not follow. Similar things might be said about the development of an acorn into an oak tree, and it does not follow that acorns are oak trees, or that we had better say they are. Arguments of this form are sometimes called "slippery slope arguments"—the phrase is perhaps self-explanatory—and it is dismaying that opponents of abortion rely on them so heavily and uncritically.

I am inclined to agree, however, that the prospects for "drawing a line" in the development of the fetus look dim. I am inclined to think also that we shall probably have to agree that the fetus has already become a human person well before birth. Indeed, it comes as a surprise when one first learns how early in its life it begins to acquire human characteristics. By the tenth week, for example, it already has a face, arms and legs, fingers and toes; it has internal organs, and brain activity is detectable. On the other hand, I think that the premise is false, that the fetus is not a person from the moment of conception. A newly fertilized ovum, a newly implanted clump of cells, is no more a person than an acorn is an oak tree. But I shall not discuss any of this. For it seems to me to be of great interest to ask what happens if, for the sake of argument, we allow the premise. How, precisely, are we supposed to get from there to the conclusion that abortion is morally impermissible? Opponents of abortion commonly spend most of their time establishing that the fetus is a person, and hardly any time explaining the step from there to the impermissibility of abortion. Perhaps they think the step too simple and obvious to require much comment. Or perhaps instead they are simply being economical in argument. Many of those who defend abortion rely on the premise that the fetus is not a person, but only a bit of tissue that will become a person at birth; and why pay out more arguments than you have to? Whatever the explanation, I suggest that the step they take is neither easy nor obvious, that it calls for closer examination than it is commonly given, and that when we do give it this closer examination we shall feel inclined to reject it.

I propose, then, that we grant that the fetus is a person from the moment of conception. How does the argument go from here? Something like this, I take it. Every person has a right to life. So the fetus has a right to life. No doubt the mother has a right to decide what shall happen in and to her body; everyone would grant that. But surely a person's right to life is stronger and more stringent than the mother's right to decide what happens in and to her body, and so outweighs it. So the fetus may not be killed; an abortion may not be performed.

It sounds plausible. But now let me ask you to imagine this. You wake up in the morning and find yourself back to back in bed with an unconscious violinist. A famous unconscious violinist. He has been found to have a fatal kidney ailment, and the Society of Music Lovers has canvassed all the available medical records and found that you alone have the right blood type to help. They have therefore kidnapped you, and last night the violinist's circulatory system was plugged into yours, so that your kidneys can be used to extract poisons from his blood as well as your own. The director of the hospital now tells you, "Look, we're sorry the Society of Music Lovers did this to you—we would never have permitted it if we had known. But still, they did it, and the violinist now is plugged into you. To unplug you would be to kill him. But never mind, it's only for nine months. By then he will have recovered from his ailment, and can safely be unplugged from you." Is it morally incumbent on you to accede to this situation? No doubt it would be very nice of you if you did, a great kindness, but do you *have* to accede to it? What if it were not nine months, but nine years? Or longer still? What if the director of the hospital says, "Tough luck, I agree, but you've now got to stay in bed, with the violinist plugged into you, for the rest of your life. Because remember this. All persons have a right to life, and violinists are persons. Granted you have a right to decide what happens in and to your body, but a person's right to life outweighs your right to decide what happens in and to your body. So you cannot ever be unplugged from him." I imagine you would regard this as outrageous, which suggests that something really is wrong with that plausible-sounding argument I mentioned a moment ago.

In this case, of course, you were kidnapped; you didn't volunteer for the operation that plugged the violinist into your kidneys. Can those who oppose abortion on the ground I mentioned make an exception for a pregnancy due to rape? Certainly. They can say that persons have a right to life only if they didn't come into existence because of rape; or they can say that all persons have a right to life, but that some have less of a right to life than others, in particular, that those who came into existence because of rape have less. But these statements have a rather unpleasant sound. Surely the question of whether you have a right to life at all, or how much of it you have, shouldn't turn on the question of whether or not you are the product of a rape. And in fact the people who oppose abortion on the ground I mentioned do not make this distinction, and hence do not make an exception in case of rape.

Nor do they make an exception for a case in which the mother has to spend the nine months of her pregnancy in bed. They would agree that would be a great pity, and hard on the mother; but all the same, all persons have a right to life, the fetus is a person, and so on. I suspect, in fact, that they would not make an exception for a case in which, miraculously enough, the pregnancy went on for nine years, or even the rest of the mother's life.

Some won't even make an exception for a case in which continuation of the pregnancy is likely to shorten the mother's life; they regard abortion as impermissible even to save the mother's life. Such cases are nowadays very rare, and many opponents of abortion do not accept this extreme view. All the same, it is a good place to begin: a number of points of interest come out in respect to it.

1. Let us call the view that abortion is impermissible even to save the mother's life "the extreme view." I want to suggest first that it does not issue from the argument I mentioned earlier with-

out the addition of some fairly powerful premises. Suppose a woman has become pregnant, and now learns that she has a cardiac condition such that she will die if she carries the baby to term. What may be done for her? The fetus, being a person, has a right to life, but as the mother is a person too, so has she a right to life. Presumably they have an equal right to life. How is it supposed to come out that an abortion may not be performed? If mother and child have an equal right to life, shouldn't we perhaps flip a coin? Or should we add to the mother's right to life her right to decide what happens in and to her body, which everybody seems to be ready to grant—the sum of her rights now outweighing the fetus' right to life?

The most familiar argument here is the following. We are told that performing the abortion would be directly killing the child, whereas doing nothing would not be killing the mother, but only letting her die. Moreover in killing the child one would be killing an innocent person, for the child has committed no crime, and is not aiming at his mother's death. And then there are a variety of ways in which this might be continued. (1) But as directly killing an innocent person is always and absolutely impermissible, an abortion may not be performed. Or, (2) as directly killing an innocent person is murder, and murder is always and absolutely impermissible, an abortion may not be performed. Or, (3) as one's duty to refrain from directly killing an innocent person is more stringent than one's duty to keep a person from dying, an abortion may not be performed. Or, (4) if one's only options are directly killing an innocent person or letting a person die, one must prefer letting the person die, and thus an abortion may not be performed.

Some people seem to have thought that these are not further premises which must be added if the conclusion is to be reached, but that they follow from the very fact that an innocent person has a right to life. But this seems to me to be a mistake, and perhaps the simplest way to show this is to bring out that while we must certainly grant that innocent persons have a right to life, the theses in (1) through (4) are all false. Take (2), for example. If directly killing an innocent person is murder, and thus is impermissible, then the mother's directly killing the innocent person inside her is murder, and thus is impermissible. But it cannot seriously be thought to be murder if the mother performs an abortion on herself to save her life. It cannot seriously be said that she *must* refrain, that she *must* sit passively by and wait for her death. Let us look again at the case of you and the violinist. There you are, in bed with the violinist, and the director of the hospital says to you, "It's all most distressing, and I deeply sympathize, but you see this is putting an additional strain on your kidneys, and you'll be dead within the month. But you *have* to stay where you are all the same. Because unplugging you would be directly killing an innocent violinist, and that's murder, and that's impermissible." If anything in the world is true, it is that you do not commit murder, you do not do what is impermissible, if you reach around to your back and unplug yourself from the violinist to save your life.

The main focus of attention in writings on abortion has been on what a third party may or may not do in answer to a request from a woman for an abortion. This is in a way understandable. Things being as they are, there isn't much a woman can safely do to abort herself. So the question asked is what a third party may do, and what the mother may do, if it is mentioned at all, is deduced, almost as an afterthought, from what it is concluded that third parties may do. But it seems to me that to treat the matter in this way is to refuse to grant to the mother that very status of person which is so firmly insisted on for the fetus. For we cannot simply read off what a person may do from what a third party may do. Suppose you find yourself trapped in a tiny house with a growing child. I mean a very tiny house, and a rapidly growing child—you are already up against the wall of the house and in a few minutes you'll be crushed to death. The child on the other hand won't be crushed to death; if nothing is done to stop him from growing he'll be hurt, but in the end he'll simply burst open the house and walk out a free man. Now I could well understand it if a bystander were to say, "There's nothing we can do for you. We cannot choose between your life and his, we cannot be the ones to decide who is to live, we cannot intervene." But it cannot be concluded that you too can do nothing, that you cannot attack it to save your life. However innocent the child may be, you do not have to wait passively while it crushes you to death. Perhaps a pregnant woman is vaguely felt to have the status of house, to which we don't allow the right of self-defense. But if the woman houses the child, it should be remembered that she is a person who houses it.

I should perhaps stop to say explicitly that I am not claiming that people have a right to do anything whatever to save their lives. I think, rather, that there are drastic limits to the right of self-defense. If someone threatens you with death unless you torture someone else to death, I think you have not the right, even to save your life, to do so. But the case under consideration here is very different. In our case there are only two people involved, one whose life is threatened, and one who threatens it. Both are innocent: the one who is threatened is not threatened because of any fault, the one who threatens does not threaten because of any fault. For this reason we may feel that we bystanders cannot intervene. But the person threatened can.

In sum, a woman surely can defend her life against the threat to it posed by the unborn child, even if doing so involves its death. And this shows not merely that the theses in (1) through (4) are false; it shows also that the extreme view of abortion is false, and so we need not canvass any other possible ways of arriving at it from the argument I mentioned at the outset.

2. The extreme view could of course be weakened to say that while abortion is permissible to save the mother's life, it may not be performed by a third party, but only by the mother herself. But this cannot be right either. For what we have to keep in mind is that the mother and the unborn child are not like two tenants in a small house which has, by an unfortunate mistake, been rented to both: the mother *owns* the house. The fact that she does adds to the offensiveness of deducing that the mother can do nothing from the supposition that third parties can do nothing. But it does more than this: it casts a bright light on the supposition that third parties can do nothing. Certainly it lets us see that a third party who says "I cannot choose between you" is fooling himself if he thinks this is impartiality. If Jones has found and fastened on a certain coat, which he needs to keep him from freezing, but which Smith also needs to keep him from freezing, then it is not impartiality that says "I cannot choose between you" when Smith owns the coat. Women have said again and again "This body is *my* body!" and they have reason to feel angry, reason to feel that it has been like shouting into the wind. Smith, after all, is hardly likely to bless us if we say to him, "Of course it's your coat, anybody would grant that it is. But no one may choose between you and Jones who is to have it."

We should really ask what it is that says "no one may choose" in the face of the fact that the body that houses the child is the mother's body. It may be simply a failure to appreciate this fact. But it may be something more interesting, namely the sense that one has a right to refuse to lay hands on people, even where it would be just and fair to do so, even where justice seems to require that somebody do so. Thus justice might call for somebody to get Smith's coat back from Jones, and yet you have a right to refuse to be the one to lay hands on Jones, a right to refuse to do physical violence to him. This, I think, must be granted. But then what should be said is not "no one may choose," but only "*I* cannot choose," and indeed not even this, but "*I* will not *act*," leaving it open that somebody else can or should, and in particular that anyone in a position of authority, with the job of securing people's rights, both can and should. So this is no difficulty. I have not been arguing that any given third party must accede to the mother's request that he perform an abortion to save her life, but only that he may.

I suppose that in some views of human life the mother's body is only on loan to her, the loan not being one which gives her any prior claim to it. One who held this view might well think it impartiality to say "I cannot choose." But I shall simply ignore this possibility. My own view is that if a human being has any just, prior claim to anything at all, he has a just, prior claim to his own body. And perhaps this needn't be argued for here anyway, since, as I mentioned, the arguments against abortion we are looking at do grant that the woman has a right to decide what happens in and to her body.

But although they do grant it, I have tried to show that they do not take seriously what is done in granting it. I suggest the same thing will reappear even more clearly when we turn away from cases in which the mother's life is at stake, and attend, as I propose we now do, to the vastly more common cases in which a woman wants an abortion for some less weighty reason than preserving her own life.

3. Where the mother's life is not at stake, the argument I mentioned at the outset seems to have a much stronger pull. "Everyone has a right to life, so the unborn person has a right to life." And isn't the child's right to life weightier than anything other than the mother's own right to life, which she might put forward as ground for an abortion?

This argument treats the right to life as if it were unproblematic. It is not, and this seems to me to be precisely the source of the mistake.

For we should now, at long last, ask what it comes to, to have a right to life. In some views having a right to life includes having a right to be given at least the bare minimum one needs for continued life. But suppose that what in fact is the bare minimum a man needs for continued life is something he has no right at all to be given? If I am sick unto death, and the only thing that will save my life is the touch of Henry Fonda's cool hand on my fevered brow, then all the same, I have no right to be given the touch of Henry Fonda's cool hand on my fevered brow. It would be frightfully nice of him to fly in from the West Coast to provide it. It would be less nice, though no doubt well meant, if my friends flew out to the West Coast and carried Henry Fonda back with them. But I have no right at all against anybody that he should do this for me. Or again, to return to the story I told earlier, the fact that for continued life that violinist needs the continued use of your kidneys does not establish that he has a right to be given the continued use of your kidneys. He certainly has no right against you that you should give him continued use of your kidneys. For nobody has any right to use your kidneys unless you give him such a right; and nobody has the right against you that you shall give him this right—if you do allow him to go on using your kidneys, this is a kindness on your part, and not something he can claim from you as his due. Nor has he any right against anybody else that *they* should give him continued use of your kidneys. Certainly he had no right against the Society of Music Lovers that they should plug him into you in the first place. And if you now start to unplug yourself, having learned that you will otherwise have to spend nine years in bed with him, there is nobody in the world who must try to prevent you, in order to *see* to it that he is given something he has a right to be given.

Some people are rather stricter about the right to life. In their view, it does not include the right to be given anything, but amounts to, and only to, the right not to be killed by anybody. But here a related difficulty arises. If everybody is to refrain from killing that violinist, then everybody must refrain from doing a great many different sorts of things. Everybody must refrain from slitting his throat, everybody must refrain from shooting him—and everybody must refrain from unplugging you from him. But does he have a right against everybody that they shall refrain from unplugging you from him? To refrain from doing this is to allow him to continue to use your kidneys. It could be argued that he has a right against us that *we* should allow him to continue to use your kidneys. That is, while he had no right against us that we should give him the use of your kidneys, it might be argued that he anyway has a right against us that we shall not now intervene and deprive him of the use of your kidneys. I shall come back to third-party interventions later. But certainly the violinist has no right against you that *you* shall allow him to continue to use your kidneys. As I said, if you do allow him to use them, it is a kindness on your part, and not something you owe him.

This difficulty I point to here is not peculiar to the right to life. It reappears in connection with all the other natural rights; and it is something which an adequate account of rights must deal with. For present purposes it is enough just to draw attention to it. But I would stress that I am not arguing that people do not have a right to life—quite to the contrary, it seems to me that the primary control we must place on the acceptability of an account of rights is that it should turn out in that account to be a truth that all persons have a right to life. I am arguing only that having a right to life does not guarantee having either a right to be given the use of or a right to be allowed continued use of another person's body—even if one needs it for life itself. So the right to life will not serve the opponents of abortion in the very simple and clear way in which they seem to have thought it would.

4. There is another way to bring out the difficulty. In the most ordinary sort of case, to deprive someone of what he has a right to is to treat him unjustly. Suppose a boy and his small brother are jointly given a box of chocolates for Christmas. If the older boy takes the box and refuses to give his brother any of the chocolates, he is unjust to him, for the brother has been given a right to half of them. But suppose that, having learned that otherwise it means nine years in bed with that violinist, you unplug yourself from him. You surely are not being unjust to him, for you gave him no right to use your kidneys, and no one else can have given him any such right. But we have to notice that in unplugging yourself, you are killing him; and violinists, like everybody else, have a right to life, and thus in the view we were considering just now, the right not to be killed. So here you do what he supposedly has a right you shall not do, but you do not act unjustly to him in doing it.

The emendation which may be made at this point is this: the right to life consists not in the right not to be killed, but rather in the right not to be killed unjustly. This runs a risk of circularity, but never mind: it would enable us to square the fact that the violinist has a right to life with the fact that you do not act unjustly toward him in unplugging yourself, thereby killing him. For if you do not kill him unjustly, you do not violate his right to life, and so it is no wonder you do him no injustice.

But if this emendation is accepted, the gap in the argument against abortion stares us plainly in the face: it is by no means enough to show that the fetus is a person, and to remind us that all persons have a right to life—we need to be shown also that killing the fetus violates its right to life, i.e., that abortion is unjust killing. And is it?

I suppose we may take it as a datum that in a case of pregnancy due to rape the mother has not given the unborn person a right to the use of her body for food and shelter. Indeed, in what pregnancy could it be supposed that the mother has given the unborn person such a right? It is not as if there were unborn persons drifting about the world, to whom a woman who wants a child says "I invite you in."

But it might be argued that there are other ways one can have acquired a right to the use of another person's body than by having been invited to use it by that person. Suppose a woman voluntarily indulges in intercourse, knowing of the chance it will issue in pregnancy, and then she does become pregnant; is she not in part responsible for the presence, in fact the very existence, of the unborn person inside her? No doubt she did not invite it in. But doesn't her partial responsibility for its being there itself give it a right to the use of her body? If so, then her aborting it would be more like the boy's taking away the chocolates, and less like your unplugging yourself from the violinist—doing so would be depriving it of what it does have a right to, and thus would be doing it an injustice.

And then, too, it might be asked whether or not she can kill it even to save her own life: If she voluntarily called it into existence, how can she now kill it, even in self-defense?

The first thing to be said about this is that it is something new. Opponents of abortion have been so concerned to make out the independence of the fetus, in order to establish that it has a right to life, just as its mother does, that they have tended to overlook the possible support they might gain from making out that the fetus is *dependent* on the mother, in order to establish that she has a special kind of responsibility for it, a responsibility that gives it rights against her which are not possessed by an independent person—such as an ailing violinist who is a stranger to her.

On the other hand, this argument would give the unborn person a right to its mother's body only if her pregnancy resulted from a voluntary act, undertaken in full knowledge of the chance a pregnancy might result from it. It would leave out entirely the unborn person whose existence is due to rape. Pending the availability of some further argument, then, we would be left with the conclusion that unborn persons whose existence is due to rape have no right to the use of their mothers' bodies, and thus that aborting them is not depriving them of anything they have a right to and hence is not unjust killing.

And we should also notice that it is not at all plain that this argument really does go even as far as it purports to. For there are cases and cases, and the details make a difference. If the room is stuffy, and I therefore open a window to air it, and a burglar climbs in, it would be absurd to say, "Ah, now he can stay, she's given him a right to the use of her house—for she is partially responsible for his presence there, having voluntarily done what enabled him to get in, in full knowledge that there are such things as burglars, and that burglars burgle." It would be still more absurd to say this if I had had bars installed outside my windows, precisely to prevent burglars from getting in, and a burglar got in only because of a defect in the bars. It remains equally absurd if we imagine it is not a burglar who climbs in, but an innocent person who blunders or falls in. Again, suppose it were like this: people-seeds drift about in the air like pollen, and if you open your windows, one may drift in and take root in your carpets or upholstery. You don't want children, so you fix up your windows with fine mesh screens, the very best you can buy. As can happen, however, and on very, very rare occasions does happen, one of the screens is defective; and a seed drifts in and takes root. Does the person-plant who now develops have a right to the use of your house? Surely not—despite the fact that you voluntarily opened your windows, you knowingly kept carpets and upholstered furniture, and you knew that screens were sometimes defective. Someone may argue that you are responsible for its rooting, that it does have a right to your house, because after all you *could* have lived out your life with bare floors and furniture, or with sealed windows and doors. But this won't do—for by the same token anyone can avoid a pregnancy due to rape by having a hysterectomy, or anyway by never leaving home without a (reliable!) army.

It seems to me that the argument we are looking at can establish at most that there are *some* cases in which the unborn person has a right to the use of its mother's body, and therefore *some* cases in which abortion is unjust killing. There is room for much discussion and argument as to precisely which, if any. But I think we should sidestep this issue and leave it open, for at any rate the argument certainly does not establish that all abortion is unjust killing.

5. There is room for yet another argument here, however. We surely must all grant that there may

be cases in which it would be morally indecent to detach a person from your body at the cost of his life. Suppose you learn that what the violinist needs is not nine years of your life, but only one hour: all you need do to save his life is to spend one hour in that bed with him. Suppose also that letting him use your kidneys for that one hour would not affect your health in the slightest. Admittedly you were kidnapped. Admittedly you did not give anyone permission to plug him into you. Nevertheless it seems to me plain you *ought* to allow him to use your kidneys for that hour—it would be indecent to refuse.

Again, suppose pregnancy lasted only an hour, and constituted no threat to life or health. And suppose that a woman becomes pregnant as a result of rape. Admittedly she did not voluntarily do anything to bring about the existence of a child. Admittedly she did nothing at all which would give the unborn person a right to the use of her body. All the same it might well be said, as in the newly emended violinist story, that she *ought* to allow it to remain for that hour—that it would be indecent in her to refuse.

Now some people are inclined to use the term "right" in such a way that it follows from the fact that you ought to allow a person to use your body for the hour he needs, that he has a right to use your body for the hour he needs, even though he has not been given that right by any person or act. They may say that it follows also that if you refuse, you act unjustly toward him. This use of the term is perhaps so common that it cannot be called wrong; nevertheless it seems to me to be an unfortunate loosening of what we would do better to keep a tight rein on. Suppose that box of chocolates I mentioned earlier had not been given to both boys jointly, but was given only to the older boy. There he sits, stolidly eating his way through the box, his small brother watching enviously. Here we are likely to say "You ought not to be so mean. You ought to give your brother some of those chocolates." My own view is that it just does not follow from the truth of this that the brother has any right to any of the chocolates. If the boy refuses to give his brother any, he is greedy, stingy, callous—but not unjust. I suppose that the people I have in mind will say it does follow that the brother has a right to some of the chocolates, and thus that the boy does act unjustly if he refuses to give his brother any. But the effect of saying this is to obscure what we should keep distinct, namely the difference between the boy's refusal in this case and the boy's refusal in the earlier case, in which the box was given to both boys jointly, and in which the small brother thus had what was from any point of view clear title to half.

A further objection to so using the term "right" that from the fact that A ought to do a thing for B, it follows that B has a right against A that A do it for him, is that it is going to make the question of whether or not a man has a right to a thing turn on how easy it is to provide him with it; and this seems not merely unfortunate, but morally unacceptable. Take the case of Henry Fonda again. I said earlier that I had no right to the touch of his cool hand on my fevered brow, even though I needed it to save my life. I said it would be frightfully nice of him to fly in from the West Coast to provide me with it, but that I had no right against him that he should do so. But suppose he isn't on the West Coast. Suppose he has only to walk across the room, place a hand briefly on my brow—and lo, my life is saved. Then surely he ought to do it, it would be indecent to refuse. Is it to be said "Ah, well, it follows that in this case she has a right to the touch of his hand on her brow, and so it would be an injustice in him to refuse"? So that I have a right to it when it is easy for him to provide it, though no right when it's hard? It's rather a shocking idea that anyone's rights should fade away and disappear as it gets harder and harder to accord them to him.

So my own view is that even though you ought to let the violinist use your kidneys for the one hour he needs, we should not conclude that he has a right to do so—we should say that if you refuse, you are, like the boy who owns all the chocolates and will give none away, self-centered and callous, indecent in fact, but not unjust. And similarly, that even supposing a case in which a woman pregnant due to rape ought to allow the unborn person to use her body for the hour he needs, we should not conclude that he has a right to do so; we should conclude that she is self-centered, callous, indecent, but not unjust, if she refuses. The compaints are no less grave; they are just different. However, there is no need to insist on this point. If anyone does wish to deduce "he has a right" from "you ought," then all the same he must surely grant that there are cases in which it is not morally required of you that you allow that violinist to use your kidneys, and in which he does not have a right to use them, and in which you do not do him an injustice if you refuse. And so also for mother and unborn child. Except in such cases as the unborn person has a right to demand it—and we were leaving open the possibility that there may be such cases—nobody is morally *required* to make large sacrifices, of health, of all other interests and concerns, of all other duties and commitments, for nine years, or even for nine months, in order to keep another person alive.

6. We have in fact to distinguish between two kinds of Samaritan: the Good Samaritan and what we might call the Minimally Decent Samaritan. The story of the Good Samaritan, you will remember, goes like this:

> A certain man went down from Jerusalem to Jericho, and fell among thieves, which stripped him of his raiment, and wounded him, and departed, leaving him half dead.
>
> And by chance there came down a certain priest that way; and when he saw him, he passed by on the other side.
>
> And likewise a Levite, when he was at the place, came and looked on him, and passed on the other side.
>
> But a certain Samaritan, as he journeyed, came where he was; and when he saw him he had compassion on him.
>
> And went to him, and bound up his wounds, pouring in oil and wine, and set him on his own beast, and brought him to an inn, and took care of him.
>
> And on the morrow, when he departed, he took out two pence, and gave them to the host, and said unto him, "Take care of him; and whatsoever thou spendest more, when I come again, I will repay thee."
>
> (Luke 10:30–35)

The Good Samaritan went out of his way, at some cost to himself, to help one in need of it. We are not told what the options were, that is, whether or not the priest and the Levite could have helped by doing less than the Good Samaritan did, but assuming they could have, then the fact they did nothing at all shows they were not even Minimally Decent Samaritans, not because they were not Samaritans, but because they were not even minimally decent.

These things are a matter of degree, of course, but there is a difference, and it comes out perhaps most clearly in the story of Kitty Genovese, who, as you will remember, was murdered while thirty-eight people watched or listened, and did nothing at all to help her. A Good Samaritan would have rushed out to give direct assistance against the murderer. Or perhaps we had better allow that it would have been a Splendid Samaritan who did this, on the ground that it would have involved a risk of death for himself. But the thirty-eight not only did not do this, they did not even trouble to pick up a phone to call the police. Minimally Decent Samaritanism would call for doing at least that, and their not having done it was monstrous.

After telling the story of the Good Samaritan, Jesus said "Go, and do thou likewise." Perhaps he meant that we are morally required to act as the Good Samaritan did. Perhaps he was urging people to do more than is morally required of them. At all events it seems plain that it was not morally required of any of the thirty-eight that he rush out to give direct assistance at the risk of his own life, and that it is not morally required of anyone that he give long stretches of his life—nine years or nine months—to sustaining the life of a person who has no special right (we were leaving open the possibility of this) to demand it.

Indeed, with one rather striking class of exceptions, no one in any country in the world is *legally* required to do anywhere near as much as this for anyone else. The class of exceptions is obvious. My main concern here is not the state of the law in respect to abortion, but it is worth drawing attention to the fact that in no state in this country is any man compelled by law to be even a Minimally Decent Samaritan to any person; there is no law under which charges could be brought against the thirty-eight who stood by while Kitty Genovese died. By contrast, in most states in this country women are compelled by law to be not merely Minimally Decent Samaritans, but Good Samaritans to unborn persons inside them. This doesn't by itself settle anything one way or the other, because it may well be argued that there should be laws in this country—as there are in many European countries—compelling at least Minimally Decent Samaritanism. But it does show that there is a gross injustice in the existing state of the law. And it shows also that the groups currently working against liberalization of abortion laws, in fact working toward having declared unconstitutional for a state to permit abortion, had better start working for the adoption of Good Samaritan laws generally, or earn the charge that they are acting in bad faith.

I should think, myself, that Minimally Decent Samaritan laws would be one thing. Good Samaritan laws quite another, and in fact highly improper. But we are not here concerned with the law. What we should ask is not whether anybody should be compelled by law to be a Good Samaritan, but whether we must accede to a situation in which somebody is being compelled by nature, perhaps—to be a Good Samaritan. We have, in other words, to look now at third-party interventions. I have been arguing that no person is morally required to make large sacrifices to sustain the life of another who has no right to demand them, and this even where the sacrifices do not include life itself; we are not morally required to be Good Samaritans or anyway Very Good Samaritans to one another. But what if a man cannot extricate himself from such a situation? What if he appeals to us to extricate him? It seems to me plain that there are cases in which we can, cases in which a Good Samaritan would extricate him. There you are, you were kidnapped, and nine years in bed with that violinist lie ahead of you. You have your own life to lead. You are sorry, but simply cannot see giving up so much of your life to the sustaining of his. You cannot extricate yourself, and ask us to do so. I should have thought that—in light of his having no right to the use of your body—it was obvious that we do not have to accede to your being forced to give up so much. We can do what you ask. There is no injustice to the violinist in our doing so.

7. Following the lead of the opponents of abortion, I have throughout been speaking of the fetus merely as a person, and what I have been asking is whether or not the argument we began with, which proceeds only from the fetus' being a person, really does establish its conclusion. I have argued that it does not.

But of course there are arguments and arguments, and it may be said that I have simply fastened on the wrong one. It may be said that what is important is not merely the fact that the fetus is a person, but that it is a person for whom the woman has a special kind of responsibility issuing from the fact that she is its mother. And it might be argued that all my analogies are therefore irrelevant—for you do not have that special kind of responsibility for that violinist, Henry Fonda does not have that special kind of responsibility for me. And our attention might be drawn to the fact that men and women both *are* compelled by law to provide support for their children.

I have in effect dealt (briefly) with this argument in section 4 above; but a (still briefer) recapitulation now may be in order. Surely we do not have any such "special responsibility" for a person unless we have assumed it, explicitly or implicitly. If a set of parents do not try to prevent pregnancy, do not obtain an abortion, and then at the time of birth of the child do not put it out for adoption, but rather take it home with them, then they have assumed responsibility for it, they have given it rights, and they cannot *now* withdraw support from it at the cost of its life because they now find it difficult to go on providing for it. But if they have taken all reasonable precautions against having a child, they do not simply by virtue of their biological relationship to the child who comes into existence have a special responsibility for it. They may wish to assume responsibility for it, or they may not wish to. And I am suggesting that if assuming responsibility for it would require large sacrifices, then they may refuse. A Good Samaritan would not refuse—or anyway, a Splendid Samaritan, if the sacrifices that had to be made were enormous. But then so would a Good Samaritan assume responsibility for that violinist; so would Henry Fonda, if he is a Good Samaritan, fly in from the West Coast and assume responsibility for me.

8. My argument will be found unsatisfactory on two counts by many of those who want to regard abortion as morally permissible. First, while I do argue that abortion is not impermissible, I do not argue that it is always permissible. There may well be cases in which carrying the child to term requires only Minimally Decent Samaritanism of the mother, and this is a standard we must not fall below. I am inclined to think it a merit of my account precisely that it does *not* give a general yes or a general no. It allows for and supports our sense that, for example, a sick and desperately frightened fourteen-year-old schoolgirl, pregnant due to rape, may *of course* choose abortion, and that any law which rules this out is an insane law. And it also allows for and supports our sense that in other cases resort to abortion is even positively indecent. It would be indecent in the woman to request an abortion, and indecent in a doctor to perform it, if she is in her seventh month, and wants the abortion just to avoid the nuisance of postponing a trip abroad. The very fact that the arguments I have been drawing attention to treat all cases of abortion, or even all cases of abortion in which the mother's life is not at stake, as morally on a par ought to have made them suspect at the outset.

Secondly, while I am arguing for the permissibility of abortion in some cases, I am not arguing for the right to secure the death of the unborn child. It is easy to confuse these two things in that up to a certain point in the life of the fetus it is not able to survive outside the mother's body; hence removing it from her body guarantees its death. But they are importantly different. I have argued that you are not morally required to spend nine months in bed, sustaining the life of that violinist; but to say this is by no means to say that if, when you unplug yourself, there is a miracle and he survives, you then have a right to turn round and slit his throat. You may detach yourself even if this costs him his life; you have no right to be guaranteed his death, by some other means, if unplugging yourself does not kill him. There are some people who will feel dissatisfied by this feature of my argument. A woman may be utterly devastated by the thought of a child, a bit of herself, put out for adoption and never seen or heard of again. She may therefore want not merely that the child be detached from her, but more, that it die. Some opponents of abortion are inclined to regard this as beneath contempt—thereby showing insensitivity to what is surely a powerful source of despair. All the same, I agree that the desire for the child's death is not one which anybody may gratify, should it turn out to be possible to detach the child alive.

At this place, however, it should be remembered that we have only been pretending throughout that the fetus is a human being from the moment of conception. A very early abortion is surely not the killing of a person, and so is not dealt with by anything I have said here.

STUDY QUESTIONS

1. Compare Thomson's treatment of the Good Samaritan story with that of Martin Luther King Jr. (chapter two, selection 8). What differences do you notice?
2. What are "slippery slope" arguments, and why does Thomson reject them?
3. Explain Thomson's famous violinist example. Do you find it convincing?
4. What are the limits, if any, to the right to self-defense?
5. How might Hauerwas (selection 48) respond to Thomson?

47

On the Moral and Legal Status of Abortion

Mary Anne Warren

Mary Anne Warren teaches at San Francisco State University. She is the author of several articles in the field of ethics, including "Do Potential People Have Moral Rights?" and "Secondary Sexism and Quota Hiring."

We will be concerned with both the moral status of abortion, which for our purposes we may define as the act which a woman performs in voluntarily terminating, or allowing another person to terminate, her pregnancy, and the legal status which is appropriate for this act. I will argue that, while it is not possible to produce a satisfactory defense of a woman's right to obtain an abortion without showing that a fetus is not a human being, in the morally relevant sense of that term, we ought not to conclude that the difficulties involved in determining whether or not a fetus is human make it impossible to produce any satisfactory solution to the problem of the moral status of abortion. For it is possible to show that, on the basis of intuitions which we may expect even the opponents of abortion to share, a fetus is not a person, and hence not the sort of entity to which it is proper to ascribe full moral rights.

Of course, while some philosophers would deny the possibility of any such proof,[1] others will deny that there is any need for it, since the moral permissibility of abortion appears to them to be too obvious to require proof. But the inadequacy of this attitude should be evident from the fact that both the friends and the foes of abortion consider their position to be morally self-evident. Because pro-abortionists have never adequately come to grips with the conceptual issues surrounding abortion, most if not all, of the arguments which they advance in opposition to laws restricting access to abortion fail to refute or even weaken the traditional antiabortion argument, i.e., that a fetus is a human being, and therefore abortion is murder.

These arguments are typically one of two sorts. Either they point to the terrible side effects of the restrictive laws, e.g., the deaths due to illegal abortions, and the fact that it is poor women who suffer the most as a result of these laws, or else they state that to deny a woman access to abortion is to deprive her of her right to control her own body. Unfortunately, however, the fact that restricting access to abortion has tragic side effects does not, in itself, show that the restrictions are unjustified, since murder is wrong regardless of the consequences of prohibiting it; and the appeal to the right to control one's body, which is generally construed as a property right, is at best a rather feeble argument for the permissibility of abortion. Mere ownership does not give me the right to kill innocent people whom I find on my property, and indeed I am apt to be held responsible if such people injure themselves while on my property. It is equally unclear that I have any moral right to expel an innocent person from my property when I know that doing so will result in his death.

Furthermore, it is probably inappropriate to describe a woman's body as her property, since it seems natural to hold that a person is something distinct from her property, but not from her body. Even those who would object to the identification of a person with his body, or with the conjunction of his body and his mind, must admit that it would be very odd to describe, say, breaking a leg, as damaging one's property, and much more appropriate to describe it as injuring one*self*. Thus it is probably a mistake to argue that the right to obtain an abortion is in any way derived from the right to own and regulate property.

But however we wish to construe the right to abortion, we cannot hope to convince those who consider abortion a form of murder of the existence of any such right unless we are able to produce a clear and convincing refutation of the traditional antiabortion argument, and this has not, to my knowledge, been done. With respect to the two most vital issues which that argument involves, i.e., the humanity of the fetus and its implication for the moral status of abortion, confusion has prevailed on both sides of the dispute.

Thus, both pro-abortionists and antiabortionists have tended to abstract the question of whether abortion is wrong to that of whether it is wrong to destroy a fetus, just as though the rights of another person were not necessarily involved. This mistaken abstraction has led to the almost universal assumption that if a fetus is a human being, with a right to life, then it follows immediately that abortion is wrong (except perhaps when necessary to save the woman's life), and that it ought to be prohibited. It has also been generally assumed that unless the question about the status of the fetus is answered, the moral status of abortion cannot possibly be determined.

Two recent papers, one by B. A. Brody,[2] and one by Judith Thomson,[3] have attempted to settle the question of whether abortion ought to be prohibited apart from the question of whether or not the fetus is human. Brody examines the possibility that the following two statements are compatible: (1) that abortion is the taking of innocent human life, and therefore wrong; and (2) that nevertheless it ought not to be prohibited by law, at least under the present circumstances.[4] Not surprisingly, Brody finds it impossible to reconcile these two statements, since, as he rightly argues, none of the unfortunate side effects of the prohibition of abortion is bad enough to justify legalizing the *wrongful* taking of human life. He is mistaken, however, in concluding that the incompatibility of (1) and (2), in itself, shows that "the legal problem about abortion cannot be resolved independently of the status of the fetus problem." . . .

What Brody fails to realize is that (1) embodies the questionable assumption that if a fetus is a human being, then of course abortion is morally wrong, and that an attack on *this* assumption is more promising, as a way of reconciling the humanity of the fetus with the claim that laws prohibiting abortion are unjustified, than is an attack on the assumption that if abortion is the wrongful killing of innocent human beings then it ought to be prohibited. He thus overlooks the possibility that a fetus may have a right to life and abortion still be morally permissible, in that the right of a woman to terminate an unwanted pregnancy might override the right of the fetus to be kept alive. The immorality of abortion is no more demonstrated by the humanity of the fetus, in itself, than the immorality of killing in self-defense is demonstrated by the fact that the assailant is a human being. Neither is it demonstrated by the *innocence* of the fetus, since there may be situations in which the killing of innocent human beings is justified.

It is perhaps not surprising that Brody fails to spot this assumption, since it has been accepted with little or no argument by nearly everyone who has written on the morality of abortion. John Noonan is correct in saying that "the fundamental question in the long history of abortion is, How do you determine the humanity of a being?"[5] He summarizes his own antiabortion argument, which is a version of the official position of the Catholic Church, as follows:

> . . . it is wrong to kill humans, however poor, weak, defenseless, and lacking in opportunity to develop their potential they may be. It is therefore morally wrong to kill Biafrans. Similarly, it is morally wrong to kill embryos.[6]

Noonan bases his claim that fetuses are human upon what he calls the theologians' criterion of humanity: that whoever is conceived of human beings is human. But although he argues at length for the appropriateness of this criterion, he never questions the assumption that if a fetus is human then abortion is wrong for exactly the same reason that murder is wrong.

Judith Thomson is, in fact, the only writer I am aware of who has seriously questioned this assumption; she has argued that, even if we grant the antiabortionist his claim that a fetus is a human being, with the same right to life as any other human being, we can still demonstrate that, in at least some and perhaps most cases, a woman is under no moral obligation to complete an unwanted pregnancy.[7] Her argument is worth examining, since if it holds up it may enable us to establish the moral permissibility of abortion without becoming involved in problems about what entitles an entity to be considered human, and accorded full moral rights. To be able to do this would be a great gain in the power and simplicity of the pro-abortion position, since, although I will argue that these problems can be solved at least as decisively as can any other moral problem, we should certainly be pleased to be able to avoid having to solve them as part of the justification of abortion.

On the other hand, even if Thomson's argument does not hold up, her insight, i.e., that it requires *argument* to show that if fetuses are human then abortion is properly classified as murder, is an extremely valuable one. The assumption she attacks is particularly invidious, for it amounts to the decision that it is appropriate, in deciding the moral status of abortion, to leave the rights of the pregnant woman out of consideration entirely, except possibly when her life is threatened. Obviously, this will not do; determining what moral rights, if any, a fetus possesses is only the first step in determining the moral status of abortion. Step two, which is at least equally essential, is finding a just solution to the conflict between whatever rights the fetus may have, and the rights of the woman who is unwillingly pregnant. While the historical error has been to pay far too little attention to the second step, Ms. Thomson's suggestion is that if we look at the second step first we may find that a woman has a right to obtain an abortion *regardless* of what rights the fetus has.

Our own inquiry will also have two stages. In Section I, we will consider whether or not it is possible to establish that abortion is morally permissible even on the assumption that a fetus is an entity with a full-fledged right to life. I will argue that in fact this cannot be established, at least not with the conclusiveness which is essential to our hopes of convincing those who are skeptical about the morality of abortion, and that we therefore cannot avoid dealing with the question of whether or not a fetus really does have the same right to life as a (more fully developed) human being.

In Section II, I will propose an answer to this question, namely, that a fetus cannot be considered a member of the moral community, the set of beings with full and equal moral rights, for the simple reason that it is not a person, and that it is personhood, and not genetic humanity, i.e., humanity as defined by Noonan, which is the basis for membership in this community. I will argue that a fetus, whatever its stage of development, satisfies none of the basic criteria of personhood, and is not even enough *like* a person to be accorded even some of the same rights on the basis of this resemblance. Nor, as we will see, is a fetus's *potential* personhood a threat to the morality of abortion, since, whatever the rights of potential people may be, they are invariably overridden in any conflict with the moral rights of actual people.

I

We turn now to Professor Thomson's case for the claim that even if a fetus has full moral rights, abortion is still morally permissible, at least sometimes, and for some reasons other than to save the woman's life. Her argument is based upon a clever, but I think faulty, analogy. She asks us to picture ourselves waking up one day, in bed with a famous violinist. Imagine that you have been kidnapped, and your bloodstream hooked up to that of the violinist, who happens to have an ailment which will certainly kill him unless he is permitted to share your kidneys for a period of nine months. No one else can save him, since you alone have the right type of blood. He will be unconscious all that time, and you will have to stay in bed with him, but after the nine months are over he may be unplugged, completely cured, that is provided that you have cooperated.

Now then, she continues, what are your obligations in this situation? The antiabortionist, if he is consistent, will have to say that you are obligated to stay in bed with the violinist: for all people have a right to life, and violinists are people, and therefore it would be murder for you to disconnect yourself from him and let him die. . . . But this is outrageous, and so there must be something wrong with the same argument when it is applied to abortion. It would certainly be commendable of you to agree to save the violinist, but it is absurd to suggest that your refusal to do so would be murder. His right to life does not obligate you to do whatever is required to keep him alive; nor does it justify anyone else in forcing you to do so. A law which required you to stay in bed with the violinist would clearly be an unjust law, since it is no proper function of the law to force unwilling people to make huge sacrifices for the sake of other people toward whom they have no such prior obligation.

Thomson concludes that, if this analogy is an apt one, then we can grant the antiabortionist his claim that a fetus is a human being, and still hold that it is at least sometimes the case that a pregnant woman has the right to refuse to be a Good Samaritan towards the fetus, i.e., to obtain an abortion. For there is a great gap between the claim that *x* has a right to life, and the claim that *y* is obligated to do whatever is necessary to keep *x* alive, let alone that he ought to be forced to do so. It is *y*'s duty to keep *x* alive only if he has somehow contracted a *special* obligation to do so; and a woman who is unwillingly pregnant, e.g., who was raped, has done nothing which obligates her to make the enormous sacrifice which is necessary to preserve the conceptus.

This argument is initially quite plausible, and in the extreme case of pregnancy due to rape it is probably conclusive. Difficulties arise, however, when we try to specify more exactly the range of cases in which abortion is clearly justifiable even on the assumption that the fetus is human. Professor Thomson considers it a virtue of her argument that it does not enable us to conclude that abortion is *always* permissible. It would, she says, be "indecent" for a woman in her seventh month to obtain an abortion just to avoid having to postpone a trip to Europe. On the other hand, her argument enables us to see that "a sick and desperately frightened schoolgirl pregnant due to rape may *of course* choose abortion, and that any law which rules this out is an insane law". . . . So far, so good; but what are we to say about the woman who becomes pregnant not through rape but as a result of her own carelessness, or because of contraceptive failure, or who gets pregnant intentionally and then changes her mind about wanting a child? With respect to such cases, the violinist analogy is of much less use to the defender of the woman's right to obtain an abortion.

Indeed, the choice of a pregnancy due to rape, as an example of a case in which abortion is permissible even if a fetus is considered a human being, is extremely significant; for it is only in the case of pregnancy due to rape that the woman's situation is adequately analogous to the violinist case for our intuitions about the latter to transfer convincingly. The crucial difference between a pregnancy due to rape and the *normal* case of an unwanted pregnancy is that in the normal case we cannot claim that the woman is in no way responsible for her predicament; she could have remained chaste, or taken her pills more faithfully, or abstained on dangerous days, and so on. If, on the other hand, you are kidnapped by strangers, and hooked up to a strange violinist, then you are free of any shred of responsibility for the situation, on the basis of which it could be argued that you are obligated to keep the violinist alive. Only when her pregnancy is due to rape is a woman clearly just as nonresponsible.[8]

Consequently, there is room for the antiabortionist to argue that in the normal case of unwanted pregnancy a woman has, by her own actions, assumed responsibility for the fetus. For if *x* behaves in a way which he could have avoided, and which he knows involves, let us say, a 1 percent chance of bringing into existence a human being, with a right to life, and does so knowing that if this should happen then that human being will perish unless *x* does certain things to keep him alive, then it is by no means clear that when it does happen *x* is free of any obligation to what he knew in advance would be required to keep that human being alive.

The plausibility of such an argument is enough to show that the Thomson analogy can provide a clear and persuasive defense of a woman's right to obtain an abortion only with respect to those cases in which the woman is in no way responsible for her pregnancy, e.g., where it is due to rape. In all other cases, we would almost certainly conclude that it was necessary to look carefully at the particular circumstances in order to determine the extent of the woman's responsibility, and hence the extent of her obligation. This is an extremely unsatisfactory outcome, from the viewpoint of the opponents of restrictive abortion laws, most of whom are convinced that a woman has a right to obtain an abortion regardless of how and why she got pregnant.

Of course a supporter of the violinist analogy might point out that it is absurd to suggest that forgetting her pill one day might be sufficient to obligate a woman to complete an unwanted pregnancy. And indeed it *is* absurd to suggest this. As we will see, the moral right to obtain an abortion is not in the least dependent upon the extent to which the woman is responsible for her pregnancy. But unfortunately, once we allow the assumption that a fetus has full moral rights, we cannot avoid taking this absurd suggestion seriously. Perhaps we can make this point more clear by altering the violinist story just enough to make it more analogous to a normal unwanted pregnancy and less to a pregnancy due to rape, and then seeing whether it is still obvious that you are not obligated to stay in bed with the fellow.

Suppose, then, that violinists are peculiarly prone to the sort of illness the only cure for which is the use of someone else's bloodstream for nine months, and that because of this there has been formed a society of music lovers who agree that whenever a violinist is stricken they will draw lots and the loser will, by some means, be made the one and only person capable of saving him. Now then, would you be obligated to cooperate in curing the violinist if you had voluntarily joined this society, knowing the possible consequences, and then your name had been drawn and you had been kidnapped? Admittedly, you did not promise ahead of time that you would, but you did deliberately place yourself in a position in which it might happen that a human life would be lost if you did not. Surely this is at least a prima facie reason for supposing that you have an obligation to stay in bed with the violinist. Suppose that you had gotten your name drawn deliberately; surely *that* would be quite a strong reason for thinking that you had such an obligation.

It might be suggested that there is one important disanalogy between the modified violinist case and the case of an unwanted pregnancy, which makes the woman's responsibility significantly less, namely, the fact that the fetus *comes into existence* as the result of the woman's actions. This fact might give her a right to refuse to keep it alive, whereas she would not have had this right had it existed previously, independently, and then as a result of her actions become dependent upon her for its survival.

My own intuition, however, is that x has no more right to bring into existence, either deliberately or as a foreseeable result of actions he could have avoided, a being with full moral rights (y), and then refuse to do what he knew beforehand would be required to keep that being alive, than he has to enter into an agreement with an existing person, whereby he may be called upon to save that person's life, and then refuse to do so when so called upon. Thus, x's responsibility for y's existence does not seem to lessen his obligation to keep y alive, if he is also responsible for y's being in a situation in which only he can save him.

Whether or not this intuition is entirely correct, it brings us back once again to the conclusion that once we allow the assumption that a fetus has full moral rights it becomes an extremely complex and difficult question whether and when abortion is justifiable. Thus the Thomson analogy cannot help us produce a clear and persuasive proof of the moral permissibility of abortion. Nor will the opponents of the restrictive laws thank us for anything less; for their conviction (for the most part) is that abortion is obviously *not* a morally serious and extremely unfortunate, even though sometimes justified act, comparable to killing in self-defense or to letting the violinist die, but rather is closer to being a morally neutral act, like cutting one's hair.

The basis of this conviction, I believe, is the realization that a fetus is not a person, and thus does not have a full-fledged right to life. Perhaps the reason why this claim has been so inadequately defended is that it seems self-evident to those who accept it. And so it is, insofar as it follows from what I take to be perfectly obvious claims about the nature of personhood, and about the proper grounds for ascribing moral rights, claims which ought, indeed, to be obvious to both the friends and foes of abortion. Nevertheless, it is worth examining these claims, and showing how they demonstrate the moral innocuousness of abortion, since this apparently has not been adequately done before.

II

The question which we must answer in order to produce a satisfactory solution to the problem of the moral status of abortion is this: How are we to define the moral community, the set of beings with full and equal moral rights, such that we can decide whether a human fetus is a member of this community or not? What sort of entity, exactly, has the inalienable rights to life, liberty, and the pursuit of happiness? Jefferson attributed these rights to all *men*, and it may or may not be fair to suggest that he intended to attribute them *only* to men. Perhaps he ought to have attributed them to all human beings. If so, then we arrive, first, at Noonan's problem of defining what makes a being human, and, second, at the equally vital question which Noonan does not consider, namely, What reason is there for identifying the moral community with the set of all human beings, in whatever way we have chosen to define that term?

On the Definition of "Human"

One reason why this vital second question is so frequently overlooked in the debate over the moral status of abortion is that the term "human" has two distinct, but not often distinguished, senses. This fact results in a slide of meaning, which serves to conceal the fallaciousness of the traditional argument that since (1) it is wrong to kill innocent human beings, and (2) fetuses are innocent human beings, then (3) it is wrong to kill fetuses. For if "human" is used in the same sense in both (1) and (2) then, whichever of the two senses is meant, one of these premises is question-begging. And if it is used in two different senses then of course the conclusion doesn't follow.

Thus, (1) is a self-evident moral truth,[9] and avoids begging the question about abortion, only if "human being" is used to mean something like "a full-fledged member of the moral community." (It may or may not also be meant to refer exclusively to members of the species *Homo sapiens*.) We may call this the *moral* sense of "human." It is not to be confused with what we will call the *genetic* sense, i.e., the sense in which *any* member of the species is a human being, and no member of any other species could be. If (1) is acceptable only if the moral sense is intended, (2) is non-question-begging only if what is intended is the genetic sense.

In "Deciding Who Is Human," Noonan argues for the classification of fetuses with human beings by pointing to the presence of the full genetic code, and the potential capacity for rational thought. . . . It is clear that what he needs to show, for his version of the traditional argument to be valid, is that fetuses are human in the moral sense, the sense in which it is analytically true that all human beings have full moral rights. But, in the absence of any argument showing that whatever is genetically human is also morally human, and he gives none, nothing more than genetic humanity can be demonstrated by the presence of the human genetic code. And, as we will see, the *potential* capacity for rational thought can at most show that an entity has the potential for *becoming* human in the moral sense.

Defining the Moral Community

Can it be established that genetic humanity is sufficient for moral humanity? I think that there are very good reasons for not defining the moral community in this way. I would like to suggest an alternative way of defining the moral community, which I will argue for only to the extent of explaining why it is, or should be, self-evident. The suggestion is simply that the moral community consists of all and only *people*, rather than all and only human beings;[10] and probably the best way of demonstrating its self-evidence is by considering the concept of personhood, to see what sorts of entity are and are not persons, and what the decision that a being is or is not a person implies about its moral rights.

What characteristics entitle an entity to be considered a person? This is obviously not the place to attempt a complete analysis of the concept of personhood, but we do not need such a fully adequate analysis just to determine whether and why a fetus is or isn't a person. All we need is a rough and approximate list of the most basic criteria of personhood, and some idea of which, or how many, of these an entity must satisfy in order to properly be considered a person.

In searching for such criteria, it is useful to look beyond the set of people with whom we are acquainted, and ask how we would decide whether a totally alien being was a person or not. (For we have no right to assume that genetic humanity is necessary for personhood.) Imagine a space traveler who lands on an unknown planet and encounters a race of beings utterly unlike any he has ever seen or heard of. If he wants to be sure of behaving morally toward these beings, he has to somehow decide whether they are people, and hence have full moral rights, or whether they are the sort of thing which he need not feel guilty about treating as, for example, a source of food.

How should he go about making this decision? If he has some anthropological background, he might look for such things as religion, art, and the manufacturing of tools, weapons, or shelters, since these factors have been used to distinguish our human from our prehuman ancestors, in what seems to be closer to the moral than the genetic sense of "human." And no doubt he would be right to consider the presence of such factors as good evidence that the alien beings were people, and morally human. It would, however, be overly anthropocentric of him to take the absence of these things as adequate evidence that they were not, since we can imagine people who have progressed beyond, or evolved without ever developing, these cultural characteristics.

I suggest that the traits which are most central to the concept of personhood, or humanity in the moral sense, are, very roughly, the following:

1. consciousness (of objects and events external and/or internal to the being), and in particular the capacity to feel pain;

2. reasoning (the *developed* capacity to solve new and relatively complex problems);
3. self-motivated activity (activity which is relatively independent of either genetic or direct external control);
4. the capacity to communicate, by whatever means, messages of an indefinite variety of types, that is, not just with an indefinite number of possible contents, but on indefinitely many possible topics;
5. the presence of self-concepts, and self-awareness, either individual or racial, or both.

Admittedly, there are apt to be a great many problems involved in formulating precise definitions of these criteria, let alone in developing universally valid behavioral criteria for deciding when they apply. But I will assume that both we and our explorer know approximately what (1)–(5) mean, and that he is also able to determine whether or not they apply. How, then, should he use his findings to decide whether or not the alien beings are people? We needn't suppose that an entity must have *all* of these attributes to be properly considered a person; (1) and (2) alone may well be sufficient for personhood, and quite probably (1)–(3) are sufficient. Neither do we need to insist that any one of these criteria is *necessary* for personhood, although once again (1) and (2) look like fairly good candidates for necessary conditions, as does (3), if "activity" is construed so as to include the activity of reasoning.

All we need to claim, to demonstrate that a fetus is not a person, is that any being which satisfies *none* of (1)–(5) is certainly not a person. I consider this claim to be so obvious that I think anyone who denied it, and claimed that a being which satisfied none of (1)–(5) was a person all the same, would thereby demonstrate that he had no notion at all of what a person is—perhaps because he had confused the concept of a person with that of genetic humanity. If the opponents of abortion were to deny the appropriateness of these five criteria, I do not know what further arguments would convince them. We would probably have to admit that our conceptual schemes were indeed irreconcilably different, and that our dispute could not be settled objectively.

I do not expect this to happen, however, since I think that the concept of a person is one which is very nearly universal (to people), and that it is common to both pro-abortionists and antiabortionists, even though neither group has fully realized the relevance of this concept to the resolution of their dispute. Furthermore, I think that on reflection even the antiabortionists ought to agree not only that (1)–(5) are central to the concept of personhood, but also that it is a part of this concept that all and only people have full moral rights. The concept of a person is in part a moral concept; once we have admitted that x is a person we have recognized, even if we have not agreed to respect, x's right to be treated as a member of the moral community. It is true that the claim that x is a *human being* is more commonly voiced as part of an appeal to treat x decently than is the claim that x is a person, but this is either because "human being" is here used in the sense which implies personhood, or because the genetic and moral senses of "human" have been confused.

Now if (1)–(5) are indeed the primary criteria of personhood, then it is clear that genetic humanity is neither necessary nor sufficient for establishing that an entity is a person. Some human beings are not people, and there may well be people who are not human beings. A man or woman whose consciousness has been permanently obliterated but who remains alive is a human being which is no longer a person; defective human beings, with no appreciable mental capacity, are not and presumably never will be people; and a fetus is a human being which is not yet a person, and which therefore cannot coherently be said to have full moral rights. Citizens of the next century should be prepared to recognize highly advanced, self-aware robots or computers, should such be developed, and intelligent inhabitants of other worlds, should such be found, as people in the fullest sense, and to respect their moral rights. But to ascribe full moral rights to an entity which is not a person is as absurd as to ascribe moral obligations and responsibilities to such an entity.

Fetal Development and the Right to Life

Two problems arise in the application of these suggestions for the definition of the moral community to the determination of the precise moral status of a human fetus. Given that the paradigm example of a person is a normal adult human being, then (1) How like this paradigm, in particular how far advanced since conception, does a human being need to be before it begins to have a right to life by virtue, not of being fully a person as of yet, but of being *like* a person? and (2) To what extent, if any, does the fact that a fetus has the *potential* for becoming a person endow it with some of the same rights? Each of these questions requires some comment.

In answering the first question, we need not attempt a detailed consideration of the moral rights of organisms which are not developed enough, aware enough, intelligent enough, etc., to be considered people, but which resemble people in some respects. It does seem reasonable to suggest that the more like a person, in the relevant respects, a being is, the stronger is the case for regarding it as having a right to life, and indeed the stronger its right to life is. Thus we ought to take seriously the suggestion that, insofar as "the human individual develops biologically in a continuous fashion . . . the rights of a human person might develop in the same way."[11] But we must keep in mind that the attributes which are relevant in determining whether or not an entity is enough like a person to be regarded as having some of the same moral rights are no different from those which are relevant to determining whether or not it is fully a person—i.e., are no different from (1)–(5)—and that being genetically human, or having recognizably human facial and other physical features, or detectable brain activity, or the capacity to survive outside the uterus, are simply not among these relevant attributes.

Thus it is clear that even though a seven- or eight-month fetus has features which make it apt to arouse in us almost the same powerful protective instinct as is commonly aroused by a small infant, nevertheless it is not significantly more personlike than is a very small embryo. It is *somewhat* more personlike; it can apparently feel and respond to pain, and it may even have a rudimentary form of consciousness, insofar as its brain is quite active. Nevertheless, it seems safe to say that it is not fully conscious, in the way that an infant of a few months is, and that it cannot reason, or communicate messages of indefinitely many sorts, does not engage in self-motivated activity, and has no self-awareness. Thus, in the *relevant* respects, a fetus, even a fully developed one, is considerably less personlike than is the average mature mammal, indeed the average fish. And I think that a rational person must conclude that if the right to life of a fetus is to be based upon its resemblance to a person, then it cannot be said to have any more right to life than, let us say, a newborn guppy (which also seems to be capable of feeling pain), and that a right of that magnitude could never override a woman's right to obtain an abortion, at any stage of her pregnancy.

There may, of course, be other arguments in favor of placing legal limits upon the stage of pregnancy in which an abortion may be performed. Given the relative safety of the new techniques of artificially inducing labor during the third trimester, the danger to the woman's life or health is no longer such an argument. Neither is the fact that people tend to respond to the thought of abortion in the later stages of pregnancy with emotional repulsion, since mere emotional responses cannot take the place of moral reasoning in determining what ought to be permitted. Nor, finally, is the frequently heard argument that legalizing abortion, especially late in the pregnancy, may erode the level of respect for human life, leading, perhaps, to an increase in unjustified euthanasia and other crimes. For this threat, if it is a threat, can be better met by educating people to the kinds of moral distinctions which we are making here than by limiting access to abortion (which limitation may, in its disregard for the rights of women, be just as damaging to the level of respect for human rights).

Thus, since the fact that even a fully developed fetus is not person-like enough to have any significant right to life on the basis of its person-likeness shows that no legal restrictions upon the stage of pregnancy in which an abortion may be performed can be justified on the grounds that we should protect the rights of the older fetus; and since there is no other apparent justification for such restrictions, we may conclude that they are entirely unjustified. Whether or not it would be *indecent* (whatever that means) for a woman in her seventh month to obtain an abortion just to avoid having to postpone a trip to Europe, it would not, in itself, be *immoral*, and therefore it ought to be permitted.

Potential Personhood and the Right to Life

We have seen that a fetus does not resemble a person in any way which can support the claim that it has even some of the same rights. But what about its *potential*, the fact that if nurtured and allowed to develop naturally it will very probably become a person? Doesn't that alone give it at least some right to life? It is hard to deny that the fact that an entity is a potential person is a strong prima facie reason for not destroying it; but we need not conclude from this that a potential person has a right to life, by virtue of that potential. It may be that our feeling that it is better, other things being equal, not to destroy a potential person is better explained by the fact that potential people are still (felt to be) an invaluable resource, not to be lightly squandered. Surely, if every speck of dust were a potential person, we would be much less apt to conclude that every potential person has a right to become actual.

Still, we do not need to insist that a potential person has no right to life whatever. There may well be something immoral, and not just imprudent, about wantonly destroying potential people, when doing so isn't necessary to protect anyone's rights. But even if a potential person does have some prima facie right to life, such a right could not possibly outweigh the right of a woman to obtain an abortion, since the rights of any actual person invariably outweigh those of any potential person, whenever the two conflict. Since this may not be immediately obvious in the case of a human fetus, let us look at another case.

Suppose that our space explorer falls into the hands of an alien culture, whose scientists decide to create a few hundred thousand or more human beings, by breaking his body into its component cells, and using these to create fully developed human beings, with, of course, his genetic code. We may imagine that each of these newly created men will have all of the original man's abilities, skills, knowledge, and so on, and also have an individual self-concept, in short that each of them will be a bona fide (though hardly unique) person. Imagine that the whole project will take only seconds, and that its chances of success are extremely high, and that our explorer knows all of this, and also knows that these people will be treated fairly. I maintain that in such a situation he would have every right to escape if he could, and thus to deprive all of these potential people of their potential lives; for his right to life outweighs all of theirs together, in spite of the fact that they are all genetically human, all innocent, and all have a very high probability of becoming people very soon, if only he refrains from acting.

Indeed, I think he would have a right to escape even if it were not his life which the alien scientists planned to take, but only a year of his freedom, or, indeed, only a day. Nor would he be obligated to stay if he had gotten captured (thus bringing all these people-potentials into existence) because of his own carelessness, or even if he had done so deliberately, knowing the consequences. Regardless of how he got captured, he is not morally obligated to remain in captivity for any period of time for the sake of permitting any number of potential people to come into actuality, so great is the margin by which one actual person's right to liberty outweighs whatever right to life even a hundred thousand potential people have. And it seems reasonable to conclude that the rights of a woman will outweigh by a similar margin whatever right to life a fetus may have by virtue of its potential personhood.

Thus, neither a fetus's resemblance to a person, nor its potential for becoming a person provides any basis whatever for the claim that it has any significant right to life. Consequently, a woman's right to protect her health, happiness, freedom, and even her life,[12] by terminating an unwanted pregnancy, will always override whatever right to life it may be appropriate to ascribe to a fetus, even a fully developed one. And thus, in the absence of any overwhelming social need for every possible child, the laws which restrict the right to obtain an abortion, or limit the period of pregnancy during which an abortion may be performed, are a wholly unjustified violation of a woman's most basic moral and constitutional rights.[13]

POSTSCRIPT ON INFANTICIDE

Since the publication of this article, many people have written to point out that my argument appears to justify not only abortion, but infanticide as well. For a newborn infant is not significantly more personlike than an advanced fetus, and consequently it would seem that if the destruction of the latter is permissible so too must be that of the former. Inasmuch as most people, regardless of how they feel about the morality of abortion, consider infanticide a form of murder, this might appear to represent a serious flaw in my argument.

Now, if I am right in holding that it is only people who have a full-fledged right to life, and who can be murdered, and if the criteria of personhood are as I have described them, then it obviously follows that killing a newborn infant isn't murder. It does *not* follow, however, that infanticide is permissible, for two reasons. In the first place, it would be wrong, at least in this country and in this period of history, and other things being equal, to kill a newborn infant, because even if its parents do not want it and would not suffer from its destruction, there are other people who would like to have it, and would, in all probability, be deprived of a great deal of pleasure by its destruction. Thus, infanticide is wrong for reasons analogous to those which make it wrong to wantonly destroy natural resources, or great works of art.

Secondly, most people, at least in this country, value infants, and would much prefer that they be preserved, even if foster parents are not immediately available. Most of us would rather be taxed to support orphanages than allow unwanted infants to be destroyed. So long as there are people who want an infant preserved, and who are willing and able to provide the means of caring for it, under reasonably humane conditions, it is, *ceteris parabis*, wrong to destroy it.

But, it might be replied, if this argument shows that infanticide is wrong, at least at this time and in this country, doesn't it also show that abortion is wrong? After all, many people value fetuses, are disturbed by their destruction, and would much prefer that they be preserved, even at some cost to themselves. Furthermore, as a potential source of pleasure to some foster family, a fetus is just as valuable as an infant. There is, however, a crucial difference between the two cases: so long as the fetus is unborn, its preservation, contrary to the wishes of the pregnant woman, violates her rights to freedom, happiness, and self-determination. Her rights override the rights of those who would like the fetus preserved, just as if someone's life or limb is threatened by a wild animal, his right to protect himself by destroying the animal overrides the rights of those who would prefer that the animal not be harmed.

The minute the infant is born, however, its preservation no longer violates any of its mother's rights, even if she wants it destroyed, because she is free to put it up for adoption. Consequently, while the moment of birth does not mark any sharp discontinuity in the degree to which an infant possesses the right to life, it does mark the end of its mother's right to determine its fate. Indeed, if abortion could be performed without killing the fetus, she would never possess the right to have the fetus destroyed, for the same reasons that she has no right to have an infant destroyed.

On the other hand, it follows from my argument that when an unwanted or defective infant is born into a society which cannot afford and/or is not willing to care for it, then its destruction is permissible. This conclusion will, no doubt, strike many people as heartless and immoral; but remember that the very existence of people who feel this way, and who are willing and able to provide care for unwanted infants, is reason enough to conclude that they should be preserved.

NOTES

1. For example, Roger Wertheimer, who in "Understanding the Abortion Argument" (*Philosophy and Public Affairs,* 1, No. 1 [Fall 1971], 67–95), argues that the problem of the moral status of abortion is insoluble, in that the dispute over the status of the fetus is not a question of fact at all, but only a question of how one responds to the facts.
2. B. A. Brody, "Abortion and the Law," *The Journal of Philosophy,* 68, No. 12 (June 17, 1971), 357–69.
3. Judith Thomson, "A Defense of Abortion," *Philosophy and Public Affairs,* 1, No. 1 (Fall 1971), 47–66.
4. I have abbreviated these statements somewhat, but not in a way which affects the argument.
5. John Noonan, "Abortion and the Catholic Church: A Summary History," *Natural Law Forum,* 12 (1967), 125.
6. John Noonan, "Deciding Who Is Human," *Natural Law Forum,* 13 (1968), 134.
7. "A Defense of Abortion."
8. We may safely ignore the fact that she might have avoided getting raped, e.g., by carrying a gun, since by similar means you might likewise have avoided getting kidnapped, and in neither case does the victim's failure to take all possible precautions against a highly unlikely event (as opposed to reasonable precautions against a rather likely event) mean that he is morally responsible for what happens.
9. Of course, the principle that it is (always) wrong to kill innocent human beings is in need of many modifications, e.g., that it may be permissible to do so to save a greater number of other innocent human beings, but we may safely ignore these complications here.
10. From here on, we will use "human" to mean genetically human, since the moral sense seems closely connected to, and perhaps derived from, the assumption that genetic humanity is sufficient for membership in the moral community.
11. Thomas L. Hayes, "A Biological View," *Commonweal,* 85 (March 17, 1967), 677–78; quoted by Daniel Callahan, in *Abortion, Law, Choice, and Morality* (London: Macmillan & Co., 1970).
12. That is, insofar as the death rate, for the woman, is higher for childbirth than for early abortion.
13. My thanks to the following people, who were kind enough to read and criticize an earlier version of this paper: Herbert Gold, Gene Glass, Anne Lauterbach, Judith Thomson, Mary Mothersill, and Timothy Binkley.

STUDY QUESTIONS

1. What, according to Warren, is the traditional antiabortion argument?
2. Why are the two usual "pro-abortion" arguments inadequate, according to Warren?
3. Explain Warren's critique of Thomson's argument.
4. Explain Warren's distinction between the genetic sense of the term "human" and the moral sense.
5. Do you agree with Warren that "defective" humans with little mental capacity or permanently comatose humans do not have moral rights?
6. In her critique of Thomson, Warren argues that an abortion for the sake of convenience (for instance, to avoid postponing a trip to Europe) is justifiable. Do you agree? Why or why not?

48

Christians and Abortion: The Narrative Context

Stanley Hauerwas

Stanley Hauerwas is a professor of religion at Duke University. He is the author of many books, including *Vision and Virtue: Essays in Christian Ethical Reflection* and *A Community of Character: Toward a Constructive Christian Social Ethic*.

. . . Christians have failed their social order by accepting too easily the terms of argument concerning abortion offered by our society. If we are to serve our society well, and on our own terms, our first task must be to address ourselves by articulating for Christians why abortion can never be regarded as morally indifferent for us. Only by doing this can we witness to our society what kind of people and what kind of society is required if abortion is to be excluded. . . .

To begin with, the first question is not, "Why do Christians think abortion is wrong?" To begin there already presupposes that we know and understand what abortion is. Rather, if we are to understand why Christians assume that by naming abortion they have already said something significant, we have to begin still a step back. We have to ask what it is about the kind of community, and corresponding world, that Christians create that makes them single out abortion in such a way as to exclude it.

For we must remember that "abortion" is not a description of a particular kind of behavior; rather it is a word that teaches us to see a singular kind of behavior from a particular community's moral perspective. The removal of the fetus from the mother's uterus before term can be called an "interruption of pregnancy," the child can be called "fetal matter," and the mother can be called a "patient." But from the Christian perspective, to see the situation in that way changes the self and the community in a decisive way. The Christian insistence on the term "abortion" is a way to remind them that what happens in the removal of the fetus from the mother in order to destroy it strikes at the heart of their community. From this perspective the attempt of Christians to be a community where the term "abortion" remains morally intelligible is a political act.

In this respect the pro-abortionists have always been at a disadvantage. For they have had to carry out the argument in a language created by the moral presuppositions of the Jewish and Christian communities. "Abortion" still carries the connotation that this is not a good thing. Thus to be "pro-abortion" seems to put one in an embarrassing position of recommending a less than good thing. It is not without reason, therefore, that pro-abortion advocates seek to redescribe both the object and act of abortion. We must remind them, however, that by doing so they not only change the description of the act, they also change themselves.

Christians insist on the significance of such a change by refusing to live in a world devoid of abortion as a moral description—a world which admittedly may, as a result, involve deep tragedy. There can be no doubt that the insistence that unjust termination of pregnancy be called "abortion" has to do with our respect for life, but this is surely too simple. Jews and Christians are taught to respect life, not as an end in itself, but as a gift created by God. Thus life is respected because all life serves God in its way. Respect for human life is but a form of our respect for all life. . . .

It is the Christian belief, nurtured by the command of Jesus, that we must learn to love one another, that we become more nearly what we were meant to be through the recognition and love of those we did not "choose" to love. Children, the weak, the ill, the dispossessed provide a particularly intense occasion for such love, as they are beings we cannot control. We must love them for what they are rather than what we want or wish them to be, and as a result we discover that we are capable of love. The existence of such love is not unique or limited to Christians. Indeed that is why we have the confidence that our Christian convictions on these matters might ring true even for those who do not share our convictions. The difference between the Christian and the non-Christian is only that what is a possibility for the non-Christian is a duty for the Christian.

But the Christian duty to welcome new life is a joyful duty, as it derives from our very being as God's people. Moreover correlative to the language of duty is the language of gift. Because children are a duty they can also be regarded as gift, for duty teaches us to accept and welcome a child into the world, not as something that is "ours," but as a gift which comes from another. As a result Christians need not resort to destructive and self-deceiving claims about the qualities they need to have, or the conditions of the world necessary to have children. Perhaps more worrisome than the moral implications of the claim "no unwanted child ought ever to be born," are the ominous assumptions about what is required for one to "want" to have a child.

Christians are thus trained to be the kind of people who are ready to receive and welcome children into the world. For they see children as a sign of the trustworthiness of God's creation and his unwillingness to abandon the world to the powers of darkness. The Christian prohibition of abortion is but the negative side of their positive commitment to welcome new life into their community: life that they know must challenge and perhaps even change their own interpretation of their tradition, but also life without which the tradition has no means to grow.

It is, of course, true that children will often be conceived and born under less than ideal conditions, but the church lives as a community which assumes that we live in an age which is always dangerous. That we live in such a time is all the more reason we must be the kind of community that can receive children into our midst. Just as we need to be virtuous, not because virtue pays but because we cannot afford to be without virtue where it does not pay, so we must learn how to be people open to new life. We can neither protect them from that suffering nor deny them the joy of participating in the adventure of God's Kingdom.

For Christians, therefore, there can be no question of whether the fetus is or is not a "human being." That way of putting the matter is far too abstract and formal. Rather, because of the kind of community we are, we see in the fetus nothing less than God's continuing creation that is destined in hope to be another citizen of his Kingdom. The question of when human life begins is of little interest to such a people, since their hope is that life will and does continue to begin time after time.

This is the form of life that brings significance to our interaction with the fetus. Our history is the basis for our "natural" sympathies, which have been trained to look forward to the joy and challenges of new life. Wertheimer may well be right that there is no corresponding "natural" welcome for life in our society that would make intelligible the recognition of the fetus as having moral status. Yet I suspect that the expectation of parents, and in particular of women, for the birth of their children remains a powerful form of life that continues to exert a force on everyone. Such an "expectation," however, in the absence of more substantive convictions about parenting, too easily becomes a destructive necessity that distorts the experience of being a parent and a child. Particularly repugnant is the assumption that women are thus primarily defined by the role of "mother," for then we forget that the role of being a parent, even for the childless, is a responsibility for everyone in the Christian community.

Nor should it be thought that the Christian commitment to welcome new life into the world stems from a sentimental fondness for babies. Rather, for Christians the having of children is one of their most significant political acts. From the world's perspective the birth of a child represents but another drain on our material and psychological resources. Children, after all, take up much of our energy that could be spent on making the world a better place and our society more just. But from the Christian perspective the birth of a child represents nothing less than our commitment that God will not have this world "bettered" by destroying life. That is why there is no more profound political act for Christians than taking the time for children. It is but an indication that God, not man, rules this existence, and we have been graciously invited to have a part in God's adventure and his Kingdom through the simple action of having children.

THE IMMEDIATE POLITICAL TASK

To some it may seem that I have argued Christians right out of the current controversy, for my argument has made appeal to religious convictions that are inadmissable in the court of our public ethos. But it has certainly not been my intention to make it implausible for Christians to continue to work in the public arena for the protection of all children; nor do I think that this implication follows from the position I have developed. Of course, Christians should prefer to live in societies that provide protection for children. And Christians should certainly wish to encourage those "natural" sentiments that would provide a basis for having and protecting children.

Moreover Christians must be concerned to develop forms of care and support, the absence of which seem to make abortion such a necessity in our society. In particular Christians should, in their own communities, make clear that the role of parent is one we all share. Thus the woman who is pregnant and carrying the child need not be the one to raise it. We must be a people who stand ready to receive and care for any child, not just as if it were one of ours, but because in fact each is one of ours.

But as Christians we must not confuse our political and moral strategies designed to get the best possible care for children in our society with the substance of our convictions. Nor should we hide the latter in the interest of securing the former. For when that is done we abandon our society to its own limits. And then our arguments fall silent in the most regrettable manner, for we forget that our most fundamental political task is to be and to point to that truth which we believe to be the necessary basis for any life-enhancing and just society.

In particular, I think that we will be wise as Christians to state our opposition to abortion in a manner that makes clear our broader concerns for the kind of people we ought to be to welcome children into the world. Therefore, rather than concentrating our energies on whether the fetus is or is not a "person," we would be better advised by example and then argument to make clear why we should hope it is a child. We must show that such a hope involves more than just the question of the status of the fetus, but indeed is the very reason why being a part of God's creation is such an extraordinary and interesting adventure.

STUDY QUESTIONS

1. What does the birth of a new life into the world mean to a Christian, according to the author?
2. How is having children a political act for Christians, according to the author?
3. How does love, seen as a duty, affect the role of the Christian in the abortion debate?
4. Discuss the differences in Hauerwas's, Warren's, and Thomson's treatments of abortion. What are the advantages and limitations of each?

FOR FURTHER STUDY

Baehr, Ninia. *Abortion without Apology: A Radical History for the 1990s*. Boston: South End Press, 1990.

Dworkin, Ronald. *Life's Dominion: An Argument about Abortion, Euthanasia, and Individual Freedom*. New York: Knopf, 1993.

Feinberg, Joel, ed. *The Problem of Abortion*. Belmont, Calif.: Wadsworth, 1984.

Gordon, Linda. *Women's Body, Women's Rights: A Social History of Birth Control in America*. New York: Penguin, 1977.

Nicholson, Susan. A*bortion and the Roman Catholic Church*. Knoxville, Tenn.: Religious Ethics, 1974.

Noonan, John T., ed. *The Morality of Abortion: Legal and Historical Perspectives*. Cambridge, Mass.: Harvard University Press, 1970.

O'Brian, Mary. *The Politics of Reproduction*. Boston: Routledge, 1981.

Overall, Christine. *Ethics and Human Reproduction: A Feminist Analysis*. London: Unwin Hyman, 1987.

Chapter Ten

Ethics of Animals and the Nonhuman Environment

49

Walking

Henry David Thoreau

Henry David Thoreau (1817–62) is regarded as one of America's greatest naturalists. His best-known work, *Walden,* continues to influence many today with its call to simplicity and spiritual liberty.

I wish to speak a word for Nature, for absolute freedom and wildness, as contrasted with a freedom and culture merely civil—to regard man as an inhabitant, or a part and parcel of Nature, rather than a member of society. I wish to make an extreme statement, if so I may make an emphatic one, for there are enough champions of civilization: the minister and the school committee and every one of you will take care of that.

I have met with but one or two persons in the course of my life who understood the art of Walking, that is, of taking walks—who had a genius, so to speak, for *sauntering*, which word is beautifully derived "from idle people who roved about the country, in the Middle Ages, and asked charity, under pretense of going *à la Sainte Terre*," to the Holy Land, till the children exclaimed, "There goes a *Sainte-Terrer*," a Saunterer, a Holy-Lander. They who never go to the Holy Land in their walks, as they pretend, are indeed mere idlers and vagabonds; but they who do go there are saunterers in the good sense, such as I mean. Some, however, would derive the word from *sans terre*, without land or a home, which, therefore, in the good sense, will mean, having no particular home, but equally at home everywhere. For this is the secret of successful sauntering. He who sits still in a house all the time may be the greatest vagrant of all; but the saunterer, in the good sense, is no more vagrant than the meandering river, which is all the while sedulously seeking the shortest course to the sea. But I prefer the first, which, indeed, is the most probable derivation. For every walk is a sort of crusade, preached by some Peter the Hermit in us, to go forth and reconquer this Holy Land from the hands of the Infidels.

It is true, we are but faint-hearted crusaders, even the walkers, nowadays, who undertake no persevering, never-ending enterprises. Our expeditions are but tours, and come round again at evening to the old hearth-side from which we set out. Half the walk is but retracing our steps. We should go forth on the shortest walk, perchance, in the spirit of undying adventure, never to return—prepared to send back our embalmed hearts only as relics to our desolate kingdoms. If you are ready to leave father and mother, and brother and sister, and wife and child and friends, and never see them again—if you have paid your debts, and made your will, and settled all your affairs, and are a free man then you are ready for a walk. . . .

But the walking of which I speak has nothing in it akin to taking exercise, as it is called, as the sick take medicine at stated hours—as the swinging of dumb-bells or chairs; but is itself the enterprise and adventure of the day. If you would get exercise, go in search of the springs of life. Think of a man's swinging dumb-bells for his health, when those springs are bubbling up in far-off pastures unsought by him!

Moreover, you must walk like a camel, which is said to be the only beast which ruminates when walking. When a traveler asked Wordsworth's servant to show him her master's study, she answered, "Here is his library, but his study is out of doors."

Living much out of doors, in the sun and wind, will no doubt produce a certain roughness of character—will cause a thicker cuticle to grow over some of the finer qualities of our nature, as on the face and hands, or as severe manual labor robs the hands of some of their delicacy of touch. So staying in the house, on the other hand, may produce a softness and smoothness, not to say thinness of skin, accompanied by an increased sensibility to certain impressions. Perhaps we should be more susceptible to some influences important to our intellectual and moral growth, if the sun had shone and the wind blown on us a little less: and no doubt it is a nice matter to proportion rightly the thick and thin skin. But methinks that is a scurf that will fall off fast enough—that the natural remedy is to be found in the proportion which the night bears to the day, the winter to the summer, thought to experience. There will be so much the more air and sunshine in our thoughts. The callous palms of the laborer are conversant with finer tissues of self-respect and heroism, whose touch thrills the heart, than the languid fingers of idleness. That is mere sentimentality that lies abed by day and thinks itself white, far from the tan and callus of experience.

When we walk, we naturally go to the fields and woods: what would become of us, if we walked only in a garden or a mall? Even some sects of philosophers have felt the necessity of importing the woods to themselves, since they did not go to the woods. "They planted groves and walks of Platanes," where they took *subdiales ambulationes* in porticos open to the air. Of course it is of no use to direct our steps to the woods, if they do not carry us thither. I am alarmed when it happens that I have walked a mile into the woods bodily, without getting there in spirit. In my afternoon walk I would fain forget all my morning occupations and my obligations to society. But it sometimes happens that I cannot easily shake off the village. The thought of some work will run in my head and I am not where my body is—I am out of my senses. In my walks I would fain return to my senses. What business have I in the woods, if I am thinking of something out of the woods? I suspect myself, and cannot help a shudder, when I find myself so implicated even in what are called good works—for this may sometimes happen.

My vicinity affords many good walks; and though for so many years I have walked almost every day, and sometimes for several days together, I have not yet exhausted them. An absolutely new prospect is a great happiness, and I can still get this any afternoon. Two or three hours' walking will carry me to as strange a country as I expect ever to see. A single farmhouse which I had not seen before is sometimes as good as the dominions of the King of Dahomey. There is in fact a sort of harmony discoverable between the capabilities of the landscape within a circle of ten miles' radius, or the limits of an afternoon walk, and the threescore years and ten of human life. It will never become quite familiar to you.

Nowadays almost all man's improvements, so called, as the building of houses and the cutting down of the forest and of all large trees, simply deform the landscape, and make it more and more tame and cheap. A people who would begin by burning the fences and let the forest stand! I saw the fences half consumed, their ends lost in the middle of the prairie, and some worldly miser with a surveyor looking after his bounds, while heaven had taken place around him, and he did not see the angels going to and fro, but was looking for an old post-hole in the midst of paradise. I looked again, and saw him standing in the middle of a boggy Stygian fen, surrounded by devils, and he had found his bounds without a doubt, three little stones, where a stake had been driven, and looking nearer, I saw that the Prince of Darkness was his surveyor.

I can easily walk ten, fifteen, twenty, any number of miles, commencing at my own door, without going by any house, without crossing a road except where the fox and the mink do: first along by the river, and then the brook, and then the meadow and the woodside. There are square miles in my vicinity which have no inhabitant. From many a hill I can see civilization and the abodes of man afar. The farmers and their works are scarcely more obvious than woodchucks and their burrows. Man and his affairs, church and state and school, trade and commerce, and manufactures and agriculture, even politics, the most alarming of them all—I am pleased to see how little space they occupy in the landscape. Politics is but a narrow field, and that still narrower highway yonder leads to it. I sometimes direct the traveler thither. If you would go to the political world, follow the great road—follow that market-man, keep his dust in your eyes, and it will lead you straight to it; for it, too, has its place merely, and does not occupy all space. I pass from it as from a bean-field into the forest, and it is forgotten. In one half-hour I can walk off to some portion of the earth's surface where a man does not stand from one year's end to another, and there, consequently, politics are not, for they are but as the cigar-smoke of a man. . . .

At present, in this vicinity, the best part of the land is not private property; the landscape is not owned, and the walker enjoys comparative freedom. But possibly the day will come when it will be partitioned off into so-called pleasure-grounds, in which a few will take a narrow and exclusive pleasure only—when fences shall be multiplied, and man-traps and other engines invented to confine men to the *public* road, and walking over the surface of God's earth shall be construed to mean trespassing on some gentleman's grounds. To enjoy a thing exclusively is commonly to exclude yourself from the true enjoyment of it. Let us improve our opportunities, then, before the evil days come.

What is it that makes it so hard sometimes to determine whither we will walk? I believe that there is a subtle magnetism in Nature, which, if we unconsciously yield to it, will direct us aright. It is not indifferent to us which way we walk. There is a right way; but we are very liable from heedlessness and stupidity to take the wrong one. We would fain take that walk, never yet taken by us through this actual world, which is perfectly symbolical of the path which we love to travel in the interior and ideal world; and sometimes, no doubt, we find it difficult to choose our direction, because it does not yet exist distinctly in our idea.

When I go out of the house for a walk, uncertain as yet whither I will bend my steps, and submit myself to my instinct to decide for me, I find, strange and whimsical as it may seem, that I finally and inevitably settle southwest, toward some particular wood or meadow or deserted pasture or hill in that direction. My needle is slow to settle—varies a few degrees, and does not always point due southwest, it is true, and it has good authority for this variation, but it always settles between west and south-southwest. The future lies that way to me, and the earth seems more unexhausted and richer on that side. The outline which would bound my walks would be, not a circle, but a parabola, or rather like one of those cometary orbits which have been thought to be non-returning curves, in this case opening westward, in which my house occupies the place of the sun. I turn round and round irresolute sometimes for a quarter of an hour, until I decide, for a thousandth time, that I will walk into the southwest or west. Eastward I go only by force; but westward I go free. Thither no business leads me. It is hard for me to believe that I shall find fair landscapes or sufficient wildness and freedom behind the eastern horizon. I am not excited by the prospect of a walk thither; but I believe that the forest which I see in the western horizon stretches uninterruptedly toward the setting sun, and there are no towns nor cities in it of enough consequence to disturb me. Let me live where I will, on this side is the city, on that the wilderness, and ever I am leaving the city more and more, and withdrawing into the wilderness. I should not lay so much stress on this fact, if I did not believe that something like this is the prevailing tendency of my countrymen. I must walk toward Oregon, and not toward Europe. And that way the nation is moving, and I may say that mankind progress from east to west. Within a few years we have witnessed the phenomenon of a southeastward migration, in the settlement of Australia; but this affects us as a retrograde movement, and, judging from the moral and physical character of the first generation of Australians, has not yet proved a successful experiment. The eastern Tartars think that there is nothing west beyond Thibet. "The world ends there," say they; "beyond there is nothing but a shoreless sea." It is unmitigated East where they live.

We go eastward to realize history and study the works of art and literature, retracing the steps of the race; we go westward as into the future, with a spirit of enterprise and adventure. The Atlantic is a Lethean stream, in our passage over which we have had an opportunity to forget the Old World and its institutions. If we do not succeed this time, there is perhaps one more chance for the race left before it arrives on the banks of the Styx; and that is in the Lethe of the Pacific, which is three times as wide. . . .

The West of which I speak is but another name for the Wild; and what I have been preparing to say is, that in Wildness is the preservation of the World. Every tree sends its fibres forth in search of the Wild. The cities import it at any price. Men plow and sail for it. From the forest and wilderness come the tonics and barks which brace mankind. Our ancestors were savages. The story of Romulus and Remus being suckled by a wolf is not a meaningless fable. The founders of every state which has risen to eminence have drawn their nourishment and vigor from a similar wild source. It was because the children of the Empire were not suckled by the wolf that they were conquered and displaced by the children of the northern forests who were.

I believe in the forest, and in the meadow, and in the night in which the corn grows. We require an infusion of hemlock spruce or arbor-vitæ in our tea. There is a difference between eating and drinking for strength and from mere gluttony. The Hottentots eagerly devour the marrow of the koodoo and other antelopes raw, as a matter of course. Some of our northern Indians eat raw the marrow of the Arctic reindeer, as well as various other parts, including the summits of the antlers, as long as they are soft. And herein, perchance, they have stolen a march on the cooks of Paris. They get what usually goes to feed the fire. This is probably better than stall-fed beef and slaughter-house pork to make a man of. Give me a wildness whose glance no civilization can endure—as if we lived on the marrow of koodoos devoured raw.

There are some intervals which border the strain of the wood thrush, to which I would migrate—wild lands where no settler has squatted; to which, methinks, I am already acclimated.

The African hunter Cumming tells us that the skin of the eland, as well as that of most other antelopes just killed, emits the most delicious perfume of trees and grass. I would have every man so much like a wild antelope, so much a part and parcel of nature, that his very person should thus sweetly advertise our senses of his presence, and remind us of those parts of nature which he most haunts. I feel no disposition to be satirical, when the trapper's coat emits the odor of musquash even; it is a sweeter scent to me than that which commonly exhales from the merchant's or the scholar's garments. When I go into their wardrobes and handle their vestments, I am reminded of no grassy plains and flowery meads which they have frequented, but of dusty merchants' exchanges and libraries rather.

A tanned skin is something more than respectable, and perhaps olive is a fitter color than white for a man—a denizen of the woods. "The pale white man!" I do not wonder that the African pitied him. Darwin the naturalist says, "A white man bathing by the side of a Tahitian was like a plant bleached by the gardener's art, compared with a fine, dark green one, growing vigorously in the open fields."

Ben Jonson exclaims,—

"How near to good is what is fair!"

So I would say,—

How near to good is what is *wild!*

Life consists with wildness. The most alive is the wildest. Not yet subdued to man, its presence refreshes him. One who pressed forward incessantly and never rested from his labors, who grew fast and made infinite demands on life, would always find himself in new country or wilderness, and surrounded by the raw material of life. He would be climbing over the prostrate stems of primitive forest-trees.

Hope and the future for me are not in lawns and cultivated fields, not in towns and cities, but in the impervious and quaking swamps. When, formerly, I have analyzed my partiality for some farm which I had contemplated purchasing, I have frequently found that I was attracted solely by a few square rods of impermeable and unfathomable bog—a natural sink in one corner of it. That was the jewel which dazzled me. I derive more of my subsistence from the swamps which surround my native town than from the cultivated gardens in the village. There are no richer parterres to my eyes than the dense beds of dwarf andromeda (*Cassandra calyculata*) which cover these tender places on the earth's surface. Botany cannot go farther than tell me the names of the shrubs which grow there—the high blueberry, panicled andromeda, lambkill, azalea, and rhodora—all standing in the quaking sphagnum. I often think that I should like to have my house front on this mass of dull red bushes, omitting other flower plots and borders, transplanted spruce and trim box, even graveled walks—to have this fertile spot under my windows, not a few imported barrowfuls of soil only to cover the sand which was thrown out in digging the cellar. Why not put my house, my parlor, behind this plot, instead of behind that meagre assemblage of curiosities, that poor apology for a Nature and Art, which I call my front yard? It is an effort to clear up and make a decent appearance when the carpenter and mason have departed, though done as much for the passer-by as the dweller within. The most tasteful front-yard fence was never an agreeable object of study to me; the most elaborate ornaments, acorn tops, or what not, soon wearied and disgusted me. Bring your sills up to the very edge of the swamp, then (though it may not be the best place for a dry cellar), so that there be no access on that side to citizens. Front yards are not made to walk in, but, at most, through, and you could go in the back way.

Yes, though you may think me perverse, if it were proposed to me to dwell in the neighborhood of the most beautiful garden that ever human art contrived, or else of a Dismal Swamp, I should certainly decide for the swamp. How vain, then, have been all your labors, citizens, for me!

My spirits infallibly rise in proportion to the outward dreariness. Give me the ocean, the desert, or the wilderness! In the desert, pure air and solitude compensate for want of moisture and fertility. The traveler Burton says of it: "Your *morale* improves; you become frank and cordial, hospitable and single-minded. . . . In the desert, spirituous liquors excite only disgust. There is a keen enjoyment in a mere animal existence." They who have been traveling long on the steppes of Tartary say, "On reëntering cultivated lands, the agitation, perplexity, and turmoil of civilization oppressed and suffocated us; the air seemed to fail us, and we felt every moment as if about to die of asphyxia." When I would recreate myself, I seek the darkest wood, the thickest and most interminable and, to the citizen, most dismal, swamp. I enter a swamp as a sacred place, a *sanctum sanctorum*. There is the strength, the marrow, of Nature. The wild-wood covers the virgin mould, and the same soil is good for men and for trees. A man's health requires as many acres of meadow to his prospect as his farm does loads of muck. There are the strong meats on which he feeds. A town is saved, not more by the righteous men in it than by the woods and swamps that surround it. A township where one primitive forest waves above while another primitive forest rots below—such a town is fitted to raise not only corn and potatoes, but poets and philosophers for the coming ages. In such a soil grew Homer and Confucius and the rest, and out of such a wilderness comes the Reformer eating locusts and wild honey.

To preserve wild animals implies generally the creation of a forest for them to dwell in or resort to. So it is with man. A hundred years ago they sold bark in our streets peeled from our own woods. In the very aspect of those primitive and rugged trees there was, methinks, a tanning principle which hardened and consolidated the fibres of men's thoughts. Ah! already I shudder for these comparatively degenerate days of my native village, when you cannot collect a load of bark of good thickness, and we no longer produce tar and turpentine.

The civilized nations—Greece, Rome, England—have been sustained by the primitive forests which anciently rotted where they stand. They survive as long as the soil is not exhausted. Alas for human culture! little is to be expected of a nation, when the vegetable mould is exhausted, and it is compelled to make manure of the bones of its fathers. There the poet sustains himself merely by his own superfluous fat, and the philosopher comes down on his marrow-bones. . . .

In literature it is only the wild that attracts us. Dullness is but another name for tameness. It is the uncivilized free and wild thinking in Hamlet and the Iliad, in all the scriptures and mythologies, not learned in the schools, that delights us. As the wild duck is more swift and beautiful than the tame, so is the wild—the mallard—thought, which 'mid falling dews wings its way above the fens. A truly good book is something as natural, and as unexpectedly and unaccountably fair and perfect, as a wild-flower discovered on the prairies of the West or in the jungles of the East. Genius is a light which makes the darkness visible, like the lightning's flash, which perchance shatters the temple of knowledge itself—and not a taper lighted at the hearth-stone of the race, which pales before the light of common day.

English literature, from the days of the minstrels to the Lake Poets—Chaucer and Spenser and Milton, and even Shakespeare, included—breathes no quite fresh and, in this sense, wild strain. It is an essentially tame and civilized literature, reflecting Greece and Rome. Her wilderness is a greenwood, her wild man a Robin Hood. There is plenty of genial love of Nature, but not so much of Nature herself. Her chronicles inform us when her wild animals, but not when the wild man in her, became extinct.

The science of Humboldt is one thing, poetry is another thing. The poet to-day, notwithstanding all the discoveries of science, and the accumulated learning of mankind, enjoys no advantage over Homer.

Where is the literature which gives expression to Nature? He would be a poet who could impress the winds and streams into his service, to speak for him; who nailed words to their primitive senses, as farmers drive down stakes in the spring, which the frost has heaved; who derived his words as often as he used them—transplanted them to his page with earth adhering to their roots; whose words were so true and fresh and natural that they would appear to expand like the buds at the approach of spring, though they lay half smothered between two musty leaves in a library—aye, to bloom and bear fruit there, after their kind, annually, for the faithful reader, in sympathy with surrounding Nature.

I do not know of any poetry to quote which adequately expresses this yearning for the Wild. Approached from this side, the best poetry is tame. I do not know where to find in any literature, ancient or modern, any account which contents me of that Nature with which even I am acquainted. You will perceive that I demand something which no Augustan nor Elizabethan age, which no *culture*, in short, can give. Mythology comes nearer to it than anything. How much more fertile a Nature, at least, has Grecian mythology its root in than English literature! Mythology is the crop which the Old World bore before its soil was exhausted, before the fancy and imagination were affected with blight; and which it still bears, wherever its pristine vigor is unabated. All other literatures endure only as the elms which overshadow our houses; but this is like the great dragon-tree of the Western Isles, as old as mankind, and, whether that does or not, will endure as long; for the decay of other literatures makes the soil in which it thrives.

The West is preparing to add its fables to those of the East. The valleys of the Ganges, the Nile, and the Rhine having yielded their crop, it remains to be seen what the valleys of the Amazon, the Plate, the Orinoco, the St. Lawrence, and the Mississippi will produce. Perchance, when, in the course of ages, American liberty has become a fiction of the past—as it is to some extent a fiction of the present—the poets of the world will be inspired by American mythology.

The wildest dreams of wild men, even, are not the less true, though they may not recommend themselves to the sense which is most common among Englishmen and Americans to-day. It is not every truth that recommends itself to the common sense. Nature has a place for the wild clematis as well as for the cabbage. Some expressions of truth are reminiscent—others merely *sensible*, as the phrase is—others prophetic. Some forms of disease, even, may prophesy forms of health. The geologist has discovered that the figures of serpents, griffins, flying dragons, and other fanciful embellishments of heraldry, have their prototypes in the forms of fossil species which were extinct before man was created, and hence "indicate a faint and shadowy knowledge of a previous state of organic existence." The Hindoos dreamed that the earth rested on an elephant, and the elephant on a tortoise, and the tortoise on a serpent; and though it may be an unimportant coincidence, it will not be out of place here to state, that a fossil tortoise has lately been discovered in Asia large enough to support an elephant. I confess that I am partial to these wild fancies, which transcend the order of time and development. They are the sublimest recreation of the intellect. The partridge loves peas, but not those that go with her into the pot.

In short, all good things are wild and free. There is something in a strain of music, whether produced by an instrument or by the human voice—take the sound of a bugle in a summer night, for instance—which by its wildness, to speak without satire, reminds me of the cries emitted by wild beasts in their native forests. It is so much of their wildness as I can understand. Give me for my friends and neighbors wild men, not tame ones. The wildness of the savage is but a faint symbol of the awful ferity with which good men and lovers meet.

I love even to see the domestic animals reassert their native rights—any evidence that they have not wholly lost their original wild habits and vigor; as when my neighbor's cow breaks out of her pasture early in the spring and boldly swims the river, a cold, gray tide, twenty-five or thirty rods wide, swollen by the melted snow. It is the buffalo crossing the Mississippi. This exploit confers some dignity on the herd in my eyes—already dignified. The seeds of instinct are preserved under the thick hides of cattle and horses, like seeds in the bowels of the earth, an indefinite period.

Any sportiveness in cattle is unexpected. I saw one day a herd of a dozen bullocks and cows running about and frisking in unwieldy sport, like huge rats, even like kittens. They shook their heads, raised their tails, and rushed up and down a hill, and I perceived by their horns, as well as by their activity, their relation to the deer tribe. But, alas! a sudden loud *Whoa!* would have damped their ardor at once, reduced them from venison to beef, and stiffened their sides and sinews like the locomotive. Who but the Evil One has cried "Whoa!" to mankind? Indeed, the life of cattle, like that of many men, is but a sort of locomotiveness; they move a side at a time, and man, by his machinery, is meeting the horse and the ox half-way. Whatever part the whip has touched is thenceforth palsied. Who would ever think of a *side* of any of the supple cat tribe, as we speak of a *side* of beef?

I rejoice that horses and steers have to be broken before they can be made the slaves of men, and that men themselves have some wild oats still left to sow before they become submissive members of society. Undoubtedly, all men are not equally fit subjects for civilization; and because the majority, like dogs and sheep, are tame by inherited disposition, this is no reason why the others should have their natures broken that they may be reduced to the same level. Men are in the main alike, but they were made several in order that they might be various. If a low use is to be served, one man will do nearly or quite as well as another; if a high one, individual excellence is to be regarded. Any man can stop a hole to keep the wind away, but no other man could serve so rare a use as the author of this illustration did. Confucius says, "The skins of the tiger and the leopard, when they are tanned, are as the skins of the dog and the sheep tanned." But it is not the part of a true culture to tame tigers, any more than it is to make sheep ferocious; and tanning their skins for shoes is not the best use to which they can be put. . . .

Here is this vast, savage, howling mother of ours, Nature, lying all around, with such beauty, and such affection for her children, as the leopard; and yet we are so early weaned from her breast to society, to that culture which is exclusively an interaction of man on man—a sort of breeding in and in, which produces at most a merely English nobility, a civilization destined to have a speedy limit.

In society, in the best institutions of men, it is easy to detect a certain precocity. When we should still be growing children, we are already little men. Give me a culture which imports much muck from the meadows, and deepens the soil—not that which trusts to heating manures, and improved implements and modes of culture only! . . .

I would not have every man nor every part of a man cultivated, any more than I would have every acre of earth cultivated: part will be tillage, but the greater part will be meadow and forest, not only serving an immediate use, but preparing a mould against a distant future, by the annual decay of the vegetation which it supports.

There are other letters for the child to learn than those which Cadmus invented. The Spaniards have a good term to express this wild and dusky knowledge, *Gramática parda*, tawny grammar, a kind of mother-wit derived from that same leopard to which I have referred.

We have heard of a Society for the Diffusion of Useful Knowledge. It is said that knowledge is power, and the like. Methinks there is equal need of a Society for the Diffusion of Useful Ignorance, what we will call Beautiful Knowledge, a knowledge useful in a higher sense: for what is most of our boasted so-called knowledge but a conceit that we know something, which robs us of the advantage of our actual ignorance? What we call knowledge is often our positive ignorance; ignorance our negative knowledge. By long years of patient industry and reading of the newspapers—for what are the libraries of science but files of newspapers?—a man accumulates a myriad facts, lays them up in his memory, and then when in some spring of his life he saunters abroad into the Great Fields of thought, he, as it were, goes to grass like a horse and leaves all his harness behind in the stable. I would say to the Society for the Diffusion of Useful Knowledge, sometimes,—Go to grass. You have eaten hay long enough. The spring has come with its green crop. The very cows are driven to their country pastures before the end of May; though I have heard of one unnatural farmer who kept his cow in the barn and fed her on hay all the year round. So, frequently, the Society for the Diffusion of Useful Knowledge treats its cattle.

A man's ignorance sometimes is not only useful, but beautiful—while his knowledge, so called, is oftentimes worse than useless, besides being ugly. Which is the best man to deal with—he who knows nothing about a subject, and, what is extremely rare, knows that he knows nothing, or he who really knows something about it, but thinks that he knows all?

My desire for knowledge is intermittent, but my desire to bathe my head in atmospheres unknown to my feet is perennial and constant. The highest that we can attain to is not Knowledge, but Sympathy with Intelligence. I do not know that his higher knowledge amounts to anything more definite than a novel and grand surprise on a sudden revelation of the insufficiency of all that we called Knowledge before—a discovery that there are more things in heaven and earth than are dreamed of in our philosophy. It is the lighting up of the mist by the sun. . . .

It is remarkable how few events or crises there are in our histories, how little exercised we have been in our minds, how few experiences we have had. I would fain be assured that I am growing apace and rankly, though my very growth disturb this dull equanimity—though it be with struggle through long, dark, muggy nights or seasons of gloom. It would be well if all our lives were a divine tragedy even, instead of this trivial comedy or farce. Dante, Bunyan, and others appear to have been exercised in their minds more than we: they were subjected to a kind of culture such as our district schools and colleges do not contemplate. Even Mahomet, though many may scream at his name, had a good deal more to live for, aye, and to die for, than they have commonly.

When, at rare intervals, some thought visits one, as perchance he is walking on a railroad, then, indeed, the cars go by without his hearing them. But soon, by some inexorable law, our life goes by and the cars return.

Gentle breeze, that wanderest unseen,
And bendest the thistles round Loira of storms,
Traveler of the windy glens,
Why hast thou left my ear so soon?

While almost all men feel an attraction drawing them to society, few are attracted strongly to Nature. In their reaction to Nature men appear to me for the most part, notwithstanding their arts, lower than the animals. It is not often a beautiful relation, as in the case of the animals. How little appreciation of the beauty of the landscape there is among us! We have to be told that the Greeks called the world Κόσμος, Beauty, or Order, but we do not see clearly why they did so, and we esteem it at best only a curious philological fact.

For my part, I feel that with regard to Nature I live a sort of border life, on the confines of a world into which I make occasional and transient forays only, and my patriotism and allegiance to the state into whose territories I seem to retreat are those of a moss-trooper. Unto a life which I call natural I would gladly follow even a will-o'-the-wisp through bogs and sloughs unimaginable, but no moon nor firefly has shown me the causeway to it. Nature is a personality so vast and universal that we have never seen one of her features. The walker in the familiar fields which stretch around my native town sometimes finds himself in another land than is described in their owners' deeds, as it were in some faraway field on the confines of the actual Concord, where her jurisdiction ceases, and the idea which the word Concord suggests ceases to be suggested. These farms which I have myself surveyed, these bounds which I have set up, appear dimly still as through a mist: but they have no chemistry to fix them; they fade from the surface of the glass, and the picture which the painter painted stands out dimly from beneath. The world with which we are commonly acquainted leaves no trace, and it will have no anniversary.

I took a walk on Spaulding's Farm the other afternoon. I saw the setting sun lighting up the opposite side of a stately pine wood. Its golden rays straggled into the aisles of the wood as into some noble hall. I was impressed as if some ancient and altogether admirable and shining family had settled there in that part of the land called Concord, unknown to me,—to whom the sun was servant,—who had not gone into society in the village,—who had not been called on. I saw their park, their pleasure-ground, beyond through the wood, in Spaulding's cranberry-meadow. The pines furnished them with gables as they grew. Their house was not obvious to vision; the trees grew through it. I do not know whether I heard the sounds of a suppressed hilarity or not. They seemed to recline on the sunbeams. They have sons and daughters. They are quite well. The farmer's cart-path, which leads directly through their hall, does not in the least put them out, as the muddy bottom of a pool is sometimes seen through the reflected skies. They never heard of Spaulding, and do not know that he is their neighbor—notwithstanding I heard him whistle as he drove his team through the house. Nothing can equal the serenity of their lives. Their coat-of-arms is simply a lichen. I saw it painted on the pines and oaks. Their attics were in the tops of the trees. They are of no politics. There was no noise of labor. I did not perceive that they were weaving or spinning. Yet I did detect, when the wind lulled and hearing was done away, the finest imaginable sweet musical hum—as of a distant hive in May—which perchance was the sound of their thinking. They had no idle thoughts, and no one without could see their work, for their industry was not as in knots and excrescences embayed.

But I find it difficult to remember them. They fade irrevocably out of my mind even now while I speak, and endeavor to recall them and recollect myself. It is only after a long and serious effort to recollect my best thoughts that I become again aware of their co-habitancy. If it were not for such families as this, I think I should move out of Concord.

We are accustomed to say in New England that few and fewer pigeons visit us every year. Our forests furnish no mast for them. So, it would seem, few and fewer thoughts visit each growing man from year to year, for the grove in our minds is laid waste—sold to feed unnecessary fires of ambition, or sent to mill—and there is scarcely a twig left for them to perch on. They no longer build nor breed with us. In some more genial season, perchance, a faint shadow flits across the landscape of the mind, cast by the *wings* of some thought in its vernal or autumnal migration, but, looking up, we are unable to detect the substance of the thought itself. Our winged thoughts are turned to poultry. . . .

We hug the earth—how rarely we mount! Methinks we might elevate ourselves a little more. We might climb a tree, at least. I found my account in climbing a tree once. It was a tall white pine, on the top of a hill; and though I got well pitched, I was well paid for it, for I discovered new mountains in the horizon which I had never seen before—so much more of the earth and the heavens. I might have walked about the foot of the tree for threescore years and ten, and yet I certainly should never have seen them. But, above all, I discovered around me—it was near the end of June—on the ends of the topmost branches only, a few minute and delicate red cone-like blossoms, the fertile flower of the white pine looking heavenward. I carried straightway to the village the topmost spire, and showed it to stranger jurymen who walked the streets—for it was court week—and to farmers and lumber-dealers and wood-choppers and hunters, and not one had ever seen the like before, but they wondered as at a star dropped down. Tell of ancient architects finishing their works on the tops of columns as perfectly as on the lower and more visible parts! Nature has from the first expanded the minute blossoms of the forest only toward the heavens, above men's heads and unobserved by them. We see only the flowers that are under our feet in the meadows. The pines have developed their delicate blossoms on the highest twigs of the wood every summer for ages, as well over the heads of Nature's red children as of her white ones; yet scarcely a farmer or hunter in the land has ever seen them.

Above all, we cannot afford not to live in the present. He is blessed over all mortals who loses no moment of the passing life in remembering the past. Unless our philosophy hears the cock crow in every barn-yard within our horizon, it is belated. That sound commonly reminds us that we are growing rusty and antique in our employments and habits of thought. His philosophy comes down to a more recent time than ours. There is something suggested by it that is a newer testament—the gospel according to this moment. He has not fallen astern; he has got up early and kept up early, and to be where he is is to be in season, in the foremost rank of time. It is an expression of the health and soundness of Nature, a brag for all the world—healthiness as of a spring burst forth, a new fountain of the Muses, to celebrate this last instant of time. Where he lives no fugitive slave laws are passed. Who has not betrayed his master many times since last he heard that note?

The merit of this bird's strain is in its freedom from all plaintiveness. The singer can easily move us to tears or to laughter, but where is he who can excite in us a pure morning joy? When, in doleful dumps, breaking the awful stillness of our wooden sidewalk on a Sunday, or, perchance, a watcher in the house of mourning, I hear a cockerel crow far or near, I think to myself, "There is one of us well, at any rate,"—and with a sudden gush return to my senses.

We had a remarkable sunset one day last November. I was walking in a meadow, the source of a small brook, when the sun at last, just before setting, after a cold, gray day, reached a clear stratum in the horizon, and the softest, brightest morning sunlight fell on the dry grass and on the stems of the trees in the opposite horizon and on the leaves of the shrub oaks on the hillside, while our shadows stretched long over the meadow eastward, as if we were the only motes in its beams. It was such a light as we could not have imagined a moment before, and the air also was so warm and serene that nothing was wanting to make a paradise of that meadow. When we reflected that this was not a solitary phenomenon, never to happen again, but that it would happen forever and ever, an infinite number of evenings, and cheer and reassure the latest child that walked there, it was more glorious still.

The sun sets on some retired meadow, where no house is visible, with all the glory and splendor that it lavishes on cities, and perchance as it has never set before—where there is but a solitary marsh hawk to have his wings gilded by it, or only a musquash looks out from his cabin, and there is some little black-veined brook in the midst of the marsh, just beginning to meander, winding slowly round a decaying stump. We walked in so pure and bright a light, gilding the withered grass and leaves, so softly and serenely bright, I thought I had never bathed in such a golden flood, without a ripple or a murmur to it. The west side of every wood and rising ground gleamed like the boundary of Elysium, and the sun on our backs seemed like a gentle herdsman driving us home at evening.

So we saunter toward the Holy Land, till one day the sun shall shine more brightly than ever he has done, shall perchance shine into our minds and hearts, and light up our whole lives with a great awakening light, as warm and serene and golden as on a bankside in autumn.

STUDY QUESTIONS

1. Explain what Thoreau means when he says, "In my walks I would fain return to my senses."
2. What arguments does Thoreau give to support his famous assertion that "in Wildness is the preservation of the World"?
3. What does Thoreau mean by the "Holy Land"? Have you ever taken a walk like the one he describes?
4. Who lives at Spaulding's Farm?

50

Christian Ecotheology and the Old Testament

Susan Power Bratton

Susan Power Bratton is a professional research biologist with the U.S. Park Service Cooperative Unit at the University of Georgia, Athens.

INTRODUCTION

The role of Judeo-Christian theology in developing environmental ethics has often been portrayed as negative or inadequate to modern problems. Historians, such as Lynn White, Jr. and Roderick Nash, have blamed either the Church or Biblical writings for encouraging abuse of nature.[1] Even modern theologians from the Christian tradition, such as John B. Cobb, Jr., find the traditional Judeo-Christian view inadequate and have suggested we must seek new theological or philosophical alternatives.[2] The question is a complex one, however, because the Western Church has, through the centuries, neglected the study of creation.[3] Interest in creation theology has been minor compared to other doctrinal issues such soteriology and Christology, and many Christian scholars have a better understanding of the Greek texts than of the older Hebrew writings. The attitude of the Church may, therefore, not have been based on a thorough analysis of Scripture. Further, the recognition of a global environmental crisis is a recent phenomenon; our current scientific understanding of the processes of environmental change was not available at the time the scriptures were written.

One possible way to develop a sound Christian ecotheology, and to determine a proper Christian approach to environmental ethics, is first to analyze scriptural texts concerning God-creation and man-creation relationships. We can then draw an accurate picture of what the Biblical writers originally meant when discussing creation. My purpose in this paper is to look at the works of modern Old Testament scholars, particularly Walther Eichrodt, Gerhard von Rad, and Claus Westermann, who have made substantial contributions to our current understanding of Hebrew theology, including theology of creation. I begin with an overview of important components of Old Testament thinking on both creation and God as creator, and discuss these ideas in relation to the development of a viable Christian ecotheology.

It should be pointed out at the beginning that modern Old Testament critics are not in agreement regarding the best methodology for analysis; nor do they all handle the question of the historical content of the texts in the same way. Some critics treat the Old Testament as if it has one central theme; others see it as presenting several themes. Some authors, such as Gerhard von Rad and Brevard Childs, attempt to include the entire canon in their work, or at least hold that all the books must be considered, while others, such as Claus Westermann, do not see all the books as equally important or interpretable in terms of central themes. (Westermann omits the wisdom literature from consideration in developing Old Testament theology.) Writers also differ greatly in how they relate the Old Testament to the New Testament: some disregard the New Testament entirely; others attempt to integrate the two sets of works, even though they are the products of different historical and cultural environments and were composed in different languages.[4] Although these disagreements among scholars are important to the detailed study of the Old Testament, they are generally beyond the scope of this paper. I attempt to avoid these conflicts by using the principles for Old Testament theology outlined by Hasel.[5] These are (in edited form):

(1) Biblical theology is to be treated as a historical-theological discipline,[6] and (2) the method must be historical and theological from the starting point.[7] These are quite different from many attempts at constructing ecotheologies or at evaluating the potential success of a Judeo-Christian ecotheology, in that most such efforts are either historical or theological, but not both.

(3) The only appropriate source for Old Testament theology is the Old Testament, not related literatures and traditions.[8] This principle is important to ecotheologies where authors have seen passages such as the Genesis accounts only as versions of myths derived from other sources. Hasel would reject this treatment as inadequate.

(4) An analysis need not follow the order of books in the canon, but should be based, as best can be determined, on the dates of the writings.[9]

(5) "An OT [Old Testament] theology not only seeks to know the theology of the various books, or groups of writings; it also attempts to draw together and present the major themes of the OT. . . . OT theology must allow its themes, motifs, and concepts to be formed for it by the OT itself."[10] We must, therefore, be careful not to do what many environmental writers have done and see the Old Testament largely from the point of view of our own current philosophical interests and cultural environment. If we are to evaluate Old Testament thought, we must do this with a recognition both of the writers' original intentions and the Hebrew world view. Old Testament theology must be based on what the Old Testament itself actually says about something. Further, we must discriminate between those concepts, events, or practices merely recorded or described in the texts and those which are affirmed or condoned. Since any discussion of creation theology must attempt to be eclectic, care must be taken not to replace the priorities of the ancient Hebrews with our own.

(6) "As the OT is interrogated for its theology, it answers first of all by yielding various theologies, namely those of the individual books and groups of writings, and then by yielding the theologies of various longitudinal themes. But the name of our discipline as theology of the OT is not only concerned to present and explicate the variety of different theologies. The concept foreshadowed by the name of the discipline has one theology in views, namely the theology of the OT."[11] For our purposes, this implies that in analyzing creation theology of the Old Testament, one has to look both at individual books and at the overall presentation of all the books. In light of Hasel's remarks, creation theology might be better termed the "creation theme" and seen as one of many theological strands, intimately connected to the other themes that combine to make Old Testament theology. In pursuing the creation theme one cannot depend solely on the first few chapters of Genesis, nor can one ignore the wisdom literature. Many writers who have tackled the question of the adequacy of Judeo-Christian environmental ethics have relied on one or two passages of Scripture and may thus have misunderstood the total thrust of the scriptural texts.[12]

(7) "The name 'theology of the Old Testament' implies the larger context of the Bible of which the New Testament is the other part. An integral OT theology must demonstrate its basic relationship to the NT or to NT theology."[13] This is, of course, critical in determining how the Old Testament should relate to Christian ecotheology.

Within this theological framework then, I attempt to develop an overview of the creation theology of the Old Testament, and try to avoid both excessive cultural distortion of the Old Testament's meaning and incomplete analysis of the Hebrew position.

THE CREATOR GOD

Although many environmental commentators begin the discussion of Judeo-Christian ecotheology with the question of man's dominion, most Old Testament commentators begin the discussion of creation theology with an investigation of God as creator. The modern reader tends to look for passages explaining man's relationship to nature, but this is of itself a poor way to start analyzing Old Testament texts, which are very theocentric. Westermann, for example, states: "A theology of the Old Testament has the task of summarizing and viewing together what the Old Testament as a whole, in all its sections, says about God."[14]

In order to answer our first question—how does the Old Testament present God as acting in the original creation?—we can begin by comparing the Hebrew presentation to those of neighboring cultures. The Old Testament has some striking parallels to Babylonian creation accounts[15] and was, of course, developed in an environment where there was considerable threat of syncretism with Caanite and Egyptian cultures. Despite some borrowing of imagery, the Hebrew picture of God as creator was quite distinct. In the Babylonian accounts, the god Marduk fights chaos and in the process creates life and order. In the Genesis accounts chaos is mentioned, but is conceptually different. The "Enuma Elish" epic of the Babylonians describes a watery chaos that is not only living matter, but is part of the first two principles, Apsu and Tiamat, "in whom all elements of the future universe were comingled."[16] Thus, in the Babylonian epic the universe is preexisting. In Genesis, God creates all matter and imparts life to His creatures via His divine breath.[17] The gods of the Babylonians arise out of the primeval chaos and are, therefore, merely deified natural forces. In the Hebrew accounts, even when Yahweh confronts chaos, "creation does not draw the deity into the flux of the world process . . . ,"[18] much less generate God or the godly. The Old Testament presents the universe as a creation of God, which He transcends. This is in marked contrast to both Babylonian and Caanite religions, where heavenly bodies, trees, and other natural objects were credited with supernatural power and thereby deified.

From the very beginning Yahweh is seen as acting spiritually and personally to create order. In the Genesis account and in the prophets, Yahweh creates through His word. These accounts provide us "with an idea of the absolute effortlessness of the divine creative action . . ." and also make clear that "if the world is the product of the creative word, it is therefore . . . sharply separated in nature from God himself—it is neither an emanation nor a mythically understood manifestation of the divine nature and power."[19] This has a number of implications for the relationship between God and creation. As Langdon Gilkey observes, no part of creation shares "divinity in any of its aspects, as if the being or substance of God had separated itself into many pieces to become the being of each creature."[20] Furthermore, the difference between God and His creation "is the result of God's creative act, not of a 'fall' or turning away from God . . ." and God's transcendence is itself a source of the "alienation" of creation from God.[21]

The spirit, or in Hebrew "Ruah" (breath of God), is instrumental in the original creative act, and is held throughout the Old Testament to be the very principle of life. Both man and animals come to life through this breath of God. If God withdraws His spirit, then "every creature must sink down in death."[22] It should be noted that this spirit is also seen as "the instrument of God in salvation history,"[23] "the consummating power of the new age,"[24] and "the power behind the life of the people of God."[25] Neither the spirit nor the creation event are independent of other major Old Testament themes. As Claus Westermann points out:

> . . . only he who is active in everything could be savior. Since God is One, the savior must also be the creator. It follows that in the Old Testament the history established by God's saving deed was expanded to include the be-

> ginning of everything that happens. The savior of Israel is the creator; the creator is the savior of Israel. What began in creation issues into Israel's history.[26]

Environmental commentators who restrict their reading to Genesis often miss the complex interweaving of the Old Testament concept of creation with other themes. Von Rad even proposes "that Israel was interested in creation not because of nature and its problems, but because of history."[27] The "history only" point of view is extreme, but a careful reading of the entire Old Testament shows creation as relating to history, salvation, the people of Israel, wisdom, and eschatological events. The references are scattered throughout the Old Testament, but are most numerous in Psalms, the Prophets, and the wisdom literature.

In the middle section of the Book of Isaiah[28] (chaps. 40–55), for example, the author combines two major Hebrew traditions, that of God the creator and of Yahweh of the Exodus as God active in history.[29] As von Rad suggests:

> A special feature in Deutero-Isaiah's thought about creation is, of course, that he does not regard creation as a work by itself, something additional to Yahweh's historical acts. . . . [F]or him creation is the first of Yahweh's miraculous historical acts and a remarkable witness to his will to save. The conclusive evidence for this 'soteriological' conception of creation is the fact that Deutero-Isaiah can at one time speak of Yahweh, the creator of the world and at another of Yahweh, the creator of Israel.

In Isaiah 40–55, the original act of creation and the creation of the people of Israel through the Exodus become types for a "new saving event" and thus are integrated into eschatology. Yahweh can, through the power of His word and His spirit, create a new kingdom of Israel. Deutero-Isaiah makes frequent use of the word *bara*, which is also used in the first chapters of Genesis to imply a creative act, such as the creation of Adam, which only God can perform. *Bara* is used not only to refer to the first creation, but also in establishing God's loving kindness toward Israel. Since both the original creation and the new saving event are accomplished by the Word and the Spirit of God, these deeds of creation are "personal, responsible" acts of God.[30]

Having established that God the creator is transcendent and that his creative acts include not only the creation of the universe via His word, but also the creation and salvation of his people, we now can ask, what are the characteristics, according to the Old Testament, of creation itself? Returning to the Genesis account we find that after the earth is separated from the seas "God saw that it was good . . . ,"[31] and that at the very end of the creation effort, "God saw everything that he had made, and behold, it was very good."[32] The English translation misses the full meaning of the Hebraic adjective *tob,* which can mean good and beautiful:

> In the concluding sentence the listener can thus also hear the echo: "Behold, it was very beautiful." The beauty of creation has its foundation in the will of the creator; beauty belongs to God's works. Whoever speaks about the work of the creator also speaks about the beautiful.[33]

The creation accounts include a judgment by God and it is a highly favorable one.

A second characteristic of creation is that it is blessed by God. When God said, "Be fruitful and multiply . . . ," he gave a blessing that continues outside of the events of salvation history.[34] Although many environmental critiques mention this statement, only in regard to humankind or actually treat the statement as if it were curse, the original intent was both universal and beneficial.

A third characteristic of creation is that it praises or glorifies God. In Psalm 148:3–10, for example, all creation is called on to praise God:

> Praise him, sun and moon,
>   praise him, all you shining stars!

Praise him you highest heavens,
and you waters above the heavens! . . .
Praise the Lord from the earth,
you sea monsters and all deeps,
fire, hail, snow and frost,
stormy wind fulfilling his command!

Mountains and all hills.
fruit trees and all cedars!
Beasts and all cattle,
creeping things and flying birds!

The same type of imagery is found in other books such as Job and Isaiah. Isaiah 55:12 reads:

For you shall go out in joy,
and be led forth in peace;
the mountains and the hills before you
shall break forth into singing,
and all the trees of the field shall
clap their hands.

Creation may also act as a party in a covenant lawsuit concerning the sins of the people of Israel, as in Micah 6:1–2:

Hear what the Lord says:
Arise, plead your case before the mountains
and let the hills hear your voice.
Hear, you mountains, the controversy of the Lord,
and you enduring foundations of the earth;
for the Lord has a controversy with his people;
and he will contend with Israel.

All this implies that God has a continuing concern for creation and that creation is continually able to respond to God. Further, in Deutero-Isaiah, creation is described as participating in the new saving event.

It should be noted that the Old Testament usually deals with creation in its entirety and there is no divine hierarchy within the whole. All is good and beautiful, while none is in any way God. For the ancient Hebrew, evil is not a necessary element in creation, and the evil now operating on and through creation will ultimately be defeated by the "new saving event" which will also be a new creative act.

ADAM IN CREATION

Having looked at the role of God, we now need to analyze how humankind relates to God in the midst of creation, and thereby relates to creation. The first problem concerns the statement in Genesis 1:26: "Then God said: 'Let us make man in our image, after our likeness. . . .'" This has been interpreted by some authors as simply setting man above creation, but it might be better interpreted as setting man in an especially close relationship to God. Von Rad states in his commentary on the passage that "God participates more intimately and intensively in this than in the earlier works of creation."[35] Westermann goes further and suggests that "this is not primarily a statement about human life, but about the creation of human life by God. The creature God is now planning is to stand in relationship to him; humans are to correspond to God so that something can happen between them and God, so that God can speak to them and they can answer."[36]

In the same verse, immediately after God declares that Adam is to be made in the divine image, we find the controversial passage: ". . . and let them have dominion over the fish of the sea, and over the birds of the air, and over cattle, and over all the earth and over every creeping thing that creeps upon the earth." Many environmental commentators have taken this as a presentation of earth to human beings as a gift to them, when in reality it is a more complex matter of setting man to work under the continuing authority of God. Even the creation in the image of God is not a gift or a declaration of simple superiority but a necessity required before Adam can rule. As von Rad suggests:

> This commission to rule is not considered as belonging to the definition of God's image; but is its consequence, i.e., that for which man is capable because of it. . . . Just as powerful earthly kings, to indicate their claim to dominion, erect an image of themselves in the

> provinces of their empire where they do not personally appear, so man is placed upon earth in God's sovereign emblem. He is really only God's representative, summoned to maintain and enforce God's claim to dominion over the earth.[37]

Eichrodt basically concurs when he writes:

> The connection between Man's creation in the image of God and his dominant position within the world of creatures is . . . indeed associated with the declaration of God's intention to create Man, being mentioned as a consequence of the especially close relationship of this creature to his Creator; but in the detailed exposition of the divine plan it is then quite clearly distinguished from this relationship as a separate item which has to be promised by a special creative act of blessing. Subjugation of the earth and dominion over its creatures bestows on the human race a common universal task, and in the execution of this task Man's special nature is to become visibly effective in that he is hereby made the responsible representative of the divine cosmic Lord.[38]

The command to take dominion was necessary for man to assume his special responsibility. That is, the command was both enabling and differentiating. Man's dominion was not a simple transfer of civil power, but was actually a spiritual transfer of authority centered in a special creative act.

After giving man dominion, God repeats the blessing given to the creatures and applies it to humankind: "And God blessed them, and God said multiply, and fill the earth and subdue it; and have dominion over the fish of the sea and over the birds of the air and over every living thing that moves upon the earth."[39] Again, environmental commentators have tended to emphasize the dominion aspect and have neglected the fact that God gives mankind exactly the same blessing as the rest of creation and that He requires that man assume the responsibility of representing God's interests. As Westermann states:

> These verses sum up what it means to be a human being; man is what he is precisely as a creature of God; his creature-state determines his capability and the meaning of his existence. What man is capable of is bestowed on him by the blessing. The blessing seen as controlling the power of fertility is a gift which man shares with the animals. It is something that binds man and beasts together.[40]

Thus, we have in this short text, man set in the image of God and therefore in special relationship to Him. Man is set above creation, but because he is given the same blessing as creation, he is therefore insured of creatureliness.

In Genesis 2, which scholars hold to be a second separate creation account combined with Genesis 1, "The Lord God took the man and put him in the garden of Eden to till it and keep it."[41] This passage does not give a portrait of man called to be despot, but presents man as called to serve. The verb *abad* translated as "to till" has the connotation not only of work, but of service, and can be translated as "to serve" or "to be a slave to." The word *shamar* "to keep" might also be translated "to watch" or "to preserve."[42] It is important that God's power placed man in Eden to serve and preserve the earth. God then allowed man to eat the fruits of the garden. Nowhere is it implied man has a right to do this, or that the earth is man's servant to be done with as he pleases.

Some authors have pointed out that the command "to take dominion" uses the Hebrew words *rada* and *kabas*, which are very strong and imply treading down or trampling.[43] All relevant texts need to be interpreted in a compatible fashion, however, and in this context some form of ravishing the earth is clearly not intended in Genesis 2:15. James Barr has suggested that nothing more is to be read into the Hebrew words of the dominion passage than "the basic needs of settlement and agriculture," including tilling the ground, and this interpretation is satisfactorily within the limits imposed by the passage on the keeping of Eden.[44]

Following Adam's placement in Eden comes the temptation and spread of sin in Genesis 3. Man, having been given a special relationship to God and a position of power over creation, breaks his relationship with God, who then reacts to the "increasingly grave violation of his order."[45] Adam's power is limited, and these limitations affect his ability to understand and know God. Adam also ceases to comprehend godly matters, such as executing dominion and receiving the blessings of Genesis 2.[46]

In the course of rebuking Adam and Eve for the transgression in Eden, God pronounces His punishment via a curse, which includes a curse of the ground. This curse puts a stumbling block in front of Adam who is still under the commission to work given in Genesis 2:15. Henceforth, "man's work is always in some way tied up with toil and effort; every area of work throws up its thorns and thistles which can not be avoided. . . ."[47] In basic recognition that what man needs must come from creation, the passage declares that the barriers to man successfully completing his tasks are found in his broken relationship with creation itself. Although theologians disagree as to whether all creation fell with Adam, nature is, at the very least, an innocent victim, under a curse because of man's sin and does not now fully produce its full fruits because of it.[48] From this it can be inferred that proper dominion is not an easy matter for man, who is struggling, because of the effects of sin, to relate not only to God, but also to other humans and all of nature. The breaking of the relationship with God and the expulsion from the garden also imply that dominion, as God intended it, can only be carried out with careful attention to the will of God and a tremendous effort. If dominion originally required God as both a lord and cooperator, God becomes even more necessary after the curse, because only God can lift it.

It should be recognized that much of the remainder of the Old Testament deals directly with the character of God, man's relationship to God, and other issues relevant to God's expectations of man. The establishment of covenant relationships, such as those made with Abraham or with Moses, present man with an opportunity to reestablish open communication with Yahweh. In the process of describing the expected man-God relationships the Prophets, for example, used a theology that included God as creator. Creation had "opened up the dimension of history and saving history" for Israel and therefore is repeatedly mentioned in her sacred texts.[49]

One last series of passages deserve analysis in regard to man's relationship to nature, and these are the references to creation and wisdom in the wisdom literature. This literature is relatively late and is the beginning of an attempt to seek out the mysteries of nature. It presents wisdom as preexisting before the rest of creation and as immanent in the world. God gave an order to his works at the very beginning and this order is separate from the activities of men. Unlike the modern who considers wisdom and knowledge to be solely the product of human endeavor, the scholars who wrote the wisdom literature considered wisdom something created by God which existed in creation, whether man was there or not. This literature also held that the way to wisdom was through fear (not literally fear, perhaps respect or awe is a better term) of Yahweh. If someone cares to pursue it, therefore, wisdom, the key not only to order in the universe, but also the key to correct behavior or proper action before God, is available.[50] A characteristic of the wisdom literature is "the determined effort to relate the phenomenon of the world, of 'nature' with its secrets of creation, to the saving revelation addressed to man."[51] These concerns are rarely discussed in the environmental literature; yet, they represent an extensive block of "how to" text which have parallels in other religions, including those of the Far East.

GOD'S CONTINUING INTERACTION WITH CREATION

Rather than stop with the Genesis accounts, we can now pose the question: does God continue to interact in creation and if so, how? Since there are relatively few direct references to creation in the New Testament and the references in the Old Testament are scattered, it is easy to concentrate on the Genesis passages and to begin to take a deist view, that is, to see God as creator only at the beginning of time. In the Old Testament God continues as creator throughout.

As mentioned previously, God acts in creation by both blessing and saving. Blessing is different from saving in that the continuing blessing of God "is a quiet, continuous, flowing, and unnoticed working . . . which can not be captured in moments or dates. . . . Evening and morning songs speak about the activity of a blessing God."[52] In addition, God also saves individuals and communities and will ultimately redeem creation as a whole. "The entire Old Testament thus speaks of God's continuous action in addition to the acts which occur once in his saving and judging deeds."[53]

Heschel makes the point that "the fundamental thought in the Bible is not creation, but God's care for his creation."[54] On one hand, we have what modern theologians call providence: the very ordering of nature is "a revelation of God's goodness, particularly his mercy and long suffering,"[55] and on the other hand, we have God working to bring about salvation. This includes miracles (or in Old Testament terms, God's mighty deeds) which may be regarded as creative acts. The Exodus, for example, was marked by a series of miraculous events, each of which may be viewed independently as a move of God the creator exercising his prerogatives with His handiwork. One may also see the entire Exodus, however, as a single new creative act of Yahweh.[56]

THE OLD TESTAMENT AND CHRISTIAN ECOTHEOLOGY

In the preceding discussion of the Old Testament, I showed that creation theology was more to the ancient Hebrew than a theology of original creative acts, it was a theology of God's continuing interaction with both humankind and nature. The concept of an ecotheology, based on relationships between God and humankind, God and nature, and humankind and nature, therefore, has a foundation in the ancient writings and is by scriptural precedent a legitimate Christian concern.

In developing a sound Christian ecotheology, we have to accept the fact that the majority of scriptural texts directly mentioning creation are in the Old Testament, and that any dependable theology of creation must be founded on extensive Hebrew scholarship.[57] We also have to accept the fact that some common criticisms of Judeo-Christian thinking—that it desacredizes nature and that it sets humankind in a special position—are basically correct interpretations of Old Testament theology. Concluding that these theological attributes of Judeo-Christian thinking produce an inadequate view of nature is an oversimplification, however.

Although the Old Testament clearly and purposefully removes any trace of divinity from nature, its discussions of creation are so spiritualized that they are difficult for the modern secular reader to comprehend fully. The very fact that nature praises God gives nature continuing intrinsic value. The Old Testament stresses the spiritual and aesthetic, neither of which can be given the definite material values our modern minds would prefer. We may actually be more comfortable with the sacred groves of the Baal worshipers, because they give individual natural features a special value and avoid the problem of having to grasp the entirety of creation as the work of God remaining under his care. The holism of the Old Testament in regard to nature presents an ironic stumbling block to categorized, materialistic modern thinking.

A second area of weakness in modern Christian interpretation concerns the ideas of "man in the image of God" and of "dominion." Many people remove these from their proper spiritual context and simply assume that the earth was placed here for the benefit of humankind. This is not, however, what the texts say. What the Genesis passages and much of the rest of the Old Testament speak for is a servitude of man to God, and as a result, to God's interests. The Old Testament records many failures in this regard, and man's inability to see his responsibilities begins when Cain asks: "Am I my brother's keeper?"[58]

The themes of servitude and of covenant relationships requiring responsibility to God are woven into the entire Old Testament. In the poetic crown of the Prophets, the second half of Isaiah, we find the "suffering servant" of Yahweh, and "might see in this description of one 'despised and rejected by men' the increasingly familiar pattern . . . dominion is servitude."[59] The Old Testament also makes clear that to serve God adequately one must be faithful, diligent, self-disciplined, giving, forgiving, etc. Dominion is not an easy task and can only be executed by continuing hard labor and overcoming major obstacles. The effort must be under God's direction and must be accomplished for God, not for personal gain.

In the United States, concepts of God and nature have had a variety of cultural associations. Barbara Novak claims that in the nineteenth century, for example, "Ideas of God's nature and of God in nature became hopelessly entangled, and only the most scrupulous theologians even tried to separate them."[60] Further, Americans have often seen the natural bounty of the continent as a special blessing, and have often extended their patriotism into a perceived divine appointment as the New Jerusalem.[61] The intent of the ancient Hebrews not withstanding, the romantic tendency to equate nature with God, on one hand, and the conservative tendency to promote civil religion as part of the national destiny, on the other, are likely to perpetuate the confusion and misinterpretation surrounding the "dominion passage."

Since the theme of creation in the Old Testament is not independent of other themes, current Christian attitudes about creation cannot be independent of other related issues such as salvation. The attitude that "the Lord will fix it all in the end" is eschatologically correct but ignores God's continuing care and blessing via his servants. Christ's parables of the householder who returns to check on the tenants working his estate and of the king who returns to see what his servants have done with the money they have been given are good models, since God has given us both a responsibility and a blessing.

If God created the cosmos as *tob*, humankind should help to maintain it as such and preserve its aesthetic values. Unfortunately, modern English translations miss the impact of the Hebrew word, and the modern reader may secularize the passage: "And God saw that it was good for something . . ." or "And God saw that it was full of material value." In "taking dominion" the Old Testament shows a concern both for the maintenance of the aesthetic values of creation and, in the Pentateuch and the writings of the prophets, for the just distribution of the resources available.

The Old Testament provides numerous texts on how one can serve God and the entire wisdom literature is dedicated to the topic of righteous action. The idea that the ancient writings are too weak and their view of the environment too primitive to be of much help today comes from superficial analysis or actual ignorance of the texts. The Old Testament attitude toward creation is so strongly spiritualized that it is hard for us to understand it. Moreover, the standards set on service to God are so high that most people, as the Old Testament so candidly illustrates in the case of the nation Israel, have no inclination to even try to meet them. Passages written centuries ago can be both difficult to understand and difficult to set in a meaningful modern context. It is important, however, that we avoid hasty judgments on one of the central roots of the Western spiritual heritage and that our approach to the Old Testament be both thoughtful and scholarly. Those interested in developing a Christian ecotheology should not be too cursory in their treatment of the Old Testament texts nor too glib in their assumptions concerning the will of God for creation. In-depth studies of specific writings and literatures, i.e., the psalms or the wisdom literature, and a search for more strands in the creation theme, will produce a better formed and sounder ecotheology and may also help to compensate for any past Christian theological neglect of God's role as creator.

NOTES

1. Lynn White, Jr., "The Historical Roots of Our Ecological Crisis," *Science* 155 (1967): 1203–1207; Roderick Nash, *Wilderness and the American Mind* (New Haven: Yale University Press, 1970).
2. John B. Cobb, Jr., *Is It Too Late? A Theology of Ecology* (Beverly Hills, Calif.: Bruce, 1972).
3. James B. Packer, "The Gospel: Its Content and Communication," in John Scott and Robert Coote, eds., *Down to Earth: Studies in Christianity and Culture* (Grand Rapids: William B. Eerdmans, 1980), pp. 97–114.
4. Gerhard Hasel, *Old Testament Theology: Basic Issues in the Current Debate* (Grand Rapids: William B. Eerdmans, 1972).
5. Ibid., pp. 169–183.
6. Ibid., p. 169.
7. Ibid., p. 171.
8. Ibid., p. 177.
9. Ibid., p. 179.
10. Ibid., p. 180.
11. Ibid., p. 181.
12. Discussions of some of the cultural results of this sort of limited interpretation may be found in Clarence Glacken, *Traces on the Rhodian Shore* (Berkeley: University of California Press, 1967) and in Keith Thomas, *Man and the Natural World: A History of Modern Sensibility* (New York: Pantheon Books, 1983).
13. Gerhard Hasel, *Old Testament Theology,* p. 183.
14. Claus Westermann, *Elements of Old Testament Theology* (Atlanta: John Knox Press, 1982), p. 9. Hereafter cited as Westermann, OTT.
15. Bernhard W. Anderson, *Creation Versus Chaos: The Reinterpretation of Mythical Symbolism in the Bible* (New York: Association Press, 1967).
16. Alexander Heidel, *The Babylonian Genesis* (Chicago: University of Chicago Press, 1951), p. 97.
17. Biblical scholars disagree on the question of whether the first chapter of Genesis really describes creation from nothing. Genesis 1:1 could also imply there was something present before creation, even if it were "chaos." Gerald Wilson has pointed out to me this is a semantic question, and alternate readings are possible.
18. Walther Eichrodt, *Theology of the Old Testament,* vol. 2 (Philadelphia: Westminster Press, 1967), p. 98.
19. Gerhard von Rad, *Old Testament Theology,* vol. 1 (New York: Harper & Row, 1962), p. 142 (hereafter cited as von Rad, OTT). This tradition is not without parallels in other cultures. The Egyptian god, Ptah, also creates by his word.
20. Langdon Gilkey, *Maker of Heaven and Earth* (New York: Doubleday and Co., 1959), p. 86.
21. Ibid., p. 87.
22. Eichrodt, *Theology,* p. 48.
23. Ibid., p. 50.
24. Ibid., p. 57.
25. Ibid., p. 60.
26. Westermann, OTT, p. 86.
27. Gerhard von Rad, *God at Work in Israel* (Nashville: Abingdon, 1980), p. 99.
28. There is some scholarly disagreement over the number of authors of the Book of Isaiah. Conservatives hold to one author. Some critics propose three or more. The term Deutero-Isaiah is used both for chapters 40–55 and the supposed author of this section.
29. Carroll Stuhlmueller, *The Prophets and the Word of God* (Notre Dame: Fides Publishers, 1964), p. 200.
30. Gerhard von Rad, *The Message of the Prophets* (New York: Harper & Row, 1962), p. 208.
31. Gen. 1:10; all translations are from *The New Oxford Annotated Bible* (New York: Oxford University Press, 1973).
32. Gen. 1:31.
33. Westermann, OTT, p. 93.
34. Gen. 1:22; Westermann, OTT, pp. 102–04.
35. Gerhard von Rad, *Genesis* (Philadelphia: Westminster Press, 1972), p. 57.
36. Westermann, OTT, p. 97.
37. Gerhard von Rad, *Genesis,* pp. 57–58.
38. Eichrodt, *Theology,* p. 127.
39. Gen. 1:28.
40. Claus Westermann, *Creation* (Philadelphia: Fortress Press, 1974), p. 49.
41. Gen. 2:15.

42. Loren Wilkinson, ed., *Earth Keeping: Christian Stewardship of Natural Resources* (Grand Rapids: Eerdmans, 1980), p. 209.
43. von Rad, *Genesis,* p. 59.
44. James Barr, "Man and Nature: The Ecological Controversy and the Old Testament," in David and Ellen Spring, eds., *Ecology and Religion in History* (New York: Harper & Row, 1974), pp. 63–64.
45. von Rad, *Genesis,* p. 155.
46. Claus Westermann, *Creation,* pp. 89–112.
47. Ibid., p. 102.
48. Paul Santmire, *Brother Earth: Nature God and Ecology in Time of Crisis* (New York: Thomas Nelson, 1970), pp. 163–68.
49. von Rad, OTT, p. 450.
50. Gerhard von Rad, *Wisdom in Israel* (Nashville: Abingdon, 1972), pp. 144–76.
51. von Rad, OTT, p. 449.
52. Westermann, OTT, p. 103.
53. Ibid.
54. Abraham Heschel, *The Prophets,* vol. 2 (New York: Harper & Row, 1962), p. 264.
55. William Dyrness, *Themes in Old Testament Theology* (Downers Grove: InterVarsity Press, 1979), p. 76.
56. Ibid., p. 77.
57. David Ehrenfeld justly criticized a draft of this paper for its lack of references to Jewish exegetes such as Rashni. Jewish interpretation of the Old Testament could not, of course, be based on Hasel's principles since Hasel accepts the New Testament as canonical. A thorough overview of Jewish scholarship on creation is a very needed addition to the environmental literature and would add further depth to our understanding of the Old Testament.
58. Gen. 4:9; Wilkinson, *Earth Keeping,* p. 212.
59. Ibid., p. 214.
60. Barbara Novak, *Nature and Culture: American Landscape Painting, 1825–1875* (New York: Oxford University Press, 1980), p. 3.
61. See, for example, Robert Linder and Richard Pierard, *Twilight of the Saints: Biblical Christianity and Civil Religion in America* (Downers Grove, Ill.: InterVarsity Press, 1978).

STUDY QUESTIONS

1. How does Bratton come to the conclusion that humanity is to represent God's interest in creation? What are God's interests, and how best are we to represent them?
2. How is God related to creation, according to the author? How are humans related to God? What is to be inferred from these relationships?
3. According to Bratton, what does "dominion" mean? What are the privileges and responsibilities inherent in dominion?
4. Is the Old Testament adequate in itself for constructing an environmental ethic? Why or why not?

51

The Rights of Animals and Unborn Generations

Joel Feinberg

Joel Feinberg teaches philosophy at the University of Arizona. He has written extensively on ethics, social philosophy, and the philosophy of law.

Every philosophical paper must begin with an unproved assumption. Mine is the assumption that there will still be a world five hundred years from now, and that it will contain human beings who are very much like us. We have it within our power now, clearly, to affect the lives of these creatures for better or worse by contributing to the conservation or corruption of the environment in which they must live. I shall assume furthermore that it is psychologically possible for us to care about our remote descendants, that many of us in fact do care, and indeed that we ought to care. My main concern then will be to show that it makes sense to speak of the rights of unborn generations against us, and that given the moral judgment that we ought to conserve our environmental inheritance for them, and its grounds, we might well say that future generations *do* have rights correlative to our present duties toward them. Protecting our environment now is also a matter of elementary prudence, and insofar as we do it for the next generation already here in the persons of our children, it is a matter of love. But from the perspective of our remote descendants it is basically a matter of justice, of respect for their rights. My main concern here will be to examine the concept of a right to better understand how that can be.

THE PROBLEM

To have a right is to have a claim *to* something and *against* someone, the recognition of which is called for by legal rules or, in the case of moral rights, by the principles of an enlightened conscience. In the familiar cases of rights, the claimant is a competent adult human being, and the claimee is an officeholder in an institution or else a private individual, in either case, another competent adult human being. Normal adult human beings, then, are obviously the sort of beings of whom rights can meaningfully be predicated. Everyone would agree to that, even extreme misanthropes who deny that anyone in fact has rights. On the other hand, it is absurd to say that rocks can have rights, not because rocks are morally inferior things unworthy of rights (that statement makes no sense either), but because rocks belong to a category of entities of whom rights cannot be meaningfully predicated. That is not to say that there are no circumstances in which we ought to treat rocks carefully, but only that the rocks themselves cannot validly claim good treatment from us. In between the clear cases of rocks and normal human beings, however, is a spectrum of less obvious cases, including some bewildering borderline ones. Is it meaningful or conceptually possible to ascribe rights to our dead ancestors? to individual animals? to whole species of animals? to plants? to idiots and madmen? to fetuses? to generations yet unborn? Until we know how to settle these puzzling cases, we cannot claim fully to grasp the concept of a right, or to know the shape of its logical boundaries.

One way to approach these riddles is to turn one's attention first to the most familiar and unproblematic instances of rights, note their most salient characteristics, and then compare the borderline cases with them, measuring as closely as possible the points of similarity and difference. In the end, the way we classify the borderline cases may depend on whether we are more impressed with the similarities or the differences between them and the cases in which we have the most confidence.

It will be useful to consider the problem of individual animals first because their case is the one that has already been debated with the most thoroughness by philosophers so that the dialectic of claim and rejoinder has now unfolded to the point where disputants can get to the end game quickly and isolate the crucial point at issue. When we understand precisely what *is* at issue in the debate over animal rights, I think we will have the key to the solution of all the other riddles about rights.

INDIVIDUAL ANIMALS

Almost all modern writers agree that we ought to be kind to animals, but that is quite another thing from holding that animals can claim kind treatment from us as their due. Statutes making cruelty to animals a crime are now very common, and these, of course, impose legal duties on people not to mistreat animals; but that still leaves open the question whether the animals, as beneficiaries of those duties, possess rights correlative to them. We may very well have duties *regarding* animals that are not at the same time duties *to* animals, just as we may have duties regarding rocks, or buildings, or lawns, that are not duties *to* the rocks, buildings, or lawns. Some legal writers have taken the still more extreme position that animals themselves are not even the directly intended beneficiaries of statutes prohibiting cruelty to animals. During the nineteenth century, for example, it was commonly said that such statutes were designed to protect human beings by preventing the growth of cruel habits that could later threaten human beings with harm too. Prof. Louis B. Schwartz finds the rationale of the cruelty-to-animals prohibition in its protection of animal lovers from affronts to their sensibilities. "It is not the mistreated dog who is the ultimate object of concern," he writes. "Our concern is for the feelings of other human beings, a large proportion of whom, although accustomed to the slaughter of animals for food, readily identify themselves with a tortured dog or horse and respond with great sensitivity to its sufferings." This seems to me to be factitious. How much more natural it is to say with John Chipman Gray that the true purpose of cruelty-to-animals statutes is "to preserve the dumb brutes from suffering." The very people whose sensibilities are invoked in the alternative explanation, a group that no doubt now includes most of us, are precisely those who would insist that the protection belongs primarily to the animals themselves, not merely to their own tender feelings. Indeed, it would be difficult even to account for the existence of such feelings in the absence of a belief that the animals deserve the protection in their own right and for their own sakes.

Even if we allow, as I think we must, that animals are the intended direct beneficiaries of legislation forbidding cruelty to animals, it does not follow directly that animals have legal rights, and Gray himself, for one, refused to draw this further inference. Animals cannot have rights, he thought, for the same reason they cannot have duties, namely, that they are not genuine "moral agents." Now, it is relatively easy to see why animals cannot have duties, and this matter is largely beyond controversy. Animals cannot be "reasoned with" or instructed in their responsibilities; they are inflexible and unadaptable to future contingencies; they are subject to fits of instinctive passion which they are incapable of repressing or controlling, postponing or sublimating. Hence, they cannot enter into contractual agreements, or make promises; they cannot be trusted; and they cannot (except within very narrow limits and for purposes of conditioning) be blamed for what would be called "moral failures" in a human being. They are therefore incapable of being moral subjects, of acting rightly or wrongly in the moral sense, of having, discharging, or breeching duties and obligations.

But what is there about the intellectual incompetence of animals (which admittedly disqualifies them for duties) that makes them logically unsuitable for rights? The most common reply to this question is that animals are incapable of *claiming* rights on their own. They cannot make motion, on their own, to courts to have their claims recognized or enforced; they cannot initiate, on their own, any kind of legal proceedings; nor are they capable of even understanding when their rights are being violated, of distinguishing harm from wrongful injury, and responding with indignation and an outraged sense of justice instead of mere anger or fear.

No one can deny any of these allegations, but to the claim that they are the grounds for disqualification of rights of animals, philosophers on the other side of this controversy have made convincing rejoinders. It is simply not true, says W. D. Lamont, that the ability to understand what a right is and the ability to set legal machinery in motion by one's own initiative are necessary for the possession of rights. If that were the case, then neither human idiots nor wee babies would have any legal rights at all. Yet it is manifest that both of these classes of intellectual incompetents have legal rights recognized and easily enforced by the courts. Children and idiots start legal proceedings, not on their own direct initiative, but rather through the actions of proxies or attorneys who are empowered to speak in their names. If there is no conceptual absurdity in this situation, why should there be in the case where a proxy makes a claim on behalf of an animal? People commonly enough make wills leaving money to trustees for the care of animals. Is it not natural to speak of the animal's right to his inheritance in cases of this kind? If a trustee embezzles money from the animal's account, and a proxy speaking in the dumb brute's behalf presses the animal's claim, can he not be described as asserting the animal's *rights*? More exactly, the animal itself claims its rights through the vicarious actions of a human proxy speaking in its name and in its behalf. There appears to be no reason why we should require the animal to understand what is going on (so the argument concludes) as a condition for regarding it as a possessor of rights.

. . . H. J. McCloskey, I believe, accepts the argument up to this point, but he presents a new and different reason for denying that animals can have legal rights. The ability to make claims, whether directly or through a representative, he implies, is essential to the possession of rights. Animals obviously cannot press their claims on their own, and so if they have rights, these rights must be assertable by agents. Animals, however, cannot be represented, McCloskey contends, and not for any of the reasons already discussed, but rather because representation, in the requisite sense, is always of interests, and animals (he says) are incapable of having interests.

Now, there is a very important insight expressed in the requirement that a being have interests if he is to be a logically proper subject of rights. This can be appreciated if we consider just why it is that mere things cannot have rights. Consider a very precious "mere thing"—a beautiful natural wilderness, or a complex and ornamental artifact, like the Taj Mahal. Such things ought to be cared for, because they would sink into decay if neglected, depriving some human beings, or perhaps even all human beings, of something of great value. Certain persons may even have as their own special job the care and protection of these valuable objects. But we are not tempted in these cases to speak of "thing-rights" correlative to custodial duties, because, try as we might, we cannot think of mere things as possessing interests of their own. Some people may have a duty to preserve, maintain, or improve the Taj Mahal, but they can hardly have a duty to help or hurt it, benefit or aid it, succor or relieve it. Custodians may protect it for the sake of a nation's pride and art lovers' fancy; but they don't keep it in good repair for "its own sake," or for "its own true welfare," or "well-being." A mere thing, however valuable to others, has no good of its own. The explanation of that fact, I suspect, consists in the fact that mere things have no conative life: no conscious wishes, desires, and hopes; or urges and impulses; or unconscious drives, aims, and goals; or latent tendencies, direction of growth, and natural fulfillments. Interests must be compounded somehow out of conations; hence mere things have no interests. *A fortiori*, they have no interests to be protected by legal or moral rules. Without interests a creature can have no "good" of its own, the achievement of which can be its due. Mere things are not loci of value in their own right, but rather their value consists entirely in their being objects of other beings' interests.

So far McCloskey is on solid ground, but one can quarrel with his denial that any animals but humans have interests. I should think that the trustee of funds willed to a dog or a cat is more than a mere custodian of the animal he protects. Rather his job is to look out for the interests of the animal and make sure no one denies it its due. The animal itself is the beneficiary of his dutiful services. Many of the higher animals at least have appetites, conative urges, and rudimentary purposes, the integrated satisfaction of which constitutes their welfare or good. We can, of course, with consistency treat animals as mere pets and deny that they have any rights; for most animals, especially those of the lower orders, we have no choice but to do so. But it seems to me, nevertheless, that in general, animals *are* among the sort of beings of whom rights can meaningfully be predicated and denied.

Now, if a person agrees with the conclusion of the argument thus far, that animals are the sort of beings that *can* have rights, and, further, if he accepts the moral judgment that we ought to be kind to animals, only one further premise is needed to yield the conclusion that some animals do in fact have rights. We must now ask ourselves for whose sake ought we to treat (some) animals with consideration and humaneness? If we conceive our duty to be one of obedience to authority, or to one's own conscience merely, or one of consideration for tender human sensibilities only, then we might still deny that animals have rights, even though we admit that they are the kinds of beings that *can* have rights. But if we hold not only that we ought to treat animals humanely but also that we should do so for the animals' own sake, that such treatment is something we owe animals as their due, something that can be claimed for them, something the withholding of which would be an injustice and a wrong, and not merely a harm, then it follows that we do ascribe rights to animals. I suspect that the moral judgments most of us make about animals do pass these phenomenological tests, so that most of us do believe that animals have rights, but are reluctant to say so because of the conceptual confusions about the notion of a right that I have attempted to dispel above.

Now we can extract from our discussion of animal rights a crucial principle for tentative use in the resolution of the other riddles about the applicability of the concept of a right, namely, that the sort of beings who *can* have rights are precisely those who have (or can have) interests. I have come to this tentative conclusion for two reasons: (1) because a right holder must be capable of being represented and it is impossible to represent a being that has no interests, and (2) because a right holder must be capable of being a beneficiary in his own person, and a being without interests is a being that is incapable of being harmed or benefitted, having no good or "sake" of its own. Thus, a being without interests has no "behalf" to act in, and no "sake" to act for. My strategy now will be to apply the "interest principle," as we can call it, to the other puzzles about rights, while being prepared to modify it where necessary (but as little as possible), in the hope of separating in a consistent and intuitively satisfactory fashion the beings who can have rights from those which cannot.

VEGETABLES

. . . Plants are not the kinds of being that can have rights. Plants are never plausibly understood to be the direct intended beneficiaries of rules designed to "protect" them. We wish to keep redwood groves in existence for the sake of human beings who can enjoy their serene beauty, and for the sake of generations of human beings yet unborn. Trees are not the sorts of beings who have their "own sakes," despite the fact that they have biological propensities. Having no conscious wants or goals of their own, trees cannot know satisfaction or frustration, pleasure or pain. Hence, there is no possibility of kind or cruel treatment of trees. In these morally crucial respects, trees differ from the higher species of animals.

Yet trees are not mere things like rocks. They grow and develop according to the laws of their own nature. Aristotle and Aquinas both took trees to have their own "natural ends." Why then do I deny them the status of beings with interests of their own? The reason is that an interest, however the concept is finally to be analyzed, presupposes at least rudimentary cognitive equipment. Interests are compounded out of *desires* and *aims*, both of which presuppose something like *belief*, or cognitive awareness. . . .

HUMAN VEGETABLES

Mentally deficient and deranged human beings are hardly ever so handicapped intellectually that they do not compare favorably with even the highest of the lower animals, though they are commonly so incompetent that they cannot be assigned duties or be held responsible for what they do. Since animals can have rights, then, it follows that human idiots and madmen can too. It would make good sense, for example, to ascribe to them a right to be cured whenever effective therapy is available at reasonable cost, and even those incurables who have been consigned to a sanatorium for permanent "warehousing" can claim (through a proxy) their right to decent treatment.

Human beings suffering extreme cases of mental illness, however, may be so utterly disoriented or insensitive as to compare quite unfavorably with the brightest cats and dogs. Those suffering from catatonic schizophrenia may be barely distinguishable in respect to those traits presupposed by the possession of interests from the lowliest vegetables. So long as we regard these patients as potentially curable, we may think of them as human beings with interests in their own restoration and treat them as possessors of rights. We may think of the patient as a genuine human person inside the vegetable casing struggling to get out, just as in the old fairy tales a pumpkin could be thought of as a beautiful maiden under a magic spell waiting only the proper words to be restored to her true self. Perhaps it is reasonable never to lose hope that a patient can be cured, and therefore to regard him always as a person "under a spell" with a permanent interest in his own recovery that is entitled to recognition and protection.

What if, nevertheless, we think of the catatonic schizophrenic and the vegetating patient with irreversible brain damage as absolutely incurable? Can we think of them at the same time as possessed of interests and rights too, or is this combination of traits a conceptual impossibility? Shocking as it may at first seem, I am driven unavoidably to the latter view. If redwood trees and rosebushes cannot have rights, neither can incorrigible human vegetables. The trustees who are designated to administer funds for the care of these unfortunates are better understood as mere custodians than as representatives of their interests since these patients no longer have interests. It does not follow that they should not be kept alive as long as possible: that is an open moral question not foreclosed by conceptual analysis. Even if we have duties to keep human vegetables alive, however, they cannot be duties *to* them. We may be obliged to keep them alive to protect the sensibilities of others, or to foster humanitarian tendencies in ourselves, but we cannot keep them alive for their own good, for they are no longer capable of having a "good" of their own. Without awareness, expectation, belief, desire, aim, and purpose, a being can have no interests; without interests, he cannot be benefited; without the capacity to be a beneficiary, he can have no rights. But there may nevertheless be a dozen other reasons to treat him as if he did.

FETUSES

If the interest principle is to permit us to ascribe rights to infants, fetuses, and generations yet unborn, it can only be on the grounds that interests can exert a claim upon us even before their possessors actually come into being, just the reverse of the situation respecting dead men where interests are respected even after their possessors have ceased to be. Newly born infants are surely noisier than mere vegetables, but they are just barely brighter. They come into existence, as Aristotle said, with the capacity to acquire concepts and dispositions, but in the beginning we suppose that their consciousness of the world is a "blooming, buzzing confusion." They do have a capacity, no doubt from the very beginning, to feel pain, and this alone may be sufficient ground for ascribing both an interest and a right to them. Apart from that, however, during the first few hours of their lives, at least, they may well lack even the rudimentary intellectual equipment necessary to the possession of interests. Of course, this induces no moral reservations whatever in adults. Children grow and mature almost visibly in the first few months so that those future interests that are so rapidly emerging from the unformed chaos of their earliest days seem unquestionably to be the basis of their present rights. Thus, we say of a newborn infant that he has a right now to live and grow into his adulthood, even though he lacks the conceptual equipment at this very moment to have this or any other desire. A new infant, in short, lacks the traits necessary for the possession of interests, but he has the capacity to acquire those traits, and his inherited potentialities are moving quickly toward actualization even as we watch him. Those proxies who make claims in behalf of infants, then, are more than mere custodians: they are (or can be) genuine representatives of the child's emerging interests, which may need protection even now if they are to be allowed to come into existence at all.

The same principle may be extended to "unborn persons." After all, the situation of fetuses one day before birth is not strikingly different from that a few hours after birth. The rights our law confers on the unborn child, both proprietary and personal, are for the most part, placeholders or reservations for the rights he shall inherit when he becomes a full-fledged interested being. The law protects a potential interest in these cases before it has even grown into actuality, as a garden fence protects newly seeded flower beds long before blooming flowers have emerged from them. The unborn child's present right to property, for example, is a legal protection offered now to his future interest, contingent upon his birth, and instantly voidable if he dies before birth. As Coke put it: "The law in many cases hath consideration of him in respect of the apparent expectation of his birth"; but this is quite another thing than recognizing a right actually to be born. Assuming that the child will be born, the law seems to say, various interests that he will come to have after birth must be protected from damage that they can incur even before birth. Thus prenatal injuries of a negligently inflicted kind can give the newly born child a right to sue for damages which he can exercise through a proxy-attorney and in his own name any time *after* he is born.

There are numerous other places, however, where our law seems to imply an unconditional right to be born, and surprisingly no one seems ever to have found that idea conceptually absurd. One interesting example comes from an article given the following headline by the *New York Times:* "Unborn Child's Right Upheld Over Religion." A hospital patient in her eighth month of pregnancy refused to take a blood transfusion even though warned by her physician that "she might die at any minute and take the life of her child as well." The ground of her refusal was that blood transfusions are repugnant to the principles of her religion (Jehovah's Witnesses). The Supreme Court of New Jersey expressed uncertainty over the constitutional question of whether a nonpregnant adult might refuse on religious grounds a blood transfusion pronounced necessary to her own survival, but the court nevertheless ordered the patient in the present case to receive the transfusion on the grounds that "the unborn child is entitled to the law's protection."

It is important to reemphasize here that the questions of whether fetuses do or ought to have rights are substantive questions of law and morals open to argument and decision. The prior question of whether fetuses are the kind of beings that can have rights, however, is a conceptual, not a moral, question, amenable only to what is called "logical analysis," and irrelevant to moral judgment. The correct answer to the conceptual question, I believe, is that unborn children are among the sort of beings of whom possession of rights can meaningfully be predicated, even though they are (temporarily) incapable of having interests, because their future interests can be protected now, and it does make sense to protect a potential interest even before it has grown into actuality. The interest principle, however, makes perplexing, at best, talk of a noncontingent fetal right to be born; for fetuses, lacking actual wants and beliefs, have no actual interest in being born, and it is difficult to think of any other reason for ascribing any rights to them other than on the assumption that they will in fact be born.

FUTURE GENERATIONS

We have it in our power now to make the world a much less pleasant place for our descendants than the world we inherited from our ancestors. We can continue to proliferate in ever greater numbers, using up fertile soil at an even greater rate, dumping our wastes into rivers, lakes, and oceans, cutting down our forests, and polluting the atmosphere with noxious gases. All thoughtful people agree that we ought not to do these things. Most would say that we have a duty not to do these things, meaning not merely that conservation is morally required (as opposed to merely desirable) but also that it is something due our descendants, something to be done for their sakes. Surely we owe it to future generations to pass on a world that is not a used up garbage heap. Our remote descendants are not yet present to claim a livable world as their right, but there are plenty of proxies to speak now in their behalf. These spokesmen, far from being mere custodians, are genuine representatives of future interests.

Why then deny that the human beings of the future have rights which can be claimed against us now in their behalf? Some are inclined to deny them present rights out of a fear of falling into obscure metaphysics, by granting rights to remote and unidentifiable beings who are not yet even in existence. Our unborn great-great-grandchildren are in some sense "potential" persons, but they are far more remotely potential, it may seem, than fetuses. This, however, is not the real difficulty. Unborn generations are more remotely potential than fetuses in one sense, but not in another. A much greater period of time with a far greater number of causally necessary and important events must pass before their potentiality can be actualized, it is true; but our collective posterity is just as certain to come into existence "in the normal course of events" as is any given fetus now in its mother's womb. In that sense the existence of the distant human future is no more remotely potential than that of a particular child already on its way.

The real difficulty is not that we doubt whether our descendants will ever be actual, but rather that we don't know who they will be. It is not their temporal remoteness that troubles us so much as their indeterminacy—their present facelessness and namelessness. Five centuries from now men and women will be living where we live now. Any given one of them will have an interest in living space, fertile soil, fresh air, and the like, but that arbitrarily selected one has no other qualities we can presently envision very clearly. We don't even know who his parents, grandparents, or great-grandparents are, or even whether he is related to us. Still, whoever these human beings may turn out to be, and whatever they might reasonably be expected to be like, they will have interests that we can affect, for better or worse, right now. That much we can and do know about them. The identity of the owners of these interests is now necessarily obscure, but the fact of their interest-ownership is crystal clear, and that is all that is necessary to certify the coherence of present talk about their rights. We can tell, sometimes, that shadowy forms in the spatial distance belong to human beings, though we know not who or how many they are; and this imposes a duty on us not to throw bombs, for example, in their direction. In like manner, the vagueness of the human future does not weaken its claim on us in light of the nearly certain knowledge that it will, after all, be human.

Doubts about the existence of a right to be born transfer neatly to the question of a similar right to come into existence ascribed to future generations. The rights that future generations certainly have against us are contingent rights: the interests they are sure to have when they come into being (assuming of course that they will come into being) cry out for protection from invasions that can take place now. Yet there are no actual interests, presently existent, that future generations, presently nonexistent, have now. Hence, there is no actual interest that they have in simply coming into being, and I am at a loss to think of any other reason for claiming that they have a right to come into existence (though there may well be such a reason). Suppose then that all human beings at a given time voluntarily form a compact never again to produce children, thus leading within a few decades to the end of our species. This of course is a wildly improbable hypothetical example but a rather crucial one for the position I have been tentatively considering. And we can imagine, say, that the whole world is converted to a strange ascetic religion which absolutely requires sexual abstinence for everyone. Would this arrangement violate the rights of anyone? No one can complain on behalf of presently nonexistent future generations that their future interests which give them a contingent right of protection have been violated since they will never come into existence to be wronged. My inclination then is to conclude that the suicide of our species would be deplorable, lamentable, and a deeply moving tragedy, but that it would violate no one's rights. Indeed if, contrary to fact, all human beings could ever agree to such a thing, that very agreement would be a symptom of our species' biological unsuitability for survival anyway.

CONCLUSION

For several centuries now human beings have run roughshod over the lands of our planet, just as if the animals who do live there and the generations of humans who will live there had no claims on them whatever. Philosophers have not helped matters by arguing that animals and future generations are not the kinds of beings who can have rights now, that they don't presently qualify for membership, even "auxiliary membership," in our moral community. I have tried in this essay to dispel the conceptual confusions that make such conclusions possible. To acknowledge their rights is the very least we can do for members of endangered species (including our own). But that is something.

STUDY QUESTIONS

1. What is the difference between a moral question and a conceptual question? How is this differentiation important to Feinberg's argument?
2. Is Feinberg correct in his criteria for rights?
3. Compare Feinberg's criteria for rights with Noonan's criteria for rights (chapter nine, selection 45). What differences do you see?
4. Why, according to Feinberg, is it important to consider the rights of future generations? Exactly what rights do future generations have against the present?

52

The Nature and Possibility of an Environmental Ethic

Tom Regan

Tom Regan teaches philosophy at North Carolina State University. Best known as a defender of animal rights, he is the author of many important books and articles on ethics, including *The Case for Animal Rights*.

I. INTRODUCTION

Is an environmental ethic possible? Answers to this question presuppose that we have an agreed upon understanding of the nature of an environmental ethic. Evidently we do not, and one fundamental problem for this burgeoning area of ethics is to say what such an ethic must be like. In this essay, I characterize and defend, although incompletely, a particular conception of an environmental ethic. My modest objective is to show that there is something worth thinking about completing.

II. TWO CONDITIONS OF AN ENVIRONMENTAL ETHIC

The conception I favor accepts the following two conditions:

1. An environmental ethic must hold that there are nonhuman beings that have moral standing.
2. An environmental ethic must hold that the class of those beings that have moral standing includes but is larger than the class of conscious beings—that is, all conscious beings and some nonconscious beings must be held to have moral standing.

If both conditions are accepted, then a theory that satisfies neither of them is not a false environmental ethic; it is not an environmental ethic at all. Any theory that satisfies (1), but does not satisfy (2) might be regarded as a theory "on the way to becoming" such an ethic, in that it satisfies a necessary condition, but, since it fails to satisfy condition (2), it fails to qualify as a genuine environmental ethic. Only theories that satisfy (2), on the conception advanced here, can properly be regarded as environmental ethics, whether true, reasonable, or otherwise.

Though only a necessary condition, (1) assists us in distinguishing between (*a*) an ethic *of* the environment, and (*b*) an ethic *for the use* of the environment. Suppose we think that only the interests of human beings matter morally. Then it certainly would be possible to develop a homocentric ethic for the use of the environment. Roughly speaking, such an ethic would declare that the environment ought to be used so that the quality of human life, including possibly that of future generations, ought to be enhanced. I do not say developing such an ethic (what I shall call "a management ethic") would be simple or unimportant, but a management ethic falls short of an ethic of the environment, given the conditions stated earlier. It restricts the loci of value to the lives and interests of *human* beings, whereas an environmental ethic requires that we recognize the moral standing of nonhumans.

L. W. Sumner advances considerations that, if accepted, would lead us to an ethical theory that satisfies condition (1) and thereby takes us beyond a management ethic. Sumner argues that the lives and interests of nonhuman animals, not just those of human beings, ought to be taken into account in their own right. Recognition of this fact, he states, marks "the beginning of a genuine environmental consciousness." Other thinkers have advanced similar arguments. Despite many differences, these thinkers share the belief that only *conscious* beings can have moral standing. I refer to theories that embody this belief as *kinship theories* because they grow out of the idea that beings resembling humans in the quite fundamental way of being conscious, and thus to this extent kin to us, have moral standing. I have more to say about kinship theories below (Section IV).

Management and kinship theories are clearly distinct. Management theories direct us, for example, to preserve wildlife if this is in the interest of human beings, including (possibly) the interest of generations yet unborn. Animals in the wild are not themselves recognized as having interests or value that ought to be taken into account. Given a kinship ethic, however, wild animals, in their own right, figure in the moral arithmetic, though precisely how we are to carry out the required computations is unclear. When, for example, there is a clash between the preservation of wild animals and the economic development of the wilderness, it is unclear how conflicting interests are to be weighed. The value of survival of how many caribou, for example, equals the disvalue of how much financial loss to oil investors in Northern Canada?

Whatever difficulties may exist for management or kinship theories in weighing conflicting claims, however, these difficulties seem to be compounded if we move beyond these theories to ones that meet condition (2), for then we are required, it appears, to deal with the possibility that human and animal interests might come into conflict with the survival or flourishing of nonconscious beings, and it is extremely doubtful whether such conflicts can *in principle* admit of rational adjudication.

I do not wish to minimize the difficulties that attend the development of an environmental ethic that is consequentialist in nature (e.g., some form of utilitarianism). There are difficulties of comparison, perhaps themselves great enough to foreclose the possibility of developing a consequentialist environmental ethic. I have more to say on this matter as we proceed. First, though, a more fundamental problem requires our attention. Is it even logically possible for a theory to meet both the conditions I have recommended for an environmental ethic? The answer clearly is no if compelling reasons can be given for limiting moral standing *only* to conscious beings. In the following section I reject three arguments that attempt to establish this restriction.

III. ARGUMENTS AGAINST THE POSSIBILITY OF AN ENVIRONMENTAL ETHIC

The first argument to be considered I call the "interest argument":

The Interest Argument

1. The only beings that can have moral standing are those beings that can have interests.
2. The only beings that can have interests are those that have the capacity for consciousness.
3. Therefore, the only beings that can have moral standing are beings having the capacity for consciousness.

Now, this argument, as I have argued elsewhere against a similar argument, has apparent plausibility because it exploits an ambiguity in the concept of something having interests. To speak of *A*'s interest in *x* might mean either (*a*) that *A* is interested in (wants, desires, hopes for, cares about, etc.) *x*, or (*b*) that *x* is in *A*'s interest (that *x* will contribute to *A*'s good, or well-being, or welfare). Clearly *if* the only beings that can have moral standing are those that can be interested in things (have desires, wants, etc.), then only conscious beings can have moral standing. The idea of nonconscious beings having desires, or wants, at least in any literal sense, seems plainly unintelligible. If, however, we mean beings that can be benefited or harmed by what is given or denied them, then it is an open question whether the class of beings which can have moral standing is coextensive with the class of beings having the capacity for consciousness. Perhaps other beings can have a good or value that can be advanced or retarded depending on what is done to them. The interest argument provides us with no resolution of this question, and so fails to demonstrate the impossibility of an environmental ethic.

A second argument, which I shall call the "sentience argument," closely resembles the interest argument and is vulnerable to the same type of objection:

The Sentience Argument

1. The only beings that can have moral standing are those that are sentient.
2. The only beings that are sentient are those that have the capacity for consciousness.
3. Therefore, the only beings that can have moral standing are those that have the capacity for consciousness.

I limit my critical remarks to step (1). How might it be supported? First, one might argue that only sentient beings have interests; that is, one might seek to support the sentience argument by invoking the interest argument, but since we have shown this latter argument is incomplete, at best, this defense of the sentience argument must bear the same diagnosis. A second defense consists in claiming that it is "meaningless" to think that nonconscious beings possibly have moral standing. This is unconvincing. *If* it is meaningless, there ought to be some way of illuminating why this is so, and this illumination is not provided by the mere charge of meaninglessness itself. Such a defense has more the aura of rhetoric than of philosophy.

A third defense consists in arguing that the only beings having moral standing are those having value in their own right, *and* that only sentient beings have value of this kind. This defense, as I argue in a moment, is a token of the argument type I call the "goodness argument." Its major liability is that by itself it provides no justification for its two central claims—namely, (*a*) that only beings that can have value in their own right can have moral standing, and (*b*) that only sentient beings have value in their own right. For reasons to which I come below, I believe (*b*) is false while (*a*) is true. Meanwhile, neither is self-evident and so each stands in need of rational defense, something not provided by the sentience argument itself.

The final argument to be considered is the goodness argument:

The Goodness Argument

1. The only beings that can have moral standing are those that can have a good of their own.
2. The only beings that can have a good of their own are those capable of consciousness.
3. Therefore, the only beings that can have moral standing are those capable of consciousness.

Premise (1) of the goodness argument seems to identify a fundamental presupposition of an environmental ethic. The importance of this premise is brought out when we ask for the grounds on which we might rest the obligation to preserve any existing *x*. Fundamentally, two types of answer are possible. First, preserving *x* is necessary to bring about future good or prevent future evil for beings other than *x*; on this account *x*'s existence has instrumental value. Second, the obligation we have might be to *x* itself, independently of *x*'s instrumental value, because x has a good or value in its own right. Given our conditions for an environmental ethic, not all of the values recognized in nonconscious nature can be instrumental. Only if we agree with premise (1) of the goodness argument, therefore, can we have a necessary presupposition of an environmental ethic. How inherent goodness or value can be intelligibly ascribed to nonconscious beings is a difficult question, one we shall return to later (Section V). At present, we must consider the remainder of the goodness argument, since if sound, it rules out the logical possibility of nonconscious beings having a good or value of their own.

"The only beings that have a good of their own," premise (2) states, "are those capable of consciousness." What arguments can be given to support this view? I have examined suggested answers elsewhere at length. What these arguments come to in the end, if I am right, is the thesis that consciousness is a logically necessary condition of having only a *certain kind* of good of one's own, happiness. Thus, though we may speak metaphorically of a "happy azalea" or a "contented broccoli," the only sorts of beings that literally can have happiness are conscious beings. There is no disputing this. What is disputable is the tacit assumption that this is the *only* kind of good or value a given x can have in its own right. Unless or until a compelling supporting argument is supplied, for limiting inherent goodness to happiness, the goodness argument falls short of limiting moral standing to just those beings capable of consciousness.

Four truths result if the argument of this section is sound. First, an environmental ethic must recognize that the class of beings having moral standing is larger than the class of conscious beings. Second, the basis on which an environmental ethic must pin this enlargement is the idea that nonconscious beings can have a good or value in their own right. Third, though it remains to be ascertained what this goodness or value is, it is not happiness; and fourth, efforts to show that nonconscious beings cannot have moral standing fail to show this. The conclusion we guardedly reach, then, is that the impossibility of an environmental ethic has not been shown.

IV. ARGUMENTS AGAINST THE NECESSITY OF AN ENVIRONMENTAL ETHIC

We turn now to a second series of objections against an environmental ethic, all of which concede that it is *possible* that nonconscious beings may have value in themselves, and thus that it is *possible* to develop an environmental ethic, but which all deny, nonetheless, that there are good enough reasons for holding that nonconscious beings *do* have a good or value in their own right. There are, these objections hold in common, alternative ways of accounting for the moral dimensions of our relationship to the environment which are rationally preferable to postulating inherent value in it. Thus, while granting the possibility of an environmental ethic, the four views about to be considered deny its necessity.

The Corruption of Character Argument

Advocates of this argument insist that it is wrong to treat nonconscious nature in certain ways—for example, unchecked strip mining—but account for this by urging that people who engage in such activities tend to become similarly ruthless in their dealings with people. Just as Kant speculated that those who act cruelly to animals develop the habit of cruelty, and so are likely to be cruel to their fellow man, so similarly those who indiscriminately destroy the natural environment will develop destructive habits that will in time wreak havoc on their neighbor. Our duties to act toward the environment in certain ways are thus explained without our having to postulate value *in* the environment.

This argument cannot be any stronger than its central empirical thesis that those who treat the environment in certain ways will be inclined to treat their fellow humans in analogous ways. I do not believe there is any hard empirical evidence at hand which supports this hypothesis. Comparing the crime rates of strip miners and accountants would probably provide much hard empirical data against it. Indeed, one cannot help wondering if the very reverse habits might not be fostered by instructing persons to do anything they want to the environment, if no person is harmed, while insisting on strict prohibitions in our dealings with persons. There would appear to be just as much (or just as little) empirical data to support this hypothesis as there is to support the hypothesis central to the corruption of character argument. On empirical grounds, the argument lacks credibility.

The Utilitarian Argument

To speak of *the* utilitarian argument is misleading. A wide variety of utilitarian arguments is possible, even including positions that hold that some nonconscious beings do have value in their own right. I restrict my attention to forms of utilitarianism that deny this, focusing mainly on hedonistic utilitarianism.

Abstractly and roughly, hedonistic utilitarianism holds that an action is right if no alternative action produces a better balance of pleasure over pain for all those affected. A theory of this type is "on the way to becoming" an environmental ethic if, as utilitarians since Bentham have argued, animals are sentient, and thus, given the utilitarian criteria, have moral standing. But hedonistic utilitarianism fails to satisfy the second condition of an environmental ethic and thus fails to qualify as an ethic of the environment. Its shortcomings are highlighted by asking, "Why not plastic trees? Why not lawns of astro-turf, or mountains of papier-mâché suitably coated with vinyl to withstand harsh weather?" Stories find their way almost daily into the popular press which illustrate that a plastic environment is increasingly within the reach of modern technology. If, as Martin Krieger argues, "the demand for rare environments is a learned one," then "conscious public choice can manipulate this learning so that the environments which people learn to use and want reflect environments which are likely to be available at low cost." Thus, as Mark Sagoff sees it, "This is the reason that the redwoods are (given Krieger's position) replaceable by plastic trees." "The advertising that created rare environments," Krieger writes, "can create plentiful (e.g., plastic) substitutes."

A hedonistic utilitarianism cannot quarrel over the *source* of environmentally based pleasures, whether they arise from real stands of redwoods or plastic replicas. Provided only that the pleasures are equal in the relevant respects (e.g., of equal duration and intensity), both are of equal value. To the suggestion that pleasures rooted in real redwoods are "higher" or "nobler" than those rooted in plastic ones, the reply must be that there is a long, untold story surrounding the idea of "higher" and "lower" pleasures, that no hedonistic utilitarian has yet succeeded in telling this story, and, indeed, that it may be inconsistent for a hedonistic utilitarian to believe this. Other things being equal, if a plastic environment can give rise to pleasures equal in value to those arising out of a natural environment, we will have just as much or as little reason to preserve the latter as to manufacture the former. Moreover, if the pleasures flowing from the manufactured environment should happen to outweigh those accompanying the natural environment, we would then have greater reason to enlarge the world of plastic trees and reduce that of living ones.

The Embodiment of Cultural Values Argument

According to this argument, the natural environment, or certain parts of it, symbolize or express certain of our culture's values. In Sagoff's words, "Our rivers, forests, and wildlife . . . serve our society as paradigms of concepts we cherish," for example, freedom, integrity, power. "A wild area may be powerful, majestic, free; an animal may express courage, innocence, purpose, and strength. As a nation we value these qualities: the obligation toward nature is an obligation toward them." Thus, we are to preserve the environment because in doing so we preserve these natural expressions of the values of our culture.

This argument is not intended to be utilitarian. The claim is not made that the consequences of natural preservation will be better, all considered, if we preserve wilderness areas, for example, than if we allow their development for commercial purposes. Whether we ought to preserve wilderness is not to be settled by cost–benefit analysis. Rather, since our obligation is to the cultural values themselves embodied in nature, our obligation to preserve the natural environment cannot be overridden by or, for that matter, based upon calculations about the comparative value of the consequences of respecting them. The propriety of respect for cultural values is not a consequence of its being useful to respect them. . . .

What the embodiment argument has in common with the other arguments considered here is the view that environmental objects have no value in their own right. This view is perhaps not so clear in this case because the embodiment argument carries with it "objectivist" presuppositions. Advocates of this argument do hold that the environment itself has certain objective qualities—for example, majesty, power, freedom. These *qualities* are *in* nature no less than are, say, chromosomes. But the *value* these qualities have is no less than are, say, chromosomes. But the *value* these qualities have is not something else that is *in them* independently of the dominant interest of a given culture ("our cultural heritage"). On the contrary, what qualities in nature are valuable is a consequence of what qualities are essential in one's cultural heritage. For example, if freedom is a dominant cultural value, then, since animals or rivers in the wild embody this quality, they have value and ought to be preserved. What *qualities* a natural object expresses is an objective question, but the *value* a natural object has is not something it has objectively in its own right, but only as it happens to embody those qualities valued by one's culture.

The embodiment argument provides an enormously important and potentially powerful basis for a political-legal argument on behalf of the preservation of American wilderness. It is easy to see how one may use it to argue for "what is best" in American society: freedom, integrity, independence, loyalty, and so on. It is the speculative developer rather than the conservationist who seems to be running roughshod over our nation's values. On this view, Disneyland, not Yosemite, seems un-American. Moreover, by insisting that such values as freedom and integrity cannot be trumped even if the consequences of doing so are utilitarian, advocates of the embodiment argument strike a blow that helps to counter the developer's argument that the commercial development of the wilderness will bring about better consequences, more pleasure to more people, than leaving it undeveloped. The embodiment argument replies that, though this may be true, it just so happens to be irrelevant. Given the nature of values such as freedom, integrity, and the like, it is inappropriate to destroy their expression in nature in the name of utilitarian consequences. The rhetorical force of such arguments can be great, and can be a powerful practical weapon in the war for the preservation of nature.

But the embodiment argument does not have comparable philosophical strength. Two problems in particular haunt it. First, how are we to establish what our culture's values are? Sagoff states that we are to do this by consulting our artistic (cultural) history. If we do this, however, we do not hear a chorus singing the same tune; on the contrary, there is much dissonance, some of which Sagoff himself mentions (e.g., the view of wilderness as an adversary to be tamed versus the view that it is to be cherished). Moreover, even if we were to arrive at a cultural consensus, the basis that Sagoff recommends is suspiciously elitist, reminding one of Ross's reference to "the judgment of the best people" in the determination of what is valuable. Implicit in Sagoff's way of establishing what our cultural values are is an evaluative estimate of whose judgment to trust. The cards are stacked against the developer from the outset, since developers normally do not have the time or inclination to dabble in arts, history, and letters. It is not surprising, therefore, that developers take a back seat to the values of freedom and integrity. The argument is indeed potentially a powerful political weapon, but fundamental questions go begging.

A second problem is no less severe. Cultural values can be relative, both between different cultures and within the same culture at different times. Thus, even were we to concede that *our* cultural values up to now call for the preservation of nature, that would entail nothing whatever about what environmental policies ought to be pushed in *other* countries (e.g., in Kenya or India, where many species of wild animals are endangered). Nor would it guarantee even in our own country that future environmental policy should continue to be protectionist. If plastic trees are possible, our culture might evolve to prefer them over real ones, in which case the embodiment of cultural values argument would sanction replacing natural with plastic flora and fauna.

Sagoff recognizes the possibility of significant changes in a culture's dominant values. He observes that we might "change the nature of our cultural heritage" and then goes on to imagine what a changed cultural heritage might be like—for example, imagining a four-lane highway painted through *Christina's World*. But I do not believe he realizes the full significance of the issues at hand. If, as he supposes, hedonistic utilitarianism falls victim to a *reductio* by allowing that a plastic environment might be just as good or better than a living one, consistency requires that we reach the same judgment *re* the embodiment of cultural values argument. That argument, too, allows that a plastic environment might be just as good or better than a natural one, *if* the dominant values of our culture were to become plasticized.

I conclude this section, therefore, not by claiming to have shown that nonconscious natural objects do have a good or value of their own, independent of human interests. I only conclude that the principal arguments that might be advanced for thinking that we can reasonably account for our duties regarding the environment short of postulating such value in nature fail to do so. Thus, neither the possibility of, nor the need for, postulating that nonconscious natural objects have a value that is independent of human interests, has been rationally undermined.

V. INHERENT GOODNESS?

In this final section, I offer some tentative remarks about the nature of inherent goodness, emphasizing their tentativeness and incompleteness. I comment first on five different but related ideas.

1. The presence of inherent value in a natural object is independent of any awareness, interest, or appreciation of it by any conscious being.

   This does not tell us what objects are inherently good or why, only that *if* an object is inherently good its value must *inhere in* (*be in*) the object itself. Inherent value is not conferred upon objects in the manner of an honorary degree. Like other properties in nature, it must be discovered. . . . There is value *in* the world, if natural objects are inherently valuable.

2. The presence of inherent value in a natural object is a consequence of its possessing those other properties that it happens to possess.

This follows from (1), given the further assumption that inherent goodness is a consequential or supervenient property. By insisting that inherent goodness depends on an object's *own* properties, the point made in (1), that inherent goodness is a value possessed by the object independently of any awareness, is reemphasized. *Its* goodness depends on its properties.

3. The inherent value of a natural object is an objective property of that object.

   This differs from but is related to Sagoff's objectivity of the freedom and majesty of natural objects. Certain stretches of the Colorado River, for example, are free, not subjectively, but objectively. The freedom expressed by (or in) the river is an objective fact. But this goes beyond Sagoff's position by insisting that *the value of the river's being free* also is an objective property of the river. If the river is inherently good, in the sense explained in (1), then it is a *fact about the river* that it is good inherently.

4. The inherent value of a natural object is such that toward it the fitting attitude is one of admiring respect.

   This brings out the appropriateness of regarding what is inherently valuable in a certain way and thus provides a way of connecting what is inherently valuable in the environment with an ideal of human nature. In part, the ideal in question bids us be appreciative of the values nature holds, not merely as a resource to be used in the name of human interests, but inherently. The ideal bids us, further, to regard what is inherently valuable with both admiration and respect. Admiration is fitting because not everything in nature is inherently valuable (what *is* is to be admired both because of its value *and* because of its comparative uniqueness). Respect is appropriate because this is a fitting attitude to have toward whatever has value in its own right. One must realize that its being valuable is not contingent on one's happening to value it, so that to treat it *merely* as a means to human ends is to mistreat it. Such treatment shows a lack of respect for its being something that has value independently of these ends. Thus, I fall short of the ideal if I gratuitously destroy what has inherent value, or even if I regard it merely as having value only relative to human desires. But half the story about ideals of human nature remains untold if we leave out the part about the value inherent in those things toward which we can act in the ideal way. So it is vital to insist that our having ideals is neither to deny nor diminish the further point that this ideal requires postulating inherent value in nature, independently of these ideals.

5. The admiring respect of what is inherently valuable in nature gives rise to the preservation principle.

   By the "preservation principle" I mean a principle of nondestruction, noninterference, and, generally, nonmeddling. By characterizing this in terms of a principle, moreover, I am emphasizing that preservation (letting be) be regarded as a moral imperative. Thus, if I regard wild stretches of the Colorado River as inherently valuable and regard these sections with admiring respect, I also think it is wrong to destroy these sections of the river; I think one ought not to meddle in the river's affairs, as it were.

A difficult question to answer is whether the preservation principle gives us a principle of absolute or of prima facie duty. It is unclear how it can be absolute, for it appears conceivable that in some cases letting be what is at present inherently good in nature may lead to value diminution or loss in the future. For example, because of various sedimentary changes, a river that is now wild and free might in time be transformed into a small, muddy creek; thus, it might be necessary to override the preservation principle to preserve or increase what is inherently valuable in nature. Even if the preservation principle is regarded as being only prima facie, however, it is still possible to agree on at least one point with those who regard it as absolute, that is, the common rejection of the "human interests principle," which says:

> Whenever human beings can benefit more from overriding the preservation principle than if they observe it, the preservation principle ought to be overridden.

This principle *must* be rejected by anyone who accepts the preservation principle because it distorts the very conception of goodness underlying that principle. If the sort of value natural objects possess is inherent, then one fails to show a proper respect for these objects if one is willing to destroy them merely on the grounds that this would benefit human beings. Since such destruction is precisely what the human interests principle commits one to, one cannot *both* accept the preservation principle, absolute or prima facie, *and* also accept the human interests principle. The common enemies of all preservationists are those who accept the human interests principle.

This brief discussion of the preservation principle may also cast some light on the problem of making intelligible cross-species value comparisons, for example, in the case of the survival of caribou versus the economic development of wilderness. The point preservationists must keep in mind is that to ask how many caribou lives equal in value the disvalue of how much economic loss is unanswerable because it is an improper question. It confounds two incommensurable kinds of good, the inherent good of the caribou with the noninherent good of economic benefits. Indeed, because these kinds of good are incommensurable, a utilitarian or consequentialist environmental ethic, which endeavors to accommodate both kinds of goodness, is doomed to fail. The inherent value of the caribou cannot be cashed in terms of human economic benefit, and such a theory ends up providing us with no clear moral direction. For the preservationist, the proper philosophical response to those who would uproot the environment in the name of human benefit is to say that they fail to understand the very notion of something being inherently good.

Two questions that I have not endeavored to answer are: (*a*) what, if anything in general, makes something inherently good, and (*b*) how can we know, if we can, what things are inherently good? The two questions are not unrelated. If we could establish that there is something (x) such that, whenever any object (y) has x it is inherently good, we could then go on to try to establish how we can know that any object has x. Unfortunately, I now have very little to say about these questions, and what little I do have to say concerns only how not to answer them.

Two possible answers to question (*a*) merit mention. The first is that an object (x) is inherently good if it is good of its kind. This is a view I have assumed and argued for elsewhere, but it now appears to me to be completely muddled. The concept of inherent goodness cannot be reduced to the notion of something being good of its kind, for though I believe that we can conceive of the goodness any x has, if x is good of its kind, as a value it has in its own right, there is no reason to believe that we ought to have the attitude of admiring respect toward what is (merely) good of its kind. A good murderer is good-of-his-kind, but is not thereby a proper object of admiring respect, and similarly in the case of natural objects. The type of inherent goodness required by an environmental ethic is conceptually distinct from being good of its kind.

The second possible answer to (*a*) is that life makes something inherently good. To what extent this view is connected with Schweitzer's famous ethic of reverence for life, or with Kenneth Goodpaster's recent argument for considering life as a necessary and sufficient condition of something being "morally considerable," I do not know, and I cannot here explore these matters in detail. But limiting the class of beings that have inherent value to the class of living beings seems to be an arbitrary decision and one that does not serve well as a basis for an environmental ethic. That it appears arbitrary is perhaps best seen by considering the case of beauty, since in nature, as in art, it is not essential to the beauty of an object to insist that something living be involved.

STUDY QUESTIONS

1. How does Regan respond to Feinberg?
2. Most would agree that conscious beings in nature have rights. How does Regan build the case for rights of the nonconscious beings?
3. How is the management theory different from the kinship theory? How do both differ from Regan's view?
4. What is the human interest principle? What are the problems with it, and how does Regan avoid this principle?

53

Economic Growth and Environmental Quality: How to Have Both

Barry Commoner

Barry Commoner, the author of a number of influential books including *The Closing Circle* and *The Politics of Energy,* is the director of the Center for the Biology of Natural Systems at Queens College of the University of New York.

There is a widespread perception that the relation between environmental quality and economic development is governed by unavoidable contradictions. Business people warn that if we insist on rigorous control of industrial pollution, plants will be closed and jobs lost. Ecologically-minded economists insist that out of respect for the inherent limits of the ecosystem, we must give up economic growth. Ecological ideologues, citing the parsimonious principles of ecology, preach against efforts to improve the standard of living.

These are familiar ideas, but I believe that they are wrong. My thesis is the reverse: that properly understood, the principles of ecology show how the economy can grow, the standard of living and jobs can be increased, and, at the same time, environmental quality can be improved. To understand why this constructive course is possible, we must undertake a *fundamental* analysis of the origin of the environmental problems that have plagued the world in recent years. To see how this goal can be achieved, we must translate this understanding into a new political direction.

THE ORIGINS OF ENVIRONMENTAL DEGRADATION

Ever since the early 1970s, when increasing pollution led to the rediscovery of the environment, there have been serious disagreements about the cause of the problem. A number of ecologists were convinced that human society behaves like any other group of organisms, in which the natural tendency toward geometric growth of the population is held in check by the resultant strains on the ecosystem that supports it. They concluded that the rapid degradation of the environment is caused by unrestrained growth of the population—and by an affluent lifestyle. According to the ecologist Paul R. Ehrlich, for example:

> The causal chain of the deterioration [of the environment] is easily followed to its source. Too many cars, too many factories, too much detergent, too much pesticide, multiplying contrails, inadequate sewage treatment plants, too little water, too much carbon dioxide—all can be traced easily to *too many people*.

And according to another ecologist, Walter S. Howard:

> The affluent society has become an effluent society. The six percent of the world's population in the United States produces 70 percent or more of the world's solid wastes.

These statements are quoted from *The Closing Circle*, in which I analyzed the actual evidence regarding the role of population and affluence in the sharp increases in environmental pollution that occurred in the United States in the 25 years after World War II. The analysis showed that neither the concurrent increase in population nor in affluence (as measured, for example, by per capita consumption of specific goods) could account for more than a very small part of the five- to ten-fold increase in pollution. Thus, in that period of time, while the United States population increased by about 42 percent, nitrogen oxides emitted by automobiles, which cause smog, increased by 63 percent; the emission of phosphate into surface waters, which causes eutrophication, increased by 700 percent; the production of non-returnable beer bottles, which contributes to trash, rose by 595 percent. Nor did affluence increase appreciably in that period of time. Per capita consumption of food—and for that matter, of beer—remained about constant; per capita consumption of textiles increased by only 9 percent; per capita housing increased by only 6 percent. Clearly, neither the increase in population, nor in affluence, nor both together could account for the very large increase in environmental pollution.

The analyses presented in *The Closing Circle* revealed the real cause of the sharp post-war increase in environmental degradation: *changes in the technology of production*. Thus, U.S. automobile engines produced much more nitrogen oxide than before because they were redesigned, after World War II, to run at high compression and temperature. This caused oxygen and nitrogen in the cylinder air to react and form nitrogen oxides, and therefore smog. The huge increase in phosphate emissions into surface waters coincided exactly with the phosphate content of detergents, which had rapidly replaced soap as cleaning agents. The sharp increase in glass trash from beer bottles resulted from the replacement of returnable bottles, which were used about 40 times before being discarded, with non-returnable ones, which are discarded after only one use.

A dramatic transformation in production technology has occurred in every industrialized country since World War II. A series of natural products—soap, cotton, wool, wood, paper and leather—have been displaced by synthetic petrochemical products: detergents, synthetic fibers and plastics. In agriculture, natural fertilizers have been displaced by chemical ones, and natural methods of pest control such as crop rotation have been displaced by synthetic pesticides. In transportation, rail freight has been displaced by truck freight. In manufacturing, the amount of energy, especially in the form of electricity, used per unit of goods produced has increased sharply. In commerce, reusable goods have been replaced by throw-aways.

These changes have intensified environmental degradation. For the benefits that farmers gain from the heavy use of nitrogen fertilizer, we pay the price of eutrophication of surface waters. Since truck freight uses four times more fuel than rail freight per ton of freight carried per mile, more fuel is burned, worsening air pollution. With the increased use of electricity comes acid rain from coal-burning plants, and radioactive hazards from nuclear plants. Throw-away plastics have sharply increased the burden of trash, which, when incinerated, generate toxic emissions.

When trash was incinerated before 1940, it contained all the components of present-day municipal waste—paper, food waste, discarded metal and glass—*except plastics*. Since then, the introduction of chlorinated plastics into the waste stream has converted incinerators into dioxin and dibenzofuran factories. The incinerator magnifies and disseminates more widely the ecological insults originally inflicted on us by the petrochemical industry's plastics.

THE LINK BETWEEN ECOLOGY AND ECONOMICS

In sum, then, in the last 40 years there has been a sweeping transformation in the technology of production, which is responsible for nearly all the environmental degradation that has occurred in that period of time. Now we can begin to see the fundamental connection between ecology and economics. The fate of the ecosystem is closely related to the nature of the system of production, which in turn is firmly linked to the economic system. Thus, the link between the economic system and the ecosystem is production.

The nature of the production system is governed almost exclusively by economic considerations. Specifically, the choice of production technology is determined by a single economic consideration—maximization of the rate of profit. In turn, as we have seen, the choice of production technology determines the impact of pollution on the ecosystem. In effect, profit maximization governs the design of the system of production and therefore the fate of the ecosystem.

This explains, I believe, why the post-war transformation of production technology has created serious economic inefficiencies as well as the severe impact on the environment. The efficiency of the overall economy is determined by the efficiencies with which resources, labor, and capital are converted by the production system into economic output. These efficiencies are generally expressed as resource productivity (goods produced per unit of resource used), labor productivity (goods produced per unit of labor used), and capital productivity (goods produced per unit of capital invested).

In the post-war transformation, production technologies with relatively high-capital and resource productivity and low-labor productivity were replaced by technologies with relatively low-capital and resource productivity and high-labor productivity. When a typical displaced product such as leather is replaced by plastics, as in shoes, the productivity of energy and capital falls, while the productivity of labor increases. In every case the new production process yielded a higher rate of profit than the one that it replaced.

It is perhaps natural to assume a direct relation between the two processes of economic growth and environmental pollution and conclude that the growth in output causes pollution because of a corresponding increase in the demand for resources. An analysis of the actual changes in the production system that have taken place in the post-war transformation invalidates this conclusion. A good example is the transformation in agriculture. It is certainly true that in this period agricultural output has increased and that the technological change responsible for much of the increase—the introduction of chemical fertilizers and pesticides—has generated intense pollution problems. But the quantitative relationship between crop production and the use of agricultural chemicals has changed.

Between 1960 and 1981 crop output in the United States increased by 67 percent, while the use of agricultural chemicals increased by 26 percent. Thus, the efficiency with which chemical inputs are converted to crop output has declined sharply. The economic productivity of agricultural chemicals—the crop output produced per unit of chemical input—has decreased by 50 percent since 1960 and is still falling. For the same reason, the environmental impact of crop production has intensified; there is now a larger environmental impact per unit of crop produced than before.

The decline in the economic efficiency of agricultural chemicals and the intensification of their environmental impact is inherent in the agricultural ecosystem. As increasing amounts of fertilizer are applied to the soil, crop growth reaches a limit, and a considerable part of the excess fertilizer is not incorporated into the crop, but leaches into rivers and lakes. In the same way, continued use of pesticides breeds resistance in the pests, so that progressively more chemicals must be used to achieve the same results. Thus, there is an inherent linkage between increased stress on the environment and reduced economic efficiency.

The manufacturing sector provides another illuminating example. As noted earlier, in this sector the post-war transformation in production technology has been characterized by a substitution of capital, in the form of machinery, for labor. This process also produces the same dual effect noted above: environmental stress increases and, in certain important aspects, economic productivity declines. The chief reason is that increased use of machinery inevitably demands more energy to drive it, so that there is a substitution of energy for labor. This relationship is particularly strong with respect to electricity, which is the preferred energy source for driving machinery. During the post-war transformation in production technology in the United States manufacturing sector, the productivity of labor, expressed as value added per man-hour, doubled, while the productivity of electricity, expressed as value added per kw.hr. of electricity, declined by nearly the same proportion.

Once again this shift is related to environmental impact: as output (in this case expressed as value-added in manufacturing) increased, larger amounts of electricity were consumed per unit of economic gain. Inevitably this was accompanied by intensified environmental impact: sulfur dioxide emissions and acid rain from coal-burning power plants, and radioactive wastes and the danger of accidents from nuclear power plants. Environmental pollution has increased per unit of goods manufactured. Once again we see the linkage between intensified impact on the environment and the declining efficiency with which a major resource, energy, is used.

The role of energy in the economy is particularly illuminating. In an ecologically balanced system, the economic cost of producing the energy needed to drive the system of production must remain in balance with the rest of the system. In most industrialized countries, about 95 percent of the energy is *non-renewable*. As they are consumed, such sources become progressively more difficult to produce, for it becomes necessary to exploit deeper, less accessible deposits of oil, natural gas, coal, and uranium. Consequently, the cost of producing a unit of energy from oil or natural gas rises exponentially with the total amount produced from a given source. In turn, this means that a progressively larger proportion of the available investment capital must be used to produce the energy needed to drive the economic system. Thus, in the United States in 1966, energy production used about 15 percent of the capital available for business investment. Since then, this figure has risen exponentially and it is now well over 30 percent.

In this way, depending on non-renewable sources of energy means that simply to make its necessary contribution to the economy, energy production will demand a progressively larger part of the economic output. In effect, a non-renewable energy system cannibalizes the economic system that it is supposed to support. The overall efficiency of the economy will rapidly decline if it is driven by a system of non-renewable energy. This process appears to be a major factor in the drop in the rate of improvement of economic productivity that has occurred in many countries since the mid-1960s.

In two crucial sectors—electric power production and petrochemicals—there is a special kind of relationship between environmental effects and the pattern of capital investment. In recent years, particularly with the introduction of nuclear power, power plants have become increasingly large, requiring capital investment in very large units, ranging up to billions of dollars per plant. To some degree, such plants have increased in size as a means of minimizing the frequency with which sites need to be chosen—a process that confronts the inherent environmental hazards associated with power production, especially from nuclear plants. In turn, the large plant size means that for a time after the plant begins to operate, there will be a considerable excess in capacity, for demand increases only gradually. This results in an inefficient use of capital, intensifying the drain on investment capital resulting from reliance on nonrenewable sources of energy.

Another link between the large capital units characteristic of the new technologies and environmental impact is illustrated by the petrochemical industry. In this case, the installations tend to be large for economic reasons. A large plant capacity reduces the need, relative to output, for the most expensive inputs: labor and process controls. The petrochemical industry's very large capacity impels it to invade very large existing markets—textiles, paper, and soap, for example—and to temporarily cut prices to ensure that sales match the large production capacity. This helps to explain the speed with which synthetic fibers, plastics, and detergents have swept into the market, generating their serious environmental problems so rapidly as to catch us unawares.

INCREASED ECONOMIC EFFICIENCY: AN ECOLOGICAL IMPERATIVE

I have sought to delineate a basic fact: that the postwar changes in the technology of production, which are largely responsible for environmental pollution, have also brought about a serious decline in the efficiency with which two major economic inputs—resources (especially energy) and capital—are used. I have argued that these economic and ecological effects are closely linked, for both are consequences of the same changes in the production system. Now it is time to turn our attention from analysis of the problem to what can be done to solve it.

Given the foregoing analysis, what steps should be taken to reduce the assault on the environment? At least in the United States, the conventional approach toward improving the quality of the environment is certainly not based on this analysis—or for that matter on any other cogent analysis of the origin of the problem. The fact that certain production technologies create pollution is simply accepted without asking *why* this should be so. Instead, reducing pollution is simply a matter of "controlling" the emissions: cars are equipped with exhaust devices; sulfur dioxide scrubbers are installed at coal-burning power plants and safety devices at nuclear power plants; toxic wastes are transferred to more secure sites; in extreme cases the offending factory is simply shut down.

It is this approach to environmental improvement that gives rise to the apparent antagonism between ecology and the economy. If cars and power plants must be equipped with environmental controls, the cost of travel and electricity increase; if petrochemical plants must give up their cheap but hazardous toxic dumps, the price of their products will rise; if the owner of a heavily polluting factory decides that it is more profitable to close the plant than improve it, the workers will lose their jobs. This approach leads to the generalization that there is always an economic cost to environmental improvement, and that the two must somehow be balanced, one against the other, by means of some sort of "cost/benefit" philosophy.

Clearly this approach is superficial; it does not address the problem at its root; it does not attempt to cure the disease but only to relieve its symptoms. This approach avoids the basic issue—the fault in the technology of production—and for that reason falls into the trap of creating a false and unnecessary conflict between ecology and the economy.

If, on the other hand, we confront the problem at its root, it becomes possible to find ways of improving *both* the environment and the economy. To support this assertion, I offer two practical examples, in agriculture and power production.

Agriculture

Like most aspects of the production system, since World War II agriculture has undergone sweeping changes in production technology that have created serious environmental problems. The chemical fertilizers, especially nitrogen, which have replaced natural sources of fertility, have leached into streams, lakes, and oceans, causing serious eutrophication.

At the same time, heavy dependence on increasing inputs of fertilizers and pesticides has become progressively less efficient; the economic return, per unit of chemicals used, has declined. In the United States, this process, together with heavy investments in equipment, has placed many farmers in a precarious economic position. Bankruptcies have become so frequent that a new, militant farmers' movement has begun to form. Thus, the post-war transformation of agriculture has created both serious environmental and economic problems. Given this understanding, it is possible to find ways of changing the technology of agricultural production that accomplish the reverse—that improve the environment *and* economic efficiency.

What are the economic consequences, for example, if, for the sake of improving the environment, farmers give up the use of the new fertilizers and pesticides? A CBNS study of Corn Belt farms provides a surprising answer. A five-year comparison between large-scale conventional farms and organic farms (which used neither chemical fertilizers nor pesticides but were otherwise very similar to conventional farms) showed that the latter's crop output was reduced by about 8.5 percent. But the resultant loss in income was exactly balanced by the savings gained by not buying agricultural chemicals. Consequently, on the average, the organic farms produced the same net income per acre as the conventional farms. In some sense this is even an economic *gain*, for it means that the farmers become less dependent on bank loans and, therefore, less vulnerable to bankruptcy.

One reason for farmers' economic difficulties is their dependence on non-renewable sources of energy, not only for fuel but also as the source of fertilizers such as ammonia and petrochemical pesticides. The price of these agricultural chemicals has risen sharply, along with the price of oil and natural gas, from which they are made. Yet, ecological principles tell us that the farm is itself a source of renewable solar energy. Can this capability be used to decrease the farm's dependence on non-renewable, progressively more costly, oil and natural gas and thereby improve its economic position?

Again, a recent CBNS study provides a surprising answer. We found that the farmers' economic position could be greatly improved, and the depletion of oil reduced, by appropriate changes in production technology. This is achieved by converting part of the farm's crop into ethanol—an excellent replacement of gasoline as a motor fuel—which is thereby a way of operating vehicles and machinery on solar energy.

The economic consequences of introducing this ecologically sound technology depend on how it is integrated into the overall agricultural system. It has often been pointed out that the use of a crop such as corn to produce ethanol will reduce the availability of food. Although the residue from ethanol fermentation can be used to feed animals, it has only 40 percent of the feed value of the original grain. If ethanol fermentation is simply added to the *present* agricultural system (which in the Corn Belt is based largely on corn and soybeans), there is no doubt that any economic gain to the farmer from selling ethanol would be outweighed by a reduction in the supply of animal feed and an increase in the price of food.

The principles of ecology, which emphasize the importance of *systems*, teach us how to overcome this difficulty. In the CBNS study we used a computer model to ask the following question: What new crop system, for the production of *both* food and ethanol, would maximize the farmers' profit without reducing food production? The answer was surprisingly simple. Recall that ethanol (which contains carbon, hydrogen, oxygen, but no nitrogen) is made from only the crop's carbohydrate. Therefore, to avoid the conflict between food and fuel, we need only increase the total carbohydrate content of the crop. This can readily be done. The study showed that by substituting sugar beets for soybeans, the farm would produce about as much protein as before but nearly twice as much carbohydrate. As a result, the extra carbohydrate could be converted to ethanol, leaving enough carbohydrate and protein to support as much animal production as before. The study showed that by 1995, such a crop system would double the farmers' profit, compared to profit from conventional agriculture. Applied to U.S. agriculture as a whole, this new system of agricultural technology could produce enough ethanol to replace about 20 percent of the national demand for gasoline without reducing the overall supply of food or significantly affecting its price.

Here, then, is a way of both improving the environmental impact of agriculture, and expanding its economic output. This approach could readily be combined with a sharp reduction in the use of fertilizers and pesticides, for any resultant loss in crop output would be far outweighed by the added production of ethanol. In sum, in agriculture it is possible to achieve economic growth *and* improve the environment—by sensibly applying the principles of ecology.

Power Production

In the United States, it is widely recognized that the electric power industry is in an economic crisis; several electric utilities have been threatened with bankruptcy. Last year a cover story in *Business Week* asked whether the industry had become "obsolete." The chief reason is that the present technology of electric power production is highly centralized and, therefore, dependent on very large capital investments. This leads to the economic inefficiencies of overcapacity and vulnerability to technological problems (as in the case of nuclear power). From the social point of view, the present technology is also inefficient because, for inescapable thermodynamic reasons, two-thirds of the energy available from the fuel is discarded into the environment as waste heat. Since the production and use of fuel causes important environmental problems, this means that the industry causes three times as much pollution per unit of useful energy produced as it would if all the wasted energy could be put to use.

The present centralized technology of power production is the source of both its thermodynamic inefficiency and environmental impact. The heat that a central power station ordinarily discards could readily be recaptured and used, for example, to heat homes. However, because heat can be distributed only over relatively short distances, this economically efficient process—cogeneration—cannot be used with the large centralized plants that are now commonly built. No one wants to live that close to a power plant, especially if it is nuclear.

Once again, by changing the technology of production in keeping with sensible, ecological principles, both the environmental and the economic situations can be improved. The basic change is to *decentralize* the production of electricity, building small cogenerator plants just large enough to meet the local energy demand. With the cogenerator supplying both heat and electricity at a high level of thermodynamic efficiency, the amount of fuel needed to meet the demand is reduced; this decreases both environmental impact and the cost of energy. For example, a recent CBNS study shows that the installation of a cogenerator in a typical New York City 50-apartment building reduces energy costs by 36 percent. Clearly, the gradual replacement of large centralized power plants by cogenerators scaled to the local demand would benefit both the environment and the economy.

The function of energy is economic; it generates the work needed to drive the production system that yields economic output. Capital must be invested in the production of energy, and if the entire system is to be stable, the efficiency with which capital yields energy must be kept in balance with the output of the economic system. As long as the economic system is driven by non-renewable energy, this balance is impossible. The very use of non-renewable energy has an influence on the resource itself: As energy is used, what remains becomes less accessible; every barrel of oil taken out of the ground makes the next barrel more costly to produce, requiring more capital investment per unit of energy produced. As indicated earlier, the cost of producing a unit amount of oil or natural gas has been rising exponentially in the United States, as these long-exploited supplies are depleted. This process progressively erodes the overall efficiency of the economy.

Solar energy can support the economy without demanding an ever-increasing investment of capital. Solar energy is derived from an energy source that is totally unaffected by the rate at which its radiation is put to use on the Earth; there is no way that the use of solar energy can influence the sun's output or make it less accessible. For that reason, unlike non-renewable sources, solar energy is not subject to escalating production costs. The transition to solar energy is, therefore, an important way of relieving the present strain of the energy system on the economy. Solar energy is both a means of improving the environment and a major source of economic growth.

The example cited earlier—replacing gasoline with ethanol produced from crops—illustrates the economic power of this transition. This process could greatly increase total agricultural output, eventually doubling agricultural profits, providing it is based on changes in production technology that integrate both food and fuel into a single system. Less is known about the economics of solar production of methane, which can replace natural gas. Exploratory studies suggest that "ocean farming," the production of marine algae in off-shore ocean areas, could produce very significant amounts of methane along with residues that can be used to feed domestic animals. Such an integrated ocean/land agricultural system could be used to significantly increase the production of both food and fuel. It could reduce the strain of natural gas production on the economy, add significantly to the net output of the production system, and at the same time improve the environment.

STRUCTURAL IMPLICATIONS OF THE NEW OPPORTUNITIES FOR ECONOMIC DEVELOPMENT

The preceding discussion shows that it is now possible to undertake a new transformation of the system of production that is designed to remedy both the environmental and economic defects imposed by the post-war transformation of production technology. Of course, this is an enormously difficult, complex task, but it is useful, nevertheless, to delineate the features of such a new transformation, so that the nature of the task can be understood clearly.

A major characteristic of the new transformation is that, as compared with the present, new capital facilities will require a higher proportion of initial capital relative to operating costs. For example, a local photovoltaic installation calls for a large initial investment but very little ongoing costs, since the solar energy input is free and the device is so simple as to require very little maintenance. On the other hand, the new production technologies will require capital investment in very much smaller units than the present technologies that they would replace. In the United States the average current cost of a coal-fired power plant is perhaps $400 million, and for a nuclear plant $3 billion. In contrast, a cogenerator for a 50-apartment building costs about $25,000; a solar collector to supply a family's home with hot water costs several thousand dollars; a photovoltaic installation for a small factory might cost about $1 million. Finally, investments in the new production technologies will represent relatively long-term investments in which returns will be slower than those of current investments.

The economic value of a new ecologically sound production technology depends a great deal on how well it is integrated into the *existing* system of production. For example, the CBNS cogenerator study found that if a cogenerator is used to supply *all* the necessary heat (i.e., meeting the winter maximum in demand), then a good deal of the investment is wasted in the summer and the savings, over a conventional system, are relatively small—about $6,000 per year. In contrast, by properly matching the cogenerator to the baseline demand for heat and using the existing system to provide additional heat at the appropriate times, the energy savings are increased to about $18,000 per year. Similarly, for the maximum economic gain from ethanol production, it must be integrated into the existing food-producing system, gradually transforming it into a system that produces both food and fuel. It is also necessary to achieve integration among several major economic sectors: agriculture, auto manufacturing, and the oil industry.

POLITICAL IMPLICATIONS

The preceding discussion has established, I believe, that there are ways of changing the present technology of production in agriculture, energy production, and transportation (which in turn will affect the types of goods produced in the manufacturing sector) that not only improve the environment but also increase the efficiency of the economic system.

Such a transformation can contribute to economic growth. For example, if, as indicated earlier, it is possible to use the same amount of land to produce, in addition to its present output of food, a very significant output of ethanol, then clearly economic growth has occurred. Similarly, if a central power plant that uses only 35 percent of the energy available from the increasingly expensive fuel that it burns is replaced by cogenerators that use fuel with an overall efficiency of 70 percent, then the net output of the economic system has grown. The same is true of changes that replace a non-renewable source of energy with a solar source, for the economy is thereby relieved of the drain of capital progressively diverted into energy production. The same can be said of a change in production technology that replaces a synthetic product of the petrochemical industry with a natural one, for society is thereby relieved of the economic burden of contending with the inevitable degradation that is inherent in petrochemical production.

Obviously this kind of economic growth cannot continue indefinitely. It takes place only during the course of the change in production technology, which remedies serious economic inefficiencies of the present system of production. The ultimate goal of the transformation is to efficiently integrate every productive process into an overall system based entirely on solar energy and on recycling of materials that is so well decentralized as to avoid the waste of capital associated with overly centralized investments. Achieving that goal will generate considerable economic growth. But when this transformation is complete, the economy may confront the limits inherent in its dependence on the ecosystem.

In the abstract sense there is, of course, an ecological limit to economic growth. The limit results from the fact that natural resources—the ecosystem that occupies the Earth's thin skin and the underlying mineral deposits—are essential to production and are finite. While the limit to the Earth's human population is set by the maximum rate of food production, the limit to economic growth is determined by the availability of minerals and energy. However, since mineral elements are indestructible, they can be recycled indefinitely, providing the necessary energy needed to collect and refine the dispersed minerals is available. (For example, perhaps 80–90 percent of all the gold ever mined remains in use.) As already pointed out, non-renewable sources of energy cannot be relied on, for they erode the economy. Hence, the ultimate limit on economic growth is imposed by the rate at which renewable solar energy can be captured and used. This in turn is limited (if we ignore the *very* long-term decrease in solar radiation) by the finite surface of the Earth, which determines how much of the energy radiated by the sun is actually intercepted and can be used.

Thus, in very general terms the ecological limit to the growth of production, and therefore the economy, is determined by the rate at which the Earth receives solar energy. How close are we to this limit at the present time? It has been estimated that the solar energy that falls annually on the Earth's land surface is more than a thousand times the amount of energy now being used to support the global economy. So even if we conclude that due to geographic inhomogeneities and unavoidable inefficiencies only one-tenth of this solar energy could be used, it still would be possible to expand our present rate of using natural resources by perhaps 100-fold before encountering the inherent limits to growth. Even if this figure should turn out to be somewhat optimistic, it seems clear that, at present, we are nowhere near the limit that natural resources will eventually impose on economic growth.

I believe, therefore, that the self-evident fact that the finiteness of the Earth's ecosystem imposes an ultimate limit on the capacity of the global system of production and, therefore, on economic growth is not relevant to current policy decisions. There are immediate opportunities for improving the efficiency of the economic system by introducing ecologically sound production technologies that yield both economic growth and environmental improvement. Once that transition is accomplished and production properly integrates human needs with ecological requirements, that balanced system could still expand very considerably before it approaches the ultimate limit imposed by the amount of solar energy that the Earth can receive. The issue that we face, then, is to determine what policies will facilitate the new transition. Both financial and political policies need to be considered.

Financial Policies

The preceding section summarized some of the financial implications of the transformation. Considerable initial capital is needed, and the overall transition will require a very large total sum of capital. Where can it come from? A useful suggestion is the more than $500 billion per year that we now literally destroy—causing more human harm than all the world's pollutants combined—by devoting it to war and the preparation of war.

Recall also that the capital is needed in relatively small units, in order to create the local decentralized facilities that are characteristic of the new production technologies. Unfortunately, it is usually difficult for relatively small local entities to accumulate the initial capital. Yet they are often the ones that are most in need of the economic returns that can be gained by the new technologies.

This paradox is illustrated by the CBNS experience with energy-conserving measures for low-income families in New York City. In recent years the cost of energy has placed a severe burden on such families. The rising price of energy has unavoidably taken a progressively larger part of the family budget, leaving less for other essential expenditures such as food or taxes; if the winter is severe, some poor families must choose between food and fuel. The remedy is to install several relatively simple but effective energy-conserving measures such as insulation and double-glazed windows. We have found that an investment of about $2,000 for a typical apartment will reduce energy bills by about 30 percent.

Nevertheless, few families can take advantage of this opportunity, simply because they do not have the needed capital. This situation applies as well to the installation of energy-conserving cogenerators in city residential buildings, or the construction of an ethanol plant in a farm community. The fact that such new, economically advantageous measures typically require a relatively large initial investment is a serious hurdle, which people who would benefit most have difficulty in overcoming. Another hurdle is the relatively slow rate of return of some of the new investments. If such an investment, for example, the restoration of impoverished soil, must compete with existing investments that yield profits quickly, it is certain to be ignored.

Obviously, none of these new investments will be made if the decision is governed by the existing "free market," which favors large-scale investments over decentralized ones and short-term over long-term returns. What is required, therefore, is an investment policy that is under social rather than private control. The key to the new transformation is social governance of the choice of production technologies, through democratic control of investment decisions.

Political Policies

The conventional approach to the questions of political policy that govern the relation between the environment and the economy, at least in the United States, is encompassed by the idea of "risk versus benefit." By this is meant the notion that the importance of reducing an environmental risk must be compared with the size of the economic benefits of the production process that creates the risk. In effect, this approach formalizes the spurious conflict between environmental quality and the economy. It is not surprising, therefore, that the efforts to develop procedures for comparing the risk with the benefit have only amplified the conflict, often to the point of absurdity.

One effort is based on the notion that the risk must be evaluated economically so that it can be compared with the benefit. Since the risk, for example of a toxic pollutant, can usually be converted to some number of human lives that may be lost, one outcome of this approach is an effort to place a dollar value on a human life. This effort leads to politically regressive results. Because this value is customarily based on a person's earning power, it turns out that a man's life is worth much more than a woman's; a black person's life is worth much less than a white's. In effect, the environmental risk is considered small if the people it kills are poor. Since many polluting industries are near neighborhoods occupied by poor people, this approach helps to diminish the importance of environmental improvement.

A more humane approach is to convert the risk into dollars by calculating the cost of the controls needed to reduce the risk. In this case it becomes necessary to decide how far the risk is to be reduced, for the cost of controlling it escalates sharply as the risk is diminished. Another version of this approach, which has become increasingly popular in the United States, is "risk assessment," in which the severity of a new risk is compared with well-established ones. This usually gives rise to a table that shows, for example, that the risk of dying of cancer from exposure to dioxin from a trash-burning incinerator is x-times less than the risk of death from riding a motorcycle or (in the case of a table prepared by the chemical industry) "going over Niagara Falls in a barrel."

In my opinion, such efforts are absurd because they are misdirected. The real problem is not to compare the risk and the benefit of the *same productive process*, but to compare the risks involved in equivalent productive processes that differ in their technology and therefore in their environmental impact. Thus, if there is a certain risk to health from the production of electricity by a nuclear power plant, then what is of interest are the alternative means of producing the same amount of electricity at a lesser risk to health and at a reasonably similar cost. This approach recognizes that the problem arises from the nature of the productive technology and that the social issue relates to the *choice* of a particular technology among the alternative ones that produce the same good.

Obviously the approach that I propose is radical; it calls for social rather than private investment decisions, for social rather than private governance of the means of production. It is curious to note, however, that this same approach is contained in a law that is usually not regarded as radical—the National Environmental Policy Act, which is the basis of all environmental legislation in the United States. According to Section 102(c) of this act, an Environmental Impact Statement must include: "(i) the environmental impact of the proposed action; (ii) any adverse environmental effects which cannot be avoided should the proposal be implemented; (iii) alternatives to the proposed action."

Thus, if the "proposed action" is the construction of a nuclear power plant, and its generation of radioactive waste is an "adverse environmental effect(s) which cannot be avoided," then, according to the law it is necessary to consider alternative, less hazardous, ways of producing electricity. The alternatives include cogenerators, photovoltaic cells, or for that matter, a well-controlled coal-burning plant. Thus, the law calls for an environmental comparison of different technological means of producing the same good; it is literally a means of exercising social control of the means of production.

Needless to say, the law has never been used in this way. Instead, American industry—and often enough, I am sorry to say, American environmental organizations—have uniformly adopted the "risk/benefit" approach or sometimes the "risk assessment" approach, out of a natural interest in avoiding confrontation with so fundamental and far-reaching a political issue.

I want to be very clear about the purpose of social governance of the means of production. It is a policy directed toward the *choice of the actual technology used to produce the goods that society needs*. I reemphasize this point because technological choices are usually regarded as outside the realm of public policy, determined instead by "objective" scientific considerations. It should be evident from the preceding discussion that this is simply not true. Certainly it is an objective scientific fact that high-compression automobile engines are particularly powerful and generate smog. But there is no objective way to determine whether it is more important to build engines that are powerful or engines that do not produce smog. Such a choice is social, not scientific. When it was decided in the United States to build high-compression engines in place of less powerful low-compression ones, a social policy was established. But the engine was regarded as a value-free piece of technology, and no questions were asked about its other attributes. The social decision was hidden from view until it was revealed, too late, by the blanket of smog that covers our cities.

The failure to deal with a technological decision as a social choice has had much wider effects than to create the false dichotomy between economic progress and environmental quality. It also affects, for example, the question of employment. Not only the decisions that substituted plastics for leather but also decisions that substitute robots for workers reduce the number of available jobs. The number of jobs created or destroyed is as important a reason for social governance of technological decisions as environmental impact. Social control of technological decisions is vital not only for environmental quality but for nearly everything else that determines how people live: employment, working conditions, the cost of transportation, energy and other necessities, and economic growth.

The Historic Transition

The argument put forward here has implications for our understanding of the relation between technology and the great historic transitions with which the world has struggled for nearly a century. Some would argue that technology is a force that develops, autonomously, from the new knowledge that the inevitable progress of science creates. This implies that, while the nature of a given technology will influence society, the reverse relation is very unlikely.

I am convinced that technology is a *social* institution that, like all others, reflects to a very large degree the governing aims of the society in which it develops. I believe that the harm generated by modern post–World War II technology is closely associated with its origin in a historic period dominated by the unresolved transition from capitalism to socialism. The basic science that gave rise to modern technology was developed in the period between World Wars I and II. The world's first socialist state, the USSR, was created at the start of that period; like the capitalist countries it developed systems of scientific research and technology. Yet, despite the fundamental difference between the two societies, after World War II both adopted essentially the same inherently harmful technologies, derived from earlier research especially in physics and chemistry. In both the socialist and capitalist countries there appeared the same dangerous nuclear power plants, the same inherently toxic industrial and agricultural chemicals, the same undegradable plastics, the same polluting cars. And the impact on the environment was the same in both societies. After all, should we expect the cars built in the USSR by an imported Fiat plant to produce less pollution in Moscow than they do in Rome, perhaps out of respect for socialism?

What does this mean? Does it prove that technology is indeed autonomous, independent of social forces? What does it tell us about the difference between the USSR and the capitalist countries? There are no brief answers to these questions, but here are some relevant thoughts.

First, it is a historic fact that nearly all of the troublesome post-war production technologies were developed and first put to commercial use in the capitalist countries, and were only later adopted by the USSR and other socialist countries. Second, the basic features of the capitalist social system in which they originated are heavily imprinted on the very nature of these technologies. For example, in keeping with the capitalist principle of unrestrained competition, petrochemical technologies were deliberately designed to create new and more highly profitable enterprises that could push older, equally (or more) socially useful enterprises out of the market. Clearly there was no concern about the economic and social consequences of these replacements: unemployment; loss of existing productive facilities such as natural rubber plantations; environmental pollution. In effect, the very technical design of the petrochemical industry was created to seize new markets and to maximize profit, regardless of the effect on public welfare.

So, the reason why modern production creates environmental and energy problems is not that there is some general fault with technology as a whole. Rather, the problem is that the particular *kinds* of technologies that are the present basis for the productive systems of *both* socialist and capitalist countries were developed in capitalist societies. And for that reason they are characterized by their ability to enhance what capitalists want—profit maximization and domination of the market—rather than the welfare of the people.

I believe that the fact that both capitalist and socialist societies alike have been burdened by the same damaging and dangerous technologies is a tragic consequence of a basic failure in the course of socialist development, as exemplified by the USSR. It is generally recognized that Soviet society has failed to adequately develop the democratic processes that are essential to the successful operation of a socialist state. What is perhaps less obvious, but equally important, is that Soviet society has also failed to create socialist technologies capable of generating means of production that, because they are deliberately designed for that purpose, serve the national interest and the people's welfare. To put this issue more concretely, the tragedy is that the Soviet Union has failed to undertake the transition to solar energy but instead leads the world in building new nuclear power plants; that it has failed to develop a chemical industry based on natural materials, but instead relies increasingly on the inherently toxic petrochemical industry. Indeed, there is a fundamental connection between the democratic and technological failures. The unwise Soviet decision to rely so heavily on nuclear power plants may be one consequence of the suppression of critics who might challenge it.

Where, then, can we look for the development of the necessary new productive technologies? We can continue to hope that the USSR and the other socialist countries will, in the course of time, learn about not only the necessity of democratic reforms, but also of technological reforms. But perhaps more immediately, I believe that this task should be undertaken by the left in capitalist countries, and especially by political parties that have already accepted the task of creating democratic socialism.

STUDY QUESTIONS

1. What, according to Commoner, has been responsible for environmental problems? What evidence does he offer for his conclusion?
2. Why is energy production crucially important to environmental quality, according to Commoner?
3. What aspects of energy production does Commoner find problematic? What improvements does he suggest, and are these convincing?
4. Efforts to improve the environment are frequently opposed because of cost, or restriction of economic growth. What strategy does Commoner recommend to overcome this problem?
5. Reconciling economic and environmental change requires sweeping changes in the way economic and environmental decisions are made. What changes does Commoner propose? What would be the benefits of these changes? What would be the costs?

54

The Power and Promise of Ecological Feminism

Karen J. Warren

Karen J. Warren teaches philosophy at Macalester College in St. Paul, Minnesota.

. . . I argue that the promise and power of ecological feminism is that *it provides a distinctive framework both for reconceiving feminism and for developing an environmental ethic which takes seriously connections between the domination of women and the domination of nature.* I do so by discussing the nature of a feminist ethic and the ways in which ecofeminism provides a feminist and environmental ethic. I conclude that any feminist theory *and* any environmental ethic which fail to take seriously the twin and interconnected dominations of women and nature is at best incomplete and at worst simply inadequate.

FEMINISM, ECOLOGICAL FEMINISM, AND CONCEPTUAL FRAMEWORKS

Whatever else it is, feminism is at least the movement to end sexist oppression. It involves the elimination of any and all factors that contribute to the continued and systematic domination or subordination of women. While feminists disagree about the nature of and solutions to the subordination of women, all feminists agree that sexist oppression exists, is wrong, and must be abolished.

A "feminist issue" is any issue that contributes in some way to understanding the oppression of women. Equal rights, comparable pay for comparable work, and food production are feminist issues wherever and whenever an understanding of them contributes to an understanding of the continued exploitation or subjugation of women. Carrying water and searching for firewood are feminist issues wherever and whenever women's primary responsibility for these tasks contributes to their lack of full participation in decision making, income producing, or high status positions engaged in by men. What counts as a feminist issue, then, depends largely on context, particularly the historical and material conditions of women's lives.

Environmental degradation and exploitation are feminist issues because an understanding of them contributes to an understanding of the oppression of women. In India, for example, both deforestation and reforestation through the introduction of a monoculture species tree (e.g., eucalyptus) intended for commercial production are feminist issues because the loss of indigenous forests and multiple species of trees has drastically affected rural Indian women's ability to maintain a subsistence household. Indigenous forests provide a variety of trees for food, fuel, fodder, household utensils, dyes, medicines, and income-generating uses, while monoculture-species forests do not.[1] Although I do not argue for this claim here, a look at the global impact of environmental degradation on women's lives suggests important respects in which environmental degradation is a feminist issue.

Feminist philosophers claim that some of the most important feminist issues are *conceptual* ones: these issues concern how one conceptualizes such mainstay philosophical notions as reason and rationality, ethics, and what it is to be human. Ecofeminists extend this feminist philosophical concern to nature. They argue that, ultimately, some of the most important connections between the domination of women and the domination of nature are conceptual. To see this, consider the nature of conceptual frameworks.

A *conceptual framework* is a set of *basic* beliefs, values, attitudes, and assumptions which shape and reflect how one views oneself and one's world. It is a socially constructed lens through which we perceive ourselves and others. It is affected by such factors as gender, race, class, age, affectional orientation, nationality, and religious background.

Some conceptual frameworks are oppressive. An *oppressive conceptual framework* is one that explains, justifies, and maintains relationships of domination and subordination. When an oppressive conceptual framework is *patriarchal,* it explains, justifies, and maintains the subordination of women by men.

I have argued elsewhere that there are three significant features of oppressive conceptual frameworks: (1) value-hierarchical thinking, i.e., "up-down" thinking which places higher value, status, or prestige on what is "up" rather than on what is "down"; (2) value dualisms, i.e., disjunctive pairs in which the disjuncts are seen as oppositional (rather than as complementary) and exclusive (rather than as inclusive), and which place higher value (status, prestige) on one disjunct rather than the other (e.g., dualisms which give higher value or status to that which has historically been identified as "mind," "reason," and "male" than to that which has historically been identified as "body," "emotion," and "female"); and (3) logic of domination, i.e., a structure of argumentation which leads to a justification of subordination.[2]

The third feature of oppressive conceptual frameworks is the most significant. A logic of domination is not *just* a logical structure. It also involves a substantive value system, since an ethical premise is needed to permit or sanction the "just" subordination of that which is subordinate. This justification typically is given on grounds of some alleged characteristic (e.g., rationality) which the dominant (e.g., men) have and the subordinate (e.g., women) lack.

Contrary to what many feminists and ecofeminists have said or suggested, there may be nothing *inherently* problematic about "hierarchical thinking" or even "value-hierarchical thinking" in contexts other than contexts of oppression. Hierarchical thinking is important in daily living for classifying data, comparing information, and organizing material. Taxonomies (e.g., plant taxonomies) and biological nomenclature seem to require *some* form of "hierarchical thinking." Even "value-hierarchical thinking" may be quite acceptable in certain contexts. (The same may be said of "value dualisms" in non-oppressive contexts.) For example, suppose it is true that what is unique about humans is our conscious capacity to radically reshape our social environments (or "societies"), as Murray Bookchin suggests.[3] Then one could truthfully say that humans are better equipped to radically reshape their environments than are rocks or plants—a "value-hierarchical" way of speaking.

The problem is not simply *that* value-hierarchical thinking and value dualisms are used, but *the way* in which each has been used *in oppressive conceptual frameworks* to establish inferiority and to justify subordination.[4] It is the logic of domination, *coupled with* value-hierarchical thinking and value dualisms, which "justifies" subordination. What is explanatorily basic, then, about the nature of oppressive conceptual frameworks is the logic of domination.

For ecofeminism, that a logic of domination is explanatorily basic is important for at least three reasons. First, without a logic of domination, a description of similarities and differences would be just that—a description of similarities and differences. Consider the claim, "Humans are different from plants and rocks in that humans can (and plants and rocks cannot) consciously and radically reshape the communities in which they live; humans are similar to plants and rocks in that they are both members of an ecological community." Even if humans are "better" than plants and rocks with respect to the conscious ability of humans to radically transform communities, one does not *thereby* get any *morally* relevant distinction between humans and nonhumans, or an argument for the domination of plants and rocks by humans. To get *those* conclusions one needs to add at least two powerful assumptions, viz., (A2) and (A4) in argument A below:

(A1) Humans do, and plants and rocks do not, have the capacity to consciously and radically change the community in which they live.
(A2) Whatever has the capacity to consciously and radically change the community in which it lives is morally superior to whatever lacks this capacity.
(A3) Thus, humans are morally superior to plants and rocks.
(A4) For any X and Y, if X is morally superior to Y, then X is morally justified in subordinating Y.
(A5) Thus, humans are morally justified in subordinating plants and rocks.

Without the two assumptions that *humans are morally superior* to (at least some) nonhumans, (A2), and that *superiority justifies subordination*, (A4), all one has is some difference between humans and some nonhumans. This is true *even if* that difference is given in terms of superiority. Thus, it is the logic of domination, (A4), which is the bottom line in ecofeminist discussions of oppression.

Second, ecofeminists argue that, at least in Western societies, the oppressive conceptual framework which sanctions the twin dominations of women and nature is a patriarchal one characterized by all three features of an oppressive conceptual framework. Many ecofeminists claim that, historically, within at least the dominant Western culture, a patriarchal conceptual framework has sanctioned the following argument B:

(B1) Women are identified with nature and the realm of the physical; men are identified with the "human" and the realm of the mental.
(B2) Whatever is identified with nature and the realm of the physical is inferior to ("below") whatever is identified with the "human" and the realm of the mental; or, conversely, the latter is superior to ("above") the former.
(B3) Thus, women are inferior to ("below") men; or, conversely, men are superior to ("above") women.
(B4) For any X and Y, if X is superior to Y, then X is justified in subordinating Y.
(B5) Thus, men are justified in subordinating women.

If sound, argument B establishes *patriarchy*, i.e., the conclusion given at (B5) that the systematic domination of women by men is justified. But according to ecofeminists, (B5) is justified by just those three features of an oppressive conceptual framework identified earlier: value-hierarchical thinking, the assumption at (B2); value dualisms, the assumed dualism of the mental and the physical at (B1) and the assumed inferiority of the physical vis-à-vis the mental at (B2); and a logic of domination, the assumption at (B4), the same as the previous premise (A4). Hence, according to ecofeminists, insofar as an oppressive patriarchal conceptual framework has functioned historically (within at least dominant Western culture) to sanction the twin dominations of women and nature (argument B), both argument B and the patriarchal conceptual framework, from whence it comes, ought to be rejected.

Of course, the preceding does not identify which premises of B are false. What is the status of premises (B1) and (B2)? Most, if not all, feminists claim that (B1), and many ecofeminists claim that (B2), have been assumed or asserted within the dominant Western philosophical and intellectual tradition.[5] As such, these feminists assert, as a matter of historical fact, that the dominant Western philosophical tradition has assumed the truth of (B1) and (B2). Ecofeminists, however, either deny (B2) or do not affirm (B2). Furthermore, because some ecofeminists are anxious to deny any ahistorical identification of women with nature, some ecofeminists deny (B1) when (B1) is used to support anything other than a strictly historical claim about what has been asserted or assumed to be true within patriarchal culture—e.g., when (B1) is used to assert that women properly are identified with the realm of nature and the physical.[6] Thus, from an ecofeminist perspective, (B1) and (B2) are properly viewed as problematic though historically sanctioned claims: they are problematic precisely because of the way they have functioned historically in a patriarchal conceptual framework and culture to sanction the dominations of women and nature.

What *all* ecofeminists agree about, then, is the way in which *the logic of domination* has functioned historically within patriarchy to sustain and justify the twin dominations of women and nature.[7] Since *all* feminists (and not just ecofeminists) oppose patriarchy, the conclusion given at (B5), all feminists (including ecofeminists) must oppose at least the logic of domination, premise (B4), on which argument B rests—whatever the truth-value status of (B1) and (B2) *outside* of a patriarchal context.

That *all* feminists must oppose the logic of domination shows the breadth and depth of the ecofeminist critique of B: it is a critique not only of the three assumptions on which this argument for the domination of women and nature rests, viz., the assumptions at (B1), (B2), and (B4); it is also a critique of patriarchal conceptual frameworks generally, i.e., of those oppressive conceptual frameworks which put men "up" and women "down," allege some way in which women are morally inferior to men, and use that alleged difference to justify the subordination of women by men. Therefore, ecofeminism is necessary to *any* feminist critique of patriarchy, and, hence, necessary to feminism (a point I discuss again later).

Third, ecofeminism clarifies why the logic of domination, and any conceptual framework which gives rise to it, must be abolished in order both to make possible a meaningful notion of difference which does not breed domination and to prevent feminism from becoming a "support" movement based primarily on shared experiences. In contemporary society, there is no one "woman's voice," no *woman* (or *human*) *simpliciter:* every woman (or human) is a woman (or human) of some race, class, age, affectional orientation, marital status, regional or national background, and so forth. Because there are no "monolithic experiences" that all women share, feminism must be a "solidarity movement" based on shared beliefs and interests rather than a "unity in sameness" movement based on shared experiences and shared victimization.[8] In the words of Maria Lugones, "Unity—not to be confused with solidarity—is understood as conceptually tied to domination."[9]

Ecofeminists insist that the sort of logic of domination used to justify the domination of humans by gender, racial or ethnic, or class status is also used to justify the domination of nature. Because eliminating a logic of domination is part of a feminist critique—whether a critique of patriarchy, white supremacist culture, or imperialism—ecofeminists insist that *naturism* is properly viewed as an integral part of any feminist solidarity movement to end sexist oppression and the logic of domination which conceptually grounds it. . . .

CLIMBING FROM ECOFEMINISM TO ENVIRONMENTAL ETHICS

Many feminists and some environmental ethicists have begun to explore the use of first-person narrative as a way of raising philosophically germane issues in ethics often lost or underplayed in mainstream philosophical ethics. Why is this so? What is it about narrative which makes it a significant resource for theory and practice in feminism and environmental ethics? Even if appeal to first-person narrative is a helpful literary device for describing ineffable experience or a legitimate social science methodology for documenting personal and social history, how is first-person narrative a valuable vehicle of argumentation for ethical decision making and theory building? One fruitful way to begin answering these questions is to ask them of a particular first-person narrative.

Consider the following first-person narrative about rock climbing:

> For my very first rock climbing experience, I chose a somewhat private spot, away from other climbers and on-lookers. After studying "the chimney," I focused all my energy on making it to the top. I climbed with intense determination, using whatever strength and skills I had to accomplish this challenging feat. By midway I was exhausted and anxious. I couldn't see what to do next—where to put my hands or feet. Growing increasingly more weary as I clung somewhat desperately to the rock, I made a move. It didn't work. I fell. There I was, dangling midair above the rocky ground below, frightened but terribly relieved that the belay rope had held me. I knew I was safe. I took a look up at the climb that remained. I was determined to make it to the top. With renewed confidence and concentration, I finished the climb to the top.
>
> On my second day of climbing, I rappelled down about 200 feet from the top of the Palisades at Lake Superior to just a few feet above the water level. I could see no one—not my belayer, not the other climbers, no one. I unhooked slowly from the rappel rope and took a deep cleansing breath. I looked all around me—really looked—and listened. I heard a cacophony of voices—birds, trickles of water on the rock before me, waves lapping against the rocks below. I closed my eyes and began to feel the rock with my hands—the cracks and crannies, the raised lichen and mosses, the almost imperceptible nubs that might provide a resting place for my fingers and toes when I began to climb. At that moment I was bathed in serenity. I began to talk to the rock in an almost inaudible, child-like way, as if the rock were my friend. I felt an overwhelming sense of gratitude for what it offered me—a chance to know myself and the rock differently, to appreciate unforeseen miracles like the tiny flowers growing in the even tinier cracks in the rock's surface, and to come to know sense of *being in relationship* with the natural environment. It felt as if the rock and I were silent conversational partners in a longstanding friendship. I realized then that I had come to care about this cliff which was so different from me, so unmovable and invincible, independent and seemingly indifferent to my presence. I wanted to be with the rock as I climbed. Gone was the determination to conquer the rock, to forcefully impose my will on it; I wanted simply to work respectfully with the rock as I climbed. And as I climbed, that is what I felt. I felt myself caring for this rock and feeling thankful that climbing provided the opportunity for me to know it and myself in this way.

There are at least four reasons why use of such a first-person narrative is important to feminism and environmental ethics. First, such a narrative gives voice to a felt sensitivity often lacking in traditional analytical ethical discourse, viz., a sensitivity to conceiving of oneself as fundamentally "in relationship with" others, including the nonhuman environment. It is a modality which *takes relationships themselves seriously*. It thereby stands in contrast to a strictly reductionist modality that takes relationships seriously only or primarily because of the nature of the *relators* or parties to those relationships (e.g., relators conceived as moral agents, right holders, interest carriers, or sentient beings). In the rock-climbing narrative above, it is the climber's relationship with the rock she climbs which takes on special significance—which is itself a locus of value—in addition to whatever moral status or moral considerability she or the rock or any other parties to the relationship may also have.[10]

Second, such a first-person narrative gives expression to a variety of ethical attitudes and behaviors often overlooked or underplayed in mainstream Western ethics, e.g., the difference in attitudes and behaviors toward a rock when one is "making it to the top" and when one thinks of oneself as "friends with" or "caring about" the rock one climbs.[11] These different attitudes and behaviors suggest an ethically germane contrast between two different types of relationship humans or climbers may have toward a rock: an imposed conqueror-type relationship, and an emergent caring-type relationship. This contrast grows out of, and is faithful to, felt, lived experience.

The difference between conquering and caring attitudes and behaviors in relation to the natural environment provides a third reason why the use of first-person narrative is important to feminism and environmental ethics: it provides a way of conceiving of ethics and ethical meaning as *emerging out of* particular situations moral agents find themselves in, rather than as being *imposed on* those situations (e.g., as a derivation or instantiation of some predetermined abstract principle or rule). This emergent feature of narrative centralizes the importance of *voice*. When a multiplicity of cross-cultural *voices* are centralized, narrative is able to give expression to a range of attitudes, values, beliefs, and behaviors which may be overlooked or silenced by imposed ethical meaning and theory. As a reflection of and on felt, lived experiences, the use of narrative in ethics provides a stance from which ethical discourse can be held accountable to the historical, material, and social realities in which moral subjects find themselves.

Lastly, and for our purposes perhaps most importantly, the use of narrative has argumentative significance. Jim Cheney calls attention to this feature of narrative when he claims, "To contextualize ethical deliberation is, in some sense, to provide a narrative or story, from which the solution to the ethical dilemma emerges as the fitting conclusion."[12] Narrative has argumentative force by suggesting *what counts* as an appropriate conclusion to an ethical situation. One ethical conclusion suggested by the climbing narrative is that what counts as a proper ethical attitude toward mountains and rocks is an attitude of respect and care (whatever that turns out to be or involve), not one of domination and conquest.

In an essay entitled "In and Out of Harm's Way: Arrogance and Love," feminist philosopher Marilyn Frye distinguishes between "arrogant" and "loving" perception as one way of getting at this difference in the ethical attitudes of care and conquest.[13] Frye writes:

> The loving eye is a contrary of the arrogant eye.
>
> The loving eye knows the independence of the other. It is the eye of a seer who knows that nature is indifferent. It is the eye of one who knows that to know the seen, one must consult something other than one's own will and interests and fears and imagination. One must look at the thing. One must look and listen and check and question.
>
> The loving eye is one that pays a certain sort of attention. This attention can require a discipline but *not* a self-denial. The discipline is one of self-knowledge, knowledge of the scope and boundary of the self. . . . In particular, it is a matter of being able to tell one's own interests from those of others and of knowing where one's self leaves off and another begins. . . .
>
> The loving eye does not make the object of perception into something edible, does not try to assimilate it, does not reduce it to the size of the seer's desire, fear and imagination, and hence does not have to simplify. It knows the complexity of the other as something which

> will forever present new things to be known. The science of the loving eye would favor The Complexity Theory of Truth [in contrast to The Simplicity Theory of Truth] and presuppose The Endless Interestingness of the Universe.[14]

According to Frye, the loving eye is not an invasive, coercive eye which annexes others to itself, but one which "knows the complexity of the other as something which will forever present new things to be known."

When one climbs a rock as a conqueror, one climbs with an arrogant eye. When one climbs with a loving eye, one constantly "must look and listen and check and question." One recognizes the rock as something very different, something perhaps totally indifferent to one's own presence, and finds in that difference joyous occasion for celebration. One knows "the boundary of the self," where the self—the "I," the climber—leaves off and the rock begins. There is no fusion of two into one, but a complement of two entities *acknowledged* as separate, different, independent, yet *in relationship;* they are in relationship *if only* because the loving eye is perceiving it, responding to it, noticing it, attending to it.

An ecofeminist perspective about both women and nature involves this shift in attitude from "arrogant perception" to "loving perception" of the nonhuman world. Arrogant perception of nonhumans by humans presupposes and maintains *sameness* in such a way that it expands the moral community to those beings who are thought to resemble (be like, similar to, or the same as) humans in some morally significant way. Any environmental movement or ethic based on arrogant perception builds a moral hierarchy of beings and assumes some common denominator of moral considerability in virtue of which like beings deserve similar treatment or moral consideration and unlike beings do not. Such environmental ethics are or generate a "unity in sameness." In contrast, "loving perception" presupposes and maintains *difference*—a distinction between the self and order, between human and at least some nonhumans—in such a way that perception of the other as other *is* an expression of love for one who/which is recognized at the outset as independent, dissimilar, different. As Maria Lugones says, in loving perception, "Love is seen not as fusion and erasure of difference but as incompatible with them."[15] "Unity in sameness" alone is an *erasure of difference.*

"Loving perception" of the nonhuman natural world is an attempt to understand what it means *for humans* to care about the nonhuman world, a world *acknowledged* as being independent, different, perhaps even indifferent to humans. Humans *are* different from rocks in important ways, even if they are also both members of some ecological community. A moral community based on loving perception of oneself *in relationship with* a rock, or with the natural environment as a whole, is one which acknowledges and respects difference, whatever "sameness" also exists.[16] The limits of loving perception are determined only by the limits of one's (e.g., a person's, a community's) ability to respond lovingly (or with appropriate care, trust, or friendship)—whether it is to other humans or to the nonhuman world and elements of it.[17]

If what I have said so far is correct, then there are very different ways to climb a mountain and *how* one climbs it and *how* one narrates the experience of climbing it matter ethically. If one climbs with "arrogant perception," with an attitude of "conquer and control," one keeps intact the very sorts of thinking that characterize a logic of domination and an oppressive conceptual framework. Since the oppressive conceptual framework which sanctions the domination of nature is a patriarchal one, one also thereby keeps intact, even if unwittingly, a patriarchal conceptual framework. Because the dismantling of patriarchal conceptual frameworks is a feminist issue, *how* one climbs a mountain and *how* one narrates—or tells the story—about the experience of climbing also are *feminist issues*. In this way, ecofeminism makes visible why, at a conceptual level, environmental ethics is a feminist issue. I turn now to a consideration of ecofeminism as a distinctively feminist and environmental ethic. . . .

All the props are now in place for seeing how ecofeminism provides the framework for a distinctively feminist and environmental ethic. It is a feminism that critiques male bias wherever it occurs in ethics (including environmental ethics) and aims at providing an ethic (including an environmental ethic) which is not male biased—and it does so in a way that satisfies the preliminary boundary conditions (the "quilt") of a feminist ethic.

First, ecofeminism is quintessentially anti-naturist. Its anti-naturism consists in the rejection of any way of thinking about or acting toward non-human nature that reflects a logic, values, or attitude of domination. Its anti-naturist, anti-sexist, anti-racist, anti-classist (and so forth, for all other "isms" of social domination) stance forms the outer boundary of the quilt: nothing gets on the quilt which is naturist, sexist, racist, classist, and so forth.

Second, ecofeminism is a contextualist ethic. It involves a shift *from* a conception of ethics as primarily a matter of rights, rules, or principles predetermined and applied in specific cases to entities viewed as competitors in the contest of moral standing, *to* a conception of ethics as growing out of what Jim Cheney calls "defining relationships," i.e., relationships conceived in some sense as defining who one is.[18] As a contextualist ethic, it is not that rights, or rules, or principles are *not* relevant or important. Clearly they are in certain contexts and for certain purposes.[19] It is just that what *makes* them relevant or important is that those to whom they apply are entities *in relationship with* others.

Ecofeminism also involves an ethical shift *from* granting moral consideration to nonhumans *exclusively* on the grounds of some similarity they share with humans (e.g., rationality, interests, moral agency, sentiency, right-holder status) *to* "a highly contextual account to see clearly what a human being is and what the nonhuman world might be, morally speaking, *for* human beings."[20] For an ecofeminist, *how* a moral agent is in relationship to another becomes of central significance, not simply *that* a moral agent is a moral agent or is bound by rights, duties, virtue, or utility to act in a certain way.

Third, ecofeminism is structurally pluralistic in that it presupposes and maintains difference—difference among humans as well as between humans and at least some elements of nonhuman nature. Thus, while ecofeminism denies the "nature/culture" split, it affirms that humans are both members of an ecological community (in some respects) and different from it (in other respects). Ecofeminism's attention to relationships and community is not, therefore, an erasure of difference but a respectful acknowledgement of it.

Fourth, ecofeminism reconceives theory as theory in process. It focuses on patterns of meaning which emerge, for instance, from the storytelling and first-person narratives of women (and others) who deplore the twin dominations of women and nature. The use of narrative is one way to ensure that the content of the ethic—the pattern of the quilt—may/will change over time, as the historical and material realities of women's lives change and as more is learned about women-nature connections and the destruction of the nonhuman world.[21]

Fifth, ecofeminism is inclusivist. It emerges from the voices of women who experience the harmful domination of nature and the way that domination is tied to their domination as women. It emerges from listening to the voices of indigenous peoples such as Native Americans who have been dislocated from their land and have witnessed the attendant undermining of such values as appropriate reciprocity, sharing, and kinship that characterize traditional Indian culture. It emerges from listening to voices of those who, like Nathan Hare, critique traditional approaches to environmental ethics as white and bourgeois, and as failing to address issues of "black ecology" and the "ecology" of the inner city and urban spaces.[22] It also emerges out of the voices of Chipko women who see the destruction of "earth, soil, and water" as intimately connected with their own inability to survive economically.[23] With its emphasis on inclusivity and difference, ecofeminism provides a framework for recognizing that what counts as ecology and what counts as appropriate conduct toward both human and nonhuman environments is largely a matter of context.

Sixth, as a feminism, ecofeminism makes no attempt to provide an "objective" point of view. It is a social ecology. It recognizes the twin dominations of women and nature as social problems rooted both in very concrete, historical, socioeconomic circumstances and in oppressive patriarchal conceptual frameworks which maintain and sanction these circumstances.

Seventh, ecofeminism makes a central place for values of care, love, friendship, trust, and appropriate reciprocity—values that presuppose that our relationships to others are central to our understanding of who we are.[24] It thereby gives voice to the sensitivity that in climbing a mountain, one is doing something in relationship with an "other," an "other" whom one can come to care about and treat respectfully.

Lastly, an ecofeminist ethic involves a reconception of what it means to be human, and in what human ethical behavior consists. Ecofeminism denies abstract individualism. Humans are who we are in large part by virtue of the historical and social contexts and the relationships we are in, including our relationships with nonhuman nature. Relationships are not something extrinsic to who we are, not an "add on" feature of human nature; they play an essential role in shaping what it is to be human. Relationships of humans to the nonhuman environment are, in part, constitutive of what it is to be a human.

By making visible the interconnections among the dominations of women and nature, ecofeminism shows that both are feminist issues and that explicit acknowledgement of both is vital to any responsible environmental ethic. Feminism *must* embrace ecological feminism if it is to end the domination of women because the domination of women is tied conceptually and historically to the domination of nature.

A responsible environmental ethic also *must* embrace feminism. Otherwise, even the seemingly most revolutionary, liberational, and holistic ecological ethic will fail to take seriously the interconnected dominations of nature and women that are so much a part of the historical legacy and conceptual framework that sanction the exploitation of nonhuman nature. Failure to make visible these interconnected, twin dominations results in an inaccurate account of how it is that nature has been and continues to be dominated and exploited and produces an environmental ethic that lacks the depth necessary to be truly *inclusive* of the realities of persons who at least in dominant Western culture have been intimately tied with that exploitation, viz., women. Whatever else can be said in favor of such holistic ethics, a failure to make visible ecofeminist insights into the common denominators of the twin oppressions of women and nature is to perpetuate, rather than overcome, the source of that oppression.

This last point deserves further attention. It may be objected that as long as the end result is "the same"—the development of an environmental ethic which does not emerge out of or reinforce an oppressive conceptual framework—it does not matter whether that ethic (or the ethic endorsed in getting there) is feminist or not. Hence, it simply is *not* the case that any adequate environmental ethic must be feminist. My argument, in contrast, has been that it *does* matter, and for three important reasons. First, there is the scholarly issue of accurately representing historical reality, and that, ecofeminists claim, requires acknowledging the historical feminization of nature and naturalization of women as part of the exploitation of nature. Second, I have shown that the conceptual connections between the domination of women and the domination of nature are located in an oppressive and, at least in Western societies, patriarchal conceptual framework characterized by a logic of domination. Thus, I have shown that failure to notice the nature of this connection leaves at best an incomplete, inaccurate, and partial account of what is required of a conceptually adequate environmental ethic. An ethic which *does not* acknowledge this is simply *not* the same as one that does, whatever else the similarities between them. Third, the claim that, in contemporary culture, one can have an adequate environmental ethic which is *not* feminist assumes that, in contemporary culture, the label *feminist* does not add anything crucial to the nature or description of environmental ethics. I have shown that at least in contemporary culture this is false, for the word *feminist* currently helps to clarify just *how* the domination of nature is conceptually linked to patriarchy and, hence, how the liberation of nature is conceptually linked to the termination of patriarchy. Thus, because it has critical bite in contemporary culture, it serves as an important reminder that in contemporary sex-gendered, raced, classed, and naturist culture, an unlabeled position functions as a privileged and "unmarked" position. That is, without the addition of the word *feminist,* one presents environmental ethics as if it has no bias, including male-gender bias, which is just what ecofeminists deny: failure to notice the connections between the twin oppressions of women and nature is male-gender bias.

One of the goals of feminism is the eradication of all oppressive sex-gender (and related race, class, age, affectional preference) categories and the creation of a world in which *difference does not breed domination*—say, the world of 4001. If in 4001 an "adequate environmental ethic" is a "feminist environmental ethic," the word *feminist* may then be redundant and unnecessary. However, this is *not* 4001, and in terms of the current historical and conceptual reality the dominations of nature and of women are intimately connected. Failure to notice or make visible that connection in 1990 perpetuates the mistaken (and privileged) view that "environmental ethics" is *not* a feminist issue, and that *feminist* adds nothing to environmental ethics.[25] . . .

NOTES

1. I discuss this in my paper "Toward an Ecofeminist Ethic."
2. The account offered here is a revision of the account given earlier in my paper "Feminism and Ecology: Making Connections." I have changed the account to be about "oppressive" rather than strictly "patriarchal" conceptual frameworks in order to leave open the possibility that there may be some patriarchal conceptual frameworks (e.g., in non-Western cultures) which are *not* properly characterized as based on value dualisms.
3. Murray Bookchin, "Social Ecology versus 'Deep Ecology'," in *Green Perspectives: Newsletter of the Green Program Project*, No. 4–5 (Summer 1987): 9.
4. It may be that in contemporary Western society, which is so thoroughly structured by categories of gender, race, class, age, and affectional orientation, there simply is no meaningful notion of "value-hierarchical thinking" which does not function in an oppressive context. For purposes of this paper, I leave that question open.
5. Many feminists who argue for the historical point that claims (B1) and (B2) have been asserted or assumed to be true within the dominant Western philosophical tradition do so by discussion of that tradition's conceptions of reason, rationality, and science. For a sampling of the sorts of claims made within that context, see "Reason, Rationality, and Gender," ed. Nancy Tuana and Karen J. Warren, a special issue of the American Philosophical Association's *Newsletter on Feminism and Philosophy* 88, No. 2 (March 1989): 17–71. Ecofeminists who claim that (B2) has been assumed to be true within the dominant Western philosophical tradition include: Gray, *Green Paradise Lost;* Griffin, *Woman and Nature: The Roaring Inside Her;* Merchant, *The Death of Nature*; Ruether, *New Woman/New Earth.* For a discussion of some of these ecofeminist historical accounts, see Plumwood, "Ecofeminism." While I agree that the historical connections between the domination of women and the domination of nature is a crucial one, I do not argue for that claim here.
6. Ecofeminists who deny (B1) when (B1) is offered as anything other than a true, descriptive, historical claim about patriarchal culture often do so on grounds that an objectionable sort of biological determinism, or at least harmful female sex-gender stereotypes, underlie (B1). For a discussion of this "split" among those ecofeminists ("nature feminists") who assert and those ecofeminists ("social feminists") who deny (B1) as anything other than a true historical claim about how women are described in patriarchal culture, see Griscom, "On Healing the Nature/History Split."
7. I make no attempt here to defend the historically sanctioned truth of these premises.

8. See. e.g., bell hooks, *Feminist Theory: From Margin to Center* (Boston: South End Press, 1984), pp. 51–52.
9. Maria Lugones, "Playfulness, 'World-Travelling,' and Loving Perception," *Hypatia* 2, No. 2 (Summer 1987): 3.
10. Suppose, as I think is the case, that a necessary condition for the existence of a moral relationship is that at least one party to the relationship is a moral being (leaving open for our purposes what counts as a "moral being"). If this is so, then the Mona Lisa cannot properly be said to have or stand in a moral relationship with the wall on which she hangs, and a wolf cannot have or properly be said to have or stand in a moral relationship with a moose. Such a necessary-condition account leaves open the question whether *both* parties to the relationship must be moral beings. My point here is simply that however one resolves *that* question, recognition of the relationships themselves as a locus of value is a recognition of a source of value that is different from and not reducible to the values of the "moral beings" in those relationships.
11. It is interesting to note that the image of being friends with the Earth is one which cytogeneticist Barbara McClintock uses when she describes the importance of having "a feeling for the organism," "listening to the material [in this case the corn plant]," in one's work as a scientist. See Evelyn Fox Keller, "Women, Science, and Popular Mythology," in *Machina Ex Dea: Feminist Perspectives on Technology*, ed. Joan Rothschild (New York: Pergamon Press, 1983), and Evelyn Fox Keller, *A Feeling for the Organism: The Life and Work of Barbara McClintock* (San Francisco: W. H. Freeman, 1983).
12. Cheney, "Eco-Feminism and Deep Ecology," p. 144.
13. Marilyn Frye, "In and Out of Harm's Way: Arrogance and Love," in *The Politics of Reality* (Trumansburg, N.Y.: The Crossing Press, 1983), pp. 66–72.
14. Ibid., pp. 75–76.
15. Maria Lugones, "Playfulness," p. 3.
16. Cheney makes a similar point in "Eco-Feminism and Deep Ecology," p. 140.
17. Ibid., p. 138.
18. Henry West has pointed out that the expression "defining relations" is ambiguous. According to West, "the 'defining' as Cheney uses it is an adjective, not a principle—it is not that ethics defines relationships; it is that ethics grows out of conceiving of the relationships that one is in as defining what the individual is."
19. For example, in relationships involving contracts or promises, those relationships might be correctly described as that of moral agent to rights holders. In relationships involving mere property, those relationships might be correctly described as that of moral agent to objects having only instrumental value, "relationships of instrumentality." In comments on an earlier draft of this paper, West suggested that possessive individualism, for instance, might be recast in such a way that an individual is defined by his or her property relationships.
20. Cheney, "Eco-Feminism and Deep Ecology," p. 144.
21. One might object that such permission for change opens the door for environmental exploitation. This is not the case. An ecofeminist ethic is anti-naturist. Hence, the unjust domination and exploitation of nature is a "boundary condition" of the ethic; no such actions are sanctioned or justified on ecofeminist grounds. What it *does* leave open is some leeway about what counts as domination and exploitation. This, I think, is a strength of the ethic, not a weakness, since it acknowledges that *that* issue cannot be resolved in any practical way in the abstract, independent of a historical and social context.
22. Nathan Hare, "Black Ecology," in *Environmental Ethics*, ed. K. S. Shrader-Frechette (Pacific Grove, Calif.: Boxwood Press, 1981), pp. 229–236.
23. For an ecofeminist discussion of the Chipko movement, see my "Toward an Ecofeminist Ethic," and Shiva's *Staying Alive*.
24. See Cheney, "Eco-Feminism and Deep Ecology," p. 122.
25. I offer the same sort of reply to critics of ecofeminism such as Warwick Fox who suggest that for the sort of ecofeminism I defend, the word *feminist* does not add anything significant to environmental ethics and, consequently, that an ecofeminist like myself might as well call herself a deep ecologist. He asks: "Why doesn't she just call it [i.e., Warren's vision of a transformative feminism] deep ecology? Why specifically attach the label *feminist* to it . . . ?" (Warwick Fox, "The Deep Ecology-Ecofeminism Debate and Its Parallels," *Environmental Ethics* 11, No. 1 [1989]: 14, n. 22). Whatever the important similarities between deep ecology and ecofeminism (or, specifically, my version of ecofeminism)—and, indeed, there are many—it is precisely my point here that the word *feminist* does add something significant to the conception of environmental ethics, and that any environmental ethic (including deep ecology) that fails to make explicit the different kinds of interconnections among the domination of nature and the domination of women will be, from a feminist (and ecofeminist) perspective such as mine, inadequate.

STUDY QUESTIONS

1. What does the author mean by the "logic of domination"?
2. What three features of "oppressive conceptual frameworks" does the author identify? Of these three, which is most significant?
3. What does the author mean by "naturism," and how is it linked to sexism?

FOR FURTHER STUDY

Callicott, J. Baird. *In Defense of the Land Ethic: Essays in Environmental Philosophy.* Albany: State University of New York Press, 1989.

Carson, Rachel. *Silent Spring*. Boston: Houghton Mifflin, 1962.

Ehrlich, Paul, and Anne Ehrlich. *Extinction: The Causes and Consequences of the Disappearance of Species*. New York: Random House, 1981.

Hughes, J. Donald. *American Indian Ecology*. Lubbock, Tex.: Texas Western Press, 1983.

McKibbon, Bill. *The End of Nature*. New York: Random House, 1989.

Merchant, Carolyn. *The Death of Nature: Women, Ecology, and the Scientific Revolution.* New York: Harper & Row, 1980.

Regan, Tom. *The Case for Animal Rights*. Berkeley: University of California Press, 1982.

——. *Earthbound: New Introductory Essays in Environmental Ethics*. New York: Random House, 1984.

Shiva, Vandana. *Staying Alive: Women, Ecology, and Development*. London: Zed, 1989.

Glossary

ALTRUISM The promotion of the good of others; as a moral principle, to consider the consequences of action for everyone except oneself.

ARETAIC ETHICS The theory, first proposed by Aristotle, that the basis of ethical judgment is character; focuses on the character and dispositions of the moral agent rather than on actions and duties.

CATEGORICAL IMPERATIVE Commands actions that are necessary in themselves, without reference to other ends. In Kant's nonconsequentialism, moral duties represent the injunctions of reason that command actions categorically.

CIVIL DISOBEDIENCE Nonviolent resistance to the law aimed at changing those laws deemed unjust.

CONSEQUENTIALISM Sometimes known as *teleological ethics;* the view that the correctness (rightness or wrongness) of moral conduct is judged in terms of its results (or consequences); *altruism, ethical egoism,* and *utilitarianism* are consequentialist ethical theories.

CULTURAL RELATIVISM The descriptive thesis (sometimes known as "diversity thesis") that different cultures have different moral rules.

DIVINE COMMAND THEORY A theory holding that moral terms are defined in terms of God's commands or that moral duties are logically dependent on God's commands.

ETHICAL ABSOLUTISM The view that there is only one answer to every moral problem; a completely absolutist ethic is made up of absolute principles that provide an answer for every possible situation in life. It is diametrically opposed to *ethical relativism* and *ethical objectivism,* which hold that moral principles, while objective, may be overridden in certain situations.

ETHICAL EGOISM A normative theory holding that we ought to act according to self-interest; our own success and happiness should be of primary and ultimate worth and all other values should flow from this.

ETHICAL HEDONISM The theory that pleasure is the only intrinsic positive value and that pain is the only thing with negative intrinsic value; all other values are derived from these two.

ETHICAL OBJECTIVISM The view that moral principles have objective validity whether or not people recognize them as such; differs from ethical relativism and also ethical absolutism, in that moral principles may be overridden in certain situations.

ETHICAL RELATIVISM The theory that the validity of moral judgments depends on subjective or cultural acceptance. It is opposed to *moral absolutism* and *moral objectivism.*

ETHICAL SKEPTICISM The theory that we cannot know whether there is any moral truth.

ETHICAL SUBJECTIVISM The theory that moral values are expressions of human emotions, feelings, wishes, or desires, and that they have no objective referent in the world.

ETHICS The systematic attempt to understand moral concepts and to justify moral principles and theories.

ETHNOCENTRISM The belief of a group or a people that their ways (values, race, religion, language, culture) are superior to all others.

FEMINIST ETHICS According to Hestor Eisenstein, a woman-centered analysis of morality that presupposes the centrality, normality, and value of women's experience and women's culture.

FORMULA OF THE END IN ITSELF Kant's first expression of the Categorical Imperative as respect for persons: Act so that you treat humanity, whether in your own person or in that of another, always as an end and never as a means only.

FORMULA OF UNIVERSAL LAW Kant's expression of the Categorical Imperative in *Fundamental Principles of the Metaphysics of Morals* (1785): Act only according to that maxim by which you can at the same time will that it should become a universal law.

INTELLECTUALISM The view that God's law is the expression of God's intellect, whose object is truth; therefore, the moral law is rational and the intellect superior to the will; opposed to *voluntarism*.

METAETHICS A theoretical study that inquires into logical, semantic, and epistemological issues in ethics. Metaethics is contrasted with *normative ethics,* which constructs moral theories based on moral principles.

MORALS Principles or rules of conduct that govern (or ought to govern) an individual or society.

MORAL SKEPTICISM The view that we cannot know whether there are valid moral principles.

NATURAL LAW THEORY The view, held by Saint Thomas Aquinas, that nature is a system of God's universal prescriptions for humankind; right and wrong can be determined by rational examination of nature and the consultation of conscience.

NONCONSEQUENTIALISM Ethical theories, such as Kant's, that deny the *consequentialist* claim that the intrinsic good and evil of consequences are the sole criteria of rightness and wrongness; sometimes called *deontological ethics.*

PSYCHOLOGICAL EGOISM A descriptive theory about human motivation stating as fact that every person always acts to satisfy his or her self-interest.

RELATIVISM See *cultural relativism* and *ethical relativism.*

SOCIAL CONTRACT THEORY The name given to a group of related and overlapping concepts and traditions in political theory and ethics that view the origin of collective society as based on an agreement; according to Thomas Hobbes, individuals agree to limit their autonomy in exchange for the peace and security that government provides. Without such an agreement, the precollective *state of nature* prevails.

STATE OF NATURE The condition of humanity without (or before) government. Hobbes portrays it as anarchy, with a continual war of all against all.

UTILITARIANISM A normative *consequentialist* ethical theory (originally esposed by Jeremy Bentham and John Stuart Mill) that holds right action to be that which maximizes utility, bringing about good consequences for all concerned—sometimes popularized as "the greatest good for the greatest number." *Act utilitarianism* holds that the right act in a given situation is that which results in the best consequences, whereas *rule utilitarianism* holds that the right act is that conforming to the set of rules that will in turn result in the best consequences.

VOLUNTARISM The view that moral law is binding simply because it is God's will. (In the example of Abraham, if God asked Abraham to sacrifice his son, then the very request makes it right; there is no independent standard of judgment for morality outside of God's will.)

CREDITS

Hannah Arendt, "Violence and Power" from *On Violence*. Copyright © 1969, 1970 by Hannah Arendt. Reprinted with the permission of Harcourt Brace and Company.

Sandra Bartky, "Foucault, Femininity, and the Modernization of Patriarchial Power" from *Feminism and Foucault: Reflections on Resistance*, edited by Irene Diamond and Lee Quinby. Copyright © 1988 by Irene Diamond and Lee Quinby. Reprinted with the permission of Northeastern University Press.

Sissela Bok, "On Lying for the Public Good" from *Lying: Moral Choice in Public and Private Lives*. Copyright © 1978 by Sissela Bok. "Kant on Peace" from *Strategy for Peace*. Copyright © 1989 by Sissela Bok. Both reprinted with the permission of Pantheon Books, a division of Random House, Inc.

Susan Power Bratton, "Christian Ecotheology and the Old Testament," *Environmental Ethics* 6. Reprinted with the permission of the author.

Barry Commoner, "Economic Growth and Environmental Quality: How to Have Both," *Social Policy* (Summer 1985). Reprinted with the permission of Social Policy Corporation.

Ronald Dworkin, "Taking Rights Seriously" from *Taking Rights Seriously*. Copyright © 1977, 1978 by Ronald Dworkin. Reprinted with the permission of Harvard University Press.

Joel Feinberg, "The Rights of Animals and Unborn Generations" from *Philosophy and the Environmental Crisis*, edited by William T. Blackstone (Athens, GA: University of Georgia Press, 1974). Reprinted with the permission of the author.

Shulamith Firestone, "Love and Women's Oppression" from *The Dialectic of Sex*. Copyright © 1970 by Shulamith Firestone. Reprinted with the permission of William Morrow & Company, Inc.

Michel Foucault, "Power, Truth, and Right" from *Power/Knowledge*. Copyright © 1972, 1975, 1976, 1977 by Michel Foucault. Reprinted with the permission of Pantheon Books, a division of Random House, Inc.

Charles Fried, "The Evil of Lying" from *Right and Wrong*. Copyright © 1978 by the President and Fellows of Harvard College. Reprinted with the permission of Harvard University Press.

Mohanda K. Gandhi, "On Satyagraha" from *The Moral and Political Writings of Mahatma Gandhi*, edited by Raghavan N. Iyer, Vol. 2 & 3. Copyright © 1986, 1987 by Raghavan N. Iyer. Reprinted with the permission of Oxford University Press.

William H. Gass, "Throw the Emptiness Out of Your Arms: Rilke's Doctrine of Nonpossessive Love." Reprinted with the permission of the author.

Carol Gilligan, "In a Different Voice: Women's Conception of the Self and of Morality," *Harvard Educational Review* 47:4. Copyright © 1977 by the President and Fellows of Harvard College. Reprinted with the permission of *Harvard Educational Review*.

Kwame Gyeke, "African Communalism" from *An Essay on African Philosophical Thought: The Akan Conceptual Scheme* (New York: Cambridge University Press, 1987). Reprinted with the permission of the author and Cambridge University Press.

Garrett Hardin, "Lifeboat Ethics: The Case Against Helping the Poor," *Psychology Today* (September 1974). Copyright © 1974 by Sussex Publishers, Inc. Reprinted with the permission of *Psychology Today*.

Stanley Hauerwas, "Christians and Abortion: The Narrative Context" from *A Community of Character: Toward a Constructive Christian Social Ethic*. Copyright © 1981 by The University of Notre Dame Press. Reprinted with the permission of the publishers.

Vacláv Havel, "Living in Truth" from *The Power of the Powerless: Citizens Against the State in Central Eastern Europe*, edited by John Keane. Copyright © 1985 by Palach Press. Reprinted with the permission of the M. E. Sharpe, Inc.

bell hooks and Cornel West, "Breaking Bread" from *Breaking Bread* (Boston: South End Press, 1991). Reprinted with the permission of South End Press.

Martin Luther King, Jr., "On Being a Good Neighbor" from *Strength to Love* (Minneapolis, MN: Augsburg Fortress, 1981). Copyright © 1963 by Martin Luther King, Jr., renewed 1991 by Coretta Scott King. Reprinted with the permission of The Heirs to the Estate of Martin Luther King, Jr., c/o Joan Daves as agent for the proprietor.

David M. Kirp, Mark G. Yudof, and Marlene Strong Franks, "Gender in the Context of Community" from *Gender Justice*. Copyright © 1986 by University of Chicago. Reprinted with the permission of David Kirp and The University of Chicago Press.

Emmanuel Levinas, "Useless Suffering," translated by Richard Cohen from *The Provocation of Levinas*, edited by Robert Bernasconi and David Wood (London: Routledge, 1988). Reprinted with the permission of the publishers.

Alasdair MacIntyre, "Tradition and the Virtues," from *After Virtue*, revised edition. Copyright © 1981, 1984 by Alasdair MacIntyre. Reprinted with the permission of the University of Notre Dame Press.

Catharine MacKinnon, "Sex and Violence" from *Feminism Unmodified: Discourses on Life and the Law*. Copyright © 1987 by the President and Fellows of Harvard College. Reprinted with the permission of Harvard University Press.

Peter Marin, "Helping and Hating the Homeless," *Harper's* (January 1987). Copyright © 1986 by Harper's. Reprinted with the permission of *Harper's*.

Lisa Newton, "Reverse Discrimination as Unjustified," *Ethics* 83 (1973). Reprinted with the permission of The University of Chicago Press.

Nel Noddings, "An Ethics of Care" from *Caring: A Feminine Approach to Ethics and Moral Education*. Copyright © 1984 by The Regents of the University of California. Reprinted with the permission of the University of California Press.

John T. Noonan, Jr., "An Almost Absolute Value in History," from *The Morality of Abortion*. Copyright © 1970 by the President and Fellows of Harvard College. Reprinted with the permission of Harvard University Press.

William V. O'Brien, "Just War Theory" from *The Conduct of Just and Limited War*. Copyright © 1981 by Praeger Publishers. Reprinted with the permission of Praeger, an imprint of Greenwood Publishing Group, Inc.

Onora O'Neill, "Kant's Ethics" from *Matters of Life and Death*, third edition, edited by Tom Regan. Copyright © 1993 by McGraw-Hill, Inc. Reprinted with the permission of the publishers.

James Rachels, "Utilitarianism" from *The Elements of Moral Philosophy*. Copyright © 1986 by Random House, Inc. Reprinted with the permission of McGraw-Hill, Inc.

John Rawls, "A Theory of Justice" from *A Theory of Justice*. Copyright © 1971 by the President and Fellows of Harvard College. Reprinted with the permission of The Belknap Press of Harvard University Press.

Tom Regan, "The Nature and Possibility of an Environmental Ethic." Reprinted with the permission of the author.

Adrienne Rich, "Women and Honor: Some Notes on Lying" from *On Lies, Secrets and Silence: Selected Prose 1966–1978*. Copyright © 1975, 1977 by Adrienne Rich. Reprinted with the permission of W. W. Norton & Company, Inc.

Cheyney C. Ryan, "Pacifism and Self-Defense" from *Ethics* (Chicago: University of Chicago Press, 1983). Reprinted with the permission of the author and The University of Chicago Press.

Peter Singer, "Famine, Affluence, and Morality" from *Philosophy and Public Affairs* (Spring 1972). Reprinted with the permission of Princeton University Press.

Robert C. Solomon, "The Virtue of (Erotic) Love" from *Midwest Studies in Philosophy XIII: Ethical Theory: Character and Virtue*, edited by Peter A. French, Theodore E. Uehling, and Howard K. Wittstein. Copyright © 1988 by the University of Notre Dame. Reprinted with the permission of the University of Notre Dame Press.

Christina Sommers, "Philosophers Against the Family" from *Virtue and Vice in Everyday Life* (New York: Harcourt Brace). Reprinted with the permission of the author.

Elizabeth V. Spelman, "Theories of Race and Gender: The Erasure of Black Women." Reprinted with the permission of the author.

Shelby Steele, "I'm Black, You're White, Who's Innocent?," *Harper's* (June 1988). Copyright © 1988 by Harper's Magazine. Reprinted with the permission of *Harper's*.

John Stoltenberg, "Rapist Ethics" from *Refusing to Be a Man: Essays on Sex & Justice* (New York: Penguin/Meridian, 1989). Copyright © 1989 by John Stoltenberg. Reprinted with the permission of the author and the Elaine Markson Literacy Agency.

Judith Jarvis Thomson, "A Defense of Abortion," *Philosophy & Public Affairs* 1, No. 1 (Fall 1971). Copyright © 1971 by Princeton University Press. Reprinted with the permission of the publishers.

Karen T. Warren, "The Power and Promise of Ecological Feminism," *Environmental Ethics* 12. Reprinted with the permission of the author and *Environmental Ethics*.

Mary Ann Warren, "On the Moral and Legal Status of Abortion," *The Monist* 57, No. 1 (January 1973). Reprinted with the permission of *The Monist*.

Richard A. Wasserstrom, "On Racism and Sexism" from *Today's Moral Problems* (New York: Macmillan, 1985). Reprinted with the permission of the author.

Cornel West, "Race Matters" and "Beyond Affirmative Action" from *Race Matters*. Copyright © 1993 by Cornel West. Reprinted with the permission of Beacon Press.